D0151164

CCDA Exam Certification Guide

A. Anthony Bruno, CCIE #2738
Jacqueline Kim, CCDA

CISCO SYSTEMS

CISCO PRESS

Cisco Press
201 W 103rd Street
Indianapolis, IN 46290

CCDA Exam Certification Guide

A. Anthony Bruno

Jacqueline Kim

Copyright© 2000 Cisco Press

Cisco Press logo is a trademark of Cisco Systems, Inc.

Published by:
Cisco Press
201 West 103rd Street
Indianapolis, IN 46290 USA

Printed in the United States of America 1 2 3 4 5 6 7 8 9 0

Library of Congress Cataloging-in-Publication Number: 99-64086

ISBN: 0-7357-0074-5

Warning and Disclaimer

This book is designed to provide information about the CCDA examination. Every effort has been made to make this book as complete and as accurate as possible, but no warranty or fitness is implied.

The information is provided on an "as is" basis. The author, Cisco Press, and Cisco Systems, Inc., shall have neither liability nor responsibility to any person or entity with respect to any loss or damages arising from the information contained in this book or from the use of the discs or programs that may accompany it.

The opinions expressed in this book belong to the authors and are not necessarily those of Cisco Systems, Inc.

Trademark Acknowledgments

All terms mentioned in this book that are known to be trademarks or service marks have been appropriately capitalized. Cisco Press or Cisco Systems, Inc., cannot attest to the accuracy of this information. Use of a term in this book should not be regarded as affecting the validity of any trademark or service mark.

Feedback Information

At Cisco Press, our goal is to create in-depth technical books of the highest quality and value. Each book is crafted with care and precision, undergoing rigorous development that involves the unique expertise of members from the professional technical community.

Readers' feedback is a natural continuation of this process. If you have any comments regarding how we could improve the quality of this book or otherwise alter it to better suit your needs, you can contact us through e-mail at **ciscopress@mcp.com**. Please make sure to include the book title and ISBN in your message.

We greatly appreciate your assistance.

Publisher	J. Carter Shanklin
Executive Editor	John Kane
Cisco Systems Program Manager	Jim LeValley
Managing Editor	Patrick Kanouse
Development Editor	Andrew Cupp
Project Editor	Dayna Isley
Copy Editors	Raymond Alexander
	Krista Hansing
Technical Editors	David Barnes
	Kevin Mahler
	Brian Melzer
CD-ROM Exam Author	David Barnes
Media Developer	Craig Atkins
Team Coordinator	Amy Lewis
Cover Designer	Louisa Klucznik
Production Team	Argosy
Indexer	Kevin Fulcher

CISCO SYSTEMS

CISCO PRESS

Corporate Headquarters
Cisco Systems, Inc.
170 West Tasman Drive
San Jose, CA 95134-1706
USA
http://www.cisco.com
Tel: 408 526-4000
      800 553-NETS (6387)
Fax: 408 526-4100

European Headquarters
Cisco Systems Europe s.a.r.l.
Parc Evolic, Batiment L1/L2
16 Avenue du Quebec
Villebon, BP 706
91961 Courtaboeuf Cedex
France
http://www-europe.cisco.com
Tel: 33 1 69 18 61 00
Fax: 33 1 69 28 83 26

American Headquarters
Cisco Systems, Inc.
170 West Tasman Drive
San Jose, CA 95134-1706
USA
http://www.cisco.com
Tel: 408 526-7660
Fax: 408 527-0883

Asia Headquarters
Nihon Cisco Systems K.K.
Fuji Building, 9th Floor
3-2-3 Marunouchi
Chiyoda-ku, Tokyo 100
Japan
http://www.cisco.com
Tel: 81 3 5219 6250
Fax: 81 3 5219 6001

Cisco Systems has more than 200 offices in the following countries. Addresses, phone numbers, and fax numbers are listed on the Cisco Connection Online Web site at http://www.cisco.com/offices.

Argentina • Australia • Austria • Belgium • Brazil • Canada • Chile • China • Colombia • Costa Rica • Croatia • Czech Republic • Denmark • Dubai, UAE Finland • France • Germany • Greece • Hong Kong • Hungary • India • Indonesia • Ireland • Israel • Italy • Japan • Korea • Luxembourg • Malaysia • Mexico • The Netherlands • New Zealand • Norway • Peru • Philippines • Poland • Portugal • Puerto Rico • Romania • Russia • Saudi Arabia • Singapore • Slovakia • Slovenia • South Africa • Spain • Sweden • Switzerland • Taiwan • Thailand • Turkey • Ukraine • United Kingdom • United States • Venezuela

About the Authors

A. Anthony Bruno is a Senior Network Systems Consultant with Lucent's NetCare Professional Services Division (formerly International Network Services). His network certifications include CCIE #2738, CCDP, CCNA-WAN, Microsoft MCSE, Nortel NNCSS, Certified Network Expert (CNX) Ethernet, Certified Network Professional, and Check Point CCSE. As a consultant, he has worked with many customers in the design, implementation, and optimization of large-scale networks. Anthony has worked on the design of large company network mergers, Voice over IP/Frame Relay, and Internet access. He formerly worked as an Air Force captain in network operations and management. He completed his Master of Science degree in Electrical Engineering from University of Missouri-Rolla in 1994 and his Bachelor of Science degree in Electrical Engineering from University of Puerto Rico-Mayaguez in 1990. Anthony is a contributor and the lead technical reviewer for the Cisco Press release *CCIE Fundamentals: Network Design and Case Studies*, Second Edition.

Jacqueline Kim is the Knowledge Resource Manager with REALTECH Systems Corporation. She designed the Knowledge Exchanged Group that has the objective of providing technical instruction to clients through instructor-led classes and Web-based training tools. She staffs and manages this group within Knowledge Management and also teaches several classes. Jacqueline has various industry certifications, including Cisco CCDA, Novell CNE, and Check Point CCSA/CCSE. She has held positions in both network engineering and pre-sales engineering, during which time she presented lectures in security for Cisco Systems and Network User Groups. Jacqueline is a technical reviewer for the Cisco Press titles *Internetworking Technologies Handbook*, Second Edition, and *Cisco Systems Networking Academy: First-Year Companion Guide*.

About the Technical Reviewers

David Barnes is a Network Consulting Engineer for Cisco Systems in Dallas, Texas. He is a Cisco Certified Design Professional, MCSE+Internet, and Master CNE. David specializes in large-scale network design and optimization. He has designed, implemented, and managed networks for numerous Fortune 500 companies during the past 10 years.

Kevin S. Mahler, CCNP and CCDA, is the National Wide-Area Network and Network Operations Center manager for the American Cancer Society. Kevin's teams are responsible for designing, deploying, maintaining, and monitoring the networks of the American Cancer Society. He also runs his own Web hosting company where he is trying to find his fortune on the Internet. He is the author of *CCNA Training Guide* published by New Riders. He also worked as a revision author on the third edition of *Internetworking Technologies Handbook* from Cisco Press. Kevin ran his own company designing, selling, and installing computer and networking systems for over ten years. Kevin has worked as a programmer, repair technician, networking consultant, database administrator, and Internetworking engineer. Today, he reminisces of when CP/M was king, everyone wanted WordStar, Microsoft was a small company, portable computers weighed just under 45 pounds, and 10 Mbps was a fast network. You can find him on the Internet at www.kmahler.com or e-mail him at kmahler@kmahler.com.

Brian Melzer is a network engineer for AT&T Solutions, where he has worked for the past three years. He is part of the Wolfpack, having earned a bachelor degree in Electrical Engineering and a master's degree in management from North Carolina State University in Raleigh, North Carolina. He is a Cisco Certified Internetworking Expert (#3981). Having managed some of the largest networks in the world, Brian has extensive experience working with Cisco routers and switches.

Dedications

This book is dedicated to my loving wife, Ivonne, my inspiration and support; and to our daughters, Joanne Nichole and Dianne Christine, my joy.—Anthony

This book is dedicated to my wonderful parents, whose love and wisdom are my guiding light; and to my lovely sister, Jeanette, whose strength I so admire.—Jacqueline

Acknowledgments

This book would not have been possible without the efforts of many dedicated people. Anthony Bruno would like to thank the following people for their contributions:

First, thanks to Andrew Cupp, Development Editor, who not only improved the book but also improved me as a writer.

I would like to thank Cisco Press Executive Editor John Kane for his vision and guidance of this book.

Thanks to the technical editors, David Barnes, Kevin Mahler, and Brian Melzer, whose advice and careful attention to detail improved the book.

Thanks to Dayna Isley, Project Editor, and Raymond Alexander and Krista Hansing, Copy Editors, for their efforts. Thanks also to Amy Lewis, Team Coordinator, for taking care of many details.

Jacqueline Kim would like to thank the following people for their contributions:

I would like to thank John Kane, Executive Editor at Cisco Press, for his continued guidance through this endeavor, and whose undying support made this project a reality. To Andrew Cupp, Development Editor, thanks for the encouragement.

To everyone at REALTECH Systems Corporation, my second family, thank you all for sharing your knowledge and visions of the future with me.

Special thanks to the founders of REALTECH, Ray LaChance and Ken Yanneck, whose foresight and entrepreneurial spirits inspire me; to my gifted friend Robert Caputo for his mentoring and support; to my friends Cuong Vu, Damon Yuhasz, Yoeng-Sen Liem, Andrew Bernardo, Cheuk Lee, and Phillip Gwon, who generously shared their technical expertise and their time; to Tom Wurst, for his wisdom; to Nancy Sanchez, for her coaching; to Mark Agovino, for his support; and to Kevin Chin, without whom I couldn't have made it through the year.

Finally, to all my coworkers and friends I could not acknowledge by name, thank you for all your support during this challenging project.

Contents at a Glance

Contents

Introduction to CCDA

So you have worked on Cisco devices for a while, designing networks for your customers, and now you want to get certified? There are several good reasons to do so. Cisco's certification program permits network analysts and engineers to demonstrate their competence in different areas of networking and at different levels. The prestige and respect that come with a Cisco certification will definitely help you in your career. Your clients, peers, and superiors will recognize you as an expert in networking.

In the Cisco Routing and Switching career certification path, there are two certification tracks: the Network Design track, with which this book is concerned, and the Network Support track. Figure I-1 illustrates the various levels of the two design tracks for Cisco Routing and Switching career certification. Note that Cisco Certified Design Associate (CCDA) is the entry-level certification in the Network Design track.

Figure I–1   *Routing and Switching Certifications*

Network Design

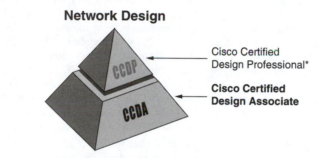

Network Support

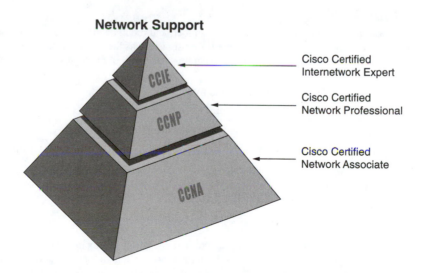

The test to obtain CCDA certification is called Designing Cisco Networks (DCN) Exam #640-441. This is a computer-based test that currently consists of between 80 and 90 questions and has a 120-minute time limit. All exam registrations are made by calling Sylvan Prometric at 1-800-204-3926. The cost for the exam is $100 USD. Throughout this book, you will see the exam referred to as the DCN exam or the CCDA exam; they are the same exam for the purposes of this text.

The DCN exam measures your ability to design networks that meet certain requirements for performance, security, capacity, and scalability. The exam is focused on small- to medium-sized networks. The candidate should have at least one year of experience in the design of small- to medium-sized networks using Cisco products. A CCDA candidate should have an understanding of internetworking technologies, including network topologies, routing, switching, WAN technologies, LAN protocols, and network management. Cisco suggests working through the Designing Cisco Networks and Internetworking Technologies course material before you take the CCDA exam. For more information on the various levels of certification, career tracks, and Cisco exams, go to the Cisco Learning Connection page of the Cisco Connection Online (CCO) Web site at http://www.cisco.com/certifications.

About This Book

CCDA Exam Certification Guide is intended to help you prepare for the design portion of the CCDA exam, recognize and improve your areas of weakness, and increase your chances of passing the test. The book is designed to provide you with mastery of the CCDA design objectives. It is strongly recommended that you take the DCN course or acquire an equivalent amount of on-the-job training before solidifying your CCDA knowledge with the elements of this book. In addition to the design information covered in this book, the CCDA exam will test you on your knowledge of internetworking technology fundamentals summarized in Appendix C, "Internetworking Technology Review." Because the scope of this book focuses on helping you master the CCDA exam design objectives, the authors assume that readers have a certain level of internetworking knowledge. If you lack experience with internetworking technologies, it is strongly recommended that you review the *Internetworking Technologies Multimedia* CD-ROM from Cisco Systems or the *Internetworking Technologies Handbook, Second Edition* from Cisco Press.

At the beginning of each chapter you will find a "Do I Know This Already?" Quiz to help you assess the degree to which you need to review the subject matter covered in that chapter. You may then read the entire chapter thoroughly or skip directly to only those sections and objectives that you need to review further. In addition, at the end of each chapter is a "Q&A" review quiz. Use this after you have read the chapter to determine your knowledge of the topics.

Objective of This Book

The objective of this book is to help you fully understand, remember, and recall details of the design topics covered on the CCDA exam. The CCDA exam will be a stepping stone for most people as they progress through the other Cisco certifications; passing the exam because of a thorough understanding and recall of the topics will be incredibly valuable at the next steps.

This book prepares you to *pass the CCDA exam* by doing the following:

- Helping you discover which design topics you have not mastered
- Providing explanations and information to fill in your knowledge gaps
- Supplying exercises and case studies that enhance your ability to recall and deduce the answers to test questions
- Providing a practice exam and exercises on the CD-ROM that will help you assess your overall progress and preparation level for the CCDA exam

Who Should Read This Book?

This book is intended to tremendously increase your chances of passing the CCDA exam. This book is intended for an audience who has taken the Designing Cisco Networks and Internetworking Technologies courses or has an equivalent level of on-the-job experience. Although others may benefit from using this book, the book is written assuming that you want to pass the exam.

So why should you want to pass CCDA? For one of many reasons: to get a raise; to show your manager you are working hard to increase your skills; to fulfill a manager's requirement (before he will spend money on another course); to enhance your résumé; because you work in a presales job at a reseller and want to eventually become CCDP certified; to prove you know the topic, if you learned via on-the-job experience rather than from taking the prerequisite classes—or one of many other reasons.

Have You Mastered All the Exam Objectives?

The exam tests you on a wide variety of topics; most people will not remember all the topics on the exam. Because some study is required, this book focuses on helping you obtain the maximum benefit from the time you spend preparing for the design portion of the exam. You can access many other sources for the information covered on the exam; for example, you could read the Cisco Documentation CD. However, this book provides effective, late-stage preparation for the exam.

You should begin your exam preparation by spending ample time reviewing the exam objectives listed in the section "DCN Exam Objectives," later in this introduction. Because exam objectives will change from time to time, check out Cisco's Web site for any future changes to the list of objectives.

How This Book Is Organized

The book begins with a chapter that generally defines the design topics that will be covered by the CCDA exam. Before you begin studying for any exam, it is important that you know the topics that could be covered. With the CCDA exam, knowing what is on the exam is seemingly straightforward; Cisco publishes a list of CCDA objectives. However, the objectives are certainly open to interpretation.

Chapters 1 through 8 follow Cisco's CCDA exam design objectives and provide detailed information on each objective. Each chapter begins with a quiz so that you can quickly determine your current level of readiness. Each chapter ends with a review "Q&A" quiz as well as case study questions.

Appendix A, "Answers to Quiz Questions," provides the answers to the various chapter quizzes. The answers to the case study questions can be found at the end of each chapter.

Finally, in the back of the book you will find an invaluable CD-ROM. It contains exercise questions on study cards and flash cards that provide answer explanations and links to the appropriate section in an electronic version of the book. The CD-ROM also enables you to take a timed practice CCDA exam that is similar in format to the actual CCDA exam you will be taking. The practice exam is complete with both general knowledge and case study questions. The practice exam has a database of more than 200 questions, so you can test yourself more than once.

Features and Conventions of This Book

This book features the following:

- **Cross-Reference to CCDA Objectives**—The beginning of each core chapter will include a reference to the CCDA design objectives discussed in that chapter. Each major section also begins with a list of the objectives covered in that section.

- **Do I Know This Already? Quiz**—This beginning section of each chapter is designed to quiz you on the topics in that chapter. This gives you an opportunity to assess just how much you need to review the subject matter covered in that chapter.

- **Foundation Topics**—This section in each chapter explains and reviews topics that will be covered in the exam. Each section in the Foundation Topics begins with a list of objectives covered in that section and then follows up with extensive review of that subject matter. Foundation Topics sections are the bulk of the material in this book.

- **Foundation Summaries**—Most of the major facts covered in each chapter are summarized in tables and charts in this section. This format enables you to review a chapter quickly, focusing on these summaries, so that you can solidify your knowledge of the major subject matter of the chapter.

- **Q&A**—Each chapter contains a section of review questions. These questions test you on your retention of the knowledge presented in the Foundation Topics for that chapter.

- **Case Studies**—Each chapter ends with case studies that include a battery of questions. These case studies are intended for use after you have reviewed the chapter and are ready to validate your mastery of the CCDA objectives presented in that chapter. Chapter 9, "Additional Case Studies," is a complete chapter of new case studies that you should read and work on after you feel you have mastered all the objectives presented in the book. The CCDA exam will most likely include some questions based on a design case study.

- **Test Questions**—Using the test engine on the CD-ROM, you can take simulated exams. You can also choose to be presented with several questions on an objective that you need more work on. This testing tool provides you with practice that will make you more comfortable when you actually take the CCDA exam.

DCN Exam Objectives

Cisco lists the objectives for CCDA Exam on its Web site at http://www.cisco.com/training. That list provides the most key information about what the test covers. Table I-1 lists the CCDA exam design objectives and the corresponding chapters in this book that cover those objectives. Each chapter and each major section of the book begins with a listing of the objectives covered. Use these references as a road map to find the exact materials you need to study to master the CCDA exam design objectives.

Table I-1   *CCDA Design Objectives and the Chapters Where They Are Covered*

Objective	Description	Chapter
Overall Objectives		
1	Design a network that meets a customer's requirements for performance, security, capacity, and scalability.	1
2	Assemble Cisco product lines into an end-to-end networking solution.	4, 5
Small- to Medium-Sized Business Solutions Framework		
3	Upon completion of this introduction, you will be able to describe a framework you can use to simplify the complexities associated with analyzing customer network problems and creating Cisco scalable solutions.	1
Identify Customer Needs—Characterize the Existing Network		
4	Identify all the data you should gather to characterize the customer's existing network.	2

Table I-1   *CCDA Design Objectives and the Chapters Where They Are Covered (Continued)*

Objective	Description	Chapter
5	Document the customer's current applications, protocols, topology, and number of users.	1, 2, 7
6	Document the customer's business issues that are relevant to a network design project.	1, 2, 7
7	Assess the health of the customer's existing network and make conclusions about the network's capability to support growth.	2
8	Determine the customer's requirements for new applications, protocols, number of users, peak usage hours, security, and network management.	2, 3, 7, 8
9	Diagram the flow of information for new applications.	2, 3
10	Isolate the customer's criteria for accepting the performance of a network.	2
11	List some tools that will help you characterize new network traffic.	2, 7
12	Predict the amount of traffic and the type of traffic caused by the applications, given charts that characterize typical network traffic.	3
Design the Network Structure		
13	Describe the advantages, disadvantages, scalability issues, and applicability of standard internetwork topologies.	4
14	Draw a topology map that meets the customer's needs and includes a high-level view of internetworking devices and interconnecting media.	4, 5
15	Recognize scalability constraints and issues for standard LAN technologies.	4
16	Recommend Cisco products and LAN technologies that will meet a customer's requirements for performance, capacity, and scalability in small to medium-sized networks.	4, 7
17	Update the network topology drawing you created in the previous section to include hardware and media.	4, 5
18	Recognize scalability constraints and issues for standard WAN technologies.	5
19	Recognize scalability constraints and performance budgets for major Cisco products.	5
20	Recommend Cisco products and WAN technologies that will meet the customer's requirements for performance, capacity, and scalability in an enterprise network.	5, 7
21	Propose an addressing model for the customer's areas, networks, subnetworks, and end stations that meets scalability requirements.	6

continues

Table I-1 *CCDA Design Objectives and the Chapters Where They Are Covered (Continued)*

Objective	Description	Chapter
22	Propose a plan for configuring addresses.	6
23	Propose a naming scheme for servers, routers, and user stations.	6
24	Identify scalability constraints and issues for IGRP, EIGRP, IP RIP, IPX RIP/SAP, NLSP, AppleTalk RTMP and AURP, static routing, and bridging protocols.	6
25	Recommend routing and bridging protocols that meet a customer's requirements for performance, security, and capacity.	6, 7
26	Recognize scalability issues for various Cisco IOS software features such as access lists, proxy services, encryption, compression, and queuing.	6
27	Recommend Cisco IOS software features that meet a customer's requirements for performance, security, capacity, and scalability.	6, 7
Build a Prototype or Pilot for the Network Structure		
28	Determine how much of the network structure must be built to prove that the network design meets the customer's needs.	8
29	List the tasks required to build a prototype or pilot that demonstrates the functionality of the network design.	8
30	List the Cisco IOS software commands you should use to determine whether a network structure meets the customer's performance and scalability goals.	8
31	Describe how to demonstrate the prototype or pilot to the customer so that the customer understands that the proposed design meets requirements for performance, security, capacity, and scalability, and that the costs and risks are acceptable.	8

Table I-2 shows which objectives are covered in each chapter.

Table I-2 *Chapter-by-Chapter Listing of CCDA Design Objectives*

Chapter	Objective
1	1, 3, 5, 6
2	4–11
3	8, 9, 12

Table I-2   *Chapter-by-Chapter Listing of CCDA Design Objectives (Continued)*

Chapter	Objective
4	2, 13-17
5	2, 14, 17–20
6	21–27
7	5, 6, 8, 11, 16, 20, 25, 27
8	8, 28–31

If you feel that your knowledge of a particular chapter's objectives is strong, you might want to proceed directly to that chapter's exercises to assess your true level of preparedness. If you are having difficulty with those exercises, make sure to read over that chapter's Foundation Topics. Also, be sure to test yourself by using the CD-ROM's test engine. Finally, if you are lacking in certain internetworking technologies knowledge, be sure to review the reference materials provided in the appendixes. No matter your background, you should begin with Chapter 1, "Design Goals."

Objectives Covered in This Chapter

The following is a list of the objectives covered in this chapter. The list of CCDA exam design objectives and the chapters in which they are covered can be found in the Introduction of this book.

1	Design a network that meets a customer's requirements for performance, security, capacity, and scalability.
3	Upon completion of this introduction, you will be able to describe a framework you can use to simplify the complexities associated with analyzing customer network problems and creating Cisco scalable solutions.
5	Document the customer's current applications, protocols, topology, and number of users.
6	Document the customer's business issues that are relevant to a network design project.

Design Goals

To get you started in your preparation for the CCDA exam, this chapter contains a framework for gathering customer objectives when designing a network. This chapter also covers the steps of network design and contains an overview of all the major topics of network design. The chapters that follow will cover in more detail each of the topics overviewed in this chapter.

"Do I Know This Already?" Quiz

The questions in the following quiz are designed to help you gauge how well you know the material covered in this chapter. Compare your answers with those found in Appendix A, "Answers to Quiz Questions." If you answered most or all of the questions thoroughly and correctly, you might want to skim the chapter and proceed to the "Q&A" section at the end of the chapter. If you find that you need to review only certain subject matter, search the chapter for those sections that cover the objectives you need to review, and then test yourself both with these questions and with the "Q&A" questions. If you find the following questions too difficult, read the chapter carefully until you feel that you can easily answers these and the "Q&A" questions.

1 What types of questions would you ask to determine a client's application requirements?

_____

_____

_____

2 What are samples of business constraints on design?

_____

_____

_____

3 What is the first step in network design?

_____

_____

_____

4 In the framework of small to medium-sized network design, what should be done if there are protocol-related problems on the network?

_____

_____

_____

5 What information is gathered in the logical assessment of the existing network?

_____

_____

_____

6 What are the three layers of hierarchical network design?

_____

_____

_____

7 If there are problems involving media contention on networks using repeaters, what should be done to resolve it?

_____

_____

_____

8 What are the five areas of network management?

_____

_____

_____

9 If you customer has a small network, what type of demonstration should be used?

_____

_____

_____

10 If higher bandwidth is required on the network, what technologies are suggested for small to medium-sized networks?

_____

_____

_____

You can find the answers to these questions in Appendix A, "Answers to Quiz Questions."

Foundation Topics

Customer Objectives

The following CCDA objectives are covered in this section:

1	Design a network that meets a customer's requirements for performance, security, capacity, and scalability.
5	Document the customer's current applications, protocols, topology, and number of users.
6	Document the customer's business issues that are relevant to a network design project.

A CCDA should design networks based on the customer's objectives. In other words, you will need to find out what the customer wants to solve. You then must create a design that solves the networking problem or issue the customer is having.

The first step in network design is to obtain the customer's requirements. To obtain a complete picture of the customer's objectives, the engineer needs to document the client's business requirements, technical requirements, and any business and political constraints.

Business Requirements of the Customer

For this aspect of determining the customer's objectives, think about the purpose of the project. Project how the business will improve. Find out if the network is affecting the company's capability or effectiveness to develop, produce, and track products. Find out if any business applications are being affected. Determine whether the company will be audited.

Scalability is a very important consideration, and it is wise for the network designer to build a network that can scale. You should figure out how much the company will grow in one year or in five years.

Technical Requirements of the Customer

Think about the type of technical problems you are trying to solve. Consider the network's topology. For example, it may be difficult to introduce Ethernet to a customer that religiously uses Token Ring. Also consider the company's use of modern technologies. Find out whether the client is willing to experiment with the latest, bleeding-edge technologies. Keep in mind scaling issues; decide whether switched Ethernet will provide the necessary bandwidth or whether Fast Ethernet is necessary to scale the network.

Technical requirements can be divided into the following areas:

- Performance requirements
- Applications requirements
- Network management requirements
- Security requirements

Performance Requirements

Determine the following performance requirements:

- Identify any issues concerning network latency and response times.
- Find out if there is high utilization on LAN segments or WAN links.
- Determine how often the WAN links go down.

Application Requirements

Consider existing application integration. The network design will need to seamlessly accommodate the existing applications. Investigate the current application flows, and incorporate those into the network design. Determine the following application requirements:

- Find out what new applications have been introduced to the network.
- Determine the number of users using these applications.
- Find out the traffic flow for these applications.
- Identify what new protocols are being introduced to the network.
- Determine what applications are used during the daytime hours and what are used during the nighttime hours.
- Determine the time of day that represents the peak usage hours of applications.

Network Management Requirements

Determine the following network management requirements:

- Determine how the network is managed.
- Determine whether there is a network management station to view network performance and faults.
- Ascertain whether there are any accounting and security management requirements.
- Find out whether the staff is training on the network management applications.
- Find out whether there is a station for configuration management.

NOTE	Remember the acronym FCAPS: fault, configuration, accounting, performance, and security management.

Security Requirements

Determine the following security requirements:

- Determine what type of security is required.

- Find out what external connections are present in the network and why they are there.

- Determine whether additional security is required on Internet connections.

Business and Political Constraints

The final aspect of determining the customer's objectives is to identify any constraints. Consider the following and ascertain whether they are constraints in your design:

- Ascertain budget or resource limitations for the project.

- Determine the timeline to complete the project.

- Determine whether any internal politics play a role in the decision-making process. Find out what different sources or groups are providing input into the requirements.

- Make sure the client's staff is able to operate and manage the new network.

- Find out whether the customer wants to reuse or trade in any existing equipment

The network design must be cost-effective and efficient. The goal is to get the best solution at a reasonable price. For example, a Catalyst 5500 may not be best solution for a remote office LAN with only 14 users.

Framework for Small- to Medium-Sized Network Design

The following CCDA objective is covered in this section:

3	Upon completion of this introduction, you will be able to describe a framework you can use to simplify the complexities associated with analyzing customer network problems and creating Cisco scalable solutions.

As you gather information from the customer, keep in mind that Cisco has proposed a framework to use when designing complex small to medium-sized networks. The framework proposes the following rules (which are summarized in Figure 1-1):

- If the problems are protocol-related, use routing. Many LAN protocols use periodic broadcasts and service advertisements and do not scale well as the network size increases. Routers can be used to further subnet your network and reduce broadcast domains. Access and security policies can be applied on routers.

- If the problem involves media contention, use LAN switching. To expand on this rule, if you have too many nodes on a shared network, you will expect to have high utilization; devices will have to compete to obtain access to the network, and application response may be slow. Introducing LAN switching will help resolve the contention on the network.

- If high bandwidth is required, consider switched Fast Ethernet. Switched Fast Ethernet offers a good cost-to-performance ratio for small to medium-sized networks. For larger networks in which high bandwidth and low latency is required, use ATM. Gigabit Ethernet now provides another option in the LAN for the backbone and for bandwidth-intensive application servers.

Figure 1-1   *Small to Medium-Sized Network Design Framework*

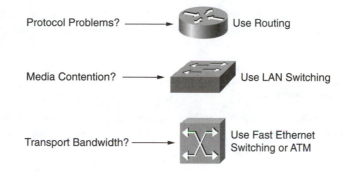

Steps for Network Design

The following CCDA objectives are covered in this section:

1	Design a network that meets a customer's requirements for performance, security, capacity, and scalability.
5	Document the customer's current applications, protocols, topology, and number of users.
6	Document the customer's business issues that are relevant to a network design project.

The steps for designing a network are as follows:

1 Gather information to support the business and technical requirements.

2 Assess the current network.

3 Consider the applications involved.

4 Design the local-area networks.

5 Design the wide-area network.

6 Design for specific network protocols.

7 Create the design document and select Cisco network management applications.

8 Test the design.

This section provides an overview of these steps. The remainder of the book fills in the details of these steps.

Gather Information to Support the Business and Technical Requirements

The section "Customer Objectives," earlier in this chapter, covers step 1. Chapter 2, "Assessing the Existing Network and Identifying Customer Objectives," covers this step in much more detail.

Assess the Current Network

This is the step during which you collect all data pertaining to physical, logical, traffic, and management information of the network. Chapter 2 covers this step in more detail. This section contains an overview of this step.

Physical Assessment

To perform a physical assessment, you need to document the physical topology of the network. Create a diagram with all routers, switches, and hubs. For example, in Figure 1-2, a list of network devices is created and the type and amount of devices is documented. Physical connectivity between devices should also be documented; also list the speed and type of media used between devices.

Figure 1-2   *Physical Assessment*

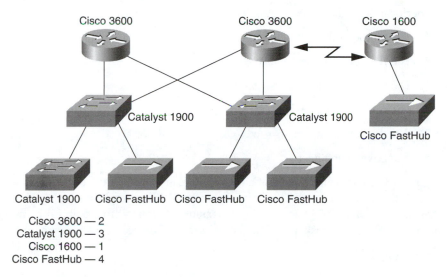

Cisco 3600 — 2
Catalyst 1900 — 3
Cisco 1600 — 1
Cisco FastHub — 4

You will also need to list the LAN technologies being used. The following is a list of possible LAN technologies:

- Ethernet

- Token Ring

- FDDI

- Fast Ethernet

- Gigabit Ethernet

Finally, document the WAN circuit information and list the WAN technologies being used. The following is a list of possible WAN technologies used:

- Frame Relay

- Private lines

- ATM

- ISDN

- X.25

Logical Assessment

To perform the logical assessment, determine the following:

- The protocols that are being routed

- The IP address assignment scheme

- The Novell IPX address assignment

- The AppleTalk address assignment

- Whether any access list is used to filter addresses or broadcasts

- The Layer 3 architecture

Figure 1-3 provides an example of a logical assessment. Here, the IP address subnet information is documented. The figure shows five Ethernet segments with 24-bit subnet masks that can support up to 254 nodes each. This figure also shows four point-to-point links with 30-bit masks. With this mask, two IP addresses are used for each router on the link.

Figure 1-3   *Logical Assessment*

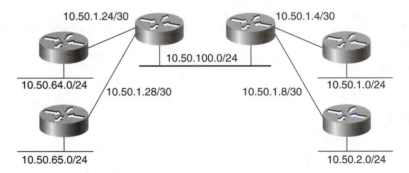

Traffic Assessment

To perform the traffic assessment, determine the following:

- Document the traffic flows on the network.

- Determine how much traffic is on each segment.

- Locate the servers.

- Determine how much traffic is local to the segment and how much traffic is external.

Determine the current tools used for network management:

- Determine whether the customer has the necessary tools to manage the network.

- Determine whether there is a management station

- Find out whether CiscoWorks is being used to manage routers and switches.

- Verify whether there are capacity or performance monitoring tools.

- Determine whether a network protocol analyzer is available for LAN segment troubleshooting.

- Find out whether any RMON probes are in use.

Consider the Applications Involved

A good designer needs to take into consideration the applications that the network supports. The only reason the network is there is to provide a highway on which application information can flow. Never ignore the applications in use. Chapter 3, "Application Considerations," covers this step in more detail. This section contains an overview of the applications to consider in this step.

Microsoft Workgroups

MS Networking uses the session-layer NetBIOS protocol for file and print sharing. NetBIOS over NetBEUI is not routable and must be bridged for all devices to communicate on the network. For this reason, NetBIOS over NetBEUI does not scale well. NetBIOS over TCP (NBT) scales better because it relies on TCP/IP for transport, thus enabling NetBIOS traffic to be routed.

Novell Application Services

Novell uses the Service Advertising Protocol (SAP) for devices to announce their services to the network. SAP broadcasts are generated by fileservers, print servers, and so on. These broadcasts are sent every minute. As required by the protocol, a router adds all SAP broadcasts to its SAP table and broadcasts it every 60 seconds to its IPX interfaces. On larger networks, these broadcasts can overwhelm the network. Consider using access lists to filter SAP broadcasts from LAN segments.

IBM Networking

Traditional SNA networking involves the use of SDLC for WAN connectivity and Token Ring for LANs. Communication between hosts and terminals is bridged. The designer needs to document the Source-Route Bridging (SRB) requirements and consider Data-Link Switching Plus (DLSw+) for transporting SNA and NetBIOS traffic over WAN links in the IP network.

Multimedia Services

The network designer should investigate requirements to support multimedia services such as video and voice. Use techniques such as multicast routing to multicast video streams to reduce the total bandwidth used on the network. Multicast routing can transmit video streams to preselected end stations and reduce bandwidth consumption when compared to broadcasting. On networks supporting Voice over IP, use techniques such as RTP header compression on WAN links to reduce overhead. RSVP, policy routing, and tag switching are techniques used in the design of these time-sensitive applications.

Design the Local-Area Network

The Cisco Certified Design Associate must be able to design local-area networks that meet the customer's objectives on performance and scalability. A CCDA must design networks in a hierarchical manner to provide scalable solutions. A CCDA also must decide where to use hubs, switches, and routers to separate broadcast and collision domains. Know the differences between Layer 2 and Layer 3 switching as well. Chapter 4, "Network Topologies and LAN Design," covers this step in more detail. This section contains an overview of this step.

Hierarchical versus Flat Designs

The CCDA should understand that there is a limit on the number of nodes in flat network designs. Network broadcasts can overcome slow serial links. Build the network in a hierarchical manner with subnetting to reduce the amount of traffic on WAN links.

The CCDA must understand the three layers of the hierarchical model for network design: the core, distribution, and access layers. Figure 1-4 provides an example of these three layers.

At the core layer, high-speed switching is used with high availability and redundancy. Apply access and distribution lists at the distribution layer, which is where the security policies are applied. Address summarization and media translations are applied in the distribution layer as well. The access layer consists of the remote office sites using ISDN, Frame Relay, and DDR, and private lines accessing the corporate network. Local-area networks end segments are also part of the access layer.

Figure 1-4   *Hierarchical Design Model*

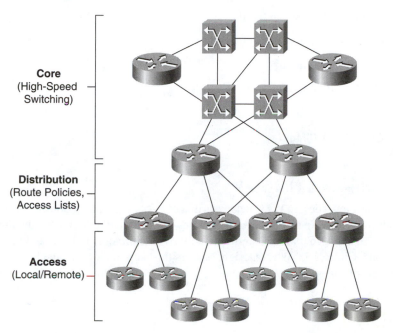

Core
(High-Speed
Switching)

Distribution
(Route Policies,
Access Lists)

Access
(Local/Remote)

LAN Protocols

You need to understand the characteristics of LAN protocols, including physical distance limitations of LAN technologies: Ethernet (10Base2, 10Base5, and 10BaseT), Fast Ethernet, Gigabit Ethernet, Token Ring, and FDDI. Use these technologies to satisfy requirements ranging from user workstations to high-bandwidth servers.

LAN Physical Design

Select the equipment to be used, keeping in mind the LAN technologies and the number of ports required for the network.

Cisco LAN solutions include repeaters and switches.

Repeaters:

- Cisco 1500 hubs
- FastHub 100, 200, and 300 families

Switches:

- Catalyst 3000 Switch family
- Catalyst 5000 Switch family
- Catalyst 5500 family
- Catalyst 1900 family
- Catalyst 2800 family
- Catalyst 2900 family

Design the Wide-Area Network

The CCDA must design WAN networks that meet the customer's objectives of performance and scalability. Design networks in a hierarchical manner. and plan for bandwidth capacity to provide scalable solutions. Determine the WAN technologies to use, and plan for Cisco router solutions. Chapter 5, "WAN Design," covers this step in more detail. This section contains an overview of this step.

Transport Selection

Decide on the WAN technology to use. The following list will help you make this decision:

- Use leased lines where traffic flows are constant between point-to-point locations.

- Use ISDN for on-demand access to remote offices and for backup for another link type.

- Use Frame Relay as a high-bandwidth, cost-effective transport. This very popular WAN protocol provides permanent virtual circuits (PVC) between routers. Frame Relay provides characteristics such as congestion notification, discard eligibility (DE) bit, bursting, and the capability to have several PVCs on a physical port. These and other features (such as cost) made Frame Relay a very popular WAN technology in the 1990s.

- Use X.25 when the reliability of the WAN links is suspect. X.25 is an older WAN technology that is still widely in use and can be found running over low-speed (9600 to 64000 bps) lines. Throughput using X.25 suffers in comparison to Frame Relay due to X.25's additional error checking.

- Use ATM when high bandwidth (155+ Mbps) is required on the core. ATM offers different Quality of Service (QoS) types, allowing traffic with varying tolerances for bandwidth and latency to travel over the same network.

Bandwidth Planning

The CCDA must look at the applications being deployed at remote sites and decide on the sizing of WAN circuits. Rely on the analysis of existing traffic flows and past experience to help determine an appropriate bandwidth size for a circuit. If WAN circuit utilization is more than 70 percent for a long period of time, the circuit bandwidth should be increased. When planning bandwidth allocation, consider the following:

- The type of servers that are located at the remote site

- Whether the applications in the hub site will be accessed remotely and whether the intranet Web sites will be accessed remotely

- Whether there are Microsoft Domain controllers or MS Exchange servers at the remote sites

- Whether there are any database applications

Physical Design

Select the equipment to be used, keeping in mind the technologies and the number of interfaces required for the network. Take into consideration that the CCDA is focused on Cisco small to medium-sized network solutions.

The small to medium-sized network solutions include the following router series:

- Cisco 760/770 series

- Cisco 1000 series

- Cisco 1600 series

- Cisco 2500 series routers

- Cisco 3600 series routers

- Cisco MC3810 router

- Cisco 4500/4700 series routers

- Cisco 5200/5300 access servers

- Cisco 7200 series router

Design for Specific Network Protocols

In this step, take into consideration the type of protocols to be used on the network. Chapter 6, "Designing for Specific Protocols," covers this step in more detail. This section contains an overview of this step.

IP

The CCDA needs to design an IP address assignment scheme based on a hierarchical model. Use VLSMs to assign networks based on the number of devices and areas on the network. A hierarchical model for address assignment with VLSMs allows the network to take advantage of routing summary features supported by protocols such as EIGRP and OSPF. Choose routing protocols that will not add significant traffic to the network. Understand the differences between distance vector and link-state routing protocols.

Novell

Create IPX addressing schemes. Consider the broadcast characteristics of Novell's distance vector Routing Information Protocol (RIP) and Service Advertising Protocol (SAP). RIP broadcasts its table every 60 seconds; SAP also broadcasts the SAP table every 60 seconds. Use access lists to filter specific SAP broadcasts. Consider the design of the distance vector IPX RIP versus NetWare Link-Services Protocol (NLSP). EIGRP can be used on WAN links to reduce IPX traffic.

AppleTalk

Consider the AppleTalk cable ranges to assign to each interface and the zones for each area. To overcome the limitations of the AppleTalk routing protocol RTMP, use methods such as AURP or EIGRP on the WAN.

Bridging

Transparent and source-route bridged networks have size limitations and do not scale well. To reduce the traffic of bridged protocols, limit the size of bridged networks.

Create the Design Document and Select Cisco Network Management Applications

After working with the LAN, WAN, and protocol design, incorporate the solutions into one design during this step. Verify that the total solution meets the customer's objectives on performance, scalability, and cost. Incorporate a proactive network management solution that satisfies the customer's network service goals. Chapter 7, "The Design Document and Cisco Network Management Applications," covers this step in more detail. This section contains an overview of this step.

The Design Document

The design document helps the designer explain how the solution meets the requirements of the project. It consists of the following primary sections:

- Executive Summary
- Design Requirements
- Design Solution
- Summary
- Appendixes
- Cost of Proposed Design (optional)

Management Applications

A CCDA must be able to select the appropriate management applications for the designed network. Chapter 7 covers several management applications with which the CCDA must be familiar and discusses which are appropriate for various networks.

Test the Design

After a design has been proposed, the next step is to verify that the design will work. For large networks, a prototype can be built; for smaller networks a pilot can be devised. Chapter 8, "Building a Prototype or Pilot," covers the steps of building prototype and pilot test networks.

Q&A

The following questions are designed to test your understanding of the topics covered in this chapter. When you have answered the questions, look up the answers in Appendix A, "Answers to Quiz Questions." After you identify the subject matter you missed, review those sections in the chapter until you feel comfortable with this material.

1 During which assessment do you find out what type of IP addressing scheme is used on the network?

_____

_____

_____

2 What would help solve a network with a high amount of broadcasts?

_____

_____

_____

3 What are the four sections of the design document, and what goes into each section?

_____

_____

_____

4 In network management, what does FCAPS stand for?

_____

_____

_____

5 You would do a prototype for what type of networks?

_____

_____

_____

6 Which section of the design document contains topology diagrams of the existing network?

_____

_____

_____

7 Briefly describe Frame Relay.

_____

_____

_____

8 Give three examples of bridged protocols.

_____

_____

_____

9 What does SAP stands for? What is it used for?

_____

_____

_____

10 List the nine steps for network design.

_____

_____

_____

11 If higher bandwidth is required on the network, what technologies are suggested for small to medium-sized networks?

_____

_____

_____

12 How often is the Novell SAP table broadcasted onto the network?

_____

_____

_____

13 What are examples of business constraints?

_____

_____

_____

Case Studies

Because passing the CCDA exam requires you to answer design questions about an ongoing case study, "Case Studies" and "Case Study Answers" sections will appear at the end of each body chapter in this book. Each "Case Studies" section asks questions based on one or more of the case studies presented in this section. Each "Case Study Answers" section answers those questions with detailed explanations. Each chapter's questions in the "Case Studies" section deal with the subject matter covered in that chapter. In some chapters, other case study background information will be presented in the question in addition to the general case study information here. This is so that you can answer that chapter's specific questions.

The remainder of this section introduces the three case studies that will be referred to at the end of each chapter. When you come across a question on a particular case study, refer back to these sections so that you can go about answering the questions on that case study.

Case Study #1: GHY Resources

Mr. Martin of GHY Resources is responsible for the company's network. He has invited you to a meeting to discuss some issues.

GHY Resources is a manufacturing company with its headquarters based in St. Louis. In the past 10 years, GHY has grown from 10 employees to more than 400. It now has a manufacturing site in Kansas City, and a new site is opening in Nashville, Tennessee, in three months. The manufacturing sites connect back to St. Louis via a 256 K circuit. Sales offices exist in more than seven cities throughout the United States. Each sales office connects back to the headquarters via a 56 K leased line. These leased lines run at more than 70 percent utilization at certain times during the day. The company currently uses a mix of routers from different vendors and wants to standardize on Cisco's if the price is right. The current routing protocol is RIPv1. Figure 1-5 shows the current topology of GHY Resources.

Novell NetWare fileservers are used throughout the company, with one server at each of the sales offices. Local offices have print servers also. The headquarters' local-area network consists of Ethernet using 10BaseT hubs. These Ethernet segments constantly run at about 45 percent utilization. There are around 10 segments connecting to a pair of Cisco 4000 routers. One of the network analysts mentioned that the protocol analyzer reported broadcast storms on some of the Ethernet segments.

Business applications run on an HP 3000 machine located on one of the segments at the headquarters. An HP 3000 is located at the manufacturing site. The manufacturing site has two NetWare file servers. Mr. Martin expects the new manufacturing site to have the same business applications. The LAN in Kansas City consists of three Ethernet segments with 30 stations each. Network utilization is at 35 percent on each segment.

Figure 1-5   *GHY Resources Logical Diagram*

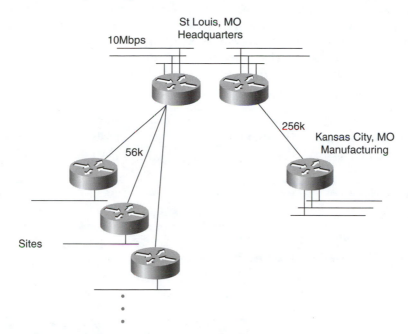

Mr. Martin has mentioned that he is interested in Frame Relay as an alternative for his WAN links. He would like to upgrade his LANs as well. He has requested a LAN/WAN solution that would help reduce the utilization problems he is having on the network. He also would like a solution to reduce the SAP traffic on the network. In addition, he wants to find a way to conserve IP addresses on his network. Mr. Martin needs to get a proposal in one week to have his managers approve the money. The design needs to be installed before the new manufacturing site becomes operational.

Look for questions on the GHY Resources case study at the end of some of the book's chapters.

Case Study #2: Pages Magazine, Inc.

Ms. Phillips is the newly appointed Director of IT at Pages Magazine, Inc. Pages Magazine realizes that to aggressively compete in its market, this company needs changes to its infrastructure that will support new applications and Internet access, allowing them to increase their productivity and to follow market trends. Pages wants to use the Internet to gain clients and find new opportunities. Ms. Phillips is faced with many options but needs your help in developing a solution that is both cost-effective and scalable. She needs to make sure that the solution will address her immediate needs and also be scalable enough to support future applications.

Pages Magazine, Inc., is a conglomerate of four periodicals. Pages Magazine is expecting at least two periodical acquisitions per year for the next three years. Each magazine acts independently and has a mix of both small and medium-sized offices throughout the continental United States. Each magazine has various access methods back to the corporate headquarters located in New York City. Table 1-1 summarizes the current layout of the Pages Magazine, Inc., offices as they are presented in Figure 1-6.

Table 1-1   *Pages Magazine, Inc., Office Layout*

Office Location	Description	# of Nodes	Access Back to HQ
New York City, New York	Corporate headquarters	100	
Newark, New Jersey	Fashion magazine	20	256 K leased line
White Plains, New York	Entertainment news magazine	10	64 K ISDN
Queens, New York	Fashion magazine	30	256 K leased line
Danbury, Connecticut	Home improvement magazine	20	128 K ISDN

Figure 1-6   *Pages Magazine, Inc., Logical Diagram*

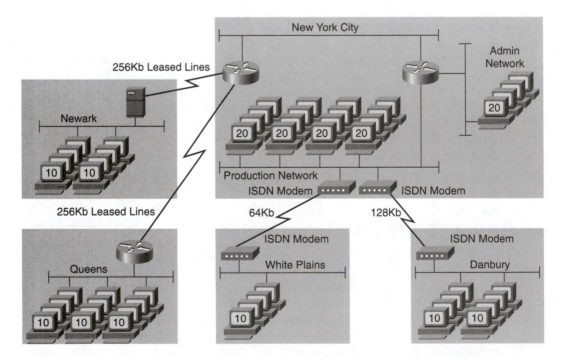

These leased lines have provided enough bandwidth to support basic e-mail and file transfer services. Each office has its own Novell servers that are currently managed independently, running on a flat 10BaseT Ethernet environment. A T1 will be installed at the NYC office to provide Internet access to the remote offices. Internet access and e-mail are the first critical applications that need to be addressed. Currently, the offices use CC:mail as their e-mail platform.

Pages Magazine has not standardized on MS Office applications and currently uses a mix of Apple and Microsoft application products. All the routers route IPX, AppleTalk, and IP; however, Pages Magazine wants to migrate to a purely IP environment with Novell GroupWise as the e-mail platform. Each office will have a GroupWise server that needs to be synchronized with the NYC office for Internet e-mail. After the two new offices go online, every office will slowly migrate to Netware 5, using native IP for transport. Until then, AppleTalk still needs to be supported as a routed protocol. The new Novell servers will also have a synchronized NDS directory structure that will manage the user access and login process.

Network manageability has been difficult since different vendor products are being used to provide WAN access. Ms. Phillips is looking for a single vendor solution that can be managed more effectively with her limited staff.

The additional offices for the new network are another concern, and she is looking to implement a network management solution that will support her staff. She has three remote IT support people in addition to three NYC-based people. One support person is located in Danbury and the other is in White Plains. The third supports Queens. Most of her staff have desktop and moderate networking skills.

The network used RIPv1, but Ms. Phillips plans to use DHCP to readdress her network so that she can conserve the valid IP address and to create a more scalable IP addressing scheme. Pages Magazine, Inc., will require a new routing protocol that will support subnetting and possible VLSM. Ms. Phillips is also interested in finding a more cost-effective WAN solution that will support the additional two offices that will go online within two months.

Ms. Phillips must present an infrastructure upgrade and Internet access plan to the CEO and CFO in three weeks. The presentation will include a network design to show how the network will scale to support new offices and to address any return on investment issues.

Look for questions on the Pages Magazine, Inc., case study at the end of some of the book's chapters.

Case Study #3: MediBill Services, Inc.

MediBill Services, Inc., started out providing billing support and services for a small community of independent medical offices. These offices used MediBill to service medical claims and provide patient data storage. After five years of service, MediBill has decided to grow and provide online medical information and Internet access to service its expanding client base. The company also is looking to provide the security for file transfers for disaster recovery purposes. MediBill is looking to ensure that the integrity of the information transferred will not going be in question.

MediBill's CIO, Mr. Lee, is responsible for approving a design strategy that would support MediBill's future goals of providing secured remote storage of medical files, as well as Internet/e-mail services and desktop support to the small to medium-sized medical offices.

MediBill currently has a T1 out to the Internet but isn't sure whether this is enough bandwidth to support its client base. The company has just acquired eight more offices that will need access within three months. MediBill has already begun the PC installation process and is waiting to coordinate the installation of the WAN connections. Prior to the WAN installations, Mr. Lee will need to purchase routers and security equipment for the Internet access.

Mr. Lee has asked several consultants to respond to the following information provided in a Request for Proposal (RFP).

MediBill has maintained an NT SQL database in its main office, which connects to the six remote doctors offices via 56 kbps dialup connections. These connections will have to be upgraded to support new services provided by the Internet. The connections will have to support Internet Web, e-mail, and file transfers as well as network management traffic. Mr. Lee is looking to implement the Microsoft Systems Management Server (SMS) for remote monitoring and management. MediBill has decided to standardize on the Microsoft platform to simplify IT management issues. MediBill has already implemented Microsoft Exchange and Outlook as the e-mail system.

MediBill is going to start by providing its clients with basic Web access, FTP, and e-mail.

After the Internet access and WAN upgrades, Mr. Lee wants to roll out a full network management solution that includes the management of each of the company's customers as well as its own network. Currently, each remote office must provide its own PC equipment, but with MediBill's new services, the company has decided to provide the PCs and all the customer premise equipment (CPE) necessary. Each office will have five to ten PCs per office, all running Microsoft Windows 98.

MediBill also won a contract with the MetroCenter Hospital, where the company will provide Internet services as well as secured disaster recovery services for data and files. The hospital will be connected to MediBill via a dedicated T1 circuit. The hospital has contracted MediBill to manage the 50 Internet workstations that will be distributed throughout the hospital, as well as the 10 data-transfer stations.

The client needs to review its WAN strategy and provide a design plan to upgrade the WAN network to support its growing client base. The client wants a demonstration of the security that his network will provide so that he can use that information in MediBill's marketing strategy.

Mr. Lee wants a proposal that will provide a baseline of the existing network and WAN connections as a comparison to a new network. Due to the large scale of changes that need to be made with MediBill, Mr. Lee is looking for a proposal that will outline how the company will migrate from its previous network to the new, more scalable network.

Additional Case Studies

Chapter 9, "Additional Case Studies," consists entirely of case studies that cover an array of CCDA topics. When you have completed all the chapters in the book, work on these case studies to fine tune your CCDA case study skills.

Objectives Covered in This Chapter

The following is a list of the objectives covered in this chapter. The list of CCDA exam design objectives and the chapters in which they are covered can be found in the Introduction of this book.

4	Identify all the data you should gather to characterize the customer's existing network.
5	Document the customer's current applications, protocols, topology, and number of users.
6	Document the customer's business issues that are relevant to a network design project.
7	Assess the health of the customer's existing network and make conclusions about the network's capability to support growth.
8	Determine the customer's requirements for new applications, protocols, number of users, peak usage hours, security, and network management.
9	Diagram the flow of information for new applications.
10	Isolate the customer's criteria for accepting the performance of a network.
11	List some tools that will help you characterize new network traffic.

CHAPTER 2

Assessing the Existing Network and Identifying Customer Objectives

To create a comprehensive design that will meet your customer's needs, you must understand the customer's objectives. This chapter is designed to help you obtain the fundamental skills necessary to determine those needs. These skills will help you formulate questions, understand what elements of the network to review, and develop a scope for the project. When a project scope has been defined, a project plan can be created to satisfy the customer's requirements. The success of the project plan and resulting design proposal will rely heavily on your ability to collect data that is both accurate and pertinent.

While the information-gathering process may seem overwhelming, guidelines introduced in this chapter can make the task more manageable. No project plan, no matter how well thought out, can anticipate every possible scenario. Use of the guidelines outlined in this chapter can provide a solid framework for a project plan that can be adapted to any unanticipated changes.

Unlike other Cisco exams, the CCDA has both a technical and a process focus. While many technical facts can be memorized, the process for developing a sound design must be understood. The various steps in the process must make sense to be useful. Eventually, as the process becomes clear, it will become easier to accurately define your customer's objectives and formulate satisfactory designs.

"Do I Know This Already?" Quiz

The questions in the following quiz are designed to help you gauge how well you know the material covered in this chapter. Compare your answers with those found in Appendix A, "Answers to Quiz Questions." If you answered most or all of the questions thoroughly and correctly, you might want to skim the chapter and proceed to the "Q&A" and "Case Study" sections at the end of the chapter. If you find that you need to review only certain subject matter, search the chapter for those sections that cover the objectives you need to review, and then test yourself both with these questions and with the "Q&A" and "Case Study" questions. If you find the following questions too difficult, read the chapter carefully until you feel that you can easily answers these and the "Q&A" and "Case Study" questions.

1 Which Cisco tool enables you to analyze interface statistics, review routing table sizes, and get a performance snapshot of the current network?

2 Identify three categories that are considered to be administrative data to help characterize the customer's network.

_____

_____

_____

3 What product can be used as a traffic analysis and protocol analysis tool?

_____

_____

4 What feature of the network design are you trying to include when you discuss future business goals with your customer?

_____

_____

_____

5 During your characterization of the network, you realize that WAN implementations and LAN networks are managed by different groups. During which data collection stage would you note this information?

_____

_____

_____

6 Broadcast/multicast behavior, supported frame sizes, flow control, and windowing are all examples of characterizing what type of behavior?

_____

_____

_____

7 What is the maximum number of recommended workstations that a flat AppleTalk network could support?

_____

_____

_____

8   True or False: Using the largest frame size that is supported by a medium has a negative impact on network performance.

_____

_____

_____

9   Identify the port used by a protocol such as SMTP.

_____

_____

_____

10 What is the purpose in documenting response time to understand and identify performance issues?

_____

_____

_____

11 True or False: Gathering budget information and resource availability for a project is a part of the process in which you are defining the manageability requirements.

_____

_____

_____

12 What is the maximum number of buffer misses a Cisco router can have in an hour?

_____

_____

_____

You can find the answers to these questions in Appendix A, "Answers to Quiz Questions."

Foundation Topics

The Necessary Data for Characterizing the Existing Network

The following CCDA objective is covered in this section:

4	Identify all the data you should gather to characterize the customer's existing network.

To help you understand and characterize your customer's network, you will review two basic areas of your customer's business. First you will review nontechnical data related to your customer's business goals, issues, and constraints—this is also known as the corporate profile information. This information is essential to understanding growth trends, corporate structure, and policies that would affect your design. The second major area you will need to review is the customer's current technical information. It is important to distinguish between business or administrative information and technical data. However, as you are collecting this data, it is important to see how they are related to each other. Remember that the goal here is to understand your customer's existing network and to uncover any problem areas you might encounter later. This section discusses basic guidelines and topics you can use to begin to profile your customer's design needs and existing network.

Assessing the Customer's Corporate Profile Information

Assessing the corporate profile information will help you characterize the type of business and your customer's business constraints. Understanding your customer's network means understanding your customer's business. The profiling data will help you determine the following:

- **Business goals and business type**—Determine what type of business your customer is engaged in and what the company's major business goals are for the future. The growth of a company will differ from one to another; try to understand how you would measure the growth of the company. Should you look for significant growth every six months, or in one year, or over the next four years? This will help you determine the scalability requirements and also help you understand the return on the investment the customer is seeking. By researching your customer's industry and the competition, you will be able to better position Cisco products to help the customer grow.

- **Corporate structure**—A network design usually resembles the corporate structure of a company by having different networks for different departments, such as Marketing, Media, Human Resources, and Accounting. An organizational chart or a similar document can help you better understand the corporate structure. An example of some information you would find includes staffing at headquarters and how regions of the company interact with each other. Of course, the best source to verify and explain the corporate structure is your customer.

- **Geographical structure**—Determine how the customer's company is spread geographically. You should always review the geographical structure of the company with the corporate structure. Doing this research helps you understand and locate major user communities.

- **Current and future staffing**—The network must have enough flexibility to address the needs of the existing staff as well as support the growth and expansion of a company. To help you determine current and future staffing needs, ask the following questions:

    — Ask the network users how these network changes will affect them.

    — Ask the network users which department or departments will be affected.

    — Ask the IS staff how much in-house internetworking expertise there is.

    — Ask the IS staff if the company plans to expand staff as required to support the new internetwork design.

    — Ask the IS staff who will help you design the internetwork.

    — Ask if the new design will cause changes in job functions or possibly eliminate jobs.

- **Policies and politics**—Provides an understanding of how the design and implementation of the new network will affect the people and policies in the company. Find out whether they have any current policies related to the infrastructure. An example would be the corporate security policy or LAN access.

Assessing the Customer's Technical Information

Before you can begin developing a design solution, you must assess the company's current network technical information. Technical data helps you identify any network bottlenecks, understand how systems work together, and determine whether there are any obvious issues in implementing the new design.

Use the business profile information to act as a guide when gathering technical information. After gathering all the business data, it is possible to start extrapolating questions you would ask to assess the customer's current technical information. For example, determining the type of business your customer is engaged in can help you determine what type of applications are used within the business. If the company provides data warehousing and administrative support, you can be sure it will have some type of database system. Also consider whether the company is in media—then you can be sure that this involves some graphic-intensive traffic. Also in this case, you might suspect that there is some AppleTalk on the network because many companies still use Apple computers for graphical design.

Another example of using the business profile information to assess technical information would be to determine what IT services your customer needs to supply its clients. What are the technical requirements to achieve this goal? If your customer wants to supply Internet services to its clients with e-mail, then you can begin to see that the WAN connections from your customer to the client will be essential; your client's services will be dependent on the Internet connection. You can use the information to start understanding how the applications and traffic flow for these applications will be affected by the bandwidth.

Technical assessment can be divided into the following areas:

- Performance
- Applications
- Network management
- Security

The following sections discuss each of these areas.

Performance Assessment

To assess the performance issues of the current network, you will want to ask the following questions:

- Is there any latency?
- What is causing that latency?
- When do the performance problems happen?
- How will performance be affected by the proposed design?
- How much traffic flows between segments?
- Are there new applications, networks, or segments that will add to the traffic?

Sometimes it might be possible to perform a baseline of the network. If that is not possible because the network is too large, consider doing the traffic analysis on the critical segments, such as the backbone.

Applications Assessment

To completely assess the applications on the current network, you will need to look at the following:

- **Applications**—Identify the customer's current applications and plans for future applications, including information such as who uses the applications.

- **Information flows**—Analyze where information flows in the company and how different applications and traffic affects that flow. If possible, try to reference existing documentation—if none is available, this process could require considerable time based on the size of the network

- **Shared data**—Determine where shared data resides and who uses it.

- **Categorize data**—This will help you understand the different types of data passed along in the company's network, such as routed protocols, nonrouted protocols, and routing protocols

Network Management Assessment

Ask the following questions to assess the company's network management situation:

- Who manages the network? Are all aspects of the network managed by the same people?

- What type of network management is the client looking to implement? Reactive versus proactive?

- What type of notification does the client want to warn it of performance or fault issues?

- Who in the company knows how to perform network management tasks?

Security Assessment

Finally, ask the following questions to assess the company's network security:

- What security risks concern the customer?

- What security risks are priorities to the customer?

- Are there any existing security policies? Are the policies documented?

- What are the different access levels a user can have?

- What is the physical security of the network? Does everyone have access to the data closet or center?

Documenting the Existing Network

The following CCDA objectives are covered in this section:

5	Document the customer's current applications, protocols, topology, and number of users.
6	Document the customer's business issues that are relevant to a network design project.

As you can see, beginning with an assessment of the customer's business goals and current network is the first step in designing the new network. The previous section gives you an idea of the sort of information you will need to look for to make this assessment. The following section explains how a CCDA can go about organizing and documenting this information to begin working on the new design. Again, a holistic approach is very important. You must thoroughly document your customer's business needs and future plans to be able to build an efficient and scalable network. You must document your customer's current network to be able to identify performance needs and problems that a new network will need to overcome.

The "Case Study" section at the end of this chapter demonstrates these documentation techniques put to use on a case study network.

Twelve Steps for Documenting Your Customer's Existing Network

The following CCDA objectives are covered in this section:

5	Document the customer's current applications, protocols, topology, and number of users.
6	Document the customer's business issues that are relevant to a network design project.
7	Assess the health of the customer's existing network and make conclusions about the network's capability to support growth.

The following list shows the 12 steps you should take to help you describe what your customer's network currently looks like. Before you alter a network, you need to know what currently exists and the impact of your design on the existing environment.

Step 1 Characterize the customer's applications.

Step 2 Characterize the network protocols.

Step 3 Document the customer's current network.

Step 4 Identify potential bottlenecks.

Step 5 Identify the business constraints and inputs into your network design.

Step 6 Characterize the existing network availability.

Step 7 Characterize the network performance.

Step 8 Characterize the existing network reliability.

Step 9 Characterize the network utilization.

Step 10   Characterize the status of the major routers.

Step 11   Characterize the existing network management tools.

Step 12   Summarize the health of the existing network.

Step 1: Characterize the Customer's Application

The existing applications are a critical part of the assessment because applications are an end-user service. This means that application documentation must be accurate and detailed because each segment and each application can have unique qualities. Create a table with the fields displayed in Table 2-1 to document the customer's applications. Remember that a good analysis of the customer's requirements can help you narrow the applications you need to document.

Table 2-1   *Fields for Documenting the Existing Applications*

Field	Definition or Explanation
Application	Identify each application that runs over the customer's network.
Application Type	Characterize the application as a database, groupware, Internet, and so on.
Number of Users	Document the number of users for each application.
Number of Hosts or Servers	Identify how many hosts or servers provide each application.
Segment	Locate which segments the applications run on.
Comments	Write any comments that would be useful later, such as key people who manage the application.

This simple chart helps you organize the applications into categories as well as determine the traffic and information flows. Mapping information flows can be accomplished by first identifying the source device and then the destination device. These devices could be end stations, such as workstations, or other devices, like application servers, routers, or CPE equipment. Note that application flows can include multiple protocols, so you need to be specific about what you are mapping. For example, you could map an application flow between a Web server and a client. One option would be to diagram the Layer 3 IP protocol associated with the HTTP application and another would be to diagram Layer 4 TCP protocol. The process of using application flows is a great tool for understanding how an application works.

Step 2: Characterize the Network Protocols

Gathering information on the network protocols can be approached much in the same manner as gathering the application information. You also want to document both routed protocols and routing protocols. Create a table using the fields displayed in Table 2-2, and use it to document the network protocols.

Table 2-2   *Fields for Documenting the Existing Network Protocols*

Field	Definition or Explanation
Protocol	Identify each protocol that runs over the customer's network
Protocol Type	Characterize each protocol as a routing protocol, a LAN protocol, a server protocol, and so on.
Number of Users	Document how many users exist for each protocol.
Number of Hosts or Servers	Identify the number of hosts or servers that use each protocol.
Comments	Write any comments that would be useful later, such as future plans for the protocol; for example, note that the customer is looking to migrate to a purely IP network.

Step 3: Document the Customer's Current Network

This step involves doing the following:

- Documenting the network topology
- Documenting the addressing schemes
- Documenting concerns about the network

Documenting the Network Topology

Having a network topology map is crucial for understanding the existing network and formulating a basis for the new network design. Usually, the client will have some sort of network topology map. If not, make sure you create one and verify that the map is accurate with the client. Two basic types of network topology maps exist: One is a logical map with generic router symbols and overall network layout. This type of map is an excellent way to overview traffic flow and LAN and WAN topologies. A more detailed physical diagram includes router specifications, network addresses, and so on. Ideally, you would want both types of network diagrams, but sometimes features of both diagrams are merged into one. The following are guidelines for the topology map or an accompanying document:

- Every segment on the customer's network should be represented.

- All segments should have the appropriate LAN or WAN topology (for example, Ethernet, Token Ring, FDDI, Frame Relay cloud, serial links, and so on).

- All segments should be identified with the correct line and segment speeds.

- Try to include addressing schemes, such as network addresses, and the corresponding subnet masks for IP.

- Include all routers and switches, along with their naming schemes, if possible.

- Document any concerns about the network diagram, including traffic-flow issues and architectural questions.

Figure 2-1 shows a simple example of a topology diagram. This logical diagram is provided so that you can see the elements discussed previously.

Figure 2-1   *Sample Network Topology Diagram*

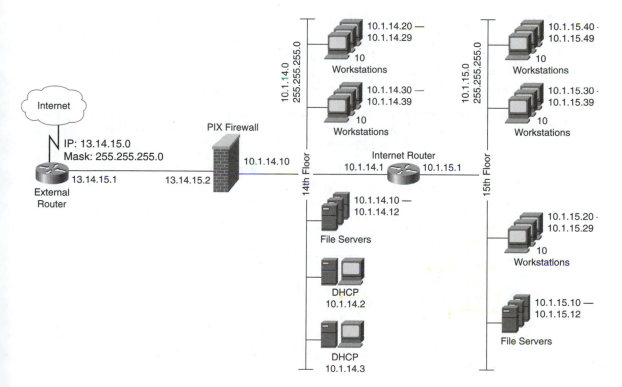

Documenting the Addressing Schemes

Addressing schemes are very important factors to consider. As long as you need network access, your devices must have addresses. IP addressing has become the most popular type of addressing. Many companies have implemented a Dynamic Host Configuration Protocol (DHCP) server, which is used to manage IP addressing within a network. This technology helps administrators quickly implement IP changes without having to track them in a spreadsheet.

Internet access and the need for network address translation (NAT) is a perfect example of how critical addressing becomes. NAT allows private addresses (those addresses not routable on the Internet) to be translated into a few public addresses. Many companies implement this technology because of the public IP address shortage. Addressing information is often included in topology diagrams.

Documenting Concerns About the Network

Document any concerns about the network diagram, including traffic-flow issues and architectural questions.

Step 4: Identify Potential Bottlenecks

When identifying potential bottlenecks, look for links or segments that are almost or completely over utilized because they are experiencing large amounts of broadcast/multicast traffic, or would be over utilized if additional application traffic were introduced. By identifying patterns in the traffic, you can redesign the infrastructure to get better response times.

A good example of traffic patterning is the 80-20 rule for LAN design. The 80-20 rule states that 80 percent of the traffic on a segment should be local to that segment. The remaining 20 percent of the traffic should be backbone traffic.

The CCDA exam covers five basic tools you can use throughout the design and testing process. These tools can be used to identify the potential bottlenecks in the existing network by looking at bandwidth utilization and traffic patterns:

- Netsys Enterprise/Solver
- NetFlow
- CiscoWorks
- Protocol analyzer/sniffer
- Scion

The exam focuses on the uses of these products more than technical details of their implementation.

The Netsys Enterprise/Solver performance tools analyze interface statistics, routing table sizes, IP/IPX accounting data, and enterprise RMON information to provide an observed performance snapshot of the current network. You can read more about Netsys tools in the "Network Management" section of Cisco's product catalog or on the Cisco Web site at http://www.cisco.com.

Cisco's NetFlow switching traffic management enables full-time monitoring of network traffic and collection of detailed statistics. It also offers advanced accounting and reporting capabilities through the NetFlow Data Export function and applications from Cisco partners. It offers advantages over many tools because it does not require an extra protocol, such as RMON.

CiscoWorks is a set of SNMP-based tools for characterizing a customer's network, monitoring the status of devices, maintaining configurations, and troubleshooting problems. Detailed information on both Cisco's NetFlow and CiscoWorks is available on the Cisco Web site and on the Cisco documentation CD-ROM.

Protocol analyzers such as Network Associate's Sniffer network analyzer capture and analyze network traffic, providing both protocol analysis and statistics. More information on Network Associate's Sniffer is available at http://www.nga.com.

The Scion software package is a freeware, turn-key Internet service provider (ISP) network statistics package developed by Merit Network, Inc. It uses SNMP to collect network management information from network routers, and it employs a standards-based client/server architecture to make the information available on the Web. More information on the Scion software package can be found at http://www.merit.edu/~netscarf/.

Step 5: Identify the Business Constraints and Inputs into Your Network Design

Now that you know what information you need to gather about a customer's company, it is time to take a step back to organize, review, and understand your data. This section offers recommendations on how to organize your data so that it will become usable information that you can apply to your design.

When you have collected the administrative data, it is time to isolate the information that is needed specifically for the network design. This section shows you how to document and identify the customer's business issues. These issues all have some impact on the network design process and will help you plan and implement your network design. The following is a checklist provided by Cisco to help you determine whether you have collected all the necessary information related to understanding your customer's business constraints. Use this checklist as a guideline to help you check your data. Remember that this list can be used as a basis for your own outline:

☐ I understand the corporate structure.

☐ I have analyzed the information flow in the corporation.

☐   The customer has identified any mission-critical data or operations.

☐   The customer has explained any policies regarding approved vendors, protocols, or platforms.

☐   The customer has explained any policies regarding open versus proprietary solutions.

☐   The customer has explained any policies regarding distributed authority for network design and implementation—for example, departments that control their own internetworking purchases.

☐   I have a good understanding of the technical expertise of my clients.

☐   I have researched the customer's industry and competition.

☐   I am aware of any politics that might affect the network design proposal.

Step 6: Characterize the Existing Network Availability

Another business constraint would be the cost associated with downtime. This is a very critical aspect of understanding the customer's business constraints. This information will affect how you plan and implement your network design. For example, if your customer is a publisher, he will have critical times during which his network cannot be down due to a publishing schedule. If this customer had a disruption in his network, it could affect whether he could publish his magazine for that month. Here are some questions to help you gather statistics on network downtime and the mean time between failure (MTBF) for the internetwork:

- What are the critical or fragile segments?

- Does any MTBF documentation exist for any network segment?

- What caused the network failure for those segments?

- How long were the network failures?

- What is the cost by department for a network outage (per hour)?

- What is the cost to the company or organization for a network outage (per hour)?

These questions will clarify the customer's requirements for redundancy and reliability in their network. The customer must weigh the cost of having a certain level of redundancy against the level of network redundancy needed. Therefore, it is important that the customer agree to the level of redundancy or reiliency being sold into the network.

Use a chart similar to the one presented in Table 2-3 to determine the impact of downtime.

Table 2-3   *Sample Chart for Determining Downtime*

Segments	Mean Time Between Failure	Date of Last Downtime	Duration of Last Downtime	Cause of Last Downtime
Backbone				
Segment 1				
Segment 2				

Step 7: Characterize the Network Performance

Characterizing network performance means measuring the response times between hosts, devices, and even applications. This information can be charted for later comparison. This is especially helpful when used as information in a baseline study because the customer can easily use this information as proof of improvement.

Step 8: Characterize the Existing Network Reliability

Both Step 8, Characterize the Existing Network Reliability, and Step 9, Characterize Network Utilization, require understanding network traffic to capture accurate data. The section "Step 4: Identify Potential Bottlenecks," earlier in this chapter, introduced some tools that help characterize the customer's network. Documenting network traffic can be the most time-consuming of all the data collections. This is primarily due to the time you need to devote to each segment to get accurate data. Determining the sampling rate depends on your analysis of network traffic cycles. Network traffic cycles are patterns in network traffic that show peak utilization, average and standard network traffic, segment-specific types of traffic, and so on. This type of analysis should be carefully planned so that you gather the critical data without compromising the delivery time of the project.

You can use a protocol analyzer or another network management tool to assess the reliability of the network. Document the following values:

- Total megabytes (MB)
- Total number of frames
- Total number of CRC errors
- Total number of MAC-layer errors (collisions, Token Ring soft errors, and FDDI ring operations)
- Total number of broadcasts/multicast frames

Cisco recommends that you document the information in the fields in Table 2-4 to track the network reliability. Each segment should be tested to yield the information necessary to complete Table 2-4. The chart includes the methods used to calculate the necessary information.

Table 2-4   *Chart for Determining Current Network Reliability*

Field	Description/Calculation Method
Average Network Utilization	Divide hourly average utilization amount it by the number of hourly averages.
Peak Network Utilization	Document the peak utilization amount. Note the time and date these peak utilizations occur.
Average Frame Size	This information can determine future bandwidth needs as well as traffic flow needs. If one segment is sending large frames to another segment, this can indicate that the devices involved need to reside on the same logical segment.
CRC Error Rate	Divide the total number of CRC errors by the number of megabytes
MAC-layer Error Rate	These errors help determine LAN problems associated with collisions. To calculate the MAC-layer error rate, divide the total number of MAC-layer errors by the total number of frames.
Broadcast/Multicast Rate	To calculate the rate of broadcasts/multicasts, just divide the total number of broadcasts/multicasts by the total number of frames.

Step 9: Characterize the Network Utilization

Characterizing the network utilization can easily be done with a network management tool. You just need to configure the monitoring tool to the time settings to gather the data, and the tool will do it for you automatically. You can gather data for every protocol and segment and even break down the sampling of protocols such as TCP/IP into TCP and UDP protocols. This would be useful in tracking different types of applications; the granularity of the sampling is really dependent on need.

Peak utilization is a very telling statistic that can help you determine the causes of excessive traffic and bandwidth constraints. On Ethernet segments, it's important to note that a 40 percent peak utilization that lasts beyond a minute can cause performance problems. If you notice a problem like this, then increase the sampling times from every hour to each minute. However, it is important to note that if you are going to be sampling each minute, you must calculate the appropriate time to do the sampling. Table 2-5 has fields that can be used in a table to characterize utilization of network protocols such as IP, IPX, and SNA.

Table 2-5   *Chart for Characterizing Utilization of Network Protocols*

Field	Description/Calculation
Relative Network Utilization	Calculate the percentage of each type of protocol on a segment. This is done by dividing the utilization amount for the segment from a specific protocol by the total bandwidth use for the segment.
Absolute Network Utilization	Note the bandwidth use of each segment relative to the size of the actual bandwidth.
Average Frame Size	Note the average frame size for each segment.
Broadcast/Multicast Rates	To calculate the rate of broadcasts/multicasts, just divide the total number of broadcasts/multicasts by the total number of frames.

Step 10: Characterize the Status of the Major Routers

Characterizing the status of the major routers can easily be done with Cisco IOS software using some basic **show** commands that should be issued every hour. Refer to the network health checklist in the section, "Step 12: Summarize the Health of the Existing Network," later in this chapter, for guidelines for determining the health of the routers. Cisco's **show** commands are powerful tools that give statistical information about the routers and the type of traffic the routers encounter. The following are three commands that can be used to show the status of routers:

- **show interfaces**—Provides statistical information on all the interfaces attached to the device, such as type of interface, identification of interface, whether the interface is up or down, and so on.

- **show processes**—Displays active processes, including CPU processes.

- **show buffers**—Shows information in main system memory to identify overutilization problems.

Step 11: Characterize the Existing Network Management Tools

The tools introduced earlier in this section represent only some of the of available network management devices. It is very possible that you will use other tools to characterize your customer's network or that the existing network already has some of these tools. This step reminds you to document the tools that already exist, as well as those you used to gather your information. It is also a good idea to document how you went about using these tools to gather your information.

Step 12: Summarize the Health of the Existing Network

The network health checklist presented in Table 2-6 can help you make some quick assessments on the overall health of the network

Although these numbers are guidelines, it's important for the exam that you refer to these guidelines when answering the questions. Many guidelines need to be tempered by taking into account the environment you are comparing. Therefore, when you compare your findings to the health list, remember to also document the reason for the deviation.

Table 2-6   *Network Health List*

Check	Condition	Actual Findings
	No shared Ethernet segments are saturated (no more than 40 percent network utilization).	
	No shared Token Ring segments are saturated (no more than 70 percent network utilization).	
	No WAN links are saturated (no more than 70 percent network utilization).	
	The response time is generally less than 100 milliseconds (1/10 of a second).	
	No segments have more than 20 percent broadcasts/multicasts.	
	No segments have more than one CRC error per million bytes of data.	
	On the Ethernet segments, less than 0.1 percent of the packets result in collisions.	
	On the Token Ring segments, less than 0.1 percent of the packets are soft errors not related to ring insertion.	
	On the FDDI segments, there has been no more than one ring operation per hour not related to ring insertion.	
	The Cisco routers are not overutilized (5-minute CPU utilization no more than 75 percent).	
	The number of output queue drops has not exceeded more than 100 in an hour on any Cisco router.	
	The number of input queue drops has not exceeded more than 50 in an hour on any Cisco router.	
	The number of buffer misses has not exceeded more than 25 in an hour on any Cisco router.	
	The number of ignored packets has not exceeded more than 10 in an hour on any interface on a Cisco router.	

Extracting the New Customer Requirements

The following CCDA objectives are covered in this section:

8	Determine the customer's requirements for new applications, protocols, number of users, peak usage hours, security, and network management.
9	Diagram the flow of information for new applications.
10	Isolate the customer's criteria for accepting the performance of a network.
11	List some tools that will help you characterize new network traffic.

Now that you have determined what the customer currently has in its network, you need to determine the customer's new design needs. Combining a thorough assessment of the existing network with complete documentation of the customer's network design needs will provide you with all the information you need to begin the customer's new network design.

Cisco provides you with the following list of steps to help you organize the customer's networking needs. Each step is followed by criteria or questions to help gather the information:

Step 1   Characterize the customer's business constraints.

- Document the customer's budget.

- List the resources available for this project, the staffing, the training level, and the timelines.

Step 2   Identify the security requirements.

- Determine the security concerns of the customer.

- Document how much security the customer needs and who will be affected.

- List the type of security the customer needs—firewalls, access lists, and so on.

- Document the type of authentication required.

- List how much node security is required, as well as information on passwords, physical security, and access rights.

Step 3   Document the customer's manageability requirements.

- Identify the specific needs for the five manageability areas: fault management, accounting management, configuration management, performance management, and security management.

Step 4   Extract the customer's application requirements.

- Document the application requirements.

- Document any new applications, including the users and the information flow.

- List any new protocols required.

Step 5   Characterize the new network traffic.

- Characterize the new network traffic using methods similar to those you would use to characterize the existing network traffic. This is done by using the analysis tools covered earlier in the chapter.

- Capture parameters such as traffic load and traffic behavior.

Step 6   Characterize the performance requirements.

- Document the customer's requirements in the following areas:

    Response time—Time it takes to respond to a service request from a node.

    Accuracy—Comparison of useful traffic to transmission errors relative to total traffic.

    Availability—Amount of time the network is running

    Maximum network utilization—The maximum capacity of the network before it is considered to be saturated.

    Throughput—Quantity of data transferred between nodes in seconds.

    Efficiency—Measurement of how much effort is required to produce a certain amount of data throughput.

    Latency—Time between a node being ready for transmission and time for successful completion of the transmission.

Step 7   Identify specific customer needs.

- Document any other customer requirements or needs.

Characterizing Network Traffic

This next section is an overview of technologies to help you characterize network traffic.

Five areas will be covered in this section:

- Broadcast behavior
- Frame size
- Windowing
- Flow control
- Error-recovery mechanisms

Each topic also includes some tables to use as a reference to compare information you would have gathered in the previous sections.

Broadcast and Multicast Behavior

Broadcast behavior is critical to understanding network traffic. Three types of broadcasts and multicasts are covered in this exam:

- Broadcasts and multicasts from desktop protocols, such as AppleTalk, IP, IPX, and NetBIOS
- Broadcasts and multicasts from servers to advertise their services
- Broadcasts and multicasts from routing protocols such as RIP

The first types of broadcasts are those caused by routed or desktop protocols such as TCP/IP, AppleTalk, NetWare, and NetBIOS. For example, when your machine looks for an IP address from the DHCP server, it sends out a broadcast looking for the addressing service.

There are also applications that send broadcasts from workstations, such as a request for printing services. These printer servers advertise their services using broadcasts. Your workstation can also broadcast requests to these print servers to find out which printer server is available to receive the print job.

Routing and bridging protocols also use broadcasts and multicasts; this topic is discussed in detail in Chapter 6, "Designing for Specific Protocols."

Routers and VLANs control broadcasts and multicasts; therefore, if you have a flat network, your broadcast and multicast traffic can adversely affect your network's performance.

All these broadcasts and multicasts also affect the CPU of network devices by causing the CPU of a machine to process the unnecessary traffic. With the right type of network design, you can separate traffic to maximize the bandwidth. The following information comes from Cisco's technical marketing group for the effects of broadcasts:

- 100 broadcasts/multicasts per second used a noticeable 2 percent of the CPU power on a Pentium 120 MHz CPU with a 3Com Fast Etherlink PCI Ethernet adapter.

- 1300 broadcasts per second used 9 percent of the CPU power.

- 3000 broadcasts per second consumed 25 percent of the CPU power.

- CPU performance was measurably affected by as few as 30 broadcasts/multicasts per second on a generic i386 PC.

- Macintosh CPUs were affected by as few as 15 broadcasts/multicasts per second.

Table 2-7 contains recommendations for the number of workstations that should populate a segment (isolated by a VLAN or a router) for different protocols. Remember that the actual number of workstations per segment will depend on other factors, such as size of frames, type of traffic, and security. As discussed later in this chapter, workstations can generate varying traffic size, depending on their function. Therefore, machines that generate more traffic, such as multimedia workstations, should be limited per segment.

Table 2-7   *Scalability Constraints for Flat (Switched and Bridged) Networks*

Protocol	Maximum Number of Workstations
IP	500
IPX	300
AppleTalk	200
NetBIOS	200
Mixed	200

Frame Size

To improve network performance, you can manipulate the frame size so that it is the largest possible maximum transmission unit (MTU) for file transfer applications on that medium. Not all protocols support MTU configuration, and you must make sure that you avoid increasing the MTU too much. This would cause network performance issues because some devices such as routers need to process the frame by fragmenting it and then reassembling it. Many vendors and industry sources recommend using the default MTU value and not modifying the MTU. Remember that the calibration of the MTU should be done with caution.

In an IP network, you might be able to use a protocol stack that supports MTU discovery, which will automatically use the largest frame size that doesn't require any fragmentation. However, make sure that you check to see whether this feature is available and enabled.

Windowing and Flow Control

Windowing and flow control are error-control methods. Network-layer protocols use windowing and flow control. Some protocols, such as Novell's traditional NetWare Core

Protocol (NCP), used a method called the ping-pong approach, in which each request generated a response that used bandwidth.

IP, however, uses burst-mode protocols. These protocols send as much data as the receiver can handle. Examples of Transmission Control Protocol (TCP) applications that use this method are presented in Table 2-8.

Table 2-8   *Examples of TCP Applications That Use Burst-Mode Protocols*

Application	Port
File Transfer Protocol	Data uses port 20
	Control uses port 21
Telnet	23
Simple Mail Transfer Protocol (SMTP)	25
Hypertext Transport Protocol (HTTP)	80

User Datagram Protocol (UDP) does not offer windowing and flow control because it is connectionless. UDP, like TCP, is a Layer 4 (transport layer) protocol. Table 2-9 shows the applications that use this protocol and the associated port numbers. This type of information is often used in access lists and firewalls.

Table 2-9   *UDP Applications and Port Numbers*

Application	Port
Simple Network Management Protocol (SNMP)	161
Domain Name System (DNS)	53
Trivial File Transfer Protocol (TFTP)	69
Remote-procedure call (RPC)	111
Both the Network File System (NFS) and Network Information Services (NIS) use RPC	
Dynamic Host Configuration Protocol (DHCP) server	67
DHCP client	68

Error Recovery

Error recovery is a method that a protocol uses to ensure successful transmission of a packet. For example, retransmission is a method of error recovery, but if the protocol retransmits the data too quickly or too often, it can cause bandwidth degradation.

Some transport-layer protocols such as UDP don't use any error-recovery methods, much like data link-layer and network-layer protocols. However, connection-oriented protocols such as TCP do use error-recovery mechanisms. You can use a protocol analyzer to see whether any of your customer's protocols use effective error-recovery methods.

Characterizing Traffic Loads and Behaviors

The tables in this section cover the different broadcasts and traffic patterns that affect the network. The information in these charts can vary depending on use, but you can use these tables to understand the relative values and to understand the impact on the network.

In comparison, plain-text information is generally smaller than multimedia or illustrative information because of the screen image. For a multimedia or illustrative application, you must transfer not only the color and the data, but also the pixels for the actual image. Therefore, a dumb terminal part of a mainframe, such as the 3270 terminal emulation application, transfers only 4000 bytes. This includes characters and the screen information.

Table 2-10 shows what is added to a data packet based on the protocols used. It is interesting to note how the behavior of the protocol, such as 802.3 versus 802.5, differs and how that difference correlates to the overhead that protocol carries.

Table 2-10   *Traffic Overhead for Various Protocols*

Protocol	Notes	Total Bytes
Ethernet	Preamble = 8 bytes Header = 14 bytes CRC = 4 bytes Interframe gap (IFG) = 12 bytes Bit times = 96	38
802.3 with 802.2	Preamble = 8 bytes Header = 14 bytes LLC = 3 or 4 bytes SNAP (if present) = 5 bytes CRC = 4 bytes IFG = 12 bytes for 10 Mbps, or 1.2 bytes for 100 Mbps Bit times = 9.6	46
802.5 with 802.2	Starting delimiter = 1 byte Header = 14 bytes LLC = 3 or 4 bytes SNAP (if present) = 5 bytes CRC = 4 bytes Ending delimiter = 1 byte Frame status = 1 byte	29
FDDI with 802.2	Preamble = 8 bytes Starting delimiter = 1 byte Header = 13 bytes LLC = 3 or 4 bytes SNAP (if present) = 5 bytes CRC = 4 bytes Ending delimiter and frame status = about 2 bytes	36

Table 2-10   *Traffic Overhead for Various Protocols (Continued)*

Protocol	Notes	Total Bytes
HDLC	Flags = 2 bytes Addresses = 2 bytes Control = 1 or 2 bytes CRC = 4 bytes	10
IP	With no options	20
TCP	With no options	20
IPX	Does not include NCP	30
DDP	Phase 2 (long extended header)	13

Traffic Caused by Workstations

The traffic data shown in the following tables is generated by specific desktop protocols. This type of traffic would be in addition to Layer 2 traffic such as Ethernet and Token Ring overhead. Keep in mind that the information in the following tables can change depending on the version used. Table 2-11 shows packet information for NetWare client initialization.

Table 2-11   *Packets for NetWare Client Initialization*

Packet	Source	Destination	Packet Size in Bytes	Number of Packets	Total Bytes
GetNearestServer	Client	Broadcast	34	1	34
GetNearestServer response	Server or router	Client	66	Depends on the number of servers	66, if one server
Find network number	Client	Broadcast	40	1	40
Find network number response	Router	Client	40	1	40
Create connection	Client	Server	37	1	37
Create connection response	Server	Client	38	1	38
Negotiate buffer size	Client	Server	39	1	39
Negotiate buffer size response	Server	Client	40	1	40

continues

Table 2-11   *Packets for NetWare Client Initialization (Continued)*

Packet	Source	Destination	Packet Size in Bytes	Number of Packets	Total Bytes
Log out old connections	Client	Server	37	1	37
Log out response	Server	Client	38	1	38
Get server's clock	Client	Server	37	1	37
Get server's clock response	Server	Client	38	1	38
Download login.exe requests	Client	Server	50	Hundreds, depending on buffer size	Depends
Download login.exe response	Server	Client	Depends on buffer size	Hundreds, depending on buffer size	Depends
Login	Client	Server	37	1	37
Login response	Server	Client	38	1	38

The behaviors of the workstations differ depending on the state of the workstation. This means that the workstation's behavior during a boot process can be different. For example, an AppleTalk workstation that had been part of the network will retain its previous network number and node and try 10 times to verify that the network.node combination is unique. If the AppleTalk station has never been on a network or has moved, it sends 20 multicasts—10 multicasts with a provisional network number, and 10 multicasts with a network number supplied by a router that responded to the ZIPGetNetInfo request. Table 2-12 shows packet information for AppleTalk client initialization.

Table 2-12   *Packets for AppleTalk Client Initialization*

Packet	Source	Destination	Packet Size, in Bytes	Number of Packets	Total Bytes
AARP for ID	Client	Multicast	28	10	280
ZIPGetNetInfo	Client	Multicast	15	1	15
GetNetInfo response	Router(s)	Client	About 44	All routers respond	44, if one router
NBP broadcast request to check uniqueness of name	Client	Router	About 65	3	195

Table 2-12 *Packets for AppleTalk Client Initialization (Continued)*

Packet	Source	Destination	Packet Size, in Bytes	Number of Packets	Total Bytes
NBP forward request	Router	Other routers	Same	Same	Same
NBP lookup	Router	Multicast	Same	Same	Same
GetZoneList	Client	Router	12	1	12
GetZoneList reply	Router	Client	Depends on number and names of zones	1	Depends
NBP broadcast request for servers in zone	Client	Router	About 65	Once a second, if Chooser is still open; decays after 45 seconds	About 3000, if Chooser is closed after 45 seconds
NBP forward request	Router	Other routers	About 65	Same	Same
NBP lookup	Router	Multicast	About 65	Same	Same
NBP reply	Server(s)	Client	About 65	Depends on number of servers	Depends
ASP open session and AFP login	Client	Server	Depends	4	About 130
ASP and AFP replies	Server	Client	Depends	2	About 90

Table 2-13 shows packet information for NetBIOS client initialization.

Table 2-13 *Packets for NetBIOS Client Initialization*

Packet	Source	Destination	Packet Size, in Bytes	Number of Packets	Total Bytes
Check name	Client	Broadcast	44	6	264
Find name for each server	Client	Broadcast	44	Depends on number of servers	44, if 1 server
Find name response	Server(s)	Client	44	Depends	44, if 1 server

continues

Table 2-13 *Packets for NetBIOS Client Initialization (Continued)*

Packet	Source	Destination	Packet Size, in Bytes	Number of Packets	Total Bytes
Session initialize for each server	Client	Server	14	Depends	14, if 1 server
Session confirm	Server	Client	14	Depends	14, if 1 server

Tables 2-14 and 2-15 show TCP/IP workstation initializations with and without DHCP. It is recommended to use a DHCP server to manage the IP network addressing information. This will ensure that there are no IP conflicts.

Table 2-14 *Packets for Traditional TCP/IP Client Initialization*

Packet	Source	Destination	Packet Size, in Bytes	Number of Packets	Total Bytes
ARP to make sure its own address is unique (optional)	Client	Broadcast	28	1	28
ARP for any servers	Client	Broadcast	28	Depends on number of servers	Depends
ARP for router	Client	Broadcast	28	1	28
ARP response	Server(s) or router	Client	28	1	28

Add the overhead of Table 2-15 to a TCP/IP workstation that needs to use DHCP services.

Table 2-15 *Packets for DHCP Client Initialization*

Packet	Source	Destination	Packet Size, in Bytes	Number of Packets	Total Bytes
DHCP discover	Client	Broadcast	576	Once every few seconds, until client hears from DHCP	Depends
DHCP offer	Server	Broadcast	328	1	328
DHCP request	Client	Broadcast	576	1	576
DHCP ACK	Server	Broadcast	328	1	328

Table 2-15 *Packets for DHCP Client Initialization (Continued)*

Packet	Source	Destination	Packet Size, in Bytes	Number of Packets	Total Bytes
ARP to make sure its own address is unique	Client	Broadcast	28	3	84
ARP for client	Server	Broadcast	28	1	1
ARP response	Client	Server	28	1	28
DHCP request	Client	Server	576	1	576
DHCP ACK	Server	Client	328	1	328

Q&A

The following questions are designed to test your understanding of the topics covered in this chapter. When you have answered the questions, look up the answers in Appendix A. After you identify the subject matter you missed, review those sections in the chapter until you feel comfortable with this material.

1 After adding the new print server to the network, you see that the workstations are experiencing performance issues. What is a likely cause of this problem?

_____

_____

_____

2 What tool could you use to verify your answer to question #1?

_____

_____

_____

3 The customer wants to determine the maximum number of multimedia workstations that should populate a segment. What information do you need to request to find out an approximate number?

_____

_____

_____

4 Which network devices are used in creating separate segments to decrease workstation broadcasts?

_____

_____

_____

5 During the planning stage, the customer wants a 30 percent improvement on the response his users get from the database. During which phase of extracting the new customer requirements would you address this information?

_____

_____

_____

6 The customer is concerned about the Token Ring traffic on his network and wants to prove that the Token Ring network must be upgraded. What is your recommendation based on finding out that the Token Ring segment has more than 60 percent utilization?

_____

_____

_____

7 Which Cisco IOS command would you use to determine if there were any output queue drops?

_____

_____

_____

8 When helping to determine the network's health, would having 25 percent of multicasts on one segment be considered healthy?

_____

_____

_____

9 What is the saturation threshold for WAN links?

_____

_____

_____

10 What tool would you use to help monitor the switching traffic?

_____

_____

_____

Case Study

The following case study questions are based on the ongoing scenarios that are presented in the "Case Studies" section of Chapter 1, "Design Goals." If you want to familiarize yourself with the entire scenario, refer to that section before working through the following questions. The answers to these questions can be found in the "Case Study Answers" section at the end of this chapter.

Case Study #2: Pages Magazine, Inc.

1 List Pages Magazine's business goals.

_____

_____

_____

2 What routed protocols are used in the current network?

_____

_____

_____

3 Which routed protocols will be needed for the new network?

_____

_____

_____

4 Describe Ms. Phillips' concerns for staffing and managing her new network.

_____

_____

_____

5 Describe some benefits of implementing a network management solution.

_____

_____

_____

6 List the traffic that would need to be routed to all remote offices.

_____

_____

_____

Case Study Answers

1 List Pages Magazine's business goals.

The company wants to use networking technology to compete in the market by increasing productivity and identifying new opportunities. The company will use its new infrastructure to support the growth of its new offices.

2 What routed protocols are used in the current network?

IPX, IP, and AppleTalk

3 Which routed protocols will be needed for the new network?

The final network will be a pure IP network, but the migration to the new network will require AppleTalk.

4 Describe Ms. Phillips' concerns for staffing and managing her new network.

Ms. Phillips is concerned that she has limited staffing and has not stated that she will increase the number of staff that will support her new network. Her new network will include new applications as well as new infrastructure, which will require experienced staff to support. She is also concerned about the geographic expansion and how she would distribute her staff to support the rapid expansion.

5 Describe some benefits of implementing a network management solution.

Ms. Phillips described her staff as having moderate networking skills. There will be a substantial implementation of new technology, such as Internet security, new routing, and new applications. The network support people will have to be trained to support the infrastructure. Therefore, a well-planned centralized network management solution would have the following results:

— Cost savings on having to hire new support staff because the IT personnel at remote offices can be supported by more experienced staff located in central office.

— Diagnosis of problems would be more effective.

— Network management can support proactive monitoring to address possible issues before affecting users.

— Increased productivity would result due to a more reliable network.

— Increased devices could be supported with the same number of IT personnel.

— Travel costs would be reduced for sending experienced IT staff to remote offices.

— The solution would be scalable for additional offices.

6 List the traffic that would need to be routed to all remote offices.

NDS synchronization traffic, e-mail traffic, Internet access traffic, and network management traffic

Objectives Covered in This Chapter

The following is a list of the objectives covered in this chapter. The list of all the CCDA exam objectives and the chapters in which they are covered can be found in the Introduction of this book.

8	Determine the customer's requirements for new applications, protocols, number of users, peak usage hours, security, and network management.
9	Diagram the flow of information for new applications.
12	Predict the amount of traffic and the type of traffic caused by the applications, given charts that characterize typical network traffic.

CHAPTER 3

Application Considerations

The purpose of this chapter is to review the different types of applications that a network architect should consider when designing a network. Some network application families cannot be routed; others can. The network must provide a way to transport the traffic across wide-area network (WAN) links. Some network operating systems produce broadcast traffic that can be filtered. A CCDA must be able to identify the types of applications your clients use and must understand how those affect the network design.

"Do I Know This Already?" Quiz

The questions in the following quiz are designed to help you gauge how well you know the material covered in this chapter. Compare your answers with those found in Appendix A, "Answers to Quiz Questions." If you answer most or all the questions thoroughly and correctly, you might want to skim the chapter and proceed to the "Q&A" and "Case Studies" sections at the end of the chapter. If you find you need to review only certain subject matter, search the chapter for those sections that cover the objectives you need to review, and then test yourself with these question again, as well as with the "Q&A" and "Case Studies" questions. If you find the following questions too difficult, read the chapter carefully, until you feel you can easily answer these and the "Q&A" and "Case Studies" questions.

1 In which bridging environment does the frame contain the routing information to the destination?

_____

_____

_____

2 Which scheme provides a way to automatically assign IP addresses to devices on the network?

_____

_____

_____

3 Which session layer protocol is very common in Windows NT environments and can be bridged or routed over IP?

_____

_____

4 With which Novell protocol do devices broadcast services to the segment, routers build a table and forward these broadcasts to all other segments, and clients use the information to know what services are available in the network?

_____

_____

_____

5 In what protocol environment do client devices automatically select a network layer address and broadcast a probe to ensure that it is unique?

_____

_____

_____

6 What are route descriptors?

_____

_____

_____

7 With what technology can you scale SRB networks over WAN links and reduce NetBIOS queries where TCP is used between peers?

_____

_____

_____

8 What is the most scalable protocol used for file and print sharing in Windows NT networking?

_____

_____

_____

9 What methods are used to assign an IP address to a workstation at bootup?

_____

_____

_____

10 What are the three components of a typical firewall system?

_____

_____

_____

You can find the answers to these questions in Appendix A, "Answers to Quiz Questions."

Foundation Topics

IBM Networking

The CCDA objectives covered in this section are:

8	Determine the customer's requirements for new applications, protocols, number of users, peak usage hours, security, and network management.
9	Diagram the flow of information for new applications.
12	Predict the amount of traffic and the type of traffic caused by the applications, given charts that characterize typical network traffic.

This section covers the protocols and design methods used when internetworking with legacy IBM devices. Source-route bridging (SRB), data-link switching plus (DLSw+), and, briefly, Advanced Peer-to-Peer Networking (APPN) are discussed in this section.

Source-Route Bridging

IBM developed SRB in the mid-eighties as a way to bridge between Token Ring local-area networks (*LANs*). In SRB, the source determines the route to arrive at the destination node before sending an information frame to it. This differs from Ethernet transparent bridging, where the bridges build and maintain tables containing paths to data-link layer destinations. In SRB, the source node acquires the routes to destinations on the network using explorer frames.

In Figure 3-1, when a source node wishes to send information to a destination that is not on the local LAN, it sends out an explorer frame. Bridges receive the explorer frame in one interface and forward the frame out all other interfaces. Bridges add route information, called route descriptors, to the frames as they travel throughout the network. The route information includes each bridge and ring number over which the explorer frame has traveled (see Figure 3-2). In Figure 3-2, when the explorer frame reaches Bridge 6, it adds information about Ring 7/Bridge 6 and the outgoing Ring 3. At Bridge 4, route information of Bridge 4 and Ring 2 is added. The bridge value of the last route descriptor is set to 0, to indicate the destination has been reached. The information gathered by the exploration process makes up the routing information field (RIF) of a Token Ring frame.

Figure 3-1   *Source-Route Bridged Network*

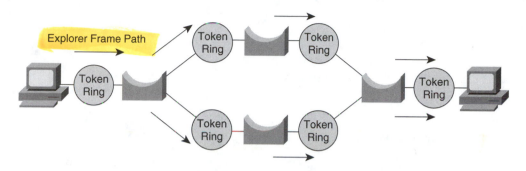

Figure 3-2   *SRB Ring/Bridge Routing Information*

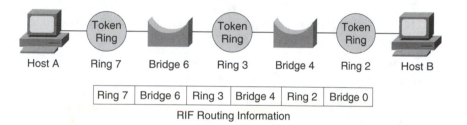

Ring 7	Bridge 6	Ring 3	Bridge 4	Ring 2	Bridge 0

RIF Routing Information

When the explorer frames arrive at the destination, the destination node sets the direction bit (also known as the D-bit) to 1 and sends the frame back to the source node via the same route it used to arrive at the destination. When multiple reply frames reach the source node, it usually uses the route of the first frame received. Other decision metrics include the minimum number of hops and the path with the largest maximum transmission unit (MTU) allowed.

Unlike transparent bridging, which uses the Spanning-Tree Protocol to form loop-free paths to data-link layer destinations, SRB is inherently loop-free and does not rely on the Spanning-Tree Protocol when delivering data. SRB can use Spanning-Tree Protocol when sending explorer frames, thus reducing the traffic generated during route discovery.

The routing information field is contained in the 802.5 frame. It is composed of a 2-byte RIF header and may contain one or more route descriptors (see Figure 3-3).

Figure 3-3 *Routing Information Field*

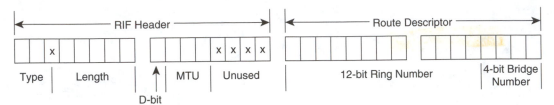

In the RIF first byte, the first 2 bits indicate the type of frame, as follows:

00—Indicates this is a regular frame that should be routed to the destination following the information in the route descriptors.

10—Indicates this is an all-rings explorer frame that should take all possible routes to the destination.

11—Indicates this is a Spanning-Tree explorer frame that should take only one path to the destination.

The next bit is unused. The 5 least significant bits in the first byte indicate the total length of the RIF field, including the 2-byte header. A RIF with only one bridge hop is 6 bytes long.

The most significant bit in the second byte is the D-bit, which determines whether the route descriptors in the RIF header are processed left-to-right or right-to-left. A value of 0 indicates left-to-right. A value of 1 indicates right-to-left.

As displayed in Figure 3-3, the next 3 bits indicate the largest frame size that can be handled along a designated route (011 indicates 4472 bytes). The lower 4 bits are not used.

As indicated in Figure 3-3, the route descriptors are 2 bytes long. The first 12 bits are used to indicate the ring number. The 4 least significant bits are used to indicate the bridge number.

SRB Design with Cisco Routers

SRB is limited in that it is a flat network topology in the data-link layer. Another limitation is the maximum hop count of seven bridges. Token Ring chipsets were originally designed to process two rings. Routers can be introduced into the network to help overcome these limitations. This is accomplished with the concept of the virtual ring (see Figure 3-4). Consider each router interface as a minibridge that connects the external ring to the internal virtual ring. The ring number is used in the RIF field as in any other physical ring. To configure the virtual ring group, use the global command **source-bridge ring-group** *virtual-ring-group-number.* Each Token Ring LAN is bridged to the virtual ring using the interface command **source-bridge** *ring-number bridge-number virtual-ring-group-number.*

Figure 3-4   *Virtual Ring*

Traffic from Ring 1 to Ring 3 flows through Bridge 1, then Ring 5, and finally Bridge 3.

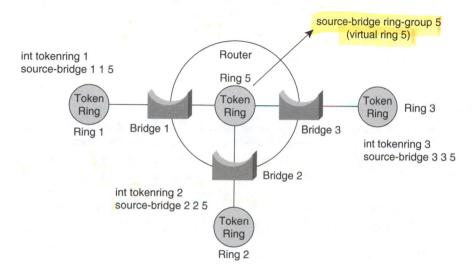

The virtual ring can be extended to several routers in a cloud, to connect remote Token Rings (see Figure 3-5). Although there are several router hops between Token Ring 1 and Token Ring 2, the RIF field for a frame will only show two bridge hops.

Figure 3-5   *Extended Virtual Ring*

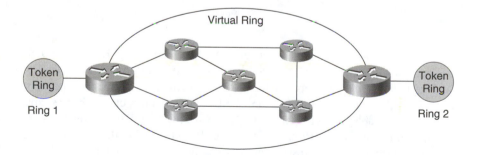

Advanced Peer-to-Peer Networking

With the limitations of Systems Network Architecture (SNA) and the growth of communications requirements, IBM introduced its second-generation SNA: Advanced Peer-to-Peer Networking (APPN). With APPN, IBM moved from the mainframe to a peer-based hierarchy composed of network nodes (NNs), end nodes (ENs), and low-entry nodes (LENs).

The CCDA test does not include detailed questions on APPN.

Data-Link Switching Plus

Data-link switching (DLSw) is documented in RFC 1795. IBM originally submitted it to the IETF as RFC 1434, to overcome some of the limitations on SRB networks, especially in WANs. The Cisco implementation of DLSw is called *DLSw Plus (DLSw+)*. Some of the benefits of implementing DLSw+ are that link-layer acknowledgements and keep-alive messages of SNA and NetBIOS traffic do not have to travel through the WAN. Also, DLSw+ traffic can be rerouted around link failures and can be prioritized on WAN links, while SRB does not provide this ability. Figure 3-6 shows an example of a DLSw+ network.

Figure 3-6   *DLSw+ Network*

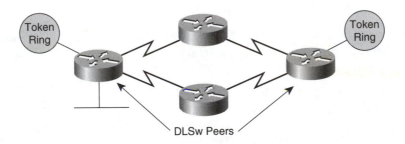

End systems can attach to the DLSw network from Token Ring, Ethernet, FDDI, Qualified Logical Link Control (QLLC), and Synchronous Data Link Control (SDLC) networks. Although there are other methods, the preferred method for establishing peer connections is using TCP. After a connection is established, the peer routers can exchange capabilities. Circuits are established between end systems (SNA and NetBIOS). NetBIOS names can be configured to prevent NetBIOS Name Queries from traversing the DLSw network; Media Access Control (MAC) addresses can be configured in the same manner, to reduce SRB explorer frames.

The basic configuration of DLSw is quite simple. Each router with attached networks is configured as a local peer. Remote peers are then configured to remote routers. It is preferable to use an IP address assigned to an internal loopback interface as the local peer address. Loopback interfaces provide a virtual interface and do not fail if a physical link fails, thus providing a stable peer address. For designs with multiple branches connecting to a hub site, the **promiscuous** keyword can be used to permit remote peers to connect without being individually specified. See Figure 3-7 for a sample configuration.

Figure 3-7   *DLSw Sample Network*

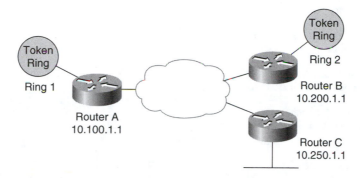

The configuration for Router A is displayed in Example 3-1.

Example 3-1   *DLSw Configuration—Router A*

```
!
source-bridge ring-group 100
!
dlsw local-peer peer-id 10.100.1.1 promiscuous
dlsw remote-peer 0 tcp 10.200.1.1
!
interface tokenring 0
source-bridge 1 1 100
!
interface loopback 0
ip address 10.100.1.1 255.255.255.255
!
```

The configuration for Router B is displayed in Example 3-2.

Example 3-2   *DLSw Configuration—Router B*

```
!
source-bridge ring-group 200
!
dlsw local-peer peer-id 10.200.1.1
dlsw remote-peer 0 tcp 10.100.1.1
!
interface tokenring 0
source-bridge 2 1 200
!
interface loopback 0
ip address 10.200.1.1 255.255.255.255
!
```

The configuration for Router C is displayed in Example 3-3.

Example 3-3 *DLSw Configuration—Router C*

```
!
bridge-group 1 protocol ieee
!
dlsw bridge-group 1
!
dlsw local-peer peer-id 10.250.1.1
dlsw remote-peer 0 tcp 10.100.1.1
!
interface loopback 0
ip address 10.250.1.1 255.255.255.255
!
interface Ethernet 0
bridge-group 1
```

Notice that Router A only defines a remote peer for Router B. It does not need to define Router C as a peer because the **promiscuous** keyword is used to accept connections from remote peers without having to define them. Router C must define Router A as a remote peer because the **promiscuous** keyword was not used.

Microsoft Windows Networking

The CCDA objectives covered in this section are as follows:

8	Determine the customer's requirements for new applications, protocols, number of users, peak usage hours, security, and network management.
9	Diagram the flow of information for new applications.
12	Predict the amount of traffic and the type of traffic caused by the applications, given charts that characterize typical network traffic.

Microsoft's network operating system is composed of Windows NT Server and several client operating systems—Windows NT Workstation, Windows 95, and Windows 98.

NT Protocols

NT uses the session layer NetBIOS protocol for file and print sharing, messaging, and name resolution. Client PCs discover other nodes on the network using NetBIOS. Users can browse the network for shares and services, but NetBIOS produces many broadcasts on the network. Services are searched for using NAME_QUERY requests and replies. In its historical environment (NetBIOS was created by IBM), NetBIOS runs over NetBEUI. NetBEUI is a data-link layer protocol that cannot be routed; it must be bridged. Large bridged networks run into high utilization caused by uncontrollable and unfiltered broadcasts. NetBIOS over NetBEUI does not scale well for large networks; it should only be used in small LANs.

NetBIOS can also run over Internetwork Packet Exchange (IPX); in NT, this is called NWLink. This solution can be used in small to medium networks or in networks that already are running the Novell IPX protocol. This implementation uses IPX packet type 20.

The most scalable solution is to run NetBIOS over TCP/IP. It is recommended for medium to large networks. With NetBIOS over TCP/IP, NetBIOS broadcasts still exist, but they run on top of TCP port 137. This provides the ability to filter NetBIOS, if necessary, using TCP port access lists.

Dynamic Host Configuration Protocol

Until the Dynamic Host Configuration Protocol (DHCP) was developed, automatic assignment of IP addresses to hosts was virtually obsolete. The only method available was BOOTP (RFC 0951), which required knowledge of the MAC layer address and preconfiguration of the IP address for a particular MAC on a BOOTP server before the station could get an address. If a station had to be moved from one subnet to another, the BOOTP server had to be reconfigured.

DHCP (RFC 2131/1541/1531) solved these problems by creating address scopes in subnets to be assigned automatically to DHCP clients. A scope is a range of subnet addresses used to dynamically assign IP addresses. This provides the benefit of being able to move a laptop from one subnet to another and be assigned an IP address.

Additional benefits are that other information, called DHCP options, can be automatically loaded to the PC client. DHCP options include subnet mask, default gateway, WINS server, Domain Name System (DNS) server, TFTP server, and others. Microsoft provides a DHCP server application as part of Windows NT. Cisco also provides a DHCP server called Cisco DNS/DHCP Manager.

A network designer must keep in mind the locations of DHCP servers in the network. Subnets without a local DHCP server require that the router forward the DHCP discover request to the DHCP servers. The **ip helper-address** command is used to accomplish this task. Looking at Figure 3-8, the interfaces Ethernet 0 and Ethernet 1 are configured to forward DHCP discover requests to the DHCP server.

The packet contains the source subnet information so that the server knows from which scope to assign IP addresses. Ethernet 2 does not need the **ip helper-address** command because the server is on the same subnet.

Figure 3-8 *DHCP Traffic Flow*

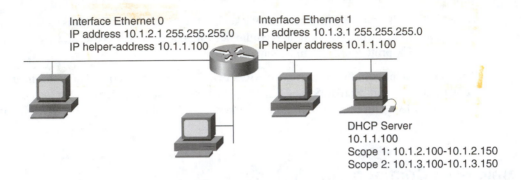

Interface Ethernet 0
IP address 10.1.2.1 255.255.255.0
IP helper-address 10.1.1.100

Interface Ethernet 1
IP address 10.1.3.1 255.255.255.0
IP helper address 10.1.1.100

DHCP Server
10.1.1.100
Scope 1: 10.1.2.100-10.1.2.150
Scope 2: 10.1.3.100-10.1.3.150

Windows Internet Naming System

Microsoft uses NetBIOS to resolve friendly device names to IP addresses in Windows. By default, Windows computers send NAME_QUERY broadcasts to all devices on a segment, and the device with the NetBIOS-friendly name being requested responds with its IP address. To reduce the number of broadcasts generated by NetBIOS devices, it is recommended that Windows network clients use the Windows Internet Naming System (WINS).

WINS is a service (included with Windows NT Server) that provides a dynamic NetBIOS name registration database similar to the service DNS provides for Internet names. WINS server IP addresses can be automatically assigned to PCs using DHCP. Windows clients register their NetBIOS names with the WINS server upon startup and then send unicast requests directly to the WINS server, to resolve NetBIOS names to IP addresses, virtually eliminating NAME_QUERY broadcasts. In Figure 3-9, in the NetBIOS over TCP/IP environment without WINS, PC A sends NetBIOS broadcasts for name resolution and will not locate remote clients unless the NetBIOS broadcast is bridged across the WAN. As shown on the right of Figure 3-9, using WINS, the unicast request generated by PC A is routed, and PC A gets the information from the WINS server.

Figure 3-9   *NetBIOS over TCP/IP and WINS Traffic Flow*

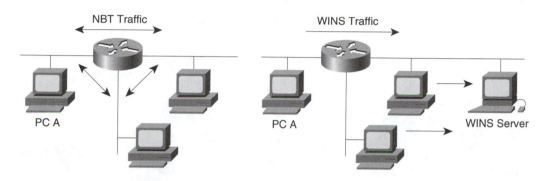

Multimedia Networking

The CCDA objectives covered in this section are as follows:

8	Determine the customer's requirements for new applications, protocols, number of users, peak usage hours, security, and network management.
9	Diagram the flow of information for new applications.
12	Predict the amount of traffic and the type of traffic caused by the applications, given charts that characterize typical network traffic.

With the introduction of technologies to integrate data with voice and video, a network designer must consider the time-sensitive nature of these applications. Packet voice introduces the ability to bypass toll charges by using the data network as a voice transport for telephone calls. When designing for video applications, consider using multicasting to reduce the amount of duplicate unicast traffic on the network.

Packet Voice

With the converging of data and voice networks, the introduction of packet voice technology provides the means for companies to save toll charges on voice telephone calls. Voice is digitized into packets, cells, or frames, is sent as data throughout the networks, and is then converted back to analog voice (see Figure 3-10). Calls are placed on telephones attached to routers. The routers digitize the voice and then forward the calls on the WAN links. If it is determined that sufficient bandwidth is not available on the data network, the call is forwarded over the Public Switched Telephone Network (PSTN). Calls placed outside the company's intranet are forwarded to the PSTN.

Figure 3-10   *Packet Voice*

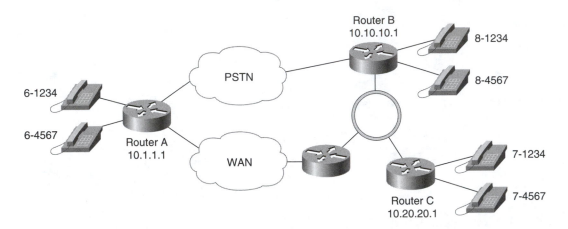

With Voice over IP (VoIP) technology, voice is digitized into IP packets. A dial plan is created to list the IP destinations of VoIP telephones and outbound telephones. When a number is dialed on a telephone attached to a router, it looks at the digits and routes the call to the appropriate destination. For example, in Figure 3-10, if a call to 8-1234 is placed from telephone 6-1234, Router A will forward the packets with voice data to Router B. Router B will convert the digitized voice into analog signals and send them out its voice interface to telephone 8-1234. Table 3-1 shows the dial plan for Router A in Figure 3-10.

Table 3-1   *Router a Dial Plan*

Phone Number	Destination
Calls to 8-*xxxx*	Forward to IP: 10.10.10.1
Calls to 7-*xxxx*	Forward to IP: 10.20.20.1
Outside calls	Forward to PSTN
6-1234	Voice port 1/0
6-4567	Voice port 1/1

In VoIP, Real-Time Transport Protocol (RTP) is used to transport audio streams. RTP runs over User Datagram Protocol (UDP), but there is no specific port assigned. The only requirement is that the data is transported on an even port and RTCP (RTP Control Protocol) is carried on the next odd port. However, ports 5004 and 5005 have been reserved for those applications that choose to use them.

UDP, in contrast to TCP, is a connectionless protocol that relies on upper layer protocols for acknowledgement and error checking. UDP is preferred to TCP for voice due to the time-sensitive nature of voice transmissions. Since voice applications are sensitive to the accumulation of delay, any Quality of Service techniques used on the network must prioritize these RTP/UDP IP packets over other traffic, such as FTP and HTTP. RTP header compression can also be used on WAN links to reduce the size of voice packets.

Video Streams

Video applications generally fall into two types—bidirectional and unidirectional. Videoconferencing between remote sites is an example of a point-to-point video application. Traffic flow is bidirectional in videoconferencing. The flow of a video stream from one source to many users on the network is an example of unidirectional flow.

Multicasting can help reduce the total amount of bandwidth used on the network (see Figure 3-11). In Figure 3-11, traffic flows through the network, and the video stream is sent to only those networks with registered clients. Note that the video stream is sent once from the server; there are no duplicate unicasts being sent. The video stream is sent to a multicast address.

Figure 3-11   *Video Stream Traffic Flow Using Multicast Routing*

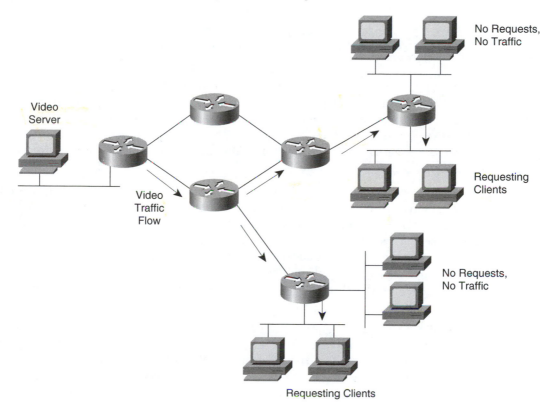

In multicast environments, a multicast server registers with its local router as a multicast group number. Clients register with the local router, requesting a multicast group. Using a multicast routing protocol, the routers determine the paths to forward the video stream through the network to only those segments that have a client that requested the multicast group. Client and server registration is done using the Internet Group Management Protocol (IGMP). More information on IGMP can be found in RFC 1112. The most current multicast routing protocol is Protocol Independent Multicast (PIM). For more information on PIM go to http://www.ietf.org/html.charters/pim-charter.html.

Novell Application Services

The CCDA objectives covered in this section are as follows:

8	Determine the customer's requirements for new applications, protocols, number of users, peak usage hours, security, and network management.
9	Diagram the flow of information for new applications.
12	Predict the amount of traffic and the type of traffic caused by the applications, given charts that characterize typical network traffic.

In the Novell IPX environment, network resources advertise their services using the Service Advertising Protocol (SAP). These resources are devices such as file and print servers. Each SAP service has a unique SAP number. For example, a file server is listed as 0004(hex), a printer server is listed as 0007(hex), and a Novell SNA gateway is listed as 010f(hex). A list of common SAP numbers can be obtained at ftp://ftp.isi.edu/in-notes/iana/assignments/novell-sap-numbers.

Routers gather the SAP information, build a SAP table, and then, every 60 seconds, forward SAP updates to other routers, out all LAN and WAN segments. Each SAP update may contain up to seven services. This traffic is in addition to the IPX Routing Information Protocol (RIP) routing table updates, which occur every 60 seconds, at 50 routes per update packet. Even if there is no change in the network and no change in the services, this traffic is still generated every 60 seconds. In large networks, this broadcast traffic may become too large and overwhelm slow WAN links or high utilization networks. There are several ways to reduce the amount of SAP traffic:

- **Use IPX SAP filters**—Apply access lists to interfaces, to filter SAP sources that are not necessary in other areas of the network. This can deny local print devices to a segment but still permit file services to other segments. This author has seen a network with a total of 1000 SAPs reduced to 300, using SAP filters. Use access lists in the range from 1000 to 1099 for SAP filters.

- **Use NetWare Link Services Protocol (NLSP) for routing IPX**—NLSP is NetWare's link-state routing protocol (IPX RIP is distance-vector) for routing IPX traffic. The benefit is that it does not send routing and service information in a periodic fashion but only when a change has occurred. This significantly reduces the amount of periodic broadcast traffic on the network. NLSP also supports hierarchical network design with route summarization.

- **Use Enhanced IGRP (EIGRP) for routing IPX**—EIGRP also reduces the amount of periodic SAP broadcasts because it sends updates only when changes occur. The design involves using IPX RIP in the LAN interfaces on the router and using EIGRP for the WAN interfaces. EIGRP automatically redistributes the routes and services to and from IPX RIP/SAP.

AppleTalk Services

The CCDA objectives covered in this section are as follows:

8	Determine the customer's requirements for new applications, protocols, number of users, peak usage hours, security, and network management.
9	Diagram the flow of information for new applications.
12	Predict the amount of traffic and the type of traffic caused by the applications, given charts that characterize typical network traffic.

AppleTalk uses the concept of zones to form a logical grouping of nodes, similar to the workgroups found in the network neighborhood of the Windows environment. Devices look for resources in their zone, so groupings are generally departmental, such as engineering, marketing, and research. Zones allow users to find resources in their workgroup, regardless of physical location, without having to browse the entire device list in the Apple Chooser. Zones can span networks and can contain nodes in multiple cable ranges on different segments.

Zones control broadcast traffic in AppleTalk networks. As the network grows, more zones can be created to control the traffic. The Zone Information Protocol (ZIP) maintains the network-to-zone mappings in AppleTalk routers. ZIP maintains a zone information table (ZIT) that can be viewed on the router. ZIP filters can be used to control access of a network to applications on a zone. For example, a GetZoneList filter can be configured to deny access to the Human Resources zone for hosts on a specific network. AppleTalk access lists are from 600 to 699.

Firewall Services

The CCDA objectives covered in this section are as follows:

8	Determine the customer's requirements for new applications, protocols, number of users, peak usage hours, security, and network management.
9	Diagram the flow of information for new applications.
12	Predict the amount of traffic and the type of traffic caused by the applications, given charts that characterize typical network traffic.

A firewall is a system of devices and applications used to protect one network from another untrusted network, such as the Internet (see Figure 3-12). Usually it is implemented using a three-layer design. On the outside there is a filtering router that implements access lists, to permit access to hosts only in the isolation LAN. In the isolation LAN, hosts are installed to provide services such as Web server, DNS, FTP servers, e-mail relays, and Telnet. These hosts are usually referred to as bastion hosts. An inside filtering router permits access from the internal network to the isolation LAN. There should be no devices communicating directly from the inside network to the outside router (no back doors).

Figure 3-12 *Firewall System*

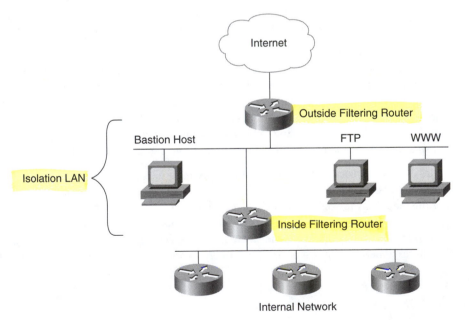

Figure 3-12 shows a diagram of a three-layer firewall system. The outside filtering router should restrict Telnet access to itself, use static routing, and encrypt passwords. It should permit access to the bastion hosts based on specific TCP/UDP port numbers. Use the **established** keyword to allow inbound TCP packets from established TCP sessions.

The inside filtering router should also allow inbound TCP packets. It should permit access to bastion hosts in the isolation LAN, such as proxy services, DNS, and Web servers.

Sites requiring strong security can use the Cisco PIX Firewall in addition to or instead of packet-filtering routers. The Cisco PIX Firewall is a hardware device that offers more robust security, provides Network Address Translation (NAT), and verifies inbound traffic state information. NAT translations can be static and/or dynamic and are verified on the command-line interface. The PIX Firewall operates on a secure real-time kernel. An architecture with a PIX Firewall could be like that shown in Figure 3-13. The PIX Firewall will control access between the outside and the isolation network and between the isolation network and the inside. NAT can be used to translate inside node IP addresses to an outside IP address pool.

Figure 3-13   *PIX Firewall*

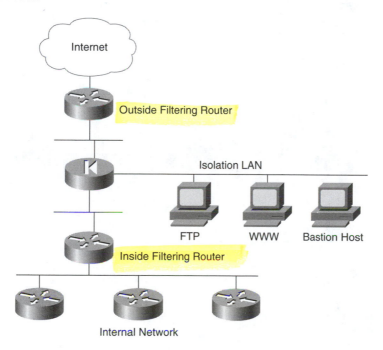

Mail Application Flow

The CCDA objectives covered in this section are as follows:

8	Determine the customer's requirements for new applications, protocols, number of users, peak usage hours, security, and network management.
9	Diagram the flow of information for new applications.
12	Predict the amount of traffic and the type of traffic caused by the applications, given charts that characterize typical network traffic.

Messaging application servers are usually deployed throughout the enterprise, based on the number of users and geographical distances. Usually, a hierarchy is used to deploy mail servers. E-mail traffic will follow the hierarchy and will be bidirectional. The Simple Mail Transfer Protocol (SMTP) gateway will reside at some point near the top of the hierarchy, providing transport to Internet messaging. Figure 3-14 shows an example of e-mail traffic flow.

Figure 3-14 *E-Mail Traffic Flow*

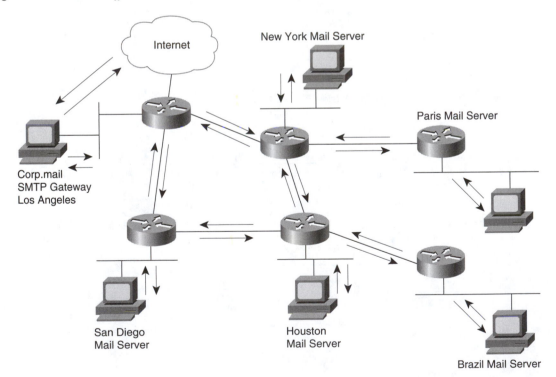

Future Application Plan

The CCDA objectives covered in this section are as follows:

8	Determine the customer's requirements for new applications, protocols, number of users, peak usage hours, security, and network management.
9	Diagram the flow of information for new applications.
12	Predict the amount of traffic and the type of traffic caused by the applications, given charts that characterize typical network traffic.

When designing for current and future applications, document the application characteristics. Include information such as the following:

- Application name.
- Application type—e-mail, file, database, and so on.
- Protocols used—IP (UDP/TCP), IPX, SNA, and so on.
- Number of users.
- Number of hosts.
- Other comments—Include information such as future requirements in Quality of Service, Network Address Translation, and scalability.

Attempt to characterize the application traffic flow as one of the following:

- **Terminal/host**—These are applications with low-volume character traffic (keyboard entries) streams being sent to the host and the host returning many characters (a screen). Telnet and TN3720 terminals are examples of this type of traffic flow.

- **Client/server**—The traffic flow is bidirectional and asymmetric. Traffic sent to the host is usually less than 100 bytes, and the return traffic from the host can be more than 1500 bytes. Examples include Windows NT, Novell NetWare, AppleShare, Banyan Vines, and HTTP.

  In HTTP, clients use a web browser, such as Netscape Navigator or MS Explorer, to access web servers. Traffic from the client to the server involves URL requests. The server sends the web page, which contains text and graphics, to the client. Traffic is bidirectional and asymmetric.

  In FTP, clients connect to an FTP server. If a **get** command is issued, files are transferred from the server to the client; if a **put** command is used, the traffic flow is the opposite.

- **Peer/peer**—This traffic flow is bidirectional and symmetric. Communications devices within a workgroup use the same types of protocols and applications. Users sharing files and directories on their workstations with others is an example of peer-to-peer traffic. Other examples include NFS and videoconferencing.

- **Server/server**—This type includes traffic between file servers for directory information (Windows NT, Novell), load balancing, and redundancy. E-mail servers also communicate, to exchange mail information.

Foundation Summary

Foundation Summary is a section presented in a concise format to provide quick reference information relating to the objectives covered in this chapter.

Table 3-2   *IBM Networking*

Source-route bridging (SRB)	• Explorer frames used to find route to destination.
	• RIF field contains ring/bridge route descriptors.
Data Link Switching Plus (DLSw+)	• Provides a way to send SNA and NetBIOS frames over an IP network.
	• Operates over TCP/IP.
	• Can control SNA explorer and NetBIOS NAME_QUERY frames.

Table 3-3   *Microsoft Networking*

NetBIOS over TCP/IP	• NetBIOS over NetBUEI cannot be routed.
	• NetBIOS over TCP/IP is more scalable than NetBIOS over NetBUEI because it runs over IP.
DHCP	• Used to automatically assign an IP address and a subnet mask to a device.
	• DHCP options include default gateway, WINS server IP address, and DNS server IP address.
	• Use **ip helper-address** command to forward DHCP requests to the DHCP server.
WINS	• Used to resolve NetBIOS names to IP addresses.
	• Clients and servers register their NetBIOS names to the WINS server.
NT Replication	• Server-to-server communication that contains NT domain information.

Table 3-4	*Multimedia*	
	Packet Voice	• Voice is digitized into packets, cells, or frames and is sent as data throughout the network. • This traffic is time sensitive. • In VoIP, voice is converted into IP packets. These packets must have priority over other non-time-sensitive traffic.
	Video	• Videoconferencing is an example of bidirectional traffic and point-to-point traffic. • Video streams are unidirectional and point-to-multipoint. Use multicasting to reduce traffic on the network.

Table 3-5	*Novell Application Services*	
	Service Advertising Protocol (SAP)	• Resources advertise their services using SAP. • Routers build an SAP table and broadcast it every 60 seconds.
	Reducing SAP traffic	• Implement SAP filters. • Use NLSP for routing IPX. • Use Enhanced IGRP for routing IPX.

Table 3-6	*Firewall Services*	
	Three-layer design	• Includes outside filtering router, isolation LAN, and inside filtering router. • No direct access from the Internet to the corporate network.
	Outside filtering router	• Provides access only to the isolation LAN devices from the Internet.
	Isolation LAN	• WWW, FTP, and e-mail servers reside on this LAN.
	Inside filtering router	• Provides access to the isolation LAN from the internal network.
	Cisco PIX Firewall	• Used to provide stateful packet inspection and Network Address Translation.

Table 3-7	*Application Characterization*	
	Document applications	• List application names, types, protocols used, numbers of hosts, and other particular information.
	Characterize application traffic flow	• Terminal/host. • Client/server. • Peer/peer. • Server/server.

Q&A

The following questions are designed to test your understanding of the topics covered in this chapter. Once you have answered the questions, you can find the answers in Appendix A, "Answers to Quiz Questions." After you identify the subject matter you missed, review those sections in the chapter until you feel comfortable with this material.

1 What session layer protocol is common in Windows NT environments when layered over TCP it can be routed?

_____

_____

_____

2 You can find WWW and FTP servers in what network that the Internet community can access?

_____

_____

_____

3 What is a method to reduce Novell SAP broadcast traffic on the network?

_____

_____

_____

4 HTTP is an example of what type of traffic flow?

_____

_____

_____

5 What access list would you use on an outside filtering router to permit access to the isolation LAN? Assume the isolation LAN is 201.201.201.0/24.

_____

_____

_____

6 What Token Ring field consists of route descriptors?

_____

_____

_____

7 What should you use to overcome the limitations of SRB in large networks?

_____

_____

_____

8 The Cisco PIX Firewall may be used to do what?

_____

_____

_____

9 What service is used to resolve NetBIOS names to IP addresses?

_____

_____

_____

10 What access list would you use on an internal filtering router to permit traffic between the isolation LAN and the internal network? Assume the isolation LAN is 201.201.201.64/26.

_____

_____

_____

11 What technique is used to reduce the amount of repetitive unicast traffic?

_____

_____

_____

12 What type of traffic flow is how small-bandwidth keyboard character streams are sent to the host?

_____

_____

_____

13 What is a logical grouping of nodes in AppleTalk to control broadcasts?

_____

_____

_____

14 What are examples of client/server traffic flow applications?

_____

_____

_____

15 With this technology a user may connect a laptop to the network and automatically have an IP address, subnet mask, default gateway, DNS server, and WINS server assigned.

_____

_____

_____

16 DHCP stands for what?

_____

_____

_____

17 What are route descriptors?

_____

_____

_____

Case Studies

The following case study questions are based on the ongoing scenarios that are presented in the "Case Studies" section of Chapter 1, "Design Goals." If you want to familiarize yourself with the entire scenario, refer to that section before working through the following questions. The answers to these questions can be found in the "Case Study Answers" section at the end of this chapter.

Case Study #1: GHY Resources

1 List the existing applications used at GHY.

_____

_____

_____

2 Diagram the traffic flow between the Novell servers.

3 Assume that each NetWare file server is also a local e-mail server. Diagram the messaging traffic flow to clients.

4 What could be a possible explanation for the broadcast storms that the protocol analyzer reports?

_____

_____

_____

5 What are possible solutions to reduce the SAP traffic on the WAN links?

_____

_____

_____

Case Study #2: Pages Magazine, Inc.

1 What applications are being used at Pages?

_____

_____

_____

2 Are there any new applications being introduced?

_____

_____

_____

Case Study Answers

Case Study #1: GHY Resources

1 List the existing applications used at GHY.

— **Office applications residing on Novell Servers.**

— **E-mail.**

— **Business applications residing on the HP 3000s.**

2 Diagram the traffic flow between the Novell servers.

Figure 3-15 shows a diagram of the traffic flow.

Figure 3-15 *The traffic flow between the Novell servers of GHY Resources*

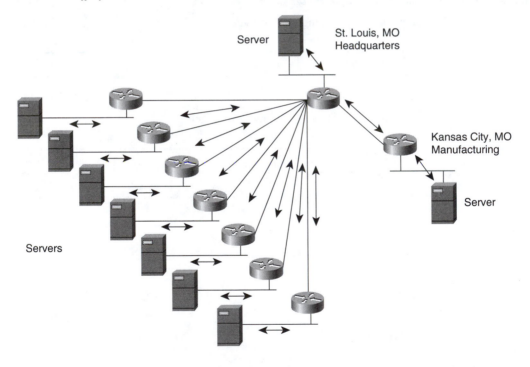

3 Assume that each NetWare file server is also a local e-mail server. Diagram the messaging traffic flow to clients.

Figure 3-16 shows a diagram of the messaging traffic flow to clients.

Figure 3-16   *The messaging traffic flow of GHY Resources*

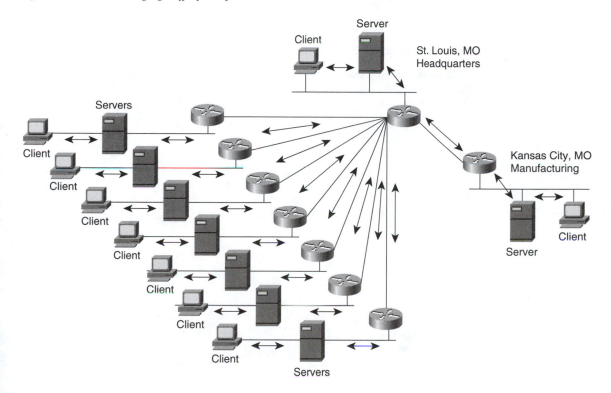

4 What could be a possible explanation for the broadcast storms that the protocol analyzer reports?

SAP broadcast traffic. Devices at each remote site are generating SAP broadcasts that are being propagated onto the WAN.

5 What are possible solutions to reduce the SAP traffic on the WAN links?

Implement SAP filters. Filter SAPs from devices at the remote sites so that they are not propagated onto the WAN unless necessary.

Case Study #2: Pages Magazine, Inc.

1 What applications are being used at Pages?

— **Novell services.**

— **AppleTalk graphics applications.**

— **cc:Mail.**

2 Are there any new applications being introduced?

With the new Internet connectivity, Novell GroupWise e-mail and HTTP traffic will be introduced.

Objectives Covered in this Chapter

The following is a list of the objectives covered in this chapter. The list of CCDA exam design objectives and the chapters in which they are covered can be found in the Introduction.

2	Assemble Cisco product lines into an end-to-end networking solution.
13	Describe the advantages, disadvantages, scalability issues, and applicability of standard internetwork topologies.
14	Draw a topology map that meets the customer's needs and includes a high-level view of internetworking devices and interconnecting media.
15	Recognize scalability constraints and issues for standard LAN technologies.
16	Recommend Cisco products and LAN technologies that will meet a customer's requirements for performance, capacity, and scalability in small- to medium-sized networks.
17	Update the network topology drawing you created in the previous section to include hardware and media.

CHAPTER 4

Network Topologies and LAN Design

This chapter reviews the topologies used in network design and covers the technologies and design approaches used when designing a local-area network (LAN). The hierarchical, redundant, and secure topology models are covered. Technologies like Ethernet, Fast Ethernet, FDDI, and Token Ring are also covered in this chapter. This chapter also discusses the characteristics of repeaters, bridges, switches, and routers, as well as how to apply these devices in a LAN environment. Finally, this chapter covers the Cisco products used in local-area networks.

"Do I Know This Already?" Quiz

The questions in the following quiz are designed to help you gauge how well you know the material covered in this chapter. Compare your answers with those found in Appendix A, "Answers to Quiz Questions." If you answer most or all of the questions thoroughly and correctly, you might want to skim the chapter and proceed to the "Q&A" and "Case Studies" sections at the end of the chapter. If you find you need to review only certain subject matter, search the chapter for only those sections that cover the objectives you need to review and then test yourself with those question again, as well as the "Q&A" and "Case Studies" questions. If you find the following questions too difficult, read the chapter carefully until you feel you can easily answers these and the "Q&A" and "Case Studies" questions.

1 What OSI layer does a bridge operate?

_____

_____

_____

2 The 10Base2 Ethernet media is commonly referred as?

_____

_____

_____

3 What is the recommended maximum number of nodes that should be used in a multi-protocol LAN segment?

_____

_____

_____

4 Bridges control collision domains, broadcast domains, or both?

_____

_____

_____

5 What is the maximum segment size in a 100BaseT network?

_____

_____

_____

6 What is the maximum segment size in a 10Base2 network?

_____

_____

_____

7 Routers operate on what OSI layer?

_____

_____

_____

8 Fast Ethernet is covered by which IEEE standard?

_____

_____

_____

9 What is 10Base5 commonly referred to as?

_____

_____

_____

10 What device controls a broadcast domain?

_____

_____

_____

You can find the answers to these questions in Appendix A, "Answers to Quiz Questions."

Foundation Topics

LAN Topology Design

The CCDA objectives covered in this section are as follows:

13	Describe the advantages, disadvantages, scalability issues, and applicability of standard internetwork topologies.
14	Draw a topology map that meets the customer's needs and includes a high-level view of internetworking devices and interconnecting media.

This section covers CCDA exam objectives about designing network topologies for the LAN. LANs provide data transfer rates that are typically much faster than wide-area networks (WANs). While most companies own their own LAN infrastructure, wide-area connections between LANs are usually leased on a monthly basis from an outside carrier. With the recent developments in Gigabit Ethernet technologies, LAN designs are now capable of 1000 Mbps speeds. High-speed Gigabit links can connect servers to LAN switches. At these speeds, the capacity is there to meet the performance requirements of current high-bandwidth applications.

Various speeds of Ethernet have evolved into the de facto standard for LANs. Ethernet uses a contention-based access method, meaning each device competes simultaneously for access to the network. All devices attached to the same Ethernet segment form a collision domain. Each device transmitting on that segment may attempt to transmit at the same time as another device on the same segment, resulting in a collision. As the number of devices in the same collision domain increases, so do the collisions, resulting in poorer performance.

Although not discussed in newer switched (bridged) networks, legacy Ethernet networks with repeaters and hubs should limit the size of the collision domain. To scale multiprotocol networks and networks with high-bandwidth applications, limit the size of collision domains using bridges, switches, and routers. This is covered in the section "LAN Hardware" later in the chapter.

Three different network topology models are discussed in the following sections:

- Hierarchical models
- Redundant models
- Secure models

Hierarchical Models

Hierarchical models enable you to design internetworks in layers. To understand the importance of layering, consider the Open System Interconnection (OSI) reference model, which is a layered model for implementing computer communications. Using layers, the OSI model simplifies the tasks required for two computers to communicate. Hierarchical models for internetwork design also use layers to simplify the tasks required for internetworking. Each layer can be focused on specific functions, allowing you to choose the right systems and features for each layer. Hierarchical models apply to both LAN and WAN design.

Benefits of Hierarchical Models

The many benefits of using hierarchical models for your network design include the following:

- Cost savings
- Ease of understanding
- Easy network growth
- Improved fault isolation

After adopting hierarchical design models, many organizations report cost savings because they are no longer trying to do it all in one routing/switching platform. The modular nature of the model enables appropriate use of bandwidth within each layer of the hierarchy, reducing wasted capacity.

Keeping each design element simple and small facilitates ease of understanding, which helps control training and staff costs. Management responsibility and network management systems can be distributed to the different layers of modular network architectures, which also helps control management costs.

Hierarchical design facilitates changes. In a network design, modularity allows creating design elements that can be replicated as the network grows, facilitating easy network growth. As each element in the network design requires change, the cost and complexity of making the upgrade is contained to a small subset of the overall network. In large, flat, or meshed network architectures, changes tend to impact a large number of systems.

Improved fault isolation is facilitated by structuring the network into small, easy-to-understand elements. Network managers can easily understand the transition points in the network, which helps identify failure points.

Today's fast-converging protocols were designed for hierarchical topologies. To control the impact of routing overhead processing and bandwidth consumption, modular hierarchical topologies must be used with protocols designed with these controls in mind, such as EIGRP.

Route summarization is facilitated by hierarchical network design. Route summarization reduces the routing protocol overhead on links in the network and reduces routing protocol processing within the routers.

Hierarchical Network Design

As Figure 4-1 illustrates, a hierarchical network design has three layers:

- The core layer provides optimal transport between sites.

- The distribution layer provides policy-based connectivity.

- The access layer provides workgroup/user access to the network.

Figure 4-1   *A Hierarchical Network Design Has Three Layers: Core, Distribution, and Access*

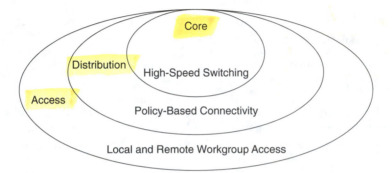

Each layer provides necessary functionality to the network. The layers do not need to be implemented as distinct physical entities. Each layer can be implemented in routers or switches, represented by a physical media, or combined in a single box. A particular layer can be omitted altogether, but for optimum performance, a hierarchy should be maintained.

Core Layer

The core layer is the high-speed switching backbone of the network, which is crucial to enable corporate communications. The core layer should have the following characteristics:

- Offer high reliability

- Provide redundancy

- Provide fault tolerance

- Adapt to changes quickly

- Offer low latency and good manageability

- Avoid slow packet manipulation caused by filters or other processes

- Have a limited and consistent diameter

NOTE   When routers are used in a network, the number of router hops from edge to edge is called the *diameter*. As noted, it is considered good practice to design for a consistent diameter within a hierarchical network. This means that from any end station to another end station across the backbone, there should be the same number of hops. The distance from any end station to a server on the backbone should also be consistent.

Limiting the diameter of the internetwork provides predictable performance and ease of troubleshooting. Distribution layer routers and client LANs can be added to the hierarchical model without increasing the diameter because neither will affect how existing end stations communicate.

Distribution Layer

The distribution layer of the network is the demarcation point between the access and core layers of the network. The distribution layer can have many roles, including implementing the following functions:

- Policy (for example, to ensure that traffic sent from a particular network should be forwarded out one interface, while all other traffic should be forwarded out another interface)
- Security
- Address or area aggregation or summarization
- Departmental or workgroup access
- Broadcast/multicast domain definition
- Routing between virtual LANs (VLANs)
- Media translations (for example, between Ethernet and Token Ring)
- Redistribution between routing domains (for example, between two different routing protocols)
- Demarcation between static and dynamic routing protocols

Several Cisco IOS software features can be used to implement policy at the distribution layer, including the following:

- Filtering by source or destination address
- Filtering on input or output ports
- Hiding internal network numbers by route filtering
- Static routing

- Quality of service mechanisms (for example, to ensure that all devices along a path can accommodate the requested parameters)

Access Layer

The access layer provides user access to local segments on the network. The access layer is characterized by switched and shared bandwidth LANs in a campus environment. Microsegmentation, using LAN switches, provides high bandwidth to workgroups by dividing collision domains on Ethernet segments and reducing the number of stations capturing the token on Token Ring LANs.

For small office/home office (SOHO) environments, the access layer provides access for remote sites into the corporate network by using WAN technologies such as ISDN, Frame Relay, and leased lines. Features such as dial-on-demand routing (DDR) and static routing can be implemented to control costs.

Hierarchical Model Examples

For small- to medium-sized companies, the hierarchical model is often implemented as a hub-and-spoke topology, as shown in Figure 4-2. Corporate headquarters forms the hub and links to the remote offices form the spokes.

Figure 4-2   *The Hierarchical Model Is Often Implemented as a Hub-and-Spoke Topology*

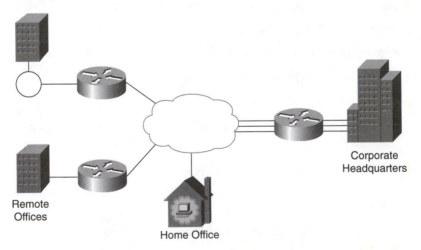

Remote
Offices

Home Office

Corporate
Headquarters

You can implement the hierarchical model by using either routers or switches. Figure 4-3 is an example of a switched hierarchical design, while Figure 4-4 shows examples of routed hierarchical designs.

Figure 4-3   *An Example of a Switched Hierarchical Design*

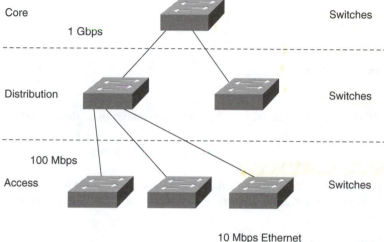

Figure 4-4   *Examples of Routed Hierarchical Designs*

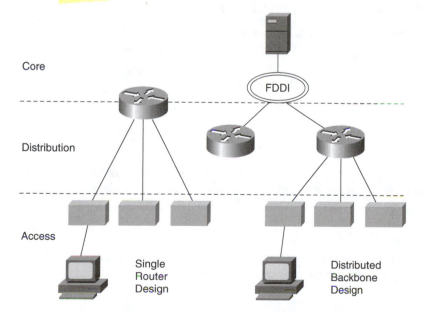

Redundant Models

When designing a network topology for a customer who has critical systems, services, or network paths, you should determine the likelihood that these components will fail and design redundancy where necessary.

Consider incorporating one of the following types of redundancy into your design:

*   Workstation-to-router redundancy
*   Server redundancy
*   Route redundancy
*   Media redundancy

Each of these types of redundancy is elaborated in the sections that follow.

Workstation-to-Router Redundancy

When a workstation has traffic to send to a station that is not local, the workstation has many possible ways to discover the address of a router on its network segment, including the following:

*   Address Resolution Protocol (ARP)
*   Explicit configuration
*   Router Discovery Protocol (RDP)
*   Routing Information Protocol (RIP)
*   Internetwork Packet Exchange (IPX)
*   AppleTalk
*   Hot Standby Router Protocol (HSRP)

The sections that follow cover each of these methods.

ARP

Some IP workstations send an ARP frame to find a remote station. A router running proxy ARP can respond with its data link layer address. Cisco routers run proxy ARP by default.

Explicit Configuration

Most IP workstations must be configured with the IP address of a default router. This is sometimes called the *default gateway*.

In an IP environment, the most common method for a workstation to find a server is via explicit configuration (default router). If the workstation's default router becomes unavailable, the workstation must be reconfigured with the address of a different router. Some IP stacks enable you to configure multiple default routers, but many other IP stacks do not support redundant default routers.

RDP

RFC 1256 specifies an extension to the Internet Control Message Protocol (ICMP) that allows an IP workstation and router to run RDP to facilitate the workstation learning the address of a router.

RIP

An IP workstation can run RIP to learn about routers. RIP should be used in passive mode rather than active mode. (Active mode means that the station sends RIP frames every 30 seconds.) The Open Shortest Path First (OSPF) protocol also supports a workstation running RIP.

IPX

An IPX workstation broadcasts a find network number message to find a route to a server. A router then responds. If the client loses its connection to the server, it automatically sends the message again.

AppleTalk

An AppleTalk workstation remembers the address of the router that sent the last Routing Table Maintenance Protocol (RTMP) packet. As long as there are one or more routers on an AppleTalk workstation's network, it has a route to remote devices.

HSRP

Cisco's HSRP provides a way for IP workstations to keep communicating on the internetwork even if their default router becomes unavailable. HSRP works by creating a phantom router that has its own IP and MAC addresses. The workstations use this phantom router as their default router.

HSRP routers on a LAN communicate among themselves to designate two routers as active and standby. The active router sends periodic hello messages. The other HSRP routers listen for the hello messages. If the active router fails and the other HSRP routers stop receiving hello messages, the standby router takes over and becomes the active router. Because the new active router assumes both the IP and MAC addresses of the phantom, end nodes see no change at all.

They continue to send packets to the phantom router's MAC address, and the new active router delivers those packets.

HSRP also works for proxy ARP. When an active HSRP router receives an ARP request for a node that is not on the local LAN, the router replies with the phantom router's MAC address instead of its own. If the router that originally sent the ARP reply later loses its connection, the new active router can still deliver the traffic.

Figure 4-5 shows a sample implementation of HSRP.

Figure 4-5   *An Example of HSRP: The Phantom Router Represents the Real Routers*

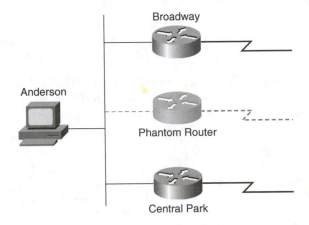

In Figure 4-5, the following sequence occurs:

1   The Anderson workstation is configured to use the Phantom router as its default router.

2   Upon booting, the routers elect Broadway as the HSRP active router. The active router does the work for the HSRP phantom. Central Park is the HSRP standby router.

3   When Anderson sends an ARP frame to find its default router, Broadway responds with the Phantom router's MAC address.

4   If Broadway goes off line, Central Park takes over as the active router, continuing the delivery of Anderson's packets. The change is transparent to Anderson. If a third HSRP router was on the LAN, that router would begin to act as the new standby router.

Server Redundancy

In some environments, fully redundant (mirrored) file servers should be recommended. For example, in a brokerage firm where traders must access data in order to buy and sell stocks, the data can be replicated on two or more redundant servers. The servers should be on different networks and power supplies.

If complete server redundancy is not feasible due to cost considerations, mirroring or duplexing of the file server hard drives is a good idea. *Mirroring* means synchronizing two disks, while *duplexing* is the same as mirroring with the additional feature that the two mirrored hard drives are controlled by different disk controllers.

Route Redundancy

Designing redundant routes has two purposes: load balancing and minimizing downtime.

Load Balancing

AppleTalk and IPX routers can remember only one route to a remote network by default, so they do not support load balancing. You can change this for IPX by using the **ipx maximum-paths** command and for AppleTalk by using the **appletalk maximum-paths** command on a Cisco router.

Most IP routing protocols can load balance across up to six parallel links that have equal cost. Use the **maximum-paths** command to change the number of links that the router will load balance over for IP; the default is four, the maximum is six. To support load balancing, keep the bandwidth consistent within a layer of the hierarchical model so that all paths have the same cost. (Cisco's IGRP and EIGRP are exceptions because they can load balance traffic across multiple routes that have different metrics by using a feature called *variance*.)

A hop-based routing protocol does load balancing over unequal bandwidth paths as long as the hop count is equal. After the slower link becomes saturated, the higher-capacity link cannot be filled; this is called *pinhole congestion*. Pinhole congestion can be avoided by designing equal bandwidth links within one layer of the hierarchy or by using a routing protocol that takes bandwidth into account.

IP load balancing depends on which switching mode is used on a router. Process switching load balances on a packet-by-packet basis. Fast, autonomous, silicon, optimum, distributed, and NetFlow switching load balance on a destination-by-destination basis because the processor caches the encapsulation to a specific destination for these types of switching modes.

Minimizing Downtime

In addition to facilitating load balancing, redundant routes minimize network downtime.

As already discussed, you should keep bandwidth consistent within a given layer of a hierarchy to facilitate load balancing. Another reason to keep bandwidth consistent within a layer of a hierarchy is that routing protocols converge much faster if multiple equal-cost paths to a destination network exist.

By using redundant, meshed network designs, you can minimize the effect of link failures. Depending on the convergence time of the routing protocols being used, a single link failure will not have a catastrophic effect.

A network can be designed as a full mesh or a partial mesh. In a full mesh network, every router has a link to every other router, as shown in Figure 4-6. A full mesh network provides complete redundancy and also provides good performance because there is just a single-hop delay between any two sites. The number of links in a full mesh is n(n–1)/2, where *n* is the number of routers. Each router is connected to every other router. (Divide the result by 2 to avoid counting Router X to Router Y and Router Y to Router X as two different links.)

Figure 4-6   *Full Mesh Network: Every Router Has a Link to Every Other Router in the Network*

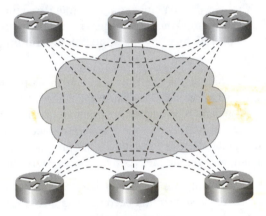

(6*5)/2=15 Circuits

A full mesh network can be expensive to implement in wide-area networks due to the required number of links. In addition, practical limits to scaling exist for groups of routers that broadcast routing updates or service advertisements. As the number of router peers increases, the amount of bandwidth and CPU resources devoted to processing broadcasts increases.

A suggested guideline is to keep broadcast traffic at less than 20 percent of the bandwidth of each link; this will limit the number of peer routers that can exchange routing tables or service advertisements. When planning redundancy, follow guidelines for simple, hierarchical design. Figure 4-7 illustrates a classic hierarchical and redundant enterprise design that uses a partial mesh rather than a full mesh architecture. For LAN designs, links between the access and distribution layer can be Fast Ethernet, with links to the core at Gigabit Ethernet speeds.

Figure 4-7   *Partial Mesh Design with Redundancy*

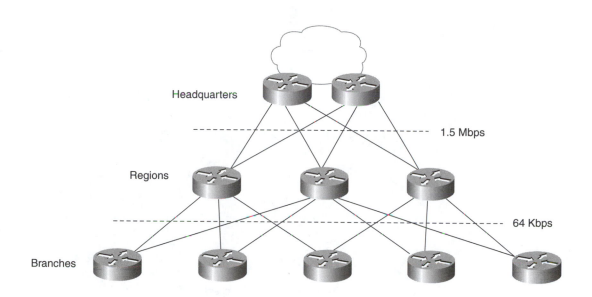

Media Redundancy

In mission-critical applications, it is often necessary to provide redundant media.

In switched networks, switches can have redundant links to each other. This redundancy is good because it minimizes downtime, but it may result in broadcasts continuously circling the network, which is called a *broadcast storm*. Because Cisco switches implement the IEEE 802.1d Spanning-Tree Algorithm, this looping can be avoided in the Spanning-Tree Protocol. The Spanning-Tree Algorithm guarantees that only one path is active between two network stations. The algorithm permits redundant paths that are automatically activated when the active path experiences problems.

Because WAN links are often critical pieces of the internetwork, redundant media is often deployed in WAN environments. As shown in Figure 4-8, backup links can be provisioned so they become active when a primary link goes down or becomes congested.

Figure 4-8 *Backup Links Can Be Used to Provide Redundancy*

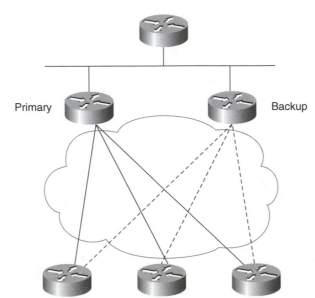

Often, backup links use a different technology. For example, a leased line can be in parallel with a backup dialup line or ISDN circuit. By using *floating static routes*, you can specify that the backup route has a higher administrative distance (used by Cisco routers to select which routing information to use) so that it is not normally used unless the primary route goes down.

NOTE   When provisioning backup links, learn as much as possible about the actual physical circuit routing. Different carriers sometimes use the same facilities, meaning that your backup path is susceptible to the same failures as your primary path. You should do some investigative work to ensure that your backup really is acting as a backup.

Backup links can be combined with load balancing and channel aggregation. *Channel aggregation* means that a router can bring up multiple channels (for example, Integrated Services Digital Network [ISDN] B channels) as bandwidth requirements increase.

Cisco supports the Multilink Point-to-Point Protocol (MPPP), which is an Internet Engineering Task Force (IETF) standard for ISDN B channel (or asynchronous serial interface) aggregation. MPPP does not specify how a router should accomplish the decision-making process to bring up extra channels. Instead, it seeks to ensure that packets arrive in sequence at the receiving router. Then, the data is encapsulated within PPP and the datagram is given a sequence number.

At the receiving router, PPP uses this sequence number to re-create the original data stream. Multiple channels appear as one logical link to upper-layer protocols.

Secure Models

This section introduces secure topology models. The information in this book is not sufficient to learn all the nuances of internetwork security. To learn more about internetwork security, you might want to read the book *Firewalls and Internet Security*, by Bill Cheswick and Steve Bellovin, published by Addison Wesley. Also, by searching for the word "security" on Cisco's web site (www.cisco.com), you can keep up to date on security issues.

Secure topologies are often designed by using a firewall. A firewall protects one network from another untrusted network. This protection can be accomplished in many ways, but in principle, a firewall is a pair of mechanisms: One blocks traffic and the other permits traffic.

Some firewalls place a greater emphasis on blocking traffic, and others emphasize permitting traffic. Figure 4-9 shows a simple firewall topology using routers.

Figure 4-9   *A Simple Firewall Network, Using Routers*

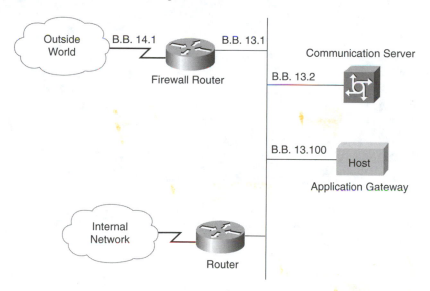

You can design a firewall system using packet-filtering routers and bastion hosts. A *bastion host* is a secure host that supports a limited number of applications for use by outsiders. It holds data that outsiders access (for example, web pages) but is strongly protected from outsiders using it for anything other than its limited purposes.

Three-Part Firewall System

The classic firewall system, called the *three-part firewall system,* has the following three specialized layers, as shown in Figure 4-10:

- An isolation LAN that is a buffer between the corporate internetwork and the outside world. (The isolation LAN is called the demilitarized zone (DMZ) in some literature.)

- A router that acts as an inside packet filter between the corporate internetwork and the isolation LAN.

- Another router that acts as an outside packet filter between the isolation LAN and the outside internetwork.

Figure 4-10   *Structure and Components of a Three-Part Firewall System*

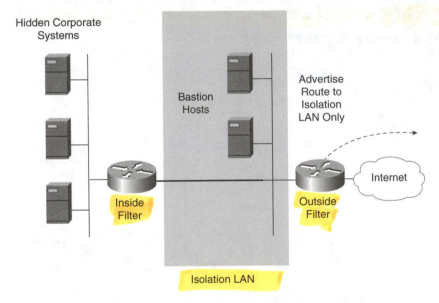

Services available to the outside world are located on bastion hosts in the isolation LAN. Example services in these hosts include:

- Anonymous FTP server
- Web server
- Domain Name System (DNS)
- Telnet
- Specialized security software such as Terminal Access Controller Access Control System (TACACS)

The isolation LAN has a unique network number that is different than the corporate network number. Only the isolation LAN network is visible to the outside world. On the outside filter, you should advertise only the route to the isolation LAN.

If internal users need to get access to Internet services, allow TCP outbound traffic from the internal corporate internetwork. Allow TCP packets back into the internal network only if they are in response to a previously sent request. All other TCP traffic should be blocked because new inbound TCP sessions could be from hackers trying to establish sessions with internal hosts.

NOTE

To determine whether TCP traffic is a response to a previously sent request or a request for a new session, the router examines some bits in the code field of the TCP header. If the acknowledgement field (ACK) is valid or reset the connection (RST) bits are set in a TCP segment header, the segment is a response to a previously sent request. The established keyword in Cisco IOS access lists (filters) is used to indicate packets with ACK or RST bits set.

The following list summarizes some *rules* for the three-part firewall system:

- The inside packet filter router should allow inbound TCP packets from established sessions.

- The outside packet filter router should allow inbound TCP packets from established TCP sessions.

- The outside packet filter router should also allow packets to specific TCP or UDP ports going to specific bastion hosts (including TCP SYN packets that are used to establish a session).

Always block traffic from coming in from between the firewall routers and hosts and the internal network. The firewall routers and hosts themselves are likely to be a jumping-off point for hackers, as shown in Figure 4-11.

Figure 4-11   *Firewall Routers and Hosts May Make Your Network Vulnerable to Hacker Attacks*

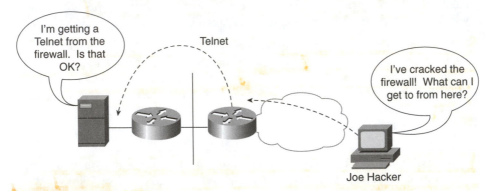

Keep bastion hosts and firewall routers simple. They should run as few programs as possible. The programs should be simple because simple programs have fewer bugs than complex programs. Bugs introduce possible security holes.

Do not enable any unnecessary services or connections on the outside filter router. A list of suggestions for implementing the outside filter router follows:

- Turn off Telnet access (no virtual terminals defined).

- Use static routing only.

- Do not make it a TFTP server.

- Use password encryption.

- Turn off proxy ARP service.

- Turn off finger service.

- Turn off IP redirects.

- Turn off IP route caching.

- Do not make the router a MacIP server (MacIP provides connectivity for IP over AppleTalk by tunneling IP datagrams inside AppleTalk).

Cisco PIX Firewall

To provide stalwart security, hardware firewall devices can be used in addition to or instead of packet-filtering routers. For example, in the three-part firewall system illustrated earlier in Figure 4-10, a hardware firewall device could be installed on the isolation LAN. A hardware firewall device offers the following benefits:

- Less complex and more robust than packet filters

- No required downtime for installation

- No required upgrading of hosts or routers

- No necessary day-to-day management

Cisco's PIX Firewall is a hardware device that offers the features in the preceding list, as well as full outbound Internet access from unregistered internal hosts. IP addresses can be assigned from the private ranges, as defined in RFC 1918 (available at http://info.internet.isi.edu/in-notes/rfc/files/rfc1918.txt). The PIX Firewall uses a protection scheme called *Network Address Translation (NAT),* which allows internal users access to the Internet while protecting internal networks from unauthorized access.

Further details on the PIX Firewall are available on Cisco's web site at www.cisco.com/warp/public/cc/cisco/mkt/security/pix/.

The PIX Firewall provides firewall security without the administrative overhead and risks associated with UNIX-based or router-based firewall systems. The PIX Firewall operates on a secure real-time kernel, not on UNIX. The network administrator is provided with complete auditing of all transactions, including attempted break-ins.

The PIX Firewall supports data encryption with the Cisco PIX Private Link, a card that provides secure communication between multiple PIX systems over the Internet using the data encryption standard (DES).

The PIX Firewall provides TCP and UDP connectivity from internal networks to the outside world by using a scheme called *adaptive security.* All inbound traffic is verified for correctness against the following connection state information:

- Source and destination IP addresses

- Source and destination port numbers

- Protocols

- TCP sequence numbers (which are randomized to eliminate the possibility of hackers guessing numbers)

LAN Types

The CCDA objective covered in this section is as follows:

14	Draw a topology map that meets the customer's needs and includes a high-level view of internetworking devices and interconnecting media.

Local-area networks can be classified as a large building LAN, campus LAN, or small/remote LAN. The large building LAN contains the major data center with high-speed access and floor communications closets; the large building LAN is usually the headquarters in larger companies. Campus LANs provide connectivity between buildings on a campus; redundancy is usually a requirement. Small/remote LANs provide connectivity to remote offices with a small number of nodes.

It is important to remember the Cisco hierarchical approach of network design. First, build a high-speed core backbone network. Second, build the distribution layer, where policy can be applied. Finally, build the access layer, where LANs provide access to the network end stations.

Large Building LANs

Large building LANs are segmented by floors or departments. Company mainframes and servers reside in a computing center. Media lines run from the computer center to the wiring closets at the various segments. From the wiring closets, media lines run to the offices and cubicles around the work areas. Figure 4-12 depicts a typical large building design.

Figure 4-12   *Large Building LAN Design*

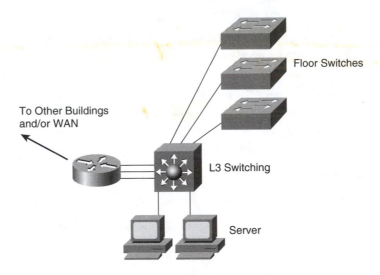

Each floor may have more than 200 users. Following a hierarchical model of access, distribution, and core, Ethernet and Fast Ethernet nodes may connect to hubs and switches in the communications closet. Uplink ports from closet switches connect back to one or two (for redundancy) distribution switches. Distribution switches may provide connectivity to server farms that provide business applications, DHCP, DNS, intranet, and other services.

Campus LANs

A campus LAN connects two or more buildings located near each other using high-bandwidth LAN media. Usually the media (for example, copper or fiber) is owned. High-speed switching devices are recommended to minimize latency. In today's networks, Gigabit Ethernet campus backbones are the standard for new installations. In Figure 4-13, campus buildings are connected by using Layer 3 switches with Gigabit Ethernet media.

Figure 4-13   *Campus LANs*

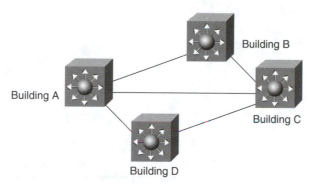

Ensure that a hierarchical design is implemented on the campus LAN and that network layer addressing is assigned to control broadcasts on the networks. Each building should have addressing assigned in such a way as to maximize address summarization. Apply contiguous subnets to buildings at the bit boundary to apply summarization and ease the design. Campus networks can support high-bandwidth applications such as video conferencing. Although most WAN implementations are configured to support only IP, legacy LANs may still be configured to support IPX and AppleTalk.

Small/Remote Site LANs

Small/remote sites usually connect back to the corporate network via a small router (Cisco 2500). The local-area network service is provided by a small hub or LAN switch (Catalyst 1900). The router filters broadcasts to the WAN circuit and forwards packets that require services from the corporate network. A server may be placed at the small/remote site to provide DHCP and other local applications such as NT backup domain controller and DNS; if not, the router will need to be configured to forward DHCP broadcasts and other types of services. Figure 4-14 shows a typical architecture of a small or remote LAN. *Building Cisco Remote Access Networks* from Cisco Press is an excellent resource for more information on remote access.

Figure 4-14 *Small/Remote Office LAN*

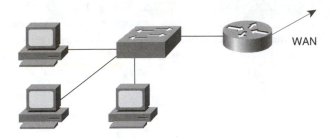

LAN Media

The CCDA objectives covered in this section are as follows:

15   Recognize scalability constraints and issues for standard LAN technologies.

16   Recommend Cisco products and LAN technologies that will meet a customer's requirements for performance, capacity, and scalability in small- to medium-sized networks.

This section identifies some of the constraints that should be considered when provisioning various LAN media types. For additional reference material on this subject, refer to Appendix D, "LAN Media Reference."

Ethernet Design Rules

Table 4-1 provides scalability information that you can use when provisioning IEEE 802.3 networks.

Table 4-1 *Scalability Constraints for IEEE 802.3*

	10Base5	10Base2	10BaseT	100BaseT
Topology	Bus	Bus	Star	Star
Maximum Segment Length (meters)	500	185	100 from hub to station	100 from hub to station

Table 4-1   *Scalability Constraints for IEEE 802.3 (Continued)*

	10Base5	10Base2	10BaseT	100BaseT
Maximum Number of Attachments per Segment	100	30	2 (hub and station or hub-hub)	2 (hub and station or hub-hub)
Maximum Collision Domain	2500 meters of 5 segments and 4 repeaters; only 3 segments can be populated	2500 meters of 5 segments and 4 repeaters; only 3 segments can be populated	2500 meters of 5 segments and 4 repeaters; only 3 segments can be populated	See the details in the section "100 Mbps Fast Ethernet Design Rules" later in this chapter.

The most significant design rule for Ethernet is that the round-trip propagation delay in one collision domain must not exceed 512 bit times, which is a requirement for collision detection to work correctly. This rule means that the maximum round-trip delay for a 10 Mbps Ethernet network is 51.2 microseconds. The maximum round-trip delay for a 100 Mbps Ethernet network is only 5.12 microseconds because the bit time on a 100 Mbps Ethernet network is 0.01 microseconds as opposed to 0.1 microseconds on a 10 Mbps Ethernet network.

To make 100 Mbps Ethernet work, distance limitations are much more severe than those required for 10 Mbps Ethernet. The general rule is that a 100 Mbps Ethernet has a maximum diameter of 205 meters when unshielded twisted-pair (UTP) cabling is used, whereas 10 Mbps Ethernet has a maximum diameter of 500 meters with 10BaseT and 2500 meters with 10Base5.

10 Mbps Fiber Ethernet Design Rules

Table 4-2 provides some guidelines to help you choose the right media for your network designs. 10BaseF is based on the fiber-optic interrepeater link (FOIRL) specification, which includes 10BaseFP, 10BaseFB, 10BaseFL, and a revised FOIRL standard. The new FOIRL allows data terminal equipment (DTE) end-node connections rather than just repeaters, which were allowed with the older FOIRL specification.

Table 4-2   *Scalability Constraints for 10 Mbps Fiber Ethernet*

	10BaseFP	10BaseFB	10BaseFL	Old FOIRL	New FOIRL
Topology	Passive star	Backbone or repeater fiber system	Link	Link	Link or star
Allows DTE (End Node) Connections?	Yes	No	No	No	Yes

continues

Table 4-2   *Scalability Constraints for 10 Mbps Fiber Ethernet (Continued)*

	10BaseFP	10BaseFB	10BaseFL	Old FOIRL	New FOIRL
Maximum Segment Length (Meters)	500	2000	1000 or 2000	1000	1000
Allows Cascaded Repeaters?	No	Yes	No	No	Yes
Maximum Collision Domains in Meters	2500	2500	2500	2500	2500

100 Mbps Fast Ethernet Design Rules

100 Mbps Ethernet, or Fast Ethernet, topologies present some distinct constraints on the network design because of their speed. The combined latency due to cable lengths and repeaters must conform to the specifications in order for the network to work properly. This section discusses these issues and provides example calculations.

Understanding Collision Domains

The overriding design rule for 100 Mbps Ethernet networks is that the round-trip collision delay must not exceed 512 bit times. However, the bit time on a 100 Mbps Ethernet network is 0.01 microseconds, as opposed to 0.1 microseconds on a 10 Mbps Ethernet network. Therefore, the maximum round-trip delay for a 100 Mbps Ethernet network is 5.12 microseconds, as opposed to the more lenient 51.2 microseconds in a 10 Mbps Ethernet network.

100BaseT Repeaters

For a 100 Mbps Ethernet to work, you must impose distance limitations based on the type of repeaters used.

The IEEE 100BaseT specification defines two types of repeaters: Class I and Class II. Class I repeaters have a latency (delay) of 0.7 microseconds or less. Only one repeater hop is allowed. Class II repeaters have a latency (delay) of 0.46 microseconds or less. One or two repeater hops are allowed.

Table 4-3 shows the maximum size of collision domains, depending on the type of repeater.

Table 4-3   *Maximum Size of Collision Domains for 100BaseT*

	Copper	Mixed Copper and Multimode Fiber	Multimode Fiber
DTE-DTE (or Switch-Switch)	100 meters		412 meters (2000 if full duplex)
One Class I Repeater	200 meters	260 meters	272 meters
One Class II Repeater	200 meters	308 meters	320 meters
Two Class II Repeaters	205 meters	216 meters	228 meters

The Cisco FastHub 316 is a Class II repeater, as are all the Cisco FastHub 300 series hubs. These hubs actually exceed the Class II specifications, which means that they have even lower latencies and therefore allow longer cable lengths. For example, with two FastHub 300 repeaters and copper cable, the maximum collision domain is 223 meters.

Example of 100BaseT Topology

Figure 4-15 shows examples of 100BaseT topologies with different media.

Figure 4-15   *Examples of 100BaseT Topologies with Various Media and Repeaters*

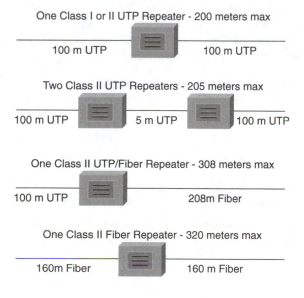

Other topologies are possible as long as the round-trip propagation delay does not exceed 5.12 microseconds (512 bit times). When the delay does exceed 5.12 microseconds, the network experiences illegal (late) collisions and CRC errors.

Checking the Propagation Delay

To determine whether configurations other than the standard ones shown in Figure 4-15 will work, use the following information from the IEEE 802.3u specification.

To check a path to make sure the path delay value (PDV) does not exceed 512 bit times, add up the following delays:

- All link segment delays
- All repeater delays
- DTE delay
- A safety margin (0 to 5 bit times)

Use the following steps to calculate the PDV:

1 Determine the delay for each link segment; this is the link segment delay value (LSDV), including interrepeater links, using the following formula. (Multiply by two so it is a round-trip delay.)

   $LSDV = 2 \times segment\ length \times cable\ delay\ for\ this\ segment.$

   For end-node segments, the segment length is the cable length between the physical interface at the repeater and the physical interface at the DTE. Use your two farthest DTEs for a worst-case calculation. For interrepeater links, the segment length is the cable length between the repeater physical interfaces.

   Cable delay is the delay specified by the manufacturer if available. When actual cable lengths or propagation delays are not known, use the delay in bit times as specified in Table 4-4.

   Cable delay must be specified in bit times per meter (BT/m).

2 Add together the LSDVs for all segments in the path.

3 Determine the delay for each repeater in the path. If model-specific data is not available from the manufacturer, determine the class of repeater (I or II).

4 MII cables for 100BaseT should not exceed 0.5 meters each in length. When evaluating system topology, MII cable lengths need not be accounted for separately. Delays attributed to the MII are incorporated into DTE and repeater delays.

5 Use the DTE delay value shown in Table 4-4 unless your equipment manufacturer defines a different value.

6 Decide on an appropriate safety margin from 0 to 5 bit times. Five bit times is a safe value.

7 Insert the values obtained from the preceding calculations into the formula for calculating the PDV:

$$PDV = link\ delays + repeater\ delays + DTE\ delay + safety\ margin$$

8 If the PDV is less than 512, the path is qualified in terms of worst-case delay.

Round-Trip Delay

Table 4-4 shows round-trip delay in bit times for standard cables and maximum round-trip delay in bit times for DTEs, repeaters, and maximum-length cables.

NOTE   Note that the values shown in Table 4-4 have been multiplied by two to provide a round-trip delay. If you use these numbers, you need not multiply by two again in the LSDV formula (LSDV = 2 × segment length × cable delay for this segment).

Table 4-4   *Network Component Delays*

Component	Round-Trip Delay in Bit Times per Meter	Maximum Round-Trip Delay in Bit Times
Two TX/FX DTEs	N/A	100
Two T4 DTEs	N/A	138
One T4 DTE and one TX/FX DTE	N/A	127
Category 3 cable segment	1.14	114 (100 meters)
Category 4 cable segment	1.14	114 (100 meters)
Category 5 cable segment	1.112	111.2 (100 meters)
STP cable segment	1.112	111.2 (100 meters)
Fiber-optic cable segment	1.0	412 (412 meters)
Class I repeater	N/A	140
Class II repeater with all ports TX or FX	N/A	92
Class II repeater with any port T4	N/A	67

Source: IEEE 802.3u—1995, "Media Access Control (MAC) Parameters, Physical Layer, Medium Attachment Units, and Repeater for 100 Mb/s Operation, Type 100BASE-T."

Example Network Cabling Implementation

See Figure 4-16 for this example. Company ABC has all UTP Category 5 cabling. Two Class II repeaters are separated by 20 meters instead of the standard 5 meters. The network administrators are trying to determine whether this configuration will work.

Figure 4-16 *An Example Network Cabling Implementation for Company ABC (Showing the Two Most Distant DTEs)*

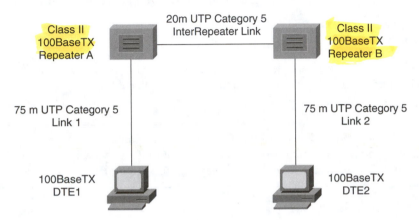

To ensure that the PDV does not exceed 512 bit times, the network administrators must calculate a worst-case scenario using DTE 1 and DTE 2, which are 75 meters from their repeaters.

Assume that DTE 1 starts transmitting a minimum-sized frame of 64 bytes (512 bits). DTE 2 just barely misses hearing DTE 1's transmission and starts transmitting also. The collision happens on the far-right side of the network and must traverse back to DTE 1. These events must occur within 512 bit times. If they take any longer than 512 bit times, then DTE 1 will have stopped sending when it learns about the collision and will not know that its frame was damaged by the collision. To calculate the link delays for the Category 5 cable segments, the repeaters, and DTEs, the administrators use the values from Table 4-4. (Remember that Table 4-4 uses round-trip delay values, so you need not multiply by two.)

To test whether this network will work, the network administrators filled in Table 4-5.

Table 4-5 *Delays of Components in Company ABC's Network*

Delay Cause	Calculation of Network Component Delay	Total (Bit Times)
Link 1	75m × 1.112 bit times/m	83.4
Link 2	75m × 1.112 bit times/m	83.4
Interrepeater link	20m × 1.112 bit times/m	22.24
Repeater A	92 bit times	92

Table 4-5   *Delays of Components in Company ABC's Network (Continued)*

Delay Cause	Calculation of Network Component Delay	Total (Bit Times)
Repeater B	92 bit times	92
DTE 1 and 2	100 bit times	100
Safety margin	5 bit times	5
Grand Total	**Add Individual Totals**	**478.04**

The grand total in Table 4-5 is fewer than 512 bit times, so this network will work.

Calculating Cable Delays

Some cable manufacturers specify propagation delays relative to the speed of light or in nanoseconds per meter (ns/m). To convert these values to bit times per meter (BT/m), use Table 4-6.

Table 4-6   *Conversion to Bit Times per Meter for Cable Delays*

Speed Relative to Speed of Light	Nanoseconds per Meter (ns/m)	Bit Times per Meter (BT/m)
0.4	8.34	0.834
0.5	6.67	0.667
0.51	6.54	0.654
0.52	6.41	0.641
0.53	6.29	0.629
0.54	6.18	0.618
0.55	6.06	0.606
0.56	5.96	0.596
0.57	5.85	0.585
0.58	5.75	0.575
0.5852	5.70	0.570
0.59	5.65	0.565
0.6	5.56	0.556
0.61	5.47	0.547
0.62	5.38	0.538

continues

Table 4-6 *Conversion to Bit Times per Meter for Cable Delays (Continued)*

Speed Relative to Speed of Light	Nanoseconds per Meter (ns/m)	Bit Times per Meter (BT/m)
0.63	5.29	0.529
0.64	5.21	0.521
0.65	5.13	0.513
0.654	5.10	0.510
0.66	5.05	0.505
0.666	5.01	0.501
0.67	4.98	0.498
0.68	4.91	0.491
0.69	4.83	0.483
0.7	4.77	0.477
0.8	4.17	0.417
0.9	3.71	0.371

Source: IEEE 802.3u — 1995, "Media Access Control (MAC) Parameters, Physical Layer, Medium Attachment Units, and Repeater for 100 Mb/s Operation, Type 100BASE-T."

Token Ring Design Rules

Table 4-7 lists some scalability concerns when designing Token Ring segments. Refer to IBM's Token Ring planning guides for more information on the maximum segment sizes and maximum diameter of a network.

Table 4-7 *Scalability Constraints for Token Ring*

	IBM Token Ring	IEEE 802.5
Topology	Star	Not specified
Maximum Segment Length (Meters)	Depends on type of cable, number of MAUs, and so on	Depends on type of cable, number of MAUs, and so on
Maximum Number of Attachments per Segment	260 for STP, 72 for UTP	250
Maximum Network Diameter	Depends on type of cable, number of MAUs, and so on	Depends on type of cable, number of MAUs, and so on

Gigabit Ethernet Design Rules

The most recent development in the Ethernet arena is Gigabit Ethernet. Gigabit Ethernet is specified by two standards: IEEE 802.3z and 802.3ab. The 802.3z standard specifies the operation of Gigabit Ethernet over fiber and coaxial cable and introduces the Gigabit Media Independent Interface (GMII). The 802.3z standard was approved in June 1998.

The 802.3ab standard specifies the operation of Gigabit Ethernet over Category 5 UTP. Gigabit Ethernet still retains the frame formats and frame sizes and it still uses CSMA/CD. As with Ethernet and Fast Ethernet, full duplex operation is possible. Differences can be found in the encoding; Gigabit Ethernet uses 8B/10B coding with simple nonreturn to zero (NRZ). Because of the 20 percent overhead, pulses run at 1250 MHz to achieve a 1000 Mbps. Table 4-8 covers Gigabit Ethernet scalability constraints.

Table 4-8   *Gigabit Ethernet Scalability Constraints*

Type	Speed	Maximum segment length	Encoding	Media
1000BaseT	1000 Mbps	100m	5-level	Cat 5 UTP
1000BaseLX (long wave)	1000 Mbps	550m	8B/10B	Single/multiple mode fiber
1000BaseSX (short wave)	1000 Mbps	62.5 micrometers: 220m 50 micrometers: 500m	8B/10B	Multimode fiber
1000BaseCX	1000 Mbps	25m	8B/10B	Shielded balanced copper

FDDI Design Rules

The FDDI specification does not actually specify the maximum segment length or network diameter. It specifies the amount of allowed power loss, which works out to the approximate distances shown in Table 4-9.

Table 4-9   *Scalability Constraints for FDDI*

	Multimode Fiber	Single-Mode Fiber	UTP
Topology	Dual ring, tree of concentrators, and others	Dual ring, tree of concentrators, and others	Star
Maximum Segment Length	2km between stations	60km between stations	100m from hub to station

continues

Table 4-9   *Scalability Constraints for FDDI (Continued)*

	Multimode Fiber	Single-Mode Fiber	UTP
Maximum Number of Attachments per Segment	1000 (500 dual-attached stations)	1000 (500 dual-attached stations)	2 (hub and station or hub-hub)
Maximum Network Diameter	200km	200km	200km

LAN Hardware

The CCDA objectives covered in this section are as follows:

13	Describe the advantages, disadvantages, scalability issues, and applicability of standard internetwork topologies.
15	Recognize scalability constraints and issues for standard LAN technologies.

This section covers the following hardware technologies as they can be applied to LAN design:

- Repeaters
- Hubs
- Bridges
- Switches
- Routers
- Layer 3 switches
- Combining hubs, switches, and routers

Repeaters

Repeaters are the basic unit used in networks to connect separate segments. Repeaters take incoming frames, regenerate the preamble, amplify the signals, and send the frame out all other interfaces. Repeaters operate in the physical layer of the OSI model. Because repeaters are not aware of packets or frame formats, they do not control broadcasts or collision domains. Repeaters are said to be protocol transparent because they are not aware of upper-layer protocols such as IP, IPX, and so on.

One basic rule of using repeaters is the 5-4-3 Rule. The maximum path between two stations on the network should not be more than 5 segments with 4 repeaters between those segments and no more than 3 populated segments. Repeaters introduce a small amount of latency, or delay, when propagating the frames. A transmitting device must be able to detect a collision with another device within the specified time after the delay introduced by the cable segments and repeaters is factored in. The 512 bit-time specification also governs segment lengths. A more detailed explanation of the specification can be found at www.cisco.com/univercd/cc/td/doc/cisintwk/ito_doc/ethernet.htm. Figure 4-17 illustrates an example of the 5-4-3 Rule.

Figure 4-17   *Repeater 5-4-3 Rule*

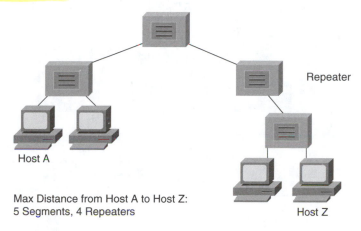

Host A

Max Distance from Host A to Host Z:
5 Segments, 4 Repeaters

Repeater

Host Z

Hubs

With the increasing density of LANs in the late 80s and early 90s, hubs were introduced to concentrate Thinnet and 10BaseT networks in the wiring closet. Traditional hubs operate on the physical layer of the OSI model and perform the same functions as basic repeaters.

Bridges

Bridges are used to connect separate segments of a network. They differ from repeaters in that bridges are intelligent devices that operate in the data link layer of the OSI model. Bridges control the collision domains on the network. Bridges also learn the MAC layer addresses of each node on each segment and on which interface they are located. For any incoming frame, bridges forward the frame only if the destination MAC address is on another port or if the bridge is not aware of its location. The latter is called *flooding*. Bridges filter any incoming frames with destination MAC addresses that are on the same segment from where the frame arrives; they do not forward the frame on.

Bridges are store and forward devices. They store the entire frame and verify the CRC before forwarding. If a CRC error is detected, the frame is discarded. Bridges are protocol transparent;

they are not aware of the upper-layer protocols like IP, IPX, and AppleTalk. Bridges are designed to flood all unknown and broadcast traffic.

Bridges implement the Spanning-Tree Protocol to build a loop free network topology. Bridges communicate with each other, exchanging information such as priority and bridge interface MAC addresses. They select a root bridge and then implement the Spanning-Tree Protocol. Some interfaces are placed in a hold state, while other bridges will have interfaces in forwarding mode. Looking at Figure 4-18, note that there is no load sharing or dual paths with bridge protocols as there is in routing.

Figure 4-18   *Spanning-Tree Protocol*

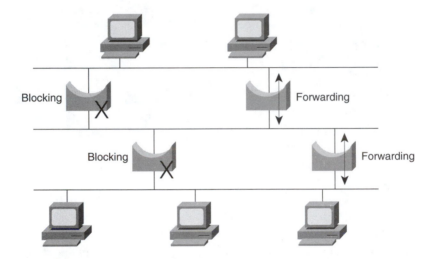

Switches

Switches are the evolution of bridges. Switches use fast integrated circuits that reduce the latency that bridges introduce to the network. Switches also enable the capability to run in cut-through mode. In cut-through mode, the switch does not wait for the entire frame to enter its buffer; instead, it forwards the frame after it has read the destination MAC address field of the frame. Cut-through operation increases the probability that error frames are propagated on the network, which increases CRC and runt frames on the network. Because of these problems, most switches today perform store-and-forward operation with CRC check as bridges do. Figure 4-19 shows a switch; note that it controls collision domains but not broadcast domains.

Figure 4-19 *Switches Control Collision Domains*

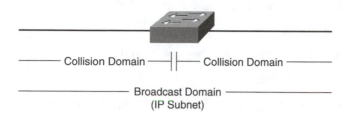

Switches have characteristics similar to bridges; however, they have more ports and run faster. Switches keep a table of MAC addresses per port, and they implement Spanning-Tree Protocol. Switches also operate in the data link layer and are protocol transparent. Each port on a switch is a separate collision domain but part of the same broadcast domain. Switches do not control broadcasts on the network.

Routers

Routers make forwarding decisions based on network layer addresses. In addition to controlling collision domains, routers control broadcast domains. Each interface of a router is a separate broadcast domain defined by a subnet and a mask. Routers are protocol aware, which means they are capable of forwarding packets of routed protocols such as IP, IPX, Decnet, and AppleTalk. Figure 4-20 describes a router; each interface is a broadcast and a collision domain.

Figure 4-20 *Routers Control Broadcast and Collision Domains*

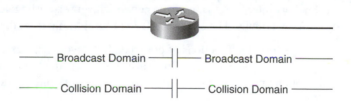

Routers exchange information about destination networks by using one of several routing protocols. The following are lists of routing protocols. The lists are divided by the protocols that can be routed.

For routing TCP/IP:

* Enhanced Interior Gateway Routing Protocol (EIGRP)

* Open Shortest Path First (OSPF)

* Routing Information Protocol (RIP)

- Intermediate System-to-Intermediate System (ISIS)
- Protocol Independent Multicast (PIM)

For routing Novell:

- Novell Routing Information Protocol (Novell RIP)
- NetWare Link Services Protocol (NLSP)
- Enhanced Interior Gateway Routing Protocol (EIGRP)

For routing AppleTalk:

- Routing Table Maintenance Protocol (RTMP)
- Enhanced Interior Gateway Routing Protocol (EIGRP)

Routing protocols are discussed in further detail in Chapter 6, "Designing for Specific Protocols."

Routers are the preferred method of forwarding packets between networks of differing media, such as Ethernet to Token Ring, Ethernet to FDDI, or Ethernet to Serial. They also provide methods to filter traffic based on the network layer address, route redundancy, load balancing, hierarchical addressing, and multicast routing.

Layer 3 Switches

LAN switches that are capable of running routing protocols are *Layer 3 switches*. These switches are capable of running routing protocols and communicating with neighboring routers. An example is a Catalyst 5500 with a Routing Switch Module (RSM). Layer 3 switches have LAN technology interfaces that perform network layer forwarding; legacy routers provide connectivity to WAN circuits. The switches off-load local traffic from the WAN routers.

Layer 3 switches perform the functions of both data link layer switches and network layer routers. Each port is a collision domain. Interfaces are grouped into broadcast domains (subnets) and a routing protocol is selected to provide network information to other Layer 3 switches and routers.

Combining Hubs, Switches, and Routers

Available in Ethernet and Fast Ethernet, hubs are best used in small networks where there are few nodes on the segment. Hubs do not control the broadcasts nor do they filter collision domains on the network. If higher bandwidth is required, use 100 Mbps hubs. When the number of nodes on the network grows, move to switches.

With the cost of switch ports comparable to hubs, use switches as the basic network connectivity devices on the network. Switches reduce collisions and resolve media contention on the network by providing a collision domain per port. Replace hubs with switches if the utilization is over 40 percent on Ethernet networks or above 70 percent on Token Ring and FDDI networks. Switches cannot resolve broadcast characteristics of protocols; use routing to resolve protocol-related problems. As you can see in the sample in Figure 4-21, the repeaters are pushed to the outer layer of the design, connecting to switches. Switches control the collision domains. Fast Layer 3 switches are used for routing between LAN segments, and the router provides access to the WAN.

Figure 4-21   *Combining Routers, Switches, and Hubs*

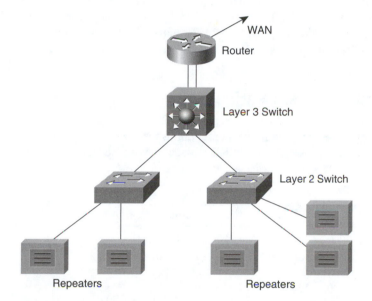

Use routers for segmenting the network into separate broadcast domains, security filtering, and access to the WAN. If broadcast traffic on the network is over 20 percent, use routing.

Cisco LAN Equipment

The CCDA objectives covered in this section are as follows:

2	Assemble Cisco product lines into an end-to-end networking solution.
16	Recommend Cisco products and LAN technologies that will meet a customer's requirements for performance, capacity, and scalability in small- to medium-sized networks.
17	Update the network topology drawing you created in the previous section to include hardware and media.

A CCDA must be familiar with Cisco products, product capabilities, and how to best apply the products to meet performance, scalability, redundancy, and cost requirements. This section lists and explains Cisco equipment for LAN requirements. A complete list of Cisco products can be found at the CCO web site.

FastHub 400

The FastHub 400 10/100 series is a full line of products that includes 12- and 24-port 10/100 Fast Ethernet repeaters in managed and manageable versions. The FastHub 400 10/100 series provides low-cost 10/100 autosensing desktop connectivity where dedicated bandwidth is not required. The Cisco 412 provides 12 UTP ports of 10/100 Fast Ethernet. The Cisco 424M provides 24 UTP ports of 10/100 Fast Ethernet in a SNMP-managed version.

Cisco Catalyst 1900/2820 Series

The Catalyst 1900 and 2820 series provide 12- or 24-switched, 10-Mbps 10BaseT ports. Different models provide Fast Ethernet uplinks in 100BaseT and 100BaseF media. Different models can keep 1KB, 2KB, or 8KB storage of MAC addresses. The specifications of the various models in these series are presented in Table 4-10.

Table 4-10   *Catalyst 1900 and 2820 Series Specifications*

Model	Specifications
WS-C1912-EN	• 12 10BaseT
	• Two 100BaseTX
	• 1KB MAC
	• Enterprise Edition
WS-C1912C-EN	• 12 10BaseT
	• One 100BaseTX
	• One 100BaseFX
	• 1KB MAC
	• Enterprise Edition
WS-C1924-EN	• 24 10BaseT
	• Two 100BaseTX
	• 1KB MAC
	• Enterprise Edition

Table 4-10   *Catalyst 1900 and 2820 Series Specifications (Continued)*

Model	Specifications
WS-C1924C-EN	• 24 10BaseT • One 100BaseTX • One 100BaseFX • 1KB MAC • Enterprise Edition
WS-C1924F-EN	• 24 10BaseT • Two 100BaseFX • 1KB MAC • Enterprise Edition
WS-C1924-EN-DC	• 24 10BaseT • Two 100BaseTX • 48-volt DC Dual-Feed Power System • 1KB MAC • Enterprise Edition
WS-C2822-EN	• 24 10BaseT • Two slots • 2KB MAC • Enterprise Edition
WS-C2828-EN	• 24 10BaseT • Two slots • 8KB MAC • Enterprise Edition

Catalyst 2900

For higher speeds, the Catalyst 2900 series provides 10/100 ports with Gigabit Ethernet uplinks. Catalyst 2948G offers 48 ports of 10/100 Ethernet with two Gigabit Ethernet uplinks.

Catalyst 3000 Series Stackable Switches

The Catalyst 3100 switch is designed for networks that require flexibility and growth with minimal initial investment. This switch contains 24 fixed 10BaseT Ethernet ports, one StackPort slot for scalability, and one expansion FlexSlot for broad media support. It is designed for a variety of campus LAN and enterprise WAN solutions; the Catalyst 3100 switch fits well in a wiring closet and branch office applications.

The Catalyst 3200 is a high port density stackable switch chassis with a modular Catalyst 3000 architecture supervisor engine and seven additional media expansion module slots. The expansion slots are backward compatible with all existing Catalyst 3000 media expansion modules. The seventh slot, called *FlexSlot*, is an expansion slot that accepts either a standard Catalyst 3000 expansion module or new doublewide expansion modules providing forward and backward investment protection.

The 3011 WAN access module for the Catalyst 3200 and Catalyst 3100 provides WAN interconnect integrated with the switch backplane. The 3011 WAN access module was the first FlexSlot module to be introduced. Based on the Cisco 2503 router, the 3011 provides two high-speed serial ports, an ISDN BRI port, and an auxiliary (AUX) port.

Catalyst 3900 Token Ring Stackable Switch

The Catalyst 3920 switch provides 24 Token Ring ports. With the Catalyst 3920 switch, you can start with a single 24-port switch and add capacity as you need it, while still managing the entire stack system as one device.

Catalyst 3500 10/100 Autosensing Switch

The Catalyst 3500 XL architecture is designed to meet the technical requirements of autosensing 10/100BaseT Ethernet interfaces. *Autosensing* enables each port to self-configure to the correct bandwidth upon determining whether it is connected to a 10- or 100-Mbps Ethernet channel. This feature simplifies setup and configuration and provides flexibility in the mix of 10 and 100 Mbps connections the switch supports. Network managers can alter connections without having to replace port interfaces.

GBIC-Based Gigabit Ethernet Ports

Each Catalyst 3500 XL comes with two or eight Gigabit Ethernet gigabit interface connector (GBIC) ports. Customers can use any of the following IEEE 802.3z-compliant GBICs based on their connection needs: 1000BaseSX, 1000BaseLX/LH, or the Cisco GigaStack stacking GBIC. These GBIC ports support standards-based, field-replaceable media modules and provide unprecedented flexibility in switch deployment while protecting customers' investments.

Catalyst 4000

The Catalyst 4912G is a 12-port dedicated Gigabit Ethernet switch featuring high-performance Layer 2 switching and intelligent Cisco OSI network (Layer 3) services for high-speed network aggregation.

The Catalyst 4003 offers 24 Gbps of switching bandwidth and provides expansion to 96 ports of 10/100 Ethernet or 36 ports of Gigabit Ethernet. Up to 96 10/100 Ethernet ports, or up to 36 Gigabit Ethernet ports, can be installed into one managed unit.

The Catalyst 4000 series provides an advanced high-performance enterprise switching solution optimized for wiring closets with up to 96 users and data center server environments that require up to 36 Gigabit Ethernet ports. New FlexiMod uplinks support up to eight 100BaseFX riser connections with EtherChannel benefits. The Catalyst 4000 series provides intelligent Layer 2 services leveraging a multiGigabit architecture for 10/100/1000-Mb Ethernet switching. The modular three-slot Catalyst 4003 system leverages the software code base from the industry-leading Catalyst 5500/5000 series to provide the rich and proven feature set that customers demand in the wiring closet for true end-to-end enterprise networking.

Catalyst 5000 Switch Series

The Cisco Catalyst 5000 series features modular chassis in 2-, 5-, 9-, and 13-slot versions. All chassis share the same set of line cards and software features, which provides scalability while maintaining interoperability across all chassis.

The Catalyst 5002 is positioned to deliver a consistent architecture and features set in a smaller package that addresses the needs of smaller wiring closets. The Catalyst 5002 switches at the 1 Mpps (million packets per second) range. The Catalyst 5002 is a fully modular, two-slot Catalyst 5000 series member, using the same architecture and software as the Catalyst 5000. The switch can deliver more than one million packets per second throughput across a 1.2-Gbps, media-independent backplane that supports Ethernet, Fast Ethernet, FDDI, Token Ring, and ATM.

The Catalyst 5000 will continue to address the needs of switched 10BaseT and group switched wiring closets with performance in the 1–3 Mpps range.

The Catalyst 5505, a five-slot chassis like the Catalyst 5000, is designed for a high-end wiring closet and data applications with performance in the 1–25 Mpps range. The Catalyst 5505 combines the size of the original Catalyst 5000 with the performance boost and added features of the Catalyst 5500 series.

The Catalyst 5509 supports high-density 10/100 Ethernet for the wiring closet, or high-density Gigabit Ethernet for backbone applications, delivering over 25-Mpps switching performance. The Catalyst 5509 provides dedicated switching for up to 384 users, making this chassis an ideal platform for wiring closet solutions. The Catalyst 5509 also supports high-density Gigabit Ethernet for switched intranet backbones and data centers.

The Catalyst 5500 is the most versatile switch in the Catalyst family, able to support LightStream 1010 ATM switching or Catalyst 8500 Layer 3 switching line cards in addition to all the Catalyst 5000 family line cards. The Catalyst 5500 is positioned as a high-capacity wiring closet or data center switch, delivering over 25-Mpps switching performance.

The Catalyst 5500 is a 13-slot chassis that is rack-mountable using the rack-mount kit. All functional components, including power supplies, fan trays, supervisors, ATM switch processors (ASPs), and interface modules are accessible and hot-swappable from the network side of the chassis. This setup ensures ease of use in tight wiring closets.

Foundation Summary

Foundation Summary is a section presented in a concise format to provide quick reference information relating to the objectives covered in this chapter.

Table 4-11   *Ethernet CSMA/CD Based Media*

Specification	Speed	Max Segment Size	Encoding	Media
10Base5	10 Mbps	500m	Manchester	0.4in 50ohm Coax (Thicknet)
10Base2	10 Mbps	185m	Manchester	0.2in 50ohm Coax (Thinnet)
10BaseT	10 Mbps	100m	Manchester	UTP
100BaseT	100 Mbps	100m	4B/5B	UTP
1000BaseT	1000 Mbps	100m	5-level	Cat 5 UTP
1000BaseLX (long wave)	1000 Mbps	550m	8B/10B	Single/multimode fiber
1000BaseSX (short wave)	1000 Mbps	62.5 micrometers: 220m 50 micrometers: 500m	8B/10B	Multimode fiber
1000BaseCX	1000 Mbps	25m	8B/10B	Shielded balanced copper

Table 4-12   *Token Access Based Media*

Type	Speed	Ring types	Encoding	Media
Token Ring	4/16 Mbps	Unidirectional single ring	Differential Manchester	UTP, STP
FDDI	100 Mbps	Dual counter rotation rings	4B/5B with nonreturn to zero inverted (NRZI)	Fiber

Table 4-13   *Network Devices*

Device	OSI Layer	Protocol	Domains	Understands
Repeaters	Layer 1: Physical	Transparent	Amplify signal	Bits
Hubs	Layer 1: Physical	Transparent	Amplify signal	Bits
Bridges	Layer 2: Data link	Transparent	Collision domain	Frames
Switches	Layer 2: Data link	Transparent	Collision domain	Frames
Routers	Layer 3: Network	Aware	Broadcast domain	Packets
Layer 3 Switches	Layer 3: Network	Aware	Broadcast domain	Packets

Table 4-14   *LAN Types*

LAN Type	Characteristics
Large building LAN	Large number of users, data center, floor closet switches
Campus LAN	High-speed backbone switching
Small/remote LAN	Small number of users, small hubs/switches

Table 4-15   *Cisco Devices*

Device	Characteristics
FastHub 400 repeater	12/24 ports of 10/100 Fast Ethernet
1900/2820 switch	12/24 ports of 10BaseT, 100 Mbps uplinks
2948G switch	48 ports of 10/100 Ethernet, 2 Gigabit Ethernet uplinks
3000 series switches	24 ports of 10BaseT stackable switches with expansion slots
3500 switch	10/100 autosensing, 2 Gigabit GBIC ports
3900 switch	24 Token Ring ports
4000 switch	Up to 24 Gigabit switched ports, plus expansion slots for up to 96 10/100 ports of 36 Gigabit Ethernet ports
5002 switch	2 slot modular chassis, 1 Mpps
5000 switch	5 slot modular chassis, 1–3 Mpps
5505 switch	5 slot modular chassis, 25 Mpps
5509 switch	9 slot modular chassis, 25 Mpps
5500 switch	13 slot modular chassis, supports Layer 3 line cards, and ATM modules

Q&A

The following questions are designed to test your understanding of the topics covered in this chapter. When you have answered the questions, you can find the answers in Appendix A, "Answers to Quiz Questions." After you identify the subject matter you missed, review those sections in the chapter until you feel comfortable with this material.

1 What is the maximum segment size in 10BaseT?

2 What is the maximum segment size in 10Base2?

3 What is the maximum segment size in 10Base5?

4 What is the maximum segment size in 100BaseT?

5 What is the maximum segment size in 1000BaseT?

6 What does the acronym DIX stands for?

7 What are the three layers of hierarchical design?

_____

_____

_____

8 At what percent utilization are Ethernets over-utilized?

_____

_____

_____

9 At what percent utilization are Token Ring networks over-utilized?

_____

_____

_____

10 At what percent utilization are FDDI networks over-utilized?

_____

_____

_____

11 What is the maximum recommended percentage of broadcasts on the network?

_____

_____

_____

12 What is the standard(s) for Gigabit Ethernet?

_____

_____

_____

13 What standard governs Token Ring?

_____

_____

_____

14 What media implements a dual-ring and forwards tokens?

_____

_____

_____

15 Routers operate on which layer of the OSI model?

_____

_____

_____

16 Switches operate on which layer of the OSI model?

_____

_____

_____

17 Repeaters operate on which layer of the OSI model?

_____

_____

_____

18 Bridges operate on which layer of the OSI model?

_____

_____

_____

19 Transceivers operate on which layer of the OSI model?

_____

_____

_____

20 Are bridges protocol transparent?

_____

_____

_____

21 When switches implement cut-through switching mode, what is not verified to check for frame errors?

_____

_____

_____

22 True or False: A repeater keeps a table of each MAC address on its ports and forwards frames accordingly.

_____

23 True or False: Routers forward frames based on the destination MAC address.

_____

24 True or False: Bridges forward frames based on the source MAC address.

_____

25 What LAN media uses dual counter rotating rings?

_____

_____

_____

26 Which Cisco device provides 48 ports of 10/100 Ethernet with 2 Gb uplinks?

_____

_____

_____

27 What are the components of the three-part firewall system?

_____

_____

_____

28 What is the encoding scheme of 10-Mbps Ethernet?

_____

_____

_____

29 What is the encoding scheme of Token Ring?

_____

_____

_____

30 100BaseT forwards frames at what speed?

_____

_____

_____

Case Studies

The following case study questions are based on the ongoing scenarios that are presented in the "Case Studies" section of Chapter 1, "Design Goals." If you want to familiarize yourself with the entire scenario, refer to that section before working through the following questions. The answers to these questions can be found in the "Case Study Answers" section at the end of this chapter.

Case Study #1: GHY Resources

1 What issues does GHY Resources have on its Ethernet segments that may cause packet loss on the network?

2 Is the LAN in Kansas City running over the recommended maximum utilization?

3 Draw the current LAN network at the headquarters in St. Louis.

4 If each sales office has less than 20 nodes but may grow to over 30, what switch would you recommend to meet the current requirements?

5 The headquarters segments have 30 users each and will not grow to over 48 nodes. Draw out the topology for a possible solution. Update the topology with Cisco products for this building LAN that uses switched ports and Fast Ethernet media.

Case Study #2: Pages Magazine, Inc.

1 What type of media is used at Pages Magazine, Inc., locations?

2 Ms. Phillips mentions that their Ethernet segments are running over 40 percent utilization during peak hours of the day. What would you suggest?

3 Is the number of nodes at the remote sites too large?

Case Study Answers

Case Study #1: GHY Resources

1 What issues does GHY Resources have on its Ethernet segments that may cause packet loss on the network?

Segments are running at 45 percent utilization.

Broadcast storms on the network.

2 Is the LAN in Kansas City running over the recommended maximum utilization?

No, the maximum is around 40 percent.

3 Draw the current LAN network at the headquarters in St. Louis.

Figure 4-22 shows a representation of the current LAN at the headquarters in St. Louis.

Figure 4-22   *Current Headquarters LAN*

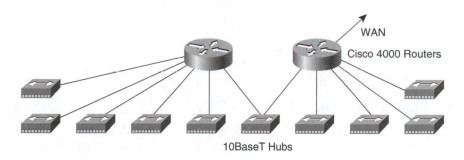

4 If each sales office has less than 20 nodes but may grow to over 30, what switch would you recommend to meet the current requirements?

Catalyst 3200 stack switch

Catalyst 2948G switch

5 The headquarters segments have 30 users each and will not grow to over 48 nodes. Draw out the topology for a possible solution. Update the topology with Cisco products for this building LAN that uses switched ports and Fast Ethernet media.

Figure 4-23 shows a strong topological solution to the customer's needs.

Figure 4-23   *GHY Headquarters LAN Solution*

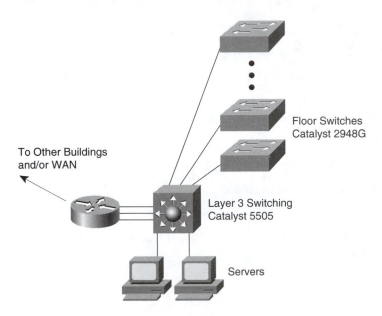

Case Study #2: Pages Magazine, Inc.

1   What type of media is used at Pages Magazine, Inc., locations?

   Unshielded twisted pair

2   Ms. Phillips mentions that Pages Magazine's Ethernet segments are running over 40 percent utilization during peak hours of the day. What would you suggest?

   A good suggestion would be to replace the 10BaseT hubs with 100BaseT switches.

3   Is the number of nodes at the remote sites too large?

   No. The number of nodes at each remote site is under the recommended maximum of 200 for multiprotocol networks.

Objectives Covered in This Chapter

The following is a list of the objectives covered in this chapter. The list of CCDA exam design objectives and the chapters in which they are covered can be found in the Introduction.

2	Assemble Cisco product lines into an end-to-end networking solution.
14	Draw a topology map that meets the customer's needs and includes a high-level view of internetworking devices and interconnecting media.
17	Update the network topology drawing you created in the previous section to include hardware and media.
18	Recognize scalability constraints and issues for standard WAN technologies.
19	Recognize scalability constraints and performance budgets for major Cisco products.
20	Recommend Cisco products and WAN technologies that will meet the customer's requirements for performance, capacity, and scalability in an enterprise network.

CHAPTER 5

WAN Design

The wide-area network (WAN) is becoming more and more critical in the design of a network. Many companies are using WANs to connect the growing number of remote offices and to share services as they would on the local-area network (LAN). With transport and switching improvements, as well as bandwidth increases, WAN design has become a critical skill needed by design consultants.

"Do I Know This Already?" Quiz

The questions in the following quiz are designed to help you gauge how well you know the material covered in this chapter. Compare your answers with those found in Appendix A, "Answers to Quiz Questions." If you answer most or all of the questions thoroughly and correctly, you might want to skim the chapter and proceed to the "Q&A" and "Case Study" sections at the end of the chapter. If you find you need to review only certain subject matter, search the chapter for only those sections that cover the objectives you need to review, and then test yourself with these question again and with the "Q&A" and "Case Study" questions. If you find the following questions too difficult, read the chapter carefully, until you feel you can easily answers these and the "Q&A" and "Case Study" questions.

1 Which WAN transport technologies use packet switching to transfer data?

_____

_____

_____

2 What is the line speed of a T3 leased line?

_____

_____

_____

3 The Cisco Product Selection Tool can be found where?

_____

_____

_____

4 If a customer is concerned about the cost of a WAN network, what technology would you recommend for a backup connection to a 128-Kb leased line?

_____

_____

_____

5 What are the two criteria for a good WAN design?

_____

_____

6 Identify the switching method on the router that has the following qualities: an inbound access list, high CPU utilization, and compression of packets.

_____

_____

_____

7 Which devices support optimum switching?

_____

_____

8 How many DS0s are there in a T1 line?

_____

_____

9 What class of Cisco routers is a 2600?

_____

_____

10 What is the first step in provisioning a Frame Relay circuit?

_____

_____

Foundation Topics

WAN Design Considerations

The CCDA objectives covered in this section are the following:

2	Assemble Cisco product lines into an end-to-end networking solution.
20	Recommend Cisco products and WAN technologies that will meet the customer's requirements for performance, capacity, and scalability in an enterprise network.

There are different requirements when choosing a technology for a WAN than when you are selecting LAN technology. The cost and speed are the critical factors for designing a WAN. WAN connections are high in cost and usually have reoccurring monthly costs. These monthly costs vary depending on the speed of the WAN connection, and sometimes even depend on usage. These charges come mostly from carriers such as MCI, AT&T, and Bell Atlantic, and they can charge different rates depending on the line speed and distance needed by the customer. WANs have traditionally been represented as an unreliable network at lower speeds than LAN connections and at a much higher cost. Recently, WAN technologies have greatly improved to support multiple services and to increase throughput. This section is an overview of the different WAN technologies and covers the hardware used to implement them.

With today's globalization of businesses, the WAN is proving to be an essential component of the network design. These changes in businesses include the growth of remote offices, increased numbers of telecommuters, and a growing business reliance on the Internet. These areas can be categorized into remote access networks and WAN access in the enterprise network.

Remote access solutions have characteristics such as lower speeds (less than T1), lower costs, and high latency due to low speeds and the fact that the connections take time to set up (nondedicated lines). These characteristics make this type of connection useful for remote offices with minimal data transfer needs, such as a remote sales office making nightly uploads of the transaction data for the day. Typical remote access solutions include analog modem access, ISDN, digital subscriber line (DSL), and cable modems.

Unlike remote access, WAN technology is the more broad term that encompasses technology used to provide remote access to the telecommuter and WAN access for an entire company. Enterprise WAN connections can vary in speed from 56 Kbps to 2.488 Gbps. Enterprise WAN technology has a broad spectrum of technologies, equipment, and services that can be implemented, such as Frame Relay, ATM, SONET, modems, routers, switches, and Quality of Service (QoS), all of which are covered in this chapter.

WAN technology goals are dependent on bandwidth considerations, Quality of Service, network topology, scalability, affordability, performance, and availability.

Steps for Designing the WAN

The following is a list of the steps a CCDA needs to take to complete a successful WAN design:

1 List the requirements for the WAN design.

2 Select a WAN technology.

3 Select the WAN hardware.

4 Provision the WAN.

The remainder of this chapter covers these steps.

Listing the Requirements for the WAN Design

The CCDA objectives covered in this section are the following:

14	Draw a topology map that meets the customer's needs and includes a high-level view of internetworking devices and interconnecting media.
17	Update the network topology drawing you created in the previous section to include hardware and media.
18	Recognize scalability constraints and issues for standard WAN technologies.
20	Recommend Cisco products and WAN technologies that will meet the customer's requirements for performance, capacity, and scalability in an enterprise network.

WAN designs should meet the following criteria:

- Reliable service
- Minimize the cost of bandwidth
- Optimize the efficiency of bandwidth

The remainder of this section covers these criteria.

Reliable Service

Reliable service can be achieved through redundancy. This section covers three basic WAN design topologies that describe the interconnection between the routers that provide redundancy:

- Star topology
- Fully meshed topology
- Partially meshed topology

Star Topology

Figure 5-1 illustrates a star topology (also known as a hub and spoke topology), which is a common design for packet-switched networks such as Frame Relay. However, this design has a single point of failure, which is the core router. The core router also acts as a bottleneck and must be able to scale to the needs of the remote offices.

Figure 5-1   *Star Topology*

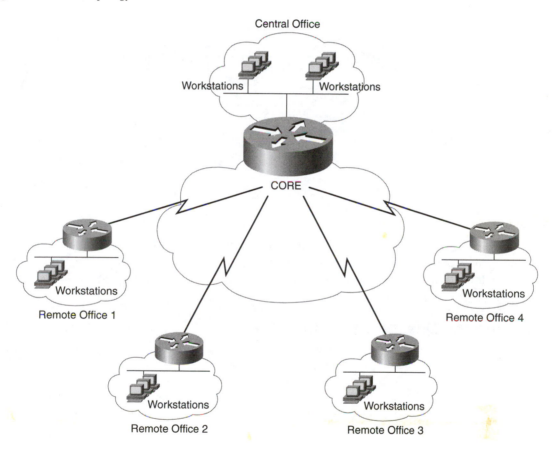

Fully Meshed Topology

Figure 5-2 illustrates a fully meshed design, which has the most redundancy. However, this design has a few problems. As the internetwork grows, each router that is added will add to the overall traffic of the existing routers. This is especially true if the traffic has a lot of broadcasts. Also, each router needs to support the performance level needed in this design, which means that the routers need to be comparable. This design is costly both in equipment and in cost for the WAN connections.

Figure 5-2   *Fully Meshed Topology*

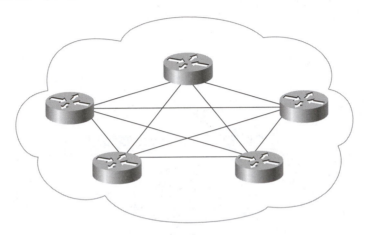

Partially Meshed Topology

Figure 5-3 illustrates a partially meshed topology that would be used in a Frame Relay network. This is often called redundant star configuration. It provides a fair amount of redundancy with a limited amount of meshing and without the negatives associated with fully meshed topologies.

Minimizing the Cost of Bandwidth

The cost of bandwidth can be minimized by choosing the proper WAN technology, such as ISDN. The customer only pays for the use of ISDN. If the service is not used, the customer does not have to pay for access. Analog modem and Frame Relay connections have similar features, but often the customer has to pay an additional monthly fee for having access to the network. In the case of Frame Relay, the customer needs to pay a reoccurring fee for T1 or partial T1 access to the carrier's Frame Relay network.

Optimizing the Efficiency of Bandwidth

Multiplexing or combining multiple services over the same bandwidth is a method of improving the efficiency of the bandwidth. Voice technology is a perfect example of using bandwidth more effectively. Now a point-to-point T1 between two offices can carry not only data, but also voice packets as well, using new hardware and compression technology. However, a critical component of this type of sharing of bandwidth is using Quality of Service techniques.

Figure 5-3   *Partially Meshed Topology*

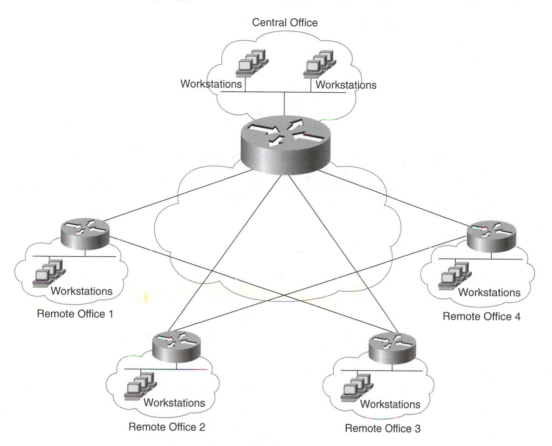

Quality of Service

QoS is a method of measuring and maintaining a level of service needed to support technologies such as voice and video. This is an important concept because technologies such as voice and video are sensitive to bandwidth congestion and errors. For example, voice data arriving in the wrong order would make conversations very difficult.

An excellent resource for more reading on QoS can be found at http://www.cisco.com/cpress/ cc/td/cpress/fund/ith2nd/it2446.htm.

Selecting a WAN Technology

The CCDA objectives covered in this section are the following:

| 18 | Recognize scalability constraints and issues for standard WAN technologies. |
| 20 | Recommend Cisco products and WAN technologies that will meet the customer's requirements for performance, capacity, and scalability in an enterprise network. |

To simplify the process for choosing the right WAN technology, Table 5-1 summarizes important aspects of common WAN technologies into a reference chart. Table 5-1 contains information on which technology is the most appropriate for certain situations, as well as important features and specifications.

Table 5-1   *Identifying the Appropriate WAN Technology*

WAN Technology	Applications
Analog modem	Used by telecommuters and dial-up mobile users.
	Average usage is less than 2 hours per day.
	Line speeds of 56 Kbps or less.
	Used for backup for another type of link.
	Can be attached to network devices such as a router for remote access and configuration.
	Customer is charged for usage of line.
DSL	Uses existing copper telephone lines to usually provide up to 1.544-Mbps speeds to the home or remote office.
	xDSL refers to the family of DSL technologies.
	An excellent reference on how DSL works can be found at http://www.netspeed.com/overview.html.
Cable modem	These are data connections through the same line as cable TV. Possible bandwidth for Internet access can be up to 27 Mbps; however, actual bandwidth would depend on how populated the cable line is.
	An excellent reference on cable modems can be found at http://www.cable-modems.org/tutorial/.

Table 5-1   *Identifying the Appropriate WAN Technology (Continued)*

WAN Technology	Applications
Leased line	Used in point-to-point networks and hub-and-spoke topologies.
	Common leased lines are fractional T1 (less than 1.544 Mbps), T1 (1.544 Mbps), and T3 (44.736 Mbps).
	Used as backup for other high-speed links.
	T1s are commonly used for corporate Internet connections.
	Customer pays for dedicated line.
ISDN	Basic Rate Interface (BRI) is composed of two 64-Kbps B (bearer) channels and one 16-Kbps D (delta) channel
	Cost-effective remote access for corporate or telecommuters.
	Supports voice and video.
	Used as backup for leased line and Frame Relay links.
	Customer is charged for usage of line.
Frame Relay	Cost-effective, high-speed, low-latency mesh or hub-and-spoke topology between remote sites.
	Used for remote offices and LANs.
	Common line speeds are fractional T1 to T1.
	Both private and carrier-provided networks.
	Customer is charged for usage of line.
X.25	WAN circuit or backbone with Layer 3 reliability features.
	Support for legacy applications.
ATM	Support for accelerating bandwidth requirements.
	Support for multiple quality of service classes for differing application requirements for delay and loss.
	Supports voice, video, and data.
	Used on top of T3, SONET, and other high-speed lines.
	Customer pays for the dedicated line.

A key design consideration for WAN implementations is cost. The costs associated with WAN connections can vary depending on the implementation. The cost associated with establishing a WAN connection can have multiple variables. For example, in the chart above, Frame Relay is described as a technology where the customer pays for the access on a usage basis. The cost of usage is charged in addition to the cost for access to the Frame Relay network. An example of this type of charge is a monthly phone bill. Every month you pay a flat access fee for having the phone service, and in addition, you are charged for certain specific phone calls. These factors contribute to the high cost of WAN access.

There are four basic methods to manage costs for WAN connections. The first is negotiating with carriers to find inexpensive and competitive pricing for bandwidth. The increase in competition within the carrier market has made shopping for inexpensive bandwidth even easier. The second method to manage costs is optimizing WAN lines by controlling traffic and by optimizing the WAN design to best use the bandwidth. The third method to manage costs is the integration of multiple services across the same bandwidth, such as voice, data, and video. The final method incorporates quality of service issues.

Frame Relay

One of the most popular WAN technologies is Frame Relay. Technology improvements and support for Frame Relay has made this WAN technology as prevalent as ATM and its use is growing. Frame Relay is being used to connect remote offices to extend the LAN and replace dial-up connections. Because Frame Relay is cost-effective and because you pay for your usage of the bandwidth, people use the Frame Relay network to deliver services such as the Internet to remote offices.

Figure 5-4 shows an example of a network that uses a Frame Relay WAN for connection to remote offices. Note that the Frame Relay network is portrayed as a cloud. The cloud is used to illustrate a network that does not use the same path between two end points. That means that the packets between the remote offices and the corporate network will most likely take different paths within the Frame Relay network.

Frame Relay is a common WAN solution for small to medium businesses because of its lower costs and scalability. Frame Relay uses a method called packet switching to transport data and operates on Layers 1 and 2 of the OSI model. Packet switching takes data and formats it into small chunks, called packets or frames, which allows you to transport different data packets over the same physical data path. A main difference between X.25 technology and Frame Relay is latency and overhead. X.25 technology assumes that the physical line is unreliable and therefore X.25 uses error checking, whereas Frame Relay does not, thereby achieving greater speeds with minimal latency.

More information on Frame Relay can be found in the section "Provisioning a Frame Relay Network" later in this chapter.

Figure 5-4   *Using A Frame Relay Network to Connect Remote Offices*

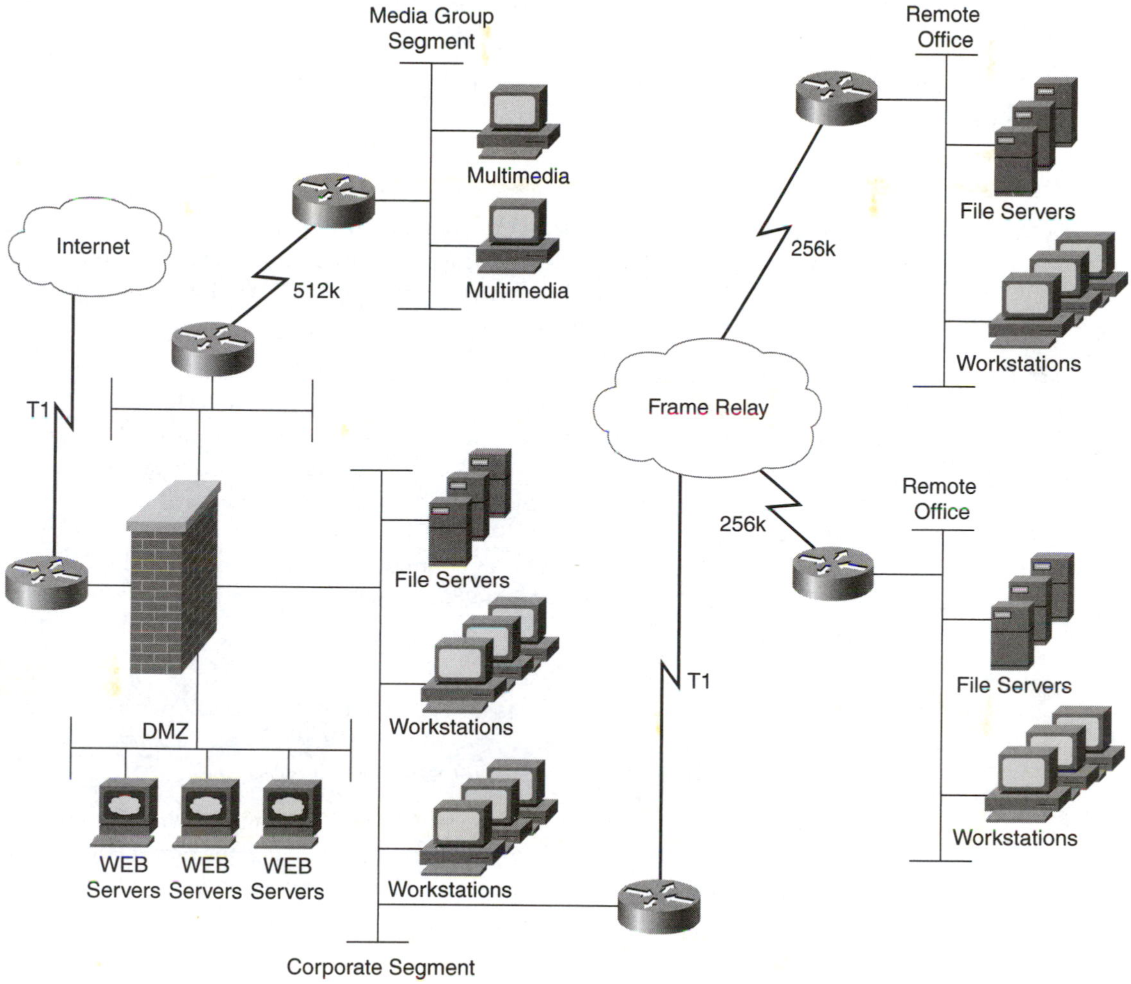

Other WAN Technologies and Design Factors

There are three basic WAN technology categories:

- Leased line
- Circuit switched
- Packet switched

Leased lines, also known as point-to-point links, are permanent connections established between two customer end points through a carrier's WAN. Usually these types of links are for private use by the customer for the duration of their lease or contract.

Circuit switching is a technology used by ISDN. This is where the carrier establishes a physical circuit for the length of the session. This type of technology is similar to establishing a phone call.

Packet switching, used by ATM, Frame Relay, Switched Multimegabit Data Service (SMDS), and X.25, can share a single physical connection through the carrier network. In these types of networks, broadcast traffic can greatly affect the network's performance. However, a technology such as X.25 and SMDS that does not support broadcasting is called a nonbroadcast multi-access (NBMA) network. Networks such as Frame Relay and ATM that do support broadcast are called multi-access networks.

Beyond meshing topologies, there are two other WAN configuration or connection types that need to be discussed. The first is a point-to-point connection. This is a description of a type of logical connection. There is a distinction between the point-to-point WAN technology and the point-to-point connection. A Frame Relay network can have one core router that only allows communication between the core and the remote offices. This means that the remote offices could not talk directly to each other, so logically the Frame Relay network is operating as multiple point-to-point connections. This type of connection is very common in T1 WAN configurations where one end system is connected to another. This connection is also seen in Frame Relay and ATM.

The other type of connection, which is often used in packet-switched networks, is the point-to-multipoint type of connection. This is similar to the star topology configuration, where one core or root device is connected to multiple end devices or leaves. These types of connections, as well as the meshing topologies, pose problems in routing because of loops.

Using the split-horizon update prevents a common problem with routing loops. Split horizon is a method of preventing a router from sending routing information out to the same interface from which it received the update. However, in the case of point-to-multipoint topologies, also known as hub-and-spoke topologies, where one central point handles all the traffic, how is this problem resolved? This problem is addressed in Frame Relay by using subinterfaces. That means that one physical interface has multiple virtual interfaces. Routing information from one virtual interface is sent out another virtual interface, thereby avoiding the split horizon problem.

After reviewing the WAN technology you want to implement, the next step is to select the right hardware.

Selecting the WAN Hardware

The CCDA objectives covered in this section are the following:

19	Recognize scalability constraints and performance budgets for major Cisco products.
20	Recommend Cisco products and WAN technologies that will meet the customer's requirements for performance, capacity, and scalability in an enterprise network.

Throughout this book there are checklists with questions and criteria to aid a designer in selecting a technology or method. Table 5-2 summarizes the criteria you need to understand to meet cost, functionality, redundancy, and scalability requirements for selecting WAN hardware.

Table 5-2   *Checklist for Selecting WAN Hardware*

Criteria	Questions
Cost	How much has the customer budgeted for access?
	Is there a possibility of consolidating services over the same WAN Technology?
Functionality	What will be the function of this router in the network?
	Is the router a backbone router?
	Is the router an Internet access router?
	What type of technologies will it have to support?
	Are there serial connections?
	Is ISDN a consideration?
	What type of modules will the router need?
	Is there a WAN interface card?
	Are there Versatile Interface Processor (VIP) cards?
	What other modules and slots will the router need?
	How much processing power will the router need (processing power depends on the complexity of the routing)?
	How fast does the processor need to be? (The processor speed can depend on complex processes such as route calculation complexity.)
	Are there other features such as encryption to consider?
	What types of ports are needed on the router, and how many ports are necessary?

continues

Table 5-2   *Checklist for Selecting WAN Hardware (Continued)*

Criteria	Questions
Redundancy	What type of redundancy is needed on this router?
	Are automatic fail-overs necessary?
	Are cold spares or off-line backups necessary?
	Are additional modules necessary?
Scalability	What is the expected growth path?
	How will this device respond to the growing needs of the company?

Cisco has anticipated the need for their hardware to have the ability for rapid changes to keep up with changes in technology and the changing needs of their customers. They have addressed the issues in Table 5-2—cost, flexibility, redundancy, and scalability—by modularizing their hardware. By creating separate components, or modules, such as IOS, VIP cards, and WAN interface cards, Cisco has devised a great way to keep up with changing needs. Now for a router to expand in functionality does not require that the entire router be replaced. The scalability issue can be addressed by changing the IOS and a module, for example. Table 5-3 is an overview of the most common of the router features and components.

Table 5-3   *Common Router Components and Their Features*

Components	Features
Cisco IOS	Software created by Cisco to give products better functionality and scalability across the hardware platforms.
High-Speed Serial Interface (HSSI)	HSSI Interface Processor (HIP) is available on the 7000, 7500, 4500, and 4700 routers.
	These interfaces support ATM, Frame Relay, and up to T3 speeds
Network modules	Used in 3600 and 2600 router families to support a wide range of both LAN and WAN technologies:
	Ethernet Fast Ethernet Token Ring ISDN WAN interface cards Asynchronous/synchronous serial Digital and analog modems ATM
	Visit the Cisco Web site at http://www.cisco.com/univercd/cc/td/doc/product/access/acs_mod/cis2600/net_mod2/index.htm for more detailed information as well as IOS compatibility.

Table 5-3   *Common Router Components and Their Features (Continued)*

Components	Features
VIP	These cards are used in 7000 and 7500 series core/high-end routers to provide multilayer switching capabilities. The latest VIPs are called VIP2.
	Supports both LAN and WAN technologies on two port adapter slots.
	They are hot-swappable components, meaning that these cards can be removed while the device is up and running.
	Visit the Cisco Web site at http://www.cisco.com/univercd/cc/td/doc/product/core/cis7505/vip1/vip2/index.htm for more detailed information.
WAN interface card	Used for 1600, 1700, 2600, and 3600 routers for versatile WAN, LAN, and voice connections.
	Supports technology such as:
	Synchronous/asynchronous serial ISDN BRI Integrated CSU/DSU in T1 and fractional T1 speeds Voice and fax interfaces
	Visit the Cisco Web site at http://www.cisco.com/univercd/cc/td/doc/product/access/acs_mod/cis2600/wan_mod/prepwanm.htm#xtocid205540 for more detailed information.

Use the following documents to help you provision the right Cisco hardware:

- Cisco Reseller Product Selection Tool can be found at http://www.cisco.com/pcgi-bin/front.x/corona/prodtool/select.pl. This tool will guide you in choosing a product by entering information such as number of LAN/WAN ports using Ethernet, Token Ring, or serial; port type, such as HSSI; integrated features, such as Integrated CSU/DSUs with T1 interfaces; and design features, such as firewalls and encryption.

- Cisco's "Small and Medium Business Solution Guide," (included as Appendix E of this book) can be found at http://www.cisco.com/univercd/cc/td/doc/product/smbsolg/smb_st.htm. This guide is organized by business cases and situations, such as recommendations for products and features associated with branch office connectivity solutions.

- Price list. To obtain a copy of the current Cisco price list, log in to the Reseller's Web site using your reseller account.

When provisioning WAN hardware, there are a few basic things you want to keep in mind. Cisco has classified their routers to help choose the right hardware.

Switching Modes

A router's ability to process packets plays a key role in the design. Once a router examines the Layer 3 information in a packet, it must switch the packet to the proper outbound interface for delivery. Cisco routers use different switching methods, outlined in the paragraphs below.

Process Switching

Process switching occurs when the packet's destination causes the router to look up the path in the routing table. This means that the packet is processed in main memory. Process switching will occur if a router has an access list, because it requires that each packet be reviewed and compared to the access list before being forwarded. Using encryption and compression also requires the use of process switching.

Fast Switching

In fast switching, incoming packets are passed based on previously cached route information derived from previous packets. These caches are stored in main memory.

With this type of switching, packets are passed to the outbound interface based on previous information. So all packets that need to go to the same location use the same switching path. Fast switching uses asynchronous interrupts, which are handled in real time. Using the route cache is more efficient than the routing table, so fast switching is faster than process switching. Fast switching can drastically reduce CPU utilization on routers. The first packet is always process switched if not already in the fast cache. Once the cache is populated, future packets are fast switched.

Silicon Switching

Silicon switching passes packets on 7000 series routers only, using information in the silicon switching engine (SSE) of the Silicon Switch Processor (SSP) module. The switching speed comes from the fact that the SSP module will make the forwarding decision without interrupting the CPU.

Optimum Switching

You will find optimum switching functionality is available only on the Route Switch Processor (RSP). Because of enhancements to the caching capability, optimum switching is almost twice as fast as silicon switching.

NetFlow Switching

NetFlow switching creates traffic flows using process switching, after which it will review the following packets for the same source, destination, encryption, and so on, and will pass them to the same destination port. When a packet meets the same criteria, it is considered part of the same flow and is passed.

NetFlow has a flow cache that makes it possible to process access lists faster than process switching. NetFlow also supports detailed traffic reporting that can be used for network management, planning, and departmental chargebacks.

Choosing a Router Platform

You need to provide your client with the right router platform, based on your customer's requirements. Remember to refer back to the Table 5-2 for selecting the right hardware. You will notice that there are many variables that can affect your choice of router platform.

For example, the section "Provisioning a Frame Relay Network" later in this chapter covers provisioning a Frame Relay network and its equipment. The equipment choice depends directly on various factors that are part of the implementation of Frame Relay.

The problem of selecting a router in this situation is no different from the process of extracting the customer's requirements for the new network. Identify existing equipment, define the requirements for the new network and apply them to features needed on the new equipment (performance, capacity, and scalability), and use tools to identify recommended equipment. This is a simplification of the process, but as you will see in the section for provisioning a Frame Relay network, the murkiness of choosing the equipment becomes clear when details of the implementation are available.

The router's ability to process packets quickly and efficiently will affect the router's overall performance. Previously, many designers were concerned about the speed at which packets were passed through the router. The following guide is a tool you can use to improve router performance.

Merike Kaeo from the Enterprise Technical Marketing group at Cisco wrote a short guide that provides information on router performance, called the "Router Performance Design and Implementation Guide." This guide is a strong overview on router performance and includes many design tips, such as recognizing design flaws. This guide is included as the following section. It has been edited here for formatting.

Router Performance Design and Implementation Guide

This Router Performance Design and Implementation Guide was originally written by Merike Kaeo from the Enterprise Technical Marketing group at Cisco. It has been edited here for formatting.

With the proliferation of Cisco router products in the past few years and the ever-increasing features and functionality available, understanding some of the intricate interworkings of these devices is necessary to design optimal performance networks. In the early days of routers, raw packet-per-second performance was a valid concern, but with the increased improvements in processor power and memory management, the increasing performance numbers are reaching a point where perception and reality are becoming blurred. This paper focuses primarily on the realities of real network performance considerations and how the varying router platforms that Cisco provides can meet the appropriate criteria for any given network.

The network performance considerations will not address issues regarding latency of routers because, in a network system as a whole, latency per switch or router has been found to be negligible when compared to normal workstation or PC disk access speeds and lower-speed media bandwidth considerations.

It is important to note that raw performance numbers in packets per second should never be the sole criterion for choosing any product because criteria based on support responsiveness, company financials, feature enhancements, software reliability, troubleshooting capability, and a variety of other criteria factor heavily into a final product decision. Performance of the varying platforms should be understood to determine what meets the user's requirement, allowing for future growth and expansion of a user's network.

A description of how to determine what a user's performance requirements may be follows, including some sample calculations that can then be used as a guideline and extrapolated to fit into specific network designs. The traffic patterns and network applications may not be well understood in new network designs, but it is important for some investigation to be done to determine approximate traffic patterns and worst-case scenarios (not to be misconstrued as theoretical worst-case scenarios). Next, the switching paths of varying Cisco router platforms are listed and platform aggregate numbers are specified to help determine the most optimal platform in a given network design scenario. The last section of the paper lists some common features that may affect switching paths and gives general guidelines for optimum network designs.

Realities of Network Performance Criteria

The bottom line of any given network is that it becomes a medium whereby users (the people relying on the network to do their work) accomplish their jobs without incurring any noticeable delays. Performance criteria are met when every user is satisfied in terms of network responsiveness. To ensure user satisfaction, every aspect of the network must be examined, from the media to the applications to the individual devices creating the network as a whole. This task is complex.

Differentiating Performance Tests Versus Real Network Performance

Three areas require classification:

- What comprises a performance test?

- How does one interpret results?

- How does one compare the results to any realistic performance requirements?

The more common performance tests include blasting traffic from an input port to an output port of a device. For a given device, injecting traffic through multiple input ports to multiple output ports on the same device gives aggregate performance numbers. Usually, these tests are performed on Ethernet because Ethernet-based testers were the first available. Aggregate performance numbers are media-independent, but the type of media used plays an important role in defining what the theoretical packet-per-second limitation is. Table 5-4 shows characteristics of some of the more common media in use today.

Table 5-4   *Media Characteristics*

	Interframe Gap	Minimum Valid Frame	Maximum Valid Frame	Bandwidth
Ethernet	96 bits	64 bytes	1518 bytes	10 Mbps
Token Ring	4 bits	32 bytes	16K bytes	16 Mbps
Fiber Distributed Data Interface (FDDI)	0	34 bytes	4500 bytes	100 Mbps
Asynchronous Transfer Mode (ATM)	0	30 bytes (AAL5)	16K bytes (AAL5)	155 Mbps
Basic Rate Interface (BRI)	0	24 bytes (PPP)	1500 bytes (PPP)	128 Kbps
Primary Rate Interface (PRI)	0	24 bytes (PPP)	1500 bytes (PPP)	1.472 Mbps
T1	0	14 bytes (HDLC)	None (Theoretical) 4500 (Real)	1.5 Mbps
Fast Ethernet	96 bits	64 bytes	1518 bytes	100 Mbps

Calculating the theoretical maximum packets per second involves all the variables listed in Table 5-4: interframe gap, bandwidth, and frame size. The formula to compute this number is:

Bandwidth/Packet Size = Theoretical Maximum Packets per Second (where packet size may incorporate interframe gap in bits)

Table 5-5 lists the theoretical packet-per-second limitations for three common media—10 Mbps Ethernet, 16 Mbps Token Ring, and FDDI—each for eight different Ethernet frame sizes. These eight frame sizes, widely used in the industry, are derived from the performance testing methodology as outlined in the Internet standard for device benchmarking in RFC 1944. The numbers are derived by using the above formula.

| NOTE | RFC 1944 has recently been made obsolete by RFC 2544. |

Table 5-5   *Packet-per-Second Limitation*

Ethernet Size (bytes)	10-Mbps Ethernet (pps)	16-Mbps Token Ring (pps)	FDDI (pps)
64	14,880	24,691	152,439
128	8,445	13,793	85,616
256	4,528	7,326	45,620
512	2,349	3,780	23,585
768	1,586	2,547	15,903
1024	1,197	1,921	11,996
1280	961	1,542	9,630
1518	812	1,302	8,138

More specific detail in how the numbers in Table 5-5 were derived for the three media (10 Mbps Ethernet, 16 Mbps Token Ring, and FDDI) follow.

10 Mbps Ethernet   The frame size needs to incorporate the data and header bytes as well as the bits used for the preamble and interframe gap, as shown in Figure 5-5.

Figure 5-5   *10 Mbps Ethernet Frames*

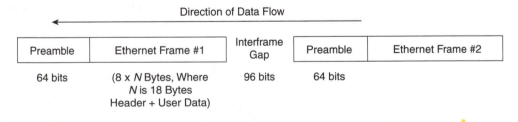

In Figure 5-5 the fields have the following lengths:

- **Preamble**—64 bits
- **Frame**—(8×*N*) bits (where *N* is Ethernet packet size in bytes, this includes 18 bytes of header)
- **Gap**—96 bits

16 Mbps Token Ring   Neither token nor idles between packets are accounted for because the theoretical minima are hard to pin down, but by using only the frame format itself the maximum theoretical packets per second can be estimated, as shown in Figure 5-6. Because we are basing our initial frame on an Ethernet frame, note that we need to subtract the Ethernet header bits for the correct calculation of the data portion. So, for a 64-byte Ethernet frame, we get 64 – 18 = 46 bytes of data for the Data portion of the Token Ring frame shown in Figure 5-6.

Figure 5-6   *16-Mbps Token Ring Frames*

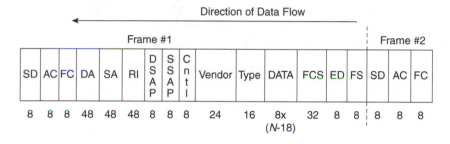

In Figure 5-6 the fields have the following lengths:

- **SD**—8 bits
- **AC**—8 bits
- **FC**—8 bits
- **DA**—48 bits
- **SA**—48 bits
- **RI**—48 bits

- **DSAP**—8 bits
- **SSAP**—8 bits
- **Control**—8 bits
- **Vendor**—24 bits
- **Type**—16 bits
- **Data**—8×(*N*–18) bits (where *N* is original Ethernet frame size)
- **FCS**—32 bits
- **ED**—8 bits
- **FS**—8 bits

FDDI   Neither token nor idles between packets are accounted for because the theoretical minima are hard to pin down, but by using only the frame format itself the maximum theoretical packets per second can be estimated, as shown in Figure 5-7. Note that, because we are basing our initial frame on an Ethernet frame, we need to subtract the Ethernet header bits for the correct calculation of the data portion. So, for a 64 byte Ethernet frame, we get 64 – 18 = 46 bytes of data for the Data portion of the FDDI frame shown in Figure 5-7.

Figure 5-7   *FDDI Frames*

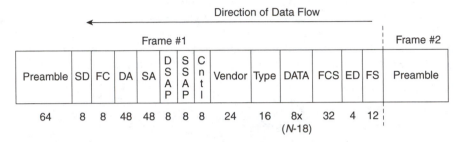

In Figure 5-7 the fields have the following lengths:

- **Preamble**—64 bits
- **SD**—8 bits
- **FC**—8 bits
- **DA**—48 bits
- **SA**—48 bits
- **DSAP**—8 bits
- **SSAP**—8 bits
- **Control**—8 bits
- **Vendor**—24 bits
- **Type**—16 bits
- **Data**—8×(N–18) bits (where N is original Ethernet frame size)
- **FCS**—32 bits
- **ED**—4 bits
- **FS**—12 bits

Frame and Packet Size   The packet size is a major factor in determining the maximum packets per second, and, in the theoretical test world, one packet size at a time is tested. Eight standard packet sizes are tested: 64-, 128-, 256-, 512-, 768-, 1024-, 1280-, and 1518-byte packets. Figure 5-8 shows a graph of the theoretical maximum packets per second for 10 Mbps Ethernet.

==It is important to note that as the frame size increases, the maximum theoretical packets per second decrease.==

Figure 5-8   *10 Mbps Ethernet Theoretical Performance*

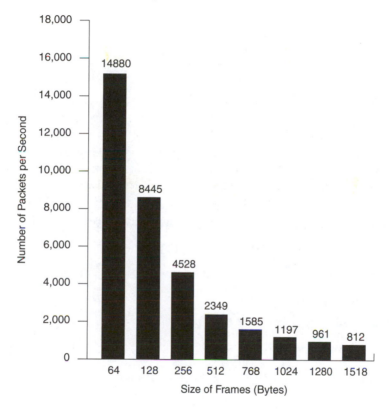

Having seen how maximum theoretical performance is determined, we now see how that data fits in with the performance requirements of real user networks. Each medium has a specific fixed-size bandwidth pipe associated with it, and each one may or may not define a minimum and maximum valid frame size. The minimum and maximum frame sizes are important because most good applications written for workstations or PCs make efficient use of bandwidth available and use maximum-sized frames. ==The smaller the frame size, the higher the percentage of overhead relative to user data; in other words, smaller frame sizes mean less effective bandwidth utilization as illustrated in Figure 5-9.==

Figure 5-9   *Bandwidth Efficiency for Small Versus Large Frames*

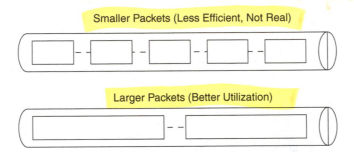

An understanding of real traffic patterns is important when designing networks. At least some typical applications should be known so that the average packet sizes on the network can be determined. Sniffer traces to look at typical packet sizes for varying applications are helpful; some of the more common ones include:

- **Hypertext Transfer Protocol (HTTP) (World Wide Web)**—400 to 1518 bytes

- **Network File System (NFS)**—64 to 1518 bytes

- **Telnet**—64 to 1518 bytes

- **NetWare**—500 to 1518 bytes

- **Multimedia**—400 to 700 bytes

For optimal network designs, an understanding of the kinds of applications that will be used is necessary to determine the typical packet sizes that will be traversing your network. The following example, taken from a real network, shows how to optimize your network design.

Example

Consider a very simple network, depicted in Figure 5-10.

Figure 5-10   *Sample Network*

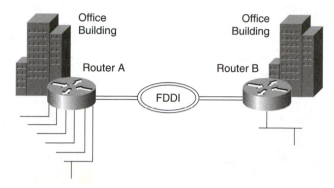

The network consists of six Ethernet networks that are interconnected via an FDDI backbone. Router A interconnects the Ethernet networks to the FDDI backbone. For simplicity, we assume that all the Ethernets have traffic characteristics similar to those shown in Figure 5-11.

Figure 5-11   *Graph of Typical Ethernet Network*

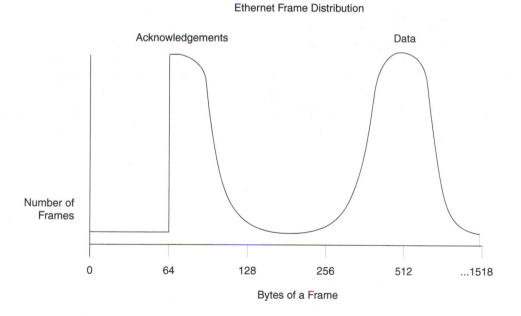

Most of the traffic falls between 256-byte and 1280-byte packets, with numerous 64-byte packets that are typically acknowledgment packets. Our calculations assume that the Ethernet network is fairly busy with average utilization at 40 percent; in other words, 4 Mbps of Ethernet bandwidth is utilized. For average traffic rates, 40 percent utilization of Ethernet bandwidth is a rather heavily utilized network because collisions are very probable and most of the traffic on the network is retransmission traffic. However, the example is intended to show a worst-case, real-world performance scenario.

For simplicity, we assume that the following traffic is on the Ethernet:

- 768-byte packets, 35%
- 1280-byte packets, 20%
- 512-byte packets, 15%
- 64-byte packets, 30%

To calculate the total packets per second that would be on the Ethernet, we need to apply the following formula for each of the different packet sizes: (Bandwidth × Percent Media Used)/ (Packet Size × bits/byte) = Packets per Second.

Using this formula yields:

- (4 Mbps × 35%)/(768 bytes × 8 bits/byte) = 228 pps
- (4 Mbps × 20%)/(1280 bytes × 8 bits/byte) = 79 pps
- (4 Mbps × 15%)/(512 bytes × 8 bits/byte) = 147 pps
- (4 Mbps × 30%)/(64 bytes × 8 bits/byte) = 2344 pps

The total, 2798 pps, is *not* the pps rate that goes through the router. If it is, the network design is not optimal and should be changed. Rather, the 80/20 rule applies to most nonswitched networks, where 80 percent of the traffic stays on the local network and 20 percent goes to a different destination. Then we have 2798 × 20% = 560 pps that the router must deal with from that single Ethernet network. If we take six Ethernets with similar characteristics, we get an aggregate of 3360 pps that the router must support.

Now consider a scenario with central servers and assume that the 80/20 rule does not apply; only 10 percent of the traffic stays local and 90 percent goes through the router to the servers that are off the backbone. In this scenario, the router must support 6 × (2798 × 90%) = 15,110 pps for our example of six Ethernets. The appropriate router platform must be chosen that will meet the traffic requirements.

This example shows how the packets-per-second requirement for varying networks is computed. As will be shown in subsequent sections, all Cisco router platforms meet and greatly exceed the pure packets-per-second requirements of real networks.

Router Platform Switching Paths

This section will list the switching paths that the various router platforms support.

Low-End/Midrange Routers

This category of routers includes the Cisco 2500, 4000, 4500, and 4700 series routers. The switching paths supported for these routers are process switching and fast switching. Fast switching is on by default for all protocols.

The aggregate performance numbers in packets per second are listed in Table 5-6.

Table 5-6 *Aggregate Maximum Performance for Low-End/Midrange Routers (in Packets-per-Second)*

Switching Paths	2500 Series	4000	4500	4700
Process Switching	1,000	1,800	10,000	11,000
Fast Switching	6,000	14,000	45,000	50,000

Features Affecting Performance

Understanding how a given feature will affect the router's switching paths is critical when designing networks. Many new features are initially incorporated into the process switching path and, in subsequent releases, incorporated into faster switching paths. The most current enhancements are listed in Cisco Connection Online (CCO) under Technical Assistance/Tech Tips: Hot Tips/IOS Information. There you will find new features for Cisco Internetwork Operating System (Cisco IOS™) releases and any performance enhancements to previously implemented features.

Low-End and Midrange Router Memory Considerations

Most performance concerns arise from the need for sufficient memory to run in certain environments and the necessity to prevent overstrain on the CPU. The memory considerations are primarily issues for the low-end and midrange platforms. Product Bulletins #284 and #290 address these issues for the Cisco 4000 and 2500 series routers, respectively. They can be accessed via the Web as follows:

- **PB # 284**—http://www.cisco.com/warp/customer/417/49.html
- **PB # 290**—http://www.cisco.com/warp/partner/synchronicd/cc/cisco/mkt/access/2500/290_pb.htm

NOTE   Only registered users can access these product bulletins on Cisco's Web site. Contact your Cisco representative for details on obtaining an account if you do not already have one.

Other Considerations

Additional features that affect CPU utilization are link-state routing protocols, such as Open Shortest Path First (OSPF) and NetWare Link Services Protocol (NLSP), tunneling, access lists, accounting, Layer 2 Forwarding (L2F), multichassis multilink Point-to-Point Protocol (MP), queuing, compression, and encryption.

No boilerplate mechanism that gives hard-and-fast platform limitations exists. What needs to be considered is that for any given platform, the number of interfaces you can support depends greatly on the encapsulations and features used. The aggregate maximum packets per second is a useful number for approximating the maximum number of interfaces to put into a given platform, as long as some real-world analysis of the traffic flow is done. If designs follow a more theoretical maximum packets-per-second approach, the Cisco routers will be greatly underutilized.

Some common rules to follow include:

- Because access lists are checked sequentially, always optimize your access lists so that most traffic meets the criteria of the first entries of the list. If a customer has extensive access lists and this problem is the major performance bottleneck, it may be time to look at a higher performance router.

- Custom, priority, and weighted-fair-queuing activate only when the serial line is congested. As of Release 11.1 they are fast-switched; as long as the serial line is not congested, the fastest switching path that the interface supports and is configured for will be used.

- For low-end and midrange router platforms, compression should be performed for serial lines running at 128 kbps or lower. At higher line rates, compression may tax the CPU.

- Encryption is very CPU- and memory-intensive, so careful consideration of appropriate platforms is necessary.

Network Design Guidelines

Some common network designs are suboptimal in terms of performance; most of these are based on media mismatch as illustrated in Figure 5-12.

This scenario shows two separate cases of common media mismatch problems. The first problem is between Router B and Router C where multiple clients are trying to access a centralized server farm. What may not be obvious at first glance is that the 56-Kbps line is the primary connection between the clients and the servers, and it will quickly become oversubscribed with traffic. At the very least, enough bandwidth to support the maximum expected peak traffic between the clients and servers should be in place. Or, if certain Ethernet segments make extensive use of a particular server, distributing servers to local Ethernet segments will greatly improve network performance.

The second performance problem is through Router A, where the server farm gets backed up to a network of backup servers. The media mismatch from 100 Mbps FDDI to 10 Mbps Ethernet is the bottleneck. To gain optimal performance for high-speed backups going through the router, the media speeds should be maximized.

Figure 5-12   *Media Mismatch*

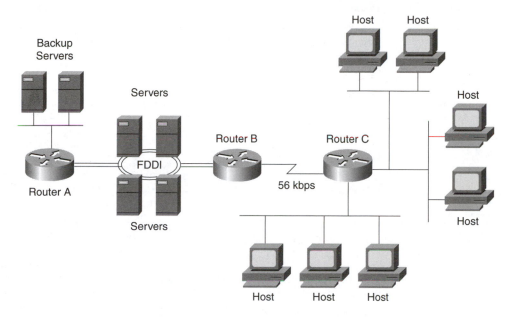

Provisioning the WAN

The CCDA objective covered in this section is the following:

20	Recommend Cisco products and WAN technologies that will meet the customer's requirements for performance, capacity, and scalability in an enterprise network.

Provisioning for WAN services means preparing to receive WAN services. The act of planning for WAN services is an essential component not only for this exam but for your internetwork design as well. This section covers line speeds, which is basic information needed for planning your WAN access. This section also includes an example of the steps needed to provision a common WAN service. Frame Relay has grown in popularity over the past five years and is essential WAN technology for a CCDA candidate to understand. Therefore, Frame Relay is used here as an example for provisioning a WAN network.

First, you must understand the different WAN speeds and the terminology surrounding them. WAN bandwidth is often provisioned in the United States using the North American digital hierarchy. The term DS, or digital signal, is based on the transmission rate of 64 Kbps, also known as DS0. This is the transmission rate usually associated with voice transmission. The T system used in the US and the E system used in Europe and Japan are multiples of the DS0, as seen in Table 5-7. The bit rate in Table 5-7 also includes circuit overhead, such as the 8K for channelizing a T1. This is what accounts for the slight variation on the total bit rate. This overhead would need to be added to the total number of DSO multiplied by 64K.

Table 5-7   *Signaling Standards*

Line Type	Signal Standard	Number of DS0s	Bit Rate (Mbps)
T1	DS1	24	1.544
T3	DS3	672	44.736
E1	2M	30	2.048
E3	3M	480	34.064
J1	Y1	30	2.048

The T1/T3 format is used primarily in North America and parts of Asia. The E1/E3 format is used in most of the rest of the world. The J1 format is used primarily in Japan.

After choosing a signaling standard, or speed, the next step is to review the components of the WAN technology you want to implement. Different WAN technologies require very different components and steps for the implementation. The following example shows how to plan for the provisioning of a Frame Relay connection. For the exam, understand each step needed for provisioning the Frame Relay network, and pay specific attention to the terminology used.

Provisioning a Frame Relay Network

This section includes details on how to provision a Frame Relay network as well as traffic shaping over the Frame Relay network. Note that provisioning means that you are prepared to request a Frame Relay service. These are not the steps needed to create a Frame Relay network. The actual network is provided by the carrier and is usually represented in a network diagram in the form of a cloud. The cloud contains the Frame Relay network, and the following steps outline information you need when provisioning for a Frame Relay network. More technical details on how to implement Frame Relay networks can be found in the section "Frame Relay" earlier in this chapter. Another excellent resource for more information on Frame Relay is a document called "Frame Relay" from Cisco Press that can be found at http://www.cisco.com/cpress/cc/td/cpress/fund/ith2nd/it2410.htm. There is also a Frame Relay Forum that has up-to-date information on Frame Relay networks and technology that is located at http://www.frforum.com/.

Provisioning a Frame Relay network involves the following steps:

1   Choose a committed information rate (CIR) based on realistic, anticipated traffic rates.

2   Aggregate all CIRs to determine core bandwidth requirements.

3 Determine the link speed and number of interfaces required on the core router.

4 Choose a router platform that can handle the job.

Step 1: Choose a CIR Based on Realistic, Anticipated Traffic Rates

A CIR is a connection's minimum bandwidth (information rate) and is specified in kilobits per second. Bandwidth in a provider's Frame Relay network is shared amng its customers. Ordering Frame Relay service with a Committed Information Rate allows the router to transmit at speeds upto the speed of the CIR without the packets being discarded in the event of congestion in the Frame Relay network. Choosing a CIR means that you need to determine what is the lowest guaranteed transmission rate needed to support your services. This step requires that you identify the WAN traffic that needs to be transferred through the Frame Relay network. The tools you use in Chapter 2, "Assessing the Existing Network and Identifying Customer Objectives," should help you to categorize and identify the traffic load that you should anticipate on your Frame Relay network. File transfers and broadcast traffic are some of the criteria that need to be determinedfor the traffic load.

Keep in mind that for nondata traffic, such as voice and video, you will need additional considerations, such as QoS. Cisco IOS Release 11.2 and later versions support a featured called traffic shaping, which is discussed later in this section.

Some Frame Relay providers claim their network has more available bandwidth than has been sold and offer a zero CIR. While a zero CIR can cut monthly reoccurring costs, all packets transmitted by the router are discard eligible. If you decide to get a zero CIR, try to get a service level agreement from your provider that will assure that you receive the bandwidth that you requested. Service level agreements (SLAs) are a set of metrics that are contracted with your carrier or Frame Relay provider. This is also a good audit trail to determine whether the provisioned network rates are obtained.

Step 2: Aggregate All CIRs to Determine Core Bandwidth Requirements

Add up all the CIRs used at each site, and if the access site has a zero CIR, use half of the link speed as the estimated speed. This information is needed to help determine the load on the core router. Frame Relay supports multiple virtual connections using the same physical devices, so it is important to know the total bandwidth needed by your services to determine which physical device can support your needs.

Step 3: Determine the Link Speed and Number of Interfaces Required on the Core Router

Determine the number of data-link connection identifiers (DLCIs) each interface will need. The DLCI identifies a logical connection between two data terminal equipment (DTE) devices; it basically identifies the virtual circuit within the Frame Relay network. Remember to decrease the number of DLCIs per interface if there are multiple protocols, because using too many

DLCIs will adversely affect the router's performance. The following are examples of factors that would affect the number of DLCIs on an interface when using multiple protocols:

- Using multiple routed protocols could result in an increase in broadcasts, which would decrease the number of DLCIs per interface.

- Size of routing protocols and updates means that for a large internetwork, these updates can be substantial, therefore, fewer DLCIs per interface should be implemented.

These examples cite routing protocols and their traffic for decreasing the amount of DLCIs per interface. However, the use of static routes would decrease the broadcast traffic and would support more DLCIs per interface.

Step 4: Choose a Router Platform That Can Handle the Job

Cisco recommends no more than 30–50 maximum DLCIs per interface that need to support broadcast traffic. This number does not define the type of router you would use in your implementation. The router type also plays a role in how many DLCIs can be supported on an interface. If the router's performance will degrade due to processing overhead, your decision for the router will need to depend on the processor, memory, and interface requirements.

For example, if you have 10 access sites, each provisioned with 64 Kbps CIR, you will need a total of 640 Kbps bandwidth. You could use one serial interface to support T1/E1 and support all ten DLCIs on that one interface. Almost all routers starting with 1600 support T1/E1 ports. However, you have to consider the type of traffic on those DLCIs. If seven out of ten DLCIs have a considerable amount of broadcasts, using a higher end router, such as a 3600 router, will have greater performance.

Traffic Shaping over Frame Relay

Cisco IOS Release 11.2 and later supports a feature called Frame Relay traffic shaping. You were briefly introduced to traffic shaping in the section that discusses the need for QoS for nondata services, such as voice and video. With traffic shaping you can virtually eliminate bottlenecks in the Frame Relay network, using these additional features:

- **Rate enforcement on a per virtual circuit basis**—Controls the loss of packets for the remote locations because the rate for outbound packets can be configured. This is especially helpful when the sending location has a higher bandwidth than a remote location.

- **Dynamic traffic throttling on a per virtual circuit basis**—This feature uses the backward explicit congestion notification (BECN) packets that indicate when there is congestion on the network. It then dynamically controls the outbound traffic rate until the congestion is relieved.

- **Enhanced queuing support on a per virtual circuit basis**—This feature uses either customer or priority queuing to guarantee bandwidth for specific traffic, such as video.

Foundation Summary

Foundation Summary is a section presented in a concise format to provide quick reference information relating to the objectives covered in this chapter.

Table 5-8 *Signaling Standards*

Line Type	Signal Standard	Number of DS0s	Bit Rate (Mbps)
T1	DS1	24	1.544
T3	DS3	672	44.736
E1	2M	30	2.048
E3	3M	480	34.064
J1	Y1	30	2.048

Table 5-9 *Identifying the Appropriate WAN Technology*

WAN Technology	Applications
Analog modem	Used by telecommuters and dial-up mobile users.
	Average usage is less than 2 hours per day.
	Line speeds of 56 Kbps or less.
	Used for backup for another type of link.
	Can be attached to network devices such as a router for remote access and configuration.
	Customer is charged for usage of line.
DSL	Uses existing copper telephone lines to usually provide up to 1.544-Mbps speeds to the home or remote office.
	xDSL refers to the family of DSL technologies.
	An excellent reference on how DSL works can be found at http://www.netspeed.com/overview.html.
Cable modem	These are data connections through the same line as cable TV. Possible bandwidth for Internet access can be up to 27 Mbps; however, actual bandwidth would depend on how populated the cable line is.
	An excellent reference on cable modems can be found at http://www.cable-modems.org/tutorial/.

continues

Table 5-9   *Identifying the Appropriate WAN Technology (Continued)*

WAN Technology	Applications
Leased line	Used in point-to-point networks and hub-and-spoke topologies.
	Common leased lines are fractional T1 (less than 1.544 Mbps), T1 (1.544 Mbps), and T3 (44.736 Mbps).
	Used as backup for other high-speed links.
	T1s are commonly used for corporate Internet connections.
	Customer pays for dedicated line.
ISDN	Basic Rate Interface (BRI) is composed of two 64-Kbps B (bearer) channels and one 16-Kbps D (delta) channel
	Cost-effective remote access for corporate or telecommuters.
	Supports voice and video.
	Used as backup for leased line and Frame Relay links.
	Customer is charged for usage of line.
Frame Relay	Cost-effective, high-speed, low-latency mesh or hub-and-spoke topology between remote sites.
	Used for remote offices and LANs.
	Common line speeds are fractional T1 to T1.
	Both private and carrier-provided networks.
	Customer is charged for usage of line.
X.25	WAN circuit or backbone with Layer 3 reliability features.
	Support for legacy applications.
ATM	Support for accelerating bandwidth requirements.
	Support for multiple quality of service classes for differing application requirements for delay and loss.
	Supports voice, video, and data.
	Used on top of T3, SONET, and other high-speed lines.
	Customer pays for the dedicated line.

Q&A

The following questions are designed to test your understanding of the topics covered in this chapter. Once you have answered the questions, you can find the answers in Appendix A, "Answers to Quiz Questions." After you identify the subject matter you missed, review those sections in the chapter until you feel comfortable with this material.

1 How many DS0s are needed to form a T1 line?

_____

_____

_____

2 When using Frame Relay, which Cisco IOS version would best support a Voice over Frame Relay (VoFR) implementation?

_____

_____

_____

3 Which traffic shaping feature would best support the VoFR implementation?

_____

_____

_____

4 When determining the Frame Relay CIR for the central office, the CCDA reviews all the traffic from the remote offices that needs to be transferred to the central office. Which step in provisioning a Frame Relay network would help determine how much bandwidth is required?

_____

_____

_____

5 Which switching method matches packets with its route cache?

_____

_____

_____

6 Which WAN technology uses the Public Switched Telephone Network (PSTN)?

_____

_____

_____

7 What term is used to describe the process of passing a packet internally from one router's interface to the other?

_____

_____

_____

8 Which packet-switching technology is used on unreliable WAN connections?

_____

_____

_____

9 Frame Relay uses which two layers of the OSI model?

_____

_____

_____

10 What router component would be used on a 2600 to provide an integrated CSU/DSU for a T1 connection?

_____

_____

_____

Case Study

The following case study questions are based on the ongoing scenarios that are presented in the "Case Studies" section of Chapter 1, "Design Goals." If you want to familiarize yourself with the entire case study, refer to that section before working through the following questions. The answers to these questions can be found in the "Case Study Answers" section at the end of this chapter.

Case Study #3: MediBill Services, Inc.

1 Characterize the traffic between the remote offices and MediBill.

_____

_____

_____

2 What type of router would you recommend for Internet access to MediBill?

_____

_____

_____

3 If the Internet access router were to be upgraded to support two T1s using Border Gateway Protocol (BGP), what would be the best choice?

_____

_____

_____

4 What type of router would you recommend for the hospital?

_____

_____

_____

5 What type of WAN topology is the hospital's connection to MediBill?

_____

_____

_____

6 If Mr. Lee wanted to implement Frame Relay connections to the six remote offices with the current bandwidth, what would be the CIR for each office?

_____

_____

_____

7 Mr. Lee has determined that MediBill will need a CIR of 1.544 Mbps. If all the remote offices need to communicate with MediBill corporate offices, would Mr. Lee's calculation cause a bottleneck?

_____

_____

_____

Case Study Answers

Case Study #3: MediBill Services, Inc.

1 Characterize the traffic between the remote offices and MediBill.

Internet traffic, email traffic, and database transfer traffic.

2 What type of router would you recommend for Internet access to MediBill?

An access router such as a 2500 or a 2600 would be ideal because there is a line speed of T1. A 2600 would be necessary over a 2500 if the client needed a CSU/DSU. The 2500 access routers do not support one.

3 If the Internet access router were to be upgraded to support two T1s using Border Gateway Protocol (BGP), what would be the best choice?

For line speeds higher than T1, you would need multiple serial interfaces. However, the key in choosing the router would be the need for the router to have enough processing power to support BGP convergence and route calculations and the additional memory to support the BGP routing tables. Therefore, a Cisco 3640 router would be recommended.

4 What type of router would you recommend for the hospital?

The hospital would also need an access router such as a 2500 or a 2600. The hospital currently has a T1 connection to MediBill but might need a redundant connection. Both routers will adequately serve the needs for the hospital; however, the 2600 is a better choice. The 2600 is a good choice for the T1 because the WAN interface card modules can support an integrated CSU/DSU component for the T1 access. Also, the WAN interface card module for the 2600 could support a backup ISDN or even a second T1, if necessary.

5 What type of WAN topology is the hospital's connection to MediBill?

This is logically a point-to-point connection because there are two end points connected together. It is a point-to-point leased line because the T1 provides a connection between two end points through the carrier's T1.

6 If Mr. Lee wanted to implement Frame Relay connections to the six remote offices with the current bandwidth, what would be the CIR for each office?

The existing offices use a 56-Kbps dial-up service, so the CIR would be 56 Kbps per office. The CIR is the guaranteed throughput rate for each connection.

7 Mr. Lee has determined that MediBill will need a CIR of 1.544 Mbps. If all the remote offices need to communicate with MediBill corporate offices, would Mr. Lee's calculation cause a bottleneck?

No. Mr. Lee's calculation should be based on adding all the CIRs for the remote offices. There are six remote offices, which means that the total of the CIRs is 336 Kbps. That is more than enough for MediBill to support the other offices and their need for greater CIRs to support their new Internet services.

Objectives Covered in This Chapter

The following is a list of the objectives covered in this chapter. The list of all the CCDA exam objectives and the chapters in which they are covered can be found in the Introduction of this book.

21	Propose an addressing model for the customer's areas, networks, subnetworks, and end stations that meets scalability requirements.
22	Propose a plan for configuring addresses.
23	Propose a naming scheme for servers, routers, and user stations.
24	Identify scalability constraints and issues for IGRP, Enhanced IGRP, IP RIP, IPX RIP/SAP, NLSP, AppleTalk RTMP and AURP, static routing, and bridging protocols.
25	Recommend routing and bridging protocols that meet a customer's requirements for performance, security, and capacity.
26	Recognize scalability issues for various Cisco IOS software features such as access lists, proxy services, encryption, compression, and queuing.
27	Recommend Cisco IOS software features that meet a customer's requirements for performance, security, capacity, and scalability.

CHAPTER 6

Designing for Specific Protocols

This chapter reviews the scalability constraints and design issues of IP, IPX, AppleTalk, and bridged networks. It also discusses device naming and addressing assignment schemes. A CCDA should know how to create an addressing scheme and assign addresses that take advantage of routing protocol features such as route summarization and VLSMs.

"Do I Know This Already?" Quiz

The questions in the following quiz are designed to help you gauge how well you know the material covered in this chapter. Compare your answers with those found in Appendix A, "Answers to Quiz Questions." If you answered most or all of the questions thoroughly and correctly, you might want to skim the chapter and proceed to the "Q&A" and "Case Study" sections at the end of the chapter. If you find that you need to review only certain subject matter, search the chapter for those sections that cover the objectives you need to review, and then test yourself both with these questions and with the "Q&A" and "Case Study" questions. If you find the following questions too difficult, read the chapter carefully until you feel that you can easily answers these and the "Q&A" and "Case Study" questions.

1 List two distance vector routing protocols for IP.

2 What is the subnet number and broadcast address for host 199.1.10.9/30?

3 How many route entries can there be in an IGRP update packet?

4 What is the default mask for 191.50.0.0?

_____

_____

_____

5 Is 001DG6Ef a valid IPX address?

_____

_____

_____

6 What is RTMP?

_____

_____

_____

7 What is NLSP?

_____

_____

_____

8 What is the broadcast address for network 192.100.7.64 with a mask of 255.255.255.192?

_____

_____

_____

9 Name three IP interior gateway routing protocols that support authentication.

_____

_____

_____

10 Which routing protocol is capable of routing IPX and AppleTalk packets in addition to IP?

_____

_____

_____

11 Which protocol advertises services by producing broadcasts every 60 seconds?

_____

_____

_____

12 Which protocol defines areas for IP networks? Which protocol defines areas for IPX networks?

_____

_____

_____

13 What is the host address of the AppleTalk address 15.4.1? What is the network address? What is the socket number?

_____

_____

_____

14 True or False: RIP version 2 sends route updates only when a change occurs on the network.

_____

_____

_____

15 What are the default metrics used by EIGRP?

_____

_____

_____

16 List three Cisco IOS features.

_____

_____

_____

Foundation Topics

Device Naming Schemes

The following CCDA objective is covered in this section:

23	Propose a naming scheme for servers, routers, and user stations.

Having the right naming scheme can help the network staff know which device they are using without having to rely on a printed spreadsheet or other outside reference.

Naming schemes can be functional or geographical, or they can just follow a random scheme, such as a movie or mythological scheme.

For very small networks, you could use a naming system such as Sneezy, Sleepy, and so on, but these names do not provide an understanding of the function of these devices. As a better solution, you could name servers based on their function or the group they serve, such as Admin01, Netman01, Finance01, IM01, and so on. End stations can also be given names.

Routers can be named by site locations—Houston, Austin, and SanAntonio, for example—in small networks. Most campus sites can use building numbers for router names, such as bldg-1001, bldg-2000, and so on. However, these schemes will not scale for larger networks that might span the globe, as some city building names may not be unique.

For larger networks, you may want to use a country-city-site-number scheme. The name US-tampa-mfg-001 gives good information about the router that is being configured. For country code, you might want to use the ISO 3166 county code standard. Including the router model within the name can also help identify router types. You could use the unique global airport codes to identify the city in which the router is located.

IP Addressing

The following CCDA objectives are covered in this section:

21	Propose an addressing model for the customer's areas, networks, subnetworks, and end stations that meets scalability requirements.
22	Propose a plan for configuring addresses.

The most important requirement that the network designer has in scaling a network is to assign addresses in a manner that can be scaled. Routing protocols cannot summarize networks if the networks are not assigned in contiguous blocks per region. This section covers IP address types, variable-length subnet masking (VLSM), and IP address assignment.

Logical IP Addresses

An IP address is a unique 32-bit logical number assigned to a network device. IP addresses are network-layer (Layer 3) addresses and are represented in dotted decimal format. With the exclusion of address ranges documented in RFC 1918 for private use, all addresses on the Internet must be unique. Each 8 bits are represented with a decimal format. In Figure 6-1, the binary IP addresses is represented in dotted decimal format as 161.8.73.84.

Figure 6-1   *Binary IP Address and Dotted Decimal Format*

10100001.00001000.01001001.01010100
161.   8.   73.   84

Five classes of IP addresses exist. The most significant bits of the first octet determine the class. Those addresses with a 0 in the most significant bit are Class A addresses. These are addresses from 00000000 (0) to 01111111 (127) in the first octet. The network numbers assigned to companies are 1.0.0.0 to 126.0.0.0, with networks 0 and 127 being reserved. For example, 127.0.0.1 is reserved for localhost. The first octet in a Class A address is the network number, and the remaining three octets are the host portion of the address, by default.

Class B addresses use 10 as the 2 most significant bits of the first octet. These are addresses from 10000000 (128) to 10111111 (191). The networks are 128.0.0.0 to 191.255.0.0. By default, the first two octets of a Class B address are the network portion of the address. The remaining two octets are the host portion.

Class C address use 110 as the 3 most significant bits of the first octet. These are address from 11000000 (192) to 11011111 (223). The networks are 192.0.1.0 to 223.255.255.0. By default, the first three octets of a Class C address are the network portion of the address. The remaining octet is the host portion.

Class D addresses use 1110 as the 4 most significant bits of the first octet. These are address from 11100000 (224) to 11101111 (239). The network addresses are from 224.0.0.1 to 239.255.255.255. These addresses are used for multicast addresses and do not have a network or host part.

Class E addresses use 11110 as the most significant bits of the first octet. These are address from 11110001 (240) to 11111110 (254). These addresses are used for experimental networks.

Private Addresses

Several addresses have been reserved for private use. Any company can use these addresses in its internal network in production or in experimental networks. The one caveat is that these addresses might not be routed to the Internet. To prevent this, Internet service providers filter out private addresses. Private addresses are described in RFC 1918; with one Class A network,

16 Class B networks, and 256 Class C networks in existence. Table 6-1 lists these private addresses.

Table 6-1   *Private Addresses*

Class Type	Start Address	End Address
Class A	10.0.0.0	10.255.255.255
Class B	172.16.0.0	172.31.255.255
Class C	192.168.0.0	192.168.255.255

Subnets

Subnetting plays an important part in IP addresses by helping to determine the network, subnetwork, and host part of an IP address. The network designer can manipulate the default mask to create subnetworks for LAN and WAN segments. From an IP address and a subnet mask, the subnetwork and broadcast address of the subnetwork can be determined; the CCDA must master these concepts.

Each A, B, and C address class has a default address mask. This mask is a 32-bit string. The mask bits are set to 1 to establish the network portion of the address. Table 6-2 shows the default mask for Class A, Class B, and Class C addresses.

Table 6-2   *Address Masks*

Class	Mask	Dotted Decimal
A	11111111000000000000000000000000	255.0.0.0
B	11111111111111110000000000000000	255.255.0.0
C	11111111111111111111111100000000	255.255.255.0

Network-layer devices use the IP address and mask to determine the network portion of the address. Table 6-3 shows that a device with an IP address of 172.17.33.1 with a mask of 255.255.240.0 is on subnetwork 172.17.32.0.

Table 6-3   *Determining the Network Portion of the Address*

IP address	172.17.33.1	10101100 00010001 00100001 00000001
Mask	255.255.240.0	11111111 11111111 **1111**0000 00000000
Subnetwork	172.17.32.0	10101100 00010001 00100000 00000000

Remember that the major network is still 172.17.0.0, a Class B network. The 255.255.240.0 mask creates 16 subnetworks (4 bolded bits in Table 6-3). The subnet mask takes the four most significant bits of the third octet for subnetwork definition. Table 6-4 shows the subnetworks defined with this mask.

Table 6-4   *Subnetworks for 172.17.0.0 with 255.255.240.0 Mask*

Third Octet	Subnetwork
00000000	172.17.0.0
00010000	172.17.16.0
00100000	172.17.32.0
00110000	172.17.48.0
01000000	172.17.64.0
01010000	172.17.80.0
01100000	172.17.96.0
01110000	172.17.112.0
10000000	172.17.128.0
10010000	172.17.144.0
10100000	172.17.160.0
10110000	172.17.176.0
11000000	172.17.192.0
11010000	172.17.208.0
11100000	172.17.224.0
11110000	172.17.240.0

The subnetwork 172.27.0.0/28 is used when the **ip subnet-zero** command is configured on the router. Each subnetwork has 12 bits for the host portion. This produces $(2^{12}) - 2 = 4096 - 2 = 4094$ hosts on each subnet. Two is subtracted for the subnet number and the broadcast address number. Looking at Table 6-5 with subnet 172.17.48.0, host addresses will range from 172.17.48.1 to 172.17.63.254, with the subnet broadcast address of 172.17.63.255. Notice that the subnetwork address has 12 0s, and the broadcast address has all 1s as the least significant bits (bolded in Table 6-5).

Table 6-5   *Subnetwork 172.17.48.0*

Type	Binary IP address	Dotted Decimal
Subnetwork	10101100 00010001 00110**000 00000000**	172.17.48.0
First host	10101100 00010001 00110000 00000001	172.17.48.1
Last host	10101100 00010001 00111111 11111110	172.17.63.254
Broadcast	10101100 00010001 00111**111 11111111**	172.17.63.255

Mask Nomenclature

Two ways exist by which to represent a subnet mask. The first format is dotted decimal—for example, 255.255.255.0. Recently, the bit mask number format has become popular. This format represents the subnet mask by using a slash with the number of bits with 1s in the mask. For example, the mask 255.255.255.0 is represented as /24. Table 6-6 shows some mask representations.

Table 6-6   *Subnet Masks*

Dotted Decimal	Bit Mask
255.0.0.0	/8
255.192.0.0	/10
255.255.0.0	/16
255.255.224.0	/19
255.255.240.0	/20
255.255.255.0	/24
255.255.255.128	/25
255.255.255.240	/28
255.255.255.248	/29
255.255.255.252	/30

Variable-Length Subnet Masks

Using one of the subnets from Table 6-4 on a point-to-point serial link would be a waste of IP addresses. Only two addresses are needed on a point-to-point serial link; therefore, more than 4000 addresses would be wasted. Variable-length subnet masks (VLSMs) provide the capability to use different masks in a network for different segments. Large LANs could use a /23 mask, for example, for 510 hosts. A serial link could use a /30 mask for two hosts (routers). Not all routing protocols support VLSM; routing protocols will be covered in the "IP Routing Protocols" section later in this chapter.

Take subnet 172.17.48.0/20 from Table 6-4. Subdividing this network using a /23 mask produces eight subnetworks. Table 6-7 displays the results of this example; the bolded bits indicate the 3 bits used to determine subnets

Table 6-7   *VLSM Subnetwork*

Third Octet	Subnetwork
0011**0000**	172.17.48.0/23
0011**0010**	172.17.50.0/23
0011**0100**	172.17.52.0/23

Table 6-7   *VLSM Subnetwork (Continued)*

Third Octet	Subnetwork
00110110	172.17.54.0/23
00111000	172.17.56.0/23
00111010	172.17.58.0/23
00111100	172.17.60.0/23
00111110	172.17.62.0/23

Now take one of these subnetworks and use it for the serial links of the internetwork. Taking 172.17.62.0/23 and subdividing it using a /30 mask produces 128 subnetworks for serial links. Table 6-8 displays the subnets created for serial links. The bolded bits indicate the bits used to determine the subnet numbers.

Table 6-8   *VLSM Subnetworks for Serial Links*

Third Octet	Fourth Octet	Subnetwork
00111110	00000000	172.17.62.0/30
00111110	00000100	172.17.62.4/30
00111110	00001000	172.17.62.8/30
00111110	00001100	172.17.62.12/30
. . .	. . .	. . .
00111111	11110100	172.17.63.244/30
00111111	11111000	172.17.63.248/30
00111111	11111100	172.17.63.252/30

To verify the addressing, take one of these subnets and break it down at the bit level. Table 6-9 shows the details for subnet 172.17.62.12/30.

Table 6-9   *Serial Link Subnet Detail*

Type	Binary IP address	Dotted Decimal
Subnetwork	10101100 00010001 00111110 00001100	172.17.62.12
Router 1	10101100 00010001 00111110 00001101	172.17.62.13
Router 2	10101100 00010001 00111110 00001110	172.17.62.14
Broadcast	10101100 00010001 00111110 00001111	172.17.62.15

Supernetting

Just as subnetting provides the capability to subdivide Class A, Class B, and Class C addresses into smaller groups, supernetting groups networks into larger supernets by borrowing bits from the network portion of the address. Say that you want a LAN network to have more than 254 hosts; a class C network is not sufficient. You can group two Class C networks using supernets to provide more IP addresses to the LAN segment without using secondary IP addresses on the router interface. Grouping classfull networks into supernets is considered classless routing.

Take networks 192.168.4.0/24 and 192.168.5.0/24, for example. These are Class C networks with a default mask of 255.255.255.0.

Notice from Table 6-10 that these networks are the same up to 23 bits. They are combined, or supernetted, into one network—192.168.4.0/**23**. The mask for the new network is 255.255.254.0. The first host address is 192.168.4.1. The last host address is 192.168.5.254. The broadcast address is 192.168.5.255.

Table 6-10   *Two Class C Networks Combined for Supernet*

Binary IP Address	Dotted Decimal
11000000 10101000 00000100 00000000	192.168.4.0
11000000 10101000 00000101 00000000	192.168.5.0

Address Aggregation

A set of classfull networks can also be summarized in routing entries by creating aggregate addresses at the supernet level. Figure 6-2 shows how address aggregation summarizes routes in which Router A sends only one route, 192.168.16.0/21, to its upstream router.

Classless Interdomain Routing

Classless interdomain routing (CIDR) is used in Internet Border Gateway Protocol (BGP) routing to reduce the number of Class C routes coming from an autonomous system. For example, ISPs can allocate blocks of 4, 8, or 16 Class C networks to a customer and use only one route for reachability. In Figure 6-3, the client has a CIDR block of four Class C networks, but Router A announces only 208.10.8.0/22 to the ISP router.

Figure 6-2   *Route Summarization*

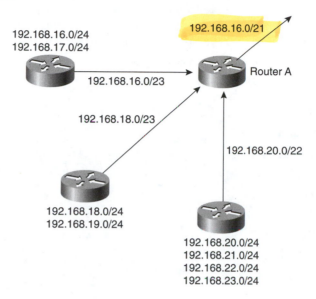

192.168.16.0/24
192.168.17.0/24

192.168.16.0/21

192.168.16.0/23

Router A

192.168.18.0/23

192.168.20.0/22

192.168.18.0/24
192.168.19.0/24

192.168.20.0/24
192.168.21.0/24
192.168.22.0/24
192.168.23.0/24

Figure 6-3   *Classless Interdomain Routing (CIDR)*

Internet Service Provider

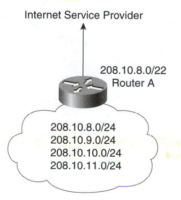

208.10.8.0/22
Router A

208.10.8.0/24
208.10.9.0/24
208.10.10.0/24
208.10.11.0/24

Addressing Scheme

When assigning addresses to areas, networks, subnetworks, and end stations, it is important to maintain an addressing scheme that can scale as the company grows. Hierarchical network design begins with the addressing scheme. Routers cannot summarize routes if the networks are not assigned within bit boundaries. Assume, for example, that network 172.17.0.0/16 will be used in a medium- to large-sized company with nine areas. Each area could have several sites.

How can the network be divided allowing at least 2000 nodes per area? One method involves dividing the network into 16 areas at the /20 bit boundary. Notice that a /19 bit boundary would provide only eight areas, which would not be sufficient for this exercise. The areas can be classified as in Table 6-11, providing sufficient room for growth.

Table 6-11   *Area Network Assignments per Geographical Region*

Area	Range
Reserved	172.17.0.0/20
North America East	172.17.16.0/20
North America West	172.17.32.0/20
North America Central	172.17.48.0/20
South America	172.17.64.0/20
Japan	172.17.80.0/20
Singapore	172.17.96.0/20
Asia	172.17.112.0/20
Europe West	172.17.128.0/20
Europe East	172.17.144.0/20
Reserved	172.17.160.0/20
Reserved	172.17.176.0/20
Reserved	172.17.192.0/20
Reserved	172.17.208.0/20
Reserved	172.17.224.0/20
Reserved	172.17.240.0/20

Networks within the areas should be assigned based on the expected number of hosts and segments on the networks. Serial links should be assigned a /30 subnet. Using the America East network, 172.17.16.0/20, subdivide into two large LANs with around 1000 hosts each, four medium LANs with 200 hosts, five small LANs with 20 hosts, and reserved addresses for serial links; leave room for future medium and small LANs. Table 6-12 shows one way of how the network can be further divided.

Table 6-12   *America East Subnetwork Assignments*

Subnetwork	Range
Large LAN1	172.17.16.0/22
Large LAN2	172.17.20.0/22
Medium LAN1	172.17.24.0/24
Medium LAN2	172.17.25.0/24

Table 6-12   *America East Subnetwork Assignments (Continued)*

Subnetwork	Range
Medium LAN3	172.17.26.0/24
Medium LAN4	172.17.27.0/24
Medium LAN5 (future)	172.17.28.0/24
Small LAN1	172.17.29.0/27
Small LAN2	172.17.29.32/27
Small LAN3	172.17.29.64/27
Small LAN4	172.17.29.96/27
Small LAN5	172.17.29.128/27
Small LAN6 (future)	172.17.29.160/27
Small LAN7 (future)	172.17.29.192/27
Small LAN8 (future)	172.17.29.224/27
Reserved	172.17.30.0/24
Serial Link1	172.17.31.0/30
Serial Link2	172.17.31.4/30
Serial Link3	172.17.31.8/30
Serial Link4	172.17.31.12/30
Serial Link5	172.17.31.16/30
. . .	. . .

LAN Addressing

It is important to design the address assignment for LAN subnets as well. Reserve addresses for the network devices, such as routers, switches, and analyzers. Set aside a range of addresses for statically assigned servers. The rest can be used for dynamically assigned Dynamic Host Configuration Protocol (DHCP) devices. Table 6-13 shows an example.

Table 6-13   *LAN Device IP Assignment for Network 172.17.26.0/24*

Range	Assignment
.1	HSRP (default gateway)
.2	Router 1
.3	Router 2
.4 to .10	LAN switches

continues

Table 6-13   *LAN Device IP Assignment for Network 172.17.26.0/24 (Continued)*

.11	Protocol analyzer
.15 to .25	Servers
.26 to .34	Printers
.35 to .225	DHCP scope
.226 to .254	Reserved

IP Routing Protocols

The following CCDA objectives are covered in this section:

24	Identify scalability constraints and issues for IGRP, Enhanced IGRP, IP RIP, IPX RIP/SAP, NLSP, AppleTalk RTMP and AURP, static routing, and bridging protocols.
25	Recommend routing and bridging protocols that meet a customer's requirements for performance, security, and capacity.

Routing is the process by which a packet is forwarded from one network to another. Routers perform this function and also maintain tables of reachable networks and corresponding interfaces used to reach those networks. Such a table can be manually entered or dynamically created using information gathered by routing protocols.

This section covers IP routing protocol characteristics and differences.

Static Versus Dynamic Routing

Static routing is the method by which the network administrator manually enters routing entries on the router. The forwarding table is not learned by speaking with other routers on the network; these entries do not change unless the administrator alters them. The main benefit of static routing is that no routing protocol traffic is generated by the router. The drawback is that routers with static routes cannot react to network changes. Static routing is recommended for hub-and-spoke topologies with low bandwidth.

Dynamic routing protocols build routing tables from information received from other routers in the internetwork. In the event of a network change, they can recalculate the best routes to a destination.

Distance Vector Versus Link-State Routing Protocols

Dynamic routing protocols are mainly divided into two types: distance vector or link-state. Distance vector protocols tend to be less complex than link-state protocols. Link-state protocols require routers to run algorithms to compute best paths to destinations, driving router CPU utilization higher.

Distance Vector Routing Protocols

The first routing protocols produced were distance vector routing protocols, and are occasionally referred to as Bellman-Ford or Ford-Fulkerson routing protocols, based on the work of R.E. Bellman, L.R. Ford, and D.R. Fulkerson. These protocols are simpler than link-state protocols. In distance vector routing protocols, distance vector routes are advertised as vectors of distance and direction. The distance metric is usually router hop count. The direction is the next-hop router to forward the packet to. The hop count is usually limited to 15 hops in distance vector routing protocols, an important scaling limitation.

Distance vector algorithms call for each router to send all or some portion of its routing table only to its neighbors. The router builds a new table and sends it to its neighbors, and so on. The table is sent in a periodic fashion. The following is a list of distance-vector routing protocols (including non-IP routing protocols):

- IP Routing Information Protocol (RIP)
- Cisco's Interior Gateway Routing Protocol (IGRP)
- IPX Routing Information Protocol (IPX RIP)
- AppleTalk Router Table Maintenance Protocol (RTMP)
- DEC DNA Phase IV
- Xerox's XNS Routing Information Protocol (XNS RIP)

Another protocol, Enhanced Interior Gateway Routing Protocol, is considered a hybrid routing protocol. This is a distance vector that acts as a link-state routing protocol.

Link-State Routing Protocols

Link-state routing protocols were developed to address some limitations of distance vector protocols. When running a link-state routing protocol, routers originate information about themselves (IP addresses), their connected links (number and type of links), and the state of each those links (up/down). The information is forwarded from router to router in the network. Each router makes a copy of the information and does not change it. Each router maintains a map of the network and independently calculates the best paths to destinations.

Link-state protocols are sometimes called *shortest path first* or *distributed-database protocols*. They are built on the Dijkstra shortest path algorithm, an algorithm from graph theory that was developed by E.W. Dijkstra. Because link-state protocols send only the state of their own links to all routers, and distance vector protocols send full routing tables to their neighbors, it can be said that link-state algorithms send small updates everywhere, while distance vector algorithms send larger updates only to neighboring routers. Link-state protocols are usually more CPU- and memory-intensive than distance vector routers. The following is a list of link-state routing protocols (including non-IP):

- IP Open Shortest Path First (OSPF)

- CLNS and IP Intermediate System-to-Intermediate System (IS-IS)

- DEC DNA Phase V

- IPX NetWare Link-Services Protocol (NLSP)

Routing Information Protocol

Routing Information Protocol (RIP) version 1 is defined in RFC 1058. This is a distance vector routing protocol that uses hop count as a metric. The maximum hop count is 15, with 16 registering as unreachable. RIP is a classfull protocol and does not support VLSM or authentication. RIP routers send updates to their neighbors every 30 seconds. RIP was designed for smaller networks, usually implemented in UNIX environments.

RIP routers expect to see routes from their neighbors every 30 seconds. An expiration timer is implemented to set a route as an invalid route. For RIP, the invalid timer is 180 seconds (six times the update timer). Another timer is used to remove the route from the routing table. This is the flush timer and it is set to 240 seconds, by default. Although not in RFC 1058, Cisco implements a hold-down timer for RIP. When a change occurs on a route, a triggered update is sent and the route is placed in holddown—no changes are accepted until the hold-down timer expires. The default hold-down timer is 180 seconds (six times the update timer).

RIP employs algorithms to prevent routing loops. These algorithms include triggered updates and split horizon with poison reverse.

Triggered Updates

A triggered update is a routing table update sent before the update timer has expired—for example, broadcasting the RIP table to neighboring routers before the normal 30-second interval. The triggered update is sent if a metric changes for a particular route, such as if a serial interface goes down.

Split Horizon with Poison Reverse

Split horizon is the technique in which routes that are learned from a neighboring router are not sent back to that neighboring router. With poison reverse, instead of suppressing the route, the route is sent with a metric of Unreachable.

RIP Version 2

RIP version 2 (RIPv2) is defined in RFC 1723. RIPv2 maintains the same distance vector characteristics of RIPv1. Updates are still sent every 30 seconds, and the 15-hop limitation still exists. However, RIPv2 becomes a classless routing protocol. The new features implemented include support for VLSM, support for authentication of route updates, and multicast updates.

RIPv2 can be used in small networks where VLSM masking is required. Authentication can be used to prevent communication from listening to UNIX stations. RFC 1723 defines simple plain-text authentication for RIPv2. In addition to plain-text passwords, Cisco's implementation provides the capability to use MD5 authentication. MD5 is the message digest algorithm defined in RFC 1321. Its algorithm takes as input a message of arbitrary length and produces as output a 128-bit fingerprint or message digest of the input, making it much more secure than plain-text passwords.

Interior Gateway Routing Protocol

Interior Gateway Routing Protocol (IGRP) was developed by Cisco Systems in the mid-1980s to overcome the limitations of RIP. IGRP is not limited to the 15-hop count limit of RIP. Although not used as a metric, IGRP keeps track of the hop count, which has an upper limit of 255 hops. As with RIP, IGRP is a distance vector routing protocol that updates its neighbors in periodic fashion. IGRP is a classfull routing protocol and cannot implement VLSM. IGRP also summarizes addresses at network boundaries. As with RIP, IGRP implements split horizon, triggered updates, and hold-down timers for stability. One benefit of IGRP is that it can load balance over unequal-cost links. As a routing protocol developed by Cisco, it is available only on Cisco routers.

The IGRP update timer is set to 90 seconds. The invalid timer is set to 270 seconds (three times the update period). The flush timer is set to 630 seconds (seven times the update period). If a triggered update is implemented, the route is placed in holddown—no new changes for the route are accepted until the hold-down timer expires. The default hold-down timer is 280 seconds (three times the update timer, plus 10 seconds).

IGRP Metrics

IGRP uses a composite metric based on bandwidth, delay, load, and reliability. Although the path maximum transmission unit (MTU) is not used for the composite metric calculation, it is also tracked. By default, interface bandwidth and delay are used to calculate the metric.

Open Shortest Path First

Open Shortest Path First (OSPF) is defined in RFC 2328 as a link-state routing protocol that uses the Dijkstra shortest path first algorithm to calculate paths to destinations. In OSPF, each router sends link-state advertisements about itself and its links to all other routers in the network. Note that it does not send routing tables, but link-state information. All routers in the internetwork receive this information and calculate the best routes to the destination by running the SPF algorithm.

OSPF is a classless routing protocol that permits the use of VLSM. It supports equal-cost load balancing and route authentication. The metric used in OSPF is cost, which is an unsigned 16-bit integer in the range of 1 to 65535. The default cost for interfaces is calculated based on the bandwidth in the formula $10^8/BW$, with BW being the bandwidth of the interface expressed as a full integer of bits per second. A 10BaseT (10Mbps = 10^7bps) interface will have a cost of $10^8/10^7 = 10$. OSPF introduces some concepts of areas, border routers, and designated routers.

Link-State Advertisement Types

OSPF defines different link-state advertisement (LSA) types for router, network, summary, external, and so on. Table 6-14 describes the major LSA types.

Table 6-14   *Major LSA Types*

Type Code	Type	Description
1	Router LSA	Produced by every router and includes all the router's links, interfaces, state of links, and cost.
2	Network LSA	Produced by every designated router (DR) on every transit broadcast or nonbroadcast multiaccess (NBMA) network. It lists all attached routers in the multiaccess network.
3	Summary LSA for ABRs	Produced by area border routers (ABRs). It is sent into an area to advertise destinations outside the area.
4	Summary LSA for ASBRs	Originated by area border routers (ARBs). It advertises autonomous system boundary routers (ASBRs).
5	Autonomous System External LSA	Originated by ASBRs. Advertises destinations external to the OSPF autonomous system (AS), flooded throughout the OSPF AS.
7	Not-so-stubby area External LSA	Originated by ASBRs in a not-so-stubby area (NSSA). It is not flooded throughout the OSPF autonomous system, only to the NSSA.

OSPF Areas

As a network grows, the initial flooding and database maintenance of LSAs can burden the CPU of a router. OSPF uses areas to reduce these effects. An area is a logical grouping of routers and links that divides the network. Routers share link-state information with only those routers in their area. This reduces the size of the database.

Area 0 is reserved for the backbone area, which is responsible for distributing routing information between areas. As you can see in Figure 6-4, communication between Area 1 and Area 2 must flow through Area 0. In intra-area traffic, packets are passed between routers in a single area. In inter-area traffic, packets are passed between routers in different areas.

Figure 6-4   *OSPF Areas*

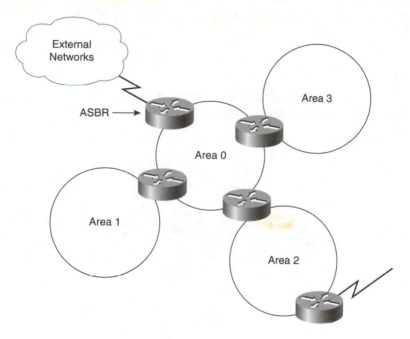

Stub Areas

Consider Area 1 in Figure 6-4. Its only path to the external routes is through Router A. All external routes are flooded to all areas in the OSPF autonomous system (AS). An area can be configured as a stub area to prevent OSPF external LSAs (type 5) from being flooded into that area. Note that network summary LSAs (type 3) from other areas will still be flooded into the area.

Totally Stubby Areas

Take the Area 1 case in Figure 6-4 one step further. The only path for Area 1 to get to Area 0 and other areas is through Router A. So, in addition to preventing external LSAs (type 5) from being flooded, in a totally stubby area network summary LSAs (type 3) are not flooded. Only a single LSA is sent for the default route.

Not-So-Stubby Areas

Notice that Area 2 in Figure 6-4 has an ASBR. If this area is configured as a Not-so-stubby area (NSSA), it will allow the external LSAs (type 7) into the OSPF system, while retaining the characteristics of a stub area to the rest of the AS. The area border router (ABR) for area 2 can be configured to convert the not-so-stubby area External LSAs (type 7) to autonomous system external LSAs (type 5) and flood the rest of the network.

OSPF Router Types

OSPF introduces several router types related to their place in the area architecture. Figure 6-5 displays a diagram of OSPF router types.

Figure 6-5   *OSPF Router Types*

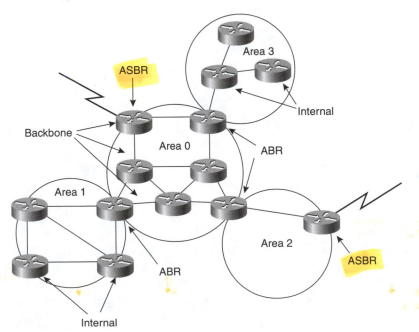

The following is a list of explanations for each router type shown in Figure 6-5:

- **Internal router**—All routers whose interfaces belong to the same OSPF area. These routers keep only one link-state database.

- **Area border router (ABR)**—Routers that are connected to more than one area. These routers maintain a link-state database for each area to which they belong.

- **Autonomous system boundary router (ASBR)**—Routers that inject external link-state advertisements into the OSPF database. These external routes are learned either via other routing protocols or as static routes.

- **Backbone router**—Routers with at least one interface attached to Area 0.

Note that a router can be an ABR, ASBR, and backbone router at the same time.

Designated Routers

On multiaccess networks (such as Ethernet or multipoint Frame Relay), OSPF routers on the network select a designated router (DR) and a backup designated router (BDR). To reduce LSAs on the multiaccess network, all routers send their LSAs to the DR and BDR. The DR forwards them to all non-DR routers. The DR also sends the Network LSA (type 2) to the rest of the internetwork. The BDR takes over the function of the DR if the DR fails.

Enhanced Interior Gateway Routing Protocol

Enhanced Interior Gateway Routing Protocol (EIGRP) was released in the early 1990s as a significant evolution toward a scalable routing protocol. EIGRP is a classless protocol that permits VLSMs and supernetting. Routing updates are not sent periodically, as in IGRP. EIGRP also allows authentication, even with MD5. Another enhancement is that EIGRP can be used to route IPX and AppleTalk over WANs. EIGRP autosummarizes networks at borders and can load balance over unequal-cost paths.

EIGRP uses the same metrics as IGRP, but scaled by 256 for finer granularity. The metrics are bandwidth, delay, load, reliability, and MTU. EIGRP implements a Diffusing Update Algorithm (DUAL) to guarantee freedom from routing loops. Work on DUAL was developed by Garcia-Luna-Aceves.

EIGRP is considered a hybrid protocol, distance vector with link-state characteristic. It advertises its routing table to its neighbors as distance vector protocols do, but it uses hellos and forms neighbor relationships as link-state protocols. EIGRP can be used only on Cisco routers.

EIGRP updates are sent only when necessary (as with link-state protocols) and are sent only to those routers requiring the new information. Hello packets are used to learn of neighboring routers. On most networks, the hello packet interval is 5 seconds. On multipoint networks with link speeds of T1 and slower, hello packets are unicast every 60 seconds.

Intermediate System-to-Intermediate System

Although not an objective for the DCN test, a CCDA should know that Intermediate System-to-Intermediate System (IS-IS) is a link-state routing protocol capable of routing IP packets. IS-IS can also route ISO's Connectionless Network Protocol (CLNP). The ISO adopted IS-IS for TCP/IP instead of the OSPF protocol that was being developed by the Internet Architecture Board. DEC also adopted IS-IS for its DECNet Phase V.

IS-IS is very similar to OSPF. It implements link-state database with SPF algorithms to calculate paths, uses the area concept and classless protocols, elects DR routers, and has authentication capabilities.

Border Gateway Protocol

Border Gateway Protocol (BGP) is an IP Exterior Gateway Protocol (EGP) used to connect different autonomous systems, and it is commonly used to connect larger organizations to the Internet. BGP performs routing among multiple autonomous systems or domains and exchanges reachability information with other BGP systems. All other routing protocols (EIGRP, OSPF, RIP, and IS-IS) are used as Interior Gateway Protocols (IGP) inside an autonomous system. The current version is BGP version 4.

IP Routing Protocol Administrative Distance

On routers running several routing protocols, the possibility exists that two different routing protocols have a route to a destination. Cisco routers assign each routing protocol an administrative distance, which by default is as show in Table 6-15. The lower the administrative distance, the more preferred that route will be.

For example, say that a router has a route in EIGRP for network 172.20.10.0/24 with the best path out Ethernet 0, and has a route in OSPF for network 172.20.10.0/24 with the best path out Ethernet 1. Because EIGRP routes have an administrative distance of 90 and OSPF routes have an administrative distance of 110, the EIGRP route will be entered into the routing table, and packets with destinations of 172.20.10.0/24 will be sent out Ethernet 0.

Table 6-15 *Default Administrative Distances for IP Routes*

IP Route	Administrative Distance
Connected interface	0
Static route using a connected interface	0
Static route using an IP address	1
EIGRP summary route	5
External BGP route	20
Internal EIGRP route	90

Table 6-15   *Default Administrative Distances for IP Routes (Continued)*

IP Route	Administrative Distance
IGRP route	100
OSPF route	110
IS-IS route	115
RIP route	120
EGP route	140
External EIGRP route	170
Internal BGP route	200
Route of unknown origin	255

Novell IPX Addressing

The following CCDA objectives are covered in this section:

21	Propose an addressing model for the customer's areas, networks, subnetworks, and end stations that meets scalability requirements.
22	Propose a plan for configuring addresses.

Novell's Network Operating System (NOS) has been popular for years. Although newer versions of this NOS uses TCP/IP for network transport, legacy implementations are still out there. Legacy Novell uses SPX/IPX protocols for transport.

IPX Addresses

IPX addresses consist of a 32-bit network part and a 48-bit host part. The 32-bit network address is represented in hexadecimal format and is configured by the network administrator. The host part of the address is the 48-bit MAC address on the network interface card of network nodes; the host part of the address is not configured by the administrator.

Figure 6-6 shows an IPX network number in binary and hexadecimal format. Every 4 bits of a binary number can be converted to hexadecimal, and vice versa. Table 6-16 shows binary-to-hexadecimal conversion.

Figure 6-6   *IPX Network Number in Binary and Hexadecimal Formats*

Binary	0000	0001	0011	1111	1100	0101	0010	1110
Hexadecimal	0	1	3	F	C	5	2	E

Table 6-16   *Binary-to-Hexadecimal Conversion*

Binary	Hexadecimal	Decimal
0000	0	0
0001	1	1
0010	2	2
0011	3	3
0100	4	4
0101	5	5
0110	6	6
0111	7	7
1000	8	8
1001	9	9
1010	A	10
1011	B	11
1100	C	12
1101	D	13
1110	E	14
1111	F	15

A host in the 013FC52E network could have the IPX address of 013FC52E.0011.022A.0245.

Some valid network addresses include 00000001, 0000DEAD, 00035A8, 0000DADA, 0ABCDEF0, and 00ADDBAD.

IPX Address Assignment

The best way to assign addresses to IPX networks is to convert the IP subnet address from dotted decimal to hexadecimal format. For example, take IP subnet 172.16.3.0 and convert it to AC0F0300. This is a proven technique that will make the IPX addresses unique and that also will provide scalability. Table 6-17 shows some samples of IPX networks.

Table 6-17   *Sample IPX Network Addresses*

IP Network	IPX Network
10.1.64.0/24	0A014000
201.50.76.12/30	C9324C0C
192.168.12.0/24	C0A80C00
172.20.4.64/192	AC140440
1.1.1.0/24	01010100

IPX Routing and Service Advertising Protocols

The following CCDA objectives are covered in this section:

24	Identify scalability constraints and issues for IGRP, Enhanced IGRP, IP RIP, IPX RIP/SAP, NLSP, AppleTalk RTMP and AURP, static routing, and bridging protocols.
25	Recommend routing and bridging protocols that meet a customer's requirements for performance, security, and capacity.

This section covers IPX routing and advertisement protocol characteristics and differences.

IPX Routing Information Protocol

IPX Routing Information Protocol (IPX RIP) is a distance vector routing protocol for Novell. IPX RIP sends periodic updates every 60 seconds and uses a tick as a metric. A tick is a delay assigned to interfaces off a router. One tick is 1/18th of a second. In the case of two paths with equal tick count, then hop count is used as a tie breaker. As in IP RIP, IPX RIP has a maximum hop count limit of 15 hops, by default.

IPX Service Advertising Protocol

IPX Service Advertising Protocol (SAP) is not a routing protocol; it is a protocol for network resources, such as file and print servers, to advertise the addresses and services they provide. SAP is the companion protocol to IPX RIP—RIP takes care of the networks, and SAP takes care of the services. As with IPX RIP updates, SAP advertisements are sent every 60 seconds. Routers gather SAP advertisements, add them to the SAP table, and broadcast the SAP table out of their interfaces.

NetWare Link-Services Protocol

IPX RIP and SAP each produce periodic broadcasts every 60 seconds, adding significant traffic to the network. NetWare Link-Services Protocol (NLSP) is a link-state routing protocol designed to overcome the limitations of RIP/SAP. NLSP has characteristics similar to other link-state protocols—link-state advertisements are generated by routers and are flooded throughout the network, and each router computes best paths to destinations. Updates are sent only when required.

NSLP also supports up to 127 hops and permits hierarchical routing with area, domain, and global internetwork components. An area is a collection of connected networks with the same area address, and a domain is a collection of areas. A global internetwork is a collection of domains.

NSLP supports hierarchical addressing, in which each area is identified by the 32-bit address and a 32-bit mask. This is similar to the masking done in IP addressing. The mask identifies the network address for an area. For example, take the address of 005A7000 with a mask of FFFFFF00. Notice that 24 bits are set to 1 in the mask. The network address for the area is 005A70. The remaining 8 bits are used for networks within this area.

AppleTalk Addressing

The following CCDA objectives are covered in this section:

21	Propose an addressing model for the customer's areas, networks, subnetworks, and end stations that meets scalability requirements.
22	Propose a plan for configuring addresses.
24	Identify scalability constraints and issues for IGRP, EIGRP, IP RIP, IPX RIP/SAP, NLSP, AppleTalk RTMP and AURP, static routing, and bridging protocols.
25	Recommend routing and bridging protocols that meet a customer's requirements for performance, security, and capacity.

AppleTalk was developed by Apple Computer in the early 1980s. This section reviews the addressing of AppleTalk networks and its routing protocols.

Address Formats and Assignment

The current implementation of AppleTalk is Phase 2. Addresses are composed of three elements:

- **Network number**—A 16-bit value assigned by the administrator using the **cable-range** command.

- **Node number**—An 8-bit value dynamically assigned that identifies the node.

- **Socket number**—This 8-bit number identifies the socket running on the node; it is similar to a port number in TCP/IP.

Addresses are written in decimal format, with periods separating the fields. Examples of AppleTalk addresses are 11.2, 100.50, and 67.10. If the socket number is included in the addresses, it is appended to the end. For AppleTalk address 11.2 with socket 7, the full address is 11.2.7. Network addresses range from 1 to 65,535, and node addresses range from 1 to 254. Sockets also range from 1 to 254.

Another particularity of AppleTalk network number assignments is that several consecutive network numbers can be assigned to an interface. This is called an extended cable range. For example, an Ethernet segment can have a cable range of 10 to 11 configured, which includes nodes from 10.1 to 11.255.

AppleTalk Zones

AppleTalk defines a zone as a logical group of nodes or networks. These nodes or networks need not be physically contiguous to belong to the same AppleTalk zone. Zones are configured to group resources together and are used to limit AppleTalk broadcasts and provide some security. Zones can be configured by function within a company, as in separating a finance department from an engineering department.

The Zone Information Protocol (ZIP) is the session-layer A protocol that maintains network number-to-zone name mappings in AppleTalk routers. Each router maintains a table with the network numbers and the zone(s) to which they belong.

AppleTalk Routing Protocols

AppleTalk's routing protocol is Routing Table Maintenance Protocol (RTMP). AppleTalk also can be routed over a WAN using EIGRP. In addition, AppleTalk can be tunneled using the AppleTalk Update-Based Routing Protocol (AURP).

Routing Table Maintenance Protocol

Routing Table Maintenance Protocol (RTMP) is the distance vector routing protocol for forwarding AppleTalk packets. RTMP is based on RIP, uses hop count as the metric, and has the same limitation of 15 hops. Routing table updates are sent in periodic fashion. The table contains the following information for each of the destination routes known to the router:

- Network cable range of the destination network

- Distance, in hops, to the destination network

- Router port that leads to the destination network

- Address of the next-hop router

- Current state of entry (good, suspect, or bad)

AppleTalk Update-Based Routing Protocol

AppleTalk Update-Based Routing Protocol (AURP) can be used to extend AppleTalk networks over a TCP/IP network, as shown in Figure 6-7. AURP encapsulates AppleTalk packets in User Datagram Protocol (UDP) headers, creating a virtual link between AppleTalk networks. AURP is the routing protocol in this virtual link and is more effective than RTMP because it does not send periodic updates through the link.

EIGRP for AppleTalk

EIGRP can be used to route AppleTalk packets over a WAN. EIGRP is configured for links between routers; RTMP is used on other interfaces. EIGRP sends updates only when changes occur, which represents a significant improvement over the periodic (10-second) RTMP updates.

Figure 6-7   *AppleTalk Update-Based Routing Protocol (AURP)*

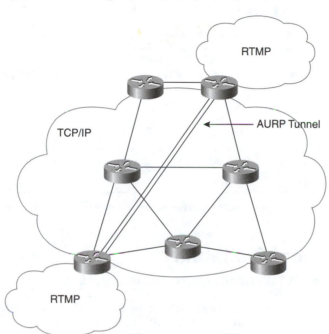

Distance Vector Routing Protocol Comparison

The following CCDA objective is covered in this section:

24   Identify scalability constraints and issues for IGRP, EIGRP, IP RIP, IPX
                            RIP/SAP, NLSP, AppleTalk RTMP and AURP, static routing, and
                            bridging protocols.

Now that all routing protocols have been covered, this section compares the traffic generated by
all distance vector routing protocols.

Distance vector routing protocols work periodically, sending updates for a specific period of
time. Each can carry a certain number of routes on a routing update. The larger the network, the

more update packets are sent every period. Table 6-18 compares distance vector protocol update times and routes per packet.

Table 6-18   *Distance Vector Routing Protocol Comparison*

Routing Protocol	Default Update Time (Seconds)	Routes per Packet
IP RIP	30	25
IP IGRP	90	104
AppleTalk RTMP	10	97
IPX SAP*	60	7
IPX RIP	60	50

*IPX SAP is not a routing protocol, but a Service Advertising Protocol. However, it is periodic by nature.

Bridging Protocol Scalability

The following CCDA objectives are covered in this section:

24	Identify scalability constraints and issues for IGRP, Enhanced IGRP, IP RIP, IPX RIP/SAP, NLSP, AppleTalk RTMP and AURP, static routing, and bridging protocols.
25	Recommend routing and bridging protocols that meet a customer's requirements for performance, security, and capacity.

This section covers the two scalability issues concerning bridging protocols.

Transparent Bridging Scalability Issues

A transparent bridge floods all multicast frames, broadcast frames, and frames with an unknown destination address out every port except the one on which the frame was received. Broadcasts and multicast create scalability issues that can be controlled only with routing.

Transparent bridges implement the Spanning-Tree Algorithm, which is specified in IEEE 802.1d. In the sample network in Figure 6-8, the Spanning-Tree Protocol states that only one active path exists between two stations. If a physical loop exists in the network, the Spanning-Tree Protocol handles this loop by disabling bridge ports.

Figure 6-8   *Spanning-Tree Protocol*

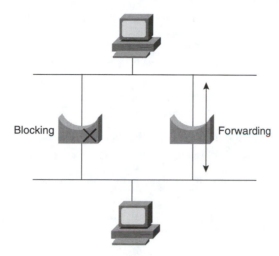

Transparent bridges send Bridge Protocol Data Unit (BPDU) frames to each other to build and maintain a Spanning Tree. The BPDU frames are sent every two seconds. The amount of traffic caused by BPDU frames can be a scalability issue on large flat networks with numerous switches and bridges. For more information on the Spanning-Tree Protocol, see Chapter 4, "Network Topologies and LAN Design."

Source-Route Bridging Scalability Issues

In source-route bridging (SRB), a source node finds another node by sending explorer packets. An all-routes explorer packet will flood the network with explorer packets. As the number of nodes grows, scalability is affected. The amount of explorer frames can also affect the destination Token Ring. Furthermore, the diameter of an SRB network is limited to seven hops. For more information on SRB, see Chapter 3, "Application Considerations." To reduce the amount of traffic on the network, do the following:

- Limit the size of flat, bridged networks
- Use routing to segment the network
- Use IP or IPX to transport NetBIOS traffic versus NetBEUI

Cisco IOS Software Features

The following CCDA objective is covered in this section:

26	Recognize scalability issues for various Cisco IOS software features such as access lists, proxy services, encryption, compression, and queuing.
27	Recommend Cisco IOS software features that meet a customer's requirements for performance, security, capacity, and scalability.

Cisco IOS provides several features that can be used to optimize and scale an internetwork. This section describes Cisco IOS features that help scale a network.

Depending on customer requirements, the following features may be implemented with Cisco IOS:

- Access lists

- Encryption

- Proxy services

- Compression

- Traffic shaping

- Queuing: custom, priority, and weighted-fair

The remainder of this section discusses these features.

Access Lists

Access lists are primarily used to control (block or forward) traffic at router interfaces. The access list defines a criteria that is applied to every packet that is processed by the router for that interface. Access lists are also used to improve the performance of a network, such as to filter unnecessary IPX Service Advertising Protocol (SAP) broadcasts, or to filter routes in routing protocol redistribution.

Two types of access lists exist: standard and extended. Standard access lists allow only simple criteria to be specified, such as packet source address. Extended access lists allow additional, more complex criteria to be specified, such as the packet destination address, upper-layer protocol, and application port number. Access lists can be defined for each protocol, with an individual specific set of criteria that can be defined.

Access lists can be applied inbound or outbound to interfaces. If the access list is applied inbound to an interface, Cisco IOS checks the access list's criteria statements for a match when the router receives a packet. If the packet is permitted, the software continues to process the packet. If the packet is denied, the software discards the packet. If the access list is applied outbound to an interface, the software checks the access list's criteria statements for a match after receiving and routing a packet to the outbound interface. If the packet is permitted, the software transmits the packet. If the packet is denied, the software discards the packet.

Certain numbers are used to define access lists. A range of numbers has been reserved for each type of access list, as shown in Table 6-19.

Table 6-19   *Access List Numbers*

Type of Access List	Range
IP standard	1 to 99
IP extended	100 to 199
Bridge type code	200 to 299
DECnet standard and extended	300 to 399
XNS standard	400 to 499
XNS extended	500 to 599
AppleTalk zone	600 to 699
Bridge MAC	700 to 799
IPX standard	800 to 899
IPX extended	900 to 999
IPX SAP	1000 to 1999
Bridge extended	1100 to 1199
NLSP route aggregation	1200 to 1299

Access List Example

The **access-group** command is used to apply an access list to an interface. The **access-list** command is used to define the criteria for the access list. The order of the access list statements is important. The Cisco IOS software tests the packets against every criteria statement in the order in which the statements were created. After a match is found, no more criteria statements are checked.

In the following configuration, an IP protocol access list is applied on the interface Ethernet 0 to inbound packets. All traffic from network 10.0.0.0/8 is denied; the rest is permitted.

```
access-list 4 deny 10.0.0.0 0.255.255.255
access-list 4 permit any
interface ethernet 0
  ip access-group 4 in
```

Encryption

To safeguard IP data, Cisco IOS 11.2 implements Cisco Encryption Technology (CET). CET provides packet-level encryption that enables you to protect the confidentiality and integrity of network data traveling between peer encrypting routers. On Cisco IOS 11.3(3)T and later versions, another encryption option, IPSec, is available. IPSec is a framework of open standards developed by the Internet Engineering Task Force (IETF). IPSec services are similar to those provided by CET; however, IPSec provides a more robust security solution and is standards-based.

More information on IP security and encryption can be found at www.cisco.com/univercd/cc/td/doc/product/software/ios120/12cgcr/secur_c/scprt4/scencove.htm.

Proxy Services

Cisco IOS has numerous proxy services that can be used to meet performance and connectivity concerns due to topology and behavior of network applications. Some examples are listed in this section.

Resource Discovery on Serverless LANs

To aid in the resource discovery on serverless LANs, the router can provide the following services:

- A router can respond to an IPX GetNearestServer request from a NetWare client if there is no local NetWare server.

- A router can forward certain types of UDP broadcast frames by configuring a helper address.

- A router can respond to an Address Resolution Protocol (ARP) request when a local IP station looks for a remote station. This is called proxy ARP.

Traffic Reduction on Bridged Networks and WANs

On bridge networks and WANs, the route provides the following services:

- A source-route bridging router can convert an all-routes explorer frame into a single-route frame, thus reducing the number of frames in a network that has many redundant paths.

- NetBIOS name caching allows a router to convert NetBIOS name-lookup frames from explorers to single-route frames.

- Watchdog spoofing on the server end of a NetWare Core protocol session answers keepalives locally, permitting DDR links to drop.

- Novell Sequenced Packet Exchange (SPX) spoofing does the same thing as watchdog spoofing, except that this is for applications that use SPX instead of NCP.

Improved Performance for Time-Sensitive Applications

The Logical Link Control (LLC) local acknowledgement feature allows a router to respond to LLC frames so that SNA and other time-sensitive applications do not time out when used on large routed networks.

Data Compression Solutions

Compression can be used to help reduce the bandwidth utilized on the network, especially on low-speed WAN links. Cisco IOS software provides the following data compression solutions:

- Van Jaconson TCP/IP header compression, which conforms to RFC 1144

- Per-interface (link) compression

- Per-virtual circuit (payload) compression

- Frame-Relay Payload Compression, from FRF.9 compression per DLCI

- Real-time Transport Protocol (RTP) header compression

Traffic Shaping

Cisco IOS 11.2 supports both generic traffic shaping and Frame Relay traffic shaping, as detailed in this section.

Generic Traffic Shaping

Generic traffic shaping helps reduce the flow of outbound traffic from a router interface into a backbone transport network when congestion is detected in the downstream portions of the downstream network or in a downstream router. Topologies that have high-speed links feeding lower-speed links often experience bottlenecks because of speed mismatch. Generic traffic shaping helps by throttling back traffic volume at the source end.

Frame Relay Traffic Shaping

Frame Relay traffic shaping uses the characteristics of Frame Relay to help shape the traffic on a PVC basis. Introduced in Cisco IOS 11.2, it offers the following capabilities:

- **Rate enforcement on a per-virtual circuit (VC) basis**—A peak rate can be configured to limit outbound traffic to either the committed information rate (CIR) or some other defined value,

- **Generalized backward explicit congestion notification (BECN) support on a per-VC basis**—The router can monitor BECNs and throttle traffic based on BECN marked packet feedback,

- **Priority and custom queuing support at the VC level**—This allows for finer granularity in the queuing of traffic, based on an individual VC.

Queuing Services

Queuing services enable a network administrator to manage the varying demand that applications put on networks. Since Cisco started supporting weighted fair queuing in IOS 11.0, there has been less need for more drastic types of queuing, such as priority and custom queuing. In some cases, however, mission-critical applications running on congested serial links might still require priority or custom queuing. The following sections describe the different queuing types.

Priority Queuing

Priority queuing is particularly useful for time-sensitive, mission-critical protocols such as SNA. It is appropriate for cases in which WAN links are congested from time to time. Priority queuing has four queues: high, medium, normal, and low. Traffic can be assigned to the various queues based on protocol, port number, or other criteria. The high-priority queue is always emptied before the lower-priority queues are serviced. Priority queuing ensures that one type of traffic will get through at the expense of all other types of traffic.

Custom Queuing

Custom queuing is a different approach for prioritizing traffic. As with priority queuing, traffic can be assigned to various queues based on protocol, port number, or other criteria. However, custom queuing handles the queues in a round-robin fashion. Custom queuing works by establishing interface output queues. The transmission size of each queue is specified in bytes. When the transmission window size has been reached by transmitting the appropriate number of frames from a queue, the next queue is checked. Custom queuing is more fair than priority queuing, although priority queuing is more powerful for prioritizing a mission-critical protocol.

Weighted Fair Queuing

Weighted fair queuing was first implemented in Cisco IOS 11.0. It is enabled by default on most low-bandwidth interfaces; no configuration is required to use weighted fair queuing. Weighted fair queuing is more fair than either priority or custom queuing because it handles the problems inherent in queuing schemes that are essentially first-come, first-served.

The main problem with first-come, first-served algorithms is that sessions using large packets can impede sessions using small packets. For example, FTP can negatively affect the performance of Telnet. The weighted fair queuing implementation looks at sizes of messages and ensures that high-volume senders do not crowd out low-volume senders. Weighted fair queuing queues packets are based on the arrival time of the last bit rather than the first bit, which ensures that applications that use large packets cannot unfairly monopolize the bandwidth.

Foundation Summary

Foundation Summary is a section presented in a concise format to provide quick reference information relating to the objectives covered in this chapter.

Table 6-20 *IP Address Types*

Class	High-Order Bits	Network Address Range
Class A	0	1.0.0.0 to 126.0.0.0
Class B	10	128.0.0.0 to 191.255.0.0
Class C	110	192.0.0.0 to 223.255.255.0
Class D[*]	1110	224.0.0.0 to 239.255.255.255
Class E[**]	1111	240.0.0.0 to 255.255.255.254

[*]Class D addresses are used for multicast.
[**]Class E addresses are experimental.

Table 6-21 *IPX and AppleTalk Address Format*

Protocol	Network	Host Portion	Format
IPX	32 bits	48 bits (MAC)	00001EAC.0010.0040.5678 mac address too long
AppleTalk	16 bits	8 bits plus 8 bits for the socket	10.5.7

Table 6-22 *Exterior and Interior Routing Protocols*

Exterior	BGP
Interior	RIP, OSPF, IGRP, IS-IS, EIGRP, IPX RIP, NLSP, RTMP

Table 6-23 *Routing Protocols per Protocol Family*

Routed Protocol	Routing Protocols
IP	RIP, IGRP, OSPF, IS-IS, EIGRP
IPX	IPX RIP, NLSP, EIGRP
AppleTalk	RTMP, AURP, EIGRP

Table 6-24 *Distance Vector Versus Link-State Routing Protocols*

Category	Routing Protocol
Distance Vector	IP RIP, IGRP, IPX RIP, RTMP
Link-State	OSPF, NLSP, ISIS
Hybrid	EIGRP

Table 6-25 *Classless Support for IP VLSMs*

Category	Routing Protocol
Classless/VLSM support	EIGRP, OSPF, ISIS, RIPv2, BGP
No VLSM	RIPv1, IGRP

Table 6-26 *Distance Vector Protocol Update Timers*

Routing Protocol	Default Update Time (Seconds)
IP RIP	30
IP IGRP	90
AppleTalk RTMP	10
IPX RIP	60

Table 6-27 *Bridging Protocols Supported by Cisco Routers and Switches*

Bridge Protocol	Description
Transparent bridging	Found in Ethernet environments; implements Spanning-Tree Protocol.
Source-route bridging (SRB)	Found in Token Ring environments; forwards explorer packets.
Translational bridging	Translates from Ethernet bridging to Token Ring bridging.
Source-route transparent bridging (SRT)	Enables a bridge to function as both a source-routing bridge and a transparent bridge.
Source-route translational bridging (SR/TLB)	Enables a bridge to function as both a source-routing and a transparent bridge, bridging between the two. Adds a Routing Information Field (RIF) to frames forwarded to the Token Ring. Removes RIFs to frames headed to the Ethernet.

Table 6-28 *Cisco IOS Features*

Cisco IOS Features	Purpose
Access lists	Used to control traffic on router interfaces; filters addresses and controls broadcasts.
Encryption	Safeguards IP data.
Proxy services	Helps with resource discovery on serverless LANs; reduces traffic on WANs; improves time-sensitive applications.
Compression	Reduces bandwidth utilized on the network.
Traffic shaping	Helps reduce the flow of outbound traffic from a router interface into a backbone transport network.
Queuing: priority, custom, and weighted fair	Priority—High, medium, normal, and low queues defined. Useful for time-sensitive, mission-critical protocols such as SNA.
	Custom—Handles the queues in a round-robin fashion. The transmission size of each queue is specified in bytes.
	Weighted fair—Default queue technique for low-speed interfaces; no configuration needed. Weighted fair queuing queues packets based on the arrival time of the last bit rather than the first bit.

Q&A

The following questions are designed to test your understanding of the topics covered in this chapter. When you have answered the questions, Look up the answers in Appendix A. After you identify the subject matter you missed, review those sections in the chapter until you feel comfortable with this material.

1 What protocol encapsulates AppleTalk packets in UDP for transport over an IP network?

2 What is the subnet address for host 150.76.78.71 with a mask of 255.255.255.224?

3 This routing protocol defines areas, domains, and supports hierarchical addressing.

4 What is an ABR?

5 Which protocol produces route updates every 10 seconds?

6 What routing protocol is used to communicate with Internet routers?

7 What routing protocol is recommended for hub-and-spoke topologies with low-bandwidth links with no route redundancy?

_____

_____

_____

8 What is the host portion of 125.240.32.45, assuming default subnet masking?

_____

_____

_____

9 This protocol supports route summarization, but it must be configured. If link flapping occurs, streams of updates are generated, causing router CPU overhead.

_____

_____

_____

10 If a customer is looking for ways to reduce WAN traffic and is also considering tunneling AppleTalk in IP, what protocol would you recommend?

_____

_____

_____

11 This protocol limits the number of route entries in a routing table update to 50 routes.

_____

_____

_____

12 What is the network portion for an NLSP area of 0020ab00 with a mask of FFFF0000?

_____

_____

_____

13 Of the following, which are valid IPX networks?

— 01010101

— DADA

— 789ABCDE

— 204A6B8CE

— 0FG3ABD4

— 10

— 0AB04

14 Is 140.176.30.31/28 a valid host address?

15 Convert the following IP address to the dotted decimal format:
00011011011011001100110000101111

16 If the client wants to use a nonproprietary routing protocol that can scale to hundreds of networks and fit in a hierarchical topology, which routing protocol can be recommended?

17 If a client wants to use a routing protocol that is easy to configure and that can scale to hundreds of networks, and if all routers are Cisco routers, which routing protocol can be recommended?

_____

_____

_____

18 What is an ASBR?

_____

_____

_____

19 What is a stub network in OSPF?

_____

_____

_____

20 What is a totally stubby network in OSPF?

_____

_____

_____

21 True or False: Bridged networks provide large scalability.

_____

_____

_____

22 True or False: To reduce the traffic in bridge networks it is recommended to limit the size of the network and use routing to segment the network.

_____

_____

_____

23 RIP uses a feature in which routes learned from a neighboring router are sent back
to that neighbor with an infinite unreachable metric. What is that feature?

_____

_____

_____

24 What is the update time in IGRP?

_____

_____

_____

25 Does EIGRP send periodic updates?

_____

_____

_____

26 Which queuing technique can be recommended to prioritize mission-critical
SNA traffic?

_____

_____

_____

27 List at least four Cisco IOS features.

_____

_____

_____

28 True or False: The order in which access list commands are configured is not
significant to the router.

_____

_____

_____

Case Studies

The following case study questions are based on the ongoing scenarios presented in the "Case Studies" section of Chapter 1, "Design Goals." If you want to familiarize yourself with the entire case study, refer to that section before working through the following questions. The answers to these questions can be found in the "Case Study Answers" section at the end of this chapter.

Case Study #1: GHY Resources

1 At GHY Resources, what routing protocols are being used? How often are routing updates sent?

_____

_____

_____

2 Mr. Martin would like a recommendation of a routing protocol that is easy to configure and will reduce traffic on the WAN. What routing protocol would you recommend?

_____

_____

_____

3 What protocol would you recommend for routing IPX?

_____

_____

_____

4 What masking would you use on the WAN links?

_____

_____

_____

Case Study #2: Pages Magazine, Inc.

1 What routing protocols are being used at Pages Magazine, Inc.?

_____

_____

_____

2 What routing protocol can be recommended to support IP and legacy Novell AppleTalk packets?

_____

_____

_____

3 If the New York City site is expected to grow to more than 150 nodes, what mask would you recommend?

_____

_____

_____

4 If all the remote sites are not expected to grow to more than 60 nodes, what subnet mask for these networks would you recommend?

_____

_____

_____

Case Study Answers

Case Study #1: GHY Resources

1   At GHY Resources, what routing protocols are being used? How often are routing updates sent?

For IP, RIPv1 is being used. RIP sends out its routing table updates every 30 seconds.

For IPX, IPX RIP is being used. IPX RIP sends routing updates every 60 seconds.

2   Mr. Martin would like a recommendation of a routing protocol that is easy to configure and will reduce traffic on the WAN. What routing protocol would you recommend?

Recommend EIGRP. It is easy to configure, VLSMs can be used to conserve address space, and routing overhead will be reduced.

3   What protocol would you recommend for routing IPX?

To reduce IPX RIP and SAP overhead, recommend routing IPX with EIGRP on the WAN links.

4   What masking would you use on the WAN links?

Use 255.255.255.252. This provides an IP address for each router on the WAN link and helps conserve address space.

Case Study #2: Pages Magazine, Inc.

1   What routing protocols are being used at Pages Magazine, Inc.?

For IP, RIPv1 is being used.

For IPX, IPX RIP is being used.

For AppleTalk, RTMP is being used.

2   What routing protocol can be recommended to support IP and legacy Novell AppleTalk packets?

Recommend EIGRP for IP, IPX, and AppleTalk. EIGRP can support VLSM subnetting and can be configured to route IPX and AppleTalk.

3 If the New York City site is expected to grow to more than 150 nodes, what mask would you recommend?

Recommend a subnet with a 255.255.255.0 mask that can support up to 254 nodes.

4 If all the remote sites are not expected to grow to more that 60 nodes, what subnet mask for these networks would you recommend?

Recommend a subnet mask of 255.255.255.192 that can support up to 62 nodes per subnet.

Objectives Covered in This Chapter

The following is a list of the objectives covered in this chapter. The list of CCDA exam design objectives and the chapters in which they are covered can be found in the Introduction of this book.

5	Document the customer's current applications, protocols, topology, and number of users.
6	Document the customer's business issues that are relevant to a network design project.
8	Determine the customer's requirements for new applications, protocols, number of users, peak usage hours, security, and network management.
11	List some tools that will help you characterize new network traffic.
16	Recommend Cisco products and LAN technologies that will meet a customer's requirements for performance, capacity, and scalability in small- to medium-sized networks.
20	Recommend Cisco products and WAN technologies that will meet the customer's requirements for performance, capacity, and scalability in an enterprise network.
25	Recommend routing and bridging protocols that meet a customer's requirements for performance, security, and capacity.
27	Recommend Cisco IOS software features that meet a customer's requirements for performance, security, capacity, and scalability.

CHAPTER 7

The Design Document and Cisco Network Management Applications

This chapter reviews the design document components and the Cisco Systems network management applications. The design document provides the customer with all the information necessary to make a decision on the proposed solution. Provided with the solution are network management applications from which the client must choose. Network management applications should be chosen based on factors such as network size and complexity, knowledge levels of the operators, and cost of the management tools.

"Do I Know This Already?" Quiz

The questions in the following quiz are designed to help you gauge how well you know the material covered in this chapter. Compare your answers with those found in Appendix A, "Answers to Quiz Questions." If you answer most or all of the questions thoroughly and correctly, you might want to skim the chapter and proceed to the "Q&A" and "Case Studies" sections at the end of the chapter. If you find that you need to review only certain subject matter, search the chapter for the sections that cover the objectives you need to review, and then test yourself both with these questions and with the "Q&A" and "Case Studies" questions. If you find the following questions too difficult, read the chapter carefully until you feel that you can easily answers these and the "Q&A" and "Case Studies" questions.

1 If a client has a small network and a staff with no UNIX experience, which network management applications would you recommend to manage Cisco routers and switches?

_____

_____

_____

2 What is the purpose of the Executive Summary in the design document?

_____

_____

_____

3 What are the five types of network management processes?

_____

_____

_____

4 The acronym SNMP stands for what?

_____

_____

_____

5 CiscoWorks is a network management application that applies to which type of network management process?

_____

_____

_____

6 The selected hardware and media for the LAN and WAN are described in which component of the design document?

_____

_____

_____

7 What is proactive network management?

_____

_____

_____

8 What is NMS?

_____

_____

_____

Foundation Topics

Design Document

The following CCDA objectives are covered in this section:

5	Document the customer's current applications, protocols, topology, and number of users.
6	Document the customer's business issues that are relevant to a network design project.
16	Recommend Cisco products and LAN technologies that will meet a customer's requirements for performance, capacity, and scalability in small- to medium-sized networks.
20	Recommend Cisco products and WAN technologies that will meet the customer's requirements for performance, capacity, and scalability in an enterprise network.
25	Recommend routing and bridging protocols that meet a customer's requirements for performance, security, and capacity.
27	Recommend Cisco IOS software features that meet a customer's requirements for performance, security, capacity, and scalability.

To communicate the combined solutions to the customer's requirements, you must create the design document. This document includes all the information about the customer's current network, requirements, and constraints, and it is used to respond to a Request for Proposals (RFP) or for unsolicited requests. For RFPs, use the format specified by the customer.

Design Document Components

The design document is divided into the following sections, all of which are covered in this section:

- Executive Summary
- Design Requirements
- Design Solution
- Summary
- Appendixes
- Cost of Proposed Design (optional)

Executive Summary

The Executive Summary is directed toward the key decision-makers for the project and should clearly articulate the strategy for the project. The Executive Summary should describe the purpose of the design document and of the project. Include strategic recommendations that outline the design strategy and the company's design objectives. Also list implementation issues for the project, such as time, training, support, and network transition. Finally, summarize the benefits of the solution and describe how it meets the customer's objectives.

Design Requirements

In the Design Requirements section, include information that characterizes the existing network. Include diagrams of the logical and the physical topologies of the existing network. Include information on the types of network devices (hubs, switches, and routers) in use. List the applications that are used across the network and the locations of application servers and clients; also list the number of nodes per segment. Provide the results on the health of network segments, and list problem segments. Be sure to include any business issues that might contribute to the requirements, such as the growth of the company.

The customer's requirements also should be part of this section. Include the performance and scalability requirements to support new applications, and add information about security policy and the capacity requirements for the new network. Also, describe the expected flow of applications for new applications, and document the expected performance so that there can be no misinterpretation of what the design will mean for user applications.

Design Solution

In the Design Solution section, describe the recommended solution, tell how it meets the customer's requirements, and detail any additional benefits it provides. Include the following components:

- **Proposed network topology**—Include and describe a topology diagram of the proposed network topology. Highlight how the network architecture best fits within the stated requirements and constraints.

- **Hardware and media for the LAN**—List the components and LAN technologies selected for the LAN. Include all hubs, switches, and routers, and describe how the components will meet the customer's requirements.

- **Hardware and media for the WAN**—List the components and WAN technologies selected for the WAN. Describe how the components will meet the customer's requirements.

- **Network-layer addressing**—Include the network-layer addressing scheme, network assignment and masking for LAN and WAN segments, and summary addressing points. Include all used network-layer protocols, including IP, Internetwork Packet Exchange (IPX), and AppleTalk. Describe how the address scheme will scale for future segments.

- **Routing and bridging protocols**—Include the recommended protocols to support the applications on the network. Include the routing protocol selected and any scalable support for nonroutable protocols. List the bridged protocols on the network. Modern routing protocols include Enhanced Interior Gateway Routing Protocol (EIGRP) and Open Shortest Path First (OSPF).

- **Software features**—Include Cisco IOS features such as access lists, policy routing, and queuing techniques that are used to meet the requirements for performance, security, capacity, and scalability.

- **Application support**—Include any requirements or restrictions for applications. An example would be no support for protocols such as NetBEUI or IPX.

- **Network scalability**—Include how the proposed solution will provide room for growth of the network. Highlight the core, distribution, and access layers of the network design. Additional scalability requirements might include an initial investment.

- **Cost of the Design Solution**—Describe how the customer can save money by purchasing devices that can scale as the company grows. You might want to summarize the costs in this section and provide a detailed, itemized list in the appendix or in a separate Cost section.

Summary

The Summary section concisely describes (often in bulleted list format) how the recommended solution meets the customer's requirements. List the various recommendations for the solution and the implementation strategy. Finally, state the benefits of the solution. If there is more than one solution that is extremely suitable, list the advantages to each option.

Appendixes

Use the appendixes to provide additional information to the customer. Appendixes can include the following:

- List of contacts for the project, including those at the customer site, at the solution provider, and at Cisco.

- Information about the Cisco products used for the solution.

- Project timeline.

- IP addressing and device naming scheme to be used in the solution.

- Information about the network management products recommended with the solution.

- List of circuits and circuit types recommended for the solution. Provide cost comparisons of the different WAN technology types and justifications of usage.

- Results from prototype tests.

- Detailed, itemized list of the cost of the proposed design.

Cost of Proposed Design

The customer might request that the cost of the design be provided separate from the other sections, especially if it is a large proposal. Provide in great detail an itemized list of the equipment to be purchased and, if necessary, installation and maintenance costs. Provide list prices and discounted pricing in a table.

Network Management

The following CCDA objectives are covered in this section:

| 8 | Determine the customer's requirements for new applications, protocols, number of users, peak usage hours, security, and network management. |
| 11 | List some tools that will help you characterize new network traffic. |

Network management becomes even more essential as networks increase in size. The recommended network management solution must help manage this growth. Beyond monitoring current network behavior and configuration, network management products must assist in identifying potential problem areas or elements that might limit future growth.

Proactive Network Management

Recommend that the customer take a proactive approach toward network management. This means monitoring the network before problems occur. The client must gather network statistics and document those as a baseline of the current status of the network. As part of the baseline, include segment utilization, router CPU utilization, and response time tests. Then define acceptable service goals for the network.

Cisco recommends that you help customers develop proactive network management strategies by assisting in the following steps:

- Determine network service goals.

- Define metrics for measuring whether the goals have been met.

- Define processes for data collecting and reporting.
- Implement network management systems.
- Collect performance data and record trends.
- Analyze results and write reports.
- Locate network irregularities and bottlenecks.
- Plan and implement network improvements.
- Review and adjust metrics and processes, if necessary.
- Document changes.

Network Management Processes

The ISO defines five types of network management processes. You can remember these processes by the acronym FCAPS (fault, configuration, accounting, performance, security):

- **Fault management**—Refers to detecting, isolating, and correcting problems (faults). HP OpenView is an example of a fault-reporting network management station. Fault events are reported to the station via Simple Network Management Protocol (SNMP) traps or regular interval polling by the management station. The station can be configured to pop a window or to send an email or page to network analysts. A cable tester must still be used to troubleshoot physical-layer errors.

- **Configuration management**—Refers to baselining, modifying, and tracking configuration changes of network devices. This facility also provides the capability of tracking versions of operating systems on the devices. CiscoWorks is an excellent example of a network application used for configuration management of Cisco devices.

- **Accounting management**—Refers to tracking the usage of segments to determine usage-based billing of service.

- **Performance management**—Refers to the measure of network behavior and effectiveness of delivering frames, packets, and segments. It includes protocol and application behavior, reachability to destinations, and the measurement of response times.

- **Security management**—Refers to the maintenance and distribution of authentication and authorization information, such as passwords and encryption keys. The use of audit logs to document logins or repeated unsuccessful attempts to log in is also part of security management. A company should have a documented security policy based on the understanding of which assets are most valuable.

Simple Network Management Protocol

The SNMP is an application-layer protocol that facilitates the exchange of management information between network devices. It is part of the TCP/IP protocol suite. SNMP enables network administrators to manage network performance, find and solve network problems, and plan for network growth.

Two versions of SNMP exist: SNMP Version 1 (SNMPv1) and SNMP Version 2 (SNMPv2). Both versions have a number of features in common, but SNMPv2 offers enhancements, such as additional protocol operations. Standardization of yet another version of SNMP—SNMP Version 3 (SNMPv3)—is pending. This section provides descriptions of the SNMPv1 and SNMPv2 protocol operations. Figure 7-1 illustrates a basic network managed by SNMP.

Figure 7-1   *SNMP Facilitates the Exchange of Network Information Between Devices*

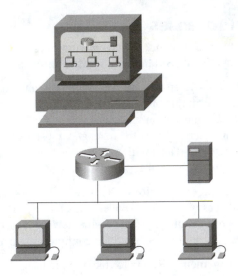

An SNMP managed network consists of three key components: *managed devices*, *agents*, and NMSs.

A managed device is a network node that contains an SNMP agent and resides on a managed network. Managed devices collect and store management information and make this information available to NMSs using SNMP. Managed devices, sometimes called network elements, can be routers and access servers, switches and bridges, hubs, computer hosts, or printers.

An agent is an NMS software module that resides in a managed device. An agent has local knowledge of management information and translates that information into a form compatible with SNMP.

An NMS executes applications that monitor and control managed devices. NMSs provide the bulk of the processing and memory resources required for network management. One or more NMSs must exist on any managed network.

Figure 7-2 illustrates the relationship between these three components.

Figure 7-2   *An SNMP Managed Network Consists of Managed Devices, Agents, and NMSs*

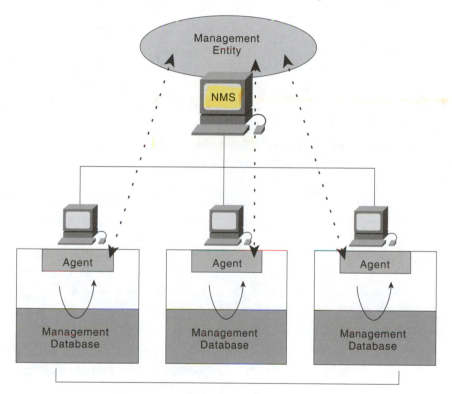

Managed Devices

SNMP Basic Commands

Managed devices are monitored and controlled using four basic SNMP commands: *read*, *write*, *trap*, and *traversal operations*.

The read command is used by an NMS to monitor managed devices. The NMS examines different variables that are maintained by managed devices.

The write command is used by an NMS to control managed devices. The NMS changes the values of variables stored within managed devices.

The trap command is used by managed devices to asynchronously report events to the NMS. When certain types of events occur, a managed device sends a trap to the NMS.

Traversal operations are used by the NMS to determine which variables a managed device supports and to sequentially gather information in variable tables, such as a routing table.

SNMP Management Information Base

A *Management Information Base (MIB)* is a collection of information that is organized hierarchically. MIBs are accessed using a network-management protocol such as SNMP. They are comprised of managed objects and are identified by object identifiers.

A managed object (sometimes called an MIB object, an object, or an MIB) is one of any number of specific characteristics of a managed device. Managed objects are comprised of one or more object instances, which are essentially variables.

Two types of managed objects exist: *scalar* and *tabular.* Scalar objects define a single object instance. Tabular objects define multiple related object instances that are grouped together in MIB tables.

An example of a managed object is *atInput*, which is a scalar object that contains a single object instance, the integer value that indicates the total number of input AppleTalk packets on a router interface.

An object identifier (or object ID) uniquely identifies a managed object in the MIB hierarchy. The MIB hierarchy can be depicted as a tree with a nameless root, the levels of which are assigned by different organizations. Figure 7-3 illustrates the MIB tree.

The top-level MIB object IDs belong to different standards organizations, while lower-level object IDs are allocated by associated organizations.

Vendors can define private branches that include managed objects for their own products. MIBs that have not been standardized typically are positioned in the experimental branch.

The managed object *atInput* can be uniquely identified either by the object name— *iso.identified-organization.dod.internet.private.enterprise.cisco.temporary variables.AppleTalk.atInput*— or by the equivalent object descriptor: 1.3.6.1.4.1.9.3.3.1.

SNMP and Data Representation

SNMP must account for and adjust to incompatibilities between managed devices. Different computers use different data-representation techniques, which can compromise the ability of SNMP to exchange information between managed devices. SNMP uses a subset of Abstract Syntax Notation One (ASN.1) to accommodate communication between diverse systems.

Figure 7-3   *The MIB Tree Illustrates the Various Hierarchies Assigned by Different Organizations*

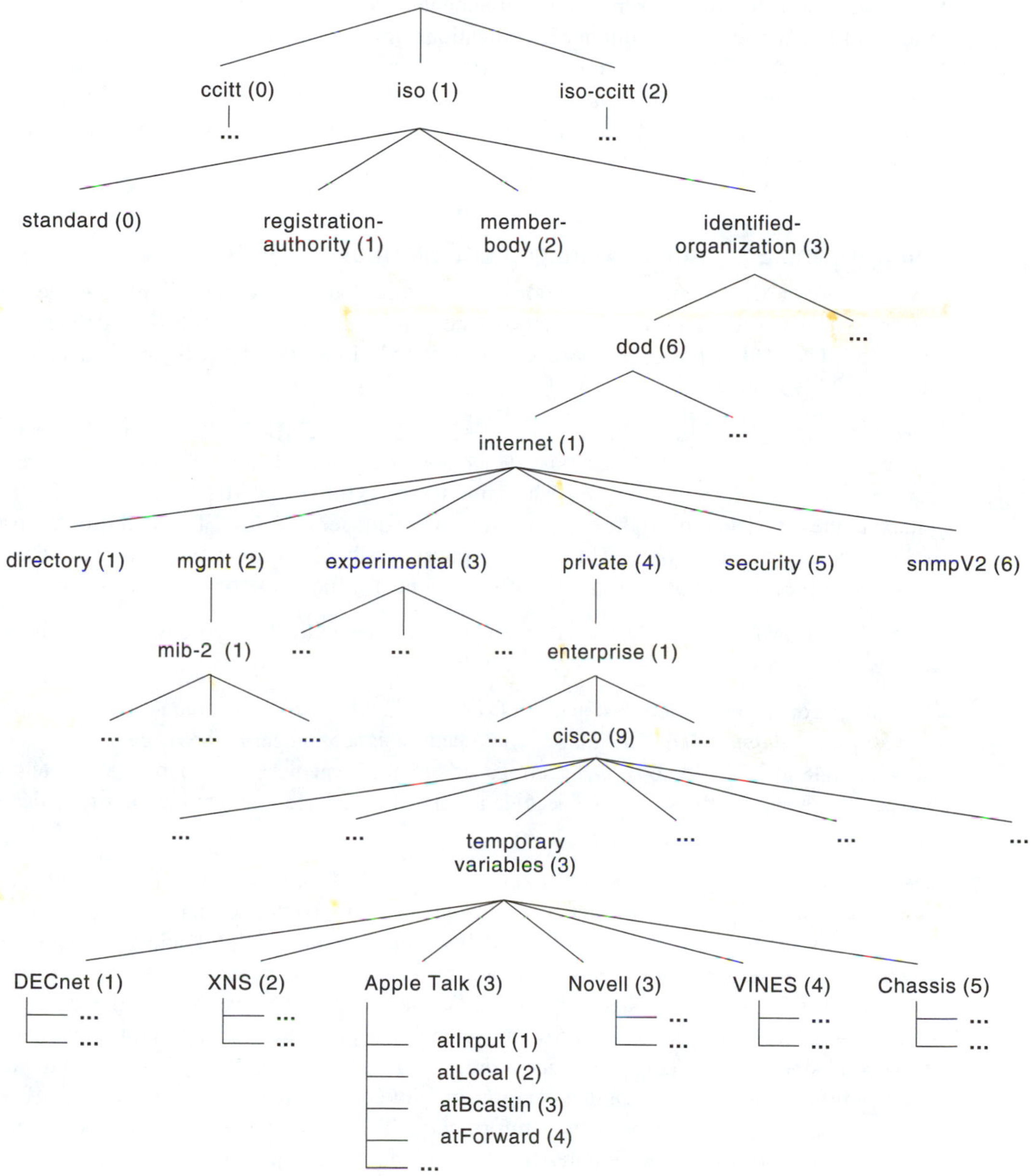

SNMP Version 1 (SNMPv1)

SNMP Version 1 (SNMPv1) is the initial implementation of the SNMP protocol. It is described in RFC 1157 and functions within the specifications of the Structure of Management Information (SMI). SNMPv1 operates over protocols such as User Datagram Protocol (UDP), IP, OSI Connectionless Network Service (CLNS), AppleTalk Datagram-Delivery Protocol (DDP), and Novell IPX. SNMPv1 is widely used and is the de facto network-management protocol in the Internet community.

SNMPv1 and Structure of Management Information (SMI)

The Structure of Management Information (SMI) defines the rules for describing management information, using Abstract Syntax Notation One (ASN.1). The SNMPv1 SMI is defined in RFC 1155. The SMI makes three key specifications: ASN.1 data types, SMI-specific data types, and SNMP MIB tables.

SNMPv1 and ASN.1 Data Types   The SNMPv1 SMI specifies that all managed objects have a certain subset of ASN.1 data types associated with them. Three ASN.1 data types are required: *name*, *syntax*, and *encoding*. The name serves as the object identifier (object ID). The syntax defines the data type of the object (for example, integer or string). The SMI uses a subset of the ASN.1 syntax definitions. The encoding data describes how information associated with a managed object is formatted as a series of data items for transmission over the network.

The SNMPv1 SMI specifies the use of a number of SMI-specific data types, which are divided into two categories: *simple data types* and *application-wide data types*.

Three simple data types are defined in the SNMPv1 SMI, all of which are unique values: *integers*, *octet strings*, and *object IDs*. The integer data type is a signed integer in the range of 2,147,483,648 to 2,147,483,647. Octet strings are ordered sequences of zero to 65,535 octets. Object IDs come from the set of all object identifiers allocated according to the rules specified in ASN.1.

Seven application-wide data types exist in the SNMPv1 SMI: *network addresses*, *counters*, *gauges*, *time ticks*, *opaques*, *integers*, and *unsigned integers*. Network addresses represent an address from a particular protocol family. SNMPv1 supports only 32-bit IP addresses. Counters are nonnegative integers that increase until they reach a maximum value and then return to zero. In SNMPv1, a 32-bit counter size is specified. Gauges are nonnegative integers that can increase or decrease but retain the maximum value reached. A time tick represents a hundredth of a second since some event. An opaque represents an arbitrary encoding that is used to pass arbitrary information strings that do not conform to the strict data typing used by the SMI. An integer represents signed integer-valued information. This data type redefines the integer data type, which has arbitrary precision in ASN.1 but bounded precision in the SMI. An unsigned integer represents unsigned integer-valued information and is useful when values are always nonnegative. This data type redefines the integer data type, which has arbitrary precision in ASN.1 but bounded precision in the SMI.

SNMP MIB Tables   The SNMPv1 SMI defines highly structured tables that are used to group the instances of a tabular object (that is, an object that contains multiple variables). Tables are composed of zero or more rows, which are indexed in a way that allows SNMP to retrieve or alter an entire row with a single Get, GetNext, or Set command.

SNMPv1 Protocol Operations

SNMP is a simple request-response protocol. The network-management system issues a request, and managed devices return responses. This behavior is implemented by using one of four protocol operations: Get, GetNext, Set, and Trap. The Get operation is used by the NMS to retrieve the value of one or more object instances from an agent. If the agent responding to the Get operation cannot provide values for all the object instances in a list, it does not provide any values. The GetNext operation is used by the NMS to retrieve the value of the next object instance in a table or list within an agent. The Set operation is used by the NMS to set the values of object instances within an agent. The Trap operation is used by agents to asynchronously inform the NMS of a significant event.

SNMP Version 2 (SNMPv2)

SNMP Version 2 (SNMPv2) is an evolution of the initial version, SNMPv1. Originally, SNMPv2 was published as a set of proposed Internet standards in 1993; currently, it is a Draft Standard. As with SNMPv1, SNMPv2 functions within the specifications of the SMI. In theory, SNMPv2 offers a number of improvements to SNMPv1, including additional protocol operations.

SNMPv2 and Structure of Management Information (SMI)

The SMI defines the rules for describing management information, using ASN.1.

The SNMPv2 SMI is described in RFC 1902. It makes certain additions and enhancements to the SNMPv1 SMI-specific data types, such as including bit strings, network addresses, and counters. Bit strings are defined only in SNMPv2 and comprise zero or more named bits that specify a value. Network addresses represent an address from a particular protocol family. SNMPv1 supports only 32-bit IP addresses, but SNMPv2 can support other types of addresses as well. Counters are non-negative integers that increase until they reach a maximum value and then return to zero. In SNMPv1, a 32-bit counter size is specified. In SNMPv2, 32-bit and 64-bit counters are defined.

SMI Information Modules   The SNMPv2 SMI also specifies information modules, which specify a group of related definitions. Three types of SMI information modules exist: *MIB modules*, *compliance statements*, and *capability statements*. MIB modules contain definitions of interrelated managed objects. Compliance statements provide a systematic way to describe a group of managed objects that must be implemented for conformance to a standard. Capability statements are used to indicate the precise level of support that an agent claims with respect to an MIB group. An NMS can adjust its behavior toward agents according to the capabilities statements associated with each agent.

SNMPv2 Protocol Operations

The Get, GetNext, and Set operations used in SNMPv1 are exactly the same as those used in SNMPv2. SNMPv2, however, adds and enhances some protocol operations. The SNMPv2 Trap operation, for example, serves the same function as that used in SNMPv1. It, however, uses a different message format and is designed to replace the SNMPv1 Trap.

SNMPv2 also defines two new protocol operations: *GetBulk* and *Inform*. The GetBulk operation is used by the NMS to efficiently retrieve large blocks of data, such as multiple rows in a table. GetBulk fills a response message with as much of the requested data as will fit. The Inform operation allows one NMS to send trap information to another NMS and receive a response. In SNMPv2, if the agent responding to GetBulk operations cannot provide values for all the variables in a list, it provides partial results.

SNMP Management

SNMP is a distributed-management protocol. A system can operate exclusively as either an NMS or an agent, or it can perform the functions of both. When a system operates as both an NMS and an agent, another NMS might require that the system query managed devices and provide a summary of the information learned, or that it report locally stored management information.

SNMP Security

SNMP lacks any authentication capabilities, which results in vulnerability to a variety of security threats. These include *masquerading, modification of information, message sequence and timing modifications*, and *disclosure*. Masquerading consists of an unauthorized entity attempting to perform management operations by assuming the identity of an authorized management entity. Modification of information involves an unauthorized entity attempting to alter a message generated by an authorized entity so that the message results in unauthorized accounting management or configuration management operations. Message sequence and timing modifications occur when an unauthorized entity reorders, delays, or copies and later replays a message generated by an authorized entity. Disclosure results when an unauthorized entity extracts values stored in managed objects, or learns of notifiable events by monitoring exchanges between managers and agents. Because SNMP does not implement authentication, many vendors do not implement Set operations, thereby reducing SNMP to a monitoring facility.

SNMP Interoperability

As presently specified, SNMPv2 is incompatible with SNMPv1 in two key areas: message formats and protocol operations. SNMPv2 messages use different header and protocol data-unit (PDU) formats than SNMPv1 messages. SNMPv2 also uses two protocol operations that are not specified in SNMPv1. Furthermore, RFC 1908 defines two possible SNMPv1/v2 coexistence strategies: proxy agents and "bilingual" network-management systems.

Proxy Agents

An SNMPv2 agent can act as a proxy agent on behalf of SNMPv1 managed devices, as follows:

- An SNMPv2 NMS issues a command intended for an SNMPv1 agent.

- The NMS sends the SNMP message to the SNMPv2 proxy agent.

- The proxy agent forwards Get, GetNext, and Set messages to the SNMPv1 agent unchanged.

- GetBulk messages are converted by the proxy agent to GetNext messages and then are forwarded to the SNMPv1 agent.

- The proxy agent maps SNMPv1 trap messages to SNMPv2 trap messages and then forwards them to the NMS.

Bilingual Network-Management System

Bilingual SNMPv2 network-management systems support both SNMPv1 and SNMPv2. To support this dual-management environment, a management application in the bilingual NMS must contact an agent. The NMS then examines information stored in a local database to determine whether the agent supports SNMPv1 or SNMPv2. Based on the information in the database, the NMS communicates with the agent using the appropriate version of SNMP.

SNMP Reference: SNMPv1 Message Formats

SNMPv1 messages contain two parts: a message header and a protocol data unit. Figure 7-4 illustrates the basic format of an SNMPv1 message.

Figure 7-4 *An SNVPv1 Message Consists of a Header and a PDU*

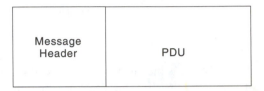

SNMPv1 Message Header

SNMPv1 message headers contain two fields: *Version Number* and *Community Name*. The following descriptions summarize these fields:

- *Version Number*—Specifies the version of SNMP used.

- *Community Name*—Defines an access environment for a group of NMSs. NMSs within the community are said to exist within the same administrative domain. Community names serve as a weak form of authentication because devices that do not know the proper community name are precluded from SNMP operations.

SNMPv1 Protocol Data Unit

SNMPv1 PDUs contain a specific command (Get, Set, and so on) and operands that indicate the object instances involved in the transaction. SNMPv1 PDU fields are variable in length, as prescribed by ASN.1. Figure 7-5 illustrates the fields of the SNMPv1 Get, GetNext, Response, and Set PDUs transactions.

Figure 7-5 *SNMPv1 Get, GetNext, Response, and Set PDUs Contain the Same Fields*

PDU Type	Request ID	Error Status	Error Index	Object 1 Value 1	Object 2 Value 2	Object x Value x

Variable Bindings

The following descriptions summarize the fields illustrated in Figure 7-5:

- *PDU Type*—Specifies the type of PDU transmitted.

- *Request ID*—Associates SNMP requests with responses.

- *Error Status*—Indicates one of a number of errors and error types. Only the response operation sets this field. Other operations set this field to zero.

- *Error Index*—Associates an error with a particular object instance. Only the response operation sets this field. Other operations set this field to zero.

- *Variable Bindings*—Serves as the data field of the SNMPv1 PDU. Each variable binding associates a particular object instance with its current value (with the exception of Get and GetNext requests, for which the value is ignored).

Trap PDU Format

Figure 7-6 illustrates the fields of the SNMPv1 Trap PDU.

Figure 7-6   *The SNMPv1 Trap PDU Consists of Eight Fields*

Enterprise	Agent Address	Generic Trap Type	Specific Trap Code	Time Stamp	Object 1 Value 1	Object 2 Value 2	Object x Value x

Variable Bindings

The following descriptions summarize the fields illustrated in Figure 7-6:

- *Enterprise*—Identifies the type of managed object generating the trap.

- *Agent Address*—Provides the address of the managed object generating the trap.

- *Generic Trap Type*—Indicates one of a number of generic trap types.

- *Specific Trap Code*—Indicates one of a number of specific trap codes.

- *Time Stamp*—Provides the amount of time that has elapsed between the last network reinitialization and generation of the trap.

- *Variable Bindings*—The data field of the SNMPv1 Trap PDU. Each variable binding associates a particular object instance with its current value.

SNMP Reference: SNMPv2 Message Format

SNMPv2 messages consist of a header and a PDU. Figure 7-7 illustrates the basic format of an SNMPv2 message.

Figure 7-7   *SNMPv2 Messages Also Consist of a Header and a PDU*

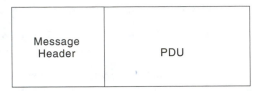

SNMPv2 Message Header

SNMPv2 message headers contain two fields: *Version Number* and *Community Name*. The following descriptions summarize these fields:

- *Version Number*—Specifies the version of SNMP that is being used.

- *Community Name*—Defines an access environment for a group of NMSs. NMSs within the community are said to exist within the same administrative domain. Community names serve as a weak form of authentication because devices that do not know the proper community name are precluded from SNMP operations.

SNMPv2 Protocol Data Unit (PDU)

SNMPv2 specifies two PDU formats, depending on the SNMP protocol operation. SNMPv2 PDU fields are variable in length, as prescribed by ASN.1.

Figure 7-8 illustrates the fields of the SNMPv2 Get, GetNext, Inform, Response, Set, and Trap PDUs.

The following descriptions summarize the fields illustrated in Figure 7-8:

- *PDU Type*—Identifies the type of PDU transmitted (Get, GetNext, Inform, Response, Set, or Trap).

- *Request ID*—Associates SNMP requests with responses.

- *Error Status*—Indicates one of a number of errors and error types. Only the response operation sets this field. Other operations set this field to zero.

- *Error Index*—Associates an error with a particular object instance. Only the response operation sets this field. Other operations set this field to zero.

- *Variable Bindings*—Serves as the data field of the SNMPv2 PDU. Each variable binding associates a particular object instance with its current value (with the exception of Get and GetNext requests, for which the value is ignored).

Figure 7-8   *SNMPv2 Get, GetNext, Inform, Response, Set, and Trap PDUs Contain the Same Fields*

PDU Type	Request ID	Error Status	Error Index	Object 1 Value 1	Object 2 Value 2	Object x Value x

                                    Variable Bindings

GetBulk PDU Format   Figure 7-9 illustrates the fields of the SNMPv2 GetBulk PDU.

Figure 7-9   *The SNMPv2 GetBulk PDU Consists of Seven Fields*

PDU Type	Request ID	Non-repeaters	Max-repetitions	Object 1 Value 1	Object 2 Value 2	Object x Value x

                                    Variable Bindings

The following descriptions summarize the fields illustrated in Figure 7-9:

- *PDU Type*—Identifies the PDU as a GetBulk operation.

- *Request ID*—Associates SNMP requests with responses.

- *Non-repeaters*—Specifies the number of object instances in the variable bindings field that should be retrieved no more than once from the beginning of the request. This field is used when some of the instances are scalar objects with only one variable.

- *Max Repetitions*—Defines the maximum number of times that other variables beyond those specified by the non-repeaters field should be retrieved.

- *Variable Bindings*—Serves as the data field of the SNMPv2 PDU. Each variable binding associates a particular object instance with its current value (with the exception of Get and GetNext requests, for which the value is ignored).

Network Management Products

This section contains a list of Cisco network management products that reside in the network management system. The CCDA should be familiar with these products.

CiscoWorks Blue

The CiscoWorks Blue suite of products is designed to simplify management of a consolidated Systems Network Architecture (SNA) and IP network.

Because many enterprises still manage their SNA networks with NetView or SOLVE:Netmaster, the Cisco IOS software includes support for native service point, which allows the Cisco routers to send alerts and to receive commands from a mainframe management application. Working with Cisco IOS, CiscoWorks Blue Internetwork Status Monitor enables router monitoring, reporting, and even configuration from a mainframe console.

In addition to host-based management tools, Cisco offers SNMP-based management with CiscoWorks Blue Maps and SNA View. These tools are ideal for managing a consolidated IP and SNA network. With one console, you can view, activate, and deactivate SNA devices (physical and logical units) and understand how they are connected to mainframe applications over a router backbone. Color-coding and the capability to drill down to the data link layer enable rapid problem isolation and resolution.

To ensure that service levels are met, Cisco offers CiscoWorks Blue Internetwork Performance Monitor, which monitors network response time on a hop-by-hop basis for both SNA and IP traffic and provides historical reporting, as well as real-time indications of problems.

CiscoWorks Windows

The CiscoWorks Windows comprehensive suite of integrated network management tools is designed to simplify the administration and maintenance of small- to medium-sized business networks or workgroups. CiscoWorks Windows provides a powerful set of configuration, monitoring, and diagnostic applications that complement the capabilities of Cisco Systems internetworking products (switches, routers, hubs, and access servers).

CiscoWorks Windows is based on the SNMP industry standard and provides an easy-to-use network management solution that seamlessly integrates with the Castle Rock Computing SNMPc and the Hewlett-Packard OpenView for Windows and OpenView Network Manager for Windows NT. The CiscoWorks Windows network management suite consists of the following applications:

- **Castle Rock SNMPc Network Management System**—This optional SNMP-based software is bundled with CiscoWorks Windows to provide network discovery, mapping, monitoring, and alarm tracking for any SNMP, Cisco, or third-party device.

- **Health Monitor**—This utility provides real-time fault and performance monitoring of device statistics, including device characteristics, CPU utilization, interface activity, errors, and protocol information.

- **Configuration Builder**—This device-configuration utility enables users to create and to distribute configuration files for multiple Cisco devices through a graphical user interface (GUI).

- **Show Commands**—This application displays detailed router system and protocol information without requiring the user to remember complex command-line languages or syntax.

- **CiscoView**—This graphical device-management technology is the standard for managing Cisco devices, providing back- and front-panel displays. These dynamic, color-coded graphical displays simplify device status monitoring, device-specific component diagnostics, and application launching. CiscoView also provides additional applets that simplify the management of Cisco devices.

CiscoView

CiscoView is a GUI-based device-management software application that provides dynamic status, statistics, and comprehensive configuration information for Cisco Systems internetworking products (switches, routers, concentrators, and adapters). CiscoView graphically displays a real-time physical view of Cisco devices. Additionally, this SNMP-based network-management tool provides monitoring functions and offers basic troubleshooting capabilities.

Using CiscoView, users can easily understand the tremendous volume of management data that is available from internetworking devices. CiscoView organizes this data into graphical device representations that are presented in a clear, consistent format.

CiscoView software can be integrated with several of the leading SNMP-based network management platforms, providing a seamless, powerful network view. It is also included within CiscoWorks, CiscoWorks for Switched Internetworks, and CiscoWorks Windows. CiscoView software can also be run on UNIX workstations as a fully functional, independent management application.

The following are features of CiscoView:

- It graphically displays Cisco products from a centralized network management location, giving network managers a complete view of Cisco products without physically checking each device at remote sites.

- It is oriented for exception reporting, enabling users to quickly grasp essential inquiry information.

- The GUI shows a continuously updated physical picture of routers, hubs, switches, or access servers.

- It can be invoked several times in the same session, to simultaneously support multiple switches, routers, hubs, or access servers.

- It can be integrated with the following network management platforms to provide a seamless and powerful system to manage Cisco devices:

  — HP OpenView

  — IBM NetView for AIX

  — Sun Microsystems Site Manager, Domain Manager, and Enterprise Manager

CiscoView Applications

Included with CiscoView software are numerous applications, or applets, that simplify the management of Cisco switches, routers, hubs, and access servers. The following information provides a brief description of each of these applications:

- **Threshold Manager**—An application that enhances the capability to set thresholds on Cisco Remote Monitoring (RMON) enabled devices, thereby reducing management overhead and improving troubleshooting capabilities.

- **StackView/StackMaker**—Features within CiscoView software that simplify management of Cisco NetBeyond devices.

- **AS5200 Manager**—Modem-management application used to monitor, configure, and troubleshoot the AS5200.

- **TN3270 Monitor**—Application for monitoring TN3270 server events and sessions on a Cisco Channel Interface Processor (CIP) card.

- **Flash File System**—System that provides file copying and editing features for Cisco 7000 routers and that provides configuration file editing and display functionality for Cisco 7000, 7010, 7200, and 7500 series high-end routers.

Netsys Connectivity Tools

The Netsys Connectivity Service Manager enables you to view, assess, and troubleshoot a full spectrum of connectivity issues, including network availability, security, and reliability. It monitors the actual network configuration data and uses built-in intelligence to verify the availability of key network services. It also enables you to establish service-level policies for connectivity, reliability, and security services, and it uses the unique VISTA (view, isolate, solve, test, apply) troubleshooting methodology to automate the diagnosis and repair of problems.

As a result, you can begin to focus more on strategic network issues, such as growth and capacity planning, and less on solving the network crisis of the moment. The Connectivity Service Manager dramatically increases the productivity of network and system administrators, thereby reducing overall network management costs.

The Connectivity Service Manager collects actual router configuration data and creates multiprotocol topologies so that you can visually navigate your network and gain a complete understanding of how it works. The topologies are drawn automatically, so you do not have to spend hours manually linking interfaces and grouping objects. All physical and logical relationships between routers and LAN switches are represented, so you focus on solving problems, not drawing pictures. You can also generate views such as campus, virtual ring group, and OSPF areas in an instant.

All multiprotocol topologies support the following:

- Visual queries, exposing devices running combinations of network or routing protocols
- Pop-up menus, accessing configuration information on each LAN, link, router, and circuit
- Graphical views of routing table coverage
- Graphical displays of round-trip paths between end systems

Netsys Performance Tools

The Netsys Performance Service Manager complements the capabilities of the Netsys Connectivity Service Manager, enabling you to define, monitor, and optimize performance service levels to make the most efficient use of existing network resources; to diagnose and solve network performance problems; to tune existing networks; and to plan network changes. This product is the only Cisco-certified performance-modeling application on the market. By providing accurate modeling of routing and flow transport over Cisco devices, you can analyze interactions among traffic flows, topologies, routing parameters, router configurations, and Cisco IOS software features.

Working interactively with the Performance Service Manager, you can ensure that service-level policies are being met, that performance problems are being solved, and that WAN costs are reduced through resource optimization. This scenario positions your company to meet future equipment and protocol migration plans and application performance requirements.

Performance Baseline

The performance baseline quickly provides a snapshot of current performance and load levels reported by router MIBs in critical areas of your network. MIB information includes interface summary and protocol statistics, buffer hits and misses, and CPU utilization. You can easily schedule MIB data collection, defining how often and at what intervals data samples should be gathered.

From this baseline, you can quickly determine overloaded or underutilized network resources and grasp general performance and loading trends. In addition, you can determine where it is safe to activate IP/IPX accounting or NetFlow switching and guide your placement of RMON agents for maximum coverage with the least impact. Where collection of end-to-end traffic data is difficult, interface statistics can also be used as a supplement.

End-to-End Traffic Baseline

The Performance Service Manager provides an accurate representation of the application-layer traffic flows between communicating subnets or host pairs. Using the end-to-end traffic baseline in combination with performance analysis enables you to better use existing resources and to more effectively plan network growth.

The Performance Service Manager can be easily scheduled to collect end-to-end traffic matrices from either Cisco router accounting or NetFlow data, or RMON data from Network General, Frontier NetScout, and Hewlett-Packard NetMetrix agents. You can also create your own traffic profiles to model the impact of new applications and users on your network. With this information, you can view and understand your network traffic flows and network-wide application breakdowns, and you can identify the volume of traffic through key devices and links or to and from remote networks or hosts.

Netsys Baseliner for Windows NT

Netsys Baseliner for Windows NT displays, debugs, and validates your network configuration. Netsys Baseliner for Windows NT enables you to do the following:

- Test configurations and changes offline, before committing them to the live network. Cisco Netsys Baseliner for Windows NT creates a model of your network and checks for configuration problems.

- Graphically view your network as configured, not as planned or discovered. It enables you to visually navigate the network and to gain a complete understanding of how it works.

- Proactively monitor configuration changes. When problems occur, recent configuration changes are often to blame.

Cisco ConfigMaker

Cisco ConfigMaker is a Microsoft Windows application used to configure a small network of Cisco routers (800, 1000, 1600, 1700, 2500, 2600, 3600, and 4000 series), switches, hubs, and other network devices from a single PC, without requiring knowledge of Cisco IOS. Cisco ConfigMaker assists in configuring IPSec, IOS Firewall, voice, Network Address Translation (NAT), Committed Access Rate (CAR), Dynamic Host Configuration Protocol (DHCP), and other Cisco IOS features.

Cisco ConfigMaker is designed for resellers and network administrators of small- to medium-size businesses who are proficient in LAN and WAN fundamentals and basic network design. More information on ConfigMaker can be found at www.cisco.com/univercd/cc/td/doc/clckstrt/cfgmkr/cmakecd1.htm.

You can download the utility after answering a survey from the Cisco Web site at www.cisco.com/warp/public/cc/cisco/mkt/enm/config/index.shtml. Click Cisco ConfigMaker Software Download.

Cisco FastStep

The Cisco FastStep configuration utility is a Microsoft Windows 95-, 98-, and NT 4.0-based software tool that simplifies the set up, monitoring, and troubleshooting of Cisco routers for home and small offices. The Cisco FastStep Setup application leads the user through a step-by-step, wizard-based procedure that simplifies the configuration of a Cisco router connected to an Internet service provider or to a remote corporate network. Cisco FastStep includes the Cisco FastStep Monitor application, which provides the user with router LAN and WAN performance statistics, fault alarms, and troubleshooting assistance.

Cisco FastStep can be used to configure Cisco 700, 800, and 1600 routers, and Cisco 2610, 2509, and 2511 dial-up routers. You can download Cisco FastStep at http://www.cisco.com/pcgi-bin/tablebuild.pl/faststep.

CiscoWorks2000

The CiscoWorks2000 family of products is based on Internet standards for managing Cisco enterprise networks and devices.

Resource Manager Essentials provides a browser-based tool set for managing Cisco devices, integrating Internet-based information, and providing links to third-party products to deliver the management intranet.

CWSI Campus adds a suite of applications that are designed for managing Cisco Catalyst and LightStream switches; it offers configuration, traffic, logical viewing, and performance management capabilities on a device and a network-wide basis, to ease network management of switched networks. The CiscoWorks2000 family also offers packages that extend the capabilities of Essentials and Campus.

For WAN environments, the CiscoWorks2000 family offers Internet Performance Monitor (IPM), a response time and availability troubleshooting application that provides wide-area monitoring solutions.

Access Control List (ACL) Manager adds access list management to Essentials, providing tools to optimize access lists, and using templates to manage usage.

User Registration Tool (URT) extends the CWSI Campus user tracking to actively identify users in the network by forming *user registration policy bindings* for policy registration, mobility, and tracking.

Other Network Management and Troubleshooting Tools

Other tools also are used to troubleshoot networks. The tools discussed in this section are not SNMP-based.

Protocol Analyzers

Protocol analyzers are devices that are placed on the network to monitor network traffic in a problem area. These devices are not SNMP-based; rather, they are placed in a problem area to monitor every frame or a filtered subset that is forwarded on the network. These devices gather information from Layer 2 up to application information. The devices are placed on SPAN ports on Cisco switches. The SPAN port is used to monitor the traffic of a certain port on the switch— for example, the port with a server connected to it. Microsoft NT includes the Network Monitor application that is a protocol analyzer; Network Associates Sniffer also is a very popular product.

Cable Testers

Cable testers are used to troubleshoot physical-layer problems. Issues include the wiring of Category 5 UTP cables (straight-through versus crossover), pinouts, and cable lengths.

Foundation Summary

Foundation Summary is a section presented in a concise format to provide quick reference information relating to the objectives covered in this chapter.

Table 7-1   *Design Document Components*

Component	Description
Executive Summary	Is directed to decision-makers. Provides an explanation of the purpose of the project, a list of strategic recommendations, and a description of how the solution meets the customer's requirements.
Design Requirements	Shows current topology, current applications, and current network health. Lists performance and scalability requirements, business requirements and constraints, and expected performance.
Design Solution	Shows the proposed network topology, selected hardware and media, suggested routing protocols, and proposed network management tools.
Summary	Provides a concise summary of the solution and a description of how the solution meets the requirements.
Appendixes	Lists contacts and provides additional information about products, circuit information, and prototype test results.
Cost	Provides an itemized and detailed cost listing of equipment to be purchased.

Table 7-2   *Network Management Processes*

Process	Description
Fault	Refers to detecting, isolating, and correcting problems (faults).
Configuration	Refers to baselining, modifying, and tracking configuration changes of network devices.
Accounting	Refers to tracking the usage of segments to determine usage-based billing of service.
Performance	Refers to the measurement of network behavior and effectiveness to deliver frames, packets, segments.
Security	Refers to the maintenance and distribution of authentication and authorization information.

Table 7-3   *Network Management Architecture*

Component	Description
Managed device	Is a router or switch with agent software.
Agent	Gathers statistics.
Network management system	Runs network management applications. Polls devices for SNMP information and configuration.

Table 7-4   *Applications*

Product	Description
CiscoWorks Blue	Suite of products designed to simplify management of a consolidated SNA and IP network.
CiscoWorks for Windows	Suite of integrated network management tools designed to simplify the administration and maintenance of small- to medium-sized business networks or workgroups. Runs on Windows NT.
CiscoView	GUI-based device-management software application that provides dynamic status, statistics, and comprehensive configuration information for Cisco Systems internetworking products (switches, routers, concentrators, and adapters). CiscoView graphically displays a real-time physical view of Cisco devices.
Netsys Connectivity Service Manager	Tool for collecting actual router configuration data and creating multiprotocol topologies so that you can visually navigate your network and gain a complete understanding of how it works.
Netsys Performance Service Manager	Modeling tool that enables you to define, monitor, and optimize performance service levels to make the most efficient use of existing network resources and to diagnose and solve network performance problems.
Netsys Baseliner for Windows NT	Tool that displays, debugs, and validates your network configuration. Tests configurations and changes offline before committing them to the live network.
Cisco ConfigMaker	An easy-to-use Microsoft Windows application used to configure a small network of Cisco routers (800, 1000, 1600, 1700, 2500, 2600, 3600, and 4000 series), switches, hubs, and other network devices from a single PC, without requiring knowledge of Cisco IOS.
Cisco FastStep	A Microsoft Windows 95-, 98-, and NT 4.0-based software tool that simplifies the set up, monitoring, and troubleshooting of Cisco routers for home and small offices. Can be used to configure Cisco 700, 800, 1600 routers and Cisco 2610, 2509, and 2511 dial-up routers.
CiscoWorks2000	A family of products based on Internet standards for managing Cisco enterprise networks and devices. It includes Resource Manager Essentials and CWSI Campus. It runs on UNIX or Windows NT.

Q&A

The following questions are designed to test your understanding of the topics covered in this chapter. When you have answered the questions, you can find the answers in Appendix A. After you identify the subject matter you missed, review those sections in the chapter until you feel comfortable with the material.

1 When writing a design document in response to a RFP, which section should you direct at the key decision-makers in a company, to clearly articulate your strategy for the project?

_____

_____

_____

2 Which application would you recommend to an IT manager if the staff are Windows NT server administrators and have little experience managing routers?

_____

_____

_____

3 As companies recognize the importance of networks, more emphasis should be placed on what form of management?

_____

_____

_____

4 Which network management application that can be installed on Windows NT can you use to test configuration changes offline?

_____

_____

_____

5 In which section of the design document would you describe the current topology of the network?

_____

_____

_____

6 Which GUI-based network management application provides dynamic status and statistics and can display a graphical view of Cisco devices?

_____

_____

_____

7 Which application is designed to simplify management of a consolidated SNA and IP network?

_____

_____

_____

8 Which network management process refers to detecting, isolating, and correcting problems?

_____

_____

_____

9 What is an agent?

_____

_____

_____

10 In which design document section would you list the recommended IP routing protocols?

_____

_____

_____

11 Which configuration utility simplifies the configuration of routers for small offices?

_____

_____

_____

12 CiscoWorks for Windows includes a utility that provides real-time fault and performance monitoring of device statistics, including device characteristics, CPU utilization, interface activity, errors, and protocol information. What is it called?

_____

_____

_____

13 Which tool can be used to diagnose and solve network performance problems, to tune existing networks, and to plan for network changes?

_____

_____

_____

14 Which tool can be used to verify the distance of the UTP cable from the wiring closet to the user end station?

_____

_____

_____

15 Which are the four operations introduced with SNMPv1?

_____

_____

_____

16 Which are the two operations introduced with SNMPv2?

_____

_____

_____

Case Studies

The following case study questions are based on the ongoing scenarios that are presented in the "Case Studies" section of Chapter 1, "Design Goals." If you want to familiarize yourself with the entire case study, refer to that section before working through the following questions. The answers to these questions can be found in the "Case Study Answers" section at the end of this chapter.

Case Study #1: GHY Resources

1 Mr. Martin mentioned that he does not have the personnel to install and configure UNIX-based management stations. Which network management applications would you recommend to manage his routers and switches?

_____

_____

_____

2 When preparing the design document, which section are managers must likely to read?

_____

_____

_____

3 What steps should GHY take to develop a proactive network management strategy?

_____

_____

_____

Case Study #2: Pages Magazine

1 Which application can Mr. Phillips use to test router configurations before committing them online?

_____

_____

_____

2 In which section of the design document would you document the current routing protocol and address its limitations?

_____

_____

_____

3 Which routing protocols that support VLSM would you mention in the Design Solution section as possible options for Pages Magazine?

_____

_____

_____

Case Study Answers

Case Study #1: GHY Resources

1 Mr. Martin mentioned that he does not have the personnel to install and configure UNIX-based management stations. Which network management applications would you recommend to manage his routers and switches?

CiscoWorks for Windows. CiscoWorks for Windows can be installed on NT platforms, so Mr. Martin does not need UNIX administrators.

2 When preparing the design document, which section are managers must likely to read?

Executive Summary. This section includes the high-level points for the project and is directed at the key decision-makers for the project.

3 What steps should GHY take to develop a proactive network management strategy?

Assign staff to proactively monitor the network and ensure that the data collecting and reporting processes are running properly. Using CiscoWorks for Windows, GHY can monitor the health of devices and links.

Case Study #2: Pages Magazine

1 Which application can Mr. Phillips use to test router configurations before committing them online?

Netsys Baseliner for NT

2 In which section of the design document would you document the current routing protocol and address its limitations?

Design Requirements

3 Which routing protocols that support VLSM would you mention in the Design Solution section as possible options for Pages Magazine?

EIGRP or OSPF. These routing protocols support VLSM and do not have the limitations of Routing Information Protocol (RIP).

Objectives Covered in This Chapter

The following is a list of the objectives covered in this chapter. The list of CCDA exam design objectives and the chapters in which they are covered can be found in the Introduction of this book.

8	Determine the customer's requirements for new applications, protocols, number of users, peak usage hours, security, and network management.
28	Determine how much of the network structure must be built to prove that the network design meets the customer's needs.
29	List the tasks required to build a prototype or pilot that demonstrates the functionality of the network design.
30	List the Cisco IOS software commands you should use to determine whether a network structure meets the customer's performance and scalability goals.
31	Describe how to demonstrate the prototype or pilot to the customer so that the customer understands that the proposed design meets requirements for performance, security, capacity, and scalability, and accepts the costs and risks.

CHAPTER 8

Building a Prototype or Pilot

The last step in creating a successful design solution is demonstrating to the customer how your design solution meets that customer's needs for performance, security, capacity, and scalability.

This chapter concentrates on methods used to finalize the customer's acceptance of the design. Often the designs proposed are complex and have many different components that must be brought together to build a complete solution. Usually a more complex design means a greater cost to the customer. Therefore, it is important that the consultant provide sound proof to the customer that the proposed design will meet the customer's needs.

Two methods demonstrate to the customer how the proposed design will solve that customer's network needs. The first method is to build a prototype, which is used for large-scale designs. The second is to construct a pilot, which is a smaller and less complicated version of the prototype that is ideal for smaller designs. This chapter covers the criteria that will help you choose the right testing method and then details the steps involved in implementing each method.

"Do I Know This Already?" Quiz

The questions in the following quiz are designed to help you gauge how well you know the material covered in this chapter. Compare your answers with those found in Appendix A, "Answers to Quiz Questions." If you answered most or all of the questions thoroughly and correctly, you might want to skim the chapter and proceed to the "Q&A" and "Case Study" sections at the end of the chapter. If you find that you need to review only certain subject matter, search the chapter for those sections that cover the objectives you need to review, and then test yourself both with these questions and with the "Q&A" and "Case Study" questions. If you find the following questions too difficult, read the chapter carefully until you feel that you can easily answers these and the "Q&A" and "Case Study" questions.

1 Which type of test plan is more appropriate for a network solution that involves a small network in which the client needs a demonstration of a basic function such as the security features on a firewall?

_____

_____

_____

2 What is the next step involved in developing a prototype after a test plan has been developed?

_____

_____

_____

3 Identify the step of the prototype development plan that includes tasks such as drawing a network and developing a list of tests.

_____

_____

_____

4 True or False: Both the prototype and the pilot require you to understand and review the competition's implementation plans.

_____

_____

_____

5 Which type of test plan requires less planning and fewer resources?

_____

_____

_____

6 Which tool could you use to avoid having to perform the test yourself?

_____

_____

_____

7 At what stage of the pilot would the designer identify the weaknesses of the competition's product, such as scalability issues?

_____

_____

_____

8 How does the designer ensure that the prototype will meet the expectations of a client?

_____

_____

_____

9 Which tool can be used to test security and capture data during the testing phase of both the pilot and the prototype?

_____

_____

_____

10 What two IOS commands can be used to troubleshoot connectivity?

_____

_____

_____

Foundation Topics

Determining the Appropriate Test Plan

The following CCDA objectives are covered in this section:

8	Determine the *customer's requirements* for new applications, protocols, number of users, peak usage hours, security, and network management.
28	Determine how much of the network structure must be built to prove that the network design meets the customer's needs.

A prototype is a complex and full trial run of the network design used to prove that the design works. A prototype is usually a large-scale, fully functional form of a new design and thus is used to prove a large implementation. The customer would have to decide whether the need to prove the design justifies the cost of setting up a prototype. If the prototype is not appropriate for your customer, you might consider recommending a pilot, which is a smaller test designed for smaller businesses. The pilot usually tests more basic functions of the design, and it also usually requires less time and fewer resources. The criteria for choosing either test plan involves comparing the cost of the test against the need to prove that the design works. Table 8-1 summarizes this criteria for choosing the pilot or the prototype.

Table 8-1   *Criteria for Choosing a Testing Plan—Pilot Versus Prototype*

	Pilot	Prototype
Size of the network design	Used on small network designs with a few segments or simple WAN networks	Used on a subset of a large network design that can span both LANs and WANs
Demonstration of functionality	Used to demonstrate basic functionality, such as connectivity	Used to prove complex functionality, such as connectivity; applications, such as e-mail; and routing
Cost	Usually small because of the simplicity of the test	More costly because it requires more equipment and resources
Customer requirements	Used when the customer requires a small test of the design	Used when the customer needs proof of full functionality of the design

After you have determined the customer's testing needs, you must perform the appropriate steps for creating a pilot or a prototype. Depending on your choice, see "Steps for Building a Prototype" or "Steps for Creating a Pilot," later in this chapter.

Steps for Building a Prototype

The following CCDA objectives are covered in this section:

8	Determine the customer's requirements for new applications, protocols, number of users, peak usage hours, security, and network management.
29	List the tasks required to build a prototype or pilot that demonstrates the functionality of the network design.

This section covers the process of building a successful prototype. The prototype can be a fully functional test either of a portion of the network or of the entire network. Therefore, as with the design of the network, the design of the prototype demands careful planning to maximize its effectiveness. The success of the prototype could help determine whether the customer will accept the project. To study for the exam, remember the steps involved in building each type of test. Remember that the purpose of both the prototype and the pilot is to validate your design to a customer.

Table 8-2 shows the steps for building a prototype. Each of these steps is covered in detail in the rest of this section.

Table 8-2   *Steps for Building a Prototype*

Step	Description
Step 1: Review the customer's requirements.	Determine the customer's major goals.
	Outline the proof required to demonstrate that your design works.
	Determine possible problem areas that might affect your design.
Step 2: Determine the extent of the prototype.	Determine how much of the design must be built into a prototype to be effective.
	Identify the tools you can use to simplify the prototype.
Step 3: Understand your competition.	Work with your sales team to determine products and designs proposed by the competition.
	If information is not available, speculate on what the competition would use.
	Research information on your competition's products by referencing Web sites, industry articles, and evaluations.

continues

Table 8-2   *Steps for Building a Prototype (Continued)*

Step	Description
Step 4: Develop a test plan.	Draw a network diagram.
	List tools for the test.
	List the plan scheduling, resources, and milestones.
	Prepare the demonstrations.
	Determine how each test will prove that the design meets the customer's requirements.
	Identify how the design shows Cisco's strengths.
	Determine how each test will show that the competitor's products do not provide the ideal solution.
Step 5: Purchase and prepare equipment.	Some or all of following equipment must be acquired and prepared:
	Network simulation tools Protocol analyzers Industry tests Cisco hardware and software Routers Switches Network-management tools Non-Cisco hardware and software Application servers File servers
Step 6: Practice.	Practice your demonstration to include the necessary elements from the previous step.
Step 7: Conduct final tests and demonstrations.	Test your configuration using the following tools: Cisco IOS software commands Protocol analyzers Simulation tools

Step 1: Review the Customer's Requirements

Having a clear goal for building your prototype is essential. In fact, the prototype design should be created using the same approach you used to determine customer requirements for the original design. Refer back to Chapter 2, "Assessing the Existing Network and Identifying Customer Objectives," if you need to review the list of requirements.

First, list the customer's major goals. Then identify the customer's requirements for performance, security, capacity, and scalability. Also consider other customer requirements such as return on investment (ROI) issues, management of the new network, equipment reuse, and cost of implementing the prototype test.

You also should determine what specific advantages for the customer you can illustrate with the prototype. These ideas should be well planned to ensure that the prototype is complete and serves as a useful vehicle to demonstrate these points.

Just as it is important to list the good ideas, you also want to be ready for any problems or issues that might negatively affect the success of the project. Take the time to list the cons to the prototype so that you are ready to address them as well.

Step 2: Determine the Extent of the Prototype

Creating the right size prototype is critical. You must determine how much of the design is necessary to be included in the prototype to meet the customer's expectations. The scope of your prototype is a factor that you and your customer must agree on before work can begin. Cost and the purpose of the prototype will often determine the size of the demonstration. For example, if one of the customer's primary concerns is time, that customer might request that you focus your test on a specific problem. The customer might need to roll out your design in multiple locations and thus might be willing to implement a full prototype in one of the company's many locations.

For the exam, it is important to remember that the customer's goals are the deciding factor in determining how much of the network design should be implemented to prove its value to the customer. When proving the effectiveness of your design, you can use tools and investigative services to simplify the development of the prototype by simulating some of the equipment and their effect on the network.

These simulations generally remove the need to purchase, install, and configure actual equipment to make the task of creating the prototype less costly. One of the tools mentioned in the exam is Network General's Sniffer network analyzer. A network analyzer can be used to simulate traffic and also works as a tool to prove the effectiveness of the network design.

Third-party industry tests also sometimes are done on competing products, and you can use these tests and their results to prove your design without building a test yourself. An example of one of these tests is the Strategic Networks Consulting, Inc. (SNCI) switch test, available from SNCI's Web site. This test was done on Cisco's Catalyst 5000 switches and Cabletron's MMAC-Plus switches. Go to SNCI's Web site at www.zdnet.com/zdtag/snci/ to review the test and other similar comparisons.

Step 3: Understand Your Competition

For a large design that requires a prototype, the customer probably is considering other designs as well. It is important to plan this particular prototype to highlight the advantages that your design can offer above the competition. Working with the account manager and sales team can help you find out about the competition's design. Taking the time to gather as much information on what the competition will propose is always a good way to double-check your own design and to make sure that you didn't miss a point.

If it isn't possible to get information on the competition, try to make some assumptions on what they would propose to meet the customer's requirements by referencing information from the client's Web site or product descriptions. You can make a comparison list of features based on the client's requirements, or draw up a list of pros and cons about the competition's products. Then use this information to build your strategy.

Step 4: Develop a Test Plan

Now that you have prepared to create the prototype, the next step is to create the test plan that will be used on the prototype. The best tool available to a designer is a topology map of the prototype test network. This one diagram can be used to view the entire network and can be the single most important document of a prototype. On this diagram, you can include major configuration parameters such as network speeds, topology information, WAN line speeds, and descriptions of specific network devices, such as firewalls.

Figure 8-1 shows a topology map of a sample network design. Notice that only the marked region of this proposed design will be the subject of the actual prototype test.

A topology map of the test environment proves invaluable. The prototype topology map can include a list of simulation tools, Cisco hardware and software, and non-Cisco hardware and software you will need for the prototype. Some of the non-Cisco hardware you might want to make use of include cables, modems, null modems, WAN connections, Internet access, workstations, servers, design simulation tools, telephone equipment simulators, and so on.

While compiling a list of the resources you will need, it is important also to list and plan the tests that you will perform on the prototype network. The test plan should reflect the goals you decided upon when the design for the prototype was created: Remember that these goals were designed to meet the customer's needs.

Performing a demonstration for the client might be complicated and might require the involvement of multiple people to ensure its success. If you require help from coworkers or collaboration from the customer's staff, remember to request the help with ample time to coordinate your resources. To make sure that everyone understands what to do for the test, be sure to develop and review a script.

Figure 8-1   *Design Topology Indicating the Prototype Area to Be Tested*

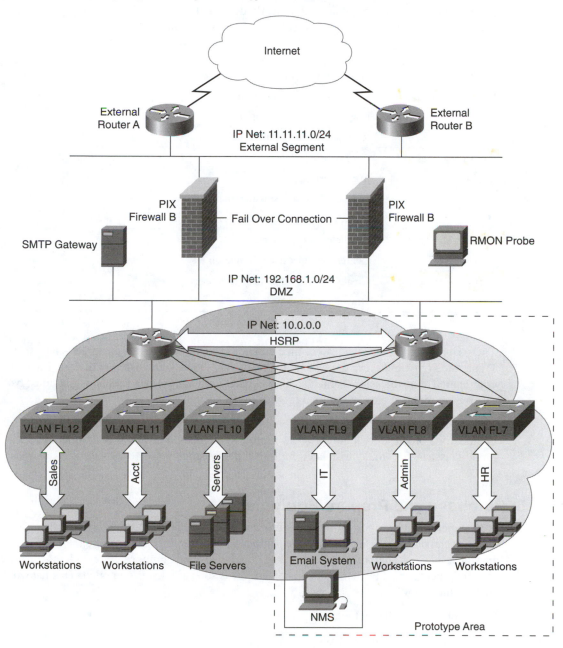

Table 8-3 shows a table included in a script that maps out the roles and responsibilities of the people involved in the presentation. By clearly defining this type of information, people are better prepared to contribute to the success of the presentation.

Table 8-3   *Creating a Script*

Role	Contributions to the Project and Script
Design Consultant	Review the design and define the customer's goals
	Provide the network diagram
	Review the benefits of the design
Project Manager	Develop a schedule
	Map milestones
	Develop an implementation plan
	Provide contact information for the client
Account Manager	Handle customer contact
	Compile competitive information
Network Engineers	Create detailed implementation plans
	Draw up testing overviews

The script should be tested ahead of time either at the Cisco lab or the customer's lab. Preparation only reinforces the testing, which in turn shows your customer that your team is coordinated and professional and also may point out any unforeseen problems that must be resolved before you present the final product to the customer.

Finally, the test should highlight the strengths of the Cisco product and point out how the competitor's product would not prove as useful. Remember to review the test plan to avoid possible issues that would arise later during the demonstration.

Step 5: Purchase and Prepare Equipment

Remember that it is important to prepare for the prototype demonstration well in advance so that you can purchase and configure the equipment with ample time. Because there are always instances in which equipment purchases can be delayed or other unforeseen problems can arise, the equipment should be gathered and configured as soon as a list is compiled. This list would include the following:

- Network simulation tools
- Cisco hardware and software
- Non-Cisco hardware and software

Remember to prepare an inventory sheet to help you track of the products as they arrive. It's also important to stage some of the equipment with basic testing. Staging is a method of setting up the equipment for basic configuration and testing the hardware. This is a good time to develop an inventory to help you sort your equipment. Table 8-4 shows a sample staging and inventory chart.

Table 8-4   *Sample Staging and Inventory Chart*

Receipt Date	Product Type	Vendor	Product	Quantity	Staging
5/10/2000	Routers	Cisco	2511	2	Burn in Configure IP address Label
5/10/2000	Routers	Cisco	3640	1	Burn in Configure IP address Label
5/10/2000	Cables	Cable Inc.	RJ 45 10FT	100	Label

Step 6: Practice

Performing the demonstration for the client will be a complex task. It's important to practice with the members of your team to coordinate your presentation—this is especially important if you are going to demonstrate the equipment. You want to make sure that your demonstration doesn't have any small surprises that would adversely affect your success. Make sure that you give yourself ample time, and practice several times.

Step 7: Conduct Final Tests and Demonstrations

This final step will be discussed in more detail later in this chapter in the section "Testing the Prototype or Pilot." That section outlines some basic tools that you can use to make your demonstrations more effective.

The steps for developing and implementing a prototype will help you prove your design. The next section shows how to develop a pilot program. As you read through the next section, note the differences in the steps and the execution of testing via pilot versus testing via prototype.

Steps for Creating a Pilot

The following CCDA objectives are covered in this section:

8	Determine the customer's requirements for new applications, protocols, number of users, peak usage hours, security, and network management.
29	List the tasks required to build a prototype or pilot that demonstrates the functionality of the network design.

Many of the same processes that apply to creating a prototype also apply to building a pilot. However, the main difference between the prototype and the pilot is that the pilot is a small demonstration of a basic feature. That makes a pilot an appropriate test for a small business or a network undergoing minimal design changes.

Unlike the prototype, developing a pilot should not require as much effort because of the smaller scale of the test. First, test the design to make sure that it meets the client's requirements. Then review the competition's proposal so that you can address any issues the client might have. This again gives you the opportunity to review the pilot to make sure that you have not missed any points you need to highlight.

After you have planned the pilot, draw up a well-practiced script to ensure a smooth presentation of the pilot. Finally, schedule time with the customer to present the demonstration when you are ready. The following list summarizes the steps involved in creating a pilot:

- Step 1: Test the design.
- Step 2: Review the competition's proposal.
- Step 3: Script the demonstration.
- Step 4: Practice.
- Step 5: Schedule time and present the demonstration to the customer.

The remainder of this section covers these steps in detail.

Step 1: Test the Design

When testing the design, make sure that you have clear objectives for the testing based on the customer's request and requirements. It will be beneficial to review the customer's requirements before engaging in the pilot so that you can ensure that your tests will be effective. For more information on how to test a pilot, see the section "Testing the Prototype or Pilot," later in this chapter.

Step 2: Review the Competition's Proposal

This step of the pilot is the same as Step 3 of prototype testing. This is important because your demonstration should point out the benefits of your design over the competition's. By understanding your competition's proposal, you will be able to address any questions that the client asks related to the competition's products and features.

Step 3: Script the Demonstration

This essential step will help you incorporate all the aspects of the project, including the design, project management, and implementation. You will want to highlight the following:

- Verify that the tests will prove that the proposed solution meets the client's requirements

- Review the strengths and benefits of the Cisco products

- Demonstrate where the competition falls short

Step 4: Practice

Be sure to practice, practice, practice. Rehearsing the presentation gives you the opportunity to coordinate all the different components involved, including the people, resources, and results you want to demonstrate. This will ensure a smooth presentation without any surprises.

Step 5: Schedule Time and Present the Demonstration to the Customer

The last step is the scheduling of the demonstration. Remember that if you use any devices (such as laptops) and presentation materials (such as projectors), you should set them up well ahead of time.

Now that you understand the differences between the processes of developing the pilot and the prototype, the next section covers the testing process. This process highlights some tools you might use to improve your design and show that your design meets the client's needs.

Testing the Prototype or Pilot

The following CCDA objectives are covered in this section:

30	List the Cisco IOS software commands you should use to determine whether a network structure meets the customer's performance and scalability goals.
31	Describe how to demonstrate the prototype or pilot to the customer so that the customer understands that the proposed design meets requirements for performance, security, capacity, and scalability, and accepts the costs and risks.

After configuring and setting up the prototype or pilot, you can use three types of tools to prove that your test meets the customer's requirements:

- Cisco IOS software commands
- Protocol analyzer
- Simulation tools

Besides using these tools to test your design, you also can use them to demonstrate your results to the customer. The remainder of this section covers these testing tools and shows how you can demonstrate your results.

When proving your design to a customer during the testing phase, it is important to consider both the cost and the practicality of the tools you will use. Good planning, including clearly defined objectives for your prototype testing and efficient resources, makes up the right formula for creating a successful test environment.

When trying to prove the functionality of a network, it is more cost effective to use tools that will generate a simulation of the type of traffic on a live network instead of purchasing the actual equipment. Protocol analyzers and simulation tools help you create the necessary environment as well as capture and present data.

Network management is evolving as quickly as the networks themselves. A common network management tool such as a probe, a device placed at a key point in the network, gathers and analyzes traffic using remote monitoring (RMON). This specification defined in RFC 1271 (Ethernet) is also supported on the Cisco Catalyst class switches and is used for traffic analysis on switched LAN networks as well as T1 WAN links. To read more on the uses of RMON for traffic analysis, refer to the white paper from Cisco at www.cisco.com/warp/public/614/4.html.

Using Cisco IOS Commands to Test the Prototype or Pilot

Table 8-5 lists the recommended IOS commands and the results they would yield. These are only a subset of the Cisco IOS commands that are available; for a full listing of Cisco IOS commands, refer to the CCO Web site or the Cisco Documentation CD-ROM.

Table 8-5 *Cisco IOS Commands Used for Testing a Prototype or Pilot*

Cisco IOS Command	Results
show interface	Shows data link layer errors, router errors (such as dropped or ignored packets), and broadcast rates
show processes	Shows router CPU usage and CPU time used by processes
show buffers	Shows buffer usage and misses
ping and **traceroute**	Is used to troubleshoot connectivity and performance problems

Table 8-5   *Cisco IOS Commands Used for Testing a Prototype or Pilot (Continued)*

Cisco IOS Command	Results
show *protocol* route	Lists the protocol routing table to troubleshoot routing problems
show access-lists	Displays access lists to help troubleshoot security problems
debug	Is used to troubleshoot and verify packets sent and received

CAUTION   The **debug** command could cause severe performance issues on the router, so use caution when using it.

Using Protocol Analyzers

Protocol analyzers are flexible tools that provide a wide range of data collection and traffic analysis methods. These are some examples of protocol analyzers and the Web sites that contain more information on them:

- Network Associate's Sniffer Suite of Products—www.nai.com/asp_set/products/tnv/tnv_literature.asp

- Network Instruments' NetSense for Observer—www.netinst.com/html/netsense_for_observer.html

- RADCOM's LAN, WAN, and ATM analyzers—www.radcom-inc.com/

This is just a tiny fraction of the protocol analyzers available. As with many technologies, you must assess the functionality by asking some questions to determine how to choose the right product. The following questions can help you select the right protocol analyzer:

- What type of environment will the protocol analyzer need to function in? LAN, WAN, ATM, switched networks, 100 Mb Ethernet, Gigabit Ethernet, T1?

- What type of protocols does it need to understand? IP, IPX/SPX, SNA, NetBEUI, Banyan Vines, AppleTalk?

- What type of network management protocols does it need to support? SNMP, RMON, RMON2?

- What type of information do you want to collect? Network utilization, protocol analysis, latency, jitter?

- What other products need to get this information? Does this involve other network management tools, such as HP Openview, CiscoWorks, Catalyst switches?

Using these questions can help you to determine what type of functionality is needed in your protocol analyzer tools.

The following are some basic steps to take when using a protocol analyzer:

- Configure for the correct LAN and WAN media
- Capture data
- Test the prototype or pilot
- Demonstrate security

Table 8-6 describes these steps in more detail.

Table 8-6 *Using a Protocol Analyzer*

Protocol Analyzer Action	Description
Configure for the correct LAN and WAN media.	Identify the correct media you are attaching.
	For WAN links, this includes leased lines, Frame Relay, HDLC, X.25, ATM, and ISDN.
	For LAN links, this includes 10 Mbps Ethernet, 100 Mbps Ethernet, Gigabit Ethernet, 4 Mbps Token Ring, and 16 Mbps Token Ring.
Capture data.	Define the criteria for capturing data:
	• Identify how many days' worth of data will give you the accurate information. Make sure that you capture data for at least one day.
	• Identify errors and irregularities.
	• Check network utilization.
	• Refer to the network health list presented in the section "Step 12: Summarize the Health of the Existing Network," in Chapter 2.
Test the prototype or pilot.	Generate traffic that replicates the customer's desired network.
Demonstrate security.	You can prove the security of your access lists by showing whether the traffic passes through your filters.

Simulation Tools

Simulation tools need to be compatible with the components necessary to affect the performance of a network. Think of all the components necessary to create a simulation of a network—the protocols, other vendor devices, the topology, application utilization on a network that fluctuates depending on time of day, and so on. Different simulation tools also test the functionality of critical devices on the network, such as a firewall. This type of simulation tool mimics different types of network attacks on a firewall or network servers to test its vulnerability.

The following are just a few links to simulation tool vendors. You will need to identify your testing needs to determine the correct product:

- Make Systems' NetMaker Suite network simulation and capacity planning tool—www.makesys.com/

- Internet Security Systems' SAFESuite products for network vulnerability testing—www.iss.net/

Demonstrating Your Findings to the Customer

After completing the tests, you need to provide proof of the results to the customer. The following are some tips to help you present the information.

- Publish your findings in a concise but comprehensive report. This report should have an organized method demonstrating how you came to your conclusions. Make sure to focus your work on the customer requirements. Include your diagrams and some of the raw data you have collected.

- Add the results of your test to the network design document or response to an RFP. For more information on writing a design document, refer to Chapter 7, "The Design Document and Cisco Network Management Applications."

- Create slides that graphically demonstrate the correlation between your test results and the customer's requirements. This should be done by examining the data you collected during your testing.

- Meet with the customer to present your findings. Be prepared to use different presentation methods to make the meeting more effective.

- Meet with the customer and reproduce your tests while the customer is watching. Do this only after you have had an opportunity to practice and replicate the results.

Conclusion

This chapter concludes the coverage of the CCDA exam objectives. The next chapter provides you with some additional case studies and questions for you to further assess your mastery of the CCDA exam objectives. You can also use the extensive assessment tools on the CD-ROM to take an entire practice CCDA exam or to test yourself on specific objectives. If you identify any objectives in which you are not completely proficient, use this book's objective cross-references, the CD-ROM electronic text links, the book's reference appendixes, and even Cisco's Web site to help you brush up on that subject matter before you take the CCDA exam.

Foundation Summary

Foundation Summary is a section presented in a concise format to provide quick reference information relating to the objectives covered in this chapter.

Table 8-7 *Criteria for Choosing a Testing Plan—Pilot Versus Prototype*

	Pilot	**Prototype**
Size of the network design	Used on small network designs with a few segments or simple WAN networks	Used on a subset of a large network design that can span both LANs and WANs
Demonstration of functionality	Used to demonstrate basic functionality, such as connectivity	Used to prove complex functionality, such as connectivity; applications, such as e-mail; and routing
Cost	Usually small because of the simplicity of the test	More costly because it requires more equipment and resources
Customer requirements	Used when the customer requires a small test of the design	Used when the customer needs proof of full functionality of the design

Table 8-8 *Steps for Building a Prototype*

Step	**Description**
Step 1: Review the customer's requirements.	Determine the customer's major goals.
	Outline the proof required to demonstrate that your design works.
	Determine possible problem areas that might affect your design.
Step 2: Determine the extent of the prototype.	Determine how much of the design needs to be built into a prototype to be effective.
	Identify the tools you can use to simplify the prototype.
Step 3: Understand your competition.	Work with your sales team to determine products and designs proposed by the competition.
	If information is not available, speculate on what the competition would use.
	Research information on your competition's products by referencing Web sites, industry articles, and evaluations.

Table 8-8   *Steps for Building a Prototype (Continued)*

Step	Description
Step 4: Develop a test plan.	Draw a network diagram.
	List tools for the test.
	List the plan scheduling, resources, and milestones.
	Prepare the demonstrations.
	Determine how each test will prove that the design meets the customer's requirements.
	Identify how the design shows Cisco's strengths.
	Determine how each test will show that the competitor's products do not provide the ideal solution.
Step 5: Purchase and prepare equipment.	Some or all of following equipment must be acquired and prepared:
	Network simulation tools Protocol analyzers Industry tests Cisco hardware and software Routers Switches Network-management tools Non-Cisco hardware and software Application servers File servers
Step 6: Practice.	Practice your demonstration to include the necessary elements from the previous step.
Step 7: Conduct final tests and demonstrations.	Test your configuration using the following tools:
	Cisco IOS software commands Protocol analyzers Simulation tools

Table 8-9   *Cisco IOS Commands Used for Testing a Prototype or Pilot*

Cisco IOS Command	Results
show interface	Shows data link layer errors, router errors (such as dropped or ignored packets), and broadcast rates
show processes	Shows router CPU usage and CPU time used by processes
show buffers	Shows buffer usage and misses
ping and **traceroute**	Is used to troubleshoot connectivity and performance problems
show *protocol* **route**	Lists the protocol routing table to troubleshoot routing problems
show access-lists	Displays access lists to help troubleshoot security problems
debug	Is used to troubleshoot and verify packets sent and received

CAUTION   The **debug** command could cause severe performance issues on the router, so use caution when using it.

Q&A

The following questions are designed to test your understanding of the topics covered in this chapter. When you have answered the questions, look up the answers in Appendix A. After you identify the subject matter you missed, review those sections in the chapter until you feel comfortable with this material.

1 Your design included multiple VLANS with similar configurations and services. The customer requested confirmation that the design is fully functional. What type of testing program would you recommend, and why?

_____

_____

_____

2 What type of testing would require more resources, including higher costs and more complexity?

_____

_____

_____

3 What stage of the prototype testing requires that you showcase the strength of Cisco's products and the areas in which the competitor's products are not as strong?

_____

_____

_____

4 When determining the customer's requirements for prototype testing, what are the four areas that should be included when making the determination?

_____

_____

_____

5 What tool can you use during testing to provide detailed information on the protocols and traffic on the network?

_____

_____

_____

6 During the practice of the pilot script, you realize that your protocol analyzer is showing that unwanted traffic is passing from an unsecured segment to your internal network. What IOS command would you use on the router to begin troubleshooting this problem?

_____

_____

_____

7 After scripting the demonstration for the client, what is the next step in the pilot testing program that would need to be implemented to ensure a smooth presentation?

_____

_____

_____

8 If the client wanted a demonstration of the connectivity between segments and routing information, which IOS commands would you use during the testing?

_____

_____

_____

9 If you are using an access list and wanted to test the security, what product could you use to demonstrate its effectiveness?

_____

_____

_____

10 How would you demonstrate your findings to your customer during the prototype testing?

_____

_____

_____

Case Study

The following case study questions are based on the ongoing scenarios presented in the "Case Studies" section of Chapter 1, "Design Goals." If you want to familiarize yourself with the entire case study, refer to that section before working through the following questions. The answers to these questions can be found in the "Case Study Answers" section at the end of this chapter.

Case Study #3: MediBill Services, Inc.

1 Draw a topology map of the existing MediBill Services, Inc., network and a topology map of the proposed new network. Include in the proposed network the traffic flow of the e-mail system.

2 What type of routed protocol will be used across the WAN to MediBill's customers?

_____

_____

_____

3 What are the two main areas of management concern for the client based on its requirements?

_____

_____

_____

4 In your design, what type of testing would you recommend for this customer?

_____

_____

_____

5 During the scripting stage of the prototype testing development, the client requested a checklist of MediBill's services. As the engineer in charge of the demonstration, list the Internet and application services MediBill will offer its customers so that you can develop a method for showcasing these applications.

_____

_____

_____

6 What tool would you use during the pilot demonstration to show the effectiveness of the security solution?

_____

_____

_____

Case Study Answers

Case Study #3: MediBill Services, Inc.

1 Draw a topology map of the existing MediBill Services, Inc., network and a topology map of the proposed new network. Include in the proposed network the traffic flow of the e-mail system.

During your demonstration, you will present the client with a topology map of the existing network. Figure 8-2 shows a topology map of the existing network.

Figure 8-3 shows a topology map of the new network, including the traffic flow of the e-mail system.

2 What type of routed protocol will be used across the WAN to MediBill's customers?

The only routed protocol necessary is IP because all of MediBill's applications, including PC network management, are IP-compliant. The client's only other type of traffic will be Internet traffic, which is also IP-based. Many companies are looking to simplify their network by standardizing to one protocol.

3 What are the two main areas of management concern for the client based on its requirements?

Security management and network management

4 In your design, what type of testing would you recommend for this customer?

Mr. Lee wants a demonstration of the security that will be implemented. Considering that certain sites can receive Internet services, a pilot is the best solution. Mr. Lee needs to see a demonstration of the security only. The test can be conducted on a subset of the existing environment to test basic connectivity and security. This is particularly true because the remote doctor offices will be duplicates of the same design.

Figure 8-2   *The Existing MediBill Services, Inc., Network*

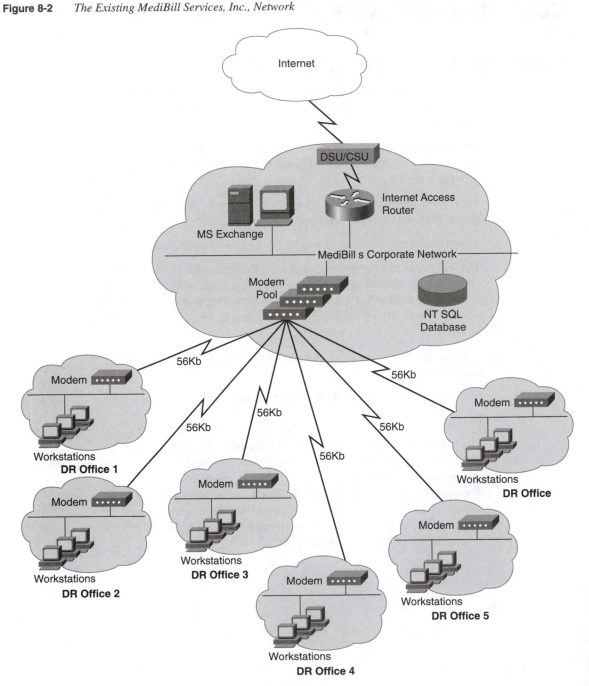

Figure 8-3   *The Proposed MediBill Services, Inc., Network with E-mail Traffic Flow*

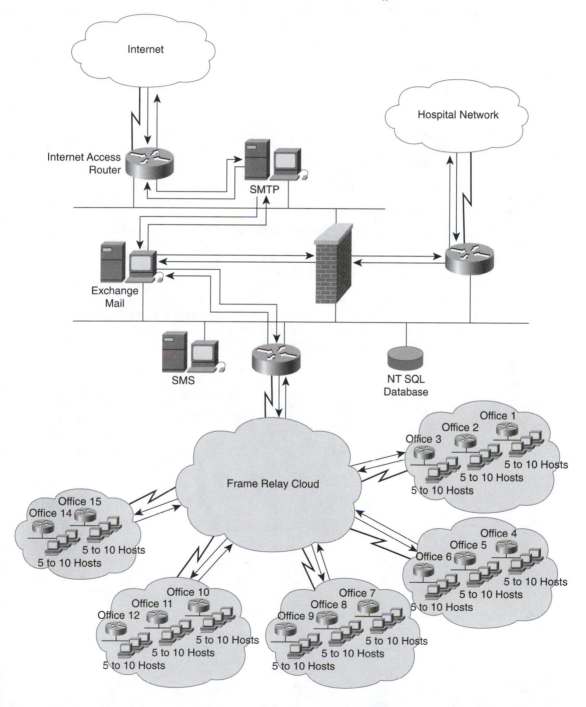

5 During the scripting stage of the prototype testing development, a checklist of MediBill's services was requested. As the engineer in charge of the demonstration, list the Internet and application services MediBill will offer its customers so that you can develop a method for showcasing these applications.

Internet services include:

— **Web access (HTTP)**

— **E-mail access (SMTP)**

— **File Transfer (FTP)**

Application services include:

— **Database storage (SQL)**

— **Network management (SMS)**

— **E-mail system (Exchange/Outlook)**

6 What tool would you use during the pilot demonstration to show the effectiveness of the security solution?

You should use a protocol analyzer, such as Network Associate's Sniffer, which will demonstrate whether these packets are passing through the router or firewall to the other network. The Sniffer can also generate traffic such as pings to test an access list rule.

The case studies and questions in this chapter draw on your knowledge of CCDA exam design objectives. Use these exercises to solidify your mastery of the objectives, as well as to identify areas you still need to review for the case study portion of the exam.

CHAPTER 9

Additional Case Studies

Your CCDA exam will probably contain questions that will require review of an accompanying case study. This chapter contains four case studies that are similar in style to the ones you might encounter on the CCDA exam. Read through each case study and answer the corresponding questions. Answers to the case study questions can be found at the end of this chapter. More than one solution can satisfy the customer's requirements. In these cases, answers presented at the end of the chapter represent the best possible solutions. An explanation of the answer will be provided where necessary.

Case Study #1: Cicala and Rosado Law Firm

Mr. Kunkel, the IT manager at Cicala and Rosado Law Firm, is responsible for updating the network to use new technologies. He has two network analysts working for him that handle the routers, hubs, clients, servers, and media for the company. The company is understaffed, and the analysts are overworked. There is no network management station monitoring the network.

The firm has two locations, one in Houston and one in Dallas, specializing in corporation legalities. A Frame Relay WAN link exists between the sites. Each office has approximately 40 workstations. The company expects only 4 percent network traffic growth in the next two years.

The current network was built in the early 1990s. Each office has a large 10BaseT concentrator with stations attached. A router in Houston provides connectivity to the Dallas office and to the Internet via a local ISP. The current routing protocol is RIP. The WAN link currently has a 256k bit rate and runs at an average of 85 percent utilization with occasional bursts. The Ethernet segments currently run at an average 45 percent utilization; occasionally, network utilization will burst to 60 percent utilization. Users complain of slow response time through the day.

The firm uses the Microsoft Office suite of applications because it does a lot of word processing and exchanging documents. E-mail and HTTP are highly used as well. The firm also uses CD-ROM servers for reference. IP is the only protocol routed on the network.

The firm recently upgraded its work stations and is now equipped with 10/100 network interface cards. Mr. Kunkel would like a proposal to upgrade the network to Fast Ethernet. He would also like a solution to integrate voice and data on the WAN link between Dallas and Houston. Mr. Kunkel mentioned that a previous network audit uncovered security issues from access to the Internet.

Case Study #1 Questions

1 What can be said about the network health of the Ethernet and WAN segments?

_____

_____

_____

2 Sketch the current network.

3 What applications are being used?

_____

_____

_____

4 What would you recommend to alleviate the WAN utilization problem?

_____

_____

_____

5 What would you recommend to improve the LAN utilization problem? What switches could you use?

_____

_____

_____

6   What Cisco device could be used to provide protection from the Internet?

_____

_____

_____

7   What Cisco devices could be used to provide an integrated voice and data solution?

_____

_____

_____

8   Would you suggest a full CiscoWorks 2000 solution with HP OpenView on a Unix workstation to Mr. Kunkel?

_____

_____

_____

9   The firm's network is small. Would you propose a pilot or a prototype to demonstrate the VoIP solution?

_____

_____

_____

10   Mr. Kunkel hands you the following IP subnet information:

Company network: 223.10.1.0, mask: 255.255.255.192

Houston LAN: 223.10.1.0/26

Dallas LAN: 223.10.1.64/26

WAN link: 223.10.1.128/26

What routing protocol would you recommend, and how would you change the addressing scheme?

_____

_____

_____

11 Draw the proposed network solution.

Case Study #2: Big Oil and Gas

Mr. Abbott is an IT manager at Big Oil and Gas. He is in charge of the network infrastructure, including routers and switches. Mr. Abbott's group includes personnel that can install and configure Cisco routers and switches. Another group manages the servers. The company currently has a Unix server with HP OpenView.

Big Oil and Gas is a medium-sized petrochemical company based in Houston. It also has operations in the Gulf and in South America.

The network includes more than 30 routers. Mr. Abbott hands you the diagram displayed in Figure 9-1, which describes the topology of the network. Although the average utilization is around 50 percent, some WAN segments are experiencing utilization peaks of 72 percent. All LAN segments are under 20 percent utilization.

Unix servers run SAP business applications, and Novell servers are used for office suite applications. IPX is routed throughout the network.

Mr. Abbott would like a solution to reduce the IPX SAP traffic on the WAN. He also would like a network management solution to better manage the router configurations.

Case Study #2 Questions

1 What possible solutions can be used to reduce SAP traffic over the WAN?

_____

_____

_____

2 If the remote locations need to see only four corporate file servers, what type of filter can be used?

_____

_____

_____

Figure 9-1   *Big Oil and Gas Existing Network*

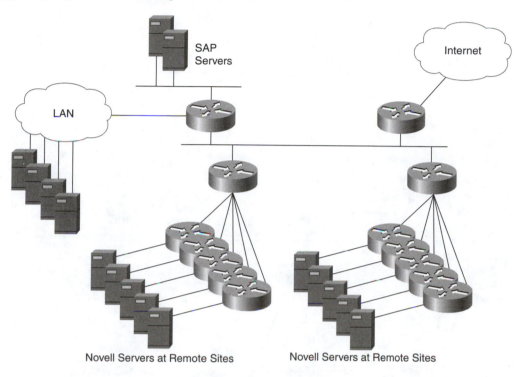

SAP
Servers

Internet

LAN

Novell Servers at Remote Sites   Novell Servers at Remote Sites

3 What network management application would you recommend for router
configuration tracking and hardware inventory management?

_____

_____

_____

4 Are there any protocols that cannot be routed on this network?

_____

_____

_____

5 What does the diagram in Figure 9-2 describe?

_____

_____

_____

Figure 9-2   *Big Oil and Gas Question #5 Diagram*

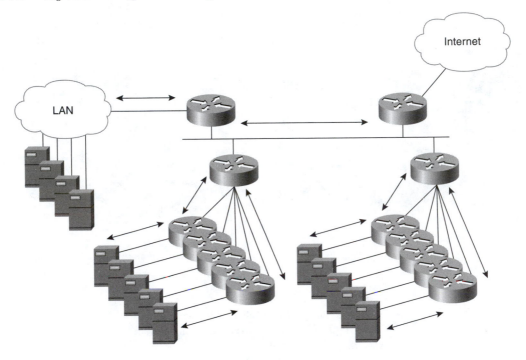

6 Do you see any utilization problems with the LAN segments?

_____

_____

_____

7 Are there any Cisco IOS features that can help prioritize the business SAP traffic
       on the WAN links?

_____

_____

_____

8 What does the diagram in Figure 9-3 describe?

_____

_____

_____

Figure 9-3   *Big Oil and Gas Question #8 Diagram*

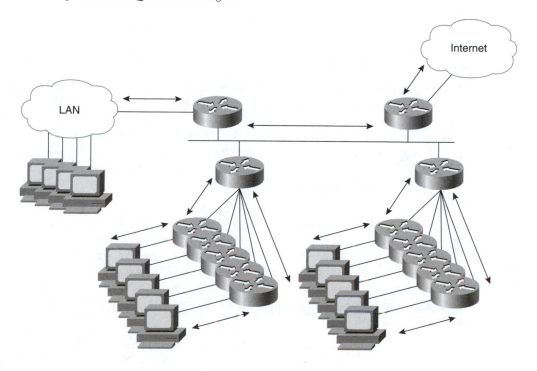

Case Study #3: CartoonWorks, Inc.

CartoonWorks, Inc., is a graphical firm specializing in animation for the advertisement and entertainment industries. This firm is growing quickly and needs to remain competitive. The firm just completed a strategy meeting to decide how each department can contribute to create a corporation that will give the company an edge in the market.

Ms. Roberts, the Director of IS for CartoonWorks, Inc., is responsible for all LAN and WAN implementations. She has proposed networking CartoonWorks' remote offices in an effort to capture and share the intellectual capital and to allow for easy communications between designers and artists to increase creativity and productivity.

The company has always operated with independent offices. Ms. Roberts has hired you to help her come up with a cost-effective plan to start connecting the different offices and to help her create this network. Ms. Roberts is interested not only in the initial design, but also in a phased implementation plan so that she can budget correctly for this upgrade.

Currently, there are two main offices, each with anywhere from 70 to 100 Apple and PC workstations, making the total hosts of the two offices no more than 200. Each office has one network segment. All administrative functions are located in CartoonWorks Main Street office. The Human Resources, Accounting, and Corporate departments all share two Novell 4.11 file servers. The Administrative and IT users have only PCs, and the Production users have a mix of PCs and Macintosh computers. The third server is the primary NDS directory for user authentication and home directories.

However, the Marketing, Production, and IT departments occupy two floors in the Oak Street office. Marketing and Production share two servers, and IT uses the secondary NDS server. The two offices are connected via a point-to-point T1 connection. Ms. Roberts has expressed concern about the redundancy for the line. All the graphical work is done on Apple computers, and the operations and administration work for the corporation is done on PCs. The network uses AppleTalk and IPX/SPX protocols. However, the new documentation management and chat room server that is designed to facilitate communication in a company is a Web-based product.

In addition, the company has been developing and testing its two new NT Web servers on the new Internet segment. These new Web servers need to communicate with the new NT SQL database at the Oak Street office. The Media Group, which is part of the Production department, will complete its testing within one month. With the new Web servers, Ms. Roberts needs to also implement a DNS solution and register a domain name. Ms. Roberts has begun the process of acquiring a domain name in preparation for the Internet access, but she needs to install and secure her DNS servers.

A new T1 Internet connection has been installed at the data center in the Oak Street office, but CartoonWorks does not have a security policy and needs to install security. Everyone in the company will have Web access, and the company is concerned about the legal implications of using the Web. Ms. Roberts wants to make changes to the network as seamlessly as possible for her users. This is especially critical due to the lack of technical support staff and the recent implementation of critical applications, such as a GroupWare system. CartoonWorks migrated to Novell's GroupWise from cc:Mail, but the company has not installed the Internet e-mail capability and has made that and security its first concern.

CartoonWorks executives know that they need to upgrade their infrastructure to work more aggressively, but they cannot disrupt production to do so. Now that you have information on what Ms. Roberts is looking to implement, use the information to help her decide on the right solution. CartoonWorks is interested in a phased solution that will address its immediate needs for connectivity to the remote users and to include the NT e-mail system.

Case Study #3 Questions

1 List the new applications that the customer wants to implement in the network.

_____

_____

_____

2 Draw a logical diagram of the existing network.

3 What type of WAN technology would you recommend as a redundant solution for the T1 line between CartoonWorks offices?

_____

_____

_____

4 What CartoonWorks services depend on the DNS server in this network?

_____

_____

_____

5 If the client were given an valid address of 199.199.199.32 with a mask of 255.255.255.224 from its ISP, what solution would you recommend to give all CartoonWorks' users access to the Internet?

_____

_____

_____

6 During the process of characterizing the network, you have found the following:

— Broadcasts are 17 percent of total traffic.

— There are 100 mixed-media workstations.

— Utilization on the segment is at 30 percent.

What would you recommend to the customer to improve the performance on this network?

_____

_____

_____

7 What are the routed protocols used in this network?

_____

_____

_____

8 What would you recommend to use as routed protocols in the new network, and why?

_____

_____

_____

9 Which routing protocol can be used to support all the routed protocols of the new network?

_____

_____

_____

Case Study #4: Martin & Martin, LLC

Mr. Jones is the Director of IT at Martin & Martin, LLC., a law firm located in downtown Chicago. He is charged with the task of planning for a network upgrade. However, Mr. Jones has decided that he would like to have a network analysis done before the upgrade so that he can find out which systems would require upgrades, and to create a three-year strategy to present to the partners. Mr. Jones is concerned about presenting the right strategy that will include the return on investment.

Martin & Martin has provided services to its clients for more than 10 years and is planning to open two new offices in the next six months. These offices will be across town, and each office will have approximately 30 people. Each office will have four senior attorneys and 10 junior attorneys, clerks, and administrative staff. To support these offices, the IT department has one support person for each remote location for desktop and level 1 support.

The law offices occupy four floors of a high-rise building in Chicago. The customer is experiencing network latency, especially in the Accounting and Finance department and in the Human Resources department, which both reside on the 22nd floor. The director of the Accounting and Finance department has raised concerns about the security of his files. To address any further security concerns with other departments, Mr. Jones met with the directors of each department, except for the attorneys. The legal department includes Research and the attorneys. Research, IT, and the Corporate Administration departments share the 23rd floor. The senior and junior partners and all attorneys with their administrative support staff occupy the 25th floor, and the 26th floor is used for reception and conference rooms. The law firm has decided that video conferencing is an essential component of its business and is looking to implement video conferencing as soon as possible so that the original firm can communicate with the two new remote offices.

The customer has four network segments for each floor but has been experiencing network latency. Each floor except the 26th has 10 to 20 printers. Each floor has a 100 Mb uplink to the Data Center on the 23rd floor. There are approximately 50 PCs on the 26th floor, 150 PCs on the 25th floor, and 40 PCs on both the 22nd and 23rd floors. The servers for each department reside on their respective floors.

Martin & Martin currently uses Microsoft Office applications and Exchange for mail. However, Martin & Martin is concerned about network security and wants a recommendation to secure the traffic of three specific departments: Human Resources, Accounting and Finance, and Corporate Administration. Mr. Jones needs to provide Internet security for the entire corporation. However, due to the sensitivity of the information in these departments, Mr. Jones wants to secure each segment so that access will be strictly defined. With the growth of the remote offices and a network audit in the near future, Mr. Jones wants to secure these networks. The senior partners are also considering the use of video and audio files in the Research department for reference. Mr. Jones is interested in a centralized IS management that can monitor devices and eventually grow to remote monitoring and proactive monitoring with the new offices. However, he is concerned that the new network would require a more experienced IS staff.

This is a critical decision for Mr. Jones to make because he needs to understand what traffic patterns he should plan for. With the need for teleconferencing looming on the horizon for each of the offices, Mr. Jones needs to take into account additional WAN capacity in his plan.

Mr. Jones has asked for a design proposal and an implementation plan for the network analysis.

Case Study #4 Questions

1 Draw the corporate structure of this client.

2 What type of testing program would you recommend to test the video conferencing among the remote offices?

_____

_____

_____

3 What network management tool would you recommend that Martin & Martin purchase to support their new network?

_____

_____

_____

4 What type of naming structure would you give to servers and endnodes in this network?

_____

_____

_____

5 The client wants to see the effect of data encryption on the router's performance during the prototype stage in which you establish connectivity among the remote offices. How would you demonstrate this effect?

_____

_____

_____

6 Describe why Mr. Jones' existing network does not provide adequate security for the data in each department.

_____

_____

_____

Case Study #1 Answers: Cicala and Rosado Law Firm

1 What can be said about the network health of the Ethernet and WAN segments?

The network health is poor. Ethernet network utilization over 40 percent is not recommended. WAN links over 70 percent utilization should be upgraded to higher speeds.

2 Sketch the current network.

Figure 9-4 shows the existing Cicala and Rosado law firm network.

Figure 9-4   _Cicala and Rosado Law Firm Existing Network_

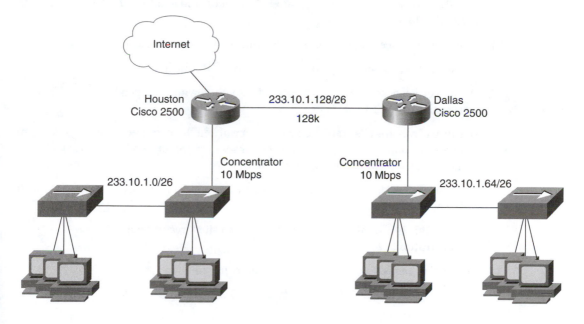

3 What applications are being used?

Microsoft Office suite applications, WWW and HTTP applications, and CD-ROM servers.

4 What would you recommend to alleviate the WAN utilization problem?

To overcome the utilization problems on the WAN link, upgrade the link to 256 Kbps and then monitor the utilization of the network.

5 What would you recommend to improve the LAN utilization problem? What switches could you use?

Because the clients have been equipped with 10/100 NIC, replace the 10 Mbps hubs with Fast Ethernet switches. The switches will also provide a separate collision domain to each device.

You could use two Cisco 2948 switches at each site, providing 96 ports for network devices.

6 What Cisco device could be used to provide protection from the Internet?

The Cisco PIX Firewall can be used to provide additional security from the Internet. The PIX Firewall provides stateful inspection of conversations and can be used for network address translation.

7 What Cisco devices could be used to provide an integrated voice and data solution?

Cisco 3600 series routers provide a Voice over IP solution.

8 Would you suggest a full CiscoWorks 2000 solution with HP OpenView on a Unix workstation to Mr. Kunkel?

Because Mr. Kunkel's staff is already overworked, learning new Unix skills might not be an option. They already run NT servers, so recommend CiscoWorks for Windows as a network management solution.

9 The firm's network is small. Would you propose a pilot or a prototype to demonstrate the VoIP solution?

Because this is a small network with only two sites, recommend a pilot demonstration.

10 Mr. Kunkel hands you the following IP subnet information:

Company network: 223.10.1.0, mask: 255.255.255.192

Houston LAN: 223.10.1.0/26

Dallas LAN: 223.10.1.64/26

WAN link: 223.10.1.128/26

What routing protocol would you recommend, and how would you change the addressing scheme?

You should recommend using a routing protocol that can do VLSMs. Possible options are RIPv2, OSPF, and Enhanced IGRP. Because both routers are Cisco, Enhanced IGRP would be most efficient. You need to place the power users with the CD-ROM servers onto another segment.

Houston main LAN: 223.10.1.0/26

Houston server LAN: 223.10.1.128/27

Dallas LAN: 223.10.1.64/26

WAN link: 223.10.1.224/30

11 Draw the proposed network solution.

Figure 9-5 shows the proposed Cicala and Rosado law firm network.

Figure 9-5   *Cicala and Rosado Law Firm Proposed Network Solution*

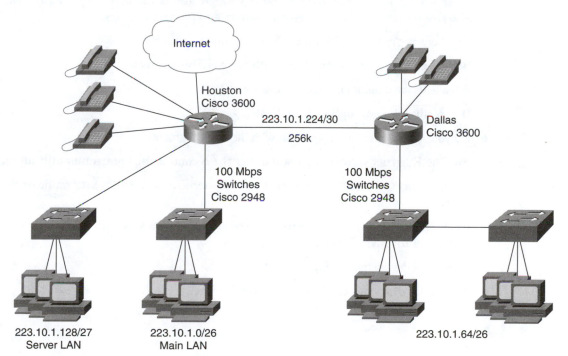

223.10.1.128/27
Server LAN

223.10.1.0/26
Main LAN

223.10.1.64/26

Case Study #2 Answers: Big Oil and Gas

1 What possible solutions can be used to reduce SAP traffic over the WAN?

   Possible solutions include the following:

   — Access lists could be used to control the broadcasted SAPs.

   — Enhanced IGRP could be used to route IPX over the WAN.

   — NLSP could be used to route IPX.

2 If the remote locations need to see only four corporate file servers, what type of filter can be used?

   An IPX SAP filter (range 1000 to 1099) should be used on outbound WAN links to permit the list of servers.

3 What network management application would you recommend for router configuration tracking and hardware inventory management?

   CiscoWorks can be used to track router configurations and inventory. CiscoWorks also can be used to make changes to routers and for viewing logs.

4 Are there any protocols that cannot be routed on this network?

   Big Oil and Gas uses IP and IPX; both are routable protocols.

5 What does the diagram in Figure 9-2 describe?

   It describes the flow of SAP broadcasts.

6 Do you see any utilization problems with the LAN segments?

   No. The Ethernet segments are still under the recommended maximum utilization.

7 Are there any Cisco IOS features that can help prioritize the business SAP traffic on the WAN links?

   Custom queuing can be configured to give priority to packets with a destination address of the SAP servers.

8 What does the diagram in Figure 9-3 describe?

   This figure describes HTTP traffic to the Internet.

Case Study #3 Answers: CartoonWorks, Inc.

1 List the new applications that the customer wants to implement in the network.

Video conferencing

Novell Internet e-mail system

Web servers

SQL database

DNS Server

2 Draw a logical diagram of the existing network.

The customer defined the network by describing the geographical locations and the services that the network provides its users. The logical diagram in Figure 9-6 is based on those services.

3 What type of WAN technology would you recommend as a redundant solution for the T1 between CartoonWorks offices?

Suggest an ISDN dial-up connection to begin with until it is determined that the client has a higher than 256K backup solution. This would require an assessment of the traffic and bandwidth utilization on the T1. However, the ISDN equipment and line are both cost-effective and can be implemented quickly.

4 What CartoonWorks services depend on the DNS server in this network?

The e-mail system depends on the DNS server because it requires a mail exchange record for Internet mail services. Web servers depend on the DNS server for name resolution. Web browsers also depend on the DNS server for name resolution.

5 If the client were given a valid address of 199.199.199.32 with a mask of 255.255.255.224 from its ISP, what solution would you recommend to give all CartoonWorks' users access to the Internet?

CartoonWorks plans to give Internet access to all its 200-plus users. The address range that the ISP had provided is not sufficient for the company's network size, so it needs to use Network Address Translation (NAT).

Figure 9-6   *Logical Diagram of the Existing CartoonWorks Network*

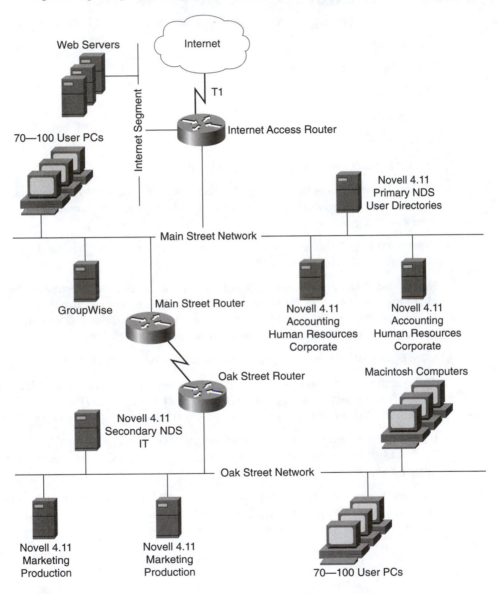

6 During the process of characterizing the network, you have found the following:

— Broadcasts are 17 percent of total traffic.

— There are 100 mixed-media workstations.

— Utilization on the segment is at 30 percent.

What would you recommend to the customer to improve the performance on this network?

Segmenting the flat network would be recommended based on the findings. The threshold for broadcasts is that broadcasts should be less than 20 percent of the total traffic. This means that a Layer 3 segmentation needs to occur to isolate the broadcast traffic. Therefore, a recommendation for creating VLANs with Catalyst switches would provide the Layer 3 segmentation and also reduce collision domains.

7 What are the routed protocols used in this network?

IPX, AppleTalk, and IP

8 What would you recommend to use as routed protocols in the new network, and why?

The client will need to implement IP to support the NT applications and the Web-based applications. However, the customer does not describe any plans to change the graphical or file systems. Therefore, the network would also include IPX and AppleTalk.

9 Which routing protocol can be used to support all the routed protocols of the new network?

Because the new network includes IP, IPX, and AppleTalk, the recommendation should be for using Enhanced IGRP. Enhanced IGRP supports all the above-mentioned routed protocols.

Case Study #4 Answers: Martin and Martin, LLC

1 Draw the corporate structure of this client.

Figure 9-7 explains the corporate structure of Martin & Martin, LLC. The diagram shows that there are two main divisions, which are the corporate functions and the legal departments. The chart reflects only information that is specifically stated.

2 What type of testing program would you recommend to test the video conferencing among the remote offices?

A prototype would be the recommended form of testing because, for the video conferencing to work, there needs to be well-tested connectivity among the offices.

3 What network management tool would you recommend Martin & Martin purchase to support its new network?

Recommend CiscoWorks for Windows. CiscoWorks is an SNMP-based tool that can provide the monitoring of devices. Martin & Martin will be opening new offices, which need to be managed remotely. The case study specifies that the remote offices will have limited IT support. Therefore, CiscoWorks' remote management and configuration capability will be useful. Also, CiscoWorks' statistical information will be useful data for comparison with the baseline.

4 What type of naming structure would you give to servers and endnodes in this network?

The server naming convention should be based on the departments that use those servers. The workstations should also be named for those departments. For example, a printer in the Research department could be named RSC_Ptr0001.

5 The client wants to see the effect of data encryption on the router's performance during the prototype stage in which you establish connectivity among the remote offices. How would you demonstrate this effect?

You can use the *show processes* command and monitor the CPU utilization.

6 Describe why Mr. Jones' existing network does not provide adequate security for the data in each department.

The network is segmented by floors, which means that people in the Accounting and Finance department share the network with those in Human Resources. If each of these departments wants security, the traffic needs to be separated.

Figure 9-7   *Corporate Structure for Martin & Martin, LLC*

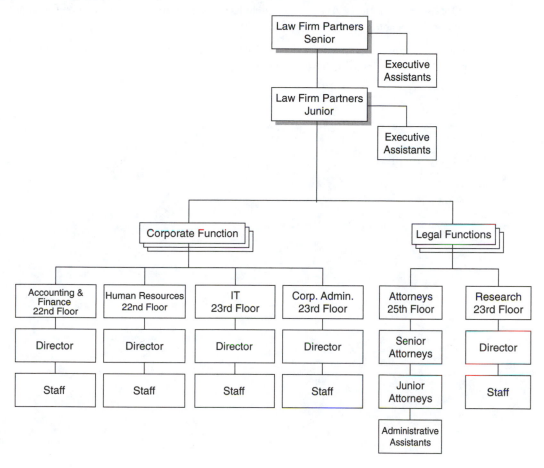

This appendix contains the answers to each chapter's "Do I Know This Already?" and "Q&A" quiz questions. Answers to a chapter's Case Study questions can be found at the end of that chapter.

Some questions can have more than one possible answer. In those cases, the author has provided the best possible answer and an explanation for that answer.

Answers to Quiz Questions

Chapter 1: Design Goals

"Do I Know This Already?" Quiz Answers

1 What types of questions would you ask to determine a client's application requirements?

   A CCDA should be prepared to ask the following questions to assess a client's application needs:

   — **What applications are being used on the network?**

   — **How many users are there per application?**

   — **What new applications are being introduced?**

   — **What are the traffic flows of these applications?**

   — **At what time of the day are these applications used?**

2 What are samples of business constraints on design?

   How the project will affect the company's ability to do business. How the new design will help the company develop, produce, and track products.

3 What is the first step in network design?

   Obtain customer requirements.

4 In the framework of small to medium-sized network design, what should be done if there are protocol-related problems on the network?

   To reduce broadcast and other protocol-related problems on small to medium-sized networks, use routers.

5 What information is gathered in the logical assessment of the existing network?

   — **Protocols used on the network**

   — **IP addressing scheme**

   — **IPX addressing**

— **Access lists and broadcast filters**

6 What are the three layers of hierarchical network design?

Access, distribution, and core

7 If there are problems involving media contention on networks using repeaters, what should be done to resolve it?

To resolve issues with node access to the media, use LAN switching to reduce the collision domains of the network.

8 What are the five areas of network management?

— **Fault management**

— **Configuration management**

— **Accounting management**

— **Performance management**

— **Security management**

9 If you customer has a small network, what type of demonstration should be used?

A pilot demonstration

10 If higher bandwidth is required on the network, what technologies are suggested for small to medium-sized networks?

To provide higher speed on small to medium-sized networks, use Switched Fast Ethernet or ATM. These technologies provide higher bandwidth than shared Ethernet or Token Ring.

Q&A Answers

1 During which assessment do you find out what type of IP addressing scheme is used on the network?

The logical assessment. IP, IPX, and other Layer 3 protocol address assignments are researched in the logical assessment.

2 What would help solve a network with a high amount of broadcasts?

Add a router. Broadcast domains are controlled by routers.

3 What are the four sections of the design document, and what goes into each section?

The Executive Summary contains the purpose of the project, strategic recommendations, implementation considerations, and the benefits of the solution.

The Design Requirements section contains information about the existing network, including topology, applications, and protocols. Also included are the new requirements for performance, security, capacity, and scalability to support new applications.

The Design Solution section contains the new proposed network topology, network addressing scheme, routing and bridging protocols, network management, and the hardware and media recommended for the LAN and WAN.

The Summary documents how your solution meets the customer's requirements.

4 In network management, what does FCAPS stand for?

FCAPS stands for fault, configuration, accounting, performance, and security management.

5 You would do a prototype for what type of networks?

For larger networks. A prototype is used to demonstrate the major goals of the new network. For smaller networks. a prototype may be too elaborate; a small pilot demonstration should be used for smaller networks to show basic functionality.

6 Which section of the design document contains topology diagrams of the existing network?

The Design Requirements section contains topology diagrams of the existing network protocols used and describes applications on the network.

7 Briefly describe Frame Relay.

Frame Relay is a WAN technology that uses permanent virtual circuits.

8 Give three examples of bridged protocols.

Bridged protocols include SNA, NetBIOS/NetBEUI, and DEC LAT.

9 What does SAP stands for? What is it used for?

SAP stands for Service Advertising Protocol. It is used by Novell devices to advertise their services to the network.

10 List the nine steps for network design.

1. Gather information to support the business and technical requirements.

2. Assess the current network.

3. Consider the applications involved.

4. Design the local-area networks.

5. Design the wide-area network.

6. Design for specific network protocols.

7. Create the design document and select Cisco network management applications.

8. Test the design.

11   If higher bandwidth is required on the network, what technologies are suggested for small to medium-sized networks?

Switched Fast Ethernet or ATM

12   How often is the Novell SAP table broadcasted onto the network?

Every 60 seconds

13   What are examples of business constraints?

Budget limitations, limited resources, and time constraints

Chapter 2: Assessing the Existing Network and Identifying Customer Objectives

"Do I Know This Already?" Quiz Answers

1   Which Cisco tool enables you to analyze interface statistics, review routing table sizes, and get a performance snapshot of the current network?

The Netsys Enterprise/Solver performance tool

2   Identify three categories that are considered to be administrative data to help characterize the customer's network.

The answer can be any combination of three of the following answers:

— **Business Goals**

— **Corporate Structure**

— **Geographical Structure**

— **Current and Future Staffing, Policies, and Politics**

3   What product can be used as a traffic analysis and protocol analysis tool?

Sniffer

4 What feature of the network design are you trying to include when you discuss future business goals with your customer?

Scalability

5 During your characterization of the network, you realize that WAN implementations and LAN networks are managed by different groups. During which data collection stage would you note this information?

This is a political issue because changes requested by one group that can potentially affect the other must be identified. Note this information when determining the policies and politics when you are assessing the customer's corporate profile information.

6 Broadcast/multicast behavior, supported frame sizes, flow control, and windowing are all examples of characterizing what type of behavior?

Traffic behavior

7 What is the maximum number of recommended workstations that a flat AppleTalk network could support?

200

8 True or False: Using the largest frame size that is supported by a medium has a negative impact on network performance.

False. Ideally, you would want to make sure that the frame size is at the maximum supported limit of the network medium.

9 Identify the port used by a protocol such as SMTP.

Port 25

10 What is the purpose in documenting response time to understand and identify performance issues?

Understanding response time will determine how much time it takes the network to respond to a request for a service.

11 True or False: Gathering budget information and resource availability for a project is a part of the process in which you are defining the manageability requirements.

False. It is a part of the business constraint defining process.

12 What is the maximum number of buffer misses a Cisco router can have in an hour?

25

Q&A Answers

1 After adding the new print server to the network, you see that the workstations are experiencing performance issues. What is a likely cause of this problem?

The print server could be advertising its services, thereby sending a lot of broadcast traffic.

2 What tool could you use to verify your answer to question #1?

Use a protocol analyzer on that segment, and see what type of traffic is generated and by what device.

3 The customer wants to determine the maximum number of multimedia workstations that should populate a segment. What information do you need to request to find out an approximate number?

You need to determine the type of LAN protocol used—IP, IPX, AppleTalk, NetBIOS, or mixed.

4 Which network devices are used in creating separate segments to decrease workstation broadcasts?

Routers and switches that have VLAN capability

5 During the planning stage, the customer wants a 30 percent improvement on the response his users get from the database. During which phase of extracting the new customer requirements would you address this information?

The customer has provided a requirement for the new network. During step 6, identify performance requirements, you would note this type of information.

6 The customer is concerned about the Token Ring traffic on his network and wants to prove that the Token Ring network must be upgraded. What is your recommendation based on finding out that the Token Ring segment has more than 60 percent utilization?

The threshold for a Token Ring network is that each segment does not exceed 70 percent. Therefore, you should recommend segmentation of the network.

7 Which Cisco IOS command would you use to determine if there were any output queue drops?

show interface

8 When helping to determine the network's health, would having 25 percent of multicasts on one segment be considered healthy?

This is unhealthy. It is recommended that none of the segments exceed 20 percent broadcasts/multicasts.

9   What is the saturation threshold for WAN links?

No more than 70 percent utilization

10   What tool would you use to help monitor the switching traffic?

NetFlow

Chapter 3: Application Considerations

"Do I Know This Already?" Quiz Answers

1   In which bridging environment does the frame contain the routing information to the destination?

Source-route bridging (SRB). SRB frames contain a routing information field (RIF) that has routing descriptors to the destination.

2   Which scheme provides a way to automatically assign IP addresses to devices on the network?

Dynamic Host Configuration Protocol (DHCP). With DHCP, clients are assigned an IP address, a subnet mask, and a default gateway by a DHCP server.

3   Which session layer protocol is very common in Windows NT environments and can be bridged or routed over IP?

NetBIOS

4   With which Novell protocol do devices broadcast services to the segment, routers build a table and forward these broadcasts to all other segments, and clients use the information to know what services are available in the network?

Service Advertising Protocol (SAP)

5   In what protocol environment do client devices automatically select a network layer address and broadcast a probe to ensure that it is unique?

AppleTalk

6   What are route descriptors?

Route descriptors are bridge/ring number fields in a routing information field. They are used to set the path that a frame should take on a source-route bridged network.

7   With what technology can you scale SRB networks over WAN links and reduce NetBIOS queries where TCP is used between peers?

Data-link switching (DLSw). DLSw is used to establish a TCP link between remote routers to transport System Network Architecture (SNA) and NetBIOS traffic.

8 What is the most scalable protocol used for file and print sharing in Windows NT networking?

NetBIOS over TCP/IP is more scalable than NetBIOS over NetBUEI.

9 What methods are used to assign an IP address to a workstation at bootup?

DHCP and BOOTP

10 What are the three components of a typical firewall system?

The three components of a typical firewall system are an outside filtering router, an isolation LAN with bastion hosts, and an inside filtering router.

Q&A Answers

1 What session layer protocol is common in Windows NT environments when layered over TCP it can be routed?

NetBIOS

2 You can find WWW and FTP servers in what network that the Internet community can access?

Isolation LAN

3 What is a method to reduce Novell SAP broadcast traffic on the network?

Use Enhanced IGRP, SAP filters, and NLSP.

4 HTTP is an example of what type of traffic flow?

Client/server

5 What access list would you use on an outside filtering router to permit access to the isolation LAN? Assume the isolation LAN is 201.201.201.0/24.

```
access-list 101 ip permit 0.0.0.0 255.255.255.255 201.201.201.0 0.0.0.255
```

6 What Token Ring field consists of route descriptors?

Routing information field (RIF)

7 What should you use to overcome the limitations of SRB in large networks?

Data-link switching over an IP network.

8 The Cisco PIX Firewall may be used to do what?

Perform Network Address Translation. Protect the internal network. Provide additional security.

9 What service is used to resolve NetBIOS names to IP addresses?

WINS

10 What access list would you use on an internal filtering router to permit traffic between the isolation LAN and the internal network? Assume the isolation LAN is 201.201.201.64/26.

```
access-list 101 ip permit 201.201.201.64 0.0.0.63 any
```

11 What technique is used to reduce the amount of repetitive unicast traffic?

Multicast routing

12 What type of traffic flow is how small-bandwidth keyboard character streams are sent to the host?

Terminal/host

13 What is a logical grouping of nodes in AppleTalk to control broadcasts?

AppleTalk zone

14 What are examples of client/server traffic flow applications?

Windows NT networking, Novell, HTTP, and AppleShare are all examples of client/server traffic flow.

15 With this technology a user may connect a laptop to the network and automatically have an IP address, subnet mask, default gateway, DNS server, and WINS server assigned.

DHCP

16 DHCP stands for what?

Dynamic Host Configuration Protocol

17 What are route descriptors?

Route descriptors are bridge ring number fields in a routing information field; they are used to set the path that a frame should take on a source-route bridged network.

Chapter 4: Network Topologies and LAN Design

"Do I Know This Already?" Quiz Answers

1 What OSI layer does a bridge operate?

Data link layer (Layer 2)

2 The 10Base2 Ethernet media is commonly referred as?

Thinnet

3 What is the recommended maximum number of nodes that should be used in a multi-protocol LAN segment?

200 nodes

4 Bridges control collision domains, broadcast domains, or both?

Collision domains

5 What is the maximum segment size in a 100BaseT network?

100 meters

6 What is the maximum segment size in a 10Base2 network?

185 meters

7 Routers operate on what OSI layer?

Network layer (Layer 3)

8 Fast Ethernet is covered by which IEEE standard?

IEEE 802.3u

9 What is 10Base5 commonly referred to as?

Thicknet

10 What device controls a broadcast domain?

Router

Q&A Answers

1 What is the maximum segment size in 10BaseT?

100 meters

2 What is the maximum segment size in 10Base2?

185 meters

3 What is the maximum segment size in 10Base5?

500 meters

4 What is the maximum segment size in 100BaseT?

100 meters

5 What is the maximum segment size in 1000BaseT?

100 meters

6 What does the acronym DIX stands for?

Digital, Intel, Xerox

7 What are the three layers of hierarchical design?

Core, distribution, and access

8 At what percent utilization are Ethernets over-utilized?

40 percent

9 At what percent utilization are Token Ring networks over-utilized?

70 percent

10 At what percent utilization are FDDI networks over-utilized?

70 percent

11 What is the maximum recommended percentage of broadcasts on the network?

20 percent

12 What is the standard(s) for Gigabit Ethernet?

IEEE 802.3z (for fiber and copper)

IEEE 802.3ab (for UTP)

13 What standard governs Token Ring?

IEEE 802.5

14 What media implements a dual-ring and forwards tokens?

Fiber Data Distributed Interface (FDDI)

15 Routers operate on which layer of the OSI model?

Network layer

16   Switches operate on which layer of the OSI model?

Data link layer

17   Repeaters operate on which layer of the OSI model?

Physical layer

18   Bridges operate on which layer of the OSI model?

Data link layer

19   Transceivers operate on which layer of the OSI model?

Physical layer

20   Are bridges protocol transparent?

Yes

21   When switches implement cut-through switching mode, what is not verified to check for frame errors?

Frame Check Sequence (FCS)

22   True or False: A repeater keeps a table of each MAC address on its ports and forwards frames accordingly.

False. Repeaters are Layer 11 devices. They do not keep a table of MAC addresses.

23   True or False: Routers forward frames based on the destination MAC address.

False. No, they forward based on Layer 3 addresses.

24   True or False: Bridges forward frames based on the source MAC address.

False. It is based on the destination MAC address.

25   What LAN media uses dual counter rotating rings?

FDDI

26   Which Cisco device provides 48 ports of 10/100 Ethernet with 2 Gb uplinks?

Catalyst 2948G

27   What are the components of the three-part firewall system?

The isolation LAN, outside filtering router, and inside filtering router.

28   What is the encoding scheme of 10-Mbps Ethernet?

Manchester

29   What is the encoding scheme of Token Ring?

Differential Manchester

30 100BaseT forwards frames at what speed?

100 Mbps

Chapter 5: WAN Design

"Do I Know This Already?" Quiz Answers

1 Which WAN transport technologies use packet switching to transfer data?

Frame Relay and X.25

2 What is the line speed of a T3 leased line?

44.736 Mbps

3 The Cisco Product Selection Tool can be found where?

The Cisco Web site (www.cisco.com) or the Cisco documentation CD-ROM

4 If a customer is concerned about the cost of a WAN network, what technology would you recommend for a backup connection to a 128-Kb leased line?

An ISDN line. An ISDN line is a common cost-effective backup solution because the customer pays on a per use basis and has minimal equipment fees. Based on the line speed, ISDN can easily support the 128-Kb requirement.

5 What are the two criteria for a good WAN design?

Minimize the cost of the bandwidth and optimize the efficient use of the bandwidth.

6 Identify the switching method on the router that has the following qualities: an inbound access list, high CPU utilization, and compression of packets.

Process switching

7 Which devices support optimum switching?

Optimum switching is available only on a Route Switch Processor (RSP).

8 How many DS0s are there in a T1 line?

24

9   What class of Cisco routers is a 2600?

Access router

10 What is the first step in provisioning a Frame Relay circuit?

Determine what the committed information rate (CIR) needs to be, based on the traffic that will use the data connection.

Q&A Answers

1   How many DS0s are needed to form a T1 line?

24 DS0s are needed. A T1 is equal to 1.544 Mbps and is a common line speed used to provide Internet access.

2   When using Frame Relay, which Cisco IOS version would best support a Voice over Frame Relay (VoFR) implementation?

Cisco IOS Release 11.2, because it supports Frame Relay traffic shaping, which has features to enhance the performance of the permanent virtual circuit (PVC).

3   Which traffic shaping feature would best support the VoFR implementation?

The enhanced queuing support on a per virtual circuit basis would provide queuing capability. This would guarantee bandwidth for the voice implementation so that the traffic would not be disrupted.

4   When determining the Frame Relay CIR for the central office, the CCDA reviews all the traffic from the remote offices that needs to be transferred to the central office. Which step in provisioning a Frame Relay network would help determine how much bandwidth is required?

Step 2: Aggregate all the CIRs to determine core bandwidth requirements. The CIR needed will depend on the total of CIRs from each remote office to transfer data with the central office.

5   Which switching method matches packets with its route cache?

Fast switching uses this method of comparing incoming packets with an entry in its fast-switching cache.

6   Which WAN technology uses the Public Switched Telephone Network (PSTN)?

An analog modem uses the existing phone system, also known as plain old telephone service (POTS).

7 What term is used to describe the process of passing a packet internally from one router's interface to the other?

Switching

8 Which packet-switching technology is used on unreliable WAN connections?

X.25 has data correcting and error checking overhead. It is used on WAN connections that are often unreliable.

9 Frame Relay uses which two layers of the OSI model?

The physical and data-link layers

10 What router component would be used on a 2600 to provide an integrated CSU/DSU for a T1 connection?

WAN interface card

Chapter 6: Designing for Specific Protocols

"Do I Know This Already?" Quiz Answers

1 List two distance vector routing protocols for IP.

Routing Information Protocol (RIP)

Interior Gateway Routing Protocol (IGRP)

2 What is the subnet number and broadcast address for host 199.1.10.9/30?

199.1.10.8 is the subnet number; 199.1.10.11 is the broadcast address.

3 How many route entries can there be in an IGRP update packet?

104

4 What is the default mask for 191.50.0.0?

255.255.0.0

5 Is 001DG6Ef a valid IPX address?

No. IPX addresses represented in hexadecimal do not have a G.

6 What is RTMP?

Routing Table Maintenance Protocol. RTMP is the distance vector routing protocol for AppleTalk networks.

7   What is NLSP?

NetWare Link-Services Protocol. NLSP is the link-state routing protocol for Novell networks.

8   What is the broadcast address for network 192.100.7.64 with a mask of 255.255.255.192?

The broadcast address is 192.100.7.127.

9   Name three IP interior gateway routing protocols that support authentication.

EIGRP, OSPF, RIPv2, and IS-IS

10   Which routing protocol is capable of routing IPX and AppleTalk packets in addition to IP?

Enhanced Interior Gateway Routing Protocol (EIGRP)

11   Which protocol advertises services by producing broadcasts every 60 seconds?

Novell's Service Advertising Protocol (SAP)

12   Which protocol defines areas for IP networks? Which protocol defines areas for IPX networks?

OSPF defines areas for IP networks.

NLSP defines areas for IPX networks.

13   What is the host address of the AppleTalk address 15.4.1? What is the network address? What is the socket number?

The host address is 4, the network address is 15, and the socket number is 1.

14   True or False: RIP version 2 sends route updates only when a change occurs on the network.

False. RIP version 2 still sends periodic updates every 30 seconds.

15   What are the default metrics used by EIGRP?

The default metrics are bandwidth and delay.

16   List three Cisco IOS features.

Cisco IOS features include access lists, encryption, proxy services, compression, traffic shaping, and queuing (custom, priority, and weighted-fair).

Q&A Answers

1   What protocol encapsulates AppleTalk packets in UDP for transport over an IP network?

AppleTalk Update-Based Tunneling Protocol (AURP)

2 What is the subnet address for host 150.76.78.71 with a mask of 255.255.255.224?

150.76.78.64

3 This routing protocol defines areas, domains, and supports hierarchical addressing.

NetWare Link-Services Protocol (NLSP); OSPF does not define domains

4 What is an ABR?

Area border router. Used in OSPF, ABRs connect OSPF areas to Area 0 and perform route summarization.

5 Which protocol produces route updates every 10 seconds?

Routing Table Maintenance Protocol (RTMP). RTMP is the distance vector routing protocol for AppleTalk.

6 What routing protocol is used to communicate with Internet routers?

Border Gateway Protocol (BGP)

7 What routing protocol is recommended for hub-and-spoke topologies with low-bandwidth links with no route redundancy?

Static routing is recommended for this topology with low bandwidth links.

8 What is the host portion of 125.240.32.45, assuming default subnet masking?

This is a Class A address with a default mask of 255.0.0.0. The host portion is 240.32.45.

9 This protocol supports route summarization, but it must be configured. If link flapping occurs, streams of updates are generated, causing router CPU overhead.

This describes a link-state protocol, such as OSPF.

10 If a customer is looking for ways to reduce WAN traffic and is also considering tunneling AppleTalk in IP, what protocol would you recommend?

AppleTalk Update-Based Tunneling Protocol

11 This protocol limits the number of route entries in a routing table update to 50 routes.

Novell's IPX RIP limits updates to 50 routes.

12 What is the network portion for an NLSP area of 0020ab00 with a mask of FFFF0000?

The network portion is 0020.

13 Of the following, which are valid IPX networks?

— 01010101

— DADA

— 789ABCDE

— 204A6B8CE

— 0FG3ABD4

— 10

— 0AB04

01010101 is a valid IPX network.

DADA is a valid IPX network.

789ABCDE is a valid IPX network.

024A6B8CE is not a valid IPX network. It is too long because IPX addresses are limited to 32 bits (4 bytes or 8 hexadecimal characters).

0FG3ABD4 is not a valid IPX network. G is not a hexadecimal character.

10 is a valid IPX network.

0AB04 is a valid IPX network.

14 Is 140.176.30.31/28 a valid host address?

No. This address is in network 140.176.30.16, with valid host addresses from 140.176.30.17 to 140.176.30.30, and where 140.176.30.31 is the broadcast address for the subnet.

15 Convert the following IP address to the dotted decimal format:
00011011011011001100110000101111

00011011 is 27.

01101100 is 108.

11001100 is 204.

00101111 is 47.

The answer is 27.108.204.47.

16 If the client wants to use a nonproprietary routing protocol that can scale to hundreds of networks and fit in a hierarchical topology, which routing protocol can be recommended?

Recommend OSPF. It is standards-based and can scale to a large network in a hierarchical topology.

17 If a client wants to use a routing protocol that is easy to configure and that can scale to hundreds of networks, and if all routers are Cisco routers, which routing protocol can be recommended?

Recommend EIGRP. It is Cisco's hybrid protocol that can scale in large networks.

18 What is an ASBR?

Autonomous system boundary router. This term is used in OSPF networks to identify those routers that have connections to external networks.

19 What is a stub network in OSPF?

A stub network does not receive External LSAs (type 5) from the ABR. A default gateway (0.0.0.0) is sent instead. Network Summary LSAs (type 3) are still sent in the area.

20 What is a totally stubby network in OSPF?

A totally stubby area does not receive External (type 5) and Network Summary (type 3) LSAs from the ABR. A default gateway (0.0.0.0) is sent instead. This significantly reduces that amount of LSAs sent into the area.

21 True or False: Bridged networks provide large scalability.

False. Bridge networks are subject to broadcasts and multicast in the entire network, limiting their size in the internetwork.

22 True or False: To reduce the traffic in bridge networks it is recommended to limit the size of the network and use routing to segment the network.

True. Use routers to segment bridged networks into smaller segments.

23 RIP uses a feature in which routes learned from a neighboring router are sent back to that neighbor with an infinite unreachable metric. What is that feature?

Split horizon with poison reverse

24 What is the update time in IGRP?

IGRP sends updates every 90 seconds.

25 Does EIGRP send periodic updates?

No. EIGRP sends updates only when a metric is changed on a route. The update includes only that route and is sent only to those routers affected by that route.

26 Which queuing technique can be recommended to prioritize mission-critical SNA traffic?

Priority queuing

27 List at least four Cisco IOS features.

Cisco IOS features include access lists, encryption, proxy services, compression, traffic shaping, and queuing (custom, priority, and weighted fair).

28 True or False: The order in which access list commands are configured is not significant to the router.

False. The order of access list statements is important. The router tests against each criteria statement in the order in which the statements were created.

Chapter 7: The Design Document and Cisco Network Management Applications

"Do I Know This Already?" Quiz Answers

1 If a client has a small network and a staff with no UNIX experience, which network management applications would you recommend to manage Cisco routers and switches?

CiscoWorks for Windows

2 What is the purpose of the Executive Summary in the design document?

The Executive Summary is directed toward the key decision-makers for the project and should clearly articulate the strategy for the project.

3 What are the five types of network management processes?

Fault management, configuration management, accounting management, performance management, and security management

4 The acronym SNMP stands for what?

Simple Network Management Protocol

5 CiscoWorks is a network management application that applies to which type of network management process?

Configuration management

6 The selected hardware and media for the LAN and WAN are described in which component of the design document?

Design Solution

7 What is proactive network management?

Proactive network management is monitoring the network before problems occur. The goal is to detect and to resolve problems before they affect end users.

8 What is NMS?

Network management system, used to manage SNMP-enabled devices

Q&A Answers

1 When writing a design document in response to a RFP, which section should you direct at the key decision-makers in a company, to clearly articulate your strategy for the project?

Executive Summary

2 Which application would you recommend to an IT manager if the staff are Windows NT server administrators and have little experience managing routers?

CiscoWorks for Windows

3 As companies recognize the importance of networks, more emphasis should be placed on what form of management?

Proactive network management

4 Which network management application that can be installed on Windows NT can you use to test configuration changes offline?

Netsys Baseliner

5 In which section of the design document would you describe the current topology of the network?

Design Requirements

6 Which GUI-based network management application provides dynamic status and statistics and can display a graphical view of Cisco devices?

CiscoView

7 Which application is designed to simplify management of a consolidated SNA and IP network?

CiscoWorks Blue

8 Which network management process refers to detecting, isolating, and correcting problems?

Fault management

9 What is an agent?

The network management software that resides in a managed device

10 In which design document section would you list the recommended IP routing protocols?

Design Solution

11 Which configuration utility simplifies the configuration of routers for small offices?

Cisco FastStep

12 CiscoWorks for Windows includes a utility that provides real-time fault and performance monitoring of device statistics, including device characteristics, CPU utilization, interface activity, errors, and protocol information. What is it called?

Health Monitor

13 Which tool can be used to diagnose and solve network performance problems, to tune existing networks, and to plan for network changes?

Netsys Performance Service Manager

14 Which tool can be used to verify the distance of the UTP cable from the wiring closet to the user end station?

Cable Tester

15 Which are the four operations introduced with SNMPv1?

Get, GetNext, Set, and Trap operations

16 Which are the two operations introduced with SNMPv2?

GetBulk and Inform operations

Chapter 8: Building a Prototype or Pilot

"Do I Know This Already?" Quiz Answers

1 Which type of test plan is more appropriate for a network solution that involves a small network in which the client needs a demonstration of a basic function such as the security features on a firewall?

Pilot

2 What is the next step involved in developing a prototype after a test plan has been developed?

Purchase necessary equipment

3 Identify the step of the prototype development plan that includes tasks such as drawing a network and developing a list of tests.

Developing a test plan

4 True or False: Both the prototype and the pilot require you to understand and review the competition's implementation plans.

True

5 Which type of test plan requires less planning and fewer resources?

Pilot

6 Which tool could you use to avoid having to perform the test yourself?

An industry test, which is a pre-existing study, such as the Strategic Networks Consulting, Inc. (SNCI) switch tests comparing the Cisco 5000 to the Cabletron MMAC-Plus switches

7 At what stage of the pilot would the designer identify the weaknesses of the competition's product, such as scalability issues?

When the designer writes a script for the demonstration

8 How does the designer ensure that the prototype will meet the expectations of a client?

When the designer reviews the information gathered by extracting the customer's requirements

9 Which tool can be used to test security and capture data during the testing phase of both the pilot and the prototype?

Network sniffer

10 What two IOS commands can be used to troubleshoot connectivity?

ping and traceroute

Q&A Answers

1 Your design included multiple VLANS with similar configurations and services. The customer requested confirmation that the design is fully functional. What type of testing program would you recommend, and why?

The design represents a complex network, with multiple services that must be demonstrated. A VLAN is a subset of that network that includes the multiple services that would exist on the other networks. Therefore, creating a prototype of one VLAN would be a sufficient demonstration of the functionality of the design.

2   What type of testing would require more resources, including higher costs and more complexity?

The prototype testing

3   What stage of the prototype testing requires that you showcase the strength of Cisco's products and the areas in which the competitor's products are not as strong?

Step 4: Develop a Test Plan

4   When determining the customer's requirements for prototype testing, what are the four areas that should be included when making the determination?

Performance, security, capacity, and scalability

5   What tool can you use during testing to provide detailed information on the protocols and traffic on the network?

A sniffer

6   During the practice of the pilot script, you realize that your protocol analyzer is showing that unwanted traffic is passing from an unsecured segment to your internal network. What IOS command would you use on the router to begin troubleshooting this problem?

If the router was configured to prevent unwanted traffic from entering a network, then the show access-list command should be used to review the access lists on the router.

7   After scripting the demonstration for the client, what is the next step in the pilot testing program that would need to be implemented to ensure a smooth presentation?

Step 4: Practice

8   If the client wanted a demonstration of the connectivity between segments and routing information, which IOS commands would you use during the testing?

The show *protocol* route and the ping and trace commands

9   If you are using an access list and wanted to test the security, what product could you use to demonstrate its effectiveness?

A protocol analyzer

10   How would you demonstrate your findings to your customer during the prototype testing?

You would meet with the customer and reproduce the test results as the customer watches.

Glossary

This glossary attempts to gather and define the terms and abbreviations of internetworking. As with any growing technical field, some terms evolve several meanings. Where necessary, multiple definitions and abbreviation expansions are presented. Multiword terms are alphabetized as if there were no spaces; hyphenated terms, as if there were no hyphens.

Terms in this glossary are typically defined under their abbreviations. Each abbreviation expansion is listed separately, with a cross-reference to the abbreviation entry. In addition, many definitions contain cross-references to related terms.

NUMERICS

4B/5B local fiber. 4-byte/5-byte local fiber. FibreChannel physical media used for FDDI and ATM. Supports speeds of up to 100 Mbps over multimode fiber. *See also* TAXI 4B/5B.

4-byte/5-byte local fiber. *See* 4B/5B local fiber.

8B/10B local fiber. 8-byte/10-byte local fiber. Fiber channel physical media that supports speeds up to 149.76 Mbps over multimode fiber.

8-byte/10-byte local fiber. *See* 8B/10B local fiber.

10Base2. 10-Mbps baseband Ethernet specification using 50-ohm thin coaxial cable. 10Base2, which is part of the IEEE 802.3 specification, has a distance limit of 185 meters per segment. *See also* Cheapernet, Ethernet, IEEE 802.3, and Thinnet.

10Base5. 10-Mbps baseband Ethernet specification using standard (thick) 50-ohm baseband coaxial cable. 10Base5, which is part of the IEEE 802.3 baseband physical layer specification, has a distance limit of 500 meters per segment. *See also* Ethernet and IEEE 802.3.

10BaseF. 10-Mbps baseband Ethernet specification that refers to the 10BaseFB, 10BaseFL, and 10BaseFP standards for Ethernet over fiber-optic cabling. *See also* 10BaseFB, 10BaseFL, 10BaseFP, and Ethernet.

10BaseFB. 10-Mbps baseband Ethernet specification using fiber-optic cabling. 10BaseFB is part of the IEEE 10BaseF specification. It is not used to connect user stations, but instead provides a synchronous signaling backbone that allows additional segments and repeaters to be connected to the network. 10BaseFB segments can be up to 2,000 meters long. *See also* 10BaseF and Ethernet.

10BaseFL. 10-Mbps baseband Ethernet specification using fiber-optic cabling. 10BaseFL is part of the IEEE 10BaseF specification and, although able to interoperate with FOIRL, is designed to replace the FOIRL specification. 10BaseFL segments can be up to 1,000 meters long if used with FOIRL, and up to 2,000 meters if 10BaseFL is used exclusively. *See also* 10BaseF, Ethernet, and FOIRL.

10BaseFP. 10-Mbps fiber-passive baseband Ethernet specification using fiber-optic cabling. 10BaseFP is part of the IEEE 10BaseF specification. It organizes a number of computers into a star topology without the use of repeaters. 10BaseFP segments can be up to 500 meters long. *See also* 10BaseF and Ethernet.

10BaseT. 10-Mbps baseband Ethernet specification using two pairs of twisted-pair cabling (Category 3, 4, or 5): one pair for transmitting data and the other for receiving data. 10BaseT, which is part of the IEEE 802.3 specification, has a distance limit of approximately 100 meters per segment. *See also* Ethernet and IEEE 802.3.

10Broad36. 10-Mbps broadband Ethernet specification using broadband coaxial cable. 10Broad36, which is part of the IEEE 802.3 specification, has a distance limit of 3,600 meters per segment. *See also* Ethernet and IEEE 802.3.

100BaseFX. 100-Mbps baseband Fast Ethernet specification using two strands of multimode fiber-optic cable per link. To guarantee proper signal timing, a 100BaseFX link cannot exceed 400 meters in length. Based on the IEEE 802.3 standard. *See also* 100BaseX, Fast Ethernet, and IEEE 802.3.

100BaseT. 100-Mbps baseband Fast Ethernet specification using UTP wiring. Like the 10BaseT technology on which it is based, 100BaseT sends link pulses over the network segment when no traffic is present. However, these link pulses contain more information than do those used in 10BaseT. Based on the IEEE 802.3 standard. *See also* 10BaseT, Fast Ethernet, and IEEE 802.3.

100BaseT4. 100-Mbps baseband Fast Ethernet specification using four pairs of Category 3, 4, or 5 UTP wiring. To guarantee proper signal timing, a 100BaseT4 segment cannot exceed 100 meters in length. Based on the IEEE 802.3 standard. *See also* Fast Ethernet and IEEE 802.3.

100BaseTX. 100-Mbps baseband Fast Ethernet specification using two pairs of either UTP or STP wiring. The first pair of wires is used to receive data; the second is used to transmit. To guarantee proper signal timing, a 100BaseTX segment cannot exceed 100 meters in length. Based on the IEEE 802.3 standard. *See also* 100BaseX, Fast Ethernet, and IEEE 802.3.

100BaseX. 100-Mbps baseband Fast Ethernet specification that refers to the 100BaseFX and 100BaseTX standards for Fast Ethernet over fiber-optic cabling. Based on the IEEE 802.3 standard. *See also* 100BaseFX, 100BaseTX, Fast Ethernet, and IEEE 802.3.

100VG-AnyLAN. 100-Mbps Fast Ethernet and Token Ring media technology using four pairs of Category 3, 4, or 5 UTP cabling. This high-speed transport technology, developed by Hewlett-Packard, can be made to operate on existing 10BaseT Ethernet networks. Based on the IEEE 802.12 standard. *See also* IEEE 802.12.

24th channel signaling. *See* A&B bit signaling.

370 block mux channel. *See* block multiplexer channel.

A

A&B bit signaling. Procedure used in T1 transmission facilities in which each of the 24 T1 subchannels devotes one bit of every sixth frame to the carrying of supervisory signaling information. *Also called* 24th channel signaling.

AAL. ATM adaptation layer. Service-dependent sublayer of the data link layer. The AAL accepts data from different applications and presents it to the ATM layer in the form of 48-byte ATM payload segments. AALs consist of two sublayers, CS and SAR. AALs differ on the basis of the source-destination timing used, whether they use CBR or VBR, and whether they are used for connection-oriented or connectionless mode data transfer. At present, the four types of AAL recommended by the ITU-T are AAL1, AAL2, AAL3/4, and AAL5. *See* AAL1, AAL2, AAL3/4, AAL5, CS, and SAR. *See also* ATM and ATM layer.

AAL1. ATM adaptation layer 1. One of four AALs recommended by the ITU-T. AAL1 is used for connection-oriented, delay-sensitive services requiring constant bit rates, such as uncompressed video and other isochronous traffic. *See also* AAL.

AAL2. ATM adaptation layer 2. One of four AALs recommended by the ITU-T. AAL2 is used for connection-oriented services that support a variable bit rate, such as some isochronous video and voice traffic. *See also* AAL.

AAL3/4. ATM adaptation layer 3/4. One of four AALs (merged from two initially distinct adaptation layers) recommended by the ITU-T. AAL3/4 supports both connectionless and connection-oriented links, but is primarily used for the transmission of SMDS packets over ATM networks. *See also* AAL.

AAL5. ATM adaptation layer 5. One of four AALs recommended by the ITU-T. AAL5 supports connection-oriented, VBR services, and is used predominantly for the transfer of classical IP over ATM and LANE traffic. AAL5 uses SEAL and is the least complex of the current AAL recommendations. It offers low bandwidth overhead and simpler processing requirements in exchange for reduced bandwidth capacity and error-recovery capability. *See also* AAL and SEAL.

AARP. AppleTalk Address Resolution Protocol. Protocol in the AppleTalk protocol stack that maps a data-link address to a network address.

AARP probe packets. Packets transmitted by AARP that determine whether a randomly selected node ID is being used by another node in a nonextended AppleTalk network. If the node ID is not being used, the sending node uses that node ID. If the node ID is being used, the sending node chooses a different ID and sends more AARP probe packets. *See also* AARP.

ABM. Asynchronous Balanced Mode. An HDLC (and derivative protocol) communication mode supporting peer-oriented, point-to-point communications between two stations, where either station can initiate transmission.

ABR. 1. available bit rate. QOS class defined by the ATM Forum for ATM networks. ABR is used for connections that do not require timing relationships between source and destination. ABR provides no guarantees in terms of cell loss or delay; it provides only best-effort service. Traffic sources adjust their transmission rates in response to information they receive describing the status of the network and its capability to successfully deliver data. *Compare with* CBR, UBR, and VBR. 2. area border router. Router located on the border of one or more OSPF areas that connects those areas to the backbone network. ABRs are considered members of both the OSPF backbone and the attached areas. They therefore maintain routing tables describing both the backbone topology and the topology of the other areas.

Abstract Syntax Notation One. *See* ASN.1.

access list. List kept by routers to control access to or from the router for a number of services (for example, to prevent packets with a certain IP address from leaving a particular interface on the router).

access method. 1. Generally, the way in which network devices access the network medium. 2. Software within an SNA processor that controls the flow of information through a network.

access server. Communications processor that connects asynchronous devices to a LAN or WAN through network and terminal emulation software. Performs both synchronous and asynchronous routing of supported protocols. Sometimes called a network access server. *Compare with* communication server.

accounting management. One of five categories of network management defined by ISO for management of OSI networks. Accounting management subsystems are responsible for collecting network data relating to resource usage. *See also* configuration management, fault management, performance management, and security management.

ACF. Advanced Communications Function. A group of SNA products that provides distributed processing and resource sharing. *See also* ACF/NCP.

ACF/NCP. Advanced Communications Function/Network Control Program. The primary SNA NCP. ACF/NCP resides in the communications controller and interfaces with the SNA access method in the host processor to control network communications. *See also* ACF and NCP.

ACK. *See* acknowledgment.

acknowledgment. Notification sent from one network device to another to acknowledge that some event (for example, receipt of a message) has occurred. Sometimes abbreviated ACK. *Compare with* NAK.

ACR. allowed cell rate. Parameter defined by the ATM Forum for ATM traffic management. ACR varies between the MCR and the PCR, and is dynamically controlled using congestion control mechanisms. *See also* MCR and PCR.

ACSE. association control service element. An OSI convention used to establish, maintain, or terminate a connection between two applications.

active hub. A multiported device that amplifies LAN transmission signals.

active monitor. A device responsible for managing a Token Ring. A network node is selected to be the active monitor if it has the highest MAC address on the ring. The active monitor is responsible for management tasks such as ensuring that tokens are not lost or that frames do not circulate indefinitely. *See also* ring monitor and standby monitor.

adapter. *See* NIC (network interface card).

adaptive differential pulse code modulation. *See* ADPCM.

adaptive routing. *See* dynamic routing.

ADCCP. Advanced Data Communications Control Protocol. An ANSI standard bit-oriented data link control protocol.

address. A data structure or logical convention used to identify a unique entity, such as a particular process or network device.

addressed call mode. A mode that permits control signals and commands to establish and terminate calls in V.25bis. *See also* V.25bis.

address mapping. A technique that allows different protocols to interoperate by translating addresses from one format to another. For example, when routing IP over X.25, the IP addresses must be mapped to the X.25 addresses so that the IP packets can be transmitted by the X.25 network. *See also* address resolution.

address mask. A bit combination used to describe which portion of an address refers to the network or subnet and which part refers to the host. Sometimes referred to simply as a mask. *See also* subnet mask.

address resolution. Generally, a method for resolving differences between computer addressing schemes. Address resolution usually specifies a method for mapping network layer (Layer 3) addresses to data link layer (Layer 2) addresses. *See also* address mapping.

Address Resolution Protocol. *See* ARP.

adjacency. A relationship formed between selected neighboring routers and end nodes for the purpose of exchanging routing information. Adjacency is based on the use of a common media segment.

adjacent nodes. 1. In SNA, nodes that are connected to a given node with no intervening nodes. 2. In DECnet and OSI, nodes that share a common network segment (in Ethernet, FDDI, or Token Ring networks).

administrative distance. A rating of the trustworthiness of a routing information source. The higher the value, the lower the trustworthiness rating.

admission control. *See* traffic policing.

ADPCM. adaptive differential pulse code modulation. The process by which analog voice samples are encoded into high-quality digital signals.

ADSL . Asymmetric Digital Subscriber Line. One of four DSL technologies. ADSL is designed to deliver more bandwidth downstream (from the central office to the customer site) than upstream. Downstream rates range from 1.5 to 9 Mbps, whereas upstream bandwidth ranges from 16 to 640 kbps. ADSL transmissions work at distances up to 18,000 feet (5,488 meters) over a single copper twisted pair.

ADSU. ATM DSU. Terminal adapter used to access an ATM network via an HSSI-compatible device. *See also* DSU.

Advanced Communications Function. *See* ACF.

Advanced Communications Function/Network Control Program. *See* ACF/NCP.

Advanced Data Communications Control Protocol. *See* ADCCP.

Advanced Peer-to-Peer Networking. *See* APPN.

Advanced Program-to-Program Communication. *See* APPC.

Advanced Research Projects Agency. *See* ARPA.

Advanced Research Projects Agency Network. *See* ARPANET.

advertising. Router process in which routing or service updates are sent at specified intervals so that other routers on the network can maintain lists of usable routes.

AEP. AppleTalk Echo Protocol. Used to test connectivity between two AppleTalk nodes. One node sends a packet to another node and receives a duplicate, or echo, of that packet.

AFI. authority and format identifier. The portion of an NSAP-format ATM address that identifies the type and format of the IDI portion of an ATM address.

agent. 1. Generally, software that processes queries and returns replies on behalf of an application. 2. In NMSs, a process that resides in all managed devices and reports the values of specified variables to management stations.

AIS. alarm indication signal. In a T1 transmission, an all-ones signal transmitted in lieu of the normal signal to maintain transmission continuity and to indicate to the receiving terminal that there is a transmission fault that is located either at, or upstream from, the transmitting terminal. *See also* T1.

alarm. A message notifying an operator or administrator of a network problem. *See also* event and trap.

alarm indication signal. *See* AIS.

a-law. The ITU-T companding standard used in the conversion between analog and digital signals in PCM systems. A-law is used primarily in European telephone networks and is similar to the North American mu-law standard. *See also* companding and mu-law.

algorithm. A well-defined rule or process for arriving at a solution to a problem. In networking, algorithms are commonly used to determine the best route for traffic from a particular source to a particular destination.

alias. *See* entity.

alignment error. In IEEE 802.3 networks, an error that occurs when the total number of bits of a received frame is not divisible by eight. Alignment errors are usually caused by frame damage due to collisions.

allowed cell rate. *See* ACR.

all-rings explorer packet. *See* all-routes explorer packet.

all-routes explorer packet. An explorer packet that traverses an entire SRB network, following all possible paths to a specific destination. Sometimes called all-rings explorer packet. *See also* explorer packet, local explorer packet, and spanning explorer packet.

alternate mark inversion. *See* AMI.

AM. amplitude modulation. Modulation technique whereby information is conveyed through the amplitude of the carrier signal. *Compare with* FM and PAM. *See also* modulation.

American National Standards Institute. *See* ANSI.

American Standard Code for Information Interchange. *See* ASCII.

AMI. alternate mark inversion. Line-code type used on T1 and E1 circuits. In AMI, zeros are represented by 01 during each bit cell, and ones are represented by 11 or 00, alternately, during each bit cell. AMI requires that the sending device maintain ones density. Ones density is not maintained independent of the data stream. Sometimes called binary coded alternate mark inversion. *See also* ones density.

amplitude. The maximum value of an analog or a digital waveform.

amplitude modulation. *See* AM.

analog transmission. Signal transmission over wires or through the air in which information is conveyed through a variation of some combination of signal amplitude, frequency, and phase.

ANSI. American National Standards Institute. A voluntary organization comprising corporate, government, and other members that coordinates standards-related activities, approves U.S. national standards, and develops positions for the United States in international standards organizations. ANSI helps develop international and U.S. standards relating to, among other things, communications and networking. ANSI is a member of the IEC and the ISO. *See also* IEC and ISO.

ANSI X3T9.5. *See* X3T9.5.

APaRT. automated packet recognition/translation. A technology that allows a server to be attached to CDDI or FDDI without requiring the reconfiguration of applications or network protocols. APaRT recognizes specific data link layer encapsulation packet types and, when these packet types are transferred from one medium to another, translates them into the native format of the destination device.

API. application programming interface. A specification of function-call conventions that defines an interface to a service.

Apollo Domain. A proprietary network protocol suite developed by Apollo Computer for communication on proprietary Apollo networks.

APPC. Advanced Program-to-Program Communication. IBM SNA system software that allows high-speed communication between programs on different computers in a distributed computing environment. APPC establishes and tears down connections between communicating programs, and consists of two interfaces: a programming interface and a data-exchange interface. The former replies to requests from programs requiring communication; the latter establishes sessions between programs. APPC runs on LU 6.2 devices. *See also* LU 6.2.

AppleTalk. A series of communications protocols designed by Apple Computer. Two phases currently exist. Phase 1, the earlier version, supports a single physical network that can have only one network number and be in one zone. Phase 2, the more recent version, supports multiple logical networks on a single physical network and allows networks to be in more than one zone. *See also* zone.

AppleTalk Address Resolution Protocol. *See* AARP.

AppleTalk Echo Protocol. *See* AEP.

AppleTalk Remote Access. *See* ARA.

AppleTalk Transaction Protocol. *See* ATP.

AppleTalk Update-Based Routing Protocol. *See* AURP.

AppleTalk zone. *See* zone.

application layer. Layer 7 of the OSI reference model. This layer provides services to application processes (such as electronic mail, file transfer, and terminal emulation) that are outside the OSI model. The application layer identifies and establishes the availability of intended communication partners (and the resources required to connect with them), synchronizes cooperating applications, and establishes agreement on procedures for error recovery and control of data integrity. Corresponds roughly with the transaction services layer in the SNA model. *See also* data link layer, network layer, physical layer, presentation layer, session layer, and transport layer.

application programming interface. *See* API.

APPN. Advanced Peer-to-Peer Networking. An enhancement to the original IBM SNA architecture. APPN handles session establishment between peer nodes, dynamic transparent route calculation, and traffic prioritization for APPC traffic. *Compare with* APPN+. *See also* APPC.

APPN+. A next-generation APPN that replaces the label-swapping routing algorithm with source routing. Also called high-performance routing. *See also* APPN.

ARA. AppleTalk Remote Access. A protocol that provides Macintosh users direct access to information and resources at a remote AppleTalk site.

ARCnet. Attached Resource Computer Network. A 2.5-Mbps token-bus LAN developed in the late 1970s and early 1980s by Datapoint Corporation.

area. A logical set of network segments (either CLNS, DECnet, or OSPF based) and their attached devices. Areas are usually connected to other areas via routers, making up a single autonomous system. *See also* autonomous system.

area border router. *See* ABR.

ARM. asynchronous response mode. An HDLC communication mode involving one primary station and at least one secondary station, where either the primary or one of the secondary stations can initiate transmissions. *See also* primary station and secondary station.

ARP. Address Resolution Protocol. An Internet protocol used to map an IP address to a MAC address. Defined in RFC 826. *Compare with* RARP. *See also* proxy ARP.

ARPA. Advanced Research Projects Agency. A research and development organization that is part of the DoD. ARPA is responsible for numerous technological advances in communications and networking. ARPA evolved into DARPA, and then back into ARPA again (in 1994). *See also* DARPA.

ARPANET . Advanced Research Projects Agency Network. A landmark packet-switching network established in 1969. ARPANET was developed in the 1970s by BBN and funded by ARPA (and later DARPA). It eventually evolved into the Internet. The term ARPANET was officially retired in 1990. *See also* ARPA, BBN, DARPA, and Internet.

ARQ. automatic repeat request. A communication technique in which the receiving device detects errors and requests retransmissions.

AS. *See* autonomous system.

ASBR. autonomous system boundary router. An ABR located between an OSPF autonomous system and a non-OSPF network. ASBRs run both OSPF and another routing protocol, such as RIP. ASBRs must reside in a non-stub OSPF area. *See also* ABR, non-stub area, and OSPF.

ASCII. American Standard Code for Information Interchange. An 8-bit code for character representation (7 bits plus parity).

ASN.1 . Abstract Syntax Notation One. An OSI language for describing data types independently of particular computer structures and representation techniques. Described by ISO International Standard 8824. *See also* BER (basic encoding rules).

association control service element. *See* ACSE.

associative memory. Memory that is accessed based on its contents, not on its memory address. Sometimes called content addressable memory (CAM).

AST. automatic spanning tree. A function that supports the automatic resolution of spanning trees in SRB networks, providing a single path for spanning explorer frames to traverse from a given node in the network to another. AST is based on the IEEE 802.1 standard. *See also* IEEE 802.1 and SRB.

ASTA. Advanced Software Technology and Algorithms. A component of the HPCC program intended to develop software and algorithms for implementation on high-performance computer and communications systems. *See also* HPCC.

Asynchronous Balanced Mode. *See* ABM.

asynchronous response mode. *See* ARM.

asynchronous time-division multiplexing. *See* ATDM.

Asynchronous Transfer Mode. *See* ATM.

asynchronous transmission. Digital signals that are transmitted without precise clocking. Such signals generally have different frequencies and phase relationships. Asynchronous transmissions usually encapsulate individual characters in control bits (called start and stop bits) that designate the beginning and end of each character. *Compare with* isochronous transmission, plesiochronous transmission, and synchronous transmission.

ATDM. asynchronous time-division multiplexing. A method of sending information that resembles normal TDM, except that time slots are allocated as needed rather than preassigned to specific transmitters. *Compare with* FDM, statistical multiplexing, and TDM.

ATM. Asynchronous Transfer Mode. An international standard for cell relay in which multiple service types (such as voice, video, or data) are conveyed in fixed-length (53-byte) cells. Fixed-length cells allow cell processing to occur in hardware, thereby reducing transit delays. ATM is designed to take advantage of high-speed transmission media such as E3, SONET, and T3.

ATM adaptation layer. *See* AAL.

ATM adaptation layer 1. *See* AAL1.

ATM adaptation layer 2. *See* AAL2.

ATM adaptation layer 3/4. *See* AAL3/4.

ATM adaptation layer 5. *See* AAL5.

ATM data service unit. *See* ADSU.

ATM Forum. An international organization jointly founded in 1991 by Cisco Systems, NET/ADAPTIVE, Northern Telecom, and Sprint that develops and promotes standards-based implementation agreements for ATM technology. The ATM Forum expands on official standards developed by ANSI and ITU-T, and develops implementation agreements in advance of official standards.

ATM layer. A service-independent sublayer of the data link layer in an ATM network. The ATM layer receives the 48-byte payload segments from the AAL and attaches a 5-byte header to each, producing standard 53-byte ATM cells. These cells are passed to the physical layer for transmission across the physical medium. *See also* AAL.

ATMM. ATM management. A process that runs on an ATM switch that controls VCI translation and rate enforcement. *See also* ATM and VCI.

ATM management. *See* ATMM.

ATM UNI. *See* UNI.

ATM user-user connection. A connection created by the ATM layer to provide communication between two or more ATM service users, such as ATMM processes. Such communication can be unidirectional, using one VCC, or bidirectional, using two VCCs. *See also* ATM layer, ATMM, and VCC.

ATP. AppleTalk Transaction Protocol. A transport-level protocol that allows reliable request-response exchanges between two socket clients.

Attached Resource Computer Network. *See* ARCnet.

attachment unit interface. *See* AUI.

attenuation. The loss of communication signal energy.

attribute. Configuration data that defines the characteristics of database objects such as the chassis, cards, ports, or virtual circuits of a particular device. Attributes might be preset or user-configurable. On a LightStream 2020 ATM switch, attributes are set using the configuration program or CLI commands.

AUI. attachment unit interface. An IEEE 802.3 interface between an MAU and a NIC (network interface card). Also called transceiver cable. *See also* IEEE 802.3, MAU, and NIC (network interface card).

AURP. AppleTalk Update-Based Routing Protocol. A method of encapsulating AppleTalk traffic in the header of a foreign protocol, allowing the connection of two or more discontiguous AppleTalk internetworks through a foreign network (such as TCP/IP) to form an AppleTalk WAN. This connection is called an AURP tunnel. In addition to its encapsulation function, AURP maintains routing tables for the entire AppleTalk WAN by exchanging routing information between exterior routers. *See also* AURP tunnel and exterior router.

AURP tunnel. A connection created in an AURP WAN that functions as a single, virtual data link between AppleTalk internetworks physically separated by a foreign network (a TCP/IP network, for example). *See also* AURP.

authority zone. A section of the domain-name tree for which one name server is the authority. Associated with DNS. *See also* DNS.

Automated Packet Recognition/Translation. *See* APaRT.

automatic call reconnect. A feature permitting automatic call rerouting away from a failed trunk line.

automatic repeat request. *See* ARQ.

automatic spanning tree. *See* AST.

autonomous confederation. A group of autonomous systems that rely on its own network reachability and routing information more than it relies on that received from other autonomous systems or confederations.

autonomous system. A collection of networks under a common administration sharing a common routing strategy. Autonomous systems are subdivided by areas. An autonomous system must be assigned a unique 16-bit number by IANA. Sometimes abbreviated AS. *See also* area and IANA.

autonomous system boundary router. *See* ASBR.

autoreconfiguration. A process performed by nodes within the failure domain of a Token Ring network. Nodes automatically perform diagnostics in an attempt to reconfigure the network around the failed areas.

available bit rate. *See* ABR.

average rate. The average rate, in kilobits per second (kbps), at which a given virtual circuit transmits.

B

B8ZS. binary 8-zero substitution. A line-code type, used on T1 and E1 circuits, in which a special code is substituted whenever eight consecutive zeros are sent through the link. This code is then interpreted at the remote end of the connection. This technique guarantees ones density independently of the data stream. Sometimes called bipolar 8-zero substitution. *Compare with* AMI. *See also* ones density.

backbone. The part of a network that acts as the primary path for traffic that is most often sourced from, and destined for, other networks.

back end. A node or software program that provides services to a front end. *See also* client, front end, and server.

backoff. The (usually random) retransmission delay enforced by contentious MAC protocols after a network node with data to transmit determines that the physical medium is already in use.

backplane. A physical connection between an interface processor or card and the data buses and power distribution buses inside a chassis.

back pressure. Propagation of network congestion information upstream through an internetwork.

backward explicit congestion notification. *See* BECN.

backward learning. An algorithmic process used for routing traffic that surmises information by assuming symmetrical network conditions. For example, if node A receives a packet from node B through intermediate node C, the backward-learning routing algorithm will assume that A can optimally reach B through C.

balanced configuration. In HDLC, a point-to-point network configuration with two combined stations.

balanced, unbalanced. *See* balun.

balun. balanced, unbalanced. A device used for matching impedance between a balanced and an unbalanced line, usually twisted-pair and coaxial cable.

bandwidth. The difference between the highest and lowest frequencies available for network signals. The term is also used to describe the rated throughput capacity of a given network medium or protocol.

bandwidth allocation. *See* bandwidth reservation.

bandwidth reservation. A process of assigning bandwidth to users and applications served by a network. It involves assigning priority to different flows of traffic based on how critical and delay sensitive they are. This makes the best use of available bandwidth, and if the network becomes congested, lower-priority traffic can be dropped. Sometimes called bandwidth allocation. *See also* call priority.

Banyan VINES. *See* VINES.

BARRNet. Bay Area Regional Research Network. A regional network serving the San Francisco Bay Area. The BARRNet backbone is composed of four University of California campuses (Berkeley, Davis, Santa Cruz, and San Francisco), Stanford University, Lawrence Livermore National Laboratory, and NASA Ames Research Center. BARRNet is now part of BBN Planet. *See also* BBN Planet.

baseband. A characteristic of a network technology in which only one carrier frequency is used. Ethernet is an example of a baseband network. Also called narrowband. *Compare with* broadband.

basic encoding rules. *See* BER.

Basic Rate Interface. *See* BRI.

Basic Research and Human Resources. *See* BRHR.

baud. Unit of signaling speed equal to the number of discrete signal elements transmitted per second. Baud is synonymous with bits per second (bps), if each signal element represents exactly 1 bit.

Bay Area Regional Research Network. *See* BARRNet.

BBN. Bolt, Beranek, and Newman, Inc. A high-technology company located in Massachusetts that developed and maintained the ARPANET (and later, the Internet) core gateway system. *See also* BBN Planet.

BBN Planet. A subsidiary company of BBN that operates a nationwide Internet access network composed in part by the former regional networks BARRNet, NEARNET, and SURAnet. *See also* BARRNet, BBN, NEARNET, and SURAnet.

Bc. Committed Burst. Negotiated tariff metric in Frame Relay internetworks. The maximum amount of data (in bits) that a Frame Relay internetwork is committed to accept and transmit at the CIR. *See also* Be and CIR.

B channel. bearer channel. In ISDN, a full-duplex, 64-kbps channel used to send user data. *Compare with* D channel, E channel, and H channel.

Be. Excess Burst. Negotiated tariff metric in Frame Relay internetworks. The number of bits that a Frame Relay internetwork attempts to transmit after Bc is accommodated. Be data is, in general, delivered with a lower probability than Bc data because Be data can be marked as DE by the network. *See also* Bc and DE.

beacon. A frame from a Token Ring or FDDI device indicating a serious problem with the ring, such as a broken cable. A beacon frame contains the address of the station assumed to be down.

bearer channel. *See* B channel.

Because It's Time Network. *See* BITNET.

BECN. backward explicit congestion notification. A bit set by a Frame Relay network in frames traveling in the opposite direction of frames encountering a congested path. DTE receiving frames with the BECN bit set can request that higher-level protocols take flow control action as appropriate. *Compare with* FECN.

Bell Communications Research. *See* Bellcore.

Bellcore. Bell Communications Research. An organization that performs research and development on behalf of the RBOCs.

Bellman-Ford routing algorithm. *See* distance vector routing algorithm.

Bell operating company. *See* BOC.

BER. 1. bit error rate. The ratio of received bits that contain errors. 2. basic encoding rules. Rules for encoding data units described in the ISO ASN.1 standard. *See also* ASN.1.

Berkeley Standard Distribution. *See* BSD.

BERT. bit error rate tester. A device that determines the BER on a given communications channel. *See also* BER (bit error rate).

best-effort delivery. Delivery in a network system that does not use a sophisticated acknowledgment system to guarantee reliable delivery of information.

BGP. Border Gateway Protocol. An interdomain routing protocol that replaces EGP. BGP exchanges reachability information with other BGP systems. It is defined in RFC 1163. *See also* BGP4 and EGP.

BGP4. BGP Version 4. Version 4 of the predominant interdomain routing protocol used on the Internet. BGP4 supports CIDR and uses route aggregation mechanisms to reduce the size of routing tables. *See also* BGP and CIDR.

BIGA. Bus Interface Gate Array. A technology that allows the Catalyst 5000 to receive and transmit frames from its packet-switching memory to its MAC local buffer memory without the intervention of the host processor.

big-endian. A method of storing or transmitting data in which the most significant bit or byte is presented first. *Compare with* little-endian.

binary . A numbering system that uses ones and zeros (1 = on, 0 = off).

binary 8-zero substitution. *See* B8ZS.

binary coded alternate mark inversion. *See* AMI.

binary synchronous communication. *See* BSC.

biphase coding. A bipolar coding scheme originally developed for use in Ethernet. Clocking information is embedded into and recovered from the synchronous data stream without the need for separate clocking leads. The biphase signal contains no direct current energy.

bipolar. An electrical characteristic denoting a circuit with both negative and positive polarity. *Compare with* unipolar.

bipolar 8-zero substitution. *See* B8ZS.

BISDN. Broadband ISDN. ITU-T communication standards designed to handle high-bandwidth applications such as video. BISDN currently uses ATM technology over SONET-based transmission circuits to provide data rates from 155 to 622 Mbps and beyond. *Compare* with N-ISDN. *See also* BRI, ISDN, and PRI.

bisync . *See* BSC.

bit . A binary digit used in the binary numbering system. Can be 0 or 1.

bit error rate. *See* BER.

bit error rate tester. *See* BERT.

BITNET. "Because It's Time" Networking Services. Low-cost, low-speed academic network consisting primarily of IBM mainframes and 9600-bps leased lines. BITNET is now part of CREN. *See also* CREN.

BITNET III. A dial-up service providing connectivity for members of CREN. *See also* CREN.

bit-oriented protocol. A class of data link layer communication protocols that can transmit frames regardless of frame content. Compared with byte-oriented protocols, bit-oriented protocols provide full-duplex operation and are more efficient and reliable. *Compare with* byte-oriented protocol.

bit rate . The speed at which bits are transmitted, usually expressed in bits per second (bps).

bits per second. Abbreviated bps.

black hole. Routing term for an area of the internetwork where packets enter, but do not emerge, due to adverse conditions or poor system configuration within a portion of the network.

blocking. In a switching system, a condition in which no paths are available to complete a circuit. The term is also used to describe a situation in which one activity cannot begin until another has been completed.

block multiplexer channel. An IBM-style channel that implements the FIPS-60 channel, a U.S. channel standard. This channel is also referred to as OEMI channel and 370-block mux channel.

BNC connector. A standard connector used to connect IEEE 802.3 10Base2 coaxial cable to an MAU.

BNN. boundary network node. In SNA terminology, a subarea node that provides boundary function support for adjacent peripheral nodes. This support includes sequencing, pacing, and address translation. Also called boundary node.

BOC. Bell operating company. *See* RBOC.

Bolt, Beranek, and Newman, Inc. *See* BBN.

BOOTP. A protocol used by a network node to determine the IP address of its Ethernet interfaces, in order to affect network booting.

boot programmable read-only memory. *See* boot PROM.

boot PROM. boot programmable read-only memory. A chip mounted on a printed circuit board used to provide executable boot instructions to a computer device.

border gateway. A router that communicates with routers in other autonomous systems.

Border Gateway Protocol. *See* BGP.

boundary function. A capability of SNA subarea nodes to provide protocol support for attached peripheral nodes. Typically found in IBM 3745 devices.

boundary network node. *See* BNN.

boundary node. *See* BNN.

BPDU. bridge protocol data unit. A Spanning-Tree Protocol hello packet that is sent out at configurable intervals to exchange information among bridges in the network. *See also* PDU.

bps. bits per second.

BRHR. Basic Research and Human Resources. A component of the HPCC program designed to support research, training, and education in computer science, computer engineering, and computational science. *See also* HPCC.

BRI. Basic Rate Interface. An ISDN interface composed of two B channels and one D channel for circuit-switched communication of voice, video, and data. *Compare with* PRI. *See also* BISDN, ISDN, and N-ISDN.

bridge. A device that connects and passes packets between two network segments that use the same communications protocol. Bridges operate at the data link layer (Layer 2) of the OSI reference model. In general, a bridge filters, forwards, or floods an incoming frame based on the MAC address of that frame. *See also* relay.

bridge forwarding. A process that uses entries in a filtering database to determine whether frames with a given MAC destination address can be forwarded to a given port or ports. Described in the IEEE 802.1 standard. *See also* IEEE 802.1.

bridge number. A number that identifies each bridge in an SRB LAN. Parallel bridges must have different bridge numbers.

bridge protocol data unit. *See* BPDU.

bridge static filtering. A process in which a bridge maintains a filtering database consisting of static entries. Each static entry equates a MAC destination address with a port that can receive frames with this MAC destination address and a set of ports on which the frames can be transmitted. Defined in the IEEE 802.1 standard. *See also* IEEE 802.1.

broadband. A transmission system that multiplexes multiple independent signals onto one cable. In telecommunications terminology, any channel having a bandwidth greater than a voice-grade channel (4 kHz). In LAN terminology, a coaxial cable on which analog signaling is used. Also called wideband. *Compare with* baseband.

Broadband ISDN. *See* BISDN.

broadcast. Data packet that is sent to all nodes on a network. Broadcasts are identified by a broadcast address. *Compare with* multicast and unicast. *See also* broadcast address.

broadcast address. A special address reserved for sending a message to all stations. Generally, a broadcast address is a MAC destination address of all ones. *Compare with* multicast address and unicast address. *See also* broadcast.

broadcast and unknown server. *See* BUS.

broadcast domain. The set of all devices that will receive broadcast frames originating from any device within the set. Broadcast domains are typically bounded by routers because routers do not forward broadcast frames.

broadcast search. A propagation of a search request to all network nodes if the location of a resource is unknown to the requester. *See also* directed search.

broadcast storm. An undesirable network event in which many broadcasts are sent simultaneously across all network segments. A broadcast storm uses substantial network bandwidth and, typically, causes network time-outs.

browser. *See* WWW browser.

BSC. binary synchronous communication. A character-oriented data link layer protocol for half-duplex applications. Often referred to simply as bisync.

BSD. Berkeley Standard Distribution. The term used to describe any of a variety of UNIX-type operating systems based on the UC Berkeley BSD operating system.

BT. burst tolerance. A parameter defined by the ATM Forum for ATM traffic management. For VBR connections, BT determines the size of the maximum burst of contiguous cells that can be transmitted. *See also* VBR.

buffer. A storage area used for handling data in transit. Buffers are used in internetworking to compensate for differences in processing speed between network devices. Bursts of data can be stored in buffers until they can be handled by slower processing devices. Sometimes referred to as a packet buffer.

burst tolerance. *See* BT.

BUS. broadcast and unknown server. A multicast server used in ELANs that is used to flood traffic addressed to an unknown destination and to forward multicast and broadcast traffic to the appropriate clients. *See also* ELAN.

bus. A common physical signal path composed of wires or other media across which signals can be sent from one part of a computer to another. Sometimes called highway. *See* bus topology.

bus and tag channel. An IBM channel developed in the 1960s that incorporates copper multiwire technology. Replaced by the ESCON channel. *See also* ESCON channel and parallel channel.

Bus Interface Gate Array. *See* BIGA.

bus topology. A linear LAN architecture in which transmissions from network stations propagate the length of the medium and are received by all other stations. *Compare with* ring topology, star topology, and tree topology.

bypass mode. An operating mode on FDDI and Token Ring networks in which an interface has been removed from the ring.

bypass relay. Allows a particular Token Ring interface to be shut down and thus effectively removed from the ring.

byte. A series of consecutive binary digits that are operated on as a unit (for example, an 8-bit byte).

byte-oriented protocol. A class of data-link communications protocols that use a specific character from the user character set to delimit frames. These protocols have largely been replaced by bit-oriented protocols. *Compare with* bit-oriented protocol.

byte reversal. A process of storing numeric data with the least-significant byte first. Used for integers and addresses on devices with Intel microprocessors.

C

cable. A transmission medium of copper wire or optical fiber wrapped in a protective cover.

cable range. A range of network numbers that is valid for use by nodes on an extended AppleTalk network. The cable range value can be a single network number or a contiguous sequence of several network numbers. Node addresses are assigned based on the cable range value.

cable television. *See* CATV.

caching. A form of replication in which information learned during a previous transaction is used to process later transactions.

California Education and Research Federation Network. *See* CERFnet.

call admission control. A traffic management mechanism used in ATM networks that determines whether the network can offer a path with sufficient bandwidth for a requested VCC.

call priority. A priority assigned to each origination port in circuit-switched systems. This priority defines the order in which calls are reconnected. Call priority also defines which calls can or cannot be placed during a bandwidth reservation. *See also* bandwidth reservation.

call setup time. The time required to establish a switched call between DTE devices.

CAM. content-addressable memory. *See* associative memory.

Canadian Standards Association. *See* CSA.

carrier. An electromagnetic wave or alternating current of a single frequency, suitable for modulation by another, data-bearing signal. *See also* modulation.

Carrier Detect. *See* CD.

carrier sense multiple access collision detect. *See* CSMA/CD.

Category 1 cabling. One of five grades of UTP cabling described in the EIA/TIA-586 standard. Category 1 cabling is used for telephone communications and is not suitable for transmitting data. *Compare with* Category 2 cabling, Category 3 cabling, Category 4 cabling, and Category 5 cabling. *See also* EIA/TIA-586 and UTP.

Category 2 cabling. One of five grades of UTP cabling described in the EIA/TIA-586 standard. Category 2 cabling is capable of transmitting data at speeds up to 4 Mbps. *Compare with* Category 1 cabling, Category 3 cabling, Category 4 cabling, and Category 5 cabling. *See also* EIA/TIA-586 and UTP.

Category 3 cabling. One of five grades of UTP cabling described in the EIA/TIA-586 standard. Category 3 cabling is used in 10BaseT networks and can transmit data at speeds up to 10 Mbps. *Compare with* Category 1 cabling, Category 2 cabling, Category 4 cabling, and Category 5 cabling. *See also* EIA/TIA-586 and UTP.

Category 4 cabling. One of five grades of UTP cabling described in the EIA/TIA-586 standard. Category 4 cabling is used in Token Ring networks and can transmit data at speeds up to 16 Mbps. *Compare with* Category 1 cabling, Category 2 cabling, Category 3 cabling, and Category 5 cabling. *See also* EIA/TIA-586 and UTP.

Category 5 cabling. One of five grades of UTP cabling described in the EIA/TIA-586 standard. Category 5 cabling is used for running CDDI and can transmit data at speeds up to 100 Mbps. *Compare with* Category 1 cabling, Category 2 cabling, Category 3 cabling, and Category 4 cabling. *See also* EIA/TIA-586 and UTP.

catenet. A network in which hosts are connected to diverse networks, which themselves are connected with routers. The Internet is a prominent example of a catenet.

CATV. cable television. A communication system in which multiple channels of programming material are transmitted to homes using broadband coaxial cable. Formerly called Community Antenna Television.

CBDS. Connectionless Broadband Data Service. A European high-speed, packet-switched, datagram-based WAN networking technology. Similar to SMDS. *See also* SMDS.

CBR. constant bit rate. A QoS class defined by the ATM Forum for ATM networks. CBR is used for connections that depend on precise clocking to ensure undistorted delivery. *Compare with* ABR (available bit rate), UBR, and VBR.

CCITT. Consultative Committee for International Telegraph and Telephone. An International organization responsible for the development of communications standards. Now called the ITU-T. *See* ITU-T.

CCS. common channel signaling. A signaling system used in telephone networks that separates signaling information from user data. A specified channel is exclusively designated to carry signaling information for all other channels in the system. *See also* SS7.

CD. Carrier Detect. A signal that indicates whether an interface is active. Also, a signal generated by a modem indicating that a call has been connected.

CDDI. Copper Distributed Data Interface. An implementation of FDDI protocols over STP and UTP cabling. CDDI transmits over relatively short distances (about 100 meters), providing data rates of 100 Mbps using a dual-ring architecture to provide redundancy. Based on the ANSI Twisted-Pair Physical Medium Dependent (TPPMD) standard. *Compare with* FDDI.

CDPD. Cellular Digital Packet Data. An open standard for two-way wireless data communication over high-frequency cellular telephone channels. Allows data transmissions between a remote cellular link and a NAP. Operates at 19.2 kbps.

CDVT. cell delay variation tolerance. A parameter defined by the ATM Forum for ATM traffic management. In CBR transmissions, it determines the level of jitter that is tolerable for the data samples taken by the PCR. *See also* CBR and PCR.

cell. The basic unit for ATM switching and multiplexing. Cells contain identifiers that specify the data stream to which they belong. Each cell consists of a 5-byte header and 48 bytes of payload. *See also* cell relay.

cell delay variation tolerance. *See* CDVT.

cell loss priority. *See* CLP.

cell relay. A network technology based on the use of small, fixed-size packets, or cells. Because cells are fixed-length, they can be processed and switched in hardware at high speeds. Cell relay is the basis for many high-speed network protocols including ATM, IEEE 802.6, and SMDS. *See also* cell.

cells per second. Abbreviated cps.

Cellular Digital Packet Data. *See* CDPD.

cellular radio. A technology that uses radio transmissions to access telephone-company networks. Service is provided in a particular area by a low-power transmitter.

central office. *See* CO.

Centrex. An AT&T PBX that provides direct inward dialing and automatic number identification of the calling PBX.

CEPT. Conference Europenne des Postes et des Telecommunications. An association of the 26 European PTTs that recommends communication specifications to the ITU-T.

CERFnet. California Education and Research Federation Network. A TCP/IP network, based in Southern California, that connects hundreds of higher-education centers internationally while also providing Internet access to subscribers. CERFnet was founded in 1988 by the San Diego Supercomputer Center and General Atomics, and is funded by the NSF.

chaining. SNA concept in which RUs are grouped for the purpose of error recovery.

Challenge Handshake Authentication Protocol. *See* CHAP.

channel. 1. A communication path. Multiple channels can be multiplexed over a single cable in certain environments. 2. In IBM, the specific path between large computers (such as mainframes) and attached peripheral devices.

channel-attached. Pertaining to attachment of devices directly by data channels (input/output channels) to a computer.

channelized E1. An access link operating at 2.048 Mbps that is subdivided into 30 B-channels and 1 D-channel. Supports DDR, Frame Relay, and X.25. *Compare with* channelized T1.

channelized T1. An access link operating at 1.544 Mbps that is subdivided into 24 channels (23 B-channels and 1 D-channel) of 64 kbps each. The individual channels or groups of channels connect to different destinations. Supports DDR, Frame Relay, and X.25. Also referred to as fractional T1. *Compare with* channelized E1.

channel service unit. *See* CSU.

CHAP. Challenge Handshake Authentication Protocol. A security feature supported on lines using PPP encapsulation that prevents unauthorized access. CHAP does not itself prevent unauthorized access; it merely identifies the remote end. The router or access server then determines whether that user is allowed access. *Compare with* PAP.

chat script. A string of text that defines the login "conversation" that occurs between two systems. It consists of expect-send pairs that define the string the local system expects to receive from the remote system and what the local system should send as a reply.

Cheapernet. An industry term used to refer to the IEEE 802.3 10Base2 standard or the cable specified in that standard. *Compare with* Thinnet. *See also* 10Base2, Ethernet, and IEEE 802.3.

checksum. A method for checking the integrity of transmitted data. A checksum is an integer value computed from a sequence of octets taken through a series of arithmetic operations. The value is recomputed at the receiving end and compared for verification.

choke packet. A packet sent to a transmitter to tell it that congestion exists and that it should reduce its sending rate.

CIA. *See* classical IP over ATM.

CICNet. A regional network that connects academic, research, nonprofit, and commercial organizations in the Midwestern United States. Founded in 1988, CICNet was a part of the NSFNET and was funded by the NSF until the NSFNET dissolved in 1995. *See also* NSFNET.

CICS. Customer Information Control System. An IBM application subsystem that allows transactions entered at remote terminals to be processed concurrently by user applications.

CIDR. classless interdomain routing. A technique supported by BGP4 and based on route aggregation. CIDR allows routers to group routes together in order to cut down on the quantity of routing information carried by the core routers. With CIDR, several IP networks appear to networks outside the group as a single, larger entity. *See also* BGP4.

CIR. committed information rate. The rate at which a Frame Relay network agrees to transfer information under normal conditions, averaged over a minimum increment of time. CIR, measured in bits per second, is one of the key negotiated tariff metrics. *See also* Bc.

circuit. A communications path between two or more points.

circuit group. A grouping of associated serial lines that link two bridges. If one of the serial links in a circuit group is in the spanning tree for a network, any of the serial links in the circuit group can be used for load balancing. This load-balancing strategy avoids data ordering problems by assigning each destination address to a particular serial link.

circuit switching. A switching system in which a dedicated physical circuit path must exist between sender and receiver for the duration of the "call." Used heavily in the telephone company network. Circuit switching can be contrasted with contention and token passing as a channel-access method, and with message switching and packet switching as a switching technique.

Class A station. *See* DAS.

Class B station. *See* SAS.

classical IP over ATM. A specification for running IP over ATM in a manner that takes full advantage of the features of ATM. Defined in RFC 1577. Sometimes called CIA.

classless interdomain routing. *See* CIDR.

class of service. *See* COS.

CLAW. Common Link Access for Workstations. A data link layer protocol used by channel-attached RISC System/6000 series systems and by IBM 3172 devices running TCP/IP off-load. CLAW improves efficiency of channel use and allows the CIP to provide the functionality of a 3172 in TCP/IP environments and support direct channel attachment. The output from TCP/IP mainframe processing is a series of IP datagrams that the router can switch without modifications.

Clear To Send. *See* CTS.

client. A node or software program (front-end device) that requests services from a server. *See also* back end, front end, and server.

client/server computing. Computing (processing) network systems in which transaction responsibilities are divided into two parts: client (front end) and server (back end). Both terms (client and server) can be applied to software programs or actual computing devices. Also called distributed computing (processing). *Compare with* peer-to-peer computing. *See also* RPC.

CLNP. Connectionless Network Protocol. OSI network layer protocol that does not require a circuit to be established before data is transmitted. *See also* CLNS.

CLNS. Connectionless Network Service. An OSI network layer service that does not require a circuit to be established before data is transmitted. CLNS routes messages to their destinations independently of any other messages. *See also* CLNP.

CLP. cell loss priority. A field in the ATM cell header that determines the probability of a cell being dropped if the network becomes congested. Cells with CLP = 0 are insured traffic, which is unlikely to be dropped. Cells with CLP = 1 are best-effort traffic, which might be dropped in congested conditions in order to free up resources to handle insured traffic.

cluster controller. 1. Generally, an intelligent device that provides the connections for a cluster of terminals to a data link. 2. In SNA, a programmable device that controls the input/output operations of attached devices. Typically, an IBM 3174 or 3274 device.

CMI. coded mark inversion. An ITU-T line coding technique specified for STS-3c transmissions. Also used in DS-1 systems. *See also* DS-1 and STS-3c.

CMIP. Common Management Information Protocol. An OSI network management protocol created and standardized by ISO for the monitoring and control of heterogeneous networks. *See also* CMIS.

CMIS. Common Management Information Services. An OSI network management service interface created and standardized by ISO for the monitoring and control of heterogeneous networks. *See also* CMIP.

CMNS. Connection-Mode Network Service. A service that extends local X.25 switching to a variety of media (Ethernet, FDDI, Token Ring). *See also* CONP.

CMT. connection management. A FDDI process that handles the transition of the ring through its various states (off, active, connect, and so on), as defined by the ANSI X3T9.5 specification.

CO. central office. A local telephone company office to which all local loops in a given area connect and in which circuit switching of subscriber lines occurs.

coaxial cable. Cable consisting of a hollow outer cylindrical conductor that surrounds a single inner wire conductor. Two types of coaxial cable are currently used in LANs: 50-ohm cable, which is used for digital signaling, and 75-ohm cable, which is used for analog signaling and high-speed digital signaling.

CODEC. coder-decoder. A device that typically uses PCM to transform analog signals into a digital bit stream and digital signals back into analog.

coded mark inversion. *See* CMI.

coder-decoder. *See* CODEC.

coding. Electrical techniques used to convey binary signals.

collapsed backbone. A nondistributed backbone in which all network segments are interconnected by way of an internetworking device. A collapsed backbone might be a virtual network segment existing in a device such as a hub, a router, or a switch.

collision. In Ethernet, the result of two nodes transmitting simultaneously. The frames from each device impact and are damaged when they meet on the physical media. *See also* collision domain.

collision detection. *See* CSMA/CD.

collision domain. In Ethernet, the network area within which frames that have collided are propagated. Repeaters and hubs propagate collisions; LAN switches, bridges, and routers do not. *See also* collision.

Committed Burst. *See* Bc.

committed information rate. *See* CIR.

common carrier. A licensed, private utility company that supplies communication services to the public at regulated prices.

common channel signaling. *See* CCS.

Common Link Access for Workstations. *See* CLAW.

Common Management Information Protocol. *See* CMIP.

Common Management Information Services. *See* CMIS.

common part convergence sublayer. *See* CPCS.

Common Programming Interface for Communications. *See* CPI-C.

common transport semantic. *See* CTS.

communication. Transmission of information.

communication controller. In SNA, a subarea node (such as an IBM 3745 device) that contains an NCP.

communication server. A communications processor that connects asynchronous devices to a LAN or WAN through network and terminal emulation software. Performs only asynchronous routing of IP and IPX. *Compare with* access server.

communications line. The physical link (such as wire or a telephone circuit) that connects one or more devices to one or more other devices.

community. In SNMP, a logical group of managed devices and NMSs in the same administrative domain.

Community Antenna Television. Now known as CATV. *See* CATV.

community string. A text string that acts as a password and is used to authenticate messages sent between a management station and a router containing an SNMP agent. The community string is sent in every packet between the manager and the agent.

companding. A contraction derived from the opposite processes of compression and expansion. Part of the PCM process whereby analog signal values are logically rounded to discrete scale-step values on a nonlinear scale. The decimal step number is then coded in its binary equivalent prior to transmission. The process is reversed at the receiving terminal, using the same nonlinear scale. *Compare with* compression and expansion. *See also* a-law and mu-law.

complete sequence number PDU. *See* CSNP.

Compressed Serial Link Internet Protocol. *See* CSLIP.

compression. The running of a data set through an algorithm that reduces the space required to store or the bandwidth required to transmit the data set. Compare with companding and expansion.

Computer Science Network. *See* CSNET.

concentrator. *See* hub.

Conference Europenne des Postes et des Telecommunications. *See* CEPT.

configuration management. One of five categories of network management defined by ISO for management of OSI networks. Configuration management subsystems are responsible for detecting and determining the state of a network. *See also* accounting management, fault management, performance management, and security management.

congestion. Traffic in excess of network capacity.

connectionless. Data transfer that occurs without the existence of a virtual circuit. Compare with connection-oriented. *See also* virtual circuit.

Connectionless Broadband Data Service. *See* CBDS.

Connectionless Network Protocol. *See* CLNP.

Connectionless Network Service. *See* CLNS.

connection management. *See* CMT.

Connection-Mode Network Service. *See* CMNS.

connection-oriented. Data transfer that requires the establishment of a virtual circuit. A Layer 4 protocol that creates with software a virtual circuit between devices to provide guaranteed transport of data. *See also* connectionless. *See also* virtual circuit.

Connection-Oriented Network Protocol. *See* CONP.

CONP. Connection-Oriented Network Protocol. An OSI protocol that provides connection-oriented operation to upper-layer protocols. *See also* CMNS.

console. A DTE through which commands are entered into a host.

constant bit rate. *See* CBR.

Consultative Committee for International Telegraph and Telephone. *See* CCITT.

content-addressable memory. *See* associative memory.

contention. An access method in which network devices compete for permission to access the physical medium. *Compare with* circuit switching and token passing.

control point. *See* CP.

convergence. The speed and ability of a group of internetworking devices running a specific routing protocol to agree on the topology of an internetwork after a change in that topology.

convergence sublayer. *See* CS.

conversation. In SNA, an LU 6.2 session between two transaction programs.

Cooperation for Open Systems Interconnection Networking in Europe. *See* COSINE.

Copper Distributed Data Interface. *See* CDDI.

core gateway. The primary routers in the Internet.

core router. In a packet-switched star topology, a router that is part of the backbone and that serves as the single pipe through which all traffic from peripheral networks must pass on its way to other peripheral networks.

Corporation for Open Systems. *See* COS.

Corporation for Research and Educational Networking. *See* CREN.

COS. 1. Class of service. An indication of how an upper-layer protocol requires that a lower-layer protocol treat its messages. In SNA subarea routing, COS definitions are used by subarea nodes to determine the optimal route to establish a given session. A COS definition comprises a virtual route number and a transmission priority field. Also called TOS (type of service). 2. Corporation for Open Systems. An organization that promulgates the use of OSI protocols through conformance testing, certification, and related activities.

COSINE. Cooperation for Open Systems Interconnection Networking in Europe. A project financed by the European Community (EC) to build a communication network between scientific and industrial entities in Europe. The project ended in 1994.

cost. An arbitrary value, typically based on hop count, media bandwidth, or other measures, that is assigned by a network administrator and used to compare various paths through an internetwork environment. Cost values are used by routing protocols to determine the most favorable path to a particular destination: The lower the cost, the better the path. Sometimes called path cost. *See also* routing metric.

count to infinity. A problem that can occur in routing algorithms that are slow to converge, in which routers continuously increment the hop count to particular networks. Typically, some arbitrary hop-count limit is imposed to prevent this problem.

CP. control point. In SNA networks, an element that identifies the APPN networking components of a PU 2.1 node, manages device resources, and can provide services to other devices. In APPN, CPs are able to communicate with logically adjacent CPs by way of CP-to-CP sessions. *See also* EN and NN.

CPCS. common part convergence sublayer. One of the two sublayers of any AAL. The CPCS is service independent and is further divided into the CS and the SAR sublayers. The CPCS is responsible for preparing data for transport across the ATM network, including the creation of the 48-byte payload cells that are passed to the ATM layer. *See also* AAL, ATM layer, CS, SAR, and SSCS.

CPE. customer premises equipment. Terminating equipment, such as terminals, telephones, and modems, supplied by the telephone company, installed at customer sites, and connected to the telephone company network.

CPI-C. Common Programming Interface for Communications. A platform-independent API developed by IBM and used to provide portability in APPC applications. *See also* APPC.

cps. cells per second.

CRC. cyclic redundancy check. An error-checking technique in which the frame recipient calculates a remainder by dividing frame contents by a prime binary divisor and compares the calculated remainder to a value stored in the frame by the sending node.

CREN. Corporation for Research and Educational Networking. The result of a merger of BITNET and CSNET. CREN is devoted to providing Internet connectivity to its members, which include the alumni, students, faculty, and other affiliates of participating educational and research institutions, via BITNET III. *See also* BITNET, BITNET III, and CSNET.

cross talk. Interfering energy transferred from one circuit to another.

CS. convergence sublayer. One of the two sublayers of the AAL CPCS, responsible for padding and error checking. PDUs passed from the SSCS are appended with an 8-byte trailer (for error checking and other control information) and padded, if necessary, so that the length of the resulting PDU is divisible by 48. These PDUs are then passed to the SAR sublayer of the CPCS for further processing. *See also* AAL, CPCS, SAR, and SSCS.

CSA. Canadian Standards Association. An agency in Canada that certifies products that conform to Canadian national safety standards.

CSLIP. Compressed Serial Link Internet Protocol. An extension of SLIP that, when appropriate, allows just header information to be sent across a SLIP connection, reducing overhead and increasing packet throughput on SLIP lines. *See also* SLIP.

CSMA/CD. carrier sense multiple access collision detect. Media-access mechanism wherein devices ready to transmit data first check the channel for a carrier. If no carrier is sensed for a specific period of time, a device can transmit. If two devices transmit at once, a collision occurs and is detected by all colliding devices. This collision subsequently delays retransmissions from those devices for some random length of time. CSMA/CD access is used by Ethernet and IEEE 802.3.

CSNET. Computer Science Network. A large internetwork consisting primarily of universities, research institutions, and commercial concerns. CSNET merged with BITNET to form CREN. *See also* BITNET and CREN.

CSNP. complete sequence number PDU. A PDU sent by the designated router in an OSPF network to maintain database synchronization.

CSU. channel service unit. A digital interface device that connects end-user equipment to the local digital telephone loop. Often referred to, together with DSU, as CSU/DSU. *See also* DSU.

CTS. 1. Clear To Send. A circuit in the EIA/TIA-232 specification that is activated when DCE is ready to accept data from DTE. 2. common transport semantic. A cornerstone of the IBM strategy to reduce the number of protocols on networks. CTS provides a single API for developers of network software and enables applications to run over APPN, OSI, or TCP/IP.

Customer Information Control System. *See* CICS.

customer premises equipment. *See* CPE.

cut-through packet switching. A packet switching approach that streams data through a switch so that the leading edge of a packet exits the switch at the output port before the packet finishes entering the input port. A device using cut-through packet switching reads, processes, and forwards packets as soon as the destination address is looked up and the outgoing port is determined. Also known as on-the-fly packet switching. *Compare with* store and forward packet switching.

cycles per second. *See* hertz.

cyclic redundancy check. *See* CRC.

D

D4 framing. *See* SF.

DAC. dual-attached concentrator. An FDDI or a CDDI concentrator capable of attaching to both rings of an FDDI or CDDI network. It can also be dual-homed from the master ports of other FDDI or CDDI concentrators.

DARPA. Defense Advanced Research Projects Agency. A U.S. government agency that funded research for and experimentation with the Internet. Evolved from ARPA, and then, in 1994, back to ARPA. *See also* ARPA.

DARPA Internet. An obsolete term referring to the Internet. *See* Internet.

DAS. dual attachment station. A device attached to both the primary and the secondary FDDI rings. Dual attachment provides redundancy for the FDDI ring; if the primary ring fails, the station can wrap the primary ring to the secondary ring, isolating the failure and retaining ring integrity. Also known as a Class A station. Compare with SAS.

database object. In general, a piece of information that is stored in a database. *See* DB connector.

data channel. *See* D channel.

data circuit-terminating equipment. *See* DCE.

data communications equipment. *See* DCE.

Data Country Code. *See* DCC.

Data Encryption Standard. *See* DES.

Data Exchange Interface. *See* DXI.

data flow control layer. Layer 5 of the SNA architectural model. This layer determines and manages interactions between session partners, particularly data flow. Corresponds to the session layer of the OSI model. *See also* data link control layer, path control layer, physical control layer, presentation services layer, transaction services layer, and transmission control layer.

datagram. A logical grouping of information sent as a network layer unit over a transmission medium without prior establishment of a virtual circuit. IP datagrams are the primary information units in the Internet. The terms frame, message, packet, and segment are also used to describe logical information groupings at various layers of the OSI reference model and in various technology circles.

Datagram Delivery Protocol. *See* DDP.

data-link connection identifier. *See* DLCI.

data link control layer. Layer 2 in the SNA architectural model. This layer is responsible for the transmission of data over a particular physical link. Corresponds roughly to the data link layer of the OSI model. *See also* data flow control layer, path control layer, physical control layer, presentation services layer, transaction services layer, and transmission control layer.

data link layer. Layer 2 of the OSI reference model. This layer provides reliable transit of data across a physical link. The data link layer is concerned with physical addressing, network topology, line discipline, error notification, ordered delivery of frames, and flow control. The IEEE has divided this layer into two sublayers: the MAC sublayer and the LLC sublayer. Sometimes simply called link layer. Roughly corresponds to the data link control layer of the SNA model. *See also* application layer, LLC, MAC, network layer, physical layer, presentation layer, session layer, and transport layer.

data-link switching. *See* DLSw.

Data Network Identification Code. *See* DNIC.

data set ready. *See* DSR.

data service unit. *See* DSU.

data sink. Network equipment that accepts data transmissions.

data stream. All data transmitted through a communications line in a single read or write operation.

data terminal equipment. *See* DTE.

data terminal ready. *See* DTR.

dB. decibels.

DB connector. data bus connector. A type of connector used to connect serial and parallel cables to a data bus. DB connector names are of the format DB-*x*, where *x* represents the number of wires within the connector. Each line is connected to a pin on the connector, but in many cases, not all pins are assigned a function. DB connectors are defined by various EIA/TIA standards.

DCA. Defense Communications Agency. A U.S. government organization responsible for DDN networks such as MILNET. Now called DISA. *See* DISA.

DCC. Data Country Code. One of two ATM address formats developed by the ATM Forum for use by private networks. Adapted from the subnetwork model of addressing, in which the ATM layer is responsible for mapping network layer addresses to ATM addresses. *See also* ICD.

DCE. data communications equipment (EIA expansion) or data circuit-terminating equipment (ITU-T expansion). The devices and connections of a communications network that comprise the network end of the user-to-network interface. The DCE provides a physical connection to the network, forwards traffic, and provides a clocking signal used to synchronize data transmission between DCE and DTE devices. Modems and interface cards are examples of DCE. Compare with DTE.

D channel. 1. data channel. Full-duplex, 16-kbps (BRI) or 64-kbps (PRI) ISDN channel. *Compare with* B channel, E channel, and H channel. 2. In SNA, a device that connects a processor and main storage with peripherals.

DDM. Distributed Data Management. Software in an IBM SNA environment that provides peer-to-peer communication and file sharing. One of three SNA transaction services. *See also* DIA and SNADS.

DDN. Defense Data Network. A U.S. military network composed of an unclassified network (MILNET) and various secret and top-secret networks. DDN is operated and maintained by DISA. *See also* DISA and MILNET.

DDP. Datagram Delivery Protocol. An Apple Computer network layer protocol that is responsible for the socket-to-socket delivery of datagrams over an AppleTalk internetwork.

DDR. dial-on-demand routing. A technique whereby a Cisco router can automatically initiate and close a circuit-switched session as transmitting stations demand. The router spoofs keepalives so that end stations treat the session as active. DDR permits routing over ISDN or telephone lines using an external ISDN terminal adapter or modem.

DE. discard eligible. *See* tagged traffic.

deadlock. 1. Unresolved contention for the use of a resource. 2. In APPN, when two elements of a process each wait for action by or a response from the other before they resume the process.

decibels. Abbreviated dB.

DECnet. Group of communications products (including a protocol suite) developed and supported by Digital Equipment Corporation. DECnet/OSI (also called DECnet Phase V) is the most recent iteration and supports both OSI protocols and proprietary Digital protocols. Phase IV Prime supports inherent MAC addresses that allow DECnet nodes to coexist with systems running other protocols that have MAC address restrictions. *See also* DNA.

DECnet routing. A proprietary routing scheme introduced by Digital Equipment Corporation in DECnet Phase III. In DECnet Phase V, DECnet completed its transition to OSI routing protocols (ES-IS and IS-IS).

decryption. The reverse application of an encryption algorithm to encrypted data, thereby restoring that data to its original, unencrypted state. *See also* encryption.

dedicated LAN. A network segment allocated to a single device. Used in LAN switched network topologies.

dedicated line. A communications line that is indefinitely reserved for transmissions, rather than switched as transmission is required. *See also* leased line.

de facto standard. A standard that exists by nature of its widespread use. Compare with de jure standard. *See also* standard.

default route. A routing table entry that is used to direct frames for which a next hop is not explicitly listed in the routing table.

Defense Advanced Research Projects Agency. *See* DARPA.

Defense Communications Agency. *See* DCA.

Defense Data Network. *See* DDN.

Defense Information Systems Agency. *See* DISA.

Defense Intelligence Agency. *See* DIA.

de jure standard. A standard that exists because of its approval by an official standards body. *Compare with* de facto standard. *See also* standard.

delay. The time between the initiation of a transaction by a sender and the first response received by the sender. Also, the time required to move a packet from source to destination over a given path.

demand priority. A media access method used in 100VG-AnyLAN that uses a hub that can handle multiple transmission requests and can process traffic according to priority, making it useful for servicing time-sensitive traffic such as multimedia and video. Demand priority eliminates the overhead of packet collisions, collision recovery, and broadcast traffic typical in Ethernet networks. *See also* 100VG-AnyLAN.

demarc. A demarcation point between carrier equipment and CPE.

demodulation. The process of returning a modulated signal to its original form. Modems perform demodulation by returning an analog signal to its original (digital) form. *See also* modulation.

demultiplexing. The separating of multiple input streams that have been multiplexed into a common physical signal back into multiple output streams. *See also* multiplexing.

dense mode PIM. *See* PIM dense mode.

Department of Defense. *See* DoD.

Department of Defense Intelligence Information System Network Security for Information Exchange. *See* DNSIX.

Dependent LU. *See* DLU.

Dependent LU Requester. *See* DLUR.

Dependent LU Server. *See* DLUS.

DES. Data Encryption Standard. A standard cryptographic algorithm developed by the U.S. NBS.

designated bridge. The bridge that incurs the lowest path cost when forwarding a frame from a segment to the route bridge.

designated router. An OSPF router that generates LSAs for a multiaccess network and has other special responsibilities in running OSPF. Each multiaccess OSPF network that has at least two attached routers has a designated router that is elected by the OSPF Hello protocol. The designated router enables a reduction in the number of adjacencies required on a multiaccess network, which in turn reduces the amount of routing protocol traffic and the size of the topological database.

destination address. The address of a network device that is receiving data. *See also* source address.

destination MAC. *See* DMAC.

destination service access point. *See* DSAP.

deterministic load distribution. A technique for distributing traffic between two bridges across a circuit group. Guarantees packet ordering between source-destination pairs and always forwards traffic for a source-destination pair on the same segment in a circuit group for a given circuit-group configuration.

Deutsche Industrie Norm. *See* DIN.

Deutsche Industrie Norm connector. *See* DIN connector.

device. *See* node.

DHCP. Dynamic Host Configuration Protocol. Provides a mechanism for allocating IP addresses dynamically so that addresses can be reused when hosts no longer need them.

DIA. Document Interchange Architecture. Defines the protocols and data formats needed for the transparent interchange of documents in an SNA network. One of three SNA transaction services. *See also* DDM and SNADS.

dial-on-demand routing. *See* DDR.

dial-up line. A communications circuit that is established by a switched-circuit connection using the telephone company network.

differential encoding. A digital encoding technique whereby a binary value is denoted by a signal change rather than a particular signal level.

differential Manchester encoding. A digital coding scheme where a mid-bit-time transition is used for clocking, and a transition at the beginning of each bit time denotes a zero. The coding scheme used by IEEE 802.5 and Token Ring networks.

Diffusing Update Algorithm. *See* DUAL.

Digital Network Architecture. *See* DNA.

digital signal level 0. *See* DS-0.

digital signal level 1. *See* DS-1.

digital signal level 3. *See* DS-3.

Dijkstra's algorithm. *See* SPF.

DIN. Deutsche Industrie Norm. A German national standards organization.

DIN connector. Deutsche Industrie Norm connector. A multipin connector used in some Macintosh and IBM PC-compatible computers, and on some network processor panels.

directed search. A search request sent to a specific node known to contain a resource. A directed search is used to determine the continued existence of the resource and to obtain routing information specific to the node. *See also* broadcast search.

direct memory access. *See* DMA.

directory services. Services that help network devices locate service providers.

DISA. Defense Information Systems Agency. A U.S. military organization responsible for implementing and operating military information systems, including the DDN. *See also* DDN.

discard eligible. *See* DE.

discovery architecture. APPN software that enables a machine configured as an APPN EN to automatically find primary and backup NNs when the machine is brought onto an APPN network.

discovery mode. A method by which an AppleTalk interface acquires information about an attached network from an operational node and then uses this information to configure itself. Also called dynamic configuration.

Distance Vector Multicast Routing Protocol. *See* DVMRP.

distance vector routing algorithm. A class of routing algorithms that iterate on the number of hops in a route to find a shortest-path spanning tree. Distance vector routing algorithms call for each router to send its entire routing table in each update, but only to its neighbors. Distance vector routing algorithms can be prone to routing loops, but are computationally simpler than link state routing algorithms. Also called Bellman-Ford routing algorithm. *See also* link state routing algorithm and SPF.

distortion delay. A problem with a communication signal resulting from nonuniform transmission speeds of the components of a signal through a transmission medium. Also called group delay.

distributed computing (processing). *See* client/server computing.

Distributed Data Management. *See* DDM.

Distributed Queue Dual Bus. *See* DQDB.

DLCI. data-link connection identifier. A value that specifies a PVC or SVC in a Frame Relay network. In the basic Frame Relay specification, DLCIs are locally significant (connected devices might use different values to specify the same connection). In the LMI extended specification, DLCIs are globally significant (DLCIs specify individual end devices). *See also* LMI.

DLSw. data-link switching. An interoperability standard, described in RFC 1434, that provides a method for forwarding SNA and NetBIOS traffic over TCP/IP networks using data link layer switching and encapsulation. DLSw uses SSP instead of SRB, eliminating the major limitations of SRB, including hop-count limits, broadcast and unnecessary traffic, timeouts, lack of flow control, and lack of prioritization schemes. *See also* SRB and SSP.

DLU. Dependent LU. An LU that depends on the SSCP to provide services for establishing sessions with other LUs. *See also* LU and SSCP.

DLUR. Dependent LU Requester. The client half of the Dependent LU Requestor/Server enhancement to APPN. The DLUR component resides in APPN ENs and NNs that support adjacent DLUs by securing services from the DLUS. *See also* APPN, DLU, and DLUS.

DLUR node. In APPN networks, an EN or NN that implements the DLUR component. *See also* DLUR.

DLUS. Dependent LU Server. The server half of the Dependent LU Requestor/Server enhancement to APPN. The DLUS component provides SSCP services to DLUR nodes over an APPN network. *See also* APPN, DLU, and DLUR.

DLUS node. In APPN networks, an NN that implements the DLUS component. *See also* DLUS.

DMA. direct memory access. The transfer of data from a peripheral device, such as a hard disk drive, into memory without that data passing through the microprocessor. DMA transfers data into memory at high speeds with no processor overhead.

DMAC. destination MAC. The MAC address specified in the Destination Address field of a packet. *Compare with* SMAC. *See also* MAC address.

DNA. Digital Network Architecture. A network architecture developed by Digital Equipment Corporation. The products that embody DNA (including communications protocols) are collectively referred to as DECnet. *See also* DECnet.

DNIC. Data Network Identification Code. Part of an X.121 address. DNICs are divided into two parts: The first specifies the country in which the addressed PSN (packet-switching node) is located and the second specifies the PSN itself. *See also* X.121.

DNS. Domain Name System. A system used in the Internet for translating names of network nodes into addresses. *See also* authority zone.

DNSIX. Department of Defense Intelligence Information System Network Security for Information Exchange. A collection of security requirements for networking defined by the U.S. Defense Intelligence Agency.

Document Interchange Architecture. *See* DIA.

DoD. Department of Defense. A U.S. government organization that is responsible for national defense. The DoD has frequently funded communication protocol development.

domain. 1. In the Internet, a portion of the naming hierarchy tree that refers to general groupings of networks based on organization type or geography. 2. In SNA, an SSCP and the resources it controls. 3. In IS-IS, a logical set of networks.

Domain. A networking system developed by Apollo Computer (now part of Hewlett-Packard) for use in its engineering workstations.

Domain Name System. *See* DNS.

domain-specific part. *See* DSP.

dot address. The common notation for IP addresses in the form *n.n.n.n*, where each number *n* represents, in decimal, 1 byte of the 4-byte IP address. Also called dotted notation, dotted-decimal notation, or four-part dotted notation.

dotted notation. *See* dot address.

downlink station. *See* ground station.

downstream physical unit. *See* DSPU.

DQDB. Distributed Queue Dual Bus. A data link layer communication protocol, specified in the IEEE 802.6 standard, designed for use in MANs. DQDB, which permits multiple systems to interconnect using two unidirectional logical buses, is an open standard that is designed for compatibility with carrier transmission standards and is aligned with emerging standards for BISDN. SIP is based on DQDB. *See also* MAN.

DRAM. dynamic random-access memory. RAM that stores information in capacitors that must be periodically refreshed. Delays can occur because DRAMs are inaccessible to the processor when refreshing their contents. However, DRAMs are less complex and have greater capacity than SRAMs. *See also* SRAM.

drop. A point on a multipoint channel where a connection to a networked device is made.

drop cable. Generally, a cable that connects a network device (such as a computer) to a physical medium. A type of AUI. *See also* AUI.

DS-0. digital signal level 0. A framing specification used in transmitting digital signals over a single channel at 64-kbps on a T1 facility. *Compare with* DS-1 and DS-3.

DS-1. digital signal level 1. A framing specification used in transmitting digital signals at 1.544 Mbps on a T1 facility (in the United States) or at 2.108 Mbps on an E1 facility (in Europe). *Compare with* DS-0 and DS-3.

DS-1 domestic trunk interface. *See* DS-1/DTI.

DS-1/DTI. DS-1 domestic trunk interface. An interface circuit used for DS-1 applications with 24 trunks.

DS-3. digital signal level 3. A framing specification used for transmitting digital signals at 44.736 Mbps on a T3 facility. *Compare with* DS-0 and DS-1. *See also* E3 and T3.

DSAP. destination service access point. The SAP of the network node designated in the Destination field of a packet. *Compare with* SSAP. *See also* SAP (service access point).

DSP. domain-specific part. The part of a CLNS address that contains an area identifier, a station identifier, and a selector byte.

DSPU. downstream physical unit. In SNA, a PU that is located downstream from the host.

DSPU concentration. *See* DSPU and PU.

DSR. data set ready. An EIA/TIA-232 interface circuit that is activated when DCE is powered up and ready for use.

DSU. data service unit. A device used in digital transmission that adapts the physical interface on a DTE device to a transmission facility such as T1 or E1. The DSU is also responsible for functions such as signal timing. Often referred to, together with CSU, as CSU/DSU. *See also* CSU.

DSX-1. A cross-connection point for DS-1 signals.

DTE. data terminal equipment. A device at the user end of a user-network interface that serves as a data source, destination, or both. DTE connects to a data network through a DCE device (for example, a modem) and typically uses clocking signals generated by the DCE. DTE includes devices such as computers, protocol translators, and multiplexers. *Compare with* DCE.

DTMF. dual tone multifrequency. The use of two simultaneous voice-band tones for dialing (such as touch tone).

DTR. data terminal ready. An EIA/TIA-232 circuit that is activated to let the DCE know when the DTE is ready to send and receive data.

DUAL. Diffusing Update Algorithm. A convergence algorithm used in Enhanced IGRP that provides loop-free operation at every instant throughout a route computation. Allows routers involved in a topology change to synchronize at the same time, while not involving routers that are unaffected by the change. *See also* Enhanced IGRP.

dual-attached concentrator. *See* DAC.

dual attachment station. *See* DAS.

dual counter-rotating rings. A network topology in which two signal paths, whose directions are opposite one another, exist in a token-passing network. FDDI and CDDI are based on this concept.

dual-homed station. A device attached to multiple FDDI rings to provide redundancy.

dual homing. A network topology in which a device is connected to the network by way of two independent access points (points of attachment). One access point is the primary connection, and the other is a standby connection that is activated in the event of a failure of the primary connection.

Dual IS-IS. *See* Integrated IS-IS.

dual tone multifrequency. *See* DTMF.

DVMRP. Distance Vector Multicast Routing Protocol. An internetwork gateway protocol, largely based on RIP, that implements a typical dense mode IP multicast scheme. DVMRP uses IGMP to exchange routing datagrams with its neighbors. *See also* IGMP.

DXI. Data Exchange Interface. An ATM Forum specification, described in RFC 1483, that defines how a network device such as a bridge, router, or hub can effectively act as an FEP to an ATM network by interfacing with a special DSU that performs packet segmentation and reassembly.

dynamic address resolution. The use of an address resolution protocol to determine and store address information on demand.

dynamic configuration. *See* discovery mode.

dynamic random-access memory. *See* DRAM.

dynamic routing. Routing that adjusts automatically to network topology or traffic changes. Also called adaptive routing.

E

E1. A wide-area digital transmission scheme used predominantly in Europe that carries data at a rate of 2.048 Mbps. E1 lines can be leased for private use from common carriers. *Compare with* T1. *See also* DS-1.

E.164. An ITU-T recommendation for international telecommunication numbering, especially in ISDN, BISDN, and SMDS. An evolution of standard telephone numbers.

E3. A wide-area digital transmission scheme, used predominantly in Europe, that carries data at a rate of 34.368 Mbps. E3 lines can be leased for private use from common carriers. *Compare with* T3. *See also* DS-3.

early token release. A technique used in Token Ring networks that allows a station to release a new token onto the ring immediately after transmitting, instead of waiting for the first frame to return. This feature can increase the total bandwidth on the ring. *See also* Token Ring.

EARN. European Academic Research Network. A European network connecting universities and research institutes. EARN merged with RARE to form TERENA. *See also* RARE and TERENA.

EBCDIC. extended binary coded decimal interchange code. Any of a number of coded character sets developed by IBM consisting of 8-bit coded characters. This character code is used by older IBM systems and telex machines. *Compare with* ASCII.

E channel. echo channel. A 64-kbps ISDN circuit-switching control channel. The E channel was defined in the 1984 ITU-T ISDN specification, but was dropped in the 1988 specification. *Compare with* B channel, D channel, and H channel.

echo channel. *See* E channel.

echoplex. A mode in which keyboard characters are echoed on a terminal screen upon return of a signal from the other end of the line indicating that the characters were received correctly.

ECMA. European Computer Manufacturers Association. A group of European computer vendors that have done substantial OSI standardization work.

EDI. electronic data interchange. The electronic communication of operational data, such as orders and invoices, between organizations.

EDIFACT. Electronic Data Interchange for Administration, Commerce, and Transport. A data exchange standard administered by the United Nations to be a multi-industry EDI standard.

EEPROM. electrically erasable programmable read-only memory. EPROM that can be erased using electrical signals applied to specific pins. *See also* EPROM.

EGP. Exterior Gateway Protocol. An Internet protocol for exchanging routing information between autonomous systems. Documented in RFC 904. Not to be confused with the general term exterior gateway protocol. EGP is an obsolete protocol that has been replaced by BGP. *See also* BGP.

EIA. Electronic Industries Association. A group that specifies electrical transmission standards. The EIA and TIA have developed numerous well-known communications standards, including EIA/TIA-232 and EIA/TIA-449. *See also* TIA.

EIA-530. Refers to two electrical implementations of EIA/TIA-449: RS-422 (for balanced transmission) and RS-423 (for unbalanced transmission). *See also* RS-422, RS-423, and EIA/TIA-449.

EIA/TIA-232. A common physical layer interface standard, developed by EIA and TIA, that supports unbalanced circuits at signal speeds of up to 64 kbps. Closely resembles the V.24 specification. Formerly known as RS-232.

EIA/TIA-449. A popular physical layer interface developed by EIA and TIA. Essentially, a faster (up to 2 Mbps) version of EIA/TIA-232 capable of longer cable runs. Formerly called RS-449. *See also* EIA-530.

EIA/TIA-586. A standard that describes the characteristics and applications for various grades of UTP cabling. *See also* Category 1 cabling, Category 2 cabling, Category 3 cabling, Category 4 cabling, Category 5 cabling, and UTP.

EIGRP. *See* Enhanced IGRP.

EISA. Extended Industry-Standard Architecture. A 32-bit bus interface used in PCs, PC-based servers, and some UNIX workstations and servers. *See also* ISA.

ELAN. emulated LAN. An ATM network in which an Ethernet or Token Ring LAN is emulated using a client/server model. ELANs are composed of an LEC, an LES, a BUS, and an LECS. Multiple ELANs can exist simultaneously on a single ATM network. ELANs are defined by the LANE specification. *See also* BUS, LANE, LEC, LECS, and LES.

electromagnetic interference. *See* EMI.

electromagnetic pulse. *See* EMP.

electrically erasable programmable read-only memory. *See* EEPROM.

electronic data interchange. *See* EDI.

Electronic Data Interchange for Administration, Commerce, and Transport. *See* EDIFACT.

Electronic Industries Association. *See* EIA.

electronic mail. A widely used network application in which mail messages are transmitted electronically between end users over various types of networks using various network protocols. Often called e-mail.

Electronic Messaging Association. *See* EMA.

electrostatic discharge. *See* ESD.

EMA. 1. Enterprise Management Architecture. A Digital Equipment Corporation network management architecture, based on the OSI network management model. 2. Electronic Messaging Association. A forum devoted to standards and policy work, education, and development of electronic messaging systems such as electronic mail, voice mail, and facsimile.

e-mail. *See* electronic mail.

EMI. electromagnetic interference. Interference by electromagnetic signals that can cause reduced data integrity and increased error rates on transmission channels.

EMIF. ESCON Multiple Image Facility. A mainframe I/O software function that allows one ESCON channel to be shared among multiple logical partitions on the same mainframe. *See also* ESCON.

EMP. electromagnetic pulse. Caused by lightning and other high-energy phenomena. Capable of coupling enough energy into unshielded conductors to destroy electronic devices. *See also* Tempest.

emulated LAN. *See* ELAN.

emulation mode. A function of an NCP that enables it to perform activities equivalent to those performed by a transmission control unit.

EN. end node. An APPN end system that implements the PU 2.1, provides end-user services, and supports sessions between local and remote CPs. ENs are not capable of routing traffic and rely on an adjacent NN for APPN services. *Compare with* NN. *See also* CP.

encapsulation. The wrapping of data in a particular protocol header. For example, Ethernet data is wrapped in a specific Ethernet header before network transit. Also, when bridging dissimilar networks, the entire frame from one network is simply placed in the header used by the data link layer protocol of the other network. *See also* tunneling.

encapsulation bridging. Bridging that carries Ethernet frames from one router to another across disparate media, such as serial and FDDI lines. *Compare with* translational bridging.

encoder. A device that modifies information into the required transmission format.

encryption. The application of a specific algorithm to data so as to alter the appearance of the data, making it incomprehensible to those who are not authorized to see the information. *See also* decryption.

end node. *See* EN.

end of transmission. *See* EOT.

endpoint. A device at which a virtual circuit or virtual path begins or ends.

end system. *See* ES.

End System-to-Intermediate System. *See* ES-IS.

Energy Sciences Network. *See* ESnet.

Enhanced IGRP. Enhanced Interior Gateway Routing Protocol. An advanced version of IGRP developed by Cisco. Provides superior convergence properties and operating efficiency, and combines the advantages of link state protocols with those of distance vector protocols. *Compare with* IGRP. *See also* IGP, OSPF, and RIP.

Enhanced Interior Gateway Routing Protocol. *See* Enhanced IGRP.

Enterprise Management Architecture. *See* EMA.

enterprise network. A large and diverse network connecting most major points in a company or other organization. Differs from a WAN in that it is privately owned and maintained.

Enterprise System Connection. *See* ESCON.

Enterprise System Connection channel. *See* ESCON channel.

entity. Generally, an individual, manageable network device. Sometimes called an alias.

EOT. end of transmission. Generally, a character that signifies the end of a logical group of characters or bits.

EPROM. erasable programmable read-only memory. Nonvolatile memory chips that are programmed after they are manufactured and, if necessary, can be erased by some means and reprogrammed. *Compare with* EEPROM and PROM.

equalization. A technique used to compensate for communications channel distortions.

erasable programmable read-only memory. *See* EPROM.

error control. A technique for detecting and correcting errors in data transmissions.

error-correcting code. A code having sufficient intelligence and incorporating sufficient signaling information to enable the detection and correction of many errors at the receiver.

error-detecting code. A code that can detect transmission errors through analysis of received data based on the adherence of the data to appropriate structural guidelines.

ES. 1. end system. Generally, an end-user device on a network. 2. end system. A nonrouting host or node in an OSI network.

ESCON. Enterprise System Connection. An IBM channel architecture that specifies a pair of fiber-optic cables, with either LEDs or lasers as transmitters and a signaling rate of 200 Mbps.

ESCON channel. An IBM channel for attaching mainframes to peripherals such as storage devices, backup units, and network interfaces. This channel incorporates FibreChannel technology. The ESCON channel replaces the bus and tag channel. *Compare with* parallel channel. *See also* bus and tag channel.

ESCON Multiple Image Facility. *See* EMIF.

ESD. electrostatic discharge. A discharge of stored static electricity that can damage electronic equipment and impair electrical circuitry, resulting in complete or intermittent failures.

ESF. Extended Superframe Format. A framing type used on T1 circuits that consists of 24 frames of 192 bits each, with the 193rd bit providing timing and other functions. ESF is an enhanced version of SF. *See also* SF.

ES-IS. End System-to-Intermediate System. An OSI protocol that defines how end systems (hosts) announce themselves to intermediate systems (routers). *See also* IS-IS.

ESnet. Energy Sciences Network. A data communications network managed and funded by the U.S. Department of Energy Office of Energy Research (DOE/OER). Interconnects the DOE to educational institutions and other research facilities.

Ethernet. A baseband LAN specification invented by Xerox Corporation and developed jointly by Xerox, Intel, and Digital Equipment Corporation. Ethernet networks use CSMA/CD and run over a variety of cable types at 10 Mbps. Ethernet is similar to the IEEE 802.3 series of standards. *See also* 10Base2, 10Base5, 10BaseF, 10BaseT, 10Broad36, and IEEE 802.3.

EtherTalk. AppleTalk protocols running on Ethernet.

ETSI. European Telecommunication Standards Institute. An organization created by the European PTTs and the European Community (EC) to propose telecommunications standards for Europe.

EUnet. European Internet. A European commercial Internet service provider. EUnet is designed to provide electronic mail, news, and other Internet services to European markets.

European Academic Research Network. *See* EARN.

European Computer Manufacturers Association. *See* ECMA.

European Telecommunication Standards Institute. *See* ETSI.

European Internet. *See* EUnet.

event. A network message indicating operational irregularities in physical elements of a network or a response to the occurrence of a significant task, typically the completion of a request for information. *See also* alarm and trap.

Excess Burst. *See* Be.

excess rate. Traffic in excess of the insured rate for a given connection. Specifically, the excess rate equals the maximum rate minus the insured rate. Excess traffic is delivered only if network resources are available and can be discarded during periods of congestion. *Compare with* insured rate and maximum rate.

exchange identification. *See* XID.

EXEC. The interactive command processor of the Cisco IOS software.

expansion. The process of running a compressed data set through an algorithm that restores the data set to its original size. *Compare with* companding and compression.

expedited delivery. An option set by a specific protocol layer telling other protocol layers (or the same protocol layer in another network device) to handle specific data more rapidly.

explicit route. In SNA, a route from a source subarea to a destination subarea, as specified by a list of subarea nodes and transmission groups that connect the two.

explorer frame. A frame sent out by a networked device in a SRB environment to determine the optimal route to another networked device.

explorer packet. A packet generated by an end station trying to find its way through a SRB network. Gathers a hop-by-hop description of a path through the network by being marked (updated) by each bridge that it traverses, thereby creating a complete topological map. *See also* all-routes explorer packet, local explorer packet, and spanning explorer packet.

Extended Binary Coded Decimal Interchange Code. *See* EBCDIC.

Extended Industry-Standard Architecture. *See* EISA.

Extended Superframe Format. *See* ESF.

exterior gateway protocol. Any internetwork protocol used to exchange routing information between autonomous systems. Not to be confused with Exterior Gateway Protocol (EGP), which is a particular instance of an exterior gateway protocol.

Exterior Gateway Protocol. *See* EGP.

exterior router. A router connected to an AURP tunnel, responsible for the encapsulation and deencapsulation of AppleTalk packets in a foreign protocol header (for example, IP). *See also* AURP and AURP tunnel.

F

failure domain. An area in which a failure has occurred in a Token Ring, defined by the information contained in a beacon. When a station detects a serious problem with the network (such as a cable break), it sends a beacon frame that includes the station reporting the failure, its NAUN, and everything in between. Beaconing in turn initiates a process called autoreconfiguration. *See also* autoreconfiguration, beacon, and NAUN.

fan-out unit. A device that allows multiple devices on a network to communicate using a single network attachment.

Fast Ethernet. Any of a number of 100-Mbps Ethernet specifications. Fast Ethernet offers a speed increase 10 times that of the 10BaseT Ethernet specification, while preserving qualities such as frame format, MAC mechanisms, and MTU. Such similarities allow the use of existing 10BaseT applications and network management tools on Fast Ethernet networks. Based on an extension to the IEEE 802.3 specification. *Compare with* Ethernet. *See also* 100BaseFX, 100BaseT, 100BaseT4, 100BaseTX, 100BaseX, and IEEE 802.3.

Fast Sequenced Transport. *See* FST.

fast switching. A Cisco feature whereby a route cache is used to expedite packet switching through a router. *Compare with* slow switching.

fault management. One of five categories of network management defined by ISO for management of OSI networks. Fault management attempts to ensure that network faults are detected and controlled. *See also* accounting management, configuration management, performance management, and security management.

FCC. Federal Communications Commission. A U.S. government agency that supervises, licenses, and controls electronic and electromagnetic transmission standards.

FCS. frame check sequence. The extra characters added to a frame for error control purposes. Used in HDLC, Frame Relay, and other data link layer protocols.

FDDI. Fiber Distributed Data Interface. A LAN standard, defined by ANSI X3T9.5, specifying a 100-Mbps token-passing network using fiber-optic cable, with transmission distances of up to 2 km. FDDI uses a dual-ring architecture to provide redundancy. *Compare with* CDDI and FDDI II.

FDDI II. An ANSI standard that enhances FDDI. FDDI II provides isochronous transmission for connectionless data circuits and connection-oriented voice and video circuits. *Compare with* FDDI.

FDM. frequency-division multiplexing. A technique whereby information from multiple channels can be allocated bandwidth on a single wire based on frequency. *Compare with* ATDM, statistical multiplexing, and TDM.

FECN. forward explicit congestion notification. A bit set by a Frame Relay network to inform DTE receiving the frame that congestion was experienced in the path from source to destination. DTE-receiving frames with the FECN bit set can request that higher-level protocols take flow-control action as appropriate. *Compare with* BECN.

Federal Communications Commission. *See* FCC.

Federal Networking Council. *See* FNC.

FEP. front-end processor. A device or board that provides network interface capabilities for a networked device. In SNA, typically an IBM 3745 device.

Fiber Distributed Data Interface. *See* FDDI.

fiber-optic cable. A physical medium capable of conducting modulated light transmission. Compared with other transmission media, fiber-optic cable is more expensive, but is not susceptible to electromagnetic interference and is capable of higher data rates. Sometimes called optical fiber.

fiber-optic interrepeater link. *See* FOIRL.

FID0. format indicator 0. One of several formats that an SNA TH can use. An FID0 TH is used for communication between an SNA node and a non-SNA node. *See also* TH.

FID1. format indicator 1. One of several formats that an SNA TH can use. An FID1 TH encapsulates messages between two subarea nodes that do not support virtual and explicit routes. *See also* TH.

FID2. format indicator 2. One of several formats that an SNA TH can use. An FID2 TH is used for transferring messages between a subarea node and a PU 2, using local addresses. *See also* TH.

FID3. format indicator 3. One of several formats that an SNA TH can use. An FID3 TH is used for transferring messages between a subarea node and a PU 1, using local addresses. *See also* TH.

FID4. format indicator 4. One of several formats that an SNA TH can use. An FID4 TH encapsulates messages between two subarea nodes that are capable of supporting virtual and explicit routes. *See also* TH.

file transfer. A popular network application that allows files to be moved from one network device to another.

File Transfer, Access, and Management. *See* FTAM.

File Transfer Protocol. *See* FTP.

filter. Generally, a process or device that screens network traffic for certain characteristics, such as source address, destination address, or protocol, and determines whether to forward or discard that traffic based on the established criteria.

firewall. A router or access server, or several routers or access servers, designated as a buffer between any connected public networks and a private network. A firewall router uses access lists and other methods to ensure the security of the private network.

firmware. Software instructions set permanently or semipermanently in ROM.

flapping. A routing problem in which an advertised route between two nodes alternates (flaps) back and forth between two paths due to a network problem that causes intermittent interface failures.

Flash memory. A technology developed by Intel and licensed to other semiconductor companies. Flash memory is nonvolatile storage that can be electrically erased and reprogrammed. Allows software images to be stored, booted, and rewritten as necessary.

flash update. A routing update sent asynchronously in response to a change in the network topology. *Compare with* routing update.

flooding. A traffic-passing technique used by switches and bridges in which traffic received on an interface is sent out all of the interfaces of that device except the interface on which the information was originally received.

flow. A stream of data traveling between two endpoints across a network (for example, from one LAN station to another). Multiple flows can be transmitted on a single circuit.

flow control. A technique for ensuring that a transmitting entity, such as a modem, does not overwhelm a receiving entity with data. When the buffers on the receiving device are full, a message is sent to the sending device to suspend the transmission until the data in the buffers has been processed. In IBM networks, this technique is called pacing.

FM. frequency modulation. A modulation technique in which signals of different frequencies represent different data values. *Compare with* AM and PAM. *See also* modulation.

FNC. Federal Networking Council. A group responsible for assessing and coordinating U.S. federal agency networking policies and needs.

FOIRL. fiber-optic interrepeater link. A fiber-optic signaling methodology based on the IEEE 802.3 fiber-optic specification. FOIRL is a precursor of the 10BaseFL specification, which is designed to replace it. *See also* 10BaseFL.

format indicator 0. *See* FID0.

format indicator 1. *See* FID1.

format indicator 2. *See* FID2.

format indicator 3. *See* FID3.

format indicator 4. *See* FID4.

forward channel. A communications path carrying information from the call initiator to the called party.

forward delay interval. The amount of time an interface spends listening for topology change information after that interface has been activated for bridging and before forwarding actually begins.

forward explicit congestion notification. *See* FECN.

forwarding. The process of sending a frame toward its ultimate destination by way of an internetworking device.

Fourier transform. A technique used to evaluate the importance of various frequency cycles in a time series pattern.

four-part dotted notation. *See* dot address.

fractional T1. *See* channelized T1.

FRAD. Frame Relay access device. Any network device that provides a connection between a LAN and a Frame Relay WAN.

fragment. A piece of a larger packet that has been broken down to smaller units.

fragmentation. The process of breaking a packet into smaller units when transmitting over a network medium that cannot support a packet of the original size. *See also* reassembly.

frame. A logical grouping of information sent as a data link layer unit over a transmission medium. Often refers to the header and trailer, used for synchronization and error control, that surround the user data contained in the unit. The terms datagram, message, packet, and segment are also used to describe logical information groupings at various layers of the OSI reference model and in various technology circles.

frame check sequence. *See* FCS.

Frame Relay. An industry-standard, switched data link layer protocol that handles multiple virtual circuits using HDLC encapsulation between connected devices. Frame Relay is more efficient than X.25, the protocol for which it is generally considered a replacement. *See also* X.25.

Frame Relay Access Device. *See* FRAD.

Frame Relay bridging. A bridging technique, described in RFC 1490, that uses the same spanning-tree algorithm as other bridging functions, but allows packets to be encapsulated for transmission across a Frame Relay network.

frame switch. *See* LAN switch.

free-trade zone. A part of an AppleTalk internetwork that is accessible by two other parts of the internetwork that are unable to directly access one another.

frequency. The number of cycles, measured in hertz, of an alternating current signal per unit time.

frequency-division multiplexing. *See* FDM.

frequency modulation. *See* FM.

front end. A node or software program that requests services of a back end. *See also* back end, client, and server.

front-end processor. *See* FEP.

FST. Fast Sequenced Transport. A connectionless, sequenced transport protocol that runs on top of IP. SRB traffic is encapsulated inside IP datagrams and is passed over an FST connection between two network devices (such as routers). Speeds up data delivery, reduces overhead, and improves the response time of SRB traffic.

FTAM. File Transfer, Access, and Management. In OSI, an application layer protocol developed for network file exchange and management between diverse types of computers.

FTP. File Transfer Protocol. An application protocol, part of the TCP/IP protocol stack, used for transferring files between network nodes. FTP is defined in RFC 959.

full duplex. The capability for simultaneous data transmission between a sending station and a receiving station. *Compare with* half duplex and simplex.

full mesh. A network in which devices are organized in a mesh topology, with each network node having either a physical circuit or a virtual circuit connecting it to every other network node. A full mesh provides a great deal of redundancy, but because it can be prohibitively expensive to implement, it is usually reserved for network backbones. *See also* mesh and partial mesh.

Fuzzball. A Digital Equipment Corporation LSI-11 computer system running IP gateway software. The NSFNET used these systems as backbone packet switches.

G

G.703/G.704. An ITU-T electrical and mechanical specifications for connections between telephone company equipment and DTE using BNC connectors and operating at E1 data rates.

G.804. An ITU-T framing standard that defines the mapping of ATM cells into the physical medium.

gateway. In the IP community, an older term referring to a routing device. Today, the term router is used to describe nodes that perform this function, and gateway refers to a special-purpose device that performs an application layer conversion of information from one protocol stack to another. *Compare with* router.

Gateway Discovery Protocol. *See* GDP.

gateway host. In SNA, a host node that contains a gateway SSCP.

gateway NCP. An NCP that connects two or more SNA networks and performs address translation to allow cross-network session traffic.

Gateway-to-Gateway Protocol. *See* GGP.

GB. gigabyte.

GBps. gigabytes per second.

Gb. gigabit.

Gbps. gigabits per second.

GDP. Gateway Discovery Protocol. A Cisco protocol that allows hosts to dynamically detect the arrival of new routers as well as determine when a router goes down. Based on UDP. *See also* UDP.

generic routing encapsulation. *See* GRE.

Get Nearest Server. *See* GNS.

GGP. Gateway-to-Gateway Protocol. A MILNET protocol specifying how core routers (gateways) should exchange reachability and routing information. GGP uses a distributed shortest-path algorithm.

GHz. gigahertz.

gigabit. Abbreviated Gb.

gigabits per second. Abbreviated Gbps.

gigabyte. Abbreviated GB.

gigabytes per second. Abbreviated GBps.

gigahertz. Abbreviated GHz.

GNS. Get Nearest Server. A request packet sent by a client on an IPX network to locate the nearest active server of a particular type. An IPX network client issues a GNS request to solicit either a direct response from a connected server or a response from a router that tells it where on the internetwork the service can be located. GNS is part of the IPX SAP. *See also* IPX and SAP (Service Advertisement Protocol).

GOSIP. Government OSI Profile. A U.S. government procurement specification for OSI protocols. Through GOSIP, the government has mandated that all federal agencies standardize on OSI and implement OSI-based systems as they become commercially available.

Government OSI Profile. *See* GOSIP.

grade of service. A measure of telephone service quality based on the probability that a call will encounter a busy signal during the busiest hours of the day.

graphical user interface. *See* GUI.

GRE. generic routing encapsulation. A tunneling protocol developed by Cisco that can encapsulate a wide variety of protocol packet types inside IP tunnels, creating a virtual point-to-point link to Cisco routers at remote points over an IP internetwork. By connecting multiprotocol subnetworks in a single-protocol backbone environment, IP tunneling using GRE allows network expansion across a single-protocol backbone environment.

ground station. A collection of communications equipment designed to receive signals from (and usually transmit signals to) satellites. Also called a downlink station.

group address. *See* multicast address.

group delay. *See* distortion delay.

guard band. An UNUSED frequency band between two communications channels that provides separation of the channels to prevent mutual interference.

GUI. graphical user interface. A user environment that uses pictorial as well as textual representations of the input and output of applications and the hierarchical or other data structure in which information is stored. Use of conventions such as buttons, icons, and windows are typical, and many actions are performed using a pointing device (such as a mouse). Microsoft Windows and the Apple Macintosh are prominent examples of platforms utilizing a GUI.

H

half duplex. The capability for data transmission in only one direction at a time between a sending station and a receiving station. *Compare with* full duplex and simplex.

handshake. A sequence of messages exchanged between two or more network devices to ensure transmission synchronization.

hardware address. *See* MAC address.

HBD3. A line code type used on E1 circuits.

H channel. high-speed channel. A full-duplex ISDN primary rate channel operating at 384 kbps. *Compare with* B channel, D channel, and E channel.

HDLC. High-Level Data Link Control. A bit-oriented synchronous data link layer protocol developed by ISO. Derived from SDLC, HDLC specifies a data encapsulation method on synchronous serial links using frame characters and checksums. *See also* SDLC.

headend. The endpoint of a broadband network. All stations transmit toward the headend; the headend then transmits toward the destination stations.

header. Control information placed before data when encapsulating that data for network transmission. *Compare with* trailer. *See also* PCI.

heartbeat. *See* SQE.

HELLO. An interior routing protocol used principally by NSFNET nodes. HELLO allows particular packet switches to discover minimal delay routes. Not to be confused with the Hello protocol.

hello packet. A multicast packet that is used by routers for neighbor discovery and recovery. Hello packets also indicate that a client is still operating and network ready.

Hello protocol. A protocol used by OSPF systems for establishing and maintaining neighbor relationships. Not to be confused with HELLO.

helper address. An address configured on an interface to which broadcasts received on that interface will be sent.

HEPnet. High-Energy Physics Network. A research network that originated in the United States, but that has spread to most places involved in high-energy physics. Well-known sites include Argonne National Laboratory, Brookhaven National Laboratory, Lawrence Berkeley Laboratory, and the Stanford Linear Accelerator Center.

hertz. A measure of frequency, abbreviated Hz. Synonymous with cycles per second.

heterogeneous network. A network consisting of dissimilar devices that run dissimilar protocols and in many cases support dissimilar functions or applications.

hierarchical routing. Routing based on a hierarchical addressing system. For example, IP routing algorithms use IP addresses, which contain network numbers, subnet numbers, and host numbers.

High-Energy Physics Network. *See* HEPnet.

High-Level Data Link Control. *See* HDLC.

High-Performance Computing and Communications. *See* HPCC.

High-Performance Computing Systems. *See* HPCS.

High-Performance Parallel Interface. *See* HIPPI.

High-Performance Routing. *See* HPR.

High-Speed Serial Interface. *See* HSSI.

highway. *See* bus.

HIPPI. High-Performance Parallel Interface. A high-performance interface standard defined by ANSI. HIPPI is typically used to connect supercomputers to peripherals and other devices.

holddown. A state into which a route is placed so that routers will neither advertise the route nor accept advertisements about the route for a specific length of time (the holddown period). Holddown is used to flush bad information about a route from all routers in the network. A route is typically placed in holddown when a link in that route fails.

homologation. Conformity of a product or specification to international standards, such as ITU-T, CSA, TUV, UL, or VCCI. Enables portability across company and international boundaries.

hop. The passage of a data packet between two network nodes (for example, between two routers). *See also* hop count.

hop count. A routing metric used to measure the distance between a source and a destination. RIP uses hop count as its sole metric. *See also* hop and RIP.

host. A computer system on a network. Similar to the term node except that host usually implies a computer system, whereas node generally applies to any networked system, including access servers and routers. *See also* node.

host address. *See* host number.

host node. An SNA subarea node that contains an SSCP.

host number. Part of an IP address that designates which node on the subnetwork is being addressed. Also called a host address.

Hot Standby Router Protocol. *See* HSRP.

HPCC. High-Performance Computing and Communications. A U.S. government funded program advocating advances in computing, communications, and related fields. The HPCC is designed to ensure U.S. leadership in these fields through education, research and development, industry collaboration, and implementation of high-performance technology. The five components of the HPCC are ASTA, BRHR, HPCS, IITA, and NREN.

HPCS. High-Performance Computing Systems. A component of the HPCC program designed to ensure U.S. technological leadership in high-performance computing through research and development of computing systems and related software. *See also* HPCC.

HPR. High-Performance Routing. A second-generation routing algorithm for APPN. HPR provides a connectionless layer with nondisruptive routing of sessions around link failures, and a connection-oriented layer with end-to-end flow control, error control, and sequencing. Compare with ISR. *See also* APPN.

HSRP. Hot Standby Router Protocol. A protocol that provides high network availability and transparent network topology changes. HSRP creates a Hot Standby router group with a lead router that services all packets sent to the Hot Standby address. The lead router is monitored by other routers in the group, and if it fails, one of these standby routers inherits the lead position and the Hot Standby group address.

HSSI. High-Speed Serial Interface. A network standard for high-speed (up to 52 Mbps) serial connections over WAN links.

HTML. hypertext markup language. A simple hypertext document formatting language that uses tags to indicate how a given part of a document should be interpreted by a viewing application, such as a WWW browser. *See also* hypertext and WWW browser.

hub. 1. Generally, a device that serves as the center of a star-topology network. 2. A hardware or software device that contains multiple independent but connected modules of network and internetwork equipment. Hubs can be active (where they repeat signals sent through them) or passive (where they do not repeat, but merely split, signals sent through them). 3. In Ethernet and IEEE 802.3, an Ethernet multiport repeater, sometimes referred to as a concentrator.

hybrid network. An internetwork made up of more than one type of network technology, including LANs and WANs.

hypertext. Electronically stored text that allows direct access to other texts by way of encoded links. Hypertext documents can be created using HTML, and often integrate images, sound, and other media that are commonly viewed using a WWW browser. *See also* HTML and WWW browser.

hypertext markup language. *See* HTML.

Hz. *See* hertz.

I

IAB. Internet Architecture Board. A board of internetwork researchers who discuss issues pertinent to Internet architecture. Responsible for appointing a variety of Internet-related groups such as IANA, IESG, and IRSG. The IAB is appointed by the trustees of ISOC. *See also* IANA, IESG, IRSG, and ISOC.

IANA. Internet Assigned Numbers Authority. An organization operated under the auspices of ISOC as a part of IAB. IANA delegates authority for IP address-space allocation and domain-name assignment to the NIC and other organizations. IANA also maintains a database of assigned protocol identifiers used in the TCP/IP stack, including autonomous system numbers. *See also* IAB, ISOC, and NIC.

ICD. International Code Designator. One of two ATM address formats developed by the ATM Forum for use by private networks. Adapted from the subnetwork model of addressing in which the ATM layer is responsible for mapping network layer addresses to ATM addresses. *See also* DCC.

ICMP. Internet Control Message Protocol. A network layer Internet protocol that reports errors and provides other information relevant to IP packet processing. Documented in RFC 792.

ICMP Router Discovery Protocol. *See* IRDP.

IDI. initial domain identifier. In OSI, the portion of the NSAP that specifies the domain.

IDN. international data number. *See* X.121.

IDP. initial domain part. The part of a CLNS address that contains an authority and format identifier and a domain identifier.

IDPR. Interdomain Policy Routing. An interdomain routing protocol that dynamically exchanges policies between autonomous systems. IDPR encapsulates interautonomous system traffic and routes it according to the policies of each autonomous system along the path. IDPR is currently an IETF proposal. *See also* policy routing.

IDRP. IS-IS Interdomain Routing Protocol. An OSI protocol that specifies how routers communicate with routers in different domains.

IEC. International Electrotechnical Commission. An industry group that writes and distributes standards for electrical products and components.

IEEE. Institute of Electrical and Electronics Engineers. A professional organization whose activities include the development of communications and network standards. IEEE LAN standards are the predominant LAN standards today.

IEEE 802.1. An IEEE specification which describes an algorithm that prevents bridging loops by creating a spanning tree. The algorithm was invented by Digital Equipment Corporation. The Digital algorithm and the IEEE 802.1 algorithm are not exactly the same, nor are they compatible. *See also* spanning tree, spanning-tree algorithm, and Spanning-Tree Protocol.

IEEE 802.12. An IEEE LAN standard that specifies the physical layer and the MAC sublayer of the data link layer. IEEE 802.12 uses the demand priority media-access scheme at 100 Mbps over a variety of physical media. *See also* 100VG-AnyLAN.

IEEE 802.2. An IEEE LAN protocol that specifies an implementation of the LLC sublayer of the data link layer. IEEE 802.2 handles errors, framing, flow control, and the network layer (Layer 3) service interface. Used in IEEE 802.3 and IEEE 802.5 LANs. *See also* IEEE 802.3 and IEEE 802.5.

IEEE 802.3. An IEEE LAN protocol that specifies an implementation of the physical layer and the MAC sublayer of the data link layer. IEEE 802.3 uses CSMA/CD access at a variety of speeds over a variety of physical media. Extensions to the IEEE 802.3 standard specify implementations for Fast Ethernet. Physical variations of the original IEEE 802.3 specification include 10Base2, 10Base5, 10BaseF, 10BaseT, and 10Broad36. Physical variations for Fast Ethernet include 100BaseT, 100BaseT4, and 100BaseX.

IEEE 802.4. An IEEE LAN protocol that specifies an implementation of the physical layer and the MAC sublayer of the data link layer. IEEE 802.4 uses token-passing access over a bus topology and is based on the token bus LAN architecture. *See also* token bus.

IEEE 802.5. An IEEE LAN protocol that specifies an implementation of the physical layer and MAC sublayer of the data link layer. IEEE 802.5 uses token passing access at 4 or 16 Mbps over STP cabling and is similar to IBM Token Ring. *See also* Token Ring.

IEEE 802.6. An IEEE MAN specification based on DQDB technology. IEEE 802.6 supports data rates of 1.5 to 155 Mbps. *See also* DQDB.

IESG. Internet Engineering Steering Group. An organization, appointed by the IAB, that manages the operation of the IETF. *See also* IAB and IETF.

IETF. Internet Engineering Task Force. A task force consisting of more than 80 working groups responsible for developing Internet standards. The IETF operates under the auspices of ISOC. *See also* ISOC.

IFIP. International Federation for Information Processing. A research organization that performs OSI prestandardization work. Among other accomplishments, IFIP formalized the original MHS model. *See also* MHS.

IGMP. Internet Group Management Protocol. A protocol used by IP hosts to report their multicast group memberships to an adjacent multicast router. *See also* multicast router.

IGP. Interior Gateway Protocol. An Internet protocol used to exchange routing information within an autonomous system. Examples of common Internet IGPs include IGRP, OSPF, and RIP. *See also* IGRP, OSPF, and RIP.

IGRP. Interior Gateway Routing Protocol. An IGP developed by Cisco to address the problems associated with routing in large, heterogeneous networks. *Compare with* Enhanced IGRP. *See also* IGP, OSPF, and RIP.

IIH. IS-IS Hello. A message sent by all IS-IS systems to maintain adjacencies. *See also* IS-IS.

IITA. Information Infrastructure Technology and Applications. A component of the HPCC program intended to ensure U.S. leadership in the development of advanced information technologies. *See also* HPCC.

ILMI. Interim Local Management Interface. A specification developed by the ATM Forum for incorporating network-management capabilities into the ATM UNI.

IMP. interface message processor. An old name for ARPANET packet switches. An IMP is now referred to as a PSN (packet-switching node). *See also* PSN (packet-switching node).

in-band signaling. A transmission within a frequency range normally used for information transmission. *Compare with* out-of-band signaling.

Industry-Standard Architecture. *See* ISA.

Information Infrastructure Technology and Applications. *See* IITA.

infrared. Electromagnetic waves whose frequency range is above that of microwaves, but below that of the visible spectrum. LAN systems based on this technology represent an emerging technology.

initial domain identifier. *See* IDI.

initial domain part. *See* IDP.

INOC. Internet Network Operations Center. A BBN group that in the early days of the Internet monitored and controlled the Internet core gateways (routers). INOC no longer exists in this form.

input/output. *See* I/O.

Institute of Electrical and Electronics Engineers. *See* IEEE.

insured burst. The largest burst of data above the insured rate that is temporarily allowed on a PVC and not tagged by the traffic policing function for dropping in the case of network congestion. The insured burst is specified in bytes or cells. *Compare with* maximum burst. *See also* insured rate.

insured rate. The long-term data throughput, in bits or cells per second, that an ATM network commits to support under normal network conditions. The insured rate is 100 percent allocated; the entire amount is deducted from the total trunk bandwidth along the path of the circuit. *Compare with* excess rate and maximum rate. *See also* insured burst.

insured traffic. Traffic within the insured rate specified for the PVC. This traffic should not be dropped by the network under normal network conditions. *See also* CLP and insured rate.

Integrated IS-IS. A routing protocol based on the OSI routing protocol IS-IS, but with support for IP and other protocols. Integrated IS-IS implementations send only one set of routing updates, making it more efficient than two separate implementations. Formerly referred to as Dual IS-IS. *Compare with* IS-IS.

Integrated Services Digital Network. *See* ISDN.

interarea routing. Term used to describe routing between two or more logical areas. *Compare with* intra-area routing.

Interdomain Policy Routing. *See* IDPR.

interface. 1. A connection between two systems or devices. 2. In routing terminology, a network connection. 3. In telephony, a shared boundary defined by common physical interconnection characteristics, signal characteristics, and meanings of interchanged signals. 4. The boundary between adjacent layers of the OSI model.

interface message processor. *See* IMP.

interference. Unwanted communication channel noise.

Interim Local Management Interface. *See* ILMI.

Interior Gateway Protocol. *See* IGP.

Interior Gateway Routing Protocol. *See* IGRP.

intermediate routing node. *See* IRN.

Intermediate Session Routing. *See* ISR.

intermediate system. *See* IS.

Intermediate System-to-Intermediate System. *See* IS-IS.

International Code Designator. *See* ICD.

International Data Number. *See* X.121.

International Electrotechnical Commission. *See* IEC.

International Federation for Information Processing. *See* IFIP.

International Organization for Standardization. *See* ISO.

International Standards Organization. An erroneous expansion of the acronym ISO. *See* ISO.

International Telecommunication Union Telecommunication Standardization Sector. *See* ITU-T.

Internet. A term that refers to the largest global internetwork, connecting tens of thousands of networks worldwide and having a "culture" that focuses on research and standardization based on real-life use. Many leading-edge network technologies come from the Internet community. The Internet evolved in part from ARPANET. At one time, called the DARPA Internet. Not to be confused with the general term internet. *See also* ARPANET.

internet. Short for internetwork. Not to be confused with the Internet. *See* internetwork.

Internet Architecture Board. *See* IAB.

Internet address. *See* IP address.

Internet Assigned Numbers Authority. *See* IANA.

Internet Control Message Protocol. *See* ICMP.

Internet Engineering Steering Group. *See* IESG.

Internet Engineering Task Force. *See* IETF.

Internet Group Management Protocol. *See* IGMP.

Internet Network Operations Center. *See* INOC.

Internet Protocol. *See* IP.

Internet protocol. Any protocol that is part of the TCP/IP protocol stack. *See* TCP/IP.

Internet Research Steering Group. *See* IRSG.

Internet Research Task Force. *See* IRTF.

Internet Society. *See* ISOC.

internetwork. A collection of networks interconnected by routers and other devices that functions (generally) as a single network. Sometimes called an internet, which is not to be confused with the Internet.

internetworking. The industry that has arisen around the problem of connecting networks together. The term can refer to products, procedures, and technologies.

Internetwork Packet Exchange. *See* IPX.

interoperability. The capability of computing equipment manufactured by different vendors to communicate with one another successfully over a network.

Inter-Switching System Interface. *See* ISSI.

intra-area routing. Routing within a logical area. *Compare with* interarea routing.

Inverse Address Resolution Protocol. *See* Inverse ARP.

Inverse ARP. Inverse Address Resolution Protocol. A method of building dynamic routes in a network. Allows an access server to discover the network address of a device associated with a virtual circuit.

I/O. input/output.

IP. Internet Protocol. A network layer protocol in the TCP/IP stack offering a connectionless internetwork service. IP provides features for addressing, type-of-service specification, fragmentation and reassembly, and security. Documented in RFC 791.

IP address. A 32-bit address assigned to hosts using TCP/IP. An IP address belongs to one of five classes (A, B, C, D, or E) and is written as four octets separated with periods (dotted decimal format). Each address consists of a network number, an optional subnetwork number, and a host number. The network and subnetwork numbers together are used for routing, and the host number is used to address an individual host within the network or subnetwork. A subnet mask is used to extract network and subnetwork information from the IP address. Also called an Internet address. *See also* IP and subnet mask.

IP multicast. A routing technique that allows IP traffic to be propagated from one source to a number of destinations or from many sources to many destinations. Rather than send one packet to each destination, one packet is sent to a multicast group identified by a single IP destination group address.

IP Security Option. *See* IPSO.

IPSO. IP Security Option. A U.S. government specification that defines an optional field in the IP packet header that defines hierarchical packet security levels on a per-interface basis.

IPX. Internetwork Packet Exchange. A NetWare network layer (Layer 3) protocol used for transferring data from servers to workstations. IPX is similar to IP and XNS.

IPXWAN. A protocol that negotiates end-to-end options for new links. When a link comes up, the first IPX packets sent across are IPXWAN packets negotiating the options for the link. When the IPXWAN options have been successfully determined, normal IPX transmission begins. Defined by RFC 1362.

IRDP. ICMP Router Discovery Protocol. A protocol that enables a host to determine the address of a router that it can use as a default gateway. Similar to ES-IS, but used with IP. *See also* ES-IS.

IRN. intermediate routing node. In SNA, a subarea node with intermediate routing capability.

IRSG. Internet Research Steering Group. A group that is part of the IAB and oversees the activities of the IRTF. *See also* IAB and IRTF.

IRTF. Internet Research Task Force. A community of network experts that consider Internet-related research topics. The IRTF is governed by the IRSG and is considered a subsidiary of the IAB. *See also* IAB and IRSG.

IS. intermediate system. A routing node in an OSI network.

ISA. Industry-Standard Architecture. A 16-bit bus used for Intel-based personal computers. *See also* EISA.

isarithmic flow control. A flow control technique in which permits travel through the network. Possession of these permits grants the right to transmit. Isarithmic flow control is not commonly implemented.

ISDN. Integrated Services Digital Network. A communication protocol, offered by telephone companies, that permits telephone networks to carry data, voice, and other source traffic. *See also* BISDN, BRI, N-ISDN, and PRI.

IS-IS. Intermediate System-to-Intermediate System. An OSI link-state hierarchical routing protocol based on DECnet Phase V routing whereby ISs (routers) exchange routing information based on a single metric to determine network topology. *Compare with* Integrated IS-IS. *See also* ES-IS and OSPF.

IS-IS Hello. *See* IIH.

IS-IS Interdomain Routing Protocol. *See* IDRP.

ISO. International Organization for Standardization. An international organization that is responsible for a wide range of standards, including those relevant to networking. ISO developed the OSI reference model, a popular networking reference model.

ISO 3309. HDLC procedures developed by ISO. ISO 3309:1979 specifies the HDLC frame structure for use in synchronous environments. ISO 3309:1984 specifies proposed modifications to allow the use of HDLC in asynchronous environments as well.

ISO 9000. A set of international quality-management standards defined by ISO. The standards, which are not specific to any country, industry, or product, allow companies to demonstrate that they have specific processes in place to maintain an efficient quality system.

ISOC. Internet Society. An international nonprofit organization, founded in 1992, that coordinates the evolution and use of the Internet. In addition, ISOC delegates authority to other groups related to the Internet, such as the IAB. ISOC is headquartered in Reston, Virginia. *See also* IAB.

isochronous transmission. An asynchronous transmission over a synchronous data link. Isochronous signals require a constant bit rate for reliable transport. *Compare with* asynchronous transmission, plesiochronous transmission, and synchronous transmission.

ISODE. ISO development environment. A large set of libraries and utilities used to develop upper-layer OSI protocols and applications.

ISO development environment. *See* ISODE.

ISP. Internet service provider. A company that provides Internet access to other companies and individuals.

ISR. Intermediate Session Routing. An initial routing algorithm used in APPN. ISR provides node-to-node connection-oriented routing. Network outages cause sessions to fail because ISR cannot provide nondisruptive rerouting around a failure. ISR has been replaced by HPR. *Compare with* HPR. *See also* APPN.

ISSI. Inter-Switching System Interface. A standard interface between SMDS switches.

ITU-T. International Telecommunication Union Telecommunication Standardization Sector. An international body that develops worldwide standards for telecommunications technologies. The ITU-T carries out the functions of the former CCITT. *See also* CCITT.

J

jabber. 1. An error condition in which a network device continually transmits random, meaningless data onto the network. 2. In IEEE 802.3, a data packet whose length exceeds that prescribed in the standard.

JANET. Joint Academic Network. An X.25 WAN connecting university and research institutions in the United Kingdom.

Japan UNIX Network. *See* JUNET.

jitter. An analog communication line distortion caused by the variation of a signal from its reference timing positions. Jitter can cause data loss, particularly at high speeds.

John von Neumann Computer Network. *See* JvNCnet.

Joint Academic Network. *See* JANET.

jumper. An electrical switch consisting of a number of pins and a connector that can be attached to the pins in a variety of different ways. Different circuits are created by attaching the connector to different pins.

JUNET. Japan UNIX Network. A nationwide, noncommercial network in Japan, designed to promote communication between Japanese and other researchers.

JvNCnet. John von Neumann Computer Network. A regional network, owned and operated by Global Enterprise Services, Inc., composed of T1 and slower serial links, providing midlevel networking services to sites in the Northeastern United States.

K

Karn's algorithm. An algorithm that improves round-trip time estimations by helping transport layer protocols distinguish between good and bad round-trip time samples.

KB. kilobyte.

Kb. kilobit.

Kbps. kilobits per second.

keepalive interval. The period of time between each keepalive message sent by a network device.

keepalive message. A message sent by one network device to inform another network device that the virtual circuit between the two is still active.

Kermit. A popular file-transfer and terminal-emulation program.

kilobit. Abbreviated Kb.

kilobits per second. Abbreviated kbps.

kilobyte. Abbreviated KB.

L

L2F Protocol. Layer 2 Forwarding Protocol. A protocol that supports the creation of secure virtual private dial-up networks over the Internet.

label swapping. A routing algorithm used by APPN in which each router that a message passes through on its way to its destination independently determines the best path to the next router.

LAN. local-area network. A high-speed, low-error data network covering a relatively small geographic area (up to a few thousand meters). LANs connect workstations, peripherals, terminals, and other devices in a single building or other geographically limited area. LAN standards specify cabling and signaling at the physical and data link layers of the OSI model. Ethernet, FDDI, and Token Ring are widely used LAN technologies. *Compare with* MAN and WAN.

LANE. LAN emulation. A technology that allows an ATM network to function as a LAN backbone. The ATM network must provide multicast and broadcast support, address mapping (MAC-to-ATM), SVC management, and a usable packet format. LANE also defines Ethernet and Token Ring ELANs. *See also* ELAN.

LAN emulation. *See* LANE.

LAN Emulation Client. *See* LEC.

LAN Emulation Configuration Server. *See* LECS.

LAN Emulation Server. *See* LES.

LAN Manager. Distributed NOS, developed by Microsoft, that supports a variety of protocols and platforms.

LAN Manager for UNIX. *See* LM/X.

LAN Network Manager. *See* LNM.

LAN Server. A server-based NOS developed by IBM and derived from LNM. *See also* LNM.

LAN switch. A high-speed switch that forwards packets between data-link segments. Most LAN switches forward traffic based on MAC addresses. This variety of LAN switch is sometimes called a frame switch. LAN switches are often categorized according to the method they use to forward traffic: cut-through packet switching or store-and-forward packet switching. Multilayer switches are an intelligent subset of LAN switches. *Compare with* multilayer switch. *See also* cut-through packet switching and store and forward packet switching.

LAPB. Link Access Procedure, Balanced. A data link layer protocol in the X.25 protocol stack. LAPB is a bit-oriented protocol derived from HDLC. *See also* HDLC and X.25.

LAPD. Link Access Procedure on the D channel. An ISDN data link layer protocol for the D channel. LAPD was derived from the LAPB protocol and is designed primarily to satisfy the signaling requirements of ISDN basic access. Defined by ITU-T Recommendations Q.920 and Q.921.

LAPM. Link Access Procedure for Modems. An ARQ used by modems implementing the V.42 protocol for error correction. *See also* ARQ and V.42.

laser. light amplification by stimulated emission of radiation. An analog transmission device in which a suitable active material is excited by an external stimulus to produce a narrow beam of coherent light that can be modulated into pulses to carry data. Networks based on laser technology are sometimes run over SONET.

LAT. local-area transport. A network virtual terminal protocol developed by Digital Equipment Corporation.

LATA. local access and transport area. A geographic telephone dialing area serviced by a single local telephone company. Calls within LATAs are called *local calls*. There are well over 100 LATAs in the United States.

latency. 1. The delay between the time a device requests access to a network and the time it is granted permission to transmit. 2. The delay between the time a device receives a frame and the time the frame is forwarded out the destination port.

LCI. logical channel identifier. *See* VCN.

LCN. logical channel number. *See* VCN.

leaf internetwork. In a star topology, an internetwork whose sole access to other internetworks in the star is through a core router.

learning bridge. A bridge that performs MAC address learning to reduce traffic on the network. Learning bridges manage a database of MAC addresses and the interfaces associated with each address. *See also* MAC address learning.

leased line. A transmission line reserved by a communications carrier for the private use of a customer. A leased line is a type of dedicated line. *See also* dedicated line.

LEC. 1. LAN Emulation Client. An entity in an end system that performs data forwarding, address resolution, and other control functions for a single ES within a single ELAN. A LEC also provides a standard LAN service interface to any higher-layer entity that interfaces to the LEC. Each LEC is identified by a unique ATM address, and is associated with one or more MAC addresses reachable through that ATM address. *See also* ELAN and LES. 2. local exchange carrier. A local or regional telephone company that owns and operates a telephone network and the customer lines that connect to it.

LECS. LAN Emulation Configuration Server. An entity that assigns individual LANE clients to particular ELANs by directing them to the LES that corresponds to the ELAN. There is logically one LECS per administrative domain, and this serves all ELANs within that domain. *See also* ELAN.

LED. light emitting diode. A semiconductor device that emits light produced by converting electrical energy. Status lights on hardware devices are typically LEDs.

LEN node. low-entry networking node. In SNA, a PU 2.1 that supports LU protocols, but whose CP cannot communicate with other nodes. Because there is no CP-to-CP session between a LEN node and its NN, the LEN node must have a statically defined image of the APPN network.

LES. LAN Emulation Server. An entity that implements the control function for a particular ELAN. There is only one logical LES per ELAN, and it is identified by a unique ATM address. *See also* ELAN.

Level 1 router. A device that routes traffic within a single DECnet or OSI area.

Level 2 router. A device that routes traffic between DECnet or OSI areas. All Level 2 routers must form a contiguous network.

light amplification by stimulated emission of radiation. *See* laser.

light emitting diode. *See* LED.

limited resource link. A resource defined by a device operator to remain active only when being used.

limited-route explorer packet. *See* spanning explorer packet.

line. 1. In SNA, a connection to the network. 2. *See* link.

line code type. One of a number of coding schemes used on serial lines to maintain data integrity and reliability. The line code type used is determined by the carrier service provider. *See also* AMI and HBD3.

line conditioning. The use of equipment on leased voice-grade channels to improve analog characteristics, thereby allowing higher transmission rates.

line driver. An inexpensive amplifier and signal converter that conditions digital signals to ensure reliable transmissions over extended distances.

line of sight. A characteristic of certain transmission systems, such as laser, microwave, and infrared systems, in which no obstructions in a direct path between transmitter and receiver can exist.

line printer daemon. *See* LPD.

line turnaround. The time required to change data transmission direction on a telephone line.

link. A network communications channel consisting of a circuit or transmission path and all related equipment between a sender and a receiver. Most often used to refer to a WAN connection. Sometimes referred to as a line or a transmission link.

Link Access Procedure, Balanced. *See* LAPB.

Link Access Procedure for Modems. *See* LAPM.

Link Access Procedure on the D channel. *See* LAPD.

link layer. *See* data link layer.

link-layer address. *See* MAC address.

link-state advertisement. *See* LSA.

link-state packet. *See* LSA.

link state routing algorithm. A routing algorithm in which each router broadcasts or multicasts information regarding the cost of reaching each of its neighbors to all nodes in the internetwork. Link state algorithms create a consistent view of the network and are therefore not prone to routing loops, but they achieve this at the cost of relatively greater computational difficulty and more widespread traffic (compared with distance vector routing algorithms). *Compare with* distance vector routing algorithm. *See also* Dijkstra's algorithm.

little-endian. A method of storing or transmitting data in which the least significant bit or byte is presented first. *Compare with* big-endian.

LLC. Logical Link Control. The higher of the two data link layer sublayers defined by the IEEE. The LLC sublayer handles error control, flow control, framing, and MAC-sublayer addressing. The most prevalent LLC protocol is IEEE 802.2, which includes both connectionless and connection-oriented variants. *See also* data link layer and MAC.

LLC2. Logical Link Control, type 2. A connection-oriented OSI LLC-sublayer protocol. *See also* LLC.

LMI. Local Management Interface. A set of enhancements to the basic Frame Relay specification. LMI includes support for a keepalive mechanism, which verifies that data is flowing; a multicast mechanism, which provides the network server with its local DLCI and the multicast DLCI; global addressing, which gives DLCIs global rather than local significance in Frame Relay networks; and a status mechanism, which provides an ongoing status report on the DLCIs known to the switch. Known as LMT in ANSI terminology.

LMT. *See* LMI.

LM/X. LAN Manager for UNIX. A monitor of LAN devices in UNIX environments.

LNM . LAN Network Manager. An SRB and Token Ring management package provided by IBM. It typically runs on a PC, and it monitors SRB and Token Ring devices and can pass alerts up to NetView.

load balancing . In routing, the ability of a router to distribute traffic over all its network ports that are the same distance from the destination address. Good load-balancing algorithms use both line speed and reliability information. Load balancing increases the utilization of network segments, thus increasing effective network bandwidth.

local access and transport area. *See* LATA.

local acknowledgment . A method whereby an intermediate network node, such as a router, responds to acknowledgments for a remote end host. Use of local acknowledgments reduces network overhead and, therefore, the risk of time-outs. Also known as local termination.

local-area network. *See* LAN.

local-area transport. *See* LAT.

local bridge. A bridge that directly interconnects networks in the same geographic area.

local exchange carrier. *See* LEC.

local explorer packet. A packet generated by an end system in an SRB network to find a host connected to the local ring. If the local explorer packet fails to find a local host, the end system produces either a spanning explorer packet or an all-routes explorer packet. *See also* all-routes explorer packet, explorer packet, and spanning explorer packet.

local loop. A line from the premises of a telephone subscriber to the telephone company CO.

Local Management Interface. *See* LMI.

LocalTalk. An Apple proprietary baseband protocol that operates at the data link and physical layers of the OSI reference model. LocalTalk uses CSMA/CD media access scheme and supports transmissions at speeds of 230 kbps.

local termination. *See* local acknowledgment.

local traffic filtering. A process by which a bridge filters out (drops) frames whose source and destination MAC addresses are located on the same interface on the bridge, thus preventing unnecessary traffic from being forwarded across the bridge. Defined in the IEEE 802.1 standard. *See also* IEEE 802.1.

logical address. *See* network address.

logical channel. A nondedicated, packet-switched communications path between two or more network nodes. Packet switching allows many logical channels to exist simultaneously on a single physical channel.

logical channel identifier. *See* LCI.

logical channel number. *See* LCN.

Logical Link Control. *See* LLC.

Logical Link Control, type 2. *See* LLC2.

logical unit. *See* LU.

Logical Unit 6.2. *See* LU 6.2.

loop. A route in which packets never reach their destination, but simply cycle repeatedly through a constant series of network nodes.

loopback test. A test in which signals are sent and then directed back toward their source from some point along the communications path. Loopback tests are often used to test network interface usability.

lossy. A characteristic of a network that is prone to lose packets when it becomes highly loaded.

low-entry networking node. *See* LEN node.

LPD. line printer daemon. A protocol used to send print jobs between UNIX systems.

LSA. link-state advertisement. A broadcast packet used by link-state protocols that contains information about neighbors and path costs. LSAs are used by the receiving routers to maintain their routing tables. Sometimes called a link-state packet (LSP).

LSP. link-state packet. *See* LSA.

LU. logical unit. A primary component of SNA, an LU is an NAU that enables end users to communicate with each other and gain access to SNA network resources.

LU 6.2. Logical Unit 6.2. In SNA, an LU that provides peer-to-peer communication between programs in a distributed computing environment. APPC runs on LU 6.2 devices. *See also* APPC.

M

MAC. Media Access Control. The lower of the two sublayers of the data link layer defined by the IEEE. The MAC sublayer handles access to shared media, such as whether token passing or contention will be used. *See also* data link layer and LLC.

MAC address. A standardized data link layer address that is required for every port or device that connects to a LAN. Other devices in the network use these addresses to locate specific ports in the network and to create and update routing tables and data structures. MAC addresses are 6 bytes long and are controlled by the IEEE. Also known as a hardware address, a MAC-layer address, or a physical address. *Compare with* network address.

MAC address learning. A service that characterizes a learning bridge, in which the source MAC address of each received packet is stored so that future packets destined for that address can be forwarded only to the bridge interface on which that address is located. Packets destined for unrecognized addresses are forwarded out every bridge interface. This scheme helps minimize traffic on the attached LANs. MAC address learning is defined in the IEEE 802.1 standard. *See also* learning bridge and MAC address.

MacIP. A network layer protocol that encapsulates IP packets in DDS or transmission over AppleTalk. MacIP also provides proxy ARP services.

MAC-layer address. *See* MAC address.

Maintenance Operation Protocol. *See* MOP.

MAN. metropolitan-area network. A network that spans a metropolitan area. Generally, a MAN spans a larger geographic area than a LAN, but a smaller geographic area than a WAN. *Compare with* LAN and WAN.

managed object. In network management, a network device that can be managed by a network management protocol.

Management Information Base. *See* MIB.

management services. SNA functions distributed among network components to manage and control an SNA network.

Manchester encoding. A digital coding scheme, used by IEEE 802.3 and Ethernet, in which a mid-bit-time transition is used for clocking, and a 1 is denoted by a high level during the first half of the bit time.

Manufacturing Automation Protocol. *See* MAP.

MAP. Manufacturing Automation Protocol. A network architecture created by General Motors to satisfy the specific needs of the factory floor. MAP specifies a token-passing LAN similar to that of IEEE 802.4. *See also* IEEE 802.4.

mask. *See* address mask and subnet mask.

MAU. media attachment unit. A device used in Ethernet and IEEE 802.3 networks that provides the interface between the AUI port of a station and the common medium of the Ethernet. The MAU, which can be built into a station or can be a separate device, performs physical layer functions including the conversion of digital data from the Ethernet interface, collision detection, and injection of bits onto the network. Sometimes referred to as a media access unit, also abbreviated MAU, or as a transceiver. In Token Ring, a MAU is known as a multistation access unit and is usually abbreviated MSAU to avoid confusion. *See also* AUI and MSAU.

maximum burst. The largest burst of data above the insured rate that is allowed temporarily on an ATM PVC but that is not dropped at the edge by the traffic policing function, even if it exceeds the maximum rate. This amount of traffic is allowed only temporarily; on average, the traffic source needs to be within the maximum rate. Specified in bytes or cells. *Compare with* insured burst. *See also* maximum rate.

maximum rate. The maximum total data throughput allowed on a given virtual circuit, equal to the sum of the insured and uninsured traffic from the traffic source. The uninsured data might be dropped if the network becomes congested. The maximum rate, which cannot exceed the media rate, represents the highest data throughput the virtual circuit will ever deliver, measured in bits or cells per second. *Compare with* excess rate and insured rate. *See also* maximum burst.

maximum transmission unit. *See* MTU.

MB. megabyte.

Mb. megabit.

MBONE. multicast backbone. The multicast backbone of the Internet. MBONE is a virtual multicast network composed of multicast LANs and the point-to-point tunnels that interconnect them.

Mbps. megabits per second.

MCA. micro channel architecture. A bus interface commonly used in PCs and some UNIX workstations and servers.

MCI. Multiport Communications Interface. A card on the AGS+ that provides two Ethernet interfaces and up to two synchronous serial interfaces. The MCI processes packets rapidly, without the interframe delays typical of other Ethernet interfaces.

MCR. minimum cell rate. A parameter defined by the ATM Forum for ATM traffic management. MCR is defined only for ABR transmissions, and specifies the minimum value for the ACR. *See also* ABR (available bit rate), ACR, and PCR.

MD5. Message Digest 5. An algorithm used for message authentication in SNMP v.2. MD5 verifies the integrity of the communication, authenticates the origin, and checks for timeliness. *See also* SNMP2.

media. Plural of medium. The various physical environments through which transmission signals pass. Common network media include twisted-pair, coaxial and fiber-optic cable, and the atmosphere (through which microwave, laser, and infrared transmission occurs). Sometimes called physical media.

Media Access Control. *See* MAC.

media access unit. *See* MAU.

media attachment unit. *See* MAU.

media interface connector. *See* MIC.

media rate. Maximum traffic throughput for a particular media type.

medium. *See* media.

medium business. This is a company that has between 100 to 500 users with a complex LAN that might include a data center with multiple Intermediate Distribution Facilities (IDFs) for LAN connectivity. Medium businesses have larger remote offices that have higher speed WANs, such as Frame Relay or T1s. Medium businesses also have complex routing protocols like OSPF or EIGRP, as well as multiple routed protocols.

megabit. Abbreviated Mb.

megabits per second. Abbreviated Mbps.

megabyte. Abbreviated MB.

mesh. A network topology in which devices are organized in a manageable, segmented manner with many, often redundant, interconnections strategically placed between network nodes. *See also* full mesh and partial mesh.

message. An application layer (Layer 7) logical grouping of information, often composed of a number of lower-layer logical groupings such as packets. The terms datagram, frame, packet, and segment are also used to describe logical information groupings at various layers of the OSI reference model and in various technology circles.

message handling system. *See* MHS.

Message Digest 5. *See* MD5.

Message Queuing Interface. *See* MQI.

message switching. A switching technique involving transmission of messages from node to node through a network. The message is stored at each node until such time as a forwarding path is available. *Compare with* circuit switching and packet switching.

message unit. A unit of data processed by any network layer.

metasignaling. A process running at the ATM layer that manages signaling types and virtual circuits.

metering. *See* traffic shaping.

metric. *See* routing metric.

metropolitan-area network. *See* MAN.

MHS. message handling system. ITU-T X.400 recommendations that provide message handling services for communications between distributed applications. NetWare MHS is a different (though similar) entity that also provides message-handling services. *See also* IFIP.

MIB . Management Information Base. A database of network management information that is used and maintained by a network management protocol such as SNMP or CMIP. The value of a MIB object can be changed or retrieved using SNMP or CMIP commands. MIB objects are organized in a tree structure that includes public (standard) and private (proprietary) branches.

MIC. media interface connector. An FDDI de facto standard connector.

micro channel architecture. *See* MCA.

microcode. The translation layer between machine instructions and the elementary operations of a computer. Microcode is stored in ROM and allows the addition of new machine instructions without requiring that they be designed into electronic circuits when new instructions are needed.

microsegmentation. The division of a network into smaller segments, usually with the intention of increasing aggregate bandwidth to network devices.

microwave. Electromagnetic waves in the range 1 to 30 GHz. Microwave-based networks are an evolving technology gaining favor due to high bandwidth and relatively low cost.

midsplit. A broadband cable system in which the available frequencies are split into two groups: one for transmission and one for reception.

Military Network. *See* MILNET.

millions of instructions per second. *See* mips.

MILNET. Military Network. An unclassified portion of the DDN. Operated and maintained by the DISA. *See also* DDN and DISA.

minimum cell rate. *See* MCR.

mips. millions of instructions per second. The number of instructions executed by a processor per second.

modem. modulator-demodulator. A device that converts digital and analog signals. At the source, a modem converts digital signals to a form suitable for transmission over analog communication facilities. At the destination, the analog signals are returned to their digital form. Modems allow data to be transmitted over voice-grade telephone lines.

modem eliminator. A device that allows connection of two DTE devices without modems.

modulation. The process by which the characteristics of electrical signals are transformed to represent information. Types of modulation include AM, FM, and PAM. *See also* AM, FM, and PAM.

modulator-demodulator. *See* modem.

monomode fiber. *See* single-mode fiber.

MOP. Maintenance Operation Protocol. A Digital Equipment Corporation protocol that provides a way to perform primitive maintenance operations on DECnet systems. For example, MOP can be used to download a system image to a diskless station.

Mosaic. A public-domain WWW browser, developed at the National Center for Supercomputing Applications (NCSA). *See also* WWW browser.

MOSPF. Multicast OSPF. An intradomain multicast routing protocol used in OSPF networks. Extensions are applied to the base OSPF unicast protocol to support IP multicast routing.

MQI. Message Queuing Interface. An international standard API that provides functionality similar to that of the RPC interface. In contrast to RPC, MQI is implemented strictly at the application layer. *See also* RPC.

MSAU. multistation access unit. A wiring concentrator to which all end stations in a Token Ring network connect. The MSAU provides an interface between these devices and the Token Ring interface. Sometimes abbreviated MAU.

MTBF. mean time between failures. This is a measurement of the reliability of a device, measured in hours.

MTU. maximum transmission unit. The maximum packet size, in bytes, that a particular interface can handle.

mu-law. A North American companding standard used in conversion between analog and digital signals in PCM systems. Similar to the European a-law. *See also* a-law and companding.

multiaccess network. A network that allows multiple devices to connect and communicate simultaneously.

multicast. Single packets copied by the network and sent to a specific subset of network addresses. These addresses are specified in the destination address field. *Compare with* broadcast and unicast.

multicast address. A single address that refers to multiple network devices. Synonymous with group address. *Compare with* broadcast address and unicast address. *See also* multicast.

multicast backbone. *See* MBONE.

multicast group. A dynamically determined group of IP hosts identified by a single IP multicast address.

Multicast OSPF. *See* MOSPF.

multicast router. A router used to send IGMP query messages on their attached local networks. Host members of a multicast group respond to a query by sending IGMP reports noting the multicast groups to which they belong. The multicast router takes responsibility for forwarding multicast datagrams from one multicast group to all other networks that have members in the group. *See also* IGMP.

multicast server. A server that establishes a one-to-many connection to each device in a VLAN, thus establishing a broadcast domain for each VLAN segment. The multicast server forwards incoming broadcasts only to the multicast address that maps to the broadcast address.

multidrop line. A communications line that has multiple cable access points. Sometimes called a multipoint line.

multihomed host. A host attached to multiple physical network segments in an OSI CLNS network.

multihoming. An addressing scheme in IS-IS routing that supports assignment of multiple area addresses.

multilayer switch. A switch that filters and forwards packets based on MAC addresses and network addresses. A subset of LAN switch. *Compare with* LAN switch.

multimode fiber. An optical fiber supporting propagation of multiple frequencies of light. *See also* single-mode fiber.

multiple domain network. An SNA network with multiple SSCPs. *See also* SSCP.

multiplexing. A scheme that allows multiple logical signals to be transmitted simultaneously across a single physical channel. *Compare with* demultiplexing.

multipoint line. *See* multidrop line.

Multiport Communications Interface. *See* MCI.

multiservice company. This is a company that would include different types of data or services that run across the same network. These data and services might include data, voice, and video. Multiservice companies include a type of network that is not judged by size, but by the complexity of information over a single infrastructure.

multistation access unit. *See* MSAU.

multivendor network. A network that uses equipment from more than one vendor. Multivendor networks pose many more compatibility problems than single-vendor networks. *Compare with* single-vendor network.

N

Nagle's algorithm. Two separate congestion control algorithms that can be used in TCP-based networks. One algorithm reduces the sending window; the other limits small datagrams.

NAK. Negative acknowledgment. A response sent from a receiving device to a sending device indicating that the information received contained errors. *Compare with* acknowledgment.

Name Binding Protocol. *See* NBP.

name caching. A method by which remotely discovered host names are stored by a router for use in future packet-forwarding decisions to allow quick access.

name resolution. Generally, the process of associating a name with a network location.

name server. A server connected to a network that resolves network names into network addresses.

NAP. network access point. A location for interconnection of Internet service providers in the United States for the exchange of packets.

narrowband. *See* baseband.

Narrowband ISDN. *See* N-ISDN.

National Bureau of Standards. *See* NBS.

National Institute of Standards and Technology. *See* NIST.

National Research and Education Network. *See* NREN.

National Science Foundation. *See* NSF.

National Science Foundation Network. *See* NSFNET.

NAU. network addressable unit. An SNA term for an addressable entity. Examples include LUs, PUs, and SSCPs. NAUs generally provide upper-level network services. *Compare with* path control network.

NAUN. nearest active upstream neighbor. In Token Ring or IEEE 802.5 networks, the closest upstream network device from any given device that is still active.

NBMA. nonbroadcast multiaccess. A multiaccess network that either does not support broadcasting (such as X.25) or in which broadcasting is not feasible (for example, an SMDS broadcast group or an extended Ethernet that is too large). *See also* multiaccess network.

NBP. Name Binding Protocol. An AppleTalk transport-level protocol that translates a character string name into an internetwork address.

NBS. National Bureau of Standards. An organization that was part of the U.S. Department of Commerce. Now known as NIST. *See also* NIST.

NCP. Network Control Program. In SNA, a program that routes and controls the flow of data between a communications controller (in which it resides) and other network resources.

NCP/Token Ring Interconnection. *See* NTRI.

NDIS. network driver interface specification. The specification for a generic, hardware- and protocol-independent device driver for NICs. Produced by Microsoft.

nearest active upstream neighbor. *See* NAUN.

NEARNET. A regional network in New England (United States) that links Boston University, Harvard University, and MIT. Now part of BBN Planet. *See also* BBN Planet.

negative acknowledgment. *See* NAK.

neighboring routers. In OSPF, two routers that have interfaces to a common network. On multiaccess networks, neighbors are dynamically discovered by the OSPF Hello protocol.

NET. network entity title. Network addresses, defined by the ISO network architecture, and used in CLNS-based networks.

net. Short for network.

NetBIOS. Network Basic Input/Output System. An API used by applications on an IBM LAN to request services from lower-level network processes. These services might include session establishment and termination, and information transfer.

NetView. An IBM network management architecture and related applications. NetView is a VTAM application used for managing mainframes in SNA networks. *See also* VTAM.

NetWare. A popular distributed NOS developed by Novell. Provides transparent remote file access and numerous other distributed network services.

NetWare Link Services Protocol. *See* NLSP.

NetWare Loadable Module. *See* NLM.

network. A collection of computers, printers, routers, switches, and other devices that are able to communicate with each other over some transmission medium.

network access point. *See* NAP.

network access server. *See* access server.

network address. A network layer address referring to a logical, rather than a physical, network device. Also called a protocol address. *Compare with* MAC address.

network addressable unit. *See* NAU.

network administrator. A person responsible for the operation, maintenance, and management of a network. *See also* network operator.

network analyzer. A hardware or software device that offers various network troubleshooting features, including protocol-specific packet decodes, specific preprogrammed troubleshooting tests, packet filtering, and packet transmission.

Network Basic Input/Output System. *See* NetBIOS.

Network Control Program. *See* NCP.

network driver interface specification. *See* NDIS.

network entity title. *See* NET.

Network File System. *See* NFS.

Network Information Center. *See* NIC.

Network Information Service. *See* NIS.

network interface. A boundary between a carrier network and a privately owned installation.

network interface card. *See* NIC.

network layer. Layer 3 of the OSI reference model. This layer provides connectivity and path selection between two end systems. The network layer is the layer at which routing occurs. Corresponds roughly with the path control layer of the SNA model. *See also* application layer, data link layer, physical layer, presentation layer, session layer, and transport layer.

network management. Systems or actions that help maintain, characterize, or troubleshoot a network.

network management system. *See* NMS.

network management vector transport. *See* NMVT.

Network-to-Network Interface. *See* NNI.

network node. *See* NN.

Network Node Interface. *See* NNI.

Network Node Server. An SNA NN that provides resource location and route selection services for ENs, LEN nodes, and LUs that are in its domain.

network number. Part of an IP address that specifies the network to which the host belongs.

network operating system. *See* NOS.

Network Operations Center. *See* NOC.

network operator. A person who routinely monitors and controls a network, performing tasks such as reviewing and responding to traps, monitoring throughput, configuring new circuits, and resolving problems. *See also* network administrator.

network service access point. *See* NSAP.

Next Hop Resolution Protocol. *See* NHRP.

NFS. Network File System. As commonly used, a distributed file system protocol suite developed by Sun Microsystems that allows remote file access across a network. In actuality, NFS is simply one protocol in the suite. NFS protocols include NFS, RPC, XDR (External Data Representation), and others. These protocols are part of a larger architecture that Sun refers to as ONC. *See also* ONC.

NHRP. Next Hop Resolution Protocol. A protocol used by routers to dynamically discover the MAC address of other routers and hosts connected to an NBMA network. These systems can then directly communicate without requiring traffic to use an intermediate hop, increasing performance in ATM, Frame Relay, SMDS, and X.25 environments.

NIC. 1. network interface card. A board that provides network communication capabilities to and from a computer system. Also called an adapter. *See also* AUI. 2. Network Information Center. An organization that serves the Internet community by supplying user assistance, documentation, training, and other services.

NIS. Network Information Service. A protocol developed by Sun Microsystems for the administration of networkwide databases. The service essentially uses two programs: one for finding a NIS server and one for accessing the NIS databases.

N-ISDN. Narrowband ISDN. A communications standards developed by the ITU-T for baseband networks. Based on 64-kbps B channels and 16- or 64-kbps D channels. *Compare with* BISDN. *See also* BRI, ISDN, and PRI.

NIST. National Institute of Standards and Technology. Formerly the NBS, a U.S. government organization that supports and catalogs a variety of standards. *See also* NBS.

NLM. NetWare Loadable Module. An individual program that can be loaded into memory and function as part of the NetWare NOS.

NLSP. NetWare Link Services Protocol. A link-state routing protocol based on IS-IS. *See also* IS-IS.

NMS. network management system. A system responsible for managing at least part of a network. An NMS is generally a reasonably powerful and well-equipped computer such as an engineering workstation. NMSs communicate with agents to help keep track of network statistics and resources.

NMVT. network management vector transport. An SNA message consisting of a series of vectors conveying network management–specific information.

NN. network node. An SNA intermediate node that provides connectivity, directory services, route selection, intermediate session routing, data transport, and network management services to LEN nodes and ENs. The NN contains a CP that manages the resources of both the NN itself and those of the ENs and LEN nodes in its domain. NNs provide intermediate routing services by implementing the APPN PU 2.1 extensions. *Compare with* EN. *See also* CP.

NNI. Network-to-Network Interface. An ATM Forum standard that defines the interface between two ATM switches that are both located in a private network or are both located in a public network. The interface between a public switch and a private one is defined by the UNI standard. Also, the standard interface between two Frame Relay switches meeting the same criteria. *Compare with* UNI.

NOC. Network Operations Center. An organization responsible for maintaining a network.

node. 1. An endpoint of a network connection or a junction common to two or more lines in a network. Nodes can be processors, controllers, or workstations. Nodes, which vary in routing and other functional capabilities, can be interconnected by links, and serve as control points in the network. Node is sometimes used generically to refer to any entity that can access a network and is frequently used interchangeably with device. *See also* host. 2. In SNA, the basic component of a network, and the point at which one or more functional units connect channels or data circuits.

noise. Undesirable communications channel signals.

nonbroadcast multiaccess. *See* NBMA.

nonreturn to zero. *See* NRZ.

nonreturn to zero inverted. *See* NRZI.

nonseed router. In AppleTalk, a router that must first obtain and then verify its configuration with a seed router before it can begin operation. *See also* seed router.

non-stub area. A resource-intensive OSPF area that carries a default route, static routes, intra-area routes, interarea routes, and external routes. Non-stub areas are the only OSPF areas that can have virtual links configured across them and are the only areas that can contain an ASBR. *Compare with* stub area. *See also* ASBR and OSPF.

nonvolatile random-access memory. *See* NVRAM.

normal response mode. *See* NRM.

Northwest Net. An NSF-funded regional network serving the Northwestern United States, Alaska, Montana, and North Dakota. Northwest Net connects all major universities in the region, as well as many leading industrial concerns.

NOS. network operating system. Distributed file systems. Examples of NOSs include LAN Manager, NetWare, NFS, and VINES.

Novell IPX. *See* IPX.

NREN. National Research and Education Network. A component of the HPCC program designed to ensure U.S. technical leadership in computer communications through research and development efforts in state-of-the-art telecommunications and networking technologies. *See also* HPCC.

NRM. normal response mode. An HDLC mode for use on links with one primary station and one or more secondary stations. In this mode, secondary stations can transmit only if they first receive a poll from the primary station.

NRZ. nonreturn to zero. Signals that maintain constant voltage levels with no signal transitions (no return to a zero-voltage level) during a bit interval. *Compare with* NRZI.

NRZI. nonreturn to zero inverted. Signals that maintain constant voltage levels with no signal transitions (no return to a zero-voltage level), but interpret the presence of data at the beginning of a bit interval as a signal transition and the absence of data as no transition. *Compare with* NRZ.

NSAP. network service access point. Network addresses, as specified by ISO. An NSAP is the point at which OSI network service is made available to a transport layer (Layer 4) entity.

NSF. National Science Foundation. A U.S. government agency that funds scientific research in the United States. The now-defunct NSFNET was funded by the NSF. *See also* NSFNET.

NSFNET. National Science Foundation Network. A large network that was controlled by the NSF and provided networking services in support of education and research in the United States, from 1986 to 1995. NSFNET is no longer in service.

NTRI. NCP/Token Ring Interconnection. A function used by ACF/NCP to support Token Ring–attached SNA devices. NTRI also provides translation from Token Ring–attached SNA devices (PUs) to switched (dial-up) devices.

null modem. A small box or cable used to join computing devices directly, rather than over a network.

NVRAM. nonvolatile RAM. RAM that retains its contents when a unit is powered off.

NYSERNet. Network in New York (United States) with a T1 backbone connecting NSF, many universities, and several commercial concerns.

O

OAM cell. operation, administration, and maintenance cell. An ATM Forum specification for cells used to monitor virtual circuits. OAM cells provide a virtual circuit–level loopback in which a router responds to the cells, demonstrating that the circuit is up, and the router is operational.

OARnet. Ohio Academic Resources Network. An Internet service provider that connects a number of U.S. sites, including the Ohio supercomputer center in Columbus, Ohio.

object instance. An instance of an object type that has been bound to a value.

OC. Optical Carrier. A series of physical protocols (OC-1, OC-2, OC-3, and so on), defined for SONET optical signal transmissions. OC signal levels put STS frames onto multimode fiber-optic line at a variety of speeds. The base rate is 51.84 Mbps (OC-1); each signal level thereafter operates at a speed divisible by that number (thus, OC-3 runs at 155.52 Mbps). *See also* SONET, STS-1, and STS-3c.

ODA. Open Document Architecture. An ISO standard that specifies how documents are represented and transmitted electronically. Formally called Office Document Architecture.

ODI. Open Data-Link Interface. A Novell specification providing a standardized interface for NICs (network interface cards) that allows multiple protocols to use a single NIC. *See also* NIC (network interface card).

OEMI channel. *See* block multiplexer channel.

Office Document Architecture. *See* ODA.

Ohio Academic Resources Network. *See* OARnet.

OIM. OSI Internet Management. A group tasked with specifying ways in which OSI network management protocols can be used to manage TCP/IP networks.

ONC. Open Network Computing. A distributed applications architecture designed by Sun Microsystems, currently controlled by a consortium led by Sun. The NFS protocols are part of ONC. *See also* NFS.

ones density. A scheme that allows a CSU/DSU to recover the data clock reliably. The CSU/DSU derives the data clock from the data that passes through it. In order to recover the clock, the CSU/DSU hardware must receive at least one 1 bit value for every 8 bits of data that pass through it. Also called pulse density.

on-the-fly packet switching. *See* cut-through packet switching.

open architecture. An architecture with which third-party developers can legally develop products and for which public domain specifications exist.

open circuit. A broken path along a transmission medium. Open circuits usually prevent network communication.

Open Data-Link Interface. *See* ODI.

Open Document Architecture. *See* ODA.

Open Network Computing. *See* ONC.

Open Shortest Path First. *See* OSPF.

Open System Interconnection. *See* OSI.

Open System Interconnection reference model. *See* OSI reference model.

operation, administration, and maintenance cell. *See* OAM cell.

Optical Carrier. *See* OC.

optical fiber. *See* fiber-optic cable.

Organizational Unique Identifier. *See* OUI.

OSI. Open System Interconnection. An international standardization program created by ISO and ITU-T to develop standards for data networking that facilitate multivendor equipment interoperability.

OSI Internet Management. *See* OIM.

OSINET. An international association designed to promote OSI in vendor architectures.

OSI reference model. Open System Interconnection reference model. A network architectural model developed by ISO and ITU-T. The model consists of seven layers, each of which specifies particular network functions such as addressing, flow control, error control, encapsulation, and reliable message transfer. The highest layer (the application layer) is closest to the user; the lowest layer (the physical layer) is closest to the media technology. The lower two layers are implemented in hardware and software, while the upper five layers are implemented only in software. The OSI reference model is used universally as a method for teaching and understanding network functionality. Similar in some respects to SNA. *See* application layer, data link layer, network layer, physical layer, presentation layer, session layer, and transport layer.

OSPF. Open Shortest Path First. A link-state, hierarchical IGP routing algorithm proposed as a successor to RIP in the Internet community. OSPF features include least-cost routing, multipath routing, and load balancing. OSPF was derived from an early version of the IS-IS protocol. *See also* Enhanced IGRP, IGP, IGRP, IS-IS, and RIP.

OUI. Organizational Unique Identifier. The three octets assigned by the IEEE in a block of 48-bit LAN addresses.

outframe. The maximum number of outstanding frames allowed in an SNA PU 2 server at any time.

out-of-band signaling. Transmission using frequencies or channels outside the frequencies or channels normally used for information transfer. Out-of-band signaling is often used for error reporting in situations in which in-band signaling can be affected by whatever problems the network might be experiencing. *Compare with* in-band signaling.

P

pacing. *See* flow control.

packet. A logical grouping of information that includes a header containing control information and (usually) user data. Packets are most often used to refer to network layer units of data. The terms datagram, frame, message, and segment are also used to describe logical information groupings at various layers of the OSI reference model and in various technology circles. *See also* PDU.

packet assembler/disassembler. *See* PAD.

packet buffer. *See* buffer.

packet internet groper. *See* ping.

packet level protocol. *See* PLP.

packet switch. A WAN device that routes packets along the most efficient path and allows a communications channel to be shared by multiple connections. Sometimes referred to as a packet-switching node (PSN), and formerly called an IMP. *See also* IMP.

packet-switched data network. *See* PSN (packet-switching node).

packet-switched network. *See* PSN (packet-switched network).

packet switching. A networking method in which nodes share bandwidth with each other by sending packets. *Compare with* circuit switching and message switching. *See also* PSN (packet-switched network).

packet switch exchange. *See* PSE.

packet-switching node. *See* PSN (packet-switching node).

PAD. packet assembler/disassembler. A device used to connect simple devices (such as character-mode terminals) that do not support the full functionality of a particular protocol to a network. PADs buffer data and assemble and disassemble packets sent to such end devices.

Palo Alto Research Center. *See* PARC.

PAM. pulse amplitude modulation. A modulation scheme in which the modulating wave is caused to modulate the amplitude of a pulse stream. *Compare with* AM and FM. *See also* modulation.

PAP. Password Authentication Protocol. An authentication protocol that allows PPP peers to authenticate one another. The remote router attempting to connect to the local router is required to send an authentication request. Unlike CHAP, PAP passes the password and host name or username in the clear (unencrypted). PAP does not itself prevent unauthorized access, but merely identifies the remote end. The router or access server then determines whether that user is allowed access. PAP is supported only on PPP lines. *Compare with* CHAP.

parallel channel. A channel that uses bus and tag cables as a transmission medium. *Compare with* ESCON channel. *See also* bus and tag channel.

parallelism. Multiple paths existing between two points in a network. These paths may be of equal or unequal cost. Parallelism is often a network design goal; if one path fails, there is redundancy in the network to ensure that an alternate path to the same point exists.

parallel transmission. A method of data transmission in which the bits of a data character are transmitted simultaneously over a number of channels. *Compare with* serial transmission.

PARC. Palo Alto Research Center. A research and development center operated by XEROX. A number of widely used technologies were originally conceived at PARC, including the first personal computers and LANs.

PARC Universal Protocol. *See* PUP.

parity check. A process for checking the integrity of a character. A parity check involves appending a bit that makes the total number of binary 1 digits in a character or word (excluding the parity bit) either odd (for odd parity) or even (for even parity).

partial mesh. A network in which devices are organized in a mesh topology, with some network nodes organized in a full mesh, but with others that are connected to only one or two other nodes in the network. A partial mesh does not provide the level of redundancy of a full mesh topology, but is less expensive to implement. Partial mesh topologies are generally used in the peripheral networks that connect to a fully meshed backbone. *See also* full mesh and mesh.

Password Authentication Protocol. *See* PAP.

path control layer. Layer 3 in the SNA architectural model. This layer performs sequencing services related to proper data reassembly. The path control layer is *also* responsible for routing. Corresponds roughly with the network layer of the OSI model. *See also* data flow control layer, data link control layer, physical control layer, presentation services layer, transaction services layer, and transmission control layer.

path control network. An SNA concept that consists of lower-level components that control the routing and data flow through an SNA network and handle physical data transmission between SNA nodes. *Compare with* NAU.

path cost. *See* cost.

path name. The full name of a UNIX, DOS, or LynxOS file or directory, including all directory and subdirectory names. Consecutive names in a path name are typically separated by a forward slash (/) or a backslash (\), as in /usr/app/base/config.

payload. The portion of a frame that contains upper-layer information (data).

PBX. private branch exchange. A digital or analog telephone switchboard located on the subscriber premises and used to connect private and public telephone networks.

PCI. protocol control information. Control information added to user data to comprise an OSI packet. The OSI equivalent of the term header. *See also* header.

PCM. pulse code modulation. The transmission of analog information in digital form through sampling and encoding the samples with a fixed number of bits.

PCR. peak cell rate. A parameter defined by the ATM Forum for ATM traffic management. In CBR transmissions, PCR determines how often data samples are sent. In ABR transmissions, PCR determines the maximum value of the ACR. *See also* ABR (available bit rate), ACR, and CBR.

PDN . public data network. A network operated either by a government (as in Europe) or by a private concern to provide computer communications to the public, usually for a fee. PDNs enable small organizations to create a WAN without all the equipment costs of long-distance circuits.

PDU. protocol data unit. An OSI term for packet. *See also* BPDU and packet.

peak cell rate. *See* PCR.

peak rate. The maximum rate, in kilobits per second, at which a virtual circuit can transmit.

peer-to-peer computing. Each network device runs both client and server portions of an application. Also, communication between implementations of the same OSI reference model layer in two different network devices. *Compare with* client/server computing.

performance management. One of five categories of network management defined by ISO for management of OSI networks. Performance management subsystems are responsible for analyzing and controlling network performance including network throughput and error rates. *See also* accounting management, configuration management, fault management, and security management.

peripheral node. In SNA, a node that uses local addresses and is therefore not affected by changes to network addresses. Peripheral nodes require boundary function assistance from an adjacent subarea node.

permanent virtual circuit. *See* PVC.

permanent virtual connection. *See* PVC.

permanent virtual path. *See* PVP.

permit processing. *See* traffic policing.

P/F. poll/final bit. A bit in bit-synchronous data link layer protocols that indicates the function of a frame. If the frame is a command, a 1 in this bit indicates a poll. If the frame is a response, a 1 in this bit indicates that the current frame is the last frame in the response.

PGP. Pretty Good Privacy. A public-key encryption application that allows secure file and message exchanges. There is some controversy over the development and use of this application, in part due to U.S. national security concerns.

phase. The location of a position on an alternating wave form.

phase shift. A situation in which the relative position in time between the clock and data signals of a transmission becomes unsynchronized. In systems using long cables at high transmission speeds, slight variances in cable construction, temperature, and other factors can cause a phase shift, resulting in high error rates.

PHY. physical sublayer. One of two sublayers of the FDDI physical layer. *See also* PMD.

physical address. *See* MAC address.

physical control layer. Layer 1 in the SNA architectural model. This layer is responsible for the physical specifications for the physical links between end systems. Corresponds to the physical layer of the OSI model. *See also* data flow control layer, data link control layer, path control layer, presentation services layer, transaction services layer, and transmission control layer.

physical layer. Layer 1 of the OSI reference model. The physical layer defines the electrical, mechanical, procedural, and functional specifications for activating, maintaining, and deactivating the physical link between end systems. Corresponds with the physical control layer in the SNA model. *See also* application layer, data link layer, network layer, presentation layer, session layer, and transport layer.

physical layer convergence procedure. *See* PLCP.

physical media. *See* media.

physical medium. *See* media.

physical medium dependent. *See* PMD.

physical sublayer. *See* PHY.

physical unit. *See* PU.

Physical Unit 2. *See* PU 2.

Physical Unit 2.1. *See* PU 2.1.

Physical Unit 4. *See* PU 4.

Physical Unit 5. *See* PU 5.

Physics Network. *See* PHYSNET.

PHYSNET.   Physics Network. A group of many DECnet-based physics research networks, including HEPnet. *See also* HEPnet.

piggybacking.   The process of carrying acknowledgments within a data packet to save network bandwidth.

PIM.   Protocol Independent Multicast. A multicast routing architecture that allows the addition of IP multicast routing on existing IP networks. PIM is unicast routing protocol independent and can be operated in two modes: dense mode and sparse mode. *See also* PIM dense mode and PIM sparse mode.

PIM dense mode.   One of the two PIM operational modes. PIM dense mode is data driven and resembles typical multicast routing protocols. Packets are forwarded on all outgoing interfaces until pruning and truncation occurs. In dense mode, receivers are densely populated, and it is assumed that the downstream networks want to receive and will probably use the datagrams that are forwarded to them. The cost of using dense mode is its default flooding behavior. Sometimes called dense mode PIM or PIM DM. *Compare with* PIM sparse mode. *See also* PIM.

PIM DM. *See* PIM dense mode.

PIM SM. *See* PIM sparse mode.

PIM sparse mode.   One of the two PIM operational modes. PIM sparse mode tries to constrain data distribution so that a minimal number of routers in the network receive it. Packets are sent only if they are explicitly requested at the RP (rendezvous point). In sparse mode, receivers are widely distributed, and the assumption is that downstream networks will not necessarily use the datagrams that are sent to them. The cost of using sparse mode is its reliance on the periodic refreshing of explicit join messages and its need for RPs. Sometimes called sparse mode PIM or PIM SM. *Compare with* PIM dense mode. *See also* PIM and RP (rendezvous point).

ping. packet internet groper. An ICMP echo message and its reply. Often used to test the reachability of a network device.

ping-ponging. The actions of a packet in a two-node routing loop.

PLCP. physical layer convergence procedure. A specification that maps ATM cells into physical media, such as T3 or E3, and defines certain management information.

plesiochronous transmission. Digital signals that are sourced from different clocks of comparable accuracy and stability. *Compare with* asynchronous transmission, isochronous transmission, and synchronous transmission.

PLP. packet level protocol. A network layer protocol in the X.25 protocol stack. Sometimes called X.25 Level 3 or X.25 Protocol. *See also* X.25.

PLU. Primary LU. The LU that is initiating a session with another LU. *See also* LU.

PMD. physical medium dependent. A sublayer of the FDDI physical layer that interfaces directly with the physical medium and performs the most basic bit transmission functions of the network. *See also* PHY.

PNNI. Private Network-Network Interface. An ATM Forum specification that describes an ATM virtual circuit routing protocol, as well as a signaling protocol between ATM switches. Used to allow ATM switches within a private network to interconnect. Sometimes called Private Network Node Interface.

point of presence. *See* POP.

Point-to-Point Protocol. *See* PPP.

poison reverse updates. Routing updates that explicitly indicate that a network or subnet is unreachable, rather than implying that a network is unreachable by not including it in updates. Poison reverse updates are sent to defeat large routing loops.

policy-based routing. *See* policy routing.

policy routing. A routing scheme that forwards packets to specific interfaces based on user-configured policies. Such policies might specify that traffic sent from a particular network should be forwarded out one interface, while all other traffic should be forwarded out another interface.

poll/final bit. *See* P/F.

polling. An access method in which a primary network device inquires, in an orderly fashion, whether secondaries have data to transmit. The inquiry occurs in the form of a message to each secondary that gives the secondary the right to transmit.

POP. point of presence. A physical access point to a long-distance carrier interchange.

port. 1. An interface on an internetworking device (such as a router). 2. In IP terminology, an upper-layer process that receives information from lower layers. 3. To rewrite software or microcode so that it will run on a different hardware platform or in a different software environment than that for which it was originally designed.

Post, Telephone, and Telegraph. *See* PTT.

PPP. Point-to-Point Protocol. A successor to SLIP that provides router-to-router and host-to-network connections over synchronous and asynchronous circuits. *See also* SLIP.

presentation layer. Layer 6 of the OSI reference model. This layer ensures that information sent by the application layer of one system will be readable by the application layer of another. The presentation layer is also concerned with the data structures used by programs and therefore negotiates data transfer syntax for the application layer. Corresponds roughly with the presentation services layer of the SNA model. *See also* application layer, data link layer, network layer, physical layer, session layer, and transport layer.

presentation services layer. Layer 6 of the SNA architectural model. This layer provides network resource management, session presentation services, and some application management. Corresponds roughly with the presentation layer of the OSI model. *See also* data flow control layer, data link control layer, path control layer, physical control layer, transaction services layer, and transmission control layer.

Pretty Good Privacy. *See* PGP.

PRI. Primary Rate Interface. ISDN interface to primary rate access. Primary rate access consists of a single 64-kbps D channel plus 23 (T1) or 30 (E1) B channels for voice or data. *Compare with* BRI. *See also* BISDN, ISDN, and N-ISDN.

primary. *See* primary station.

Primary LU. *See* PLU.

Primary Rate Interface. *See* PRI.

primary ring. One of the two rings that make up an FDDI or CDDI ring. The primary ring is the default path for data transmissions. *Compare with* secondary ring.

primary station. In bit-synchronous data link layer protocols such as HDLC and SDLC, a station that controls the transmission activity of secondary stations and performs other management functions, such as error control, through polling or other means. Primary stations send commands to secondary stations and receive responses. Also called, simply, a primary. *See also* secondary station.

print server. A networked computer system that fields, manages, and executes (or sends for execution) print requests from other network devices.

priority queuing. A routing feature in which frames in an interface output queue are prioritized based on various characteristics, such as packet size and interface type.

private branch exchange. *See* PBX.

Private Network-Network Interface. *See* PNNI.

Private Network Node Interface. *See* PNNI.

process switching. An operation that provides full route evaluation and per-packet load balancing across parallel WAN links. Involves the transmission of entire frames to the router CPU, where they are repackaged for delivery to or from a WAN interface, with the router making a route selection for each packet. Process switching is the most resource-intensive switching operation that the CPU can perform.

programmable read-only memory. *See* PROM.

PROM. programmable read-only memory. ROM that can be programmed using special equipment. A PROM can be programmed only once. *Compare with* EPROM.

propagation delay. The time required for data to travel over a network, from its source to its ultimate destination.

protocol. The formal description of a set of rules and conventions that govern how devices on a network exchange information.

protocol address. *See* network address.

protocol control information. *See* PCI.

protocol converter. A device or software that enables equipment with different data formats to communicate by translating the data transmission code of one device to the data transmission code of another device.

protocol data unit. *See* PDU.

Protocol Independent Multicast. *See* PIM.

protocol stack. A set of related communications protocols that operate together and, as a group, address communication at some or all of the seven layers of the OSI reference model. Not every protocol stack covers each layer of the model, and often a single protocol in the stack addresses a number of layers at once. TCP/IP is a typical protocol stack.

protocol translator . A network device or software that converts one protocol into another, similar, protocol.

proxy. An entity that, in the interest of efficiency, essentially stands in for another entity.

proxy Address Resolution Protocol. *See* proxy ARP.

proxy ARP. proxy Address Resolution Protocol. A variation of the ARP protocol in which an intermediate device (for example, a router) sends an ARP response on behalf of an end node to the requesting host. Proxy ARP can lessen bandwidth use on slow-speed WAN links. *See also* ARP.

proxy explorer. A technique that minimizes exploding explorer packet traffic propagating through an SRB network by creating an explorer packet reply cache, the entries of which are reused when subsequent explorer packets need to find the same host.

proxy polling. A technique that alleviates the load across an SDLC network by allowing routers to act as proxies for primary and secondary nodes, thus keeping polling traffic off the shared links. Proxy polling has been replaced by SDLC transport.

PSDN. packet-switched data network. *See* PSN (packet-switched network).

PSE. packet switch exchange. Essentially, a switch. The term PSE is generally used in reference to a switch in an X.25 PSN (packet-switching node). *See also* switch.

PSN. 1. packet-switched network. A network that utilizes packet-switching technology for data transfer. Sometimes called a packet-switched data network (PSDN). *See* packet switching. 2. packet-switching node. A network node capable of performing packet switching functions. *See also* packet switching.

PSTN. Public Switched Telephone Network. The variety of telephone networks and services in place worldwide.

PTT. Post, Telephone, and Telegraph. A government agency that provides telephone services. PTTs exist in most areas outside North America and provide both local and long-distance telephone services.

PU. physical unit. An SNA component that manages and monitors the resources of a node, as requested by an SSCP. There is one PU per node.

PU 2. Physical Unit 2. An SNA peripheral node that can support only DLUs that require services from a VTAM host and that are only capable of performing the secondary LU role in SNA sessions.

PU 2.1. Physical Unit type 2.1. An SNA network node used for connecting peer nodes in a peer-oriented network. PU 2.1 sessions do not require that one node reside on VTAM. APPN is based on PU 2.1 nodes, which can also be connected to a traditional hierarchical SNA network.

PU 4. Physical Unit 4. A component of an IBM FEP capable of full-duplex data transfer. Each such SNA device employs a separate data and control path into the transmit and receive buffers of the control program.

PU 5. Physical Unit 5. A component of an IBM mainframe or host computer that manages an SNA network. PU 5 nodes are involved in routing within the SNA path control layer.

public data network. *See* PDN.

Public Switched Telephone Network. *See* PSTN.

pulse amplitude modulation. *See* PAM.

pulse code modulation. *See* PCM.

pulse density. *See* ones density.

PUP. PARC Universal Protocol. A protocol similar to IP, developed at PARC.

PVC. permanent virtual circuit. A virtual circuit that is permanently established. PVCs save bandwidth associated with circuit establishment and tear down in situations where certain virtual circuits must exist all the time. Called a permanent virtual connection in ATM terminology. *Compare with* SVC.

PVP. permanent virtual path. A virtual path that consists of PVCs. *See also* PVC and virtual path.

Q

Q.920/Q.921. ITU-T specifications for the ISDN UNI data link layer. *See also* UNI.

Q.922A. An ITU-T specification for Frame Relay encapsulation.

Q.931. An ITU-T specification for signaling to establish, maintain, and clear ISDN connections. *See also* Q.93B.

Q.93B. An ITU-T specification signaling to establish, maintain, and clear BISDN network connections. An evolution of ITU-T recommendation Q.931. *See also* Q.931.

QLLC. Qualified Logical Link Control. A data link layer protocol defined by IBM that allows SNA data to be transported across X.25 networks.

QoS. Quality of Service. A measure of performance for a transmission system that reflects its transmission quality and service availability.

QoS parameters. Quality of Service parameters. The parameters that control the amount of traffic the source router in an ATM network sends over an SVC. If any switch along the path cannot accommodate the requested QoS parameters, the request is rejected, and a rejection message is forwarded to the originator of the request.

Qualified Logical Link Control. *See* QLLC.

Quality of Service. *See* QoS.

quartet signaling. A signaling technique used in 100VG-AnyLAN networks that allows data transmission at 100 Mbps over four pairs of UTP cabling at the same frequencies used in 10BaseT networks. *See also* 100VG-AnyLAN.

query. A message used to inquire about the value of some variable or set of variables.

queue. 1. Generally, an ordered list of elements waiting to be processed. 2. In routing, a backlog of packets waiting to be forwarded over a router interface.

queuing delay. The amount of time that data must wait before it can be transmitted onto a statistically multiplexed physical circuit.

queuing theory. Scientific principles governing the formation or lack of formation of congestion on a network or at an interface.

R

RACE. Research on Advanced Communications in Europe. A project sponsored by the European Community (EC) for the development of broadband networking capabilities.

radio frequency. *See* RF.

radio frequency interference. *See* RFI.

RAM. random-access memory. Volatile memory that can be read and written by a microprocessor.

random-access memory. *See* RAM.

Rapid Transport Protocol. *See* RTP.

RARE. RÈseaux AssociÈs pour la Recherche EuropÈenne. Association of European universities and research centers designed to promote an advanced telecommunications infrastructure in the European scientific community. RARE merged with EARN to form TERENA. *See also* EARN and TERENA.

RARP. Reverse Address Resolution Protocol. A protocol in the TCP/IP stack that provides a method for finding IP addresses based on MAC addresses. Compare with ARP.

rate enforcement. *See* traffic policing.

rate queue. A value that is associated with one or more virtual circuits and that defines the speed at which an individual virtual circuit transmits data to the remote end. Each rate queue represents a portion of the overall bandwidth available on an ATM link. The combined bandwidth of all configured rate queues should not exceed the total bandwidth available.

RBHC. Regional Bell Holding Company. One of seven telephone companies created by the AT&T divestiture in 1984.

RBOC. Regional Bell Operating Company. A local or regional telephone company that owns and operates telephone lines and switches in one of seven U.S. regions. The RBOCs were created by the divestiture of AT&T. Also called Bell Operating Company (BOC).

rcp. remote copy. A protocol that allows users to copy files to and from a file system residing on a remote host or server on the network. The rcp protocol uses TCP to ensure the reliable delivery of data.

rcp server. A router or another device that acts as a server for rcp. *See also* rcp.

read-only memory. *See* ROM.

Ready To Send. *See* RTS.

reassembly. The putting back together of an IP datagram at the destination after it has been fragmented either at the source or at an intermediate node. *See also* fragmentation.

redirect. The part of the ICMP and ES-IS protocols that allows a router to tell a host that using another router would be more effective.

redirector. Software that intercepts requests for resources within a computer and analyzes them for remote access requirements. If remote access is required to satisfy the request, the redirector forms an RPC and sends the RPC to lower-layer protocol software for transmission through the network to the node that can satisfy the request.

redistribution. Allowing routing information discovered through one routing protocol to be distributed in the update messages of another routing protocol. Sometimes called route redistribution.

redundancy. 1. In internetworking, the duplication of devices, services, or connections so that, in the event of a failure, the redundant devices, services, or connections can perform the work of those that failed. *See also* redundant system. 2. In telephony, the portion of the total information contained in a message that can be eliminated without loss of essential information or meaning.

redundant system. A computer, router, switch, or other computer system that contains two or more of each of the most important subsystems, such as two disk drives, two CPUs, or two power supplies.

Regional Bell Holding Company. *See* RBHC.

Regional Bell Operating Company. *See* RBOC.

registered jack connector. *See* RJ connector.

relay. OSI terminology for a device that connects two or more networks or network systems. A data link layer (Layer 2) relay is a bridge; a network layer (Layer 3) relay is a router. *See also* bridge and router.

reliability. The ratio of expected to received keepalives from a link. If the ratio is high, the line is reliable. Used as a routing metric.

remote bridge. A bridge that connects physically disparate network segments via WAN links.

remote copy . *See* rcp.

remote job entry. *See* RJE.

remote login. *See* rlogin.

Remote Monitoring. *See* RMON.

Remote Operations Service Element. *See* ROSE.

remote-procedure call. *See* RPC.

remote shell protocol. *See* rsh.

remote source-route bridging. *See* RSRB.

rendezvous point. *See* RP.

repeater. A device that regenerates and propagates electrical signals between two network segments. *See also* segment.

Request For Comments. *See* RFC.

request/response unit. *See* RU.

Research on Advanced Communications in Europe. *See* RACE.

RÈseaux AssociÈs pour la Recherche EuropÈenne. *See* RARE.

Reverse Address Resolution Protocol. *See* RARP.

Reverse Path Multicasting. *See* RPM.

RF. radio frequency. A frequency that corresponds to radio transmissions. Cable TV and broadband networks use RF technology.

RFC. Request For Comments. A document series used as the primary means for communicating information about the Internet. Some RFCs are designated by the IAB as Internet standards. Most RFCs document protocol specifications such as Telnet and FTP, but some are humorous or historical. RFCs are available online from numerous sources.

RFI. radio frequency interference. A radio frequency that creates noise that interferes with information being transmitted across unshielded copper cabling.

RIF. Routing Information Field. A field in the IEEE 802.5 header that is used by a source-route bridge to determine through which Token Ring network segments a packet must transit. A RIF is made up of ring and bridge numbers as well as other information.

RII. Routing Information Identifier. A bit used by SRT bridges to distinguish between frames that should be transparently bridged and frames that should be passed to the SRB module for handling.

ring. A connection of two or more stations in a logically circular topology. Information is passed sequentially between active stations. Token Ring, FDDI, and CDDI are based on this topology.

ring latency. The time required for a signal to propagate once around a ring in a Token Ring or IEEE 802.5 network.

ring monitor. A centralized management tool for Token Ring networks based on the IEEE 802.5 specification. *See also* active monitor and standby monitor.

ring topology. A network topology that consists of a series of repeaters connected to one another by unidirectional transmission links to form a single closed loop. Each station on the network connects to the network at a repeater. Although logically a ring, ring topologies are most often organized in a closed-loop star. *Compare with* bus topology, star topology, and tree topology.

RIP. Routing Information Protocol. An IGP supplied with UNIX BSD systems. The most common IGP in the Internet. RIP uses hop count as a routing metric. *See also* Enhanced IGRP, hop count, IGP, IGRP, and OSPF.

RJ connector. registered jack connector. Standard connectors originally used to connect telephone lines. RJ connectors are now used for telephone connections and for 10BaseT and other types of network connections. RJ-11, RJ-12, and RJ-45 are popular types of RJ connectors.

RJE. remote job entry. An application that is batch oriented, as opposed to interactive. In RJE environments, jobs are submitted to a computing facility, and output is received later.

rlogin. remote login. A terminal emulation program, similar to Telnet, offered in most UNIX implementations.

RMON. Remote Monitoring. An MIB agent specification described in RFC 1271 that defines functions for the remote monitoring of networked devices. The RMON specification provides numerous monitoring, problem detection, and reporting capabilities.

ROM. read-only memory. Nonvolatile memory that can be read, but not written, by the microprocessor.

root account. A privileged account on UNIX systems used exclusively by network or system administrators.

root bridge. A bridge that exchanges topology information with designated bridges in a spanning-tree implementation in order to notify all other bridges in the network when topology changes are required. This prevents loops and provides a measure of defense against link failure.

ROSE. Remote Operations Service Element. An OSI RPC mechanism used by various OSI network application protocols.

round-trip time. *See* RTT.

route. A path through an internetwork.

routed protocol. A protocol that can be routed by a router. A router must be able to interpret the logical internetwork as specified by that routed protocol. Examples of routed protocols include AppleTalk, DECnet, and IP.

route extension. In SNA, a path from the destination subarea node, through peripheral equipment, to a NAU.

route map. A method of controlling the redistribution of routes between routing domains.

route summarization. The consolidation of advertised addresses in OSPF and IS-IS. In OSPF, this causes a single summary route to be advertised to other areas by an ABR (area border router).

router. A network layer device that uses one or more metrics to determine the optimal path along which network traffic should be forwarded. Routers forward packets from one network to another based on network layer information. Occasionally called a gateway (although this definition of gateway is becoming increasingly outdated). *Compare with* gateway. *See also* relay.

route redistribution. *See* redistribution.

routing. The process of finding a path to a destination host. Routing is very complex in large networks because of the many potential intermediate destinations a packet might traverse before reaching its destination host.

routing domain. A group of end systems and intermediate systems operating under the same set of administrative rules. Within each routing domain is one or more areas, each uniquely identified by an area address.

Routing Information Field. *See* RIF.

Routing Information Identifier. *See* RII.

Routing Information Protocol. *See* RIP.

routing metric. A method by which a routing algorithm determines that one route is better than another. This information is stored in routing tables. Metrics include bandwidth, communication cost, delay, hop count, load, MTU, path cost, and reliability. Sometimes referred to simply as a metric. *See also* cost.

routing protocol. A protocol that accomplishes routing through the implementation of a specific routing algorithm. Examples of routing protocols are IGRP, OSPF, and RIP.

routing table. A table stored in a router or some other internetworking device that keeps track of routes to particular network destinations and, in some cases, metrics associated with those routes.

Routing Table Maintenance Protocol. *See* RTMP.

Routing Table Protocol. *See* RTP.

routing update. A message sent from a router to indicate network reachability and associated cost information. Routing updates are typically sent at regular intervals and after a change in network topology. *Compare with* flash update.

RP. 1. rendezvous point. A router specified in PIM sparse mode implementations to track membership in multicast groups and to forward messages to known multicast group addresses. *See also* PIM sparse mode. 2. route processor. A processor module in the Cisco 7000 series routers that contains the CPU, system software, and most of the memory components that are used in the router. Sometimes called a supervisory processor.

RPC. remote-procedure call. The technological foundation of client/server computing. RPCs are procedure calls that are built or specified by clients and executed on servers, with the results returned over the network to the clients. *See also* client/server computing.

RPM. Reverse Path Multicasting. A multicasting technique in which a multicast datagram is forwarded out of all but the receiving interface if the receiving interface is one used to forward unicast datagrams to the source of the multicast datagram.

RS-232. A popular physical layer interface. Now known as EIA/TIA-232. *See* EIA/TIA-232.

RS-422. A balanced electrical implementation of EIA/TIA-449 for high-speed data transmission. Now referred to collectively with RS-423 as EIA-530. *See also* EIA-530 and RS-423.

RS-423. An unbalanced electrical implementation of EIA/TIA-449 for EIA/TIA-232 compatibility. Now referred to collectively with RS-422 as EIA-530. *See also* EIA-530 and RS-422.

RS-449. A popular physical layer interface. Now known as EIA/TIA-449. *See* EIA/TIA-449.

rsh. remote shell protocol. A protocol that allows a user to execute commands on a remote system without having to log in to the system. For example, rsh can be used to remotely examine the status of a number of access servers without connecting to each communication server, executing the command, and then disconnecting from the communication server.

RSRB. remote source-route bridging. An SRB over WAN links. *See also* SRB.

RSVP. Resource Reservation Protocol. A protocol that supports the reservation of resources across an IP network. Applications running on IP end systems can use RSVP to indicate to other nodes the nature (bandwidth, jitter, maximum burst, and so forth) of the packet streams they want to receive. RSVP depends on IPv6. Also known as Resource Reservation Setup Protocol.

RTCP. RTP Control Protocol. A protocol that monitors the QOS of an IPv6 RTP connection and conveys information about the on-going session.

RTMP. Routing Table Maintenance Protocol. An Apple Computer proprietary routing protocol. RTMP was derived from RIP. *See also* RIP.

RTP. 1. Routing Table Protocol. A VINES routing protocol based on RIP. Distributes network topology information and aids VINES servers in finding neighboring clients, servers, and routers. Uses delay as a routing metric. *See also* SRTP. 2. Rapid Transport Protocol. A protocol that provides pacing and error recovery for APPN data as it crosses the APPN network. With RTP, error recovery and flow control are done end-to-end rather than at every node. RTP prevents congestion rather than reacts to it.

RTS. Ready To Send. An EIA/TIA-232 control signal that requests a data transmission on a communications line.

RTT. round-trip time. The time required for a network communication to travel from the source to the destination and back. RTT includes the time required for the destination to process the message from the source and generate a reply. RTT is used by some routing algorithms to aid in calculating optimal routes.

RU. request/response unit. The request and response messages exchanged between NAUs in an SNA network.

S

SAC. single-attached concentrator. An FDDI or CDDI concentrator that connects to the network by being cascaded from the master port of another FDDI or CDDI concentrator.

sampling rate. The rate at which samples of a particular waveform amplitude are taken.

SAP. 1. service access point. A field defined by the IEEE 802.2 specification that is part of an address specification. Thus, the destination plus the DSAP define the recipient of a packet. The same applies to the SSAP. *See also* DSAP and SSAP. 2.

Service Advertisement Protocol. An IPX protocol that provides a means of informing network clients, via routers and servers, of available network resources and services. *See also* IPX.

SAR. segmentation and reassembly. One of the two sublayers of the AAL CPCS, responsible for dividing (at the source) and reassembling (at the destination) the PDUs passed from the CS. The SAR sublayer takes the PDUs processed by the CS and, after dividing them into 48-byte pieces of payload data, passes them to the ATM layer for further processing. *See also* AAL, ATM layer, CPCS, CS, and SSCS.

SAS. single attachment station. A device attached only to the primary ring of an FDDI ring. Also known as a Class B station. *Compare with* DAS. *See also* FDDI.

satellite communication. The use of orbiting satellites to relay data between multiple earth-based stations. Satellite communications offer high bandwidth and a cost that is not related to distance between earth stations, long propagation delays, or broadcast capability.

SBus. A bus technology used in Sun SPARC-based workstations and servers. The SBus specification has been adopted by the IEEE as a new bus standard.

SCR. sustainable cell rate. A parameter defined by the ATM Forum for ATM traffic management. For VBR connections, SCR determines the long-term average cell rate that can be transmitted. *See also* VBR.

SCTE. serial clock transmit external. A timing signal that DTE echoes to DCE to maintain clocking. SCTE is designed to compensate for clock phase shift on long cables. When the DCE device uses SCTE instead of its internal clock to sample data from the DTE, it is better able to sample the data without error, even if there is a phase shift in the cable. *See also* phase shift.

SDH. Synchronous Digital Hierarchy. A European standard that defines a set of rate and format standards that are transmitted using optical signals over fiber. SDH is similar to SONET, with a basic SDH rate of 155.52 Mbps, designated at STM-1. *See also* SONET and STM-1.

SDLC. Synchronous Data Link Control. An SNA data link layer communications protocol. SDLC is a bit-oriented, full-duplex serial protocol that has spawned numerous similar protocols, including HDLC and LAPB. *See also* HDLC and LAPB.

SDLLC. A feature that performs translation between SDLC and IEEE 802.2 type 2.

SDSU. SMDS DSU. A DSU for access to SMDS via HSSIs and other serial interfaces.

SDU. service data unit. A unit of information from an upper-layer protocol that defines a service request to a lower-layer protocol.

SEAL. simple and efficient AAL. A scheme used by AAL5 in which the SAR sublayer segments CS PDUs without adding additional fields. *See also* AAL, AAL5, CS, and SAR.

secondary. *See* secondary station.

secondary ring. One of the two rings that makes up an FDDI or CDDI ring. The secondary ring is usually reserved for use in the event of a failure of the primary ring. *Compare with* primary ring.

secondary station. In bit-synchronous data link layer protocols such as HDLC, a station that responds to commands from a primary station. Sometimes referred to simply as a secondary. *See also* primary station.

security management. One of five categories of network management defined by ISO for management of OSI networks. Security management subsystems are responsible for controlling access to network resources. *See also* accounting management, configuration management, fault management, and performance management.

seed router. A router that responds to configuration queries from nonseed routers on its connected AppleTalk network, allowing those routers to confirm or modify their configurations accordingly. *See also* nonseed router.

segment. 1. A section of a network that is bounded by bridges, routers, or switches. 2. In a LAN using a bus topology, a continuous electrical circuit that is often connected to other such segments with repeaters. 3. In the TCP specification, a single transport layer unit of information. The terms datagram, frame, message, and packet are also used to describe logical information groupings at various layers of the OSI reference model and in various technology circles.

segmentation and reassembly. *See* SAR.

Sequenced Packet Exchange. *See* SPX.

Sequenced Packet Protocol. *See* \SPP.

Sequenced Routing Update Protocol. *See* SRTP.

serial clock transmit external. *See* SCTE.

Serial Line Internet Protocol. *See* SLIP.

serial transmission . A method of data transmission in which the bits of a data character are transmitted sequentially over a single channel. *Compare with* parallel transmission.

server. A node or software program that provides services to clients. *See also* back end, client, and front end.

Server Message Block. *See* SMB.

service access point. *See* SAP.

Service Advertisement Protocol. *See* SAP.

service data unit. *See* SDU.

service point. An interface between non-SNA devices and NetView that sends alerts from equipment unknown to the SNA environment.

service profile identifier. *See* SPID.

service-specific convergence sublayer. *See* SSCS.

session. 1. A related set of communications transactions between two or more network devices. 2. In SNA, a logical connection enabling two NAUs to communicate.

session layer. Layer 5 of the OSI reference model. This layer establishes, manages, and terminates sessions between applications and manages data exchange between presentation layer entities. Corresponds to the data flow control layer of the SNA model. *See also* application layer, data link layer, network layer, physical layer, presentation layer, and transport layer.

SF. Super Frame. A common framing type used on T1 circuits. SF consists of 12 frames of 192 bits each, with the 193rd bit providing error checking and other functions. SF has been superseded by ESF, but is still widely used. Also called D4 framing. *See also* ESF.

SGMP. Simple Gateway Monitoring Protocol. A network management protocol that was considered for Internet standardization and later evolved into SNMP. Documented in RFC 1028. *See also* SNMP.

shaping. *See* traffic shaping.

shielded cable. A cable that has a layer of shielded insulation to reduce EMI.

shielded twisted-pair. *See* STP.

shortest path first algorithm. *See* SPF.

shortest-path routing. Routing that minimizes distance or path cost through application of an algorithm.

signaling. The process of sending a transmission signal over a physical medium for purposes of communication.

signaling packet. A packet generated by an ATM-connected device that wants to establish a connection with another such device. The signaling packet contains the ATM NSAP address of the desired ATM endpoint, as well as any QoS parameters required for the connection. If the endpoint can support the desired QoS, it responds with an accept message, and the connection is opened. *See also* QoS.

Signaling System number 7. *See* SS7.

signal quality error. *See* SQE.

simple and efficient AAL. *See* SEAL.

Simple Gateway Monitoring Protocol. *See* SGMP.

Simple Mail Transfer Protocol. *See* SMTP.

Simple Multicast Routing Protocol. *See* SMRP.

Simple Network Management Protocol. *See* SNMP.

simplex. The capability for data transmission in only one direction between a sending station and a receiving station. *Compare with* full duplex and half duplex

single-attached concentrator. *See* SAC.

single attachment station. *See* SAS.

single-mode fiber. Fiber-optic cabling with a narrow core that allows light to enter only at a single angle. Such cabling has higher bandwidth than multimode fiber, but requires a light source with a narrow spectral width (for example, a laser). Also called monomode fiber. *See also* multimode fiber.

single-route explorer packet. *See* spanning explorer packet.

single-vendor network. A network using equipment from only one vendor. Single-vendor networks rarely suffer compatibility problems. *See also* multivendor network.

SIP. SMDS Interface Protocol. A protocol used in communications between CPE and SMDS network equipment. Allows the CPE to use SMDS service for high-speed WAN internetworking. Based on the IEEE 802.6 DQDB standard. *See also* DQDB.

sliding window flow control. A method of flow control in which a receiver gives a transmitter permission to transmit data until a window is full. When the window is full, the transmitter must stop transmitting until the receiver advertises a larger window. TCP, other transport protocols, and several data link layer protocols use this method of flow control.

SLIP. Serial Line Internet Protocol. A standard protocol for point-to-point serial connections using a variation of TCP/IP. A predecessor of PPP. *See also* CSLIP and PPP.

slotted ring. A LAN architecture based on a ring topology in which the ring is divided into slots that circulate continuously. Slots can be either empty or full, and transmissions must start at the beginning of a slot.

slow switching. Packet processing performed at process level speeds, without the use of a route cache. *Compare with* fast switching.

SMAC. source MAC. A MAC address specified in the Source Address field of a packet. *Compare with* DMAC. *See also* MAC address.

small business. A company that has 1 to 100 users. This type of company might have a small remote offices with some telecommuters. The network is made of simple LANs with low-speed WAN connections such as fractional T1s, Frame Relay, ISDN, or modem connections. Small businesses usually have simple routing protocols, such as static routing or RIP.

SMB. Server Message Block. A file-system protocol used in LAN Manager and similar NOSs to package data and exchange information with other systems.

SMDS. Switched Multimegabit Data Service. A high-speed, packet-switched, datagram-based WAN networking technology offered by the telephone companies. *See also* CBDS.

SMDS Interface Protocol. *See* SIP.

SMI. Structure of Management Information. A document (RFC 1155) specifying rules used to define managed objects in the MIB. *See also* MIB.

smoothing. *See* traffic shaping.

SMRP. Simple Multicast Routing Protocol. A specialized multicast network protocol for routing multimedia data streams on enterprise networks. SMRP works in conjunction with multicast extensions to the AppleTalk protocol.

SMT. Station Management. An ANSI FDDI specification that defines how ring stations are managed.

SMTP. Simple Mail Transfer Protocol. An Internet protocol that provides electronic mail services.

SNA. Systems Network Architecture. A large, complex, feature-rich network architecture developed in the 1970s by IBM. Similar in some respects to the OSI reference model, but with a number of differences. SNA is essentially composed of seven layers. *See* data flow control layer, data link control layer, path control layer, physical control layer, presentation services layer, transaction services layer, and transmission control layer.

SNA Distribution Services. *See* SNADS.

SNA Network Interconnection. *See* SNI.

SNADS. SNA Distribution Services. Consists of a set of SNA transaction programs that interconnect and cooperate to provide asynchronous distribution of information between end users. One of three SNA transaction services. *See also* DDM and DIA.

SNAP. Subnetwork Access Protocol. An Internet protocol that operates between a network entity in the subnetwork and a network entity in the end system. SNAP specifies a standard method of encapsulating IP datagrams and ARP messages on IEEE networks. The SNAP entity in the end system makes use of the services of the subnetwork and performs three key functions: data transfer, connection management, and QOS selection.

SNI. 1. Subscriber Network Interface. An interface for SMDS-based networks that connects CPE and an SMDS switch. *See also* UNI. 2. SNA Network Interconnection. An IBM gateway connecting multiple SNA networks.

SNMP. Simple Network Management Protocol. A network management protocol used almost exclusively in TCP/IP networks. SNMP provides a means to monitor and control network devices, and to manage configurations, statistics collection, performance, and security. *See also* SGMP and SNMP2.

SNMP communities. Authentication scheme that enables an intelligent network device to validate SNMP requests from sources such as the NMS. *See also* SNMP.

SNMP2. SNMP Version 2. Version 2 of the popular network management protocol. SNMP2 supports centralized as well as distributed network management strategies, and includes improvements in the SMI, protocol operations, management architecture, and security. *See also* SNMP.

SNPA. subnetwork point of attachment. A data link layer address (such as an Ethernet address, an X.25 address, or a Frame Relay DLCI address). SNPA addresses are used to configure a CLNS route for an interface.

socket. A software structure operating as a communications endpoint within a network device.

SONET. Synchronous Optical Network. A high-speed (up to 2.5 Gbps) synchronous network specification developed by Bellcore and designed to run on optical fiber. STS-1 is the basic building block of SONET. Approved as an international standard in 1988. *See also* SDH, STS-1, and STS-3c.

source address. The address of a network device that is sending data. *See also* destination address.

source MAC. *See* SMAC.

source-route bridging. *See* SRB.

source-route translational bridging. *See* SR/TLB.

source-route transparent bridging. *See* SRT.

source service access point. *See* SSAP.

Southeastern Universities Research Association Network. *See* SURAnet.

span. A full-duplex digital transmission line between two digital facilities.

spanning explorer packet. A packet that follows a statically configured spanning tree when looking for paths in an SRB network. Also known as a limited-route explorer packet or a single-route explorer packet. *See also* all-routes explorer packet, explorer packet, and local explorer packet.

spanning tree. A loop-free subset of a network topology. *See also* spanning-tree algorithm and Spanning-Tree Protocol.

spanning-tree algorithm. An algorithm used by the Spanning-Tree Protocol to create a spanning tree. Sometimes abbreviated STA. *See also* spanning tree and Spanning-Tree Protocol.

Spanning-Tree Protocol. A bridge protocol that utilizes the spanning-tree algorithm, enabling a learning bridge to dynamically work around loops in a network topology by creating a spanning tree. Bridges exchange BPDU messages with other bridges to detect loops, and then remove the loops by shutting down selected bridge interfaces. Refers to both the IEEE 802.1 Spanning-Tree Protocol standard and the earlier Digital Equipment Corporation Spanning-Tree Protocol on which it is based. The IEEE version supports bridge domains and allows the bridge to construct a loop-free topology across an extended LAN. The IEEE version is generally preferred over the Digital version. Sometimes abbreviated STP. *See also* BPDU, learning bridge, MAC address learning, spanning tree, and spanning-tree algorithm.

sparse mode PIM. *See* PIM sparse mode.

speed matching. A feature that provides sufficient buffering capability in a destination device to allow a high-speed source to transmit data at its maximum rate, even if the destination device is a lower-speed device.

SPF. shortest path first. A routing algorithm that iterates on length of path to determine a shortest-path spanning tree. Commonly used in link-state routing algorithms. Sometimes called Dijkstra's algorithm. *See also* link state routing algorithm.

SPID. service profile identifier. A number that some service providers use to define the services to which an ISDN device subscribes. The ISDN device uses the SPID when accessing the switch that initializes the connection to a service provider.

split-horizon updates. A routing technique in which information about routes is prevented from exiting the router interface through which that information was received. Split-horizon updates are useful in preventing routing loops.

spoofing. A packet illegally claiming to be from an address from which it was not actually sent. Spoofing is designed to foil network security mechanisms such as filters and access lists.

spooler. An application that manages requests or jobs submitted to it for execution. Spoolers process the submitted requests in an orderly fashion from a queue. A print spooler is an example of a spooler.

SPP. Sequenced Packet Protocol. A protocol that provides reliable, connection-based, flow-controlled packet transmission on behalf of client processes. Part of the XNS protocol suite.

SPX. Sequenced Packet Exchange. A reliable, connection-oriented protocol that supplements the datagram service provided by network layer (Layer 3) protocols. Novell derived this commonly used NetWare transport protocol from the SPP of the XNS protocol suite.

SQE. signal quality error. A transmission sent by a transceiver to the controller to let the controller know whether the collision circuitry is functional. Also called heartbeat.

SRAM. A type of RAM that retains its contents for as long as power is supplied. SRAM does not require constant refreshing, as does DRAM. *Compare with* DRAM.

SRB. source-route bridging. A method of bridging originated by IBM and popular in Token Ring networks. In an SRB network, the entire route to a destination is predetermined, in real time, prior to the sending of data to the destination. *Compare with* transparent bridging.

SRT. source-route transparent bridging. An IBM bridging scheme that merges the two most prevalent bridging strategies, SRB and transparent bridging. SRT employs both technologies in one device to satisfy the needs of all ENs. No translation between bridging protocols is necessary. *Compare with* SR/TLB.

SR/TLB. source-route translational bridging. A method of bridging in which source-route stations can communicate with transparent bridge stations with the help of an intermediate bridge that translates between the two bridge protocols. *Compare with* SRT.

SRTP. Sequenced Routing Update Protocol. A protocol that assists VINES servers in finding neighboring clients, servers, and routers. *See also* RTP (Routing Table Protocol).

SS7. Signaling System number 7. A standard CCS system used with BISDN and ISDN. Developed by Bellcore. *See also* CCS.

SSAP. source service access point. The SAP of the network node designated in the Source field of a packet. *Compare with* DSAP. *See also* SAP (service access point).

SSCP. system services control points. The focal points within an SNA network for managing network configuration, coordinating network operator and problem determination requests, and providing directory services and other session services for network end users.

SSCP-PU session. A session used by SNA to allow an SSCP to manage the resources of a node through the PU. SSCPs can send requests to and receive replies from individual nodes in order to control the network configuration.

SSCS. service-specific convergence sublayer. One of the two sublayers of any AAL. SSCS, which is service dependent, offers insured data transmission. The SSCS can be null as well, in classical IP over ATM or LAN emulation implementations. *See also* AAL, ATM layer, CPCS, CS, and SAR.

SSP. Switch-to-Switch Protocol. A protocol specified in the DLSw standard that routers use to establish DLSw connections, locate resources, forward data, and handle flow control and error recovery. *See also* DLSw.

STA. *See* spanning-tree algorithm.

stack. *See* protocol stack.

standard. A set of rules or procedures that are either widely used or officially specified. *See also* de facto standard and de jure standard.

standby monitor. A device placed in standby mode on a Token Ring network in case an active monitor fails. *See also* active monitor and ring monitor.

StarLAN. CSMA/CD LAN, based on IEEE 802.3, developed by AT&T.

star topology. A LAN topology in which endpoints on a network are connected to a common central switch by point-to-point links. A ring topology that is organized as a star implements a unidirectional closed-loop star, instead of point-to-point links. *Compare with* bus topology, ring topology, and tree topology.

start-stop transmission. *See* asynchronous transmission.

static route. A route that is explicitly configured and entered into the routing table. Static routes take precedence over routes chosen by dynamic routing protocols.

Station Management. *See* SMT.

statistical multiplexing . A technique whereby information from multiple logical channels can be transmitted across a single physical channel. Statistical multiplexing dynamically allocates bandwidth only to active input channels, making better use of available bandwidth and allowing more devices to be connected than with other multiplexing techniques. Also referred to as statistical time-division multiplexing or stat mux. *Compare with* ATDM, FDM, and TDM.

statistical time-division multiplexing. *See* statistical multiplexing.

stat mux. *See* statistical multiplexing.

STM-1. Synchronous Transport Module level 1. One of a number of SDH formats that specifies the frame structure for the 155.52-Mbps lines used to carry ATM cells. *See also* SDH.

store and forward packet switching. A packet-switching technique in which frames are completely processed before being forwarded out the appropriate port. This processing includes calculating the CRC and checking the destination address. In addition, frames must be temporarily stored until network resources (such as an unused link) are available to forward the message. *Compare with* cut-through packet switching.

STP. 1. shielded twisted-pair. A two-pair wiring medium used in a variety of network implementations. STP cabling has a layer of shielded insulation to reduce EMI. *Compare with* UTP. *See also* twisted pair. 2. *See* Spanning-Tree Protocol.

Structure of Management Information. *See* SMI.

STS-1. Synchronous Transport Signal level 1. A basic building block signal of SONET, operating at 51.84 Mbps. Faster SONET rates are defined as STS-*n*, where *n* is a multiple of 51.84 Mbps. *See also* SONET.

STS-3c. Synchronous Transport Signal level 3, concatenated. A SONET format that specifies the frame structure for the 155.52-Mbps lines used to carry ATM cells. *See also* SONET.

stub area. An OSPF area that carries a default route, intra-area routes, and interarea routes, but does not carry external routes. Virtual links cannot be configured across a stub area, and they cannot contain an ASBR. *Compare with* non-stub area. *See also* ASBR and OSPF.

stub network. A network that has only a single connection to a router.

subarea. A portion of an SNA network that consists of a subarea node and any attached links and peripheral nodes.

subarea node. An SNA communication controller or host that handles complete network addresses.

subchannel. In broadband terminology, a frequency-based subdivision creating a separate communications channel.

subinterface. One of a number of virtual interfaces on a single physical interface.

subnet. *See* subnetwork.

subnet address. A portion of an IP address that is specified as the subnetwork by the subnet mask. *See also* IP address, subnet mask, and subnetwork.

subnet mask. A 32-bit address mask used in IP to indicate the bits of an IP address that are being used for the subnet address. Sometimes referred to simply as mask. *See also* address mask and IP address.

subnetwork. 1. In IP networks, a network sharing a particular subnet address. Subnetworks are networks arbitrarily segmented by a network administrator in order to provide a multilevel, hierarchical routing structure while shielding the subnetwork from the addressing complexity of attached networks. Sometimes called a subnet. *See also* IP address, subnet address, and subnet mask. 2. In OSI networks, a collection of ESs and ISs under the control of a single administrative domain and using a single network access protocol.

Subnetwork Access Protocol. *See* SNAP.

subnetwork point of attachment. *See* SNPA.

Subscriber Network Interface. *See* SNI.

subvector. A data segment of a vector in an SNA message. A subvector consists of a length field, a key that describes the subvector type, and subvector-specific data.

Super Frame. *See* SF.

supervisory processor. *See* RP (route processor).

SURAnet. Southeastern Universities Research Association Network. A network connecting universities and other organizations in the Southeastern United States. SURAnet, originally funded by the NSF and a part of NSFNET, is now part of BBN Planet. *See also* BBN Planet, NSF, and NSFNET.

sustainable cell rate. *See* SCR.

SVC. switched virtual circuit. A virtual circuit that is dynamically established on demand and is torn down when transmission is complete. SVCs are used in situations where data transmission is sporadic. Called a switched virtual connection in ATM terminology. *Compare with* PVC.

switch. 1. A network device that filters, forwards, and floods frames based on the destination address of each frame. The switch operates at the data link layer of the OSI model. 2. An electronic or mechanical device that allows a connection to be established as necessary and terminated when there is no longer a session to support.

switched LAN. A LAN implemented with LAN switches. *See* LAN switch.

Switched Multimegabit Data Service. *See* SMDS.

switched virtual circuit. *See* SVC.

switched virtual connection. *See* SVC.

Switch-to-Switch Protocol. *See* SSP.

synchronization. Establishment of common timing between sender and receiver.

Synchronous Data Link Control. *See* SDLC.

Synchronous Digital Hierarchy. *See* SDH.

Synchronous Optical Network. *See* SONET.

synchronous transmission. Digital signals that are transmitted with precise clocking. Such signals have the same frequency, with individual characters encapsulated in control bits (called start bits and stop bits) that designate the beginning and end of each character. *Compare with* asynchronous transmission, isochronous transmission, and plesiochronous transmission.

Synchronous Transport Module level 1. *See* STM-1.

Synchronous Transport Signal level 1. *See* STS-1.

Synchronous Transport Signal level 3, concatenated. *See* STS-3c.

sysgen. system generation. The process of defining network resources in a network.

system generation. *See* sysgen.

system services control points. *See* SSCP.

Systems Network Architecture. *See* SNA.

T

T1. A digital WAN carrier facility. T1 transmits DS-1–formatted data at 1.544 Mbps through the telephone-switching network, using AMI or B8ZS coding. *Compare with* E1. *See also* AMI, B8ZS, and DS-1.

T3. A digital WAN carrier facility. T3 transmits DS-3–formatted data at 44.736 Mbps through the telephone switching network. *Compare with* E3. *See also* DS-3.

TAC. Terminal Access Controller. An Internet host that accepts terminal connections from dial-up lines.

TACACS. Terminal Access Controller Access Control System. An authentication protocol, developed by the DDN community, that provides remote access authentication and related services, such as event logging. User passwords are administered in a central database rather than in individual routers, providing an easily scalable network security solution.

tag switching. A high-performance, packet-forwarding technology that integrates network layer (Layer 3) routing and data link layer (Layer 2) switching and provides scalable, high-speed switching in the network core. Tag switching is based on the concept of label swapping, in which packets or cells are assigned short, fixed-length labels that tell switching nodes how data should be forwarded.

tagged traffic. ATM cells that have their CLP bit set to 1. If the network is congested, tagged traffic can be dropped to ensure delivery of higher-priority traffic. Sometimes called DE (discard eligible) traffic. *See also* CLP.

TAXI 4B/5B. Transparent Asynchronous Transmitter/Receiver Interface 4-byte/5-byte. An encoding scheme used for FDDI LANs, as well as for ATM. Supports speeds of up to 100 Mbps over multimode fiber. TAXI is the chipset that generates 4B/5B encoding on multimode fiber. *See also* 4B/5B local fiber.

T-carrier. A TDM transmission method usually referring to a line or cable carrying a DS-1 signal.

TCP. Transmission Control Protocol. A connection-oriented transport layer protocol that provides reliable full-duplex data transmission. TCP is part of the TCP/IP protocol stack. *See also* TCP/IP.

TCP/IP. Transmission Control Protocol/Internet Protocol. A common name for the suite of protocols developed by the U.S. DoD in the 1970s to support the construction of worldwide internetworks. TCP and IP are the two best-known protocols in the suite. *See also* IP and TCP.

TCU. trunk coupling unit. In Token Ring networks, a physical device that enables a station to connect to the trunk cable.

TDM. time-division multiplexing. A technique in which information from multiple channels can be allocated bandwidth on a single wire based on preassigned time slots. Bandwidth is allocated to each channel, regardless of whether the station has data to transmit. *Compare with* ATDM, FDM, and statistical multiplexing.

TDR. time domain reflectometer. A device capable of sending signals through a network medium to check cable continuity and other attributes. TDRs are used to find physical layer network problems.

Technical Assistance Center. *See* TAC.

Technical Office Protocol. *See* TOP.

telco. Abbreviation for telephone company.

telecommunications. Communications (usually involving computer systems) over the telephone network.

Telecommunications Industry Association. *See* TIA.

telephony. The science of converting sound to electrical signals and transmitting it between widely removed points.

telex. A teletypewriter service that allows subscribers to send messages over PSTN.

Telnet. A standard terminal emulation protocol in the TCP/IP protocol stack. Telnet is used for remote terminal connection, enabling users to log in to remote systems and use resources as if they were connected to a local system. Telnet is defined in RFC 854.

Tempest. A U.S. military standard. Electronic products adhering to the Tempest specification are designed to withstand EMP. *See also* EMP.

TERENA. Trans-European Research and Education Networking Association. An organization that promotes information and telecommunications technologies development in Europe. Formed by the merging of EARN and RARE. *See also* EARN and RARE.

termid. SNA cluster controller identification. Termid is meaningful only for switched lines. Also called Xid.

terminal. A simple device at which data can be entered or retrieved from a network. Generally, a terminal has a monitor and a keyboard, but no processor or local disk drive.

Terminal Access Controller. *See* TAC.

Terminal Access Controller Access System. *See* TACACS.

terminal adapter. A device used to connect ISDN BRI connections to existing interfaces such as EIA/TIA-232. Essentially, an ISDN modem.

terminal emulation. A network application in which a computer runs software that makes it appear to a remote host as a directly attached terminal.

terminal server. A communications processor that connects asynchronous devices such as terminals, printers, hosts, and modems to any LAN or WAN that uses TCP/IP, X.25, or LAT protocols. Terminal servers provide the internetwork intelligence that is not available in the connected devices.

terminator. A device that provides electrical resistance at the end of a transmission line to absorb signals on the line, thereby keeping them from bouncing back and being received again by network stations.

Texas Higher Education Network. *See* THEnet.

TFTP. Trivial File Transfer Protocol. A simplified version of FTP that allows files to be transferred from one computer to another over a network.

TH. transmission header. An SNA header that is appended to the SNA basic information unit (BIU). The TH uses one of a number of available SNA header formats. *See also* FID0, FID1, FID2, FID3, and FID4.

THEnet. Texas Higher Education Network. A regional network comprising more than 60 academic and research institutions in the Texas area.

Thinnet. A thinner, less expensive version of the cable specified in the IEEE 802.3 10Base2 standard. *Compare with* Cheapernet. *See also* 10Base2, Ethernet, and IEEE 802.3.

throughput. The rate of information arriving at, and possibly passing through, a particular point in a network system.

TIA. Telecommunications Industry Association. An organization that develops standards relating to telecommunications technologies. Together, the TIA and the EIA have formalized standards, such as EIA/TIA-232, for the electrical characteristics of data transmission. *See also* EIA.

TIC. Token Ring interface coupler. A controller through which an FEP connects to a Token Ring.

time-division multiplexing. *See* TDM.

time domain reflectometer. *See* TDR.

Time Notify. *See* TNotify.

time-out. An event that occurs when one network device expects to hear from another network device within a specified period of time, but does not. The resulting time-out usually results in a retransmission of information or the dissolving of the session between the two devices.

Time To Live. *See* TTL.

TN3270. Terminal emulation software that allows a terminal to appear to an IBM host as a 3278 Model 2 terminal.

TNotify. Time Notify. Specifies how often SMT initiates neighbor notification broadcasts. *See also* SMT.

token. A frame that contains control information. Possession of the token allows a network device to transmit data onto the network. *See also* token passing.

token bus. A LAN architecture that uses token passing access over a bus topology. This LAN architecture is the basis for the IEEE 802.4 LAN specification. *See also* IEEE 802.4.

token passing. An access method by which network devices access the physical medium in an orderly fashion based on possession of a small frame called a token. *Compare with* circuit switching and contention. *See also* token.

Token Ring. A token-passing LAN developed and supported by IBM. Token Ring runs at 4 or 16 Mbps over a ring topology. Similar to IEEE 802.5. *See also* IEEE 802.5, ring topology, and token passing.

Token Ring interface coupler. *See* TIC.

TOP. Technical Office Protocol. An OSI-based architecture developed for office communications.

topology. The physical arrangement of network nodes and media within an enterprise networking structure.

TOS. type of service. *See* COS (class of service).

TP0. Transport Protocol Class 0. An OSI connectionless transport protocol for use over reliable subnetworks. Defined by ISO 8073.

TP4. Transport Protocol Class 4. An OSI connection-based transport protocol. Defined by ISO 8073.

traffic policing . A process used to measure the actual traffic flow across a given connection and compare it to the total admissible traffic flow for that connection. Traffic outside the agreed on flow can be tagged (where the CLP bit is set to 1) and can be discarded en route if congestion develops. Traffic policing is used in ATM, Frame Relay, and other types of networks. Also know as admission control, permit processing, rate enforcement, and UPC (usage parameter control). *See also* tagged traffic.

traffic shaping. The use of queues to limit surges that can congest a network. Data is buffered and then sent into the network in regulated amounts to ensure that the traffic will fit within the promised traffic envelope for the particular connection. Traffic shaping is used in ATM, Frame Relay, and other types of networks. Also known as metering, shaping, and smoothing.

trailer. Control information appended to data when encapsulating the data for network transmission. *Compare with* header.

transaction. A result-oriented unit of communication processing.

transaction services layer. Layer 7 in the SNA architectural model. Represents user application functions, such as spreadsheets, word processing, or electronic mail, by which users interact with the network. Corresponds roughly with the application layer of the OSI reference model. *See also* data flow control layer, data link control layer, path control layer, physical control layer, presentation services layer, and transmission control layer.

transceiver. *See* MAU.

transceiver cable. *See* AUI.

Trans-European Research and Education Networking Association. *See* TERENA.

transit bridging. Bridging that uses encapsulation to send a frame between two similar networks over a dissimilar network.

translational bridging. Bridging between networks with dissimilar MAC sublayer protocols. MAC information is translated into the format of the destination network at the bridge. *Compare with* encapsulation bridging.

transmission control layer. Layer 4 in the SNA architectural model. This layer is responsible for establishing, maintaining, and terminating SNA sessions, sequencing data messages, and controlling session level flow. Corresponds to the transport layer of the OSI model. *See also* data flow control layer, data link control layer, path control layer, physical control layer, presentation services layer, and transaction services layer.

Transmission Control Protocol. *See* TCP.

Transmission Control Protocol/Internet Protocol. *See* TCP/IP.

transmission group. In SNA routing, one or more parallel communications links treated as one communications facility.

transmission header. *See* TH.

transmission link. *See* link.

TRANSPAC. A major packet data network run by France Telecom.

Transparent Asynchronous Transmitter/Receiver Interface 4-byte/5-byte. *See* TAXI 4B/5B.

transparent bridging. A bridging scheme often used in Ethernet and IEEE 802.3 networks in which bridges pass frames one hop at a time based on tables associating end nodes with bridge ports. Transparent bridging is so named because the presence of bridges is transparent to network end nodes. *Compare with* SRB.

transport layer. Layer 4 of the OSI reference model. This layer is responsible for reliable network communication between end nodes. The transport layer provides mechanisms for the establishment, maintenance, and termination of virtual circuits, transport fault detection and recovery, and information flow control. Corresponds to the transmission control layer of the SNA model. *See also* application layer, data link layer, network layer, physical layer, presentation layer, and session layer.

Transport Protocol Class 0. *See* TP0.

Transport Protocol Class 4. *See* TP4.

trap. A message sent by an SNMP agent to an NMS, console, or terminal to indicate the occurrence of a significant event, such as a specifically defined condition or a threshold that has been reached. *See also* alarm and event.

tree topology. A LAN topology similar to a bus topology, except that tree networks can contain branches with multiple nodes. Transmissions from a station propagate the length of the medium and are received by all other stations. *Compare with* bus topology, ring topology, and star topology.

Trivial File Transfer Protocol. *See* TFTP.

trunk. A physical and logical connection between two ATM switches across which traffic in an ATM network travels. An ATM backbone is composed of a number of trunks.

trunk coupling unit. *See* TCU.

trunk up-down. *See* TUD.

TTL. Time To Live. A field in an IP header that indicates how long a packet is considered valid.

tunneling. An architecture that is designed to provide the services necessary to implement any standard point-to-point encapsulation scheme. *See also* encapsulation.

TUD. trunk up-down. A protocol used in ATM networks that monitors trunks and detects when one goes down or comes up. ATM switches send regular test messages from each trunk port to test trunk line quality. If a trunk misses a given number of these messages, TUD declares the trunk down. When a trunk comes back up, TUD recognizes that the trunk is up, declares the trunk up, and returns it to service. *See also* trunk.

TUV. A German test agency that certifies products to European safety standards.

twisted pair. A relatively low-speed transmission medium consisting of two insulated wires arranged in a regular spiral pattern. The wires can be shielded or unshielded. Twisted pair is common in telephony applications and is increasingly common in data networks. *See also* STP and UTP.

two-way simultaneous. *See* TWS.

TWS. two-way simultaneous. A mode that allows a router configured as a primary SDLC station to achieve better utilization of a full-duplex serial line. When TWS is enabled in a multidrop environment, the router can poll a secondary station and receive data from that station while it sends data to or receives data from a different secondary station on the same serial line.

TYMNET. *See* XStream.

Type 1 operation. IEEE 802.2 (LLC) connectionless operation.

Type 2 operation. IEEE 802.2 (LLC) connection-oriented operation.

type of service. *See* TOS.

U

UART. Universal Asynchronous Receiver/Transmitter. An integrated circuit, attached to the parallel bus of a computer, used for serial communications. The UART translates between serial and parallel signals, provides transmission clocking, and buffers data sent to or from the computer.

UB Net/One. Ungermann-Bass Net/One. A routing protocol, developed by UB Networks, that uses hello packets and a path-delay metric, with end nodes communicating using the XNS protocol. There are a number of differences between the manner in which Net/One uses the XNS protocol and the usage common among other XNS nodes.

UBR. unspecified bit rate. A QOS class defined by the ATM Forum for ATM networks. UBR allows any amount of data up to a specified maximum to be sent across the network, but there are no guarantees in terms of cell loss rate and delay. *Compare with* ABR (available bit rate), CBR, and VBR.

UDP. User Datagram Protocol. A connectionless transport layer protocol in the TCP/IP protocol stack. UDP is a simple protocol that exchanges datagrams without acknowledgments or guaranteed delivery, requiring that error processing and retransmission be handled by other protocols. UDP is defined in RFC 768.

UL. Underwriters Laboratories. An independent agency within the United States that tests product safety.

ULP. upper-layer protocol. A protocol that operates at a higher layer in the OSI reference model than other layers. ULP is sometimes used to refer to the next-highest protocol (relative to a particular protocol) in a protocol stack.

unbalanced configuration. HDLC configuration with one primary station and multiple secondary stations.

Underwriters Laboratories. *See* UL.

Ungermann-Bass Net/One. *See* UB Net/One.

UNI. User-Network Interface. An ATM Forum specification that defines an interoperability standard for the interface between ATM-based products (a router or an ATM switch) located in a private network and the ATM switches located within the public carrier networks. Also used to describe similar connections in Frame Relay networks. *See also* NNI, Q.920/Q.921, and SNI (Subscriber Network Interface).

unicast. A message sent to a single network destination. *Compare with* broadcast and multicast.

unicast address. An address that specifies a single network device. *Compare with* broadcast address and multicast address. *See also* unicast.

uninsured traffic. Traffic within the excess rate (the difference between the insured rate and maximum rate) for a VCC. This traffic can be dropped by the network if congestion occurs. *See also* CLP, insured rate, and maximum rate.

unipolar. One polarity (literally), the fundamental electrical characteristic of internal signals in digital communications equipment. *Compare with* bipolar.

unity gain. In broadband networks, the balance between signal loss and signal gain through amplifiers.

Universal Asynchronous Receiver/Transmitter. *See* UART.

Universal Resource Locator. *See* URL.

UNIX. An Operating system developed in 1969 at Bell Laboratories. UNIX has gone through several iterations since its inception. These include UNIX 4.3 BSD (Berkeley Standard Distribution), developed at the University of California at Berkeley, and UNIX System V, Release 4.0, developed by AT&T.

UNIX-to-UNIX Copy Program. *See* UUCP.

unnumbered frame. An HDLC frame used for a specific control or management purposes, including link startup and shutdown, and mode specification.

unshielded twisted-pair. *See* UTP.

unspecified bit rate. *See* UBR.

UPC. usage parameter control. *See* traffic policing.

upper-layer protocol. *See* ULP.

URL. Universal Resource Locator. A standardized addressing scheme for accessing hypertext documents and other services using a WWW browser. *See also* WWW browser.

usage parameter control. *See* traffic policing.

USENET. Initiated in 1979, one of the oldest and largest cooperative networks, with more than 10,000 hosts and a quarter million users. Its primary service is a distributed conferencing service called *news*.

User Datagram Protocol. *See* UDP.

User-Network Interface. *See* UNI.

UTP. unshielded twisted-pair. A four-pair wire medium used in a variety of networks. UTP does not require the fixed spacing between connections that is necessary with coaxial-type connections. There are five types of UTP cabling commonly used: Category 1 cabling, Category 2 cabling, Category 3 cabling, Category 4 cabling, and Category 5 cabling. *Compare with* STP. *See also* EIA/TIA-586 and twisted pair.

UUCP. UNIX-to-UNIX Copy Program. A protocol stack used for point-to-point communication between UNIX systems.

V

V.24. An ITU-T standard for a physical layer interface between DTE and DCE. V.24 is essentially the same as the EIA/TIA-232 standard. *See also* EIA/TIA-232.

V.25bis. An ITU-T specification describing procedures for call setup and teardown over the DTE-DCE interface in a PSDN.

V.32. An ITU-T standard serial line protocol for bidirectional data transmissions at speeds of 4.8 or 9.6 kbps. *See also* V.32bis.

V.32bis. An ITU-T standard that extends V.32 to speeds up to 14.4 kbps. *See also* V.32.

V.34. An ITU-T standard that specifies a serial line protocol. V.34 offers improvements to the V.32 standard, including higher transmission rates (28.8 kbps) and enhanced data compression. *Compare with* V.32.

V.35. An ITU-T standard describing a synchronous, physical layer protocol used for communications between a network access device and a packet network. V.35 is most commonly used in the United States and in Europe and is recommended for speeds up to 48 kbps.

V.42. An ITU-T standard protocol for error correction using LAPM. *See also* LAPM.

variable bit rate. *See* VBR.

variable-length subnet mask. *See* VLSM.

VBR. variable bit rate. A QOS class defined by the ATM Forum for ATM networks. VBR is subdivided into a real time (RT) class and a non-real time (NRT) class. VBR (RT) is used for connections in which there is a fixed timing relationship between samples. VBR (NRT) is used for connections in which there is no fixed timing relationship between samples, but that still need a guaranteed QOS. *Compare with* ABR (available bit rate), CBR, and UBR.

VC. *See* virtual circuit.

VCC. virtual channel connection. A logical circuit, made up of VCLs, that carries data between two endpoints in an ATM network. Sometimes called a virtual circuit connection. *See also* VCI, VCL, and VPI.

VCI. virtual channel identifier. A 16-bit field in the header of an ATM cell. The VCI, together with the VPI, is used to identify the next destination of a cell as it passes through a series of ATM switches on its way to its destination. ATM switches use the VPI/VCI fields to identify the next network VCL that a cell needs to transit on its way to its final destination. The function of the VCI is similar to that of the DLCI in Frame Relay. *Compare with* DLCI. *See also* VCL and VPI.

VCL. virtual channel link. A connection between two ATM devices. A VCC is made up of one or more VCLs. *See also* VCC.

VCN. virtual circuit number. A 12-bit field in an X.25 PLP header that identifies an X.25 virtual circuit. Allows DCE to determine how to route a packet through the X.25 network. Sometimes called LCI (logical channel identifier) or LCN (logical channel number).

VDSL. Very-High-Data-Rate Digital Subscriber Line. One of four DSL technologies. VDSL delivers 13 to 52 Mbps downstream and 1.5 to 2.3 Mbps upstream over a single twisted copper pair. The operating range of VDSL is limited to 1,000 to 4,500 feet (304.8 to 1,372 meters).

vector. A data segment of an SNA message. A vector consists of a length field, a key that describes the vector type, and vector-specific data.

VINES. Virtual Integrated Network Service. A NOS developed and marketed by Banyan Systems.

virtual address. *See* network address.

virtual channel. *See* virtual circuit.

virtual channel connection. *See* VCC.

virtual channel identifier. *See* VCI.

virtual channel link. *See* VCL.

virtual circuit. A logical circuit created to ensure reliable communication between two network devices. A virtual circuit is defined by a VPI/VCI pair, and can be either permanent (a PVC) or switched (an SVC). Virtual circuits are used in Frame Relay and X.25. In ATM, a virtual circuit is called a virtual channel. Sometimes abbreviated VC. *See also* PVC, SVC, VCI, virtual route, and VPI.

virtual circuit connection. *See* VCC.

virtual circuit number. *See* VCN.

Virtual Integrated Network Service. *See* VINES.

virtualization. The process of implementing a network based on virtual network segments. Devices are connected to virtual segments independent of their physical location and their physical connection to the network.

virtual LAN. *See* VLAN.

virtual LAN internetwork. *See* VLI.

virtual path. A logical grouping of virtual circuits that connect two sites. *See also* virtual circuit.

virtual path connection. *See* VPC.

virtual path identifier. *See* VPI.

virtual path identifier/virtual channel identifier. *See* VPI/VCI.

virtual path link. *See* VPL.

virtual ring. An entity in an SRB network that logically connects two or more physical rings either locally or remotely. The concept of virtual rings can be expanded across router boundaries.

virtual route. In SNA, a logical connection between subarea nodes that is physically realized as a particular explicit route. SNA terminology for virtual circuit. *See also* virtual circuit.

virtual telecommunications access method. *See* VTAM.

Virtual Terminal Protocol. *See* VTP.

VLAN. virtual LAN. A group of devices on a LAN that are configured (using management software) so that they can communicate as if they were attached to the same wire, when in fact they are located on a number of different LAN segments. Because VLANs are based on logical instead of physical connections, they are extremely flexible.

VLI. virtual LAN internetwork. An internetwork composed of VLANs. *See* VLAN.

VLSM. variable-length subnet mask. The ability to specify a different subnet mask for the same network number on different subnets. VLSM can help optimize available address space.

VPC. virtual path connection. Grouping of VCCs that share one or more contiguous VPLs. *See also* VCC and VPL.

VPI. virtual path identifier. An 8-bit field in the header of an ATM cell. The VPI, together with the VCI, is used to identify the next destination of a cell as it passes through a series of ATM switches on its way to its destination. ATM switches use the VPI/VCI fields to identify the next VCL that a cell needs to transit on its way to its final destination. The function of the VPI is similar to that of the DLCI in Frame Relay. *Compare with* DLCI. *See also* VCI and VCL.

VPI/VCI. *See* VCI and VPI.

VPL. virtual path link. Within a virtual path, a group of unidirectional VCLs with the same endpoints. Grouping VCLs into VPLs reduces the number of connections to be managed, thereby decreasing network control overhead and cost. A VPC is made up of one or more VPLs.

VPN. virtual private network. A network that enables IP traffic to travel securely over a public TCP/IP network by encrypting all traffic from one network to another. A VPN uses tunneling to encrypt all information at the IP level.

VTAM. virtual telecommunications access method. A set of programs that control communication between LUs. VTAM controls data transmission between channel-attached devices and performs routing functions.

VTP. Virtual Terminal Protocol. An ISO application for establishing a virtual terminal connection across a network.

W

WAN. wide-area network. A data communications network that serves users across a broad geographic area and often uses transmission devices provided by common carriers. Frame Relay, SMDS, and X.25 are examples of WANs. *Compare with* LAN and MAN.

watchdog packet. A packet used to ensure that a client is still connected to a NetWare server. If the server has not received a packet from a client for a certain period of time, it sends that client a series of watchdog packets. If the station fails to respond to a predefined number of watchdog packets, the server concludes that the station is no longer connected and clears the connection for that station.

watchdog spoofing. A subset of spoofing that refers specifically to a router acting for a NetWare client by sending watchdog packets to a NetWare server to keep the session between client and server active. *See also* spoofing.

watchdog timer. 1. A hardware or software mechanism that is used to trigger an event or an escape from a process unless the timer is periodically reset. 2. In NetWare, a timer that indicates the maximum period of time a server will wait for a client to respond to a watchdog packet. If the timer expires, the server sends another watchdog packet (up to a set maximum). *See also* watchdog packet.

waveform coding. Electrical techniques used to convey binary signals.

wide-area network. *See* WAN.

wideband. *See* broadband.

wildcard mask. A 32-bit quantity used in conjunction with an IP address to determine which bits in an IP address should be ignored when comparing that address with another IP address. A wildcard mask is specified when setting up access lists.

wiring closet. A specially designed room used for wiring a data or voice network. Wiring closets serve as a central junction point for the wiring and wiring equipment that is used for interconnecting devices.

WISCNET. A TCP/IP network in Wisconsin connecting University of Wisconsin campuses and a number of private colleges. Links are 56 kbps and T1.

workgroup. A collection of workstations and servers on a LAN that are designed to communicate and exchange data with one another.

workgroup switching. A method of switching that provides high-speed (100-Mbps) transparent bridging between Ethernet networks and high-speed translational bridging between Ethernet and CDDI or FDDI.

World Wide Web. *See* WWW.

wrap. An action taken by an FDDI or CDDI network to recover in the event of a failure. The stations on each side of the failure reconfigure themselves, creating a single logical ring out of the primary and secondary rings.

WWW. World Wide Web. A large network of Internet servers providing hypertext and other services to terminals running client applications such as a WWW browser. *See also* WWW browser.

WWW browser. A GUI-based hypertext client application, such as Mosaic, used to access hypertext documents and other services located on innumerable remote servers throughout the WWW and Internet. *See also* hypertext, Internet, Mosaic, and WWW.

X

X.121. An ITU-T standard describing an addressing scheme used in X.25 networks. X.121 addresses are sometimes called IDNs.

X.21. An ITU-T standard for serial communications over synchronous digital lines. The X.21 protocol is used primarily in Europe and Japan.

X.21bis. An ITU-T standard that defines the physical layer protocol for communication between DCE and DTE in an X.25 network. Virtually equivalent to EIA/TIA-232. *See also* EIA/TIA-232 and X.25.

X.25. An ITU-T standard that defines how connections between DTE and DCE are maintained for remote terminal access and computer communications in PDNs. X.25 specifies LAPB, a data link layer protocol, and PLP, a network layer protocol. Frame Relay has to some degree superseded X.25. *See also* Frame Relay, LAPB, and PLP.

X.25 Level 3. *See* PLP.

X.25 Protocol. *See* PLP.

X.28. An ITU-T recommendation that defines the terminal-to-PAD interface in X.25 networks. *See also* PAD and X.25.

X.29. An ITU-T recommendation that defines the form for control information in the terminal-to-PAD interface used in X.25 networks. *See also* PAD and X.25.

X.3. An ITU-T recommendation that defines various PAD parameters used in X.25 networks. *See also* PAD and X.25.

X3T9.5. A number assigned to the ANSI Task Group of Accredited Standards Committee for their internal, working document describing FDDI.

X.400. An ITU-T recommendation specifying a standard for electronic mail transfer.

X.500. An ITU-T recommendation specifying a standard for distributed maintenance of files and directories.

X.75. An ITU-T specification that defines the signaling system between two PDNs. X.75 is essentially an NNI. *See also* NNI.

X Display Manager Control Protocol. *See* XDMCP.

xDSL. x digital subscriber line. A group term used to refer to ADSL, HDSL, SDSL, and VDSL. All are emerging digital technologies using the existing copper infrastructure provided by the telephone companies. xDSL is a high-speed alternative to ISDN.

Xerox Network Systems. *See* XNS.

XID. exchange identification. Request and response packets exchanged prior to a session between a router and a Token Ring host. If the parameters of the serial device contained in the XID packet do not match the configuration of the host, the session is dropped.

Xid. *See* termid.

XDMCP. X Display Manager Control Protocol. A protocol used to communicate between X terminals and workstations running UNIX.

XNS. Xerox Network Systems. A protocol suite originally designed by PARC. Many PC networking companies, such as 3Com, Banyan, Novell, and UB Networks, used or currently use a variation of XNS as their primary transport protocol.

XRemote. A protocol developed specifically to optimize support for X Window over a serial communications link.

XStream. A major public PSN (packet-switched network) in the United States operated by MCI. Formerly called TYMNET.

X terminal. A terminal that allows a user simultaneous access to several different applications and resources in a multivendor environment through implementation of X Window. *See also* X Window.

X Window. A distributed, network-transparent, device-independent, multitasking windowing and graphics system originally developed by MIT for communication between X terminals and UNIX workstations. *See also* X terminal.

Z

zero code suppression. A line coding scheme used for transmission clocking. Zero line suppression substitutes a one in the seventh bit of a string of eight consecutive zeros. *See also* ones density.

ZIP. Zone Information Protocol. An AppleTalk session layer protocol that maps network numbers to zone names. *See also* ZIP storm and zone.

ZIP storm. A broadcast storm that occurs when a router running AppleTalk propagates a route for which it currently has no corresponding zone name. The route is then forwarded by downstream routers, and a ZIP storm ensues. *See also* ZIP.

zone. In AppleTalk, a logical group of network devices. *See also* ZIP.

Zone Information Protocol. *See* ZIP.

This appendix provides a review of key internetworking technology information. In addition to the design information covered in this book, the DCN exam will test you on your knowledge of internetworking technology fundamentals.

It is assumed that you have working knowledge of internetworking and Cisco products before reading this book. If you lack experience with internetworking technologies and Cisco products, it is recommended that you review Cisco's interactive, self-paced *Internetworking Multimedia CD-ROM* or read the *Internetworking Technologies Handbook*, Second Edition, from Cisco Press before starting this course. This review appendix includes some information from these sources to serve as a reminder and/or summary of important points on specific topics relevant to this book.

Internetworking Technology Review

An internetwork is a collection of individual networks, connected by intermediate networking devices, which functions as a single large network. *Internetworking* refers to the industry, products, and procedures that meet the challenge of creating and administering internetworks.

The first networks were time-sharing networks that used mainframes and attached terminals. Such environments were implemented by both IBM's System Network Architecture (SNA) and Digital's network architecture.

Local-area networks (LANs) evolved around the PC revolution. LANs enabled multiple users in a relatively small geographical area to exchange files and messages, as well as access shared resources such as file servers.

Wide-area networks (WANs) interconnect LANs across normal telephone lines (and other media), thereby interconnecting geographically dispersed users.

Today, high-speed LANs and switched internetworks are becoming widely used, largely because they operate at high speeds and support high-bandwidth applications such as voice and video conferencing.

Protocols

Computers need to agree on a set of traffic rules to successfully communicate. Such a set of rules is known as a *protocol*. Two computers use the same protocol if they want to communicate. Two computers trying to use different protocols would be like speaking French to a German—it wouldn't work.

There are many different networking protocols in use. In the past, each networking vendor would invent their own protocol; today, standard protocols exist so that devices can communicate with each other. For example, TCP/IP is the most widely used *routed protocol*, but Novell's IPX and Apple Computer's AppleTalk are also used.

The OSI Model

Because sending data, like an e-mail, involves doing so many things, a standards committee—the International Organization for Standardization (ISO)—came up with a list of these functions and divided them into seven categories. These categories are collectively known as the Open Systems Interconnection (OSI) seven-layer model. It represents everything that must happen in order to send data. It doesn't say *how* these things are to be done, just *what* needs to be done. Figure C-1 illustrates the seven layers of the OSI model.

Figure C-1   *Each Layer of the Seven-Layer OSI Model Represents a Function that Is Needed When Devices Communicate*

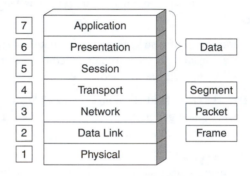

Different vendors will implement the functions at these layers differently. For example, there are different physical layers (wires)—copper and fiber optic are two common ones.

As data is sent through the functions at each of the layers, information is added to allow the data to go through the network. The data is *encapsulated*, or wrapped in, the appropriate information. This encapsulated information includes addressing and error checking.

At Layer 4, the transport layer, the data is encapsulated in a *segment*.

At Layer 3, the network layer, this segment is then encapsulated in a *packet* or *datagram*. At Layer 3, *routed protocols* are used to send data through the network. There are different types of packets for each of the routed protocols at Layer 3; examples include IP and IPX packets.

At Layer 2, the data link layer, this packet is then encapsulated in a *frame*. The data link layer used is determined by the type of LAN or WAN you are connected to. There are different types of frames for each type of LAN or WAN. For example, the frames sent out on Ethernet are different than those sent out on Frame Relay because there are different protocols to be followed.

At Layer 1, the physical layer, the frame is sent out on the wire in bits.

When data is received at the other end of the network, it must have the additional information removed. Thus the data is *decapsulated*, or unwrapped, until the original data sent arrives at its destination.

LAN Protocols

A LAN typically has the following characteristics:

- Interconnects devices over a "short" distance (hence the term "local area")
- Is fast
- Belongs to you
- Is there all the time

There are a number of different LAN technologies. Ethernet is the most common. Ethernet runs at 10 million bits per second (10 Mbps). New versions, known as Fast Ethernet and Gigabit Ethernet, run at 100 Mbps and 1 Gbps, respectively.

Other LAN technologies include Token Ring and FDDI. Token Ring is an IBM invention and is found mainly at IBM sites. FDDI is based on optical fiber and runs at 100 Mbps.

LAN protocols function at the lowest two layers of the OSI reference model: the physical layer and data link layer.

LAN Physical Network Access

LAN protocols typically use one of two methods to access the physical network medium:

- In the *carrier sense multiple access/collision detect (CSMA/CD)* scheme, network devices contend for the use of the physical network. CSMA/CD is sometimes called contention access. Examples of LANs that use the CSMA/CD media access scheme are Ethernet/IEE 802.3 networks.

- In the *token passing media access* scheme, network devices access the physical medium based on possession of a token. Examples of LANs that use the token passing media access scheme are Token Ring/IEEE 802.5 and FDDI.

LAN Data Transmission Types

LAN data transmissions fall into three classifications:

- In a *unicast* transmission, a single packet is sent from the source to a destination on a network. The source node addresses the packet by using the address of the destination node. The packet is then sent to the network, and finally, the network passes the packet to its destination.

- A *multicast* transmission consists of a single data packet that is copied and sent to a specific subset of nodes on the network. The source node addresses the packet by using a multicast address. The packet is then sent to the network, which makes copies of the packet and sends a copy to each node that is part of the multicast address.

- A *broadcast* transmission consists of a single data packet that is copied and sent to all nodes on the network. In these types of transmissions, the source node addresses the packet by using the broadcast address. The packet is then sent to the network, which makes copies of the packet and sends a copy to every node on the network.

WAN Protocols

A WAN interconnects devices located at different geographical locations. A WAN typically

- Interconnects devices over a "long" distance (hence "wide-area")
- Is slow (compared to a LAN)
- Belongs to someone else (the "service provider")
- Is there only when you want to send something

WAN protocols function at the lowest two layers of the OSI reference model, the physical layer and data link layer. (X.25 is an exception to this; it functions at layer three also.)

WAN Categories

WANs can be categorized as follows:

- **Point-to-point links**—Provide a single, preestablished WAN communication path from the customer premises through a carrier network, such as the telephone company, to a remote network. A point-to-point link is also known as a leased line because its established path is permanent and fixed for each remote network reached through the carrier facilities.

- **Circuit switching**—A WAN switching method in which a dedicated physical circuit is established, maintained, and terminated through a carrier network for each communication session. Used extensively in telephone company networks, circuit switching operates much like a normal telephone call. Integrated Services Digital Network (ISDN) is an example of a circuit-switched WAN technology.

- **Packet switching**—A WAN switching method in which network devices share a single point-to-point link to transport packets from a source to a destination across a carrier network. Statistical mulitplexing is used to enable devices to share these circuits. Asynchronous Transfer Mode (ATM), Frame Relay, Switched Multimegabit Data Service (SMDS), and X.25 are examples of packet-switched WAN technologies.

WAN Virtual Circuits

Virtual circuits are logical circuits created to ensure reliable communication between two network devices. Two types of virtual circuits exist:

- **Switched virtual circuits (SVCs)**—Virtual circuits that are dynamically established on demand and terminated when transmission is complete. Communication over an SVC consists of three phases: circuit establishment, data transfer, and circuit termination.

- **Permanent virtual circuits (PVCs)**—Permanently established virtual circuits that consist of one mode: data transfer.

WAN Dialup Services

Dialup services offer cost-effective methods for connectivity across WANs. Two popular dialup implementations follow:

- **Dial-on-demand routing (DDR)**—A technique whereby a router can dynamically initiate and close a circuit-switched session as transmitting end stations demand. A router is configured to consider certain traffic interesting (such as traffic from a particular protocol) and other traffic uninteresting. When the router receives interesting traffic destined for a remote network, a circuit is established, and the traffic is transmitted normally. If the router receives uninteresting traffic and a circuit is already established, that traffic also is transmitted normally. The router maintains an idle timer that is reset only when interesting traffic is received. If the router receives no interesting traffic before the idle timer expires, the circuit is terminated. Likewise, if uninteresting traffic is received and no circuit exists, the router drops the traffic.

- **Dial backup**—A service that activates a backup serial line under certain conditions. The secondary serial line can act as a backup link that is used when the primary link fails or as a source of additional bandwidth when the load on the primary link reaches a certain threshold.

WAN Devices

Devices used in WAN environments include:

- **WAN switch**—A multiport internetworking device used in carrier networks. These devices typically switch such traffic as Frame Relay, X.25, and SMDS and operate at the data link layer.

- **Access server**—Acts as a concentration point for dial-in and dial-out connections.

- **Modem**—A device that interprets digital and analog signals, enabling data to be transmitted over voice-grade telephone lines.

- **Channel service unit/digital service unit (CSU/DSU)**—A digital-interface device (or sometimes two separate digital devices) that adapts the physical interface on a data terminal equipment (DTE) device (such as a terminal) to the interface of a data circuit-terminating (DCE) device (such as a switch) in a switched-carrier network. The CSU/DSU also provides signal timing for communication between these devices.

- **ISDN terminal adapter (TA)**—A device used to connect ISDN Basic Rate Interface (BRI) connections to other interfaces, such as EIA/TAI-232. A terminal adapter is essentially an ISDN modem.

Defining the type of WAN and the specifications and options desired is called *provisioning* the network.

Internetwork Addressing

Internetwork addresses identify devices separately or as members of a group. Addressing schemes vary depending on the protocol family and the OSI layer.

MAC Addresses

Media Access Control (MAC) addresses identify network entities in LANs. MAC addresses are unique for each LAN interface on a device. MAC addresses are 48 bits in length and are expressed as 12 hexadecimal digits. The first 6 hexadecimal digits, which are administered by the IEEE, identify the manufacturer or vendor and thus comprise the Organizational Unique Identifier (OUI). The last 6 hexadecimal digits comprise the interface serial number, or another value administered by the specific vendor. MAC addresses sometimes are called burned-in addresses (BIAs) because they are burned into read-only memory (ROM) and are copied into random-access memory (RAM) when the interface card initializes.

Network Layer Addresses

A network layer address identifies an entity at the OSI network layer. Network addresses usually exist within a hierarchical address space and sometimes are called *virtual* or *logical* addresses.

Network layer addresses have two parts: the *network* that the device is on and the *device* (or *host*) number of that device on that network. Devices on the same logical network must have addresses with the same network part; however they will have unique device parts.

This is analogous to the postal "network" addresses: one part indicates the street, city, province/state, and so on, whereas the other part identifies the building number on that street. For example, a building at 27 Main Street is on the same "network" as a building at 35 Main Street. The "network" portion of their addresses, Main Street, is identical, whereas the "device" portions are unique.

Network Devices

The main devices used in networking are as follows:

- Hubs

- Bridges and switches

- Routers

Hubs

A hub is used to connect devices so that they are on one LAN, as shown in Figure C-2. The cables normally used for Ethernet have RJ-45 connectors. Because only two devices can be connected with these cables, we need a hub if we want to interconnect more than two devices on one LAN.

Figure C-2   *A Hub Connects Devices So that They Are on One LAN*

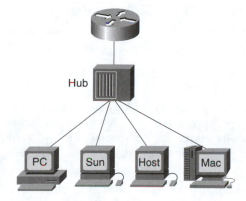

A hub is not a "smart" device. A hub sends all the data from a device on one port to all the other ports. When devices are connected via a hub, the devices all hear everything that the other devices send, whether it was meant for them or not. This is analogous to being in a room with lots of people—if you speak, everyone will hear you. If more than one person speaks at a time, there will just be noise. Rules must be put in place if real conversations are to happen; in networking, these rules are the protocols.

Bridges and Switches

To improve performance, LANs are usually divided into smaller multiple LANs. These LANs are then interconnected by a LAN switch or by a bridge, as shown in Figure C-3.

Figure C-3 *LANs Are Split into Many Smaller LANs, Using Switches or Bridges to Improve Performance*

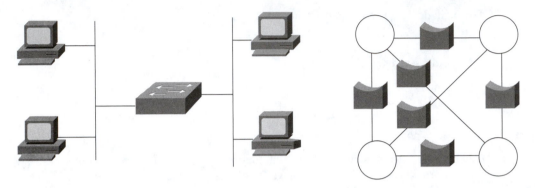

Switches and bridges have some "smarts." When devices are connected via a switch or a bridge, a device will only hear the following:

- Everything that the other devices on its port send

- Any information from devices on other ports that was meant for *everyone* (a *broadcast*)

- Any information from devices on other ports that was meant for devices on its port

A device connected to a switch or bridge will *not* hear any of the information meant just for devices on other ports of the switch.

Upper-layer protocol transparency is a primary advantage of both bridging and switching. Because both device types operate at the data link layer, they are not required to examine upper-layer information. This means that they can rapidly forward traffic representing any network layer protocol. It is not uncommon for a bridge to move AppleTalk, DECnet, TCP/IP, XNS, and other traffic between two or more networks.

By dividing large networks into self-contained units, bridges and switches provide several advantages. Because only a certain percentage of traffic is forwarded, a bridge or switch diminishes the traffic experienced by devices on all connected segments. Bridges and switches extend the effective length of a LAN, permitting the attachment of distant stations that were not previously permitted.

Bridging Protocols

Switches and bridges may communicate with each other by using a bridging protocol. Several types of bridging protocols are supported by Cisco routers (acting as bridges) and switches, including the following:

- **Transparent bridging**—Found primarily in Ethernet environments.

- **Source-route bridging (SRB)**—Found primarily in Token Ring environments.

- **Translational bridging**—Translates from Ethernet bridging to Token Ring bridging.

- **Encapsulating bridging**—Allows packets to cross a bridged backbone network.

- **Source-route transparent (SRT) bridging**—Allows a bridge to function as both a source-routing and transparent bridge.

- **Source-route translational (SR/TLB) bridging**—Allows a bridge to function as both a source-routing and transparent bridge, and to bridge between the two.

NOTE   In SRB terminology, Layer 2 *frames* are also known *as packets.*

Transparent bridges send Bridge Protocol Data Unit (BPDU) frames to each other to build and maintain a spanning tree, as specified in IEEE 802.1d. The Spanning-Tree Algorithm states that there is one and only one active path between two stations. If a physical loop exists in the network (for redundancy reasons), the Spanning-Tree Algorithm handles this loop by disabling bridge ports. This prevents *broadcast storms* in networks with redundancy, which occurs when broadcasts continuously circle the network.

Bridges Versus Switches

Although bridges and switches share most relevant attributes, several distinctions differentiate these technologies. Switches are significantly faster because they switch in hardware, whereas bridges switch in software. Switches can interconnect LANs of unlike bandwidth; a 10-Mbps Ethernet LAN and a 100-Mbps Ethernet LAN, for example, can be connected using a switch. Switches also can support higher port densities than bridges. Some switches support cut-through switching, which reduces latency and delays in the network, whereas bridges support only store-and-forward traffic switching.

Switches also support virtual LANs (VLANs). A VLAN is a *logical,* rather than *physical,* grouping of devices. The devices are grouped using switch management software so that they can communicate as if they were attached to the same wire, when in fact they might be located on a number of different physical LAN segments.

Cisco switches are known as Catalyst switches (because Cisco bought a company called Catalyst). Catalyst switches include the following series:

Catalyst 1900	Catalyst 4000
Catalyst 2820	Catalyst 5000
Catalyst 2900	Catalyst 5500
Catalyst 2900XL	Catalyst 6000
Catalyst 3000	Catalyst 3900
Catalyst 8500 multiservice switch routers	

Generally the bigger the series number, the more LAN ports the switch has.

Routers

A router connects devices on LANs to devices on other LANs, usually via WANs, as shown in Figure C-4.

Figure C-4 *A Router Connects Devices on LANs to Devices on Other LANs, Usually Via WANs*

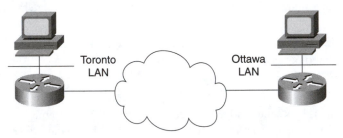

A router has a lot of "smarts." When companies started deploying PCs and connecting them via LANs, they soon wanted to go one step further and interconnect LANs and PCs located at geographically separate locations. The router provides this facility. The router will connect to a local LAN and then connect over a longer distance to another router, which in turn is connected to the remote LAN. Two PCs located hundreds of miles apart can now exchange data.

A router's job is comprised of the following tasks:

- Segment LANs and WANs

- Figure out the best way to send data to its destination

- Talk to other routers to learn from them and tell them what it knows

- Send the data the best way, over a LAN or a WAN

When devices are connected via a router, a device will hear only the following:

- Everything that the other devices on its port send

- Any information from devices on other ports that was meant for devices on its port

A device connected to a router will not hear any of the information meant just for devices on other ports, nor any information from devices on other ports that was meant for *everyone*.

Cisco has a large selection of routers, including the following series:

Cisco 700	Cisco 3600
Cisco 800	Cisco MC3810 multiservice concentrator
Cisco 1000	Cisco 4000
Cisco 1600	Cisco AS5200/AS5300/AS5800 access servers
Cisco 1720	Cisco 7200
Cisco 2500	Cisco 12000
Cisco 2600	
Cisco 7500	

Generally the bigger the series number, the more LAN and WAN ports the router has and the better performance it provides.

Routing

Routing is the act of moving information across an internetwork from a source to a destination. Along the way, at least one intermediate node typically is encountered. Routing occurs at Layer 3, the network layer.

The book *Introduction to Cisco Router Configuration* (Cisco Press) defines *routed protocols* and *routing protocols:*

- A **routed protocol** is a protocol that contains enough network-layer addressing information for user traffic to be directed from one network to another network. Routed protocols define the format and use of the fields within a packet. Packets that use a routed protocol are conveyed from end system to end system through an internetwork.

- A **routing protocol** supports a routed protocol by providing mechanisms for sharing routing information. Routing protocol messages move between the routers. A routing protocol allows the routers to communicate with other routers to update and maintain routing tables. Routing protocol messages do not carry end-user traffic from network to network. A routing protocol uses the routed protocol to pass information between routers. (pg. 79)

A *metric* is a standard of measurement, such as path length, that is used by routing algorithms to determine the optimal path to a destination. To aid the process of path determination, routing algorithms initialize and maintain *routing tables*, which contain route information. Route information varies depending on the routing algorithm used.

Routing algorithms can be classified by type. Key differentiators include:

- **Static versus dynamic**—Static routing algorithms are hardly algorithms at all, but are table mappings established by the network administrator prior to the beginning of routing. These mappings do not change unless the network administrator alters them.

- **Single-path versus multipath**—Some sophisticated routing protocols support multiple paths to the same destination.

- **Flat versus hierarchical**—In a flat routing system, the routers are peers of all others. In a hierarchical routing system, some routers form what amounts to a routing backbone. Routing systems often designate logical groups of nodes, called domains, autonomous systems, or areas.

- **Host-intelligent versus router-intelligent**—Some routing algorithms assume that the source end-node will determine the entire route. This is usually referred to as *source routing*. Other algorithms assume that hosts know nothing about routes. In these algorithms, routers determine the path through the internetwork based on their own calculations.

- **Intradomain versus interdomain**—Some routing algorithms work only within domains; others work within and between domains.

- **Link-state versus distance-vector versus hybrid**—Link-state algorithms (also known as *shortest path first* algorithms) flood routing information to all nodes in the internetwork. Each router, however, sends only the portion of the routing table that describes the state of its own links. Distance-vector algorithms (also known as *Bellman-Ford* algorithms) call for each router to send all or some portion of its routing table, but only to its neighbors. In essence, link-state algorithms send small updates everywhere, whereas distance-vector algorithms send larger updates only to neighboring routers. Hybrid, or advanced, routing protocols have attributes associated with both distance-vector and link-state protocols; hybrid protocols send small updates only to neighboring routers.

There are many *suites* of protocols that define protocols corresponding to the functions defined in the OSI seven layers, including routed protocols, a selection of routing protocols, applications, and so forth. They are called protocol *suites* because they have protocols for doing many different things included in their suites. Protocol suites are also known as protocol *stacks*. This section provides a brief overview of some of these protocol suites.

TCP/IP Protocol Suite

TCP/IP is by far the most widely used protocol suite; it is the only one used in the Internet. TCP/IP is short for Transmission Control Protocol/Internet Protocol, after two of the protocols in the suite. It was not invented by any single vendor but evolved as the Internet grew.

TCP/IP Network Layer

The network layer (Layer 3) includes the following protocols:

- **Internet Protocol (IP)**—Defines a set of rules for communicating across a network. IP contains addressing information and some control information that enables packets to be routed. IP has two primary responsibilities: providing connectionless, best-effort delivery of datagrams through an internetwork, and providing fragmentation and reassembly of datagrams to support data links with different maximum transmission unit (MTU) sizes.

- **Address Resolution Protocol (ARP)**—Allows a host to dynamically discover the MAC-layer address corresponding to a particular IP network layer address. In order for two machines on a given network to communicate, they must know the other machine's physical addresses.

- **Reverse Address Resolution Protocol (RARP)**—Used to map MAC-layer addresses to IP addresses. RARP, which is the logical inverse of ARP, might be used by diskless workstations that do not know their IP addresses when they boot. RARP relies on the presence of a RARP server with table entries of MAC layer-to-IP address mappings.

- **Internet Control Message Protocol (ICMP)**—Used to report errors and other information regarding IP packet processing back to the source.

TCP/IP Transport Layer

At the transport layer (Layer 4), two transport protocols are defined:

- **Transmission Control Protocol (TCP)**—Provides connection-oriented, end-to-end reliable transmission of data in an IP environment. Connection establishment is performed by using a "three-way handshake" mechanism. A three-way handshake synchronizes both ends of a connection by allowing both sides to agree upon initial sequence numbers. This mechanism also guarantees that both sides are ready to transmit data and know that the other side is ready to transmit as well. This is necessary so that packets are not transmitted or retransmitted during session establishment or after session termination.

- **User Datagram Protocol (UDP)**—A connectionless protocol that is basically an interface between IP and upper-layer processes. Unlike the TCP, UDP adds no reliability, flow-control, or error-recovery functions to IP. Because of UDP's simplicity, UDP headers contain fewer bytes and consume less network overhead than TCP.

TCP and UDP use protocol *port numbers* to distinguish multiple applications (described in the next section) running on a single device from one another. The port number is part of the TCP or UDP segment and is used to identify the application to which the data in the segment belongs. There are well-known, or standardized, port numbers assigned to applications, so that different implementations of the TCP/IP protocol suite can interoperate. Examples of these well-known port numbers include the following:

- **File Transfer Protocol (FTP)**—TCP port 20 (data) and port 21 (control)
- **Telnet**—TCP port 23
- **Trivial File Transfer Protocol (TFTP)**—UDP port 69

TCP/IP Application Layer

In the TCP/IP protocol suite, the upper three layers of the OSI model are combined together into one layer, called the application layer. This suite includes many application layer protocols that represent a wide variety of applications, including the following:

- **File Transfer Protocol (FTP) and Trivial File Transfer Protocol (TFTP)**—To move files between devices

- **Simple Network-Management Protocol (SNMP)**—Primarily reports anomalous network conditions and sets network threshold values

- **Telnet**—Serves as a terminal emulation protocol

- **Simple Mail Transfer Protocol (SMTP)**—Provides electronic mail services

- **Domain Name System (DNS)**—Translates the names of network nodes into network addresses

IP Addressing

As mentioned, network layer addresses have two parts: the *network* that the device is on and the *device* (or *host*) number of that device on that network. Devices on the same logical network must have addresses with the same network part; however, they will have unique device parts.

IP addresses are 32 bits, as shown in Figure C-5. The 32 bits are grouped into four sets of 8 bits (octets), separated by dots, and represented in decimal format; this is known as *dotted decimal* notation. Each bit in the octet has a binary weight (128, 64, 32, 16, 8, 4, 2, 1). The minimum value for an octet is 0, and the maximum decimal value for an octet is 255.

Figure C-5   *IP Addresses Are 32 Bits, Written in Dotted Decimal Format*

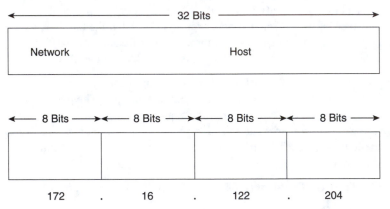

IP Address Classes

IP addressing defines five address classes: A, B, C, D, and E. Only classes A, B, and C are available for addressing devices; class D is used for multicast groups, and class E is reserved for experimental use.

The first octet of an address defines its class, as illustrated in Table C-1. This table also shows the format of the addresses in each class as defined by the network bits (N) and host bits (H).

Table C-1   *IP Address Classes A, B, and C Are Available for Addressing Devices*

Class	Format (N=network number, H=host number)	Higher-Order Bit(s)	Address Range
Class A	N.H.H.H	0	1.0.0.0 to 126.0.0.0
Class B	N.N.H.H	10	128.0.0.0 to 191.255.0.0
Class C	N.N.N.H	110	192.0.0.0 to 223.255.255.0

Reference: RFC 1700, available at http://info.internet.isi.edu/in-notes/rfc/files/rfc1700.txt

IP Subnets

IP networks can be divided into smaller networks called *subnetworks* (or *subnets*). Subnetting provides the network administrator with several benefits, including extra flexibility, more efficient use of network addresses, and the capability to contain broadcast traffic (a broadcast will not cross a router).

Subnets are under local administration. As such, the outside world sees an organization as a single network and has no detailed knowledge of the organization's internal structure.

A subnet address is created by "borrowing" bits from the host field and designating them as the subnet field. A *subnet mask* is a 32-bit number that is associated with an IP address; each bit in the subnet mask indicates how to interpret the corresponding bit in the IP address. In binary, a subnet mask bit of *one* indicates that the corresponding bit in the IP address is a network or subnet bit; a subnet mask bit of *zero* indicates that the corresponding bit in the IP address is a host bit. The subnet mask then indicates how many bits have been borrowed from the host field for the subnet field.

The *default subnet mask* for an address depends on its address class. Referring to Table C-1, class A addresses have one octet, or 8 bits, of network and 3 octets or 24 bits of host; therefore the default subnet mask for a class A address is 255.0.0.0, indicating 8 bits of network (binary ones in the mask) and 24 bits of host (binary zeros in the mask). Similarly, the default subnet mask for a class B address is 255.255.0.0 and for a class C address is 255.255.255.0.

Subnet mask bits come from the high-order (left-most) bits of the host field.

When all the host bits of an address are zero, the address is for the wire (or subnet); when all the host bits of an address are one, the address is the broadcast on that wire.

As an example, a class B network 172.16.0.0 with 8 bits of subnet would have 8 of the available 16 host bits "borrowed" for subnet bits; the subnet mask would be 255.255.255.0. With these 8 subnet bits, there are $2^8 - 2 = 254$ subnets; each subnet has 8 host bits, so there are $2^8 - 2 = 254$ hosts available on each subnet. (The two hosts and subnets are subtracted in the above calculations because of the network address and broadcast address.) The subnets would be

172.16.1.0, 172,16.2.0, 172.16.3.0, and so on. On the first subnet, the available host addresses would be 172.16.1.1, 172.16.1.2, 172.16.1.3, and so on.

Usually within the same "major" network (a class A, B, or C network), the subnet mask used is the same for all subnets of that network. Using *variable length subnet masking* (VLSM) means using a different mask in some parts of the network.

Tables C-2 and C-3 indicate the number of bits of subnetting, associated subnet mask, and resulting number of subnets and hosts available for class B and C networks, respectively.

Table C-2   *Class B Subnetting*

Number of Subnet Bits	Subnet Mask	Number of Subnets	Number of Hosts
2	255.255.192.0	2	16382
3	255.255.224.0	6	8190
4	255.255.240.0	14	4094
5	255.255.248.0	30	2046
6	255.255.252.0	62	1022
7	255.255.254.0	126	510
8	255.255.255.0	254	254
9	255.255.255.128	510	126
10	255.255.255.192	1022	62
11	255.255.255.224	2046	30
12	255.255.255.240	4094	14
13	255.255.255.248	8190	6
14	255.255.255.252	16382	2

Table C-3   *Class C Subnetting*

Number of Subnet Bits	Subnet Mask	Number of Subnets	Number of Hosts
2	255.255.255.192	2	62
3	255.255.255.224	6	30
4	255.255.255.240	14	14
5	255.255.255.248	30	6
6	255.255.255.252	62	2

How Subnet Masks Are Used to Determine the Network Number

The router performs a set process to determine the network (or more specifically, the subnetwork) address to which a packet should be forwarded. First, the router extracts the IP destination address from the incoming packet and retrieves the internal subnet mask. It then performs a *logical AND* operation to obtain the network number. This causes the host portion of the IP destination address to be removed, while the destination subnetwork number remains. The router then looks up the destination subnetwork number in its routing table and matches it with an outgoing interface. Finally, it forwards the frame to the destination IP address.

Three basic rules govern logically "ANDing" two binary numbers. First, 1 "ANDed" with 1 yields 1. Second, 1 "ANDed" with 0 yields 0. Finally, 0 "ANDed" with 0 yields 0. The truth table provided in Table C-4 illustrates the rules for logical AND operations.

Table C-4 *Rules for Logical AND Operations*

Input	Input	Output
1	1	1
1	0	0
0	1	0
0	0	0

Two simple guidelines exist for remembering logical AND operations: Logically "ANDing" a 1 with any number yields that number, and logically "ANDing" a 0 with any number yields 0.

Table C-5 illustrates an example of the logical "ANDing" of a destination IP address and the subnet mask. The subnetwork number remains, which the router uses to forward the packet.

Table C-5 *Example Calculation of Subnet Number*

		Network	Subnet	Host	Host
Destination IP Address	172.16.1.2	10101100	00010000	00000001	00000010
Subnet Mask	255.255.255.0	11111111	11111111	11111111	00000000
Subnet Number	172.16.1.0	10101100	00010000	00000001	00000000

TCP/IP Routing Protocols

The TCP/IP suite defines a selection of routing protocols:

- **Routing Information Protocol (RIP)**—A distance-vector protocol that uses hop count as its metric. RIP is widely used for routing traffic and is an *Interior Gateway Protocol* (IGP), which means it performs routing within a single autonomous system. The latest enhancement to RIP is the RIP 2 specification, which allows more information to be included in RIP packets and provides a simple authentication mechanism.

- The **Interior Gateway Routing Protocol (IGRP)**—A routing protocol that was developed in the mid-1980s by Cisco Systems, Inc. Cisco's principal goal in creating IGRP was to provide a robust protocol for routing within an autonomous system (AS). IGRP is a distance vector interior gateway protocol. IGRP uses a combination (vector) of metrics. *Internetwork delay, bandwidth, reliability,* and *load* are all factored into the routing decision.

- **Enhanced Internet Gateway Routing Protocol (EIGRP)**—Represents an evolution from its predecessor IGRP. Enhanced IGRP is a hybrid routing protocol. It integrates the capabilities of link-state protocols into distance-vector protocols. EIGRP incorporates the *Diffusing Update Algorithm* (DUAL). Key capabilities that distinguish Enhanced IGRP from other routing protocols include fast convergence, support for VLSM, support for partial updates, and support for multiple network layer protocols (EIGRP supports IPX and AppleTalk, as well as IP).

- **Open Shortest Path First (OSPF)**—A link-state routing protocol that calls for the sending of *link-state advertisements* (LSAs) to all other routers within the same hierarchical area. Information on attached interfaces, metrics used, and other variables is included in OSPF LSAs. As OSPF routers accumulate link-state information, they use the *shortest path first* (SPF) algorithm to calculate the shortest path to each node. Unlike RIP, OSPF can operate within a hierarchy. The largest entity within the hierarchy is the *autonomous system* (AS), which is a collection of networks under a common administration that share a common routing strategy. OSPF is an interior gateway routing protocol, although it is capable of receiving routes from and sending routes to other ASs. An AS can be divided into a number of *areas*, which are groups of contiguous networks and attached hosts.

- **Border Gateway Protocol (BGP)**—An exterior gateway protocol (EGP), which means that it performs routing between multiple autonomous systems or domains and exchanges routing and reachability information with other BGP systems. BGP was developed to replace its predecessor, the now obsolete *Exterior Gateway Protocol* (EGP), as the standard exterior gateway routing protocol used in the global Internet. BGP solves serious problems with EGP and scales to Internet growth more efficiently.

Resource Reservation Protocol

The Resource Reservation Protocol (RSVP) is a network control protocol that enables Internet applications to obtain special qualities of service (QoSs) for their data flows. RSVP is not a routing protocol; instead, it works in conjunction with routing protocols and installs the equivalent of dynamic access lists along the routes that routing protocols calculate. RSVP occupies the place of a transport protocol in the OSI seven-layer model.

In RSVP, a data flow is a sequence of messages that have the same source, destination (one or more), and quality of service. QoS requirements are communicated through a network via a *flow specification*, which is a data structure used by internetwork hosts to request special services from the internetwork. A flow specification often guarantees how the internetwork will handle some of its host traffic.

RSVP supports three traffic types: *best-effort*, *rate-sensitive*, and *delay-sensitive*. The type of data flow service used to support these traffic types depends on QoS implemented:

- **Best-effort** traffic is traditional IP traffic. Applications include file transfer, mail transmissions, disk mounts, interactive logins, and transaction traffic. The service supporting best-effort traffic is called *best-effort service*.

- **Rate-sensitive** traffic is willing to give up timeliness for guaranteed rate. Rate-sensitive traffic, for example, might request 100 kbps of bandwidth. If it actually sends 200 kbps for an extended period, a router can delay traffic. An example of such an application is H.323 videoconferencing, which is designed to run on ISDN (H.320) or ATM (H.310) but is found on the Internet. H.323 encoding is a constant, or nearly constant, rate and it requires a constant transport rate. The RSVP service supporting rate-sensitive traffic is called *guaranteed bit-rate service*.

- **Delay-sensitive** traffic is traffic that requires timeliness of delivery and varies its rate accordingly. MPEG-II video, for example, averages about 3 to 7 Mbps, depending on the amount of change in the picture. MPEG-II video sources send key and delta frames. Typically, one or two key frames per second describe the whole picture, and 13 or 28 frames describe the change from the key frame. Delta frames are usually substantially smaller than key frames. As a result, rates vary quite a bit from frame to frame. A single frame, however, requires delivery within a frame time or the CODEC (coder-decoder) is unable to do its job. A specific priority must be negotiated for delta-frame traffic. RSVP services supporting delay-sensitive traffic are referred to as *controlled-delay service* (non-real-time service) and *predictive service* (real-time service).

RSVP data flows are generally characterized by *sessions*, over which data packets flow. A session is a set of data flows with the same unicast or multicast destination, and RSVP treats each session independently.

In the context of RSVP, quality of service is an attribute specified in flow specifications that is used to determine the way in which data interchanges are handled by participating entities (routers, receivers, and senders). RSVP is used to specify the QoS by both hosts and routers. Hosts use RSVP to request a QoS level from the network on behalf of an application data stream. Routers use RSVP to deliver QoS requests to other routers along the path(s) of the data stream. In doing so, RSVP maintains the router and host state to provide the requested service.

To initiate an RSVP multicast session, a receiver first joins the multicast group specified by an IP destination address by using the Internet Group Membership Protocol (IGMP). In the case of a unicast session, unicast routing serves the function that IGMP, coupled with Protocol-Independent Multicast (PIM), serves in the multicast case. After the receiver joins a group, a potential sender starts sending RSVP path messages to the IP destination address. The receiver application receives a path message and starts sending appropriate reservation request messages specifying the desired flow descriptors using RSVP. After the sender application receives a reservation request message, the sender starts sending data packets.

NetWare Protocol Suite

NetWare is a network operating system (NOS) that provides transparent remote file access and numerous other distributed network services, including printer sharing and support for various applications, such as electronic mail transfer and database access. NetWare specifies the upper five layers of the OSI reference model and, as such, runs on virtually any media-access protocol (layer 2). Additionally, NetWare runs on virtually any kind of computer system, from PCs to mainframes. Introduced in the early 1980s, NetWare was developed by Novell, Inc. It was derived from Xerox Network Systems (XNS), which was created by Xerox Corporation in the late 1970s, and is based on a client-server architecture. *Clients* (sometimes called workstations) request services, such as file and printer access, from *servers*.

Internetwork Packet Exchange (IPX) is the original NetWare network layer (Layer 3) protocol used to route packets through an internetwork. IPX is a connectionless datagram-based network protocol and, as such, is similar to the Internet Protocol found in TCP/IP networks.

The *Sequenced Packet Exchange* (SPX) protocol is the most common NetWare transport protocol at Layer 4 of the OSI model. SPX resides on top of IPX in the NetWare Protocol Suite. SPX is a reliable, connection-oriented protocol that supplements the datagram service provided by the IPX protocol. SPX was derived from the Xerox Networking Systems (XNS) Sequenced Packet Protocol (SPP).

NetWare supports a wide variety of upper-layer protocols, including the following:

- **NetWare shell**—Runs on clients and intercepts application input/output (I/O) calls to determine whether they require network access for completion. Client applications are unaware of any network access required for completion of application calls.

- **NetWare Remote Procedure Call (NetWare RPC)**—Another more general redirection mechanism similar in concept to the NetWare shell supported by Novell.

- **NetWare Core Protocol (NCP)**—A series of server routines designed to satisfy application requests coming from, for example, the NetWare shell. The services provided by NCP include file access, printer access, name management, accounting, security, and file synchronization.

- **Network Basic Input/Output System (NetBIOS)**—A session layer interface specification from IBM and Microsoft. NetWare's NetBIOS emulation software allows programs written to the industry-standard NetBIOS interface to run within NetWare system.

NetWare application layer services include:

- **NetWare message-handling service (NetWare MHS)**—A message-delivery system that provides electronic mail transport.

- **Btrieve**—Novell's implementation of the binary tree (btree) database-access mechanism.

- **NetWare loadable modules (NLMs)**—Add-on modules that attach into a NetWare system. NLMs currently available from Novell and third parties include alternate protocol stacks, communication services, and database services.

- **IBM Logical Unit (LU) 6.2 network-addressable units (NAUs)**—Support to allow peer-to-peer connectivity and information exchange across IBM networks. NetWare packets are encapsulated within LU 6.2 packets for transit across an IBM network.

IPX Addressing

As with other network addresses, Novell IPX network addresses must be unique. These addresses are represented in hexadecimal format and consist of two parts: a network number and a node number. The IPX network number, which is assigned by the network administrator, is 32 bits long. The node number, which usually is the Media Access Control (MAC) address for one of the system's network interface cards (NICs), is 48 bits long.

NetWare Routing and Service Advertisement Protocols

IPX uses the following protocols for routing and service advertisement:

- **IPX Routing Information Protocol (RIP)**—A distance vector routing protocol that sends routing updates every 60 seconds. To make best-path routing decisions, IPX RIP uses a *tick* as the metric, which in principle is the delay expected when using a particular length. One tick is 1/18th of a second. In the case of two paths with an equal tick count, IPX RIP uses the hop count as a tie breaker.

- **Service Advertisement Protocol (SAP)**—An IPX protocol through which network resources, such as file servers and print servers, advertise their addresses and the services they provide. Advertisements are sent via SAP every 60 seconds. Services are identified by a hexadecimal number, which is called a SAP identifier (for example, 4 = file server and 7 = print server). SAP is pervasive in current networks based on NetWare 3.11 and earlier but is utilized less frequently in NetWare 4.0 networks because workstations can locate services by consulting a NetWare Directory Services (NDS) Server. SAP, however, still is required in NetWare 4.0 networks for workstations when they boot up to locate an NDS server.

- **NetWare Link-Services Protocol (NLSP)**—A link-state routing protocol from Novell designed to overcome some of the limitations associated with the IPX RIP and SAP. As compared to RIP and SAP, NLSP provides improved routing, better efficiency, and scalability. In addition, NLSP-based routers are backward-compatible with RIP-based routers. NLSP-based routers use a reliable delivery protocol, so delivery is guaranteed. NLSP is based on the OSI Intermediate System-to-Intermediate System (IS-IS) protocol and is similar to IS-IS except that a hierarchical topology was not defined until Version 1.1 of NLSP was specified (which is supported in Cisco IOS™ Release 11.1). NLSP now supports hierarchical routing with area, domain, and global internetwork components.

AppleTalk Protocol Suite

AppleTalk, a protocol suite developed by Apple Computer in the early 1980s, was developed in conjunction with the Macintosh computer. AppleTalk's purpose was to allow multiple users to share resources, such as files and printers. The devices that supply these resources are called *servers*, whereas the devices that make use of these resources (such as a user's Macintosh computer) are called *clients*.

AppleTalk was designed with a transparent network interface. That is, the interaction between client computers and network servers requires little interaction from the user. In addition, the actual operations of the AppleTalk protocols are invisible to end users, who see only the result of these operations. Two versions of AppleTalk exist: AppleTalk Phase 1 and AppleTalk Phase 2.

Four main media-access implementations exist in the AppleTalk protocol suite: EtherTalk, LocalTalk, TokenTalk, and FDDITalk. These data link layer implementations perform address translation and other functions that allow proprietary AppleTalk protocols to communicate over industry-standard interfaces, which include IEEE 802.3 (using EtherTalk), Token Ring/IEEE 802.5 (using TokenTalk), and FDDI (using FDDITalk). In addition, AppleTalk implements its own network interface, known as LocalTalk.

AppleTalk Network Components

AppleTalk networks are arranged hierarchically. Four basic components form the basis of an AppleTalk network: sockets, nodes, networks, and zones.

- An AppleTalk **socket** is a unique, addressable location in an AppleTalk node. It is the logical point at which upper-layer AppleTalk software processes and the network layer Datagram-Delivery Protocol (DDP) interact.

- An AppleTalk **node** is a device that is connected to an AppleTalk network. This device might be a Macintosh computer, a printer, an IBM PC, a router, or some other similar device.

- A *nonextended* AppleTalk **network** is a physical-network segment that is assigned only a single network number, which can range between 1 and 1,024. An *extended* AppleTalk network is a physical-network segment that can be assigned multiple network numbers. This configuration is known as a **cable range**.

- An AppleTalk **zone** is a logical group of nodes or networks that is defined when the network administrator configures the network. The nodes or networks need not be physically contiguous to belong to the same AppleTalk zone.

AppleTalk Protocols

There are two protocols at the network layer:

- **AppleTalk Address-Resolution Protocol (AARP)**—Associates AppleTalk network addresses with hardware addresses

- **Datagram Delivery Protocol (DDP)**—Provides a best-effort connectionless datagram service between AppleTalk sockets

Five key implementations exist at the transport layer of the AppleTalk protocol suite:

- **Routing Table Maintenance Protocol (RTMP)**—Responsible for establishing and maintaining routing tables for AppleTalk routers. RTMP is a distance-vector protocol typically used in AppleTalk LANs; it uses hop count as its metric.

- **Name-Binding Protocol (NBP)**—Maps the addresses used at lower layers to AppleTalk names.

- **AppleTalk Update-Based Routing Protocol (AURP)**—Allows two or more AppleTalk internetworks to be interconnected through a TCP/IP network to form an AppleTalk WAN. AURP encapsulates packets in User Datagram Protocol (UDP) headers, allowing them to be transported transparently through a TCP/IP network; this creates a virtual data link between the AppleTalk networks. AURP is also the routing protocol used on this virtual data link; in this capacity, it is similar to distance vector routing protocols but is designed to handle routing update traffic over WAN links more efficiently than RTMP by only sending changed information.

- **AppleTalk Transaction Protocol (ATP)**—Handles transactions between two AppleTalk sockets.

- **AppleTalk Echo Protocol (AEP)**—Generates packets that test the reachability of network nodes.

The session layer protocol implementations supported by AppleTalk include:

- **AppleTalk Data-Stream Protocol (ADSP)**—Establishes and maintains full-duplex communication between two AppleTalk sockets

- **Zone-Information Protocol (ZIP)**—Maintains network number-to-zone name mappings in AppleTalk routers

- **AppleTalk Session Protocol (ASP)**—Establishes and maintains sessions between AppleTalk clients and servers

- **Printer-Access Protocol (PAP)**—Allows client workstations to establish connections with servers, particularly printers

The **AppleTalk Filing Protocol (AFP)** is implemented at the presentation and application layers of the AppleTalk protocol suite. AFP permits AppleTalk workstations to share files across a network.

AppleTalk Addressing

AppleTalk utilizes addresses to identify and locate devices on a network in a manner similar to the process utilized by protocols such as TCP/IP and IPX. These addresses, which are assigned dynamically, are composed of three elements:

- **Network number**—A 16-bit value that identifies a specific AppleTalk network (either a nonextended network or from an extended cable range)

- **Node number**—An 8-bit value that identifies a particular AppleTalk node attached to the specified network

- **Socket number**—An 8-bit number that identifies a specific socket running on a network node

AppleTalk addresses usually are written as decimal values separated by a period. For example, 10.1.50 means network 10, node 1, socket 50. This also might be represented as 10.1, socket 50.

IBM Systems Network Architecture Protocols

IBM networking today consists of essentially two separate architectures that branch from a common origin. Before contemporary networks existed, IBM's *Systems Network Architecture* (SNA) ruled the networking landscape, so it is often referred to as traditional or legacy SNA.

With the rise of personal computers, workstations, and client/server computing, the need for a peer-based networking strategy was addressed by IBM with the creation of *Advanced Peer-to-Peer Networking* (APPN) and *Advanced Program-to-Program Computing* (APPC).

Traditional SNA Environments

SNA was developed in the 1970s with an overall structure that parallels the OSI reference model. With SNA, a mainframe running *Advanced Communication Facility/Virtual Telecommunication Access Method* (ACF/VTAM) serves as the hub of an SNA network. ACF/VTAM is responsible for establishing all sessions and for activating and deactivating resources. In this environment, resources are explicitly predefined, thereby eliminating the requirement for broadcast traffic and minimizing header overhead.

IBM SNA model components map closely to the OSI reference model, as shown in Figure C-6.

Figure C-6   *The IBM SNA Model Maps Closely to the OSI Model*

SNA	OSI
Transaction Services	Application
Presentation Services	Presentation
Data Flow Control	Session
Transmission Control	Transport
Path Control	Network
Data Link Control	Data Link
Physical	Physical

The SNA layers are:

- **Data-link control**—Defines several protocols, including the *Synchronous Data Link Control* (SDLC) protocol for hierarchical communication, and the Token Ring Network communication protocol for LAN communication between peers.

- **Path control**—Performs many OSI network-layer functions, including routing and datagram *segmentation and reassembly* (SAR).

- **Transmission control**—Provides a reliable end-to-end connection service, as well as encrypting and decrypting services.

- **Data flow control**—Manages request and response processing, determines whose turn it is to communicate, groups messages together, and interrupts data flow on request.

- **Presentation services**—Specifies data-transformation algorithms that translate data from one format to another, coordinate resource sharing, and synchronize transaction operations.

- **Transaction services**—Provides application services in the form of programs that implement distributed processing or management services.

Traditional SNA physical entities assume one of the following four forms:

- **Hosts**—In SNA, control all or part of a network and typically provide computation, program execution, database access, directory services, and network management. (An example of a host device within a traditional SNA environment is an S/370 mainframe.)

- **Communications controllers**—Manage the physical network and control communication links. In particular, communications controllers (also called *front-end processors* [FEPs]) are relied upon to route data through a traditional SNA network. (An example of a communications controller is a 3745.)

- **Establishment controllers**—Commonly called *cluster controllers*, these devices control input and output operations of attached devices, such as terminals. (An example of an establishment controller is a 3174.)

- **Terminals**—Also referred to as workstations, terminals provide the user interface to the network. (A typical example would be a 3270.)

IBM Peer-Based Networking

Changes in networking and communications requirements caused IBM to evolve (and generally overhaul) many of the basic design characteristics of SNA. The emergence of peer-based networking entities (such as routers) resulted in a number of significant changes in SNA. Internetworking among SNA peers hinges on several IBM-developed networking components.

Advanced Peer-to-Peer Networking (APPN) represents IBM's second-generation SNA. In creating APPN, IBM moved SNA from a hierarchical, mainframe-centric environment to a peer-based networking environment. At the heart of APPN is an IBM architecture that supports peer-based communications, directory services, and routing between two or more Advanced Program-to-Program Computing (APPC) systems that are not directly attached.

Network Management

In general, network management is a service that employs a variety of tools, applications, and devices to assist human network managers in monitoring and maintaining networks.

Most network management architectures use the same basic structure and set of relationships. End stations (*managed devices*), such as computer systems and other network devices, run software that enables them to send alerts when they recognize problems (for example, when one or more user-determined thresholds are exceeded). Upon receiving these alerts, *management entities* are programmed to react by executing one, several, or a group of actions, including operator notification, event logging, system shutdown, and automatic attempts at system repair.

Management entities also can poll end stations to check the values of certain variables. Polling can be automatic or user-initiated, but *agents* in the managed devices respond to all polls. Agents are software modules that first compile information about the managed devices in which they reside, store this information in a *management database*, and finally provide it (proactively or reactively) to management entities within *network management systems* (NMSs) via a *network management protocol*. The Simple Network Management Protocol (SNMP) is a well-known network management protocol. *Management proxies* are entities that provide management information on behalf of other entities.

Simple Network Management Protocol

The Simple Network Management Protocol is an application layer protocol that facilitates the exchange of management information between network devices. It is part of the TCP/IP protocol suite. SNMP enables network administrators to manage network performance, find and solve network problems, and plan for network growth.

Two versions of SNMP exist: SNMP Version 1 (SNMPv1) and SNMP Version 2 (SNMPv2). Both versions have a number of features in common, but SNMPv2 offers enhancements, such as additional protocol operations.

Managed devices are monitored and controlled using four basic SNMP commands:

- The **read** command is used by a network management system (NMS) to monitor managed devices. The NMS examines different variables that are maintained by managed devices.

- The **write** command is used by an NMS to control managed devices. The NMS changes the values of variables stored within managed devices.

- The **trap** command is used by managed devices to asynchronously report events to the NMS. When certain types of events occur, a managed device sends a trap to the NMS.

- **Traversal operations** are used by the NMS to determine which variables a managed device supports and to sequentially gather information in variable tables (such as a routing table).

A Management Information Base (MIB) is a collection of information that is organized hierarchically. MIBs are accessed using a network management protocol such as SNMP. MIBs are composed of managed objects and are identified by object identifiers. A managed object (sometimes called a MIB object, an object, or a MIB) is one of any number of specific characteristics of a managed device. Managed objects are composed of one or more object instances, which are essentially variables. An object identifier (or object ID) uniquely identifies a managed object in the MIB hierarchy.

SNMP is a simple request-response protocol. The NMS issues a request, and managed devices return responses. This behavior is implemented by using one of four protocol operations in SNMPv1:

- The **Get** operation is used by the NMS to retrieve the value of one or more object instances from an agent.

- The **GetNext** operation is used by the NMS to retrieve the value of the next object instance in a table or list within an agent.

- The **Set** operation is used by the NMS to set the values of object instances within an agent.

- The **Trap** operation is used by agents to asynchronously inform the NMS of a significant event.

The Get, GetNext, and Set operations used in SNMPv1 are exactly the same as those used in SNMPv2. SNMPv2, however, adds and enhances some protocols operations. The SNMPv2 Trap operation, for example, serves the same function as that used in SNMPv1; however, it uses a different message format and is designed to replace the SNMPv1 Trap. SNMPv2 also defines two new protocol operations:

- The **GetBulk** operation is used by the NMS to efficiently retrieve large blocks of data, such as multiple rows in a table.

- The **Inform** operation allows one NMS to send trap information to another NMS and receive a response.

Remote Monitoring

Remote Monitoring (RMON) is a standard monitoring specification that enables various network monitors and console systems to exchange network-monitoring data. The RMON specification defines a set of statistics and functions that can be exchanged between RMON-compliant console managers and network probes. As such, RMON provides network administrators with comprehensive network-fault diagnosis, planning, and performance-tuning information. RMON delivers information in nine RMON *groups* of monitoring elements, each providing specific sets of data to meet common network-monitoring requirements. Each group is optional so that vendors do not need to support all the groups within the Management Information Base (MIB).

LAN Media Reference

To supplement the material in Chapter 4, "Network Topologies and LAN Design," this appendix covers Ethernet, Fast Ethernet, Gigabit Ethernet, FDDI, and Token Ring technologies. This appendix covers the frame formats and the specifications for each LAN technology.

Ethernet Standards

Today's Ethernet networks are based on the Ethernet development by Digital, Intel, and Xerox (DIX). Version 1 of the standard was created in 1980. It used unbalanced signaling (0,+5). In 1982, Version 2 of Ethernet was introduced. It added the *heartbeat signal* to transceivers and moved to balanced signaling (-5,0,+5). The heartbeat is used as a link test pulse. Version 2 is the basis of Ethernet that is used today.

Carrier sense multiple access/collision detect (CSMA/CD) is the media access method on Ethernet networks. In this scheme, nodes listen to the network for activity. If there is none, they can transmit a frame onto the network. While transmitting, they listen to the network for any collisions with other transmitting nodes. If a collision is detected, the node waits a random amount of time, listens for traffic on the segment, and if there is none, attempts to send the frame, again. It attempts 16 times before sending an error message to the upper-layer protocol.

Manchester encoding was selected to code signals on the wire on Ethernet. In Manchester encoding, a 0 is represented as a transition from high to low in the middle of the clocking time interval. A 1 is represented as a transition from low to high in the middle of the time interval. Figure D-1 shows a sample of Manchester encoding.

Figure D-1   *Manchester Encoding*

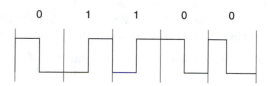

After the DIX Ethernet Version 2 standard was published, an effort went into producing an IEEE standard for Ethernet. The IEEE produced their 802.3 and 802.3 SNAP frame formats. Novell also produced their frame format for their network operating system. As a result, these different groups produced different frame formats for the Ethernet wire, but the signaling, encoding, and frame maximum and minimum sizes remain the same; therefore, these four frame formats can reside on the same segment:

- Ethernet Version 2

- Novell 802.3 raw

- IEEE 802.3

- IEEE 802.3 SNAP

Ethernet Version 2 Frame Format

Figure D-2 shows the Ethernet Version 2 frame format. The remainder of this section discusses the fields in the Ethernet Version 2 frame format.

Figure D-2   *Ethernet Version 2 Frame Format*

Preamble 8 bytes	DA 6 bytes	SA 6 bytes	Type 2 bytes	Data+pad 46—1500 bytes	FCS 4 bytes

The *preamble* is a string of 1s and 0s, ending with 11, to indicate the beginning of the *destination address* (DA) field. The string of 1s and 0s is used by the transceiver to sync up to the receiving signal. The preamble is as follows:

```
10101010 10101010 10101010 10101010 10101010 10101010 10101010 10101011
```

The DA field contains the 48-bit MAC layer Ethernet address of the destination host.

The *source address* (SA) field contains the 48-bit MAC layer Ethernet address of the host that sent the frame.

The *type* field contains the Ethernet type (Ethertype) number that indicates the upper-layer protocol that this frame should be sent to. This number is greater than 1500 (05DC hex). Examples of Ethertypes are 0800 for the IP protocol and 6004 for Dec LAT. A list of Ethernet types can be viewed at http://www.standards.ieee.org/regauth/ethertype/type-pub.html.

The *data* field contains the upper-layer protocol information. If the information is less than 46 bytes, padding is used to reach the minimum frame size of 64 bytes (header plus data).

The *frame check sequence* (FCS) field contains the CRC data to check for errors when receiving the frame.

The minimum frame size on Ethernet is 64 bytes, and the maximum is 1518. When calculating the frame size, do not include the preamble. The Version 2 frame format conforms to the following specification:

- The minimum frame size is 6+6+2+46+4 = 64 bytes

- The maximum frame size is 6+6+2+1500+4 = 1518 bytes

Novell 802.3 Raw Frame Format

Prior to the IEEE 802.3 specification, Novell needed a frame format for their NetWare Internetwork Packet Exchange (IPX) network operating system. The IEEE was going to change the Type field to a Length field, but no other work was completed. Novell went ahead with their frame format to run on CSMA/CD networks.

Figure D-3 shows the Novell 802.3 raw frame format. The remainder of this section discusses the fields in the Novell 802.3 raw frame format.

Figure D-3   *Novell 802.3 Raw Frame Format*

Preamble 8 bytes	DA 6 bytes	SA 6 bytes	Length 2 bytes	FFFF	Data+pad 46—1500 bytes	FCS 4 bytes

The preamble field is exactly the same as in Ethernet Version 2 frame format.

The DA field contains the MAC address of the destination.

The SA field contains the MAC address of the source.

The length field contains the length of the data field. Values are from 3 to 1500 bytes.

The FCS contains the CRC information.

Novell frames are unique in that the data field begins with FFFF hex (at the beginning of the IPX protocol header).

IEEE 802.3 Frame Format

The IEEE produced their Ethernet standard in June 1983. They changed the type field to a length field and added the *Logical Link Control* (LLC) layer.

Figure D-4 shows the IEEE 802.3 frame format. The remainder of this section discusses the fields in the IEEE 802.3 frame format.

Figure D-4 *IEEE 802.3 Frame Format*

Preamble 7 bytes	SFD 1 byte	DA 6 bytes	SA 6 bytes	Length 2 bytes	LLC 3 bytes	Data+pad 43—1497 bytes	FCS 4 bytes

The IEEE defined the preamble to be a string of 1s and 0s that is 7 bytes long. The following byte is the *Start Frame Delimiter* (SFD):

    10101011

Following the SFD are the DA and SA fields, with MAC addresses.

The length field contains the length of the LLC plus the data field. Its values range from 3 to 1500.

The LLC layer is added by the IEEE to indicate the upper-layer protocol. It is divided into three fields, as shown in Figure D-5.

Figure D-5 *IEEE LLC Layer Fields*

DSAP 1 byte	SSAP 1 byte	Control 1 or 2 bytes

The *destination service access point* (DSAP) indicates the destination upper-layer protocol. The *source service access point* (SSAP) indicates the source upper-layer protocol. Examples of SAPs are as follows:

- NetBios = F0
- Bridge PDU = 42
- SNA = 04,05,0C
- SNAP = AA
- X.25 = 7E

The data field (see Figure D-4) contains the upper-layer protocol information, as in other frame formats. The FCS field (see Figure D-4) contains the CRC

IEEE 802.3 SNAP Frame Format

The problem the IEEE faced when developing the IEEE frame format was, by then, protocols using DIX Version 2 had been in use for three years. To transition to an IEEE 802.3-compliant frame, the *SNAP* field was added to 802.3, to provide transition. The SNAP field includes the Ethernet type information used in DIX Version 2. Figure D-6 shows the IEEE 802.3 SNAP frame format. The remainder of this section discusses the fields in the IEEE 802.3 SNAP frame format.

Figure D-6   *IEEE 802.3 SNAP Frame Format*

Preamble 7 bytes	SFD 1 byte	DA 6 bytes	SA 6 bytes	Length 2 bytes	LLC 3 bytes	SNAP 5 bytes	Data+pad 38–1492 bytes	FCS

All fields are the same as in IEEE 802.3. The SNAP field is added. It contains two fields, including a 3-byte vendor code field that is unique to different vendors. The next field in the SNAP is the 2-byte Ethernet type field, used in Ethernet Version 2. The SNAP fields are displayed in Figure D-7.

Figure D-7   *IEEE SNAP Fields*

Vendor code 3 bytes	Type 2 bytes

What has happened in the years following these standards is that IP and DEC protocols use Ethernet Version 2, Novell IPX (3.x) uses its 802.3 raw format, and SNA uses 802.3. In multi-protocol networks today, there is a mix of frame formats on the network.

The following sections cover Ethernet physical specifications.

10Base5

Commonly referred as Thick Ethernet or Thicknet, this specification uses 0.4-inch, 50-ohm coaxial cable. The specifications for Thicknet are as follows:

- 0.4-inch, 50-ohm coax cable
- Maximum segment length is 500 m
- Maximum number of attachments per segment is 100
- Maximum attachment unit interface (AUI) cable length is 50 m
- Minimum separation between media attachment units (MAUs) is 2.5 m
- Cable ends terminate with 50-ohm terminators
- MAUs attach workstations
- Maximum network length is 5 segments and 2500 m
- Maximum number of stations on the network is 1024

Figure D-8 shows a sample 10Base5 Ethernet network.

Figure D-8   *Sample 10Base5 Network*

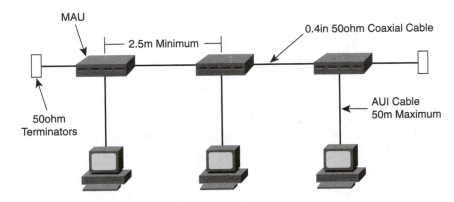

10Base2

Commonly referred to as Thinnet, this specification uses 0.2-inch, 50-ohm coaxial cable. Thinnet specifications are as follows:

- 0.2-inch, RG58-U, 50-ohm coax cable
- Maximum segment length is 185 m
- Maximum number of attachments per segment is 30
- Minimum separation per segment is 0.5 m
- T-connectors attach workstations

Figure D-9 shows a sample 10Base2 Ethernet network.

Figure D-9   *Sample 10Base2 Network*

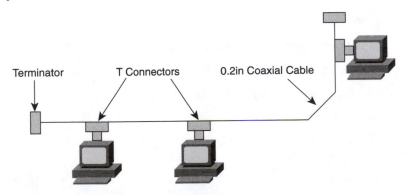

10BaseT

Unshielded twisted-pair (UTP) has become a very popular medium for LAN systems. 10BaseT was made an IEEE standard in 1990. The 10BaseT specifications are as follows:

- 24 AWG UTP 0.4-/0.6-mm cable

- Maximum segment length is 100 m

- One device per cable

Figure D-10 shows a sample 10BaseT Ethernet network.

Figure D-10   *Sample 10BaseT Network*

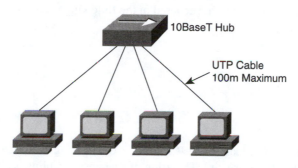

100BaseT Fast Ethernet

The IEEE developed the 802.3u in 1995 to provide Ethernet speeds of 100 Mbps over UTP and fiber cabling. The 100BaseT standard is similar to 10 Mbps Ethernet in that it uses CSMA/CD; runs on Cat 3, 4, and 5 UTP cable; and the frame formats are preserved. Connectivity still uses hubs, repeaters, and bridges.

The difference is that the encoding changed from Manchester to 4B/5B with nonreturn to zero (NRZ), the new speed is 100 Mbps, and the Media Independent Interface (MII) was introduced as a replacement to the AUI.

The 4B/5B coding takes 4 bits of data and expands it into a 5-bit code for transmission on the physical channel. Because of the 20 percent overhead, pulses run at 125 MHz on the wire, to achieve 100 Mbps. Table D-1 shows how some data numbers are converted to 4B/5B code.

Table D-1   *Converting Data to 4B/5B Code*

Data	Binary	4B/5B Code
0	0000	11110
1	0001	01001

continues

Table D-1   *Converting Data to 4B/5B Code (Continued)*

Data	Binary	4B/5B Code
2	0010	10100
...	...	...
D	1101	11011
E	1110	11100
F	1111	11101

The following specifications are covered in the following sections:

- 100BaseTX
- 100BaseT4
- 100BaseFX

100BaseTX

The 100BaseTX specification uses Category 5 UTP wiring. Like 10BaseT, Fast Ethernet uses only two pairs of the four-pair UTP wiring. If Category 5 cabling is already in place, upgrading to Fast Ethernet only requires a hub or switch and NIC upgrades. Because of the low cost, most of today's installations use switches. The specifications are as follows:

- Transmission over Cat 5 UTP or Cat 1 STP wire
- RJ-45 connector (same as in 10BaseT)
- Punchdown blocks in the wiring closet must be Category 5 certified
- 4B/5B coding

100BaseT4

The 100BaseT4 specification was developed to support UTP wiring at the Category 3 level. This implementation is not widely deployed. The specifications are as follows:

- Transmission over Cat 3, 4, or 5 UTP wiring
- Three wires used for transmission, and the fourth wire is used for collision detection
- No separate transmit and receive pairs are present, so full-duplex operation is not possible
- 8B/6T coding

100BaseFX

The 100BaseFX specifications for fiber are as follows:

- Operates over two strands of multi-mode or single-mode fiber cabling
- Can transmit over greater distances than copper media
- Uses MIC, ST, or SC fiber connectors defined for FDDI and 10BaseFX networks
- 4B/5B coding

1000 Mbps Gigabit Ethernet

The most recent development in the Ethernet arena is Gigabit Ethernet. Gigabit Ethernet is specified by two standards: IEEE 802.3z and 802.3ab. The 802.3z standard specifies the operation of Gigabit Ethernet over fiber and coaxial cable and introduces the Gigabit Media Independent Interface (GMII). The 802.3z standard was approved in July 1998. The 802.3ab standard specifies the operation of Gigabit Ethernet over Category 5 UTP. It was approved in June 1999. Gigabit Ethernet still retains the frame formats and frame sizes of 10 Mbps Ethernet, along with the use of CSMA/CD. As with Ethernet and Fast Ethernet, full-duplex operation is possible. Differences can be found in the encoding; Gigabit Ethernet uses 8B/10B coding with simple NRZ. Because of the 20 percent overhead, pulses run at 1250 MHz to achieve 1000 Mbps. Gigabit Ethernet includes the following methods to achieve 1 Gbps speed:

- 8B/10B coding
- Bytes are encoded as 10-bit symbols
- Run-length limited (no long sequences of 1s or 0s)
- Pulses on the wire run at 1250 MHz to achieve 1000 Mbps speed

Table D-2 shows how data is converted into 8B/10B code for transmission.

Table D-2   *8B/10B Encoding*

Data	Binary	8B/10B code
00	00000000	0110001011
01	00000001	1000101011
02	00000010	0100101011
03	00000011	1100010100
04	00000100	0010101011

The following specifications are covered in the following sections:

- 1000BaseLX
- 1000BaseSX
- 1000BaseCX
- 1000BaseT

1000BaseLX

The IEEE 1000BaseLX uses long-wavelength optics over a pair of fiber strands. The specifications are as follows:

- Uses long wave (1300nm)
- Use on multi-mode or single-mode fiber
- Maximum lengths for multi-mode fiber are:
    - 62.5-micron: 550m
    - 50-micron: 550m
- Maximum length for a 9-micron, single-mode fiber is 9 microns: 5km
- Uses 8B/10B encoding with simple NRZ

1000BaseSX

The IEEE 1000BaseSX uses short-wavelength optics over a pair of multi-mode fiber strands. The specifications are as follows:

- Uses short wave (850nm)
- Use on multi-mode fiber
- Maximum lengths:
    - 62.5-micron: 220m
    - 50-micron: 500m
- Uses 8B/10B encoding with simple NRZ

1000BaseCX

The IEEE 1000BaseCX standard is intended for short copper runs between servers. The specifications are as follows:

- Used on short copper runs
- Over a pair of 150-ohm balanced coaxial cables (twinax)
- Maximum length is 25m
- Mainly for server connections
- Uses 8B/10B encoding with simple NRZ

1000BaseT

The IEEE standard for 1000 Mbps Ethernet over Category 5 UTP is IEEE 802.3ab. This standard uses the four pairs in the cable (Fast and 10BaseT Ethernet use only two pairs). The specifications are as follows:

- Category 5, four-pair UTP
- Maximum length is 100m
- Encoding defined as a 5-level coding scheme
- 1 byte is sent over the four pairs at 1250 MHz
- Standard was approved in June 1999

Token Ring

Token Ring was developed by IBM for the forwarding of data on a logical unidirectional ring; the physical connectivity can be a star. The IEEE standard for Token Ring is IEEE 802.5; the differences with IBM's specification are minor. Devices connect to a *multistation access unit* (MSAU). MSAUs can be connected together with patch cables, to form a ring. The MSAU can also bypass stations that are defective on the ring. Figure D-11 shows the connectivity in the Token Ring network. The MSAUs are connected in a physical ring.

Token Ring uses *Differential Manchester* as a coding scheme. In Differential Manchester, a 0 is represented as a transition at the beginning of the clock time interval. A 1 is indicated as an absence of a transition. Access is controlled by using a token. A token is passed along the network from station to station; if a station has no data to transmit, it forwards the token to the next station. If the station wants to transmit data, it seizes the token, produces a data frame, and sends it to the destination. The receiving station reads the frame and forwards it along the ring, back to the source station. The source station verifies that the data frame was read and releases a token back onto the network.

Figure D-11 *Token Ring*

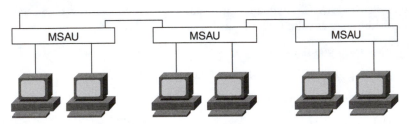

One station on the Token Ring is selected to be the *active monitor*. This station acts as a centralized source of timing information for other ring stations and performs a variety of ring-maintenance functions. The active monitor can remove continuously circulating frames that are not removed by a fault sender.

Token Ring Frame Format

There are two types of frame formats: data/command frames and token frames. These frames are displayed in Figures D-12 and D-13. Tokens are 3 bytes in length and consist of a start delimiter, an access control byte, and an end delimiter. Data/command frames vary in size, depending on the size of the information field. Command frames contain control information and do not carry upper-layer protocols.

Figure D-12 *Data/Command Frame*

SD 1 byte	AC 1 byte	FC 1 byte	DA 6 bytes	SA 6 bytes	Data	FCS 4 bytes	ED 1 byte	FS 1 byte

Figure D-13 *Token Frame (no data)*

SD 1 byte	AC 1 byte	ED 1 byte

The following is an explanation of the fields in Figures D-12 and D-13:

- **SD (starting delimiter)**—Used to alert a station on the arrival of a frame.

- **AC (access control)**—Contains the token bit that is used to differentiate a token from a data/command frame. Also contains priority and reservation fields.

- **FC (frame control)**—Used to indicate whether the frame contains data or is a command frame with control information.

- **DA (destination address)**—Contains the 48-bit Token Ring MAC address of the destination node.

- **SA (source address)**—Contains the 48-bit Token Ring MAC address of the source node.

- **Data**—Contains the upper-layer protocol information; this field is of variable size.

- **FCS (frame check sequence)**—Contains the CRC to verify for frame errors.

- **ED (end delimiter)**—Used to indicate the end of the Token Ring frame or the last frame in a logical sequence.

- **FS (frame status)**—Used to terminate a data/command frame.

Token Ring Physical Specifications

The following are the Token Ring physical specifications:

- **Data rates**—4 and 16 Mbps

- **Maximum stations per segment**—250

- **Topology**—Logical ring, physical star

- **Media**—Twisted pair

- **Access method**—Token passing

- **Encoding**—Differential Manchester

Fiber Distributed Data Interface

Fiber Distributed Data Interface (FDDI) was developed for the transmission of data over fiber at 100 Mbps. The standard is governed by the American National Standards Institute (ANSI). FDDI is deployed in a dual-ring topology. Each dual-attached station (DAS) attaches to both rings; the second ring is on standby. If there is a failure of a station or a link on the ring, a ring wrap occurs, creating a single ring for continued communication. Access to the ring is by the use of a token (as in Token Ring). Figure D-14 shows a sample FDDI network.

Figure D-14 *Sample FDDI Network*

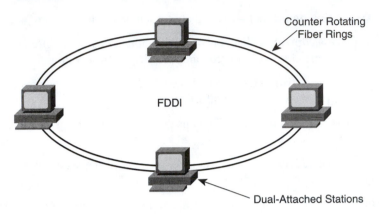

FDDI Frame Format

The FDDI frame format is similar to the format of a Token Ring frame. FDDI frames can be as large as 4500 bytes. There is a token and a data frame format. Figures D-15 and D-16 show these formats.

Figure D-15 *FDDI Data Frame*

Preamble	SD 1 byte	FC 1 byte	DA 6 bytes	SA 6 bytes	Data	FCS 4 bytes	ED 1 byte	FS 1 byte

Figure D-16 *FDDI Token (no data)*

Preamble	SD	FC	ED

The following is an explanation of the fields in Figures D-15 and D-16:

- **Preamble**—Used to prepare a station for an incoming frame.

- **SD (starting delimiter)**—Used to indicate that an incoming frame follows.

- **FC (frame control)**—Contains control information. Used to indicate whether this is a data or token frame.

- **DA (destination address)**—Contains the 48-bit MAC layer destination address.

- **SA (source address)**—Contains the 48-bit MAC layer source address.

- **Data**—Contains upper-layer protocol information.
- **FCS (frame check sequence)**—Contains the CRC to verify for frame errors.
- **ED (end delimiter)**—Indicates the end of the frame.
- **FS (frame status)**—Used by the source station to determine whether the frame was copied by the destination or whether errors occurred.

This appendix covers Ethernet, Fast Ethernet, Gigabit Ethernet, Token Ring, and FDDI. The frame formats of these LAN technologies and their scalability specifications are reviewed.

This appendix is an excerpt from the *Small and Medium Business Solution Guide*, which is located at www.cisco.com/univercd/cc/td/doc/product/smbsolg/smb_st.htm on the CCO Web site. It has been edited slightly so that it can be presented here in book format. Some sales-oriented information has been omitted.

This appendix summarizes the Cisco product solutions for small and medium-sized business networking needs. The following is a list of the solutions covered in this appendix:

- Cisco Business Solutions
- Cisco Access Routers and Servers Overview
- Cisco Internet Security and Scalability Overview
- Cisco Ethernet and Fast Ethernet Switches Overview
- Cisco Ease of Use and Network Management Overview

Cisco Small and Medium Business Solution Guide

Cisco Business Solutions

In today's competitive environment, small- to medium-sized businesses need powerful networking solutions to enhance productivity, increase business opportunities, and sustain a competitive edge. Cisco Systems solutions are tailored to meet the needs of customers who want networking solutions that are easy to install, use, and manage.

Cost-effective branch office connectivity solutions help increase productivity, allowing small- and medium-sized businesses to stay competitive. These solutions combine application availability with fast, timely access to business information; low cost of ownership to control wide-area connections and ongoing management costs; and scalability to protect investments and allow for expansion.

Telecommuting can reduce office costs, increase employee productivity, and improve morale and job satisfaction while enhancing a company's capability to recruit top talent in a competitive job market. By employing innovative remote user solutions, growing businesses can provide their field employees with remote access to e-mail, network resources, and up-to-date pricing, product, and inventory information. The result is dramatically improved customer service.

Highly integrated end-to-end solutions for the Internet offer an alternative channel for reaching new customers and for providing cost-effective customer support.

High-performance LAN solutions can minimize network congestion, substantially improving performance to the desktop, server, and backbone as well as increasing employee productivity.

Cisco Networked Office Stack is a flexible suite of products designed for small and medium-sized businesses to provide secure access to the Internet. It also links users and offices so that they can easily share resources such as information, documents, and printers.

Cisco Branch Office Connectivity Solutions

Communication becomes challenging for small- and medium-sized companies with branch offices, warehouses, or business partners located in various geographical areas. These companies frequently need to share customer information, check inventory, look up sales data, transfer files, process invoices, and exchange e-mail. The integration of voice and data traffic over shared WAN lines can save companies significant amounts of money. Still, a dispersed organization cannot communicate effectively and efficiently without the right technology.

Customers in need of branch office connectivity solutions require the following:

- Cost-effective branch office connectivity solutions that combine application availability with fast and timely access to business information, to increase productivity and stay competitive

- Low cost of ownership to control wide-area connections and ongoing management costs

- Scalability to protect investments and allow for expansion

- Reduction of WAN line costs by integrating voice and data traffic over shared lines

Branch Office Connectivity Considerations

This section covers branch office connectivity considerations.

WAN Connectivity Flexibility

A central site solution should have a modular design that can accommodate many different types of WAN connections with remote locations. In addition, this solution should meet bandwidth and usage connection time requirements.

WAN service options for branch office connectivity include these:

- ISDN leased lines for a high-bandwidth, cost-effective solution for companies requiring light or sporadic high-speed access to either a central office or a branch office

- Frame Relay or X.25 for companies needing more permanent connections

- Leased-line solutions in which higher connection times and shorter distances are generally more cost-effective

WAN Optimization Features

Because some WAN charges (such as ISDN) are based on usage, it is important that companies have a solution that can implement features to optimize bandwidth and help keep WAN costs to a minimum. Bandwidth-on-demand (BOD), dial-on-demand routing (DDR), snapshot routing, Internetwork Packet Exchange (IPX) spoofing, and compression keep WAN costs to a minimum.

Security

Ensuring that central site and branch office data remains secure is an important consideration for these reasons:

- Access lists can filter out unauthorized data flow between offices.

- Point-to-Point Protocol (PPP) network links, Password Authentication Protocol (PAP), and Challenge Handshake Authentication Protocol (CHAP) can identify the remote entity to prevent unauthorized network connections.

Branch Office to Central Site Solutions

For simplified management and to ensure full interoperability, customers should consider vendors that have solutions for both the branch office and the central site. Figure E-1 shows sample branch office connectivity solutions.

Figure E-1   *Cisco Branch Office Connectivity Solutions*

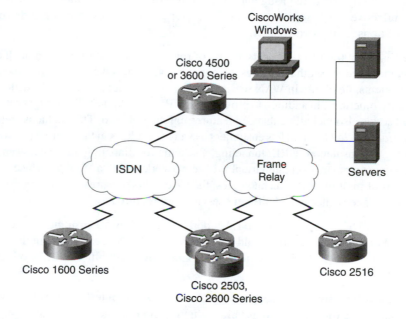

Cisco Solutions for Branch Offices

Cisco offers a wide range of router products that are perfect for the branch office. These branch office routers support the same comprehensive set of Cisco IOS features that are available with the central site routers.

The Cisco 2600 router provides a cost-effective solution for extending data/voice integration, dial concentration, and virtual private network (VPN) access to remote branch offices.

The Cisco 2500 series of access routers is the world's most popular line of branch office routers. Its broad range of models provides a wide variety of connectivity options, level of technology integration, and price points.

The multifunctional Cisco 2505, 2507, and 2516 models deliver the capabilities of a manageable Ethernet 10BaseT hub and router in the same box. By eliminating multiple standalone network devices, clumsy cabling, and complicated installations, these versatile routers are ideal for deployment in remote office locations. The Cisco 2516 also offers an ISDN BRI port that can be used as a backup link, to allow flexibility for disaster recovery and additional BOD.

The Cisco 2501-4 and 252x models offer the flexibility, performance, and redundancy of dual serial interfaces and the option of ISDN BRI.

The Cisco 2513, 2514, and 2515 models double the LAN interfaces of the Cisco 2501-4 models to two Ethernet or Token Ring interfaces, or one of each. These models give branch offices a cost-effective way to segment existing LANs for faster network response and to provide firewall applications to improve security.

The Cisco 1600 series represents a class of routers optimized for small branch offices. It contains a feature set that matches the concerns customers have today over the need to protect investments, flexibility in WAN service choices, feature support for multimedia, and enhanced security functions. In addition to providing IP, IPX, and AppleTalk routing protocols, the Cisco 1600 series also includes enhanced features unique to Cisco: This includes *Network Address Translation (NAT)*, which lets customers use any IP address in the internal network; and generic routing encapsulation (GRE) tunneling, a scheme for tunneling traffic between networks, allowing customers to create virtual private networks. With a WAN interface card slot and support of multiple WAN technologies, the Cisco 1600 ensures investment protection as customer needs change and different services are required.

The Cisco 1605-R router has two LAN ports, which allows a customer to securely segment a LAN. For example, a school could have the student LAN separated from the administration's LAN. The Cisco 1605-R is also ideal for connecting small offices with two Ethernet LANs to the Internet.

The Cisco 1600 series also supports the Cisco ClickStart interface, a Web browser application that makes the routers easy to install, configure, and manage. In addition, it supports ConfigMaker, an easy-to-use Windows application for initial configuration of a single device or multiple 1600s.

Both the Cisco 2600 and 1600 series routers offer a range of optional WAN cards, including serial (asynchronous and synchronous), ISDN BRI (with or without an integrated NT1), 56/64 kbps four-wire DSU/CSU, and T1/Fractional T1 DSU/CSU.

The Cisco IOS Firewall feature set, available on Cisco 1600 and 2500 router platforms, provides an advanced security solution for Cisco IOS software, with rich application support, failover, and encryption in a single device. The Cisco IOS Firewall feature set provides full multiprotocol routing, WAN access capabilities, and seamless integration with existing Cisco IOS environments.

Cisco Solutions for the Central Site

Cisco Systems offers a range of central site products ideal for connecting branch offices. The Cisco 4500/4700 series and the Cisco 3600 series offer network administrators modular, flexible solutions that will meet changing needs as a company grows while also preserving its investment. In addition, these routers support extensive features to increase WAN security and reduce WAN costs.

The Cisco 4500 and 4700 series access routers are high-performance, modular central site routers that support the most comprehensive set of LAN and WAN technologies with network interface modules (NIMs). Their modular design allows easy reconfiguration as needs change. A full range of high-speed connectivity options are available, including Fast Ethernet, ATM, High-Speed Serial Interface (HSSI), and FDDI.

The highly modular Cisco 3600 series access servers provide amazing versatility to support branch/central site dial access applications, LAN-to-LAN or routing applications, and multiservice applications in a single chassis.

The Cisco 3640 has four network module slots, and the Cisco 3620 access router is equipped with two slots that accept a variety of mixed-media or WAN network modules, including one slot that supports dual Ethernet and dual WAN ports. Multiservice applications are supported by integrated voice network modules.

The Cisco 3600 series routers offer a range of optional WAN cards, including serial (asynchronous and synchronous), ISDN BRI (with or without an integrated NT1), 56/64 kbps four-wire DSU/CSU, and T1/Fractional T1 DSU/CSU.

All Cisco access routers incorporate the industry-leading Cisco IOS software.

Cisco IOS software supports robust multiprotocol routing and provides enhanced support for multimedia and features to reduce WAN connection costs. Data compression and multiple traffic prioritization techniques ensure that critical data is accommodated. Dialup costs are minimized with features such as protocol spoofing, snapshot routing, NSLP route aggregation, DDR, and BOD. Comprehensive authentication and authorization allow only approved traffic onto the network, and event logging, audit trails, encryption, virtual private networking functions, and NAT provide additional network security. Support for protocols such as Internet Group Management Protocol (IGMP) and Resource Reservation Protocol (RSVP) makes Cisco routers ideally suited to meet the demanding needs of audio and video services.

Cisco Management Solutions for Branch Office Connectivity

All Cisco access routers are manageable by the CiscoWorks Windows software, a comprehensive, Windows-based network management system with these characteristics:

- Based on the Simple Network Management Protocol (SNMP) industry standard

- A powerful set of network management tools for easily managing Cisco products

ConfigMaker is a free GUI-based Windows 95/NT tool for initial configuration of Cisco 1000, 1600, 2500, 2600, and 3600 series routers.

Cisco Telecommuting and Remote User Solutions

As advances in digital communications shrink time and distance, a new model of the workplace is taking shape. The modern office is no longer contained within a structure—instead, it is mobile and geographically scattered. The twenty-first century workplace is becoming any place where work is done. Companies must provide remote access to e-mail and other network resources to telecommuters and remote users. Telecommuting can be a valuable tool for recruiting and retaining key personnel in today's tight labor market.

Small- and medium-sized businesses in need of integrated telecommuting and remote user solutions need to take the following actions:

- Integrate dialup connectivity with traditional, remote user to LAN access

- Support the higher levels of performance required for new applications, such as Internet access, intranet communications, and multimedia

- Ensure security, data privacy, and availability as users connect from any location, including branch offices, home offices, and hotel rooms

- Integrate products powerful enough to handle today's needs and flexible enough to grow and to adapt to tomorrow's requirements.

Telecommuting and Remote User Considerations

This section covers telecommuting and remote user considerations.

Scalability

Scalability and modularity are key requirements—as a company grows, it can leverage its investment in existing equipment.

For telecommuting and remote access solutions, it is critical that the central office solution allows system administrators to scale their network capacities.

Security

When implementing telecommuting and remote user solutions, it is critical that security for the central site be preserved; user authentication features prove a user's true identity to prevent unauthorized use of network resources.

WAN Optimization

Because most ISDN charges are based on usage, it is important that ISDN telecommuting users have a solution that can implement dial-on-demand routing, enabling users to initiate a WAN connection only when there is network traffic destined for a remote location.

Bandwidth-on-demand is another important feature that allows ISDN users to dynamically aggregate multiple B channels for high bandwidth when required.

Configuration Flexibility

Today, two popular WAN services for telecommuters are modem dialup via basic telephone service and ISDN modem dialup is a cost-effective solution for users who need occasional access to the corporate network to transfer relatively small amounts of data, or for mobile users who need to connect from customer sites, hotel rooms, or other locations. ISDN offers an attractive alternative for users who need high-speed access to network resources and large files. In addition, Frame Relay is growing in popularity as a WAN service for full-time telecommuters. It is important that a central site solution for telecommuting have a modular design that can accommodate all three types of connections from a single device.

Telecommuter to Central Site Solutions

A vendor that provides both home office and central site products offers a solution that simplifies network management and that ensures full interoperability. The correct solution depends on the needs of the user:

- Does the user need additional analog interfaces that allow devices such as fax machines to share the ISDN BRI line?

- Does the user need an integrated four-port hub?

- Does the user require support for multiprotocol routing or synchronous serial WAN connectivity?

Figure E-2 shows Cisco telecommuting and remote user solutions.

Figure E-2   *Cisco Telecommuting and Remote User Solutions*

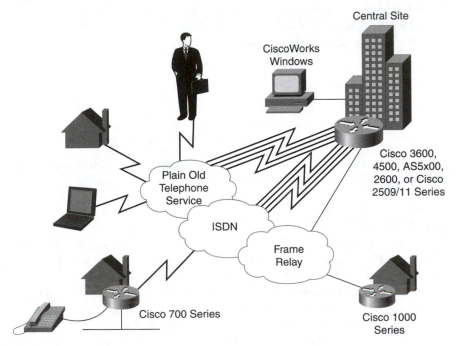

Cisco Solutions for the Home Office

Cisco offers a variety of solutions for the home office.

The Cisco 700 series ISDN access routers offer a cost-effective solution for telecommuters with multiple computers or network devices that require transparent, high-speed access to a company network.

The Cisco 760 and 770 series feature two analog telephone interfaces that allow devices such as standard telephones, fax machines, and modems to share the ISDN BRI line, eliminating the need for multiple telephone lines or expensive ISDN telephones. The Cisco 770 series offers an integrated four-port 10BaseT hub. All the routers in this family of products include the Cisco Fast Step application, a Windows 95 and NT 4.0 graphical user interface (GUI) that makes the routers easy to install, configure, and manage. In addition, the Cisco 770 series can be managed from a central site.

The Cisco 1000 series of compact, easily installed and managed fixed-configuration desktop routers provides low-cost, high-speed connectivity for branch and small offices, as well as telecommuters. These products can be installed by nontechnical people at remote sites.

The Cisco 1000 routers are ideal for home telecommuters who need AppleTalk capability or for connecting small remote sites with Ethernet LANs to regional and central sites. The Cisco 1000 family offers ISDN, leased line, Frame Relay, X.25, and Switched Multimegabit Data Service (SMDS) WAN services.

Cisco Solutions for the Central Site

Cisco Systems offers a range of central site products ideal for telecommuting and remote user solutions. All the following series of products are scalable and modular, and they offer the utmost in configuration flexibility. In addition, they all support features to increase WAN security and to reduce WAN costs.

The Cisco AS5x00 family of universal integrated access servers provides superior density, price, and performance to accommodate the needs of general remote access users and high-bandwidth telecommuters. The AS5x00 series is extremely popular because it integrates the functions of standalone channel service units (CSUs), channel banks, modems, communication servers, switches, and routers into a single chassis. By terminating both analog modem and ISDN calls on the same chassis from the same trunk line, the AS5x00 meets traditional analog dial-in needs while supporting the growing demands for high-speed ISDN access.

The Cisco 4500 and 4700 series access routers are high-performance, modular central site routers that support the most comprehensive set of LAN and WAN technologies with NIMs. Their modular design allows easy reconfiguration as needs change. A full range of high-speed connectivity options are available, including Fast Ethernet, ATM, HSSI, and FDDI.

The highly modular Cisco 3600 series access servers provide amazing versatility to support branch/central site dial access applications, LAN-to-LAN or routing applications, and multiservice applications in a single chassis.

The Cisco 3640 has four network module slots, and the Cisco 3620 access router is equipped with two slots that accept a variety of mixed-media or WAN network modules, including one slot that supports dual Ethernet and dual WAN ports. Multiservice applications are supported by integrated voice network modules.

The Cisco 2600 provides a cost-effective solution for extending data/voice integration, dial concentration, and VPN access to remote branch offices.

The Cisco 2509 and 2511 and the AS2509-RJ and AS2511-RJ access server models are dialup remote access servers with integrated routing. They provide high-speed synchronous and asynchronous serial line connections that are perfect for telecommuting and remote access solutions to the corporate LAN from a single platform. These fixed-configuration access server models provide Ethernet or Token Ring LAN connections for 8 and 16 simultaneous dialup users.

All Cisco access routers incorporate the industry-leading Cisco IOS software. Cisco IOS software supports robust multiprotocol routing and provides enhanced support for multimedia and features, to reduce WAN connection costs. Data compression and multiple traffic prioritization techniques ensure that critical data is accommodated. Dialup costs are minimized with features such as protocol spoofing, snapshot routing, NSLP route aggregation, DDR, and BOD. Comprehensive authentication and authorization allow only approved traffic onto the network; event logging, audit trails, encryption, virtual private networking functions, and NAT provide additional network security. Support for protocols such as IGMP and RSVP makes the Cisco routers ideally suited to meet the demanding needs of audio and video services.

Cisco Management Solutions for Telecommuting and Remote Users

All Cisco access routers are manageable by the CiscoWorks Windows software, a comprehensive, Windows-based network management system with the following characteristics:

- Based on the SNMP industry standard

- A powerful set of network management tools for easily managing Cisco products

The Fast Step utility is used for configuration, troubleshooting, and monitoring of Cisco 700 series routers.

ConfigMaker is used for initial configuration of Cisco 1000, 1600, 2500, 2600, and 3600 series routers.

Cisco Internet and Intranet Solutions

Small- and medium-sized companies seeking to remain competitive must leverage the Internet as a business asset. From simple electronic mail to marketing and customer service information, the Internet is changing the way everyone does business. Cisco solutions support a variety of Internet and intranet applications.

Internet Access

At its most basic, Internet access is the process of connecting a private local-area network to the Internet. Most small- and medium-sized businesses rely upon an Internet service provider (ISP) to provide technical expertise to set up and manage an Internet access point. Small and medium-sized businesses require an access router to link their Ethernet or Token Ring LANs to ISP sites via dialup or dedicated WAN lines.

Intranets

An intranet is a private communications network based on TCP/IP and Web technologies, and it resembles a private version of the Internet. Intranets can span a single network segment, a building, or all offices of a company. Familiar, easy-to-use Web browsers act as interfaces to existing network applications and databases. Users no longer have to know where a server is located or how to connect to it. Older, powerful mainframe or client/server applications are easier to use with simplified Web interfaces.

Internet Marketing

Internet marketing uses World Wide Web sites and other means (such as e-mail and File Transfer Protocol [FTP] sites) to market companies. The Internet has been called the great equalizer between giant corporations and small businesses. With Internet marketing, customers do not know how small or large a company is because Web sites focus on the product or service. Web sites can also help small- and medium-sized businesses build stronger customer and partner relationships by providing easy access to company information from anywhere and at any time.

Extranets and Electronic Commerce

Extranets are an extension of a company network or a collaborative Internet connection to key customers, suppliers, and partners. Extranets use private WAN lines or virtual private networks (VPNs) to provide access to specific company information and to build closer business relationships. VPNs use the Internet to create secure pathways between a company and its extranet partners. VPNs provide the same types of network services you expect in your private network, but they do it over the Internet, thus saving money. A typical extranet solution requires a router at each end, a firewall, authentication software, a server, and a dedicated WAN line or VPN over the Internet.

Electronic commerce is the act of purchasing goods and services online and requires the electronic exchange of funds, usually by credit card. E-commerce can build customer satisfaction by receiving orders and fulfilling them more quickly, with less hassle and greater accuracy. E-commerce applications require a commerce application deployed on a Web site, an access router, a firewall, and a full-time Internet connection.

Security

What most concerns customers about any Internet solution is security. Good security solutions reduce costs, enable new applications and services, and make the Internet a low-cost, ubiquitous access media. Cisco offers a comprehensive security solution through Cisco IOS software and dedicated firewall appliances that enable customers to securely take advantage of the Internet.

Internet and Intranet Customer Needs

Customers in need of integrated Internet solutions are taking these actions:

- Seeking ways to provide excellent and timely service and information to a customer and prospect base that is increasing exponentially

- Facing the challenge of keeping pace with the demands and costs of integrating multiple systems and tools from different vendors

- Facing increasing complexity with the rapid growth in new technology and products

- Seeking to ensure that the security of company data and applications is not compromised, while allowing access to its information resources as well as its network path

Internet and Intranet Considerations

This section covers Internet and intranet considerations.

Security

Internet access solutions should provide features such as these:

- User authentication

- Dynamic access control

- Data encryption

- NAT to prevent unauthorized use and access of network resources

- Firewall solutions, available as separate components or integrated into router software

WAN Optimization

An Internet access solution that optimizes bandwidth and reduces WAN costs is accomplished using features such as these:

- Bandwidth-on-demand

- Dial-on-demand routing

- Snapshot routing

- Protocol spoofing

- Compression

Scalability

Scalability is a key requirement so that, as a company grows, it can leverage its investment in existing equipment.

For Web hosting applications, it is critical that the solution be scalable to accommodate increased traffic quickly, easily, and cost-effectively.

Guide to Internet and Intranet Solutions

Figure E-3 shows Cisco Internet and intranet solutions.

Figure E-3   *Cisco Internet and Intranet Solutions*

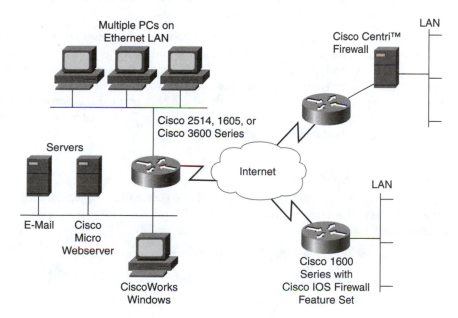

Cisco Central Site, Branch Office, and Home Office Internet Connectivity Solutions

Cisco offers a range of central site, branch office, and home office solutions that provide access to the Internet.

The Cisco 3600 series multiservice access servers/routers offer a modular solution for dialup connectivity over asynchronous, synchronous, and ISDN lines. They offer industry-leading price-for-performance value.

The Cisco 2500 series access routers are the world's most popular line of branch office routers. There is a broad range of models from which to choose to provide a wide variety of connectivity options, level of technology integration, and price points.

The Cisco 1600 series access routers represent inexpensive, easy-to-use, multiprotocol routers ideal for Internet access from small branch offices or professional offices.

The Cisco 1605-R and 2514 access routers offer a dual-LAN architecture ideal for Internet access, network segmentation, and firewall applications.

The Cisco 700 series provides easy-to-use ISDN routers for telecommuters.

All Cisco access routers incorporate the industry-leading Cisco IOS software. Cisco IOS software supports robust multiprotocol routing and provides enhanced support for multimedia and features, to reduce WAN connection costs.

Data compression and multiple traffic prioritization techniques ensure that critical data is accommodated. Dialup costs are minimized with features such as protocol spoofing, snapshot routing, NSLP route aggregation, DDR, and BOD. Comprehensive authentication and authorization allow only approved traffic onto the network; event logging, audit trails, encryption, virtual private networking functions, and NAT provide additional network security. Support for protocols such as IGMP and RSVP makes the Cisco routers ideally suited to meet the demanding needs of audio and video services.

Cisco Security Solutions

Cisco offers a range of security solutions. The Cisco Centri Firewall provides a strong security solution that is tightly integrated with Windows NT and that is easy to set up and administer. It features the following:

- Easy-to-use graphical policy builder for designing security policies

- High-performance kernel proxy for scalability

- Capability to run third-party server applications such as Web, Domain Name System (DNS), and e-mail servers securely on the firewall system

The Cisco IOS Firewall feature set extends Cisco IOS security features. It offers the following:

- Context-Based Access Control (CBAC)

- Support for a rich set of applications, such as standard TCP and UDP applications and multimedia applications, including H.323, CUSeeMe, and VDO Live

- Audit trails and real-time alerts

- Java blocking

The Cisco PIX Firewall, a dedicated firewall appliance, is suited for medium-sized businesses with high-performance site requirements. It offers the following:

- An enterprise-class integrated hardware and software firewall

- Rich application support

- Virtual private network capabilities

Cisco Internet Marketing Solutions

Cisco also offers a range of solutions to address Internet marketing. The Cisco Micro Webserver is a versatile Web server appliance that is easy to install and also cost-effective. It can be used for entry-level World Wide Web hosting, to set up a corporate workgroup intranet, or as a documentation server. It features the following:

- A standalone or stackable Web hosting and publishing solution

- A Java-based configuration utility and network wizard for easy setup

- CGI support for forms data interaction and exchange and TCI scripting on the server.

Cisco LocalDirector provides an integrated solution for load balancing TCP/IP traffic across multiple servers, such as database applications, intranet, or TN3270 mainframe services. It offers the following:

- A redundant fault-tolerant server system ideal for mission-critical applications

- Simple setup, with little disruption to network configuration

- Increased network uptime by providing high availability architecture

Cisco Management Solutions for Internet/Intranet Connectivity

All Cisco access routers are manageable by CiscoWorks Windows software, a comprehensive, Windows-based network management system with these characteristics:

- Based on the SNMP industry standard

- A powerful set of network management tools for easily managing Cisco products

Cisco High-Performance LAN Solutions

Networks are a vital business asset. Small- and medium-sized businesses must be sure that their networks provide quick, reliable access to applications and data, which are the keys to success in today's highly competitive, increasingly global economy. Today's business applications require high-bandwidth networks. Businesses also require more powerful network technologies that are capable of intelligently and efficiently managing traffic flow.

Traditional hub-centric LANs can no longer support the bandwidth needed for companies to conduct business. Small- and medium-sized businesses often connect remote or branch offices, mobile users, and telecommuters. Internet usage to support marketing and commerce applications also places demand on LANs once isolated from the rest of the world.

Customers need the additional bandwidth of high-performance LANs in these circumstances:

- Users are sitting idle while tasks complete over the network.

- File transfers become a productivity bottleneck.

- Project schedules are compromised by an incapability to quickly access and share data.

- Vital business activities are interrupted by repeated network failures.

High-Performance LAN Considerations

This section covers high-performance LAN considerations.

High Performance

Cisco LAN components have the power to support advanced applications and heavy traffic. Powerful processors, nonblocking bus and backplane architectures, Fast Ethernet support, and industry-leading reliability features contribute performance characteristics to an end-to-end network architecture unmatched in the industry.

Ease of Use

Plug-and-play features simplify installation, configuration, and network management, and they also enhance reliability. Features such as autosensing 10/100 Ethernet enable port configuration changes without requiring the user to buy more equipment.

Modularity and Versatility

Port expansion modules offer cost-effective, high-speed uplinks to Fast Ethernet, FDDI, ATM, and future Gigabit Ethernet backbones.

Interoperability

Cisco solutions are completely interoperable with existing standards-based Ethernet equipment. Migration capabilities to new technologies and services are already built in, further protecting current investments.

Scalability

Capacity can easily be added to support more users, applications, and servers as business requirements change. Consider high-performance LAN solutions when you need technologies supporting scalability, including VLAN and multicast application support. Cisco IOS technologies provide many features supporting a wide array of services to configure networks and to meet company requirements.

Manageability

Effective monitoring provides usage statistics for maximum network visibility. Management features include Remote Monitoring (RMON) agents, SNMP support, Hypertext Transfer Protocol (HTTP), Cisco Discovery Protocol (CDP), and TFTP. Administrators can monitor and configure networks from a central location, including software downloading to devices in branch offices.

Guide to High-Performance LAN Solutions

Cisco offers two complementary solutions for increasing LAN performance: the FastHub line of Fast Ethernet repeaters and the Catalyst line of Ethernet and Fast Ethernet switches. Figure E-4 shows Cisco high-performance LAN solutions.

Figure E-4   *Cisco High-Performance LAN Solutions*

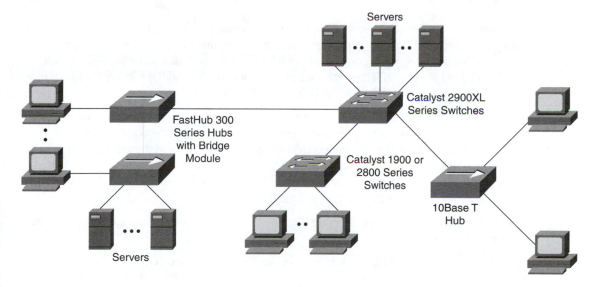

Cisco Catalyst Line of Ethernet Switches

Cisco Catalyst Ethernet and Fast Ethernet switches combine configuration flexibility with exceptional affordability for applications from the desktop to the corporate backbone. These best-of-class switches are ideal for Ethernet workgroups and individual users requiring increased performance and 100BaseT, FDDI, or ATM connectivity to servers and backbones at a very low cost per port. This line of switches also lets you choose between lowest price and maximum flexibility.

The Catalyst 2900 series XL (2908 XL, 2916M XL, 2924 XL, and 2924C XL) is a full line of affordable 10/100 autosensing Fast Ethernet switches, offering outstanding performance, versatile modularity, and superior manageability. The Cisco advanced architecture incorporates a switch fabric of 3.2 Gbps and a forwarding rate of more than 3 Mpps (million packets per second) to deliver wire-speed performance across all ports. The Catalyst 2916M XL has two versatile modular slots that provide expansion capabilities, higher-speed connectivity, and future support for feature modules, granting users the flexibility to upgrade their networks and to preserve their initial investment. Catalyst 2900 series XL switches deliver easy-to-use management and advanced security features. In addition, integrated Cisco IOS technologies provide superior functionality for end-to-end integration, including bandwidth aggregation, networked multimedia support, and future virtual LAN support.

The Catalyst 1900 series Ethernet switches offer four fixed-port models: 24 10BaseT ports with either two fixed 100BaseTX ports or one 100BaseTX and 100BaseFX port; or for smaller networks, 12 10BaseT ports with either two fixed 100BaseTX ports or one 100BaseTX and 100BaseFX port.

The versatile Catalyst 2820 series Ethernet switches also provide 24 10BaseT ports but have two expansion slots for a choice of high-speed modules, including switched 100BaseTX, switched 100BaseFX, eight-port shared 100BaseTX, four-port shared 100BaseFX, FDDI unshielded twisted-pair (UTP) single attachment station (SAS), FDDI Fiber SAS, FDDI Fiber dual-attachment station (DAS), ATM UTP, and ATM Multimode fiber.

The Catalyst 1900 and 2820 series switches use the same award-winning architecture and large 3 MB shared buffer as their predecessors, consistently surpassing the competition in key throughput and latency tests by independent analysts. Like the FastHub repeaters, the switches are manageable via SNMP, Telnet, RMON, and an out-of-band console. Enterprise Edition models offer enhanced network services for customers who require end-to-end VLANs and bandwidth aggregation with Fast EtherChannel.

For higher performance and higher port density, the Catalyst 5000 series rounds out the system solutions.

Catalyst switches support Cisco IOS technologies, including Cisco Group Management Protocol (CGMP), to selectively forward routed IP multicast traffic to targeted multimedia end stations. CGMP prevents multimedia traffic from being forwarded to all devices on the switches, reducing overall network traffic and optimizing bandwidth usage. CGMP is based on the standard IGMP that is supported in Cisco routers.

Cisco FastHub Line of Fast Ethernet and 10/100 Class II Hubs

The FastHub 100, 200, and 300 series 100BaseT and 10/100 hubs features a range of functionality and price points to meet today's network needs for affordable, easy-to-use, shared Fast Ethernet connectivity.

Cisco FastHub 100 series 10/100 hubs are standalone hubs with a choice of fixed 12 or 24 10BaseT/100BaseTX ports for UTP attachment. These cost-effective hubs are ideal for providing 10 or 100 Mbps performance for users with multiple workstations, small workgroups, or switch aggregation when management is not a requirement.

Cisco FastHub 200 series Fast Ethernet hubs deliver the lowest-cost, managed 100BaseT hub solution for midsize workgroups and server farms. These standalone hubs combine 100 Mbps performance and integrated management with Cisco IOS technologies in an extremely affordable solution.

When manageability and scalability are required, the FastHub 300 series is the optimal solution. The FastHub 300 series combines all the benefits of stackable hubs with unmatched configuration flexibility, exceptional affordability, and integrated Cisco IOS software.

The FastHub 300 series is the only Fast Ethernet hub available that lets you add users and management in a single unit.

The FastHub 300 series hubs offer richer management options than any other Fast Ethernet hub. A single, optional network management module provides comprehensive manageability and simplified troubleshooting on a per-port, per-hub, and per-stack basis using SNMP, Telnet, RMON, or an out-of-band console.

The 10/100 bridge module with integrated management extends cabling for the FastHub 300 series and provides Ethernet/Fast Ethernet connectivity.

Catalyst switches and FastHub repeaters can be used alone or together to improve network performance.

Existing Ethernet users can be attached to the switches directly through their existing adapter cards, and new users or high-bandwidth users with 10/100 network interface cards are connected to the FastHubs.

Servers can be attached to high-speed switch ports, or the FastHub repeater can act as both a server farm and a high-speed local backbone for the switches.

As traffic increases, 10/100 Fast Ethernet switches can be added to prevent backbone congestion and to provide dedicated Fast Ethernet connections for individual users.

Cisco Management Solutions for High-Performance LANs

All Cisco Ethernet switches are manageable by CiscoWorks Windows software, a comprehensive, Windows-based network management system with the following characteristics:

- Based on the SNMP industry standard

- A powerful set of network management tools for easily managing Cisco products

Cisco Networked Office Stack

Cisco Networked Office Stack is a flexible suite of products designed for small offices to provide secure access to the Internet and to link users and offices so that they can easily share resources such as applications, documents, and printers. The Cisco Networked Office Stack extends a company's reach to customers and suppliers and accelerates the sharing of information and resources, making the office network a strategic competitive asset. The Cisco Networked Office Stack products work together to meet the specific communication requirements that small or remote offices with 20 to 100 employees have, including the following:

- File and print sharing between computers

- Accessing e-mail within a LAN

- Accessing the Internet for e-mail, competitive information, advertising, and commerce

- Accessing corporate headquarters for database information

- Accessing suppliers and customers electronically for inventory information, orders, sales, and file sharing

- Web serving, to create and manage content of a Web site

- Protecting private network information while accessing the Internet or another site

- Using an existing LAN more effectively or enlarging a LAN using higher-speed technologies, including autosensing Fast Ethernet

The Cisco Networked Office Stack works with a company's existing equipment. As the organization's needs grow, it can easily add network functions, technologies, and users while preserving the initial investment.

Cisco Networked Office Stack Products

Cisco Networked Office Stack products include the following:

- Cisco 1600 series routers

- Cisco 1500 series hubs

- Cisco 1528 Micro Hub 10/100

- Cisco 1548 Micro Switch 10/100

- Cisco Micro Webserver

- Centri Firewall

- Cisco IOS Firewall feature set for the Cisco 1600 and 2500 series routers

- ConfigMaker

For more information on these products, see the individual product sections of this guide.

Cisco Networked Office Stack Solutions

Cisco Networked Office Stack is best when a customer needs the following:

- A complete small-office integrated solution to connect five or more desktops and devices

- A complete desktop networking solution for small businesses or branch offices with no wiring closet

- An Internet access solution for small businesses

- A solution to connect branch offices to a central site

Application-Specific Solution Kits

The application-specific solution kits are as follows:

- **Secure Internet Access (CNOSECURE)**—Ideal for small businesses and branch offices requiring secure access to the Internet and high-performance LAN connectivity. Includes the following:

  - Cisco 1601 access router

  - Cisco 1548 Micro Switch 10/100

  - Cisco IOS Firewall feature set

- **High-Performance LAN (CNOLAN)**—Ideal for eliminating network bottlenecks in small businesses and branch offices. Includes the following:

  - Two Cisco 1501 Micro Hubs

  - Cisco 1548 Micro Switch 10/100

- **Internet Marketing (CNOINTERNET)**—Enables businesses to market and sell products and services over the Internet. Includes the following:

  — Cisco 1605-R access router

  — Cisco IOS Firewall Feature Set

  — Cisco Micro Webserver 200

- **ISDN Internet Access (CNOISDN)**—Designed for small businesses upgrading from desktop modems to a router solution. Includes the following:

  — Cisco 1603 or 1604 access router

  — Cisco 1528 Micro Hub 10/100

Cisco Access Routers and Servers Overview

The full line of Cisco routers ranges from home office access routers to central site access servers. The scope of Cisco products supports a significant number of solution scenarios.

Key Features of Cisco IOS Software Supported by Cisco Routers and Servers

This section summarizes the features of the Cisco IOS software.

Bandwidth Optimization

Cisco IOS technologies deliver bandwidth optimization with these features:

- **Dial-on-demand routing**—Minimizes ownership cost by allowing a router to automatically initiate and close a circuit-switched session.

- **Bandwidth-on-demand**—Dynamically increases network throughput by allowing a router to automatically establish a new, load-sharing connection to the destination in response to a definable load level.

- **Snapshot routing**—Serves as a routing update mechanism that minimizes ownership costs by eliminating the need for configuring and maintaining large static tables, allowing dynamic routing protocols to be used on DDR lines.

- **Virtual bandwidth reservation and priority queuing**—Enhances throughput by reserving bandwidth and prioritizing traffic based on the type of application, its source, or its destination.

- **IPX protocol spoofing**—Optimizes Novell networking by responding to server Watchdog requests on behalf of a remote client.

- **Cisco IOS compression solutions**—Accomplished with header compression for TCP/IP, per-interface compression (one set of dictionaries per hardware link), and per-virtual circuit compression (one set of dictionaries per compressed virtual circuit).

Security

The powerful suite of Cisco security technologies includes the following:

- **Network address translation and port address translation (PAT)**—Hides private topology and IP addresses from an external network.

- **Digital Signature Standard (DSS) and digital certification**—Positively authenticates users or devices.

- **Data Encryption Standard (DES)**—Enables 40-/56-bit encryption.

- **Terminal Access Controller Access Control System Plus (TACACS+)**—Provides complete network access security (NAS) for dial-in connections.

- **Password Authentication Protocol authentication**—Allows a remote node to establish its identity using a two-way handshake.

- **Challenge Handshake Authentication Protocol authentication**—Allows a remote node to establish its identity using a three-way handshake.

- **Calling line identification**—Uses calling line identification to compare the ISDN number of a calling device against a list of known callers.

- **Access lists**—Checks source address of packets (standard access lists) and checks source and destination addresses and other parameters (extended access lists).

- **Lock and Key**—Allows per-user authorization in a shared-media environment.

Multimedia Features

Cisco IOS network services that support multimedia applications with multimedia and multicast capabilities include these:

- **Resource Reservation Protocol**—Dynamically reserves end-to-end bandwidth for delay-sensitive IP traffic.

- **IP Multicast-Protocol Independent Multicast (PIM)**—Serves as a multicast protocol that can be used in conjunction with all unicast IP routing protocols.

- **Internet Group Management Protocol**—Indicates to the router whether any hosts on a given physical network belong to a multicast group.

- **AppleTalk Simple Multicast Routing Protocol (SMRP)**—Provides connectionless, best-effort delivery of multicast datagrams.

Quality of Service

Cisco IOS Quality of Service network services readily support bandwidth-intensive traffic:

- **Resource Reservation Protocol**—Establishes priority bandwidth allocation.

- **Weighted Fair Queuing (WFQ)**—Adds new levels of control to previous queuing methods.

- **Random Early Detection (RED)**—Monitors traffic levels on very large networks to prevent congestion and to guarantee priority traffic delivery.

- **Cisco IOS technologies that manage resource allocation**—Includes PIM, Private Network-Network Interface (PNNI), and available bit rate (ABR).

Ease of Use and Management

Cisco IOS management services are designed to meet the needs of today's distributed networks:

- **Management services**—Support for AutoInstall, SNMP, Telnet, RMON, Management Information Bases (MIBs), and HTTP server interface.

- **Fast Step for Cisco 700 series routers**—A new Windows 95- or NT 4.0-based configuration and monitoring tool targeted at small office and home office users.

- **Cisco ConfigMaker**—The new Windows 95 or NT 4.0 graphical tool enabling a reseller or network administrator to configure Cisco 1000, 1600, 2500, and 3600 series routers and to design networks for LAN-to-LAN and user-to-LAN internetworking solutions.

- **Cisco ClickStart**—The Web-based software solution embedded in Cisco IOS software that enables users to install Cisco 700, 1000, or 1600 series routers in minutes.

- **Cisco ISDN Support Service**—A single point of contact to assist users with setting up an ISDN connection to Cisco 700, 1003, 1004, 1600, 2503, 2524, 2525, 3600, and 4000 series routers and Cisco AS5x00 series access servers.

Cisco Access Router and Access Server Summarization

Tables E-1, E-2, and E-3 summarize the uses and specifications of the various routers and access servers covered in this section.

Table E-1   *Telecommuter, Small Office, and Home Office Dialup Access Routers*

User Count	Data Type	Platform Type	Product Name	Product Description
1 to 4+	ISDN/POTS	Standalone	Cisco 760	Small office multiprotocol router for remote access
1 to 4+	ISDN/POTS with integrated hub	Standalone	Cisco 770	Small office multiprotocol router with integrated hub
1 LAN	ISDN/Serial	Standalone	Cisco 1000	Fixed-configuration desktop router

Table E-2   *Remote Office, Branch Office, and Central Site Access Routers*

Port Count	LAN Technology	Configuration Design	Product Name	Product Description
1 LAN 1 WAN	Ethernet	Fixed configuration	Cisco 1000, 1600, 2500	Fixed-configuration desktop routers
1 LAN 1 to 2 WANs	Ethernet	Modular	Cisco 1600	Modular desktop routers with LAN-to-WAN connectivity
1 to 2 LANs 2 WANs	Ethernet or Token Ring	Modular, fixed configuration	Cisco 1600, 2500, 2600	Modular or fixed-configuration routers with Ethernet or Token Ring connectivity
Configurable by module	Ethernet, Fast Ethernet, Token Ring, FDDI	Fully modular	Cisco 3620, 3640, 4500/4700	Modular high-performance central site routers

Table E-3   *Central Site Access Servers*

Simultaneous User Count (ISDN)	Simultaneous User Count (Analog)	Dialup Connectivity	Product Name	Product Description
0	8 or 16	Analog only	Cisco 2509, 2511, AS2509-RJ, AS2511-RJ	Analog access servers for up to 16 lines
20*	32*	ISDN and async via separate lines	Cisco 3620	Modular access router/ server
52*	96*	ISDN and async via separate lines	Cisco 3640	Modular access router/ server
48 (T1)** 60 (E1)**	48 (T1)** 60 (E1)**	ISDN and async via same line	Cisco 3640	Modular access router/ server
48 (T1)** 60 (E1)**	48 (T1)** 60 (E1)**	ISDN and async via same line	Cisco AS5200	Universal access server for mobile, telecommuter, and branch office access
96 (T1)** 120 (E1)**	96 (T1)** 120 (E1)**	ISDN and async via same line	Cisco AS5300	High-density universal access server for mobile, telecommuter, and branch office access

*Assumes that at least one module is a LAN port
**Maximum of 48 (AS5200) or 96 (AS5300) simultaneous users (in Europe, 60 or 120 simultaneous users with E1/PRI)

Cisco 700 Series Access Routers

The Cisco 700 series is the next generation of low-cost and easy-to-manage multiprotocol ISDN access routers. These devices provide small professional offices, home offices, and telecommuters with high-speed remote access to enterprise networks and the Internet. Table E-4 lists the products in the 700 series.

Table E-4   *Cisco 700 Series Product Family*

	Integrated NT1	Analog Telephone Ports	4-Port Ethernet Hub
Cisco 761M	No	0	No
Cisco 762M	Yes	0	No
Cisco 765M	No	2	No

Table E-4   *Cisco 700 Series Product Family (Continued)*

	Integrated NT1	Analog Telephone Ports	4-Port Ethernet Hub
Cisco 766M	Yes	2	No
Cisco 771M	No	0	Yes
Cisco 772M	Yes	0	Yes
Cisco 775M	No	2	Yes
Cisco 776M	Yes	2	Yes

Cisco 700 Series Key Features

Key features of the 700 series include the following:

- Fast Step configuration utility software, enabling Cisco 700 series router installation in minutes using a Windows 95 desktop or NT platform

- Dynamic addressing of the Cisco 700 series and remote workstations for ease of configuration and network management

- PAT, for creating a private network and an additional layer of network security

- Dual-tone multifrequency (DTMF) support, enabling basic network configuration of the Cisco 700 series with a push-button telephone, after which a network manager can dial into the Cisco 700 router to complete the installation (Cisco 765M, 766M, 775M, 776M)

- MP, for standards-based B-channel aggregation (RFC 1717)

- Call connect/disconnect switch for manual call initiation (Cisco 770 series)

- Dynamic Host Configuration Protocol (DHCP) relay agent and server for dynamic addressing of attached workstations

- IOS-700, a suite of software features targeted at small office, home office (SOHO), and telecommuting users

Cisco 700 Series Customers

This section breaks down the 700 series by customer needs.

Cisco 760 series (Cisco 761M, 762M, 765M, 766M)

This series is best when a customer needs the following:

- Internet or main office LAN access for telecommuters or home offices

- Built-in NT1 for the United States and Canada (Cisco 762M, 766M)

- Two plain old telephone service (POTS) interfaces to allow a standard telephone, fax, or modem to share an ISDN line (Cisco 765M, 766M)

Cisco 770 series (Cisco 771M, 772M, 775M, 776M)

This series is best when a customer needs the following:

- Internet or main office LAN access for small professional offices or home offices

- A cost-effective, unmanaged hub

- Built-in NT1 for the United States and Canada (Cisco 772M, 776M)

- Two POTS interfaces to allow a standard telephone, fax, or modem to share an ISDN line (Cisco 775M, 776M)

Software Feature Packs

These are best when a customer needs the following:

- IP routing for up to four devices with compression (Internet Router Pack)

- IP and IPX routing for up to 1500 devices with compression (Remote Office Feature Pack)

Cisco 1000 Series Access Routers

The Cisco 1000 series of compact, easily installed and managed, fixed-configuration desktop routers provides low-cost, high-speed connectivity for branch and small offices. These products offer a range of synchronous and asynchronous WAN options to address a variety of needs and fit seamlessly into any networking environment. Table E-5 lists the products in the Cisco 1000 series.

Table E-5   *Cisco 1000 Series Product Family*

	ISDN BRI	NT1 Device	Sync Serial	Ethernet Port
Cisco 1003	Yes	No	No	Yes
Cisco 1004	Yes	Yes	No	Yes
Cisco 1005	No	–	Yes	Yes

Cisco 1000 Series Key Features

Key features of the Cisco 1000 series include the following:

- Support for Cisco IOS software

- Integration with enterprise networks that are based on asynchronous serial lines, leased lines, Frame Relay, Switched 56, and X.25 services (Cisco 1005) or ISDN (Cisco 1003 and 1004)

- Flash Memory (PC Card) and primary memory upgrade capability for easy software image maintenance

- Products tailored for easy inventory, installation, operation, and maintenance

- ClickStart configuration utility software enabling installation of Cisco 1000 series routers in minutes using any Web browser from any desktop platform

- CiscoWorks Windows for centralized router management and remote maintenance

Cisco 1000 Series Customers

This section breaks down the 1000 series by customer needs.

Cisco 1003

This series is best when a customer needs the following:

- Inexpensive, easy-to-install and manage multiprotocol routing for small remote sites

- ISDN (BRI) port, 10BaseT Ethernet port, console port, and slot for a Flash ROM card

- Software features that extend to support IP, IPX, and AppleTalk routing

Cisco 1004

This series is best when a customer needs the following:

- The same features as Cisco 1003, plus an integrated NT1 device, reducing the number of devices needed to connect to ISDN lines in North America

Cisco 1005

This series is best when a customer needs the following:

- Inexpensive, fixed-configuration, easy-to-install and manage multiprotocol routing for small remote sites

- Serial port with synchronous speeds up to 2.048 Mbps, 10BaseT Ethernet port, console port, and slot for Flash ROM card

- Software features that extend to support IP, IPX, and AppleTalk routing

Cisco 1600 Series Access Routers

The Cisco 1600 series, with modular features, is optimized to meet the needs of small remote offices. Cisco 1600 series routers connect small offices with Ethernet LANs to the Internet and to company intranets using several WAN technologies: ISDN, asynchronous serial, and synchronous serial, including Frame Relay, leased lines, Switched 56, SMDS, and X.25. Optional WAN interface cards add flexibility and growth opportunities. The Cisco 1600 series routers are part of the Cisco Networked Office Stack, a flexible suite of products that enables small businesses to easily take advantage of the Internet to attract new customers, improve communications, lower ongoing expenses, and increase productivity. Table E-6 lists the products in the 1600 series.

Table E-6   *Cisco 1600 Series Product Family*

	Ethernet Fixed Port	Serial Fixed Port	ISDN Basic Rate Interface	WAN Interface Card Slot[*]
Cisco 1601	1	1	0	1
Cisco 1602	1	1, with integrated 56 Kbps Data Service Unit/ Channel Service Unit (DSU/CSU)	0	1
Cisco 1603	1	0	1, with S/T interface	1[**]
Cisco 1604	1	0	1, with integrated NT1; U interface	1[**]
Cisco 1605-R	2	0	0	1

[*]Cisco 1600 series WAN interface cards: Serial (asynchronous and synchronous), ISDN BRI (S/T interface), ISDN BRI with integrated NT1 (U interface), 56/64 Kbps four-wire DSU/CSU, T1/Fractional T1 DSU/CSU
[**]Supports serial WAN interface cards

Cisco 1600 Series Key Features

Key features of the 1600 series include the following:

- Support for Cisco IOS software
- Modular WAN interface card slot for adding and changing WAN connections, for flexibility and investment protection
- Optional firewall and virtual private network software
- Integrated DSU/CSU up to T1 speed and integrated NT1 for North American market
- Flash Memory (PC Card) and primary memory upgrade capability for easy software image maintenance

- ClickStart, Web browser-based software for simplified configuration
- ConfigMaker, Windows 95 and NT 4.0 ease-of-use tool for simplified configuration
- Part of the Cisco Networked Office Stack solution

Cisco 1600 Series Customers

This section breaks down the 1600 series by customer needs.

Cisco 1601 Series

This series is best when a customer needs the following:

- One serial port with synchronous performance up to T1/E1 speeds for Frame Relay, leased line, Switched 56, SMDS, and X.25 WAN services, or async performance up to 115.2 kbps
- Higher speeds than ISDN or Switched 56 Kbps

Cisco 1602 Series

This series is best when a customer needs the following:

- A 56 Kbps serial port (Frame Relay, leased line, Switched 56, SMDS, and X.25)
- Low-cost integrated CSU/DSU at 56 Kbps
- Capability to get CSU/DSU diagnostics information and configuration remotely via Cisco IOS command-line interface

Cisco 1603 and 1604 Series

These are best when a customer needs the following:

- ISDN (BRI) and ISDN leased-line connectivity
- Built-in NT1 for the United States and Canada (Cisco 1604)

Cisco 1605-R Series

This series is best when a customer needs the following:

- Two Ethernets, to isolate an internal secure LAN from a perimeter LAN (exposed to Internet)
- Single, flexible WAN connection (any WIC card)

Software Feature Packs

These are best when a customer needs the following:

- IP routing (IP Feature Pack)

- IP, IPX, and AppleTalk routing (IP/IPX/AppleTalk)

- NAT, RSVP, and Open Shortest Path First (OSPF) (All Plus Feature Packs)

- 40- or 56-bit DES encryption (All Plus Encryption Feature Packs)

Cisco 2500 Series Access Routers/Servers

The Cisco 2500 series of routers is the world's most popular brand of branch office router, providing a variety of models designed for branch office and remote site environments.

Cisco 2500 Series Key Features

Cisco 2500 series key features include the following:

- Full suite of Cisco IOS software

- ClickStart software, providing installation in minutes using any Web browser from any desktop platform

- CiscoWorks Windows software, allowing remote management and maintenance from a central location

- Flash and DRAM memory upgrade capability for easy software image maintenance

- A range of connectivity options, from standard LAN/WAN connectivity to models that can maximize networking budget value by combining functionalities such as integrated hub or asynchronous line support in a single package

- ConfigMaker, Windows 95 and NT 4.0 ease-of-use tool for simplified configuration

Cisco 2500 Series Single LAN Routers Product Family

- The Cisco 2500 series of single-LAN access routers combines LAN routing capability with either two fixed synchronous serial ports or user-configurable WAN options. Table E-7 lists the products in this family.

Table E-7   *Cisco 2500 Series Single-LAN Routers Product Family*

	LAN Connections	**WAN Connections**	**ISDN Port**
Cisco 2501	1 Ethernet	2 Sync Serial	0
Cisco 2502	1 Token Ring	2 Sync Serial	0
Cisco 2503	1 Ethernet	2 Sync Serial	1
Cisco 2504	1 Token Ring	2 Sync Serial	1
Cisco 2524	1 Ethernet	User-configurable	User-configurable
Cisco 2525	1 Token Ring	User-configurable	User-configurable

Note: All Cisco 2500 series routers have an AUX port that supports async communications through 38.4 Kbps.

Cisco 2500 Series Dual-LAN Routers Product Family

The Cisco 2500 series of dual-LAN access routers combines LAN routing capability with two synchronous WAN options. With a dual-LAN architecture, these routers are ideal to serve as firewalls. Table E-8 lists the products in this family.

Table E-8   *Cisco 2500 Series Dual-LAN Routers Product Family*

	LAN Connections	**WAN Connections**	**ISDN Port**
Cisco 2513	1 Ethernet 1 Token Ring	2 Sync Serial	0
Cisco 2514	2 Ethernet	2 Sync Serial	0
Cisco 2515	2 Token Ring	2 Sync Serial	0

Cisco 2500 Series High-Density Serial Routers Product Family

The Cisco 2500 series high-density serial access routers are optimized to provide maximum performance for high-speed WAN connections and low-speed serial connections. Table E-9 lists the products in this family.

Table E-9   *Cisco 2500 Series High-Density Serial Routers Product Family*

	LAN Connection	**WAN Connections**	**Serial Lines**	**ISDN Port**
Cisco 2520	1 Ethernet	2 high-speed serial	2 low-speed sync/async	1
Cisco 2521	1 Token Ring	2 high-speed serial	2 low-speed sync/async	1

continues

Table E-9   *Cisco 2500 Series High-Density Serial Routers Product Family (Continued)*

	LAN Connection	WAN Connections	Serial Lines	ISDN Port
Cisco 2522	1 Ethernet	2 high-speed serial	8 low-speed sync/async	1
Cisco 2523	1 Token Ring	2 high-speed serial	8 low-speed sync/async	1

Cisco 2500 Series Access Routers/Hubs Product Family

Cisco 2500 series access routers/hubs integrate routing and wiring hub operations in a single device, providing remote offices with both LAN and internetwork connectivity. Table E-10 lists the products in this family.

Table E-10   *Cisco 2500 Series Access Routers/Hubs Product Family*

	LAN Connection	WAN Connections	ISDN Port	Hub Ports
Cisco 2505	1 Ethernet	2 Sync serial	0	8
Cisco 2507	1 Ethernet	2 Sync serial	0	16
Cisco 2516	1 Ethernet	2 Sync serial	1	14

Cisco 2500 Series Access Servers Product Family

The Cisco 2500 access server series is a low-cost entry into the access server marketplace. These products give users the capability to connect asynchronous devices, such as modems, terminals, router consoles, ISDN terminal adapters, and so on, into a routed network. These products also enable users to backhaul routed traffic through T1/E1 lines. Table E-11 lists the products in this family.

Table E-11   *Cisco 2500 Series Access Servers Product Family*

	LAN Connection	WAN Connections	Asynchronous Lines
Cisco 2509	1 Ethernet	2 Sync serial	8
Cisco 2511	1 Ethernet	2 Sync serial	16
AS2509-RJ	1 Ethernet	1 Sync serial	8
AS2511-RJ	1 Ethernet	1 Sync serial	16

Cisco 2500 Series Customers

This section breaks down the 2500 series by customer needs.

Cisco 2501, 2502, 2503, 2504

These are best when a customer needs the following:

- Multiprotocol routing between WAN and LANs
- A single Ethernet LAN and dual serial ports (Cisco 2501, 2503)
- A single Token Ring LAN and dual serial ports (Cisco 2502, 2504)
- An ISDN BRI interface (Cisco 2503, 2504)

Cisco 2513, 2514, 2515

These are best when a customer needs the following:

- Dual-LAN configuration for network segmentation or security (physical firewall)
- A single Ethernet port, a single Token Ring port, and dual serial ports (Cisco 2513)
- Dual Ethernet ports and dual serial ports (Cisco 2514)
- Dual Token Ring and dual serial ports (Cisco 2515)

Cisco 2505, 2507, 2516

These are best when a customer needs the following:

- Multiprotocol routing with integrated 10BaseT hubs and dual serial ports
- An ISDN BRI interface (Cisco 2516)

Cisco 2509, 2511, AS2509-RJ, AS2511-RJ

These are best when a customer needs the following:

- An access server combining a terminal server, a protocol translator, and a router in a single device
- A single Ethernet LAN and dual serial ports
- Eight or 16 asynchronous ports
- External cable assembly (Cisco 2509, 2511)
- RJ11 jacks integrated in unit (AS2509-RJ, AS2511-RJ)

Cisco 2520, 2521, 2522, 2523

These are best when a customer needs the following:

- WAN aggregation routers that can be used as communication servers

- A single Ethernet LAN, ISDN BRI, and dual sync/multiple sync/async serial ports (Cisco 2520, 2522)

- A single Token Ring LAN, ISDN BRI, and dual sync/multiple sync/async serial ports (Cisco 2521, 2523)

- High-density asynchronous ports (Cisco 2522, 2523)

Cisco 2524, 2525

These are best when a customer needs modular WAN connectivity for flexibility to support Switched 56, Fractional T1/T1, sync serial, and ISDN

Software Feature Packs

These are best when a customer needs the following:

- IP routing (IP Feature Pack)

- IP, IPX, AppleTalk (AT), and DEC routing for the desktop (IP/IPX/AT/DEC Feature Pack)

- The broadest set of routing features (Enterprise Feature Pack)

- RAS, NAT, RMON, and IBM features (Plus Feature Pack)

- 40- or 56-bit DES network-layer encryption (Encryption Feature Pack)

Cisco 2600 Series Access Routers

The Cisco 2600 series modular access router offers a new level of flexibility and investment protection for the remote branch office. The Cisco 2600 series offers network managers and service providers an attractively priced solution for extending the versatility, integration, and power of the Cisco 3600 series to smaller, remote branch offices. The Cisco 2600 shares modular interfaces with the Cisco 1600 and 3600 series, offering a solution both for today's remote branch office needs and for increasing demands for applications such as multiservice data, voice, and video integration; departmental dial services; and extranet/VPN access. Table E-12 lists the products in the 2600 family.

Table E-12   *Cisco 2600 Series Product Family*

	LAN Ports	WAN Interface Card Slots	Network Module Slot	Advanced Integration Module Slot
Cisco 2610	1 Ethernet	2	1	1
Cisco 2611	2 Ethernet	2	1	1

Cisco 2600 Series Key Features

Key features of the 2600 series include the following:

- High-performance RISC architecture

- Full Cisco IOS support

- Modular WAN interface cards and network modules for flexibility and investment protection

- Advanced Integration Module (AIM) slot that offers expandability to support advanced services such as hardware-assisted data compression and encryption

- Multiservice voice/data integration

- Wire-speed LAN-to-LAN routing (packet-forwarding rates of up to 15,000 pps)

- Integrated CSU/DSU and ISDN NT1 options that enable remote management

- Optional redundant power supply

- WAN interface cards compatible with Cisco 1600 and Cisco 3600 routers

Cisco 2600 Series Customers

This section breaks down the 2600 series by customer needs.

Cisco 2600 Series

This series is best when a customer needs the following:

- Multiservice voice/data integration

- Departmental dial services

- Extranet/VPN access

Cisco 2610

The Cisco 2610 is best when a customer needs one Ethernet port.

Cisco 2611

The Cisco 2611 is best when a customer needs two Ethernet ports to isolate an internal secure LAN from a perimeter LAN.

Telephony/Packet Gateway Network Modules

These are best when a customer needs the following:

- Integrated messaging
- Web-based call centers
- Desktop video with audio

Async/Sync Serial Network Modules

These are best when a customer needs the following:

- Synchronous Data Link Control (SDLC) controllers concentrator
- Point-of-sale (POS) devices concentrator
- Automated teller machines concentrator
- Connecting fire and alarm services

High-Density Async Network Modules

These are best when a customer needs the following:

- Dial services in the branch office, using their own modems
- Remote control of async devices
- Async device concentration

Software Feature Packs

These are best when a customer needs the following:

- IP routing (IP Feature Pack)
- IP, IPX, AppleTalk, and DEC routing (IP/IPX/AT/DEC Feature Pack)
- The broadest set of routing features (Enterprise Plus Feature Pack)
- Advanced IBM services (Enterprise/Advanced Peer-to-Peer Networking [APPN] Feature Pack)
- Full remote access services (RAS Feature Pack)

- NAT, RMON, IBM, Multichassis Multilink Point-to-Point Protocol (MMP), VPDN/L2F, and voice features (Plus Feature Pack)

- 40- or 56-bit DES network-layer encryption (All Plus Encryption Feature Packs)

Cisco 3600 Series Modular Access Routers/Servers

The Cisco 3600 series is designed to accommodate the growing numbers of dialup branch and remote office users who need dial access to corporate intranets and the public Internet. The Cisco 3600 series of access dialup servers offers an unprecedented degree of support flexibility for dialup applications across both ISDN and asynchronous media. The Cisco 3600 series also supports synchronous serial communication and is fully supported by the Cisco IOS software. Table E-13 lists the products in the 3600 family.

Table E-13   *Cisco 3600 Series Product Family*

	Network Module Slots	DRAM Memory	Processor (CPU)
Cisco 3620	2	16 MB, upgradeable to 64 MB	80 MHz IDT R4700 RISC
Cisco 3640	4	16 MB, upgradeable to 128 MB	100 MHz IDT R4700 RISC

Cisco 3600 Series Key Features

Key features of the 3600 series include the following:

- Combined dial access, advanced LAN-to-LAN routing services, and multiservice integration of voice, video, data, and future technologies into a single platform

- Modular design that supports a wide array of network modules for scalability and flexibility

- Industry-leading ISDN price/port and price/performance in high-end branch/regional offices

- Integrated Cisco IOS software for extensive security features, reduced WAN service costs, enhanced multimedia support, and guaranteed interoperability across all Cisco routers

- SNMP, Telnet, and a console port for remote management and monitoring

- Flash and primary memory upgrade capability for easy software image maintenance

Cisco 3600 Series Modules

The modules in the 3600 series are as follows:

- **LAN Network Modules**
    - 1- and 4-port 10BaseT Ethernet
    - 1-port 10/100BaseTX Fast Ethernet
    - 1-port 100BaseFX Fast Ethernet
- **WAN Network Modules**
    - 16- and 32-port asynchronous serial
    - 4-port synchronous serial
    - 1- and 2-port channelized T1/E1 ISDN Primary Rate Interface (PRI) (with optional CSU)
    - 4- and 8-port ISDN BRI (with optional NT1)
    - 4- and 8-port sync/async low-speed serial
- **Mixed Media Network Modules (includes one LAN and two WAN interface slots)**
    - 1-port Token Ring and 1-port Ethernet mixed media
    - 2-port Ethernet mixed media
    - 1-port Ethernet mixed media
- **Modem Modules**
    - 6, 12, 18, 24, and 30 digital modems
    - 6 digital modems upgrade
- **Voice/Fax Network Modules**
    - 1- and 2-slot voice/fax
- **Other**
    - Compression

Cisco 3600 Series Customers

This section breaks down the 3600 series by customer needs.

Cisco 3620

The 3620 is best when a customer needs the following:

- Medium-density WAN and dialup connectivity with:
    - Up to eight ISDN BRI ports with optional integrated NT1
    - Up to two ISDN PRI ports with optional integrated CSU
    - Up to eight async/sync serial ports
    - Up to four sync serial ports
    - Up to 32 async serial ports
    - Or a combination thereof
- Medium-density LAN connectivity with:
    - Up to eight Ethernet ports
    - Up to four Token Ring ports
    - One Fast Ethernet port

Cisco 3640

The 3640 is best when a customer needs the following:

- High-density WAN and dialup connectivity with:
    - Up to 24 ISDN BRI ports with optional integrated NT1
    - Up to six ISDN PRI ports with optional integrated CSU
    - Up to 24 async/sync serial ports
    - Up to eight sync serial ports
    - Up to 96 async serial ports
    - Or a combination thereof
- Medium- to high-density LAN connectivity with:
    - Up to 12 Ethernet ports
    - Up to 12 Token Ring ports
    - Two Fast Ethernet ports

Software Feature Packs

These are best when a customer needs the following:

- IP routing (IP Feature Pack)

- IP, IPX, AppleTalk, and DECnet routing (IP/IPX/AT/DEC Feature Pack)

- The broadest set of routing features (Enterprise Feature Pack)

- NAT, RSVP, and IBM features (All Plus Feature Packs)

- 40- or 56-bit DES network-layer encryption (All Plus Encryption Feature Packs)

Cisco 4000 Series Access Routers

The Cisco 4000 series routers are highly cost-effective, modular platforms that reduce network costs and complexity by aggregating multiple LANs into a single multiprotocol network. The Cisco 4500M is optimized for low- to medium-bandwidth LAN/WAN/ISDN applications. The Cisco 4700M, with its faster CPU, excels in process-level tasks demanded by high-bandwidth, fast-switching applications. Table E-14 lists the products in the 4000 family.

Table E-14 *Cisco 4000 Product Family*

	Network Module Slots	DRAM Memory	Processor (CPU)
Cisco 4500	3	16 MB, upgradeable to 32 MB	100 MHz IDT Orion RISC
Cisco 4700	3	16 MB, upgradeable to 64 MB	133 MHz IDT Orion RISC

Cisco 4000 Series Key Features

Key features of the 4000 series include the following:

- Supports the full suite of Cisco IOS software

- Provides high-performance modular architecture

- Segregates users on different networks for increased security management

- Supports a wide range of WAN services and routing protocols with Cisco IOS software

- Allows easy and reliable software upgrades via PC Flash memory card

Cisco 4000 Series Modules

The modules in the 4000 series are as follows:

- **LAN Network Modules**
    - 2- and 6-port 10BaseT Ethernet
    - 1-port 100BaseTX Fast Ethernet
    - 1- and 2-port Token Ring
- **WAN Network Modules**
    - 1-port single-attachment and 1-port dual-attachment multimode FDDI
    - 1-port dual-attachment single-mode FDDI
    - 2- and 4-port synchronous serial
    - 4- and 8-port ISDN BRI
    - 1- and 2-port channelized T1 ISDN PRI
    - 1-port E1 ISDN PRI (balanced and unbalanced)
    - 1-port E1 G.703 (balanced and unbalanced)
    - 1-port High-Speed Serial Interface (HSSI)
    - 2-port high-speed serial and 16-port sync/async

Cisco 4000 Series Customers

This section breaks down the 4000 series by customer needs.

Cisco 4000 Series (Cisco 4500, 4700)

The 4000 series is best when a customer needs the following:

- High-density LAN connectivity: Up to 18 Ethernet ports, or 6 Token Ring ports, or 2 Fast Ethernet ports, or a combination thereof
- Medium-density WAN and dialup connectivity: Up to 16 ISDN BRI ports, or 2 ISDN PRI ports, or up to 32 async/sync serial ports, or up to 8 sync serial ports, or a combination thereof
- FDDI or IBM internetworking connectivity

Software Feature Packs

These are best when a customer needs the following:

- IP routing (IP Feature Pack)

- IP, IPX, AppleTalk, and DECnet routing (IP/IPX/AT/DEC Feature Pack)

- The broadest set of routing features (Enterprise Feature Pack)

- NAT, RSVP, and IBM features (All Plus Feature Packs)

- 40- or 56-bit DES network-layer encryption (All Plus Encryption Feature Packs)

Cisco AS5x00 Universal Access Server Series

The AS5x00 series products are high-performance, medium- to high-density universal access servers that deliver hybrid asynchronous serial and ISDN line service to accommodate both mobile users and high-bandwidth dedicated telecommuters. By terminating both analog modem and ISDN calls on the same chassis from the same trunk line, the AS5x00 enables ISPs and enterprise network managers to meet traditional analog dial access needs while supporting the growing demand for high-speed ISDN access. The AS5x00 contains the functionality of CSUs, channel banks, communication servers, switches, routers, ISDN capabilities, and up to 120 56K digital modems tightly integrated in one standalone chassis, making it ideal for mixed-media environments. The AS5x00 does the following:

- Reduces costs by providing universal access via one trunk line for all calls (async and ISDN)

- Protects investment through modular design that can change and grow

- Protects investment in legacy systems by offering easy integration and support for a wide range of protocols through Cisco IOS software

- Minimizes security issues through multiprotocol security levels

Table E-15 lists the products in the AS5200 product family.

Table E-15 *Cisco AS5200 Series Product Family*

	LAN Connection	WAN Connectivity	Network Interface Card Slots	Dual T1/ E1/PRI Card	Modems
AS5224	1 10BaseT	2 High-speed serial	3	Bundled	24 Microcom or MICA bundled
AS5248	1 10BaseT	2 High-speed serial	3	Bundled	48 Microcom or MICA bundled

Table E-16 lists the products in the AS5300 product family.

Table E-16 *Cisco AS5300 Series Product Family*

	LAN Connection	**WAN Connectivity**	**MICA Modems**
AS5348	1 10/100BaseT	Quad T1/PRI	48 Bundled
AS5396	1 10/100BaseT	Quad T1/PRI	96 Bundled
AS53108	1 10/100BaseT	Quad T1/PRI	108 Bundled

Cisco AS5x00 Series Key Features

Key features of the AS5x00 series include the following:

- Supports the full suite of Cisco IOS software

- Services and terminates asynchronous and digital (ISDN) calls with one standalone AS5x00 and one phone number

- Combines LAN, WAN, and asynchronous line support in a single package

- Supports up to 60 (AS5200 in E1 configuration) or 120 (AS5300 in E1 configuration) integrated modems

- Supports all protocols and services on all asynchronous ports, as well as asynchronous routing and reverse Telnet connections for dialing out from the network

- Supports a wide range of WAN services and routing protocols through Cisco IOS software

- Has two PRI/T1 lines with integrated CSUs that are terminated in the AS5200, meaning that a network manager can have up to 48 simultaneous callers terminated in one box

- Has two PRI/E1 lines (most services outside North America are terminated in the AS5200 for up to 60 simultaneous calls).

- An Ethernet port that provides the capability to route data locally

- Two synchronous serial ports that provide the capability to route data to other sites (backhaul)

- Modems that come with a choice of management functionality levels

- A router engine that is based on the reliable and proven Cisco 2500 (more than 1,000,000 of these router engines are deployed in the field)

- Full remote management of the integrated CSUs, router, and modems via the router command-line interface, SNMP, MIBs, or a CiscoView graphical user interface applet

- Modular design that allows easy implementation of future technology

Cisco AS5x00 Series Customers

The AS5x00 is best when a customer needs the following:

- Hybrid combination of analog and ISDN dial access
- Integrated modems
- Managed Internet connectivity
- Flexible and robust remote access
- Manageability (SNMP, RMON, Telnet, out-of-band modem management)
- Security, scalability, and resiliency
- For higher density, use the AS5300

Software Feature Packs

These are best when a customer needs the following:

- IP routing (IP Feature Pack)
- IP, IPX, and AppleTalk for the desktop (Desktop Feature Pack)
- The broadest set of routing features (Enterprise Feature Pack)
- NAT, RMON, and Virtual Private Dialup Network, Multichassis
- MMP, V.120, and modem management features (All Plus Feature Packs)

Cisco Internet Security and Scalability Overview

In providing Internet connectivity, a company faces the challenge of keeping pace with the demands and costs of integrating multiple systems and tools from different vendors. This complexity is increasing continuously with the rapid growth in new technology and products, prompting small and medium-sized businesses to seek highly integrated end-to-end solutions.

Cisco Internet security and scalability products enhance Internet productivity and reduce costs. Cisco products address issues such as network and data security, difficult access and slow performance, migration of legacy networks, scalable network administration, and support for emerging applications.

Firewall Functionality

A critical part of an overall security solution is a network firewall, which monitors traffic crossing network perimeters and imposes restrictions according to security policy. The Cisco firewall family offers a comprehensive range of security features, meeting requirements for perimeter policy enforcement, extending to more complex virtual private networks, content filtering, and denial of service detection and prevention. When deployed in combination, Cisco firewall products let network managers realize even more powerful security architectures by implementing a layered security strategy. No other vendor offers this kind of flexibility in its security solutions:

- The Centri Firewall provides a strong security solution that is tightly integrated with Windows NT and that is easy to setup and administer.

- The PIX Firewall delivers enterprise-class firewall functionality as an integrated hardware and software solution. This dedicated appliance provides the broadest range of firewall features with unsurpassed performance.

- The Cisco IOS Firewall feature set provides rich application support that complements the full routing and WAN access capabilities offered by Cisco IOS software. This optional feature set affords seamless integration with existing Cisco IOS software-based environments and strengthens the Cisco end-to-end security offering by providing access list policy enforcement within the network infrastructure.

- Cisco 1605-R and 2514 access routers and Cisco 3600 series modular dialup access servers feature a dual-LAN architecture, which is ideal to serve as a firewall.

Cisco Firewall Solution Summarization

Table E-17 summarizes the uses and specifications of the various Cisco firewall solutions covered in this section.

Table E-17   *Firewall Solutions*

Platform Type	WAN Connectivity	Product Name	Product Description
Software; NT operating system	Up to T1	Cisco Centri Firewall	High-performance, flexible Windows NT-based security software with intuitive user-based policy rules; easy to install, configure, and manage.
Software; network infrastructure integrated	Up to T1	Cisco IOS Firewall feature set	Advanced, rich security option for Cisco IOS software, with full routing and WAN access capabilities; integrates seamlessly with existing Cisco IOS software-based environments.
Dedicated appliance	Up to multiple T3	Cisco PIX Firewall	Highest performance, enterprise-class, scalable, dedicated security appliance with most advanced features and application support.

Centri Firewall

The Cisco Centri Firewall provides smal-l to medium-sized businesses a strong security solution that is tightly integrated with Windows NT and that is easy to set up and administer. Centri innovative ease-of-use features make it possible to have expert-level security without the expense of onsite security experts. The powerful combination of the Centri Firewall Natural Network Viewer and Policy Builder features make securing a network truly simple for the first time. Security policies can be applied to users and groups in a Windows NT domain.

Centri also comes with preconfigured support for popular network applications and services. In addition to these out-of-box services, Centri helps you to safely and easily customize support for any network application or service.

The Centri Firewall can allow other network services, such as Web, e-mail, and DNS servers, to reside securely on the same Windows NT system. This setup allows companies to maximize existing resources and to reduce the cost of securely connecting to the Internet.

The Centri Firewall is part of the Cisco Networked Office Stack, a flexible suite of compatible products that provides secure access to the Internet and that links users and offices so that employees can easily share resources such as information, documents, and printers.

Centri Firewall Key Features

Key features of the Cisco Centri Firewall include the following:

- Integration with Windows NT domain
- Secure kernel proxy architecture
- Graphical user interface for creating security policies
- Drag-and-drop security policies
- ActiveX, Java applets, JavaScript, and VBscript blocking
- Universal Resource Locator (URL) blocking
- Transparent and proxy support for all common TCP/IP applications, including WWW, FTP, Telnet, and e-mail

Centri Firewall Customers

The Centri Firewall is best when a customer needs the following:

- Windows NT platform preference
- Secure, easy connection to the Internet
- Additional services (Web, e-mail, DNS) to run on the firewall platform

The Centri Firewall key benefits include the following:

- Strong security and performance with kernel proxy architecture running in the kernel and the Windows NT operating system.

- Easy to administer with security Policy Builder; an installation wizard walks nonsecurity experts through setup with easy-to-answer questions.

- Seamless integration with Windows NT to maximize the NT security features.

- Reduced Internet connection costs by running multiple services (Web, e-mail, DNS) on the same system as the Centri Firewall.

Cisco IOS Firewall Feature Set

The Cisco IOS Firewall feature set adds greater depth and flexibility to existing Cisco IOS security solutions for the Cisco 1600 and 2500 series routers. The Cisco IOS Firewall feature set is particularly appropriate for dual-LAN routers, such as the Cisco 2514 or Cisco 1605-R routers, which can be used to secure a remote office internal LAN while allowing public access to a second LAN segment containing, for example, Web servers.

The Cisco IOS Firewall feature set is part of the Cisco Networked Office Stack, the suite of stackable desktop products designed to deliver secure Internet access; high-speed, local-area networking; and "plug-and-play" Web hosting.

Cisco IOS Firewall Feature Set Key Features

The key features of the Cisco IOS Firewall feature set include the following:

- CBAC provides secure, application-based filtering and supports the latest protocols for advanced applications.

- Java blocking controls downloading of potentially malicious applets.

- Denial of service detection and prevention adds to existing functionality for greater protection against attackers.

- Real-time alerts send syslog error messages to central management consoles upon detecting suspicious activity.

- TCP/UDP transaction logs track user access by source/destination address and port pairs.

- Configuration and management features integrate smoothly with existing management applications.

The existing Cisco IOS perimeter security technologies are as follows:

- Traffic filters, or access control lists, control whether routed traffic is forwarded or blocked at router interfaces based on information embedded in the traffic itself.

- Route authentication provides a method of authenticating routing table updates using the Message Digest 5 (MD5) encryption algorithm so that routers are not vulnerable to disguised attackers.

- Network-layer encryption safeguards information exchanged end-to-end between sites.

- Layer 2 Forwarding (L2F) and GRE provide tunneling techniques for deploying virtual private networks and virtual private dialup networks.

- NAT secures networks by hiding internal, unregistered IP addresses from public view, also simplifying IP address management and conserving legal IP addresses.

- TCP Intercept prevents SYN flooding-type denial of service attacks by tracking, optionally intercepting and validating TCP connection requests.

- Lock and Key provides dynamic access control lists (ACLs) that can be tied to Layer 3 user authentication.

- ACL violation logging uses existing router logging facilities to log ACL violations whenever a packet matches a particular access entry.

Cisco IOS Firewall Feature Set Customers

The Cisco IOS Firewall feature set is best when a customer needs or prefers the following:

- Secure, low-cost Internet access for remote or branch offices

- Cisco IOS software-based environments

- One box to manage; router integrated with firewall

- Integration of enhanced security capabilities into the infrastructure of their network

- Rich application support, including multimedia

Cisco PIX Firewall

The Cisco PIX Firewall series products are stateful firewalls that deliver high security and fast performance to corporate networks. These firewalls allow users to thoroughly protect their internal networks from the outside world, providing full firewall security policy and protection. Unlike typical CPU-intensive proxy servers that perform extensive processing on each data packet, the Cisco PIX Firewalls use a secure, real-time, embedded system. The Cisco adaptive security algorithm (ASA) and cut-through proxy allow the Cisco PIX Firewall series to deliver outstanding performance for more than 16,000 simultaneous connections, dramatically greater than any UNIX system-based firewall.

Cisco PIX Firewall Key Features

The Cisco PIX Firewall key features are as follows:

- Located between the corporate network and the Internet access router; includes Ethernet, Fast Ethernet, or Token Ring LAN connectivity options.

- Protection scheme based on the adaptive security algorithm (ASA) to ensure the utmost in security—no other firewall provides this level of protection.

- Patent-pending cut-through proxy for authentication and authorization.

- Support for 64 simultaneous outbound connections; scalable to more than 16,000 as a business grows.

- Unrestricted inbound connections to support large-scale Internet commerce sites.

- Graphical user interface for configuration and management.

- Alert and alarm notification via e-mail and pager.

- Virtual private network support with Private Link encryption card.

Cisco PIX Firewall Customers

The PIX Firewall is best when a customer needs the following:

- Strongest security for corporate networks

- Highest performance, enterprise-class firewall

- Failover/hot standby for network reliability; mission-critical applications

- Support for sophisticated use of multimedia over the Internet

PIX Firewall key benefits include these:

- Strongest security based on the adaptive security algorithm, which offers stateful connection-oriented security

- Greatest authentication performance with cut-through proxy that allows PIX Firewalls to perform faster than proxy servers

- Lowest cost of ownership from simple installation, configuration, maintenance, and scalability

- Platform extensibility so that publicly accessible Web, e-mail, and DNS servers can be protected

Cisco Micro Webserver

Many small- and medium-sized businesses recognize the potential of Internet marketing. A Web site can market a company and enhance communication. The Cisco Micro Webserver is a Web server appliance that gives small- to medium-sized businesses and branch office customers an easy way to establish an Internet presence or to provide intranet-based intraoffice communications.

The Micro Webserver packages both hardware and the embedded Web software kernel within a small footprint for content storage and Web authoring. The simple and intuitive graphical installation and configuration utilities enable nontechnical users to rapidly and easily connect Micro Webserver to the network. Its user-friendly graphical user interface and extensibility make the Cisco Micro Webserver appliance the ideal choice for a wide variety of customers and mission-specific applications.

The Cisco Micro Webserver has excellent price per performance, with more than 50 connections per second. The Micro Webserver reduces cost of ownership by making deployment easy and reduces administration overhead with the embedded operating system. The Micro Webserver is priced at a fraction of the cost of traditional server-based systems that require an investment in separate server hardware, software, and system management personnel.

The Cisco Micro Webserver is offered as part of the Cisco Networked Office Stack. This is a flexible suite of products that enables small businesses to easily take advantage of the Internet to attract new customers, improve communications, lower ongoing expenses, and increase productivity.

Cisco Micro Webserver Key Features

The following are the Cisco Micro Webserver key features:

- Stackable, small footprint; can be used standalone or stacked with other Cisco Networked Office Stack products.

- Easy to set up and install, with color-coded cables, Quick Start flow chart, and Administrative Wizard.

- Real-time HTTP 1.1-compliant kernel that prevents hacking and adds no operating system management overhead.

- 2.1 GB internal hard drive that enhances Web authoring, content creation, and information dissemination and transfer.

- Platform independence that eliminates complexity of traditional Web server, for minimal management.

- CGI support for forms data interaction and exchange and TCI scripting on the server.

- Support for multiple SCSI devices, such as CD-ROMs and hard drives.

- Superior performance; more than 6 Mbps throughput and more than 50 connections per second.

Cisco Micro Webserver Customers

The Cisco Micro Webserver is best when a customer needs to accomplish the following:

- To host a Web site on the Internet

- To publish Web pages on the Internet

- To facilitate intraoffice communications (Micro Webserver acts as an intranet server)

- To share information with clients and partners (Micro Webserver acts as an extranet server)

- To create a Web-based document server

- To achieve minimal management

- To achieve low cost of ownership

- To achieve quick and easy setup and configuration

Key benefits of the Cisco Micro Webserver include the following:

- Cost-effective, plug-and-play Web server appliance with an easy-to-use, Java-based configuration utility and Network Wizard, allowing setup and installation within minutes.

- An embedded HTTP 1.1-compliant microkernel that prevents hacking, making it less prone to file corruption. The built-in configuration management application provides password protection for multiple users.

- Scalability for growing businesses by supporting up to six SCSI devices, such as CD-ROMs and hard drives, and by providing an easy upgrade path to future software enhancements.

LocalDirector

Cisco LocalDirector is a high-availability Internet appliance for mission-critical TCP/IP applications such as database applications, intranet, and TN3270 services. It is an integrated solution with a secure, real-time embedded operating system that intelligently load balances TCP/IP traffic across multiple servers. Appearing as a single virtual server, it delivers optimized performance by distributing client requests across a cluster of low-cost servers. As a result, it dramatically reduces the cost of providing large-scale Internet services.

The LocalDirector session distribution algorithm (SDA) library provides a flexible and adaptable method for directing TCP/IP traffic. It enables users to intelligently distribute load and to maximize the number of TCP/IP connections a server farm can manage. It also allows them to direct TCP/IP traffic to different servers based on service, speed, or quantity of connections. A maximum connection limit can be set to ensure that servers do not fail from traffic overload.

LocalDirector is a high-availability system that ensures maximum client access. Servers can be automatically and transparently placed in or out of service, providing fault tolerance. LocalDirector itself is equipped with a hot standby failover mechanism, eliminating all points of failure for the server system. Virtual and real servers can back up one another.

LocalDirector is a high-performance Internet appliance with more than 80 Mbps throughput. It supports up to 8000 virtual IP addresses and domain names. It also can direct traffic to 8000 servers that can be a collection of heterogeneous hardware platforms and operating systems, and it efficiently handles more than 700,000 simultaneous TCP connections. Effortless setup, with no network address changes, frees up valuable system administration time.

LocalDirector Key Features

LocalDirector key features are as follows:

- Hot standby failover that enables configuration of highly redundant, fault-tolerant systems
- Scalability, to meet the needs of the largest Web sites
- Simple setup, with little disruption to existing network configuration
- Configurable to a total of 8000 virtual and real servers, with flexibility in domain names and network configuration
- Transparent support for all common TCP/IP Internet services such as Web FTP, Telnet, Gopher, and Simple Mail Transfer Protocol (SMTP)
- Easy server configuration by adding and removing servers transparently as traffic grows
- Compatibility with any server operating system, to retain IS investment
- Support of Secure Socket Layer (SSL), which allows secure Internet commerce

LocalDirector Customers

LocalDirector is best when the customer needs the following:

- Load-balancing TCP/IP servers
- Web-based distribution of high-traffic Web sites
- High availability for mission-critical applications
- TN3270 sessions in an IBM environment

Key benefits of LocalDirector are as follows:

- Simple setup, with little disruption to network

- Scalable, to meet needs of the largest Web sites

- Elimination of all points of failure in a server farm

- Capability to add and remove servers transparently, for high availability

Cisco Ethernet and Fast Ethernet Switches Overview

The Catalyst line of switches spans the entire user spectrum, from small companies and branch offices to central site backbone applications. The Catalyst switch family includes switches for the desktop and workgroup and multilayer-capable switches for scalable enterprise applications in the wiring closet, data center, and backbone. The Catalyst line of switching solutions offers scalability, breadth, performance, and manageability.

Cisco IOS software delivers advanced network services to Catalyst platforms and networked applications. Cisco IOS technologies, optimized for switching and available on all Catalyst switches, include Fast EtherChannel for bandwidth aggregation, CGMP support for optimized performance with multicast and multimedia traffic, and extensive management features. Cisco IOS software also provides support for VLAN configuration and management, IP address management, and secure access to network services.

Administrators manage Cisco intranets with a combination of embedded RMON agents and Switched Port Analyzer (SPAN) support in every Catalyst switch, and network management software, including CiscoWorks Windows and CiscoWorks UNIX.

Key Features of Cisco IOS Software Supported by Catalyst Ethernet Switches

The following are key features of Cisco IOS software supported by Catalyst Ethernet switches:

- CiscoView GUI-based network management support, allowing easy point-and-click discovery of device status, statistics, and comprehensive per-port configuration and performance information. CiscoView is an application within CiscoWorks.

- Web-based interface for installation and administration.

- Telnet and SNMP support for in-band and out-of-band management console.

- Embedded RMON for four groups of RMON and a SPAN port, supporting an RMON probe for complete traffic monitoring.

- LEDs for monitoring the activities and status of the switches.

- IEEE 802.1d spanning tree for network loop detection and disabling, and for fault-tolerant connectivity.

- CDP, to deliver network topology discovery and mapping, allowing devices to discover other Cisco devices on the network.

- Multicast address registration and packet filtering.

- Intranet multimedia and multicast support through CGMP.

Key Features of Cisco IOS Software Supported by Catalyst 1900, 2820, and 5000 Series Ethernet Switches

The following are key features of Cisco IOS software supported by Catalyst 1900, 2820, and 5000 series Ethernet switches:

- VLANs ease network administration by enabling users to be logically grouped, regardless of physical interface location, for performance and security considerations.

- Virtual Trunking Protocol (VTP) allows VLAN configuration changes made on one switch to be automatically updated to the other switches within the network.

- Inter-Switch Link (ISL) protocol dynamically configures trunk ports between Catalyst switches.

- Fast EtherChannel provides bandwidth aggregation, enabling parallel bandwidth links between switches.

Cisco Ethernet and Fast Ethernet Switches Summarization

Table E-18 summarizes Ethernet and Fast Ethernet switches for the workgroup or desktop.

Table E-18   *Ethernet and Fast Ethernet Switches—Workgroup/Desktop*

Configura-tion Design	Switched 10BaseT Port Count	Switched 100BaseT X Port Count	Switched 10/100 BaseT Port Count	Other Technolo-gies	Product Name	Product Description
Fixed	0	0	8	100BaseTX	Cisco 1548 Micro Switch 10/100	Low-cost, small workgroup 10/100 switch (unmanaged)
Fixed	12	2	0	0	Catalyst 1912	Affordable workgroup switch for lower-density requirements

Table E-18   *Ethernet and Fast Ethernet Switches—Workgroup/Desktop (Continued)*

Configura-tion Design	Switched 10BaseT Port Count	Switched 100BaseT X Port Count	Switched 10/100 BaseT Port Count	Other Technolo-gies	Product Name	Product Description
Fixed	12	1	0	100BaseFX (1 port)	Catalyst 1912C	Affordable workgroup switch for lower-density requirements with 100BaseFX
Fixed	24	2	0	0	Catalyst 1924	Lowest cost per port workgroup switch with 100BaseTX
Fixed	24	1	0	100BaseFX (1 port)	Catalyst 1924C	Lowest cost per port workgroup switch with 100BaseFX
Modular	24	0–2	0	Switched 100BaseFX, Shared 100BaseTX and 100BaseFX, FDDI, ATM	Catalyst 2820	Affordable workgroup switch with flexible high-speed media modules
Modular	0	0	16–24	100BaseFX, Future: Gigabit Ethernet, ATM, ISL VLANs	Catalyst 2916M XL	Flexible 10/100 workgroup switch
Fixed	0	0	24	0	Catalyst 2924 XL	Low cost per port 10/100 desktop switch
Fixed	0	0	22	100BaseFX	Catalyst 2924C XL	Low cost per port 10/100 desktop switch with 100BaseFX

Table E-19 summarizes Ethernet and Fast Ethernet switches for the backbone.

Table E-19 *Ethernet and Fast Ethernet Switches—Backbone*

Configura-tion Design	Switched 10BaseT Port Count	Switched 10/100 BaseT Port Count	Switched 100BaseT Port Count	Other Technolo-gies	Product Name	Product Description
Fixed	0	8	0		Catalyst 2908 XL	10/100 autosensing backbone switch
Modular	0	16–24	0	100BaseFX Future: Gigabit Ethernet, ATM, ISL VLANs	Catalyst 2916M XL	Standalone 10/100 LAN aggregation switch
Chassis-based	48	24	2	100BaseFX FDDI, ATM, Gigabit Ethernet, WAN module, Ethernet group switching	Catalyst 5002	Modular 10/100 workgroup switch with media flexibility
Chassis-based	192	96	2	100BaseFX FDDI, ATM, Gigabit Ethernet, WAN module, Ethernet group switching	Catalyst 5000	Modular switching system; widest range of LAN connections

The remainder of this section covers the Cisco Ethernet and Fast Ethernet Switches summarized in Tables E-18 and E-19.

Cisco 1548 Micro Switch 10/100

The Cisco 1548 Micro Switch 10/100 is an affordable plug-and-play desktop Ethernet switch for creating high-performance LANs in small offices and workgroups. A single Cisco 1548 Micro Switch comes with eight 10BaseT/100BaseTX autosensing, autonegotiating switch ports, making it ideal to aggregate users, workgroups, and servers in a small network office environment. The Cisco 1548 Micro Switch 10/100 can be used as a standalone switch for server farms, workgroups, or users who require switched Fast Ethernet performance. Its optimal port density, high performance, and flexibility allow the Cisco 1548 Micro Switch 10/100 to be a perfect LAN backbone for small to medium-sized businesses.

The Cisco 1548 Micro Switch 10/100 is an integral member of the Cisco Networked Office Stack of network solutions designed for small and medium-sized businesses. The Cisco 1548 Micro Switch 10/100, combined with the Cisco 1600 series routers and other products in the Cisco Networked Office Stack, provides reliable and affordable Internet access, high-performance local-area networking, and secure remote access solutions.

Cisco 1548 Micro Switch 10/100 Key Features

The following are the Cisco 1548 Micro Switch 10/100 key features:

- Eight 10BaseT/100BaseTX Fast Ethernet switch ports, supporting connections at Ethernet and Fast Ethernet speeds

- 800 Mbps switching capacity, with up to a 1.19 Mpps forwarding rate

- Autosensing of communications speed and autonegotiation of duplex mode

- Full-duplex operation on each switched 10/100 port, delivering up to 200 Mbps of bandwidth to end stations or servers and between switches

- Automatic configuration and self-test on startup

- Extensive array of LEDs for convenient visual management

- Operation as a standalone device or connected to other hubs, switches, or routers to form a larger network

Cisco 1548 Micro Switch 10/100 Customers

The Cisco 1548 Micro Switch 10/100 is best when a customer needs the following:

- The higher performance of a 10/100 autosensing Fast Ethernet switch to serve users in a small office or workgroup

- A LAN backbone in larger small-office networks

Cisco Catalyst 1900 Series Ethernet Switches

The Catalyst 1900 series switches, available in Standard and Enterprise Editions, provide industry-leading performance and Cisco end-to-end network integration at an exceptionally affordable price. For an extremely low price per port, these switches offer an affordable high-performance alternative to shared 10BaseT hubs. The Catalyst 1900 series switches are equipped with 12 or 24 switched 10BaseT ports for attachment to individual workstations, or 10BaseT hubs and two 100BaseT ports for high-speed connectivity to servers and backbones.

Enterprise Edition software enables these switches to deliver unmatched network configuration flexibility and scalability through embedded Cisco IOS technologies, delivering comprehensive management and security, bandwidth optimization, networked multimedia, and VLAN support.

Table E-20 summarizes the products in the Catalyst 1900 series.

Table E-20 *Catalyst 1900 Series Product Family*

	Fixed Ports	MAC Addresses
Catalyst 1912	12 10BaseT 2 100BaseTX 1 AUI	1024
Catalyst 1912C	12 10BaseT 1 100BaseTX 1 100BaseFX 1 AUI	1024
Catalyst 1924	24 10BaseT 2 100BaseTX 1 AUI	1024
Catalyst 1924C	24 10BaseT 1 100BaseTX 1 100BaseFX 1 AUI	1024

Cisco Catalyst 1900 Series Key Features

The following are the Catalyst 1900 series key features:

- 10BaseT ports that use RJ-45 connectors to connect to single workstations, 10BaseT hubs, or any 10BaseT compatible device.

- Two fixed 100BaseT ports for server or backbone connectivity. One or both of these ports can be set to CollisionFree full-duplex mode, providing up to 200 Mbps bandwidth and extended distances using fiber cabling.

- 1024 Media Access Control (MAC) address cache shared dynamically among all ports.

- Web-based interface for ease of installation and administration.

- CiscoWorks device management support.

- Up to 370 Mbps maximum forwarding bandwidth and 550,000 pps aggregate packet-forwarding rate (64-byte packets).

- Telnet and SNMP support for in-band management and a menu-driven out-of-band management console.

- CGMP for dynamic and selective forward-routed IP multicast traffic to target multimedia end stations, reducing overall network traffic.

- Embedded RMON software agents supporting four RMON groups (history, statistics, alarms, and events) and SPAN port for connection to RMON probe.

- Support for up to four overlapping bridge groups to manage bandwidth and to provide added security through broadcast control.

Enterprise Edition Software Features

The following are the features of the Enterprise Edition software:

- Cisco IOS command-line interface for consistent management across Cisco switches and routers

- Up to 1024 port-based VLANs with Inter-Switch Link trunking on 100BaseT ports

- Enhanced security through TACACS+ authentication of usernames and passwords

- Bandwidth aggregation through Fast EtherChannel, which enhances fault tolerance and offers up to 400 Mbps of bandwidth between switches and routers and individual servers

Cisco Catalyst 2820 Series Ethernet Switches

The Catalyst 2820 series switches, available in Standard and Enterprise Editions, provide industry-leading performance and Cisco end-to-end network integration at an exceptionally affordable price. The Catalyst 2820 series are the most flexible workgroup switches available. These switches have 24 switched 10BaseT ports and two high-speed uplink expansion slots. High-speed modules provide configuration, wiring, and backbone flexibility, with a choice of 100BaseT, FDDI modules supporting Category 5 UTP or fiber-optic cabling, and ATM modules supporting Category 5 UTP or fiber-optic cabling.

Enterprise Edition software enables these switches to deliver unmatched network configuration flexibility and scalability through embedded Cisco IOS technologies, delivering comprehensive management and security, bandwidth optimization, networked multimedia, and virtual LAN support.

Table E-21 summarizes the products in the Catalyst 2820 series.

Table E-21 *Catalyst 2820 Series Product Family*

	Fixed Ports/ Slots	MAC Addresses	100BaseT Port Modules	Other Modules
Catalyst 2822	24 10BaseT 1 AUI 2 high-speed module slots	2048	1-Port 100BaseTX* 8-Port 100BaseTX**	FDDI UTP SAS FDDI Fiber SAS, DAS ATM 155 MM fiber ATM 155 UTP ATM SM fiber (15 Km) ATM SM fiber (40 Km)
Catalyst 2828	24 10BaseT 1 AUI 2 high-speed module slots	8192	1-Port 100BaseFX* 4-Port 100BaseFX**	

*Switched
**Shared

Cisco Catalyst 2820 Series Key Features

The following are the Cisco Catalyst 2820 series key features:

- Increased performance of Ethernet workgroups requiring 100BaseT, FDDI, or ATM connectivity to servers and backbones

- 10BaseT ports that use RJ-45 connectors to connect to single workstations, 10BaseT hubs, or any 10BaseT-compatible device

- Two high-speed expansion slots that are compatible with Catalyst 2820 100BaseT, FDDI, and ATM modules and that provide high-bandwidth connections to backbones, servers, and other high-performance devices

- CollisionFree operation for full-duplex 100BaseT, providing up to 200 Mbps bandwidth and extended distances using fiber cabling

- Web-based interface for ease of installation and administration

- Up to 370 Mbps maximum forwarding bandwidth and 550,000 pps aggregate packet-forwarding rate (64-byte packets)

- Telnet and SNMP support for in-band management and a menu-driven out-of-band management console

- CGMP for dynamic and selective forward-routed IP multicast traffic to target multimedia end stations, reducing overall network traffic

- Embedded RMON software agents supporting four RMON groups (history, statistics, alarms, and events)

Enterprise Edition Software Features

The following are features of the Enterprise Edition software:

- Cisco IOS command-line interface for consistent management across Cisco switches and routers

- Up to 1024 port-based VLANs with ISL trunking on 100BaseT ports

- Enhanced security through TACACS+ authentication of usernames and passwords

- Bandwidth aggregation through Fast EtherChannel, which enhances fault tolerance and offers up to 400 Mbps of bandwidth between switches and routers and individual servers

- Up to 64 ATM Emulated LANs (ELANs) with ATM modules

Cisco Catalyst 2820 Series Customers

This section breaks down the Catalyst 2820 series by customer needs.

Cisco Catalyst 2820 Series Standard Edition

The Standard Edition is best when a customer needs the following:

- Affordable switched Ethernet for larger workgroups

- High-speed module choices with switched and shared 100BaseT, switched FDDI, and ATM

- Dynamic multicast management support (CGMP)

- Software upgradeability to Enterprise Edition features

Cisco Catalyst 2820 Series Enterprise Edition

The Enterprise Edition is best when a customer needs the following:

- End-to-end ISL VLANs

- Bandwidth aggregation with Fast EtherChannel

- Up to 64 emulated LANs

Cisco Catalyst 2900 Series XL 10/100 Switches

The Cisco Catalyst 2900 Series XL is a full line of 10/100 autosensing Fast Ethernet switches that offers outstanding performance, versatile modularity, and easy-to-use management. The Catalyst 2900 series XL includes four models with different port densities, configuration options, and pricing designed to meet a broad range of network design requirements.

Table E-23 summarizes the products in the Catalyst 2900 series.

Table E- 23   *Catalyst 2900 Series XL Product Family*

	Fixed Ports/Slots	**Modules**
Catalyst 2908 XL	8 10/100 Mbps autosensing ports	–
Catalyst 2916M XL	16 10/100 Mbps autosensing ports 2 versatile module slots	4-port 10BaseT/100BaseT 2-port 100BaseFX Future: Gigabit Ethernet, ATM, and ISL modules
Catalyst 2924 XL	24 10/100 Mbps autosensing ports	–
Catalyst 2924C XL	22 10/100 Mbps autosensing ports 2 100Base FX ports	–

Cisco Catalyst 2900 Series Key Features

The following are the Cisco Catalyst 2900 series key features:

- Eight, 16, 22, or 24 autosensing switched 10BaseT/100BaseT ports

- Two switched 100BaseFX ports (Catalyst 2924C XL)

- Switch fabric of 3.2 Gbps, a forwarding rate of more than 3.0 Mpps, and a maximum forwarding bandwidth of 1.6 Gbps, delivering wire-speed performance across all ports

- Two versatile module slots on Catalyst 2916 M Xl, providing expansion capabilities, fiber connectivity over extended distances, higher-speed connectivity, and future support for feature modules

- Web-based interface for switch management from anywhere on the network through a standard Web browser

- Multilevel security on console access, preventing unauthorized users from altering switch configuration

- Autoconfiguration of multiple switches across a network from a single boot server

- Up to 800 Mbps bandwidth among routers, switches, and servers with Fast EtherChannel

- CGMP, enabling a switch to dynamically and selectively forward routed IP multicast traffic to target end stations, reducing overall network traffic and improving multimedia performance

- Future support for VLANs, using ISL trunking for broadcast control, security, and simplified adds, moves, and changes

Cisco Catalyst 2900 Series Customers

This section breaks down the Catalyst 2900 series by customer needs.

Cisco Catalyst 2908 XL

The Catalyst 2908 XL is best when a customer needs the following:

- Switch for connecting smaller Ethernet and Fast Ethernet workgroups or servers
- Low entry price

Cisco Catalyst 2924 XL or Catalyst 2924C XL

The Catalyst 2924 XL or Catalyst 2924C XL are best when a customer needs the following:

- Dedicated 10 Mbps or 100 Mbps connections to individual PCs, servers, and other systems
- High-speed uplink flexibility over extended distances with 100BaseFX connections (Catalyst 2924C XL only)
- Low per-port cost

Cisco Catalyst 2916M XL

The Catalyst 2916M XL is best when a customer needs the following:

- Any combination of dedicated 10 Mbps or 100 Mbps connections to individual PCs, servers, and other systems, or connectivity between existing Ethernet and Fast Ethernet workgroups
- The option to easily increase the switch port density and to provide inexpensive higher-speed uplinks through bandwidth aggregation (Fast EtherChannel)
- Future Gigabit Ethernet and ATM interface modules for higher-speed links
- VLAN support through a future ISL feature module
- Maximum flexibility

Cisco Catalyst 5000 Series Ethernet Switches

Cisco Systems flagship Catalyst 5000 series switches are the industry's most powerful switching solutions in the wiring closet, data center, or backbone. This series features a Gigabit Ethernet and ATM-ready platform, offering users high-speed trunking technologies and media-rate performance with a broad variety of interface modules.

The Catalyst 5500 is a high-end modular switching platform that scales to more than 50 Gbps and throughput of tens of millions of packets per second, providing the scalability, flexibility, and redundancy required for building large, switched intranets. The Catalyst 5500 can be used in both wiring closet and backbone applications. The new Catalyst 5505 extends many of the same high-end features of the 5500 in a five-slot form factor.

Table E-24 summarizes the products in the Catalyst 5000 series.

Table E-24   *Catalyst 5000 Series Product Family*

	Slots	System Multicast Throughput	Redundant Supervisors	Switch Fabric	Redundant Power Supply
Catalyst 5002	2	1 Mpps	No	Standard	Yes
Catalyst 5000	5	25 Mpps	No	Standard	Optional
Catalyst 5505	5	38 Mpps	Yes	Enhanced[*]	Optional
Catalyst 5500	13	>50 Mpps	Yes	Enhanced[*]	Optional

[*]With Supervisor III

Table E-25 summarizes the Catalyst 5000 series supervisor engines.

Table E-25   *Catalyst 5000 Supervisor Engines*

	Switch Fabric Speed	Uplinks	Fast Ethernet	Gigabit Ethernet
Supervisor I	1.2 Gbps	Fixed	2	0
Supervisor II	1.2 Gbps	Fixed	2	0
Supervisor III	3.6 Gbps	Modular	2 or 4[*]	2 (optional)

[*]4 Fast Ethernet—future

Cisco Catalyst 5000 Series Modules

The 10BaseT/100BaseT port modules are listed here:

- 48-port 10BaseT[*]
- 48-port 10BaseT (RJ-21)
- 24-port 10BaseT (RJ-21)
- 24-port 10BaseT (RJ-45)
- 12-port 10BaseFL
- 24-port 100BaseTX[*]

[*]Group Switched

[**]ISL and FEC models available

- 12-port 10/100BaseT[**]
- 12-port 100BaseFX[**]
- 24-port10/100BaseTX
- Fast EtherChannel, 100BaseFX (12MM SC)
- Fast EtherChannel, 10/100BaseFX (12 RJ-45)

Other modules are these:

- 1-port CDDI/FDDI
- 16-port copper Token Ring
- 2-port ATM LAN Emulation OC-3 (MMF)
- 2-port ATM LAN Emulation OC-3 (SMF)
- 2-port ATM LAN Emulation OC-3 (UTP)

Cisco Catalyst 5000 Series Key Features

The following are Cisco Catalyst 5000 series key features:

- High-speed connectivity, using standard Fast Ethernet, FDDI, or ATM interfaces
- Fast EtherChannel supported on Supervisor Engine II ports and Fast Ethernet line cards, providing up to 800 Mbps of load-sharing, redundant, point-to-point connections
- Support for all Supervisor Engines, including the NetFlow Switching feature card option on Supervisor Engine II, which scales to multimillion packets per second forwarding across campus
- Dual redundant switching engines, power supplies, and a passive backplane design to ensure full system redundancy for mission-critical environments
- Cisco VTP, which supports dynamic VLANs and dynamic trunk configuration across all switches
- Support for all advanced switching features of Cisco IOS software
- Support for advanced multicasting with CGMP
- Advanced IOS features
- Modular investment protection
- Extreme throughput (1 MM pps)
- Backbone applications
- Wiring closet applications

[*]Group Switched
[**]ISL and FEC models available

Cisco FastHub Line of 100BaseT Class II Hubs

The Cisco FastHub line delivers exceptionally affordable 100 Mbps performance for enterprise power workgroups, server farms, or an entire small- or medium-sized business network. Available in managed, unmanaged, or manageable versions; stackable or standalone; and in a range of port densities, the FastHub line lets you choose among a variety of models for lowest cost or maximum flexibility.

The FastHub line is an integral element in Cisco small- and medium-sized business solutions. The Fast Hub 100 series, available in 12-, 16-, and 24-port configurations, provides the lowest-cost solution for networks in which management is not critical. The standalone FastHub 200 series hub delivers the most cost-effective managed solution. The FastHub 300 series offers both manageability and the flexibility of a modular, stackable solution.

Table E-26 summarizes the products in the Cisco FastHub product family.

Table E-26   *Cisco FastHub Product Family*

	Ports/Slots	Network Management	Wiring	Configuration/ Collision Domain
FastHub 112T	12 10/100 autosensing Fast Ethernet ports	Unmanaged	UTP	Standalone/up to 22 ports
FastHub 116T	16 100BaseTX ports	Unmanaged	UTP	Standalone/up to 30 ports
FastHub 124T	24 10/100 autosensing Fast Ethernet ports	Unmanaged	UTP	Standalone/up to 46 ports
FastHub 216T	16 100BaseTX ports	Integrated management port	UTP	Standalone/up to 30 ports
FastHub 316C	15 100BaseTX ports 1 100BaseFX port 1 16-100BaseTX slot	1 NMM or BMM slot	UTP/Fiber	Stackable/up to 254 ports
FastHub 316T	16 100BaseTX ports 1 16-100BaseTX slot	1 NMM or BMM slot	UTP	Stackable/up to 254 ports

Cisco FastHub Key Features

The following are Cisco FastHub key features:

- High-performance, 100 Mbps bandwidth, using Category 5 UTP and fiber cabling

- Class II design for direct interconnection of geographically distributed hubs or stacks without intermediate switch, bridge, or router

- Integrated management for monitoring all ports or the entire unit on the FastHub 200

- SNMP, Telnet, terminal-based out-of-band console, and RMON support for comprehensive management and simplified troubleshooting (FastHub 200 and 300 series)

- Optional network management module (NMM) that provides management statistics on a per-port, per-unit, or per-stack basis (FastHub 300 series)

- Optional bridge management module (BMM) that extends cabling distances for 100BaseT networks (FastHub 300 series)

- Stackable up to four hubs, for 128 ports in a single logical repeater (FastHub 300)

- Only 100BaseT hub providing the addition of port expansion and management modules in one unit (FastHub 300 series)

- Built-in growth path and scalability with support for both 10BaseT and 100BaseTX (FastHub 112T and 124T)

Cisco FastHub Customers

This section breaks down the Cisco FastHub series by customer needs.

FastHub 100 Series (112T, 116T, 124T)

The FastHub 100 series is best when a customer needs the following:

- Fast Ethernet performance for power workgroups and users

- Lowest cost

- Scalability, but management and expandability are not critical

- Smooth migration from 10BaseT to 100BaseTX (FastHub 112T and 124T)

- Power supply redundancy

FastHub 200 Series (216T)

The FastHub 200 series is best when a customer needs the following:

- Fast Ethernet performance for smaller workgroups or server farms
- Integrated management (SNMP, RMON, Telnet, out-of-band console)
- Power supply redundancy

FastHub 300 Series (316T, 316C)

The FastHub 300 series is best when a customer needs the following:

- Fast Ethernet performance for enterprise power workgroups or an entire small to medium-sized business network
- Manageability (SNMP, RMON, Telnet, out-of-band console)
- Expandability, scalability
- Bridging 100BaseT to legacy 10BaseT networks
- Hub interconnections and backbone connections over extended cabling distances
- Power supply redundancy

Cisco 1500 Series Micro Hubs

The Cisco 1500 series Micro Hub family provides economical, scalable 10 Mbps hubs for creating LANs in small offices. A single Cisco 1500 Micro Hub can create a LAN that connects up to eight devices. Up to five 10 Mbps hubs can be stacked to create a single manageable stack.

The Cisco 1500 series Micro Hub is a member of the Cisco Networked Office Stack, which is designed for small businesses.

Table E-27 summarizes the products in the Cisco 1500 series.

Table E-27   *Cisco 1500 Series Micro Hub Product Family*

	User Ports	Technology	Console Port	In/Out Cascade Port	Management
Cisco 1501	8	10BaseT	No	No	None
Cisco 1502	8	10BaseT	No	Yes	Via connection to a Cisco 1503 hub
Cisco 1503	8	10BaseT	Yes	Yes	Local or remote

Cisco 1500 Series Micro Hub Key Features

The following are Cisco 1500 Series Micro Hub key features:

- Automatic configuration and self-test on startup

- Color-coded ports on the rear panel of the unit

- Flash memory in the Cisco 1502 and 1503, for software updates through Xmodem file transfer or via TFTP

- Cisco 1503 and 1502 models support for CiscoWorks Windows management system

- Automatic partitioning and reconnection to the LAN when excessively long packets are detected

Cisco 1500 Series Micro Hub Customers

This section breaks down the Cisco 1500 Series Micro Hub series by customer needs.

Cisco 1501

The Cisco 1501 is best when a customer needs the following:

- The most economical solution for creating a LAN

- No management capabilities

- Additional units for a Micro Hub stack

Cisco 1502

The Cisco 1502 is best when a customer needs the following:

- Remote management only (via a Cisco 1503)

- Capability to create a manageable stack for up to five hubs, supporting 40 users and devices

Cisco 1503

The Cisco 1503 is best when a customer needs the following:

- Remote and local management capabilities

- Capability to create a manageable stack for up to five hubs, supporting 40 users and devices

Cisco 1528 Micro Hub 10/100

The Cisco 1528 Micro Hub 10/100 provides an affordable, simple, autosensing Fast Ethernet solution for creating high-performance LANs in small offices and workgroups. A single Cisco 1528 Micro Hub 10/100 can create a LAN that connects up to eight PCs, printers, servers, and other devices at either 10 Mbps Ethernet or 100 Mbps Fast Ethernet speeds. The hub is unmanaged but provides easy-to-read LED indicators for visual monitoring and troubleshooting.

The Cisco 1528 Micro Hub 10/100 supports Ethernet and Fast Ethernet users simultaneously and provides a cost-effective way to migrate to Fast Ethernet. This hub delivers high-speed data communications necessary for bandwidth-intensive applications.

The Cisco 1528 Micro Hub 10/100 is an integral component of the Cisco Networked Office Stack.

Table E-28 summarizes the Cisco 1528 Micro Hub 10/100.

Table E-28 *Cisco 1528 Micro Hub 10/100*

	User Port	Technology	Console Port	In/Out Cascade Port	Management
Cisco 1528	8	10BaseT/ 100BaseT	No	No	None

Cisco 1528 Micro Hub 10/100 Key Features

The following are Cisco 1528 Micro Hub 10/100 key features:

- Eight 10BaseT/100BaseTX autosensing hub ports

- 10 Mbps and 100 Mbps peak aggregate throughput

- Internal bridge function, for connecting both 10 Mbps and 100 Mbps devices

- Automatic configuration and self-test on startup

- Extensive LEDs, for visual management

- One user-selectable MDI/MDI-X port, for connecting a compatible hub or switch without a crossover cable

- Standalone operation or connection with another 1528 Micro Hub that supports up to 14 Ethernet or Fast Ethernet ports in a single collision domain

Cisco 1528 Customers

The Cisco 1528 is best when a customer needs the following:

- A simple, unmanaged, 10/100 autosensing Fast Ethernet hub for LAN connections in a small office

- Future-proof LANs in anticipation of adding network-intensive applications

- Shared 10/100 network connections to the Cisco 1600 series router for WAN access

HP 10Base-T Hub-16M

Developed by Hewlett-Packard and integrated with Cisco IOS technologies, the HP 10Base-T Hub-16M combines cost-effective LAN connectivity, security, and integrated management with the benefits of Cisco IOS technologies. The 10 Mbps shared hub is the ideal complement to the Cisco Catalyst 1900 and 2820 series Ethernet switches for small- and medium-sized businesses and enterprise branch offices.

The HP 10Base-T Hub-16M has 16 10BaseT ports for workgroup connectivity and one attachment unit interface (AUI) port to connect coaxial or fiber Ethernet cable. The hub also features a MDI/MDI-X switch on port 16 for inter-hub connectivity without special crossover cables. Up to four HP 10Base-T Hub-16M units can be cascaded together to create a single collision domain of up to 58 10BaseT ports. The hub can be connected upstream to a Catalyst 1900 or 2820 series Ethernet switch in a high-performance network or can be installed as a standalone solution in a small business environment.

The HP 10Base-T Hub-16M has comprehensive hub-level and port-level security features, including intruder prevention, auto port disabling, network management alarm, eavesdrop prevention, and password protection to prevent unauthorized network access. The hub also provides intelligent error monitoring through automatic port/segment partitioning and reconnection for ports experiencing excessive collision problems.

The HP 10Base-T Hub-16M is fully integrated with Cisco 3600 series routers, Catalyst 1900 and 2820 series switches, Catalyst 2900 XL series 10/100 autosensing switches, and FastHub 200 and 300 series system of modular, stackable LAN and WAN products through Cisco IOS technologies for guaranteed product interoperability and unified management. The hub is also equipped with a connector for the Cisco 600-Watt AC Redundant Power System (RPS) to guarantee maximum uptime.

HP 10Base-T Hub-16M Key Features

The following are the HP 10Base-T Hub-16M key features:

- One AUI connection for workgroup connectivity to coaxial or fiber Ethernet cable and 16 10BaseT connections for workstations

- MDI/MDI-X switch for inter-hub connectivity without special crossover cables

- Support for up to four units cascaded together

- Full integration with Catalyst 1900 and 2820 series switches

- SNMP, Telnet, and terminal out-of-band management console for comprehensive management and troubleshooting

- Manageable by CiscoWorks and other SNMP-compatible management systems on a per-port and per-hub basis

- Comprehensive security features, including intruder prevention, eavesdrop prevention, network management alarm, auto port disabling, and password protection

- Per-port and per-hub status LEDs

- Rack-mount kit (19-inch) included

Cisco 1516M Customers

The Cisco 1516M is best when a customer needs the following:

- An economical solution for creating a LAN

- Cisco IOS technologies for seamless integration with other Cisco switches and routers

- Capability to create a manageable collision domain supporting up to 58 users and devices

Cisco Ease of Use and Network Management Overview

Ease of use and network management are important to small- and medium-sized companies and SOHO customers because these businesses are not highly technical or because occasional or infrequent users might be put off by the complexities of networking.

Many of the router solutions on the market today for small- to medium-sized businesses have installation instructions requiring a high level of network understanding. All the cables look alike, and configuring the router requires use of non-user-friendly command-line interfaces. Cisco has developed two Windows NT/95 wizard-based tools to specifically address configuring and installing routers designed for small companies and SOHO users.

Network management is also of growing concern because of the increasing number of difficulties and high expense that arise due to seemingly uncontrollable problems. Network managers are faced with many problems regarding creating and maintaining their LAN and WAN environments, including lack of network management expertise; decreasing management resources; unintegrated, dissimilar management tools; and the increased cost of network downtime. CiscoWorks Windows offers network managers a comprehensive management solution based on a common, integrated set of PC (Windows-based) applications that assists network managers in conducting their daily business while providing Cisco device- and task-specific expertise.

Cisco ISDN Support Service adds a single point of contact to assist users with setting up an ISDN connection to Cisco 700, 1003, 1004, 1600, 2503, 2524, 2525, 3600, and 4000 series routers and Cisco AS5x00 series servers.

Cisco IOS software provides an array of network management capabilities designed to meet the needs of today's distributed networks.

Key Management Services of Cisco IOS Software

Cisco IOS software provides a range of management services, including these:

- **MIBs**—Provides databases of information that can be changed or retrieved using either SNMP or Common Management Information Protocol (CMIP) commands.

- **Remote Monitoring**—Gathers monitoring, problem detection, and reporting data for retrieval.

- **Hypertext Transfer Protocol server interface to Cisco routers**—Eliminates the need to use the command-line interface through hot links, using any Web browser application.

- **Cisco ClickStart**—Is a Web-based software solution embedded in Cisco IOS software that enables users to install Cisco 760, 1000, or 1600 series routers:

  — Allows Cisco ISDN access routers to be accessed by any Web browser from any desktop platform

  — Enables configuration of the router and ISDN connection after the user completes an initial setup form

  — Enables centralized router management, allowing remote fine-tuning and upgrades

  — Allows remote management and monitoring via SNMP, Telnet, and console port

CiscoWorks Windows 3.1

CiscoWorks Windows 3.1 is comprehensive network management software that provides a powerful set of tools to easily manage your small to medium-sized business network or workgroup. Information such as dynamic status, statistics, and comprehensive configuration information is available for Cisco routers, switches, hubs, and access servers.

Based on the SNMP industry standard, CiscoWorks Windows provides complete management of Cisco solutions within diverse, heterogeneous networks using the powerful embedded features of the industry-leading Cisco IOS software.

CiscoWorks Windows provides easy-to-use network management that seamlessly integrates with the Castle Rock Computing SNMPc and the Hewlett-Packard OpenView Professional Suite and OpenView Network Node Manager. CiscoWorks Windows leverages investments in software and manages Cisco devices, when installed, to complement any third-party network management platform.

CiscoWorks Windows Key Features

CiscoWorks Windows provides the following features when used in conjunction with Castle Rock SNMPc or Hewlett-Packard OpenView for Windows:

- Automatic discovery process for networked devices that creates a network topology map using a color-coded, hierarchical view of the network for IP and IPX networks

- Access to extensive data on port status, bandwidth utilization, traffic statistics, protocol information, and other network performance statistics for Cisco devices

- Flexible graphing capabilities for quickly recording and analyzing historical data that can be exported to files for use by spreadsheets or other tools

- MIB compiler and browser for managing third-party SNMP devices

- Tools to simplify device configuration and management for Cisco routers, switches, hubs, and access servers

- Threshold management features that can be set for many performance variables to generate an alarm or event notifications

- Event filters that condense events into useful information to speed troubleshooting

- Device configuration features for configuring simple virtual LANs within Cisco switches

CiscoWorks Windows Components

CiscoWorks Windows is a suite of network management applications and is composed of the following tools:

- **Castle Rock SNMPc Network Management System (optional)**—SNMP-based software provides network discovery, mapping, monitoring, and alarm tracking for any SNMP, Cisco, or third-party device.

- **CiscoView**—Graphical device-management technology provides back- and front-panel displays. Dynamic, color-coded graphical displays simplify device status monitoring, device-specific component diagnostics, and application launching. Table E-29 describes the applets contained within CiscoView.

Table E-29   *Applets Contained Within CiscoView*

Application	Description
Threshold Manager	Enhances the capability to set thresholds on Cisco RMON-enabled devices, reducing management overhead and improving troubleshooting capabilities
StackView/StackMaker	Provides features within CiscoView that simplify device configuration, monitoring, and management of Cisco extended network system
Flash File System	Provides file copying and editing features to simplify router configuration for the Cisco 7000, 7010, 7204, 7406, 7505, 7507, and 7513 routers

- **Health Monitor**—This provides real-time fault and performance monitoring of device statistics, including device characteristics, CPU utilization, interface activity, errors, and protocol information.

- **Configuration Builder**—This device-configuration utility allows users to create and distribute configuration files for multiple Cisco devices through a graphical user interface.

- **Show Commands**—This displays detailed router system and protocol information without requiring the user to remember complex command-line languages or syntax.

CiscoWorks Windows System Requirements

This section overviews the CiscoWorks Windows system requirements.

Hardware requirements are as follows:

- Dedicated, Pentium-based IBM PC or compatible computer

- 24 MB RAM total (32 MB RAM recommended)

- 45 MB of free disk space for standard installation (130 MB may be needed if SNMPc third-party device support files are installed)

- CD-ROM drive for installation

- Super video graphics adapter (SVGA) and color (1024-by-768 pixels and 256 colors are recommended)

- Network driver interface (NDI) or Open Data-Link Interface (ODI)-compliant network interface card

Software requirements are as follows:

- Windows 95 or Windows NT 3.51, 4.0

- WinSock-compliant TCP/IP stack (Windows resident TCP/IP stack recommended)

The following are the network management platforms supported:

- Castle Rock SNMPc V4.2 (optionally bundled with the product)

- Hewlett-Packard OpenView Professional Suite D.01.00, D.01.02

- Hewlett-Packard OpenView Network Node Manager 5.0, 5.01 (for Windows NT only)

Cisco ConfigMaker V2

ConfigMaker is a key easy-to-use Windows 95/Windows NT 4.0 network and device configuration tool for small- to medium-sized business environments. This tool enables fast and efficient configurations of Cisco routers, access servers, Micro Hubs, Micro Switches, or Micro Webservers, with no dependency on LAN or WAN connectivity. As part of the Cisco Networked Office Stack, Cisco ConfigMaker enables stackable devices to be configured for operation on the network.

Cisco ConfigMaker Key Features

The following are Cisco ConfigMaker key features:

- Multiple protocol support, including support for IP, IPX, and AppleTalk routed protocols and Frame Relay, High-Level Data Link Control (HDLC), ISDN (BRI or PRI), and PPP connections

- Address Network Wizard that enables supplied address ranges to be assigned to selected devices or the entire network

- AutoDetect Device Wizard that provides automatic detection of devices attached to the COM port of the PC running ConfigMaker

- Insert Network that allows use of network diagrams created in earlier versions of ConfigMaker

- WAN configuration worksheets that itemize necessary service provider information

- Advanced capability that appends command-line interface commands to autogenerated configuration files

Fast Step

The Cisco Fast Step configuration utility for 700 series routers simplifies the setup and monitoring of Cisco routers for small office and home office users. It enables people with no technical experience to have a Cisco 700 series router up, tested, and connected in less than 15 minutes.

This is done via a combination of new packaging, such as Open Me First bag; match-the-colors cabling design; new, clear, and colorful documentation; and Cisco Fast Step software.

The software provides a familiar Windows hardware wizard interface to radically simplify setting up and testing the product. In addition, when setup is complete, the Fast Step monitoring facility provides instant status, ISDN connection times, and on-demand troubleshooting.

Fast Step Key Features

The following are the Fast Step key features:

- Enables auto-discovery of the router
- Loads the initial IP address
- Prefills fields with most common defaults
- Guides user through entry of LAN/WAN parameters, ISDN parameters, and security parameters
- Tests configuration
- Makes initial connection to Internet or intranet
- Monitors items such as call duration, errors, and disconnected calls

Numerics

C

D

F

G

M

P-Q

R

U

V

W

X

Z

CCIE Professional Development

Cisco LAN Switching

Kennedy Clark, CCIE; Kevin Hamilton, CCIE

1-57870-094-9 • AVAILABLE NOW

This volume provides an in-depth analysis of Cisco LAN switching technolo gies, architectures, and deployments, including unique coverage of Catalyst network design essentials. Network designs and configuration examples are incorporated throughout to demonstrate the principles and enable easy translation of the material into practice in production networks.

Advanced IP Network Design

Alvaro Retana, CCIE; Don Slice, CCIE; and Russ White, CCIE

1-57870-097-3 • AVAILABLE NOW

Network engineers and managers can use these case studies, which highligh various network design goals, to explore issues including protocol choice, network stability, and growth. This book also includes theoretical discussio on advanced design topics.

Large-Scale IP Network Solutions

Khalid Raza, CCIE; and Mark Turner

1-57870-084-1 • AVAILABLE NOW

Network engineers can find solutions as their IP networks grow in size and complexity. Examine all the major IP protocols in-depth and learn about scalability, migration planning, network management, and security for large-scale networks.

Routing TCP/IP, Volume I

Jeff Doyle, CCIE

1-57870-041-8 • AVAILABLE NOW

This book takes the reader from a basic understanding of routers and routing protocols through a detailed examination of each of the IP interior routing protocols. Learn techniques for designing networks that maximize the efficiency of the protocol being used. Exercises and review questions provide core study for the CCIE Routing and Switching exam.

www.ciscopress.

Cisco Career Certifications

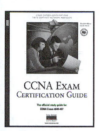

CCNA Exam Certification Guide

Wendell Odom, CCIE

0-7357-0073-7 • AVAILABLE NOW

This book is a comprehensive study tool for CCNA Exam #640-407 and part of a recommended study program from Cisco Systems. *CCNA Exam Certification Guide* helps you understand and master the exam objectives. Instructor-developed elements and techniques maximize your retention and recall of exam topics, and scenario-based exercises help validate your mastery of the exam objectives.

Advanced Cisco Router Configuration

Cisco Systems, Inc., edited by Laura Chappell

1-57870-074-4 • AVAILABLE NOW

Based on the actual Cisco ACRC course, this book provides a thorough treatment of advanced network deployment issues. Learn to apply effective configuration techniques for solid network implementation and management as you prepare for CCNP and CCDP certifications. This book also includes chapter-ending tests for self-assessment.

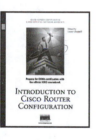

Introduction to Cisco Router Configuration

Cisco Systems, Inc., edited by Laura Chappell

1-57870-076-0 • AVAILABLE NOW

Based on the actual Cisco ICRC course, this book presents the foundation knowledge necessary to define Cisco router configurations in multiprotocol environments. Examples and chapter-ending tests build a solid framework for understanding internetworking concepts. Prepare for the ICRC course and CCNA certification while mastering the protocols and technologies for router configuration.

Cisco CCNA Preparation Library

Cisco Systems, Inc., Laura Chappell, and Kevin Downes, CCIE

1-57870-125-2 • AVAILABLE NOW • CD-ROM

This boxed set contains two Cisco Press books—*Introduction to Cisco Router Configuration* and *Internetworking Technologies Handbook,* Second Edition—and the *High-Performance Solutions for Desktop Connectivity* CD.

CISCO SYSTEMS

CISCO PRESS

www.ciscopress.com

Cisco Press Solutions

Enhanced IP Services for Cisco Networks
Donald C. Lee, CCIE

1-57870-106-6 • AVAILABLE NOW

This is a guide to improving your network's capabilities by understanding the new enabling and advanced Cisco IOS services that build more scalable, intelligent, and secure networks. Learn the technical details necessary to de[p] Quality of Service, VPN technologies, IPsec, the IOS firewall and IOS Intru[s] Detection. These services will allow you to extend the network to new fron[t] securely, protect your network from attacks, and increase the sophistication network services.

Developing IP Multicast Networks, Volume I
Beau Williamson, CCIE

1-57870-077-9 • AVAILABLE NOW

This book provides a solid foundation of IP multicast concepts and explain[s] how to design and deploy the networks that will support appplications suc[h] audio and video conferencing, distance-learning, and data replication. Inclu[des] an in-depth discussion of the PIM protocol used in Cisco routers and detai[l] coverage of the rules that control the creation and maintenance of Cisco m[ulticast] state entries.

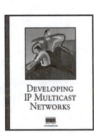

OpenCable Architecture
Michael Adams

1-57870-135-X • AVAILABLE NOW

Whether you're a television, data communications, or telecommunications [pro] fessional, or simply an interested business person, this book will help you understand the technical and business issues surrounding interactive televis[ion] services. It will also provide you with an inside look at the combined effor[t] the cable, data, and consumer electronics industries' efforts to develop tho[se] new services.

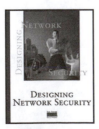

Designing Network Security
Merike Kaeo

1-57870-043-4 • AVAILABLE NOW

Designing Network Security is a practical guide designed to help you understand the fundamentals of securing your corporate infrastructure. Th[is] book takes a comprehensive look at underlying security technologies, the process of creating a security policy, and the practical requirements necess[ary] implement a corporate security policy.

CISCO SYSTEMS

CISCO PRESS

www.ciscopress.

Cisco Press Solutions

OSPF Network Design Solutions

Thomas M. Thomas II

1-57870-046-9 • **AVAILABLE NOW**

This comprehensive guide presents a detailed, applied look into the workings of the popular Open Shortest Path First protocol, demonstrating how to dramatically increase network performance and security, and how to most easily maintain large-scale networks. OSPF is thoroughly explained through exhaustive coverage of network design, deployment, management, and troubleshooting.

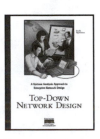

Top-Down Network Design

Priscilla Oppenheimer

1-57870-069-8 • **AVAILABLE NOW**

Building reliable, secure, and manageable networks is every network professional's goal. This practical guide teaches you a systematic method for network design that can be applied to campus LANs, remote-access networks, WAN links, and large-scale internetworks. Learn how to analyze business and technical requirements, examine traffic flow and Quality of Service requirements, and select protocols and technologies based on performance goals.

Internetworking SNA with Cisco Solutions

George Sackett and Nancy Sackett

1-57870-083-3 • **AVAILABLE NOW**

This comprehensive guide presents a practical approach to integrating SNA and TCP/IP networks. It provides readers with an understanding of internetworking terms, networking architectures, protocols, and implementations for internetworking SNA with Cisco routers.

For the latest on Cisco Press resources and Certification and Training guides, or for information on publishing opportunities, visit **www.ciscopress.com**.

CISCO SYSTEMS
CISCO PRESS

Cisco Press books are available at your local bookstore, computer store, and online booksellers.

Cisco Press

Staying Connected to Networkers

We want to hear from **you**! Help Cisco Press **stay connected** to the issues and challenges you face on a daily basis by registering your book and filling out our brief survey.

Complete and mail this form, or better yet, jump to **www.ciscopress.com** and do it online. Each complete entry will be eligible for our monthly drawing to **win a FREE book** from the Cisco Press Library.

Thank you for choosing Cisco Press to help you work the network.

Name _____

Address _____

City _____ State/Province _____

Country _____ Zip/Post code _____

E-mail address _____

May we contact you via e-mail for product updates and customer benefits?
❒ Yes   ❒ No

Where did you buy this product?
❒ Bookstore   ❒ Computer store   ❒ Electronics store
❒ Online retailer   ❒ Office supply store   ❒ Discount store
❒ Mail order   ❒ Class/Seminar
❒ Other _____

When did you buy this product? _____ **Month** _____ **Year**

What price did you pay for this product?
❒ Full retail price   ❒ Discounted price   ❒ Gift

How did you learn about this product?
❒ Friend   ❒ Store personnel   ❒ In-store ad
❒ Catalog   ❒ Postcard in the mail   ❒ Saw it on the shelf
❒ Magazine ad   ❒ Article or review   ❒ Used other products
❒ School   ❒ Professional Organization
❒ Other _____

What will this product be used for?
❒ Business use   ❒ Personal use   ❒ School/Education
❒ Other _____

How many years have you been employed in a computer-related industry?
❒ 2 years or less   ❒ 3-5 years   ❒ 5+ years

www.ciscopress.com

www.ciscopress.com

Which best describes your job function?

❏ Corporate Management   ❏ Systems Engineering   ❏ IS Management
❏ Network Design   ❏ Network Support   ❏ Webmaster
❏ Marketing/Sales   ❏ Consultant   ❏ Student
❏ Professor/Teacher

❏ Other _____

What is your formal education background?

❏ High school   ❏ Vocational/Technical degree   ❏ Some college
❏ College degree   ❏ Masters degree   ❏ Professional or Doctoral degree

Have you purchased a Cisco Press product before?

❏ Yes   ❏ No

On what topics would you like to see more coverage?

_____

_____

Do you have any additional comments or suggestions?

_____

_____

CCDA Exam Certification Guide (0-7357-0074-5)

Cisco Press

201 West 103rd Street
Indianapolis, IN 46290

www.ciscopress.com

Place
Stamp
Here

Cisco Press
Customer Registration
P.O. Box 189014
Battle Creek, MI 49018-9947

Cisco Systems®

IF YOU'RE USING

CISCO PRODUCTS,

YOU'RE QUALIFIED

TO RECEIVE A

FREE SUBSCRIPTION

TO CISCO'S

PREMIER PUBLICATION,

PACKET™ MAGAZINE.

Packet delivers complete coverage of cutting-edge networking trends and innovations, as well as current product updates. A magazine for technical, hands-on Cisco users, it delivers valuable information for enterprises, service providers, and small and midsized businesses.

Packet is a quarterly publication. To qualify for the upcoming issue, simply click on the URL and follow the prompts to subscribe: www.cisco.com/warp/public/784/packet/subscribe/request.shtml

PACKET

Packet magazine serves as the premier publication linking customers to Cisco Systems, Inc. Delivering complete coverage of cutting-edge networking trends and innovations, *Packet* is a magazine for technical, hands-on users. It delivers industry-specific information for enterprise, service provider, and small and midsized business market segments. A toolchest for planners and decision makers, *Packet* contains a vast array of practical information, boasting sample configurations, real-life customer examples, and tips on getting the most from your Cisco Systems' investments. Simply put, *Packet* magazine is straight talk straight from the worldwide leader in networking for the Internet, Cisco Systems, Inc.

We hope you'll take advantage of this useful resource. I look forward to hearing from you!

Jennifer Biondi
Packet Circulation Manager
packet@cisco.com
www.cisco.com/go/packet

☐ **YES!** I'm requesting a **free** subscription to *Packet*™ magazine.

☐ No. I'm not interested at this time.

☐ Mr.
☐ Ms.

First Name (Please Print) _____ Last Name _____

Title/Position (Required) _____

Company (Required) _____

Address _____

City _____ State/Province _____

Zip/Postal Code _____ Country _____

Telephone (Include country and area codes) _____ Fax _____

E-mail _____

Signature (Required) _____ Date _____

☐ I would like to receive additional information on Cisco's services and products by e-mail.

1.0 Do you or your company:
- A ☐ Use Cisco products
- B ☐ Resell Cisco products
- C ☐ Both
- D ☐ Neither

1. Your organization's relationship to Cisco Systems:
- A ☐ Customer/End User
- B ☐ Prospective Customer
- C ☐ Cisco Reseller
- D ☐ Cisco Distributor
- DI ☐ Non-Authorized Reseller
- E ☐ Integrator
- G ☐ Cisco Training Partner
- I ☐ Cisco OEM
- J ☐ Consultant
- K ☐ Other (specify): _____

2. How would you classify your business?
- A ☐ Small/Medium-Sized
- B ☐ Enterprise
- C ☐ Service Provider

3. Your involvement in network equipment purchases:
- A ☐ Recommend
- B ☐ Approve
- C ☐ Neither

4. Your personal involvement in networking:
- A ☐ Entire enterprise at all sites
- B ☐ Departments or network segments at more than one site
- C ☐ Single department or network segment
- F ☐ Public network
- D ☐ No involvement
- E ☐ Other (specify): _____

5. Your Industry:
- A ☐ Aerospace
- B ☐ Agriculture/Mining/Construction
- C ☐ Banking/Finance
- D ☐ Chemical/Pharmaceutical
- E ☐ Consultant
- F ☐ Computer/Systems/Electronics
- G ☐ a. Education (K–12)
- ☐ b. Education (College/Univ.)
- H ☐ Government—Federal
- I ☐ Government—State
- J ☐ Government—Local
- K ☐ Health Care
- L ☐ Telecommunications
- M ☐ Utilities/Transportation
- N ☐ Other (specify): _____